The Sunday Telegraph
GOOD WINE GUIDE

1 9 9 5

The Sunday Telegraph

GOOD
WINE
Guide
1995

ROBERT JOSEPH

MACMILLAN REFERENCE BOOKS

Editor: Robert Joseph
Senior Editorial Assistants: Justin Howard-Sneyd, Alex Watson,
Editorial Assistants: David Lindsay, Karen Menzies, Paul Henry.
Editorial Production/Coordination: Sheila Keating
Author photograph: Patrick Mark

Published in Great Britain 1994
by the Sunday Telegraph
1 Canada Square, Canary Wharf
London E14 5DT
in association with Macmillan Reference Books

First edition published 1983
Copyright © Robert Joseph and
The Sunday Telegraph 1994

ISBN 0 333 618769

Designed by Peter Ward
Typeset by R J Publishing Services
Printed and bound in Great Britain by
BPC Hazell Books Ltd
A member of
The British Printing Company Ltd

CONTENTS

ACKNOWLEDGEMENTS

A couple of editions ago, I described the putting together of that year's Guide as like building a skyscraper in a month. Little did I imagine the efforts which would be required to create the 1995 edition with its wholly new 2000-entry A-Z encyclopedia. This time it was more like creating a whole town.

In my efforts to ensure that all of the information in the *Guide* was as comprehensive, as accurate and as up-to-date as possible, I was lucky to have a team of extraordinarily dedicated helpers.

Paul Henry, Karen Menzies and particularly David Lindsay all worked long hours at a bank of Apple Macintoshes while, in the crucial final stages of production, Justin Howard-Sneyd and Alexander Watson sacrificed themselves almost totally to the book.

Francis Jago of MPA Fingal performed his customary miracle of turning computer discs into camera-ready film despite power cuts and rail strikes.

Despite all these efforts, Catherine Hurley, Ingrid Connell and the production department at Pan Macmillan were faced with the task of getting this book onto the shelves within weeks of the last words having been written. Their success in doing so says a great deal for their publishing expertise.

Mark Hughes-Morgan, my editor at the Sunday Telegraph deserves special thanks for his indulgence and I am grateful to Ruth Arnold, Jane Hughes, Sophie Wybrew-Bond and Damien Riley-Smith, all of WINE Magazine, for their support and for allowing me, once again, to include the results of the International Wine Challenge Wine and Wine Merchant of the Year Awards.

I would also like to thank John Gowers and Paul Elmes for adapting the design of the book, sub-editors, Di Spencer and Tony Russell and, for their various forms of help, Marilyn Warnick of Telegraph Books, Piers Russell-Cobb, Clare Anderson and John Clay. Just as important for their forbearance at times when the Guide monopolised more time than a newly-born child were Tim and Liam White and Sue Cannelle.

Most crucial of all, though, as ever, was Sheila Keating, without whose friendship, commitment, support and 20-hour days the *Guide* would never have appeared at all.

All of these people share any credit for this book; the blame should be pointed directly at my shoulders.

INTRODUCTION

Today it is hard to name a country where grapes are grown whose wines are not on sale in Britain. If you want to try a Brazilian fizz or a Zimbabwean red, they're out there somewhere – along with organic and low-alcohol wines and wines made specifically to go with particular types of fish.

The range of grapes is extraordinary too – from the Arneis and the Airèn to the Xarel-Lo and Zinfandel. But all this choice is bewildering: the wine department of a supermarket can be the vinous equivalent of the paint section at B & Q. With every month, the range develops at such a rate that it's easy to understand why so many people take the 'safe' option and carry home a bottle of Muscadet or a gallon of Magnolia Vinyl-Silk.

But these are exciting times for anybody who feels adventurous enough to try something new. A combination of improved skills in the vineyards and cellars and tougher standards among the professional buyers has all but removed the risk of buying an expensive bottle of vinegar. Now the challenge lies in finding the particular styles of wine you enjoy.

From the outset, the *Guide* has sought to help every wine drinker, from the person with the most casual interest to the keenest buff, to find his or her way to the most interesting and the best value wines on the market, whatever their style.

Over the last few years, the *Guide* has performed this task so effectively that it has become a victim of its own success. As sales of the book have risen, it has inevitably become increasingly difficult to find some of the recommended 500 wines; often they have sold out within weeks of publication.

Which is why, with this edition, I have taken the plunge and created a new 110-page A-Z encyclopedia containing over 2500 wine recommendations, from the humblest Vin de Pays to the grandest of Grands Crus and Newest Wave superstars.

Faithful to the traditions of the *Guide* however, I also include a wholly updated review of over 175 of Britain's best high street merchants, supermarkets and specialists, and list what I think are some of their best buys.

The result is a *Guide* which is more comprehensive than ever before – and unashamedly quirkier, more personal and often more controversial. I hope you enjoy it.

Robert Joseph, July 1994

HOW TO USE THIS BOOK

There are various wine books and guides on the market, but this one is unique in that through its key section, the A-Z, it allows readers simply to look up St. Emilion, Semillon or Santa Rita, etc and find a description of the region, wine style, grape or producer, together with information on vintages, a set of recommended examples and an indication of what each will cost and where it can be bought. All this plus a round up of what is happening in the wine world, everything you need to know about buying wine, and a selection of the best wine merchants to be found in Britain.

To help you use it easily, the *Guide* is divided into four main sections: The Awards, The Wine World, The A-Z and The Merchants.

THE AWARDS

Following this year's WINE magazine International Wine Challenge, two panels of judges were convened to choose the Wine Merchants and Wines of the Year. Over three pages we present the best of the best. At the end of this section, beginning on page 12 you will find listed over 250 codes representing all the wine merchants referred to throughout this year's *Guide.*, followed by a regional guide to help you find those nearest to you.

THE WINE WORLD

In this section I take a personal look back at some of the developments in the world of wine over the last twelve months and introduce some of the characters who have made their mark. I also suggest some of the best places to learn about wine, give some pointers on investing in it or storing it, and recommend the ideal glasses, corkscrews etc. There is a section on organic wines, entertaining with wine and food, and my selection of the bottles which I think currently represent especially good value.

THE A-Z

The core of the *Guide* : a wholly new encyclopedia of wines, grapes, producers, regions and terms, which is unique in that not only does it provide definitions and descriptions, but it also recommends over 2500 representative wines, graded from * to ***** according to their value for money.

THE MERCHANTS

Perhaps you buy your wine at the same time – and in the same shop – as you pick up your soap powder and cat food, perhaps you prefer to browse through specialist catalogues or among the shelves of your local Oddbins or independent merchant. If, like an increasing number of wine drinkers, you like to shop around, chasing the best bargains and the most interesting bottles, this section is for you: you'll find descriptions and details of 200 of the very best independent merchants, wine shop chains, supermarkets and specialists throughout the country.

THE WINE MAGAZINE/INTERNATIONAL WINE CHALLENGE
WINE MERCHANTS AND WINES OF THE YEAR

Every year, following the International Wine Challenge – the world's biggest wine competition, of which this Guide's editor is Chairman — WINE Magazine convenes two panels of judges whose responsibility it is to choose the Wine Merchants and Wines of the Year.

The team of judges who assessed the short-listed Wine Merchants of the Year comprised Julian Brind MW of Waitrose, Robert Joseph, Charles Metcalfe of Granada Television's 'This Morning', Chris Pugh-Morgan of Thos Peatling, Joanna Simon of the Sunday Times and Kim Tidy of Thresher/Wine Rack/Bottoms Up. The judges (who dropped out of the discussion and voting when they had an interest to declare) were presided over by Ken White, a District Judge and keen amateur wine enthusiast. While several of the category and regional awards were hotly contested, there was little question over the four most highly rated merchants, and even less over the winner.

WINE MERCHANT OF THE YEAR

Winner: Adnams
Short List: Justerini & Brooks, Oddbins, Winecellars.

CATEGORY AWARDS

Small Independent Wine Merchant of the Year
Winner: The Nobody Inn
Short List: Ameys, Croque-en-Bouche, Derek Smedley, Helen Verdcourt.

National High Street Chain Wine Merchant of the Year
Winner: Oddbins
Short List: Bottoms Up, Thresher, Wine Rack

Supermarket Wine Merchant of the Year
Winner: J. Sainsbury
Short List: Safeway, Tesco, Waitrose

Regional Wine Merchant of the Year
Winners: Adnams/Justerini & Brooks
Short List: Anthony Byrne, The Nobody Inn

Wine List of the Year:
Winner: Oddbins
Short List: Adnams, Bottoms Up, Lay & Wheeler, Winecellars

REGIONAL AWARDS

Scotland
Winners: Raeburn Fine Wines/Ubiquitous Chip
Short List: Bute Wines, Valvona & Crolla

North of England
Winner: BH Wines
Short List: Corn Road Vintners, Great Northern Wine Co, Wright Wine Co.

Central England
Winner: Anthony Byrne Fine Wines
Short List: Noble Rot Wine Warehouse, Tanners, Windrush

East of England:
Winner: Adnams
Short List: Lay & Wheeler, Thos Peatling, T&W

London and the South East
Winner: Justerini & Brooks
Short List: Bibendum, Roberson, Winecellars

West of England
Winner: The Nobody Inn
Short List: Averys of Bristol, Hicks & Don, Christopher Piper

Northern Ireland
Winner: James Nicholson
Short List: Direct Wine Shipments, Winemark

SPECIALIST AWARDS

Spanish
Winner: Moreno Fine Wines
Short List: Bottoms Up, Laymont & Shaw, Oddbins

German
Winner: Lay & Wheeler
Short List: Adnams, Justerini & Brooks, OW Loeb

Italian
Winner: Winecellars
Short List: Adnams, Lea & Sandeman, Valvona & Crolla

New World
Winners: Adnams/Oddbins
Short List: Australian Wine Club (check), Lay & Wheeler

Fine & Rare
Winner: T & W
Short List: Farr Vintners, Justerini & Brooks, La Vigneronne

Bordeaux
Winner: The Wine Society
Short List: Justerini & Brooks, Lay & Wheeler, Thos Peatling

Burgundy
Winner: Howard Ripley
Short List: Justerini & Brooks, Oddbins

Rhone
Winner: Yapp Bros.
Short List: Croque en Bouche, Gauntleys of Nottingham, Justerini & Brooks

WINES OF THE YEAR

The wines selected for consideration must meet the following criteria: they must be of exceptional standard (silver or ideally gold medallists in the International Wine Challenge), affordable (entered in the under £5 and £8 categories for table wines; under £10 for sparkling) and widely available (in quantities of over 10,000 cases).

The judges had a heavy responsibility, given the award's track record of predicting vinous trends. Past winners have included such wines as the Montana Marlborough Sauvignon Blanc, Mumm Cuvée Napa Sparkling Wine and Tinto da Anfora from Portugal.

The tasters who chose the Wines of the Year were Tim Atkin of The Observer, John Avery MW, Hew Blair of Justerini and Brooks, Oz Clarke, Rosemary George MW, Jane Hunt MW, Robert Joseph of WINE and The Sunday Telegraph, Maggie McNie MW, Charles Metcalfe of WINE and Granada TV's 'This Morning', Angela Muir MW, Michael Peace MW, Anthony Rose of The Independent, Derek Smedley MW, Jo Standen MW, Kit Stevens MW, Tom Stevenson, author of the Sothebys World Wine Encyclopedia, and Stuart Walton of BBC Good Food Magazine.

WHITE WINES OF THE YEAR

La Serre Sauvignon Blanc, Vin de Pays d'Oc 1993
(Victoria Wine £4.99)Made in Southern France by the ubiquitous Hugh Ryman. A brilliant alternative to the Loire and New Zealand.

Cafayate Torrontes by Arnaldo Etchart 1993
(Thresher £3.99) A dry-but-grapey wine produced in Argentina from the local Muscat-like Torrontes grape.

RED WINES OF THE YEAR

Penfolds Coonawarra Cabernet 1990 and 1991
(Oddbins et al £7.99) Two winning vintages of the same intensely blackcurranty wine from Australia's leading red wine region.

Rosemount Cabernet-Shiraz 1993
(Tesco et al £4.49) The Aussie wine we've been waiting for. A delicious Down-Under-Beaujolais.

Solana Cencibel Valdepeñas 1993
(Oddbins et al £4.99) Yet another Australian success story – a juicy young Tempranillo made by Don Lewis of Mitchelton in Victoria.

SPARKLING WINES OF THE YEAR

Pongràcz Bergkelder
(Safeway et al £6.99) A gorgeously rich, great value wine from one of the biggest producers in South Africa.

Yalumba Cuvée 1 Prestige Pinot Noir-Chardonnay
(Sainsbury et al £7.99) Winning its second award as Sparkling Wine of the Year, this Champage Method wine is made by one of Australia's leading fizz producers.

MERCHANTS CODES

Merchants listed throughout this *Guide* are referred to using the
following codes. Those who do not appear in The Merchants section
(beginning on page 159) are listed with their telephone numbers.

A	Asda	CAR	C. A.Rookes
A&A	A&A Wines		0789 297777
	0483 274666	CAX	Caxton Tower Wines
A&N	Army & Navy Store		081 758 4500
	081 527 3735	CC	Chiswick Cellar
ABY	Anthony Byrne Fine Wines	CCL	Cockburns of Leith
ADB	Addison Bagot Page	CEB	Croque-en-Bouche
ADN	Adnam Wine Merchants	CEL	Cellar 5 Ltd.
AF	Alexr Findlater & Co.		0925 444555
AL	A. L.Vose & Co. Ltd.	CHF	Chippendale Fine Wines
	05395 33328	CNL	Connolly's
AMA	Amathus	COK	Corkscrew Wines
AMW	Amey's Wines	COR	Corn Road Vintners
AUC	Australian Wine Club	CPS	C P A's Wine Ltd.
A	Avery's of Bistol	CPW	Christopher Piper Wines
BAB	Bablake Wines	CRL	The Wine Centre
	0203 228272	CT	Charles Taylor
BAK	Barkham Manor Vineyard	CTL	Continental Wine & Food
	0825 722103		0484 538333
BAL	Ballantyne's of Cowbridge	CUM	Cumbrian Wine Cellar
BAR	Barwell & Jones	CWI	A Case Of Wine
BBR	Berry Bros. & Rudd	CWN	Cornwall Wine Merchants
BD	Bordeaux Direct	CWS	The CO-OP
BE	Bin Ends of Rotherham	CWW	Classic Wines & Spirits
BEN	Bennetts	D	Davison
BGC	Borg Castel	D&F	D & F Wine Shippers
BG	Berwick Glebe Vineyard		081 969 2277
	05806 4996	DAL	Tom Tiddlers
BH	B H Wines		0628 30295
BI	Bibendum	DBW	DavidBaker Wines
BIN	Bin '89 Wine Warehouse	DBY	DavidByrne
BKW	Berkeley Wines	DD	Domaine Direct
BNK	The Bottleneck	DHM	DouglasHenn-McCrae
	0843 60195	DIR	Direct Wine Shipments
BOD	Bodegas Direct	DN	Deinhard
	0243 773474		071 261 1111
BOO	Booths of Stockport	DWC	Dorking Wine Cellars
BP	Boutinot Prince	DWL	Sunday Times Wine Club
	0925 444555		0734 481711
BTH	E H Booth	ECK	Eckington
BU	Bottoms Up	EEL	Electric Eel Limited
BUD	Budgens 081 422 9511		071 736 1523
BUT	The Butler's Wine Cellar	EOO	Evertons of Ombersley
BVL	David Burns Ltd.		0905 620282
	0202 823411	EOR	Ellis of Richmond
BWC	Berkmann		081 943 4033
BWI	Bute Wines	EP	Eldridge Pope
BWL	Berkeley Wines	ES	Edward Sheldon
BWS	Barnes Wine Shop	ET	Elliot & Tatham Fine Wines
C&B	Corney & Barrow		0451 870555
CAC	Cachet	EUR	Europa Stores Ltd
CAP	Cape Province Wines		081 845 1255

EV	El Vino	JFD	John Ford Wines /
EVI	Evingtons		See York House Wines
EWC	English Wine Centre	JMC	James E.McCabe
	0323 870532		0762 333 102
F& M	Fortnum & Mason	JN	James Nicholson
FAR	Farr Vintners	JS	Sainsbury
FDL	Findlater Mackie Todd	KS	Kwiksave
FSW	Frank E.Stainton	L&S	Laymont & Shaw
FUL	Fuller Smith & Turner Plc.	L&W	Lay & Wheeler
FV	Fernlea Vintners	LAV	Les Amis Du Vin /
G	Gateway - See Somerfield		See The Winery
G & M	Gordon & Macphail	LAY	Laytons Wine Merchants
GAR	Garland Wines Ltd	LEA	Lea & Sandeman
	0372 275241	LEF	Le Fleming
GEL	Gelston Castle Fine Wines	LES	Leos
	0556 3012		061 832 8152
GH	Goedhuis & Co. Ltd.	LU	Luigi's Delicatessan
GHS	Gerard Harris Fine Wines	LV	La Vigneronne
	0296 631041	LWE	London Wine Emporium
GI	Grape Ideas	LWL	London Wine Ltd
GM	G M Vintners		071 351 6856
	0392 218186	M&S	Marks & Spencer
GNW	Great Northern Wine Co.	M&V	Morris & Verdin
GON	Gauntleys of Nottingham	MAR	Marco's Wine
GRO	Grog Blossom	MG	Mathew Gloag & Sons Ltd.
GRT	Great Western	MHC	Manor House Wine
GWC	Greek Wine Centre		0446 775 591
GWI	General Wine Company	MM	MichaelMenzel
	0428 722201	MOR	Morenos
H&D	Hicks & Don	MRN	Wm Morrison
H&H	Hector & Honorez Ltd.	MRT	Martinez Fine Wine
HAL	Hall Batson & Co		0943 603241
	0603 415115	MTL	Mitchells
HAM	Hampden Wine	MWW	Majestic Wine Warehouse
HAR	Harrods	MYS	Mayor Sworder
HHC	Haynes Hanson & Clarke	N&P	Nickolls & Perks
HLV	Halves Ltd	NAD	The Nadder Wine Co. Ltd.
	See The Wine Treasury	NGF	Norman Goodfellow
HN	Harvey Nichols	NI	Nobody Inn
HOL	Holland Park Wine Co.	NIC	Nicolas
HOT	House of Townsend	NRW	Noble Rot Wines
HOU	Hoult's Wine Merchants	NY	NoelYoung
HPD	Harpenden Wines	OD	Oddbins
HR	Howard Ripley	OLS	The Old Street Wine Co.
HV	John Harvey & Sons		071 729 1768
	0272 268882	OWL	O.E.Loeb
HVW	Helen Verdcourt		071 928 7750
HW	Hedley Wright	P	Parfrements
HWM	Harvest Wine Group	PAG	Pagendam Pratt & Partners
IRV	Irvine Robertson Ltd.		0937 844711
	031 553 3521	PEA	Peake Wine Associates
J & B	Justerini & Brooks		071 733 5657
JAG	J. A.Glass	PEY	Philip Eyres Wine Merchant
JAR	John Armit Wines	PF	PercyFox
JAV	John Arkle Vintners		0279 626801
JEF	John E.Fells & Sons	PHI	Philglas & Swiggot
	081 749 3661	PLA	Playford Ros
JEH	J. E.Hogg	PMR	Premier Wine Warehouse

POL	Pol Roger	VR	Vintage Roots
	0531 6111	VW	Victoria Wine
PON	Le Pont de la Tour	W	Waitrose
POR	The Portland Wine Co.	WAC	Waters of Coventry Ltd.
PST	Penistone Court Wine Cellars	WAW	Waterloo Wine Co.
PTR	Peter Green	WBM	Wine Byre Merchants
PWY	Peter Wylie Fine Wines		0334 53215
R	R. S. Wines	WCE	Winecellars
RAE	Raeburn Fine Wines	WDW	Windrush Wines
RAM	Ramsbottom Victuallers	WES	Wessex Wines Ltd.
RAV	Ravensbourne Wine	WG	Wines Galore
RBS	Roberson		081 858 6014
RD	Reid Wines	WGW	Woodgate Wines
RDW	Rodney Densem Wines Ltd.	WHC	Whiclar & Gordon Wines Ltd.
RES	La Reserve Group		0306 885711
RIB	Ribble Vintners	WIN	The Winery
RN	Rex Norris	WL	William Low & Co. Ltd.
ROB	T.M.Robertson & Son	WLA	Wine Talk of Lytham St.Annes
	PROB	WMK	Winemark
ROG	Roger Harris	WNS	Winos
RTW	Rose Tree Wines	WOC	Whitesides of Clitheroe Ltd.
RWC	Rioja Wine Co.	WOI	Wines of Interest
RWW	Richmond Wine Warhouse	WOW	Wines of Westhorpe
S&J	Simpkin & James		0283 820285
	0533 623 132	WR	Wine Rack
SAC	Le Sac à Vin	WRW	Wright Wine Co.
	See La Reserve	WSC	Wine Schoppen
SAF	Safeway	WSG	Walter S Siegel Ltd.
SAN	Sandiway Wine Co.		071 627 2720
SAS	Sherston Wine Co.	WSO	Wine Society
SB	Sainsbury Brothers	WTR	Wine Treasur
	0225 460481	WWI	Woodhouse Wines
SEL	Selfridges		0258 452141
SHJ	S. H.Jones & Co. Ltd	WWT	Whitebridge Wines
SK	Seckford Wines	YAP	Yapp Brothers
SMF	Somerfield	YHW	York House Wines
SOB	Stones of Belgravia	j	
	071 235 1612		
SOM	Sommelier Wine Co. Ltd.		
SPG	Springfield Wines		
SPR	Spar		
SUM	Summerlee Wines Ltd.		
SV	Smedley Vintners		
SWB	Satchells of Burnham Market		
T&T	Thierry & Tatham		
	0794 515500		
T&W	T & W Wines		
TAN	Tanners Wines Ltd.		
TDS	Thresher Drink Stores		
TH	Thresher		
THP	Thomas Peatling		
TO	Tesco		
TOJ	Tony Jeffries		
TP	Terry Platt Wine Merchant		
TVW	Turville Valley Wines		
U	Unwins		
UDC	Ubiquitous Chip		
V&C	Valvona & Crolla		
VDV	Vin du Van		
VER	Vinceremos		

MERCHANTS BY REGION

The following will help you to find the nearest wine merchant in any part of the country. Companies marked in red are regional chains and the area they cover is indicated in brackets after the company name.

LONDON
EC1
Corney & Barrow
EC4
El Vino's
N7
Berkmanns
Alex Findlater
N13
Amathus
N21
Howard Ripley
NW1
Bibendum
Laytons
NW6
Grog Blossom
NW10
Les Amis du Vin
SE1
Le Pont de la Tour
Morris & Verdin
Waterloo Wine Co
SE10
Ravensbourne
SE11
London Wine
Emporium Ltd
Mayor Sworder
SW1
Berry Brothers &
Rudd
Farr Vintners
Justerini & Brooks
Harrods
Harvey Nichols
SW3
La Réserve
SW6
Wine Treasury
Premier Wine
Warehouse
SW7
La Vigneronne
SW8
Goedhuis & Co
SW10
Luigi's
Delicatessen
Lea & Sandeman
SW11
Philglas &
Swiggot
SW12
Fernlea Vintners

SW13
Barnes Wine Shop
SW18
Marco's
Winecellars
SW19
Findlater Mackie
Todd
W1
Fortnum & Mason
Selfridges
Norman
Goodfellows
W2
Moreno
W4
Chiswick Cellars
Fullers (South
East)
W8
Bute Wines
Haynes Hanson &
Clarke
Nicolas
W9
Moreno
The Winery
W11
John Armit Wines
Holland Park
Wine Co
W14
Roberson
WC1
Domaine Direct

AVON
Bath
Great Western
Bristol
Averys of Bristol
R S Wines
Reid Wines

BEDFORDSHIRE
Luton
Smedley Vintners

BERKSHIRE
Maidenhead
Helen Verdcourt
Reading
Bordeaux Direct
The Sunday Times
Wine Club

Wargrave
Vintage Roots

**BUCKINGHAM-
SHIRE**
Amersham
Philip Eyres
Great Missenden
Turville Valley

**CAMBRIDGE-
SHIRE**
Cambridge
Noel Young
Kimbolton
H & H Wines Ltd
Ramsay
Anthony Byrne

CHESHIRE
AlderleyEdge
Addison-Bagot
Chester
Classic Wine
Warehouses
Nantwich
Rodney Densem
Sale
Portland Wine Co
Sandiway
Sandiway Wine
Co
Stockport
Booths of
Stockport
Warrington
Berkeley Wines
Cellar 5 (Midlands
and North-West)

CORNWALL
Camborne
Cornwall Wine
Merchants
Truro
Laymont & Shaw

CUMBRIA
Carlisle
Corkscrew
B H Wines
Kendall
Frank E Stainton
Lowick
Woodgate Wines

Penrith
The Cumbrian
Cellar

DEVON
**Doddiscomb-
sleigh**
The Nobody Inn
Ottery St Mary
Christopher Piper
Plymtree
Peter Wylie
Tavistock
The Wine Centre

DORSET
**Blandford St
Mary**
Hicks & Don
Bridport
Wessex Wines
Dorchester
Eldridge Pope
(South)

ESSEX
Colchester
Lay & Wheeler

**GLOUCESTER-
SHIRE**
Cheltenham
The Rose Tree
Wine Co
Windrush Wines
Chipping Norton
Bennetts
Stow on the Wold
Haynes, Hanson
and Clarke

**HEREFORD &
WORCESTER**
Bromsgrove
Noble Rot Wine
Warehouse
Malvern Wells
Croque en Bouche

**HERTFORD-
SHIRE**
Bishops Stortford
Hedley Wright
Harpenden
Harpenden Wine

Le Fleming Wines
St Albans
Sherston Wine Co
Stevenage
The Wine Society

HUMBERSIDE
Hull
House of
Townend
(Humberside)

KENT
Appledore
Vin du Van
Aylesford
Douglas Henn-
Macrae
Dartford
Unwins (South
East)

LANCASHIRE
Bury
The Ramsbottom
Victuallers Co
Clitheroe
D Byrne & Co
Whitesides of
Clitheroe
Lytham St Annes
Wine Talk of
Lytham St Annes
Oldham
Winos Wine Shop
Preston
Borg Castel
E H Booth (North
West)
Ribble Vintners

LEICESTERSHIRE
Leicester
Evingtons

MIDDLESEX
Staines
Cape Province

NORFOLK
Burnham Market
Satchells
Norwich
Adnams
Thetford
T&W Wines
Weston Longville
Roger Harris

NORTHAMPTON
-SHIRE
Northampton
Tony Jeffries
Summerlee Wines
Ltd

NORTHUMBER-
LAND
Morpeth
Corn Road
Vintners

NOTTINGHAM-
SHIRE
Nottingham
Gauntley's of
Nottingham

OXFORDSHIRE
Banbury
S H Jones & Co
Oxford
Grape Ideas
Thame
The Hampden
Wine Co

SHROPSHIRE
Shrewsbury
Greek Wine
Centre
Tanners (Central
England and
Wales)

STAFFORDSHIRE
Stone
Whitebridge
Wines

SUFFOLK
Bury St Edmunds
Thos Peatling (E.
Anglia)
Ipswich
Barwell & Jones
(East Anglia)
Wines of Interest
**Martlesham
Heath**
Seckford Wines
Newmarket
Corney & Barrow
Southwold
Adnams
Sudbury
Amey's Wines

SURREY
Croydon
Davisons (South
East)
Dorking
Dorking Wine
Cellars
Epsom
Charles Taylor
Fine Wines
Richmond
Richmond Wine
Warehouse

SUSSEX (East)
Haywards Heath
Rex Norris
Brighton
The Butlers Wine
Cellar
Hove
York House Wines

WARWICKSHIRE
Coventry
Parfrements
Shipston on Stour
Edward Sheldon
Warwick
Waters of
Coventry Ltd

WEST
MIDLANDS
Birmingham
Connolly's

Stourbridge
Nickolls & Perks

WILTSHIRE
Mere
Yapp Brothers
Salisbury
Hicks & Don
Nadder Wine Co
Swindon
John Arkell
Vintners

YORKSHIRE
(North)
Skipton
Wright Wine Co
Thirsk
Playford Ros Ltd
York
Cachet Wines

YORKSHIRE
(South)
Rotherham
Bin Ends
Sheffield
Bin 89
Eckington Wines
Michael Menzel
Mitchells
Penistone Court
Wine Schoppen

YORKSHIRE
(West)
Huddersfield
Hoults
Springfield Wines
Otley
Chippendale
Springfield

Leeds
Great Northern
Wine Co
Hoults
Vinceremos
Wakefield
Wm Morrison
(North)

N IRELAND
Co Down
James Nicholson
Belfast
Direct Wine
Shipments
Winemark
(N. Ireland)

SCOTLAND
Dundee
William Low & Co
(Scotland)
Edinburgh
Peter Green
J E Hogg
Justerini & Brooks
Raeburn Fine
Wines
Valvona & Crolla
Cockburns of
Leith
Fife
J A Glass
Glasgow
The Ubiquitous
Chip
Isle of Bute
Bute Wines
Moray
Gordon & McPhail
Perth
Matthew Gloag &
Son

WALES
Clwyd
Rioja Wine
Company
Dyfed
A Case Of Wine
Llandudno
Terry Platt
Bridgend
David Baker
South Glamorgan
Ballantynes of
Cowbridge
Swansea
CPA's Wine

CHANNEL
ISLANDS
Guernsey
Sommelier Wine
Co

THIS YEAR

In a corrupt world, it's good to live in a country with an honest government whose Chancellor freely admits that he's going to go on stinging us every time we buy a bottle of wine. Until so many of us do our booze-buying across the Channel that the Treasury begins to feel the pinch. And that's why, unlike the Danes, whose masters are reducing their duty rates, we are sentenced to go on paying more for our wine than almost any other country in Europe. Unless of course we have the time and wherewithal to go shopping in France where, as true patriots, we now have the choice of spending our francs with Sainsbury, Tesco, the Wine Society, Marco's and East Enders.

Meanwhile, back home, posters vigorously urge us to turn in those friendly bootleggers who are so heartily welcomed in housing estates and car boot sales throughout the land. For my part, I'm glad the police and customs officers have so few other calls on their time.

GOLIATH 2 DAVID 0

This year, however, there was some suspiciously cheap wine *legally* on sale. How did some of Britain's biggest retailers profitably contrive to sell bottles of wine at £1.99 and £2.19 a throw when the Chancellor's duty and VAT, shipping, bottles, corks and labels all add up to at least £1.75 before the producer takes a single penny for the stuff we are supposed to drink?

The answer lay in a price war which led the supermarketeers to behave like Casablanca carpet salesmen. What good this did them individually it's impossible to say; it certainly didn't do much for the small independent merchants whose number this year shrank still further. Whatever the reasons Winecellars had for selling out to a major Italian wholesaler, at least the transaction left the award-winning specialist in operation. Two other award-winners, the Fulham Road Wine Centre and The Hermitage, simply gave up the struggle against discounting giants and cross-Channel trade.

The point to be made about those cheap supermarket wines is that they weren't bad. And that will be my enduring memory of 1994: a year full of 'not bad' wines and disappointingly light on good, interesting ones. Looking back over hundreds of notes, I seem to have tasted a long series of wines labelled 'Chardonnay', 'Sauvignon' and 'Dry White' which were almost interchangeable. For every over-oaked Aussie blockbuster with which some wine drinkers claim to be bored, there are countless wines which defy you to detect any kind of taste. For less than a fiver, you really have to go looking for flavour.

Often, while struggling to keep awake as I sniffed, sipped and spat my way through yet another anonymous set of wines, I recalled the words of Lalou Bize Leroy, for many years one of Burgundy's best merchants: 'I detest the "not bad" wines – I'd much rather have to deal with the frankly horrible. At least they taste of something.'

But nobody really wants to drink horrible wines, however interesting their flavours. Despite the risk of boredom, we should be grateful for the way in which vinegar has more or less been banished from British wine racks.

The improvement in quality can be directly attributed to the efforts made by the buyers for Britain's major retail chains. Unlike their Gallic counterparts who shamelessly buy and sell *Appellation Contrôlée* 'labels', almost irrespective of their quality, retailers like Sainsbury's, Victoria Wine and even Spar and Kwik Save really do scour the world for the best value they can find. And when their traditional producers fail to deliver the goods, they almost always know a man who can.

HUGH RYMAN'S FLYING CIRCUS

That man's name might well be Hugh Ryman. But it could just as easily be Kym Milne, Jacques Lurton, Nick Butler, Peter Bright, Don Lewis or Geoff Merrill – all of whom last year worked as flying winemakers in one country or another. The idea of asking a supplier to let you make your own wine using his grapes, presses and tanks is as bizarre as proposing to your local Italian restaurant that you cook your own osso bucco in his kitchen, but money talks. It is a rare cooperative that will turn down the offer of labour-free cash.

In 1993, there were at least 120 flying winemakers at work in Southern France, Bordeaux, Burgundy, Spain, Italy, Chile, Argentina, South Africa and throughout Eastern Europe, flitting from one country to another like the conference-going academics in a David Lodge novel. The results are already impressing the wine world – in the way that the first Skoda with operational brakes and steering impressed motoring journalists. As Liz Robertson of Safeway says, a flying winemaker wine may not be brilliant but it is almost invariably better than the stuff it replaces.

These vinous mercenaries are now as big a part of professional wine buying as disposable nappies are to a home with a new baby. And for much the same reasons: they are reliable and hygienic. Or, as one of them wrily explained after a tough day in a southern French winery: 'All you have to do to improve the quality of the wine in the average European cooperative winery by about 50% is wash the pipes through and keep the grapes fresh and clean. Until these guys get the message for themselves I'll not be short of work.'

In Italy, as Geoff Merrill one of the best-known winemakers in South Australia's McLaren Vale discovered when making wine for Sainsbury's, 'lunch' can last for hours - during which newly picked grapes are routinely left to cook in the sun. His compatriot Nick Butler suffered a similar culture clash in Spain when he wanted to work during the weekend. 'Here', he was told, 'it is not customary'. 'In Australia', he replied, 'it bloody well is. We work 24 hours a day during the harvest when necessary. Maybe that's why our wines sell for higher prices in Britain than yours.'

But that's only part of the story. It is no accident that so many of the flying winemakers are Australian. Their experience in an industry where Value For Money and Quality-Control are joint monarchs teaches them to do the best they can with the grapes they are given, irrespective of the price of the finished wine. In this, they are very different both from the Californians who treat their cheapest wines with as much respect as Marco Pierre White would afford an order for baked beans – and from many of the Europeans who would rather blame nature for not letting them make a better wine than put in the extra effort themselves.

In Bergerac, in September 1993, I stood with a young Australian looking at a vatful of newly picked grapes. It was a sorry sight, with almost as much rot and rainwater as fruit. 'Back home', he said, 'we wouldn't dream of turning stuff like that into wine. We probably wouldn't even distil it for industrial alcohol.' But he'd been brought half way across the globe to do a job and, 12 months later, there's Bergerac on sale which proves that unlike others in that region, he managed to turn a rotten sow's ear into a reasonably acceptable cotton purse.

Elsewhere, throughout France, a great many producers were less successful. But all too often the local authorities turned a blind eye to the poor quality of the wines set before them and happily gave them the stamp of *Appellation Contrôlée* approval. Thus raising the heat beneath the simmering argument over what is supposed to be the mark of quality for a French wine.

APPELLATION SCHMAPPELLATION

A few months after that trip to Bergerac, I spent a couple of hours with Alain Berger, a (very) civil servant who readily – if conservatively – agrees that at least 15% of *Appellation Contrôlée* wine is sub-standard. He ought to know; he runs the *Institut National des Appellations d'Origine Contrôlée* which more or less governs the French wine industry.

M. Berger would like to improve the quality of France's *Appellation Contrôlée* wine and intends to do so by means of what he opaquely calls 'intellectual terrorism'.

While we await the results – or at least an explanation of this very Gallic concept – the words *Appellation Contrôlée* remain as trustworthy as a politician's promise. In France, consumers may still believe that bottles labelled Bordeaux, Côtes du Rhône and Mâcon Blanc are implicitly better than 'Vin de Pays d'Oc' made from the same grape varieties. In this country, we know better. Which is why Sainsbury's Aussie-made Vin de Pays d'Oc Sauvignon sells for more than its Bordeaux Blanc.

BRAVE NEW WORLD 1

Today, despite the effort – and the hard cash – that has been put into persuading us all to drink *Appellation Contrôlée* wines, the focus of interest in Britain remains on Vins de Pays in general and Vin de Pays d'Oc in particular, for the simple reason that this is where the value and the flavour are most easily found. If you want Chardonnay, Sauvignon, Cabernet or Shiraz, they're all so plentiful that, this year, even the makers of Piat d'Or acknowledged the fact with Vin de Pays Merlot, Cabernet and Chardonnay. None of these was brilliant; all were a million times better than the vin de table previously to be found in those skittle-shaped bottles.

But that's not all. Over the last few years, other varieties have been planted which will give Languedoc Roussillon even more of a marketing edge. Until now, if you wanted to experience the extraordinary floral flavour of the Viognier grape, you had to dig deeply into your pocket to buy a bottle of Condrieu or Château-Grillet, two of France's priciest white wines.

Today those two Rhône appellations have lost their hold on the variety; now Georges Duboeuf and Robert Skalli have planted it by the mile – and produced inexpensive wines which would put Chateau-Grillet to shame even if it didn't cost four times as much.

The last three harvests have not been easy in France. While there have been a few honourable exceptions in the Rhône and Bordeaux, the only region which can claim a success in the early 1990s was Burgundy where 1992 was a truly great vintage. The people who bought these wines when they first hit the streets will not be disappointed – whether they drink them young, or in a few years.

Whether the same can be said for the buyers of 1993 *en primeur* claret is another question. While many chateaux did produce good wines, the zeal shown by British merchants to to sell them in barrel smacked more of an eagerness to pull in a bit of cash than a sincere effort to supply their customers with good value for money.

DEUTSCHLAND UNTER ALLES

Despite harvests in 1992 and 1993 which should have yielded some of Europe's better wines, Germany, like the South Africa of the 1970s and 1980s, still demonstrates what happens when politicians subsidize lazy, inefficient wine farmers in return for their votes. When Sainsbury's proudly set out 200 wines for the press, at the beginning of the day, there were just two Germans. But then the buyers tasted them – and withdrew both as faulty. At Safeway there were some German wines – made at the supposedly state of the art St. Ursula winery by the Aryan-looking but fully British Hugh Ryman, who was given the brief to produce an Australian Riesling.

Even when some of the very best estates do make the kind of wine I want to buy, they use enough sulphur dioxide to fumigate the Augean stables. I have no nostalgia for my schooldays and certainly don't wish to be reminded of chemistry lessons every time I pull the cork from a £7.50 bottle of wine. Honourable exceptions to the rule persevere and the new generation of producers like Dr Loosen, Kurt Darting, Müller Catoir and Karl Lingenfelder offer hope for the future, but two facts remain: few serious bottles of German wine are sold to Britons of under 40 and the best way to sell a Riesling is to say it comes from Down Under.

It cannot be much fun for Germany's producers and importers to face this kind of criticism yet again, let alone to witness the excitement with which Austria's winemakers and their wines are now being greeted in Britain. For the moment at least, the number of wines being imported is laughably small and prices ludicrously high, but the anti-freeze scandal of a decade ago is long forgotten. This was the year when Alois Kracher did sufficiently well in the International Wine Challenge to become the first ever Austrian white winemaker of the year.

MANANA FROM HEAVEN

While the Germans languish in their vinous doldrums the ghost of that implacable economist Adam Smith has been busy at work among the Spaniards and Italians. In Spain, until very recently, conservatism ruled with an iron hand. Visitors – even visitors with active tastebuds and loaded cheque books – found little readiness among producers to cast off the bad habits of generations. Change was coming, they were told. Tomorrow. Or the day after that.

Today, the insult to Hispanic pride caused by the arrival of a squadron of flying winemakers has forced at least a few to listen. So far this is an activity which has yet to exert widespread appeal, but, for the first time new styles of wine and examples from new producers are arriving in British shops. Mañana really does seem to be at hand.

Mind you, like a magician producing a rabbit from nowhere, the Spanish revolutionaries are rarely making their new wines in regions like Rioja or even the supposedly up-and-coming Penedes. For a taste of the future, go to Navarra, to Ribera del Duero or even to the former vinous wasteland of Valdepeñas. Despite the efforts of producers like Martinez Bujanda and Remelluri, Rioja will have to fight hard to keep its present role as Spain's top wine area.

(NOT SO) DOLCE VITA

There were parallels in Italy. One of the trophy winners in the 1994 International Wine Challenge, the red which beat a long list of big names from Tuscany and Piedmont, came from Sardinia. Some of the best inexpensive Italians on sale this year were made in Puglia, a region which once had as much to do with drinkable wine as most of Italy's recent political leaders have to do with financial probity.

Adam Smith hit Italy hard, teaching its winemakers laws of economics they had happily ignored for years. Until very recently a seemingly endless queue of wine drinkers had seemed ready to pay almost any price for a bottle of red or white, provided it came in a smart bottle and with the requisite amount of hype.

Over the last couple of years, while Italian voters began to notice the flaws in their government, they started to realise that, once you stripped them of their designer-chic packaging, many wines represented the same sort of value for money as strawberries at Wimbledon. Even in New York, sales of $50 Tuscan reds slowed to a trickle and in Rome, restaurant customers thought twice before spending a day's wages on a bottle.

The result is good news for anyone interested in flavour; Italian wines represent better value today than they have for many years.

BRAVE NEW WORLD 2

In Eastern Europe, while the flying winemakers gadded about, making inexpensive reds and whites, in Hungary, several teams of heavy-hitting French investors collaborated and competed in Tokay, revealing one of the big differences in attitude between the French and the British. When we go looking for vinous challenges, we tend to explore regions like Moldova and southern France where there is no proven history of quality winemaking. The French believe in 'heritage'; when they leave home, they are happiest in places like Tokay with centuries of winemaking history and a ready-made reputation as the 'wine of kings'. Which explains why Gallic cash is creating impressive results in Hungary far more quickly than it has in places like California, Chile, Australia and New Zealand, where it is easy to imagine that they have not really tried to achieve any kind of greatness. (If you don't believe

me, just try Lafite Rothschild's white Los Vascos from Chile or the
wines Moët & Chandon make in California and South America.)

BRAVE NEW WORLDS 3, 4, 5 AND 6

In front of me, there's a bottle of wine from discounters Kwik Save. At
first and even second glance, it looks just like an inexpensive Aussie
red. The name ('Steep Ridge') the grape varieties (Grenache-Shiraz)
and the water-colour of red-soil hillsides beneath an ochre sky are all as
Antipodean as Crocodile Dundee. The only incongruous note is struck
by the words 'Vin de Pays d'Oc'. It's just like the range of budget
British-made hi fi one of Britain's biggest high street shops launched a
few years ago; they gave it a Japanese-sounding name – because that's
what people buying hi fi are looking for. And when they want a
reliable wine it had better be Australian.

In the US, if a wine needs that kind of cachet, the word that has to go
on the label, thanks to one of the world's most effective marketing
campaigns, is Napa. On this side of the water, we are less receptive to
hype. E & J Gallo have proved that marketing works by spending an
estimated £3,000,000 to persuade us to drink their – at best –
unexceptional wines, but they have still had to cut prices.

Sadly for all those great winemakers in California whose wines I'd
love to see more readily on sale here, far too many British wine
drinkers now imagine that Gallo's bottles are typical of the state as a
whole - a situation which will hardly be helped by the announcement
that California is to cut its promotional budget in the UK by almost
half. Only a cynic would wonder about the influence E&J Gallo
California's biggest producer, has on such matters.

Ironically, a much-needed piece of encouragement for California's
other producers may come in 1995, when Hugh Ryman hits the world
with his first effort at transatlantic flying winemaking.

If it seems strange that the high-tech Californians need help from
outsiders, it's worth taking a look at the impact the flying circus
members have had in South Africa. After the years of isolation when
South Africa's wines were either ignored or over-praised, depending
largely on the politics of the taster, the Cape producers really are
beginning to make wines of international quality. Judged objectively,
most of South Africa's wines are far from ready to compete with those
of Australia and New Zealand, but for many wine drinkers they enjoy
a stylistic advantage over the Antipodes. At their best and worst, they
are more European in style. Bad examples – especially the reds – are
full of winemaking faults the most stubborn Italians and Spaniards
grew out of years ago; when they get it right, however, Cape producers
like Danie de Wet make wines of a subtlety rarely achieved Down
Under.

Chile, by contrast, still has to recall some of the lessons it learned and
forgot years ago. Maybe Chile's customers in North America demand
tough, tannic, inexpensive reds; we don't need them. Any more than
we want the sweet Chardonnays favoured by many producers in
California. Chile's potential is for producing great value, accessible
wines pitched in style between the Old and New Worlds. Fortunately,
there's a growing band of new-wave producers like Cono Sur,
Casablanca and Viallard who seem to have got that message.

THE GRAPEVINE ...

WINE AND HEALTH

Rabbits thrive on wine. And that's official, according to researchers in New York who gave a number of them the same kind of diet as most humans: plenty of fatty foods, and drinks ranging from red and white wine to water, beer and whisky. Apparently, the red-sipping bunnies suffered fewer than half as many aortic and coronary lesions as the water-drinkers.

The INSERM health institute in Lyon reports that half as many cheese-loving Frenchmen and women die of heart disease as the Anglo-Saxons who daily debate whether to put skimmed or semi-skimmed in their coffee.

It has already been proved that red wine raises the levels of (good) HDL cholesterol while reducing those of (bad) LDL cholesterol, making blood clots less likely. But that's not all it can do; research in the UK suggests that wine can deter the common cold and according to the American Cancer Society, red wine drinkers are subject to 15-20% fewer deaths *from all causes*...

But what's the ideal dosage? In Italy where they've studied 15,000 people for over 20 years, the prescription is a quarter of a bottle a day, a slightly more generous figure than the BMA weekly maximum of 21 and 14 'units' for men and women respectively. Though whether the stuff in the glass should be a 14% Aussie Shiraz or a 11.5% Bardolino is still far from clear. I guess they'll just have to go on subjecting rabbits to the good life.

ORGANIC WINES

What could be more organic than fermented grape juice? Even when winegrowers used bull's blood and fish scales as fining agents, no one could accuse them of not being organic. It was only when they began to fight mould, pests and bacteria that 'chemicals' began to be used. For the most part the products involved were far more harmless than many of the ones used by other farmers and food processors. Even so, the idea of winemakers as unscrupulous alchemists persists. Hence the growing interest in organic wines.

Sadly, good, organic intentions are no substitute for winemaking skills. It is no accident that the winners at the Safeway/WINE Magazine Organic Wine Challenge were all from the New World. Nor that some of the best genuinely organic winemakers are very happy not to join any kind of organic association or bandwagon.

A selection of top class organic wines: Fetzer Bonterra Chardonnay, California 1991 (SAF*); Penfolds Chardonnay-Sauvignon Blanc 1993 (TH*); The Millton Vineyard Semillon-Chardonnay, New Zealand 1993 (SAF*); Botobolar Red, Mudgee, Australia 1992 (AUC*); Domaine Richeaume Syrah Côtes de Provence (SAF*); Tesco Organic White, Entre Deux Mers (TO*) For codes see page 12

LEARNING ABOUT WINE

Following the closure of the Fulham Road Wine Centre and the abandonment of Roberson's courses, Londoners who want to become clued-up winos have had rather fewer options open to them this year. As we go to press, the Wine Treasury proposes to launch a series of tastings focusing on the wines of France and WINE Magazine has plans to run courses and dinners. For the moment, however, the only accessible 'fun' courses we can recommend are the ones run by Leith's School of Food and Wine.

For those who want more classical training, Michael Schuster runs first class technical courses while Christie's and Sotheby's hold emphatically serious tastings usually hosted by Masters of Wine.

Out of London, Lay & Wheeler now run Saturday Wine Trails which are educative bargains at £6.50 a time and Château Loudenne and Château Gratien both boast UK-trained lecturers. Anyone wanting to join the wine trade, however, should make for the Wine & Spirit Education Trust, where you can take the basic (very basic) 'Certificate', the useful 'Higher Certificate' and the testing two-part 'Diploma'. Only after you have cleared all three hurdles may you try the real high jump, the Master of Wine written and tasting exams. But be warned: it's now a two-year course, and fewer than 200 people have earned this qualification in three decades. Incidentally, if you know of good local authority courses and lecturers – then let us know.

> Recommended wine courses: Christie's Wine Course (Tel 071- 839 9060; Fax 071-839 1611); Ecole de Vin, Chateau Loudenne (Tel 010 33 56 09 05 03; Fax 010 33 56 09 02 87); German Wine Academy (Tel 010 39 61 31 28 29 50); Grants of St James's (Tel 081-542 5879; mobile 0850 995718); International Wine School (Tel 0582 713290); Lay & Wheeler (Tel 0206 764446; Fax 0206 564488); Leith's School of Food and Wine (Tel 071-229 0177; Fax 071-937 5257); Michael Schuster (Tel 071-254 9734); Sotheby's (Tel 071-924 3287); Fax 071-493 8080); Wine & Spirit Education Trust (Tel 071-236 3551; Fax 071-329 0298).

TASTINGS

For many people, a course is quite unnecessary, as much can be learned by attending tutored tastings given by wine merchants, writers or winemakers. Whether you attend a structured class or simply a tutored tasting, what you get out of it will depend largely on your teacher. The following people are especially worth travelling some way to hear.

> Liz Berry MW, Michael Broadbent MW, Tony Brown MW, Nick Clarke MW, Oz Clarke, Clive Coates MW, Nancy Gilchrist, David Gleave MW, Richard Harvey MW, Jane Hunt MW, Patrick McGrath MW, Richard Mayson, Maggie McNie MW, Charles Metcalfe, David Molyneux-Berry MW, Angela Muir MW, Jethro Probes, John Radford, Michael Schuster, Steven Spurrier, Serena Sutcliffe MW, Richard Hobson MW Pamela Vandyke Price, John Vaughan Hughes MW, Roger Voss.

THE CASE FOR JOINING A WINE CLUB

Before joining a club, check carefully how much you are going to have to pay and what you are being offered in return. In particular, beware of so-called clubs run by merchants as part of their business; often these offer little if anything one could not find for nothing elsewhere.

The Sunday Times Wine Club offers an enjoyable annual tasting in London and good wine tours, but very few vinous bargains for those whose only contact with the club is by mail. The Wine Society, which genuinely belongs to its members, is worth joining, if only to benefit from its depot in northern France. If, however, you want a club whose existence is not geared towards purchasing, there are all sorts of local wine appreciation societies that organise tastings presented by merchants and producers, plus theme dinners. In addition to those listed below, clubs with vacancies for new members are listed in the diary pages of both *WINE* and *Decanter* magazines.

The following mostly meet monthly, charging £15-20 per year membership (those in italics are associated with wine merchants).

Amersham Wine Appreciation Society (Tel 0494 721961); Association of Wine Cellarmen (Tel 081-944 5979); Bramhope Wine Tasting Group (Tel 0532 666322); Cambridge Food and Wine Society (Tel 0954 780438); Carlisle Wine Tasting Society (Tel 0228 576711); Chandlers Cross Wine Society (Tel 0923 264718); *Châteaux Wines* (Tel 0454 613959); Chiltern Wine Society (Tel 0582 414803); Civil Service Wine Society (Tel 0634 848345); Cleveland Wine Society (Tel 0287 624459); Coopers Hill Wine Club; (Tel 0628 25577); Cornwall Wine Tasting Group (Tel 0726 882616); Eastbourne District Wine Society (Tel 0323 725528); *Evington Wine Appreciation Society* (Tel 0533 314760); Garforth Wine Group (Tel 0532 666322); Guild of Sommeliers (Tel 061 928 0852); Harrogate Medical Wine Society (Tel 0423 884426); Hatfield Wine Apreciation Society (Tel 0707 263129); Herefordshire Fine Wine Society (Tel 0432 275656); Hertfordshire Fine Wine Society (Tel 0582 794867); Hextable Wine Club (Tel 0732 823345); Leicester Grand Union Wine Society (Tel 0533 871662); Lincoln Wine Society (Tel 0522 680388); Lymington Wine Society (Tel 0590 677498); *Maidenhead Wine Circle* (Tel 0628 25577); Newcastle Upon Tyne Wine Appreciation Group (Tel 0921 264 3489); North East Wine Tasting Society (Tel 091 438 4107); North Hampshire Wine Society (Tel 0734 815358); Opimian Wine School (Tel 0625 611542); *Penfolds Wine Club* (Tel 081-200 5152); Perth Area Wine Tasters (Tel 0738 233308); Petersham Wine Society (Tel 0932 348720); Rochester Wine Society (Tel 0634 848345); Roseberry Wine & Food Society (Tel 0325 721071); Sittingbourne Fine Wine Society (Tel 0795 478818); *Treasury Wine Club* (Tel 071-371 7131); *The Vintner* (Tel 0923 51585; Fax 0923 251585); *Vin de Garde/ Vintage Expectations* (Tel 0372 463251); Welland Vale Wine and Food Society (Tel 0604 811993); Wessex Wine Society (Tel 0985 214578); West Country Wine Club (Tel 0209 715765); West Hampstead Wine Club (Tel 071-794 3926); Whitewater Valley Wine Society (Tel 0252 844948); The Wine and Dine Society (Tel 081-673 4439; Fax 071-274 9484); The Winetasters (Tel 081-997 1252).

BUYING AT AUCTION

As we went to press in the Summer of 1994, a prominent wine merchant-turned-wine-writer sold the contents of his cellar at Christies. To the surprise of many of his former colleagues, the wines sold well, in many instances at ludicrously high prices. The success of that sale and the enthusiasm of the Hong Kong businessman who helped to make it such a success, however, are not typical of the market as a whole. Despite the arrival of easier times, there are still plenty of Lloyds 'names' who are likely to become unwilling cellar-sellers, and restaurants and merchants who will be calling. All of which should make auction houses a better than ever source of all sorts of wine. But don't get carried away. It's still worth keeping a check on what you end up paying per bottle. Auctions are not inevitably cheaper than wine merchants.

For details of the 'right' prices for top-flight wines, check WINE Magazine's Fine Wine section. Remember, too, that a 'bargain' £50 case of Chablis can be less of a snip by the time you have added the 10% buyer's premium, £1 a bottle duty and 17.5% VAT – and driven to Edinburgh to collect it.

Among fine wines today, my tip would be to go for the 1985s, which have always been undervalued, and the best 1986s and 1988s – provided you are prepared to gamble on both vintages losing their currently unattractive toughness. Fairly priced 1982s are worth buying, as are 1978s and 1979s from good chateaux, but I would be wary of 1983s, many of which are already looking distinctly too ready for drinking.

Auction Houses: Christie's Auction House (Wine Department) (Tel 071-839 9060; Fax 071-839 1611); Sotheby's (Tel 071-924 3287; Fax 071-924 3287); Bigwood Auctioneers (Tel 0789 269 415; Fax 0789 294168); Lacy Scott (Tel 0284 763531; Fax 0284 704713); Lithgow Sons and Partners (Tel 0642 710158; Fax 0642 712641); Phillips (Tel 0865 723524; Fax 0865 791064); Jean Pierre et Fils (Tel 0273 308 422).

Specialists in fine, rare and old wines: Bibendum, The Wine Society; Laytons, Lay & Wheeler; Thos Peatling; Turville Valley, Farr Vintners and Berry Bros & Rudd (see The Merchants) and Pat Simon (Tel 081-455 8255; Fax 081-458 6825).

BUYING EN PRIMEUR/INVESTING IN WINE

If you imagined that buying wine as a 'future' was any kind of wise investment, we have one word of advice: don't. At least not if you want to avoid the plight of the people who invested tens of thousands of their hard-earned pounds in the late and much-lamented Hungerford Wine Co.

Even those who have restricted their dealings to firms with stronger foundations (including members of a recently constituted group called 'The Bunch' will have almost certainly noticed that they might have been better advised to wait until the same wines made their way onto the shelves of Oddbins Fine Wine shops. If you absolutely must put your money into wine, either go for otherwise hard-to-find wines such as the 1992 white Burgundies that you are sure to enjoy, whatever happens to their market value – or stick to 'blue chip' first growths which always seem to find buyers.

WINE TOURS AND WINE BREAKS

With the shaky climb out of recession, wine tours and weekends have begun to attract greater interest. Wine tours and weekends are rather like any other holiday organised for a group of apparently like-minded people. They can be enormously successful – or they can be extraordinarily tedious.

In our experience, enjoyment depends only partly on one's fellow travellers. How well the trip has been organised has a much greater bearing. Make sure you know the name of the 'expert' leading the trip and, in the case of tours, the producers to be visited. A quality-conscious tour operator will take the trouble to choose high-quality winemakers; while travel agents who are playing at wine tours will often opt for 'big names' irrespective of their worth. Before making your booking, be sure to check that you are protected through some kind of bond.

And if you fancy setting up your own tour, it may be worth asking a wine merchant from whom you buy if they can help with letters of introduction. Some may even be organising their own trips – as Oddbins did to Australia during the 1994 harvest.

From personal experience, we can recommend the following: Alternative Travel Group (now comprising World Wine Tours) (Tel 0865 310399; Fax 0865 310299); Arblaster & Clarke (Tel 0730 893344; Fax 0730 892888) and The Sunday Times Wine Club (see The Stockists). Other companies and hotels include: Accompanied Cape Tours (Tel 0531 660210); Blackheath Wine Trails (Tel 081-463 0012); California Wine Country (Tel 0425 655022); Chateau Latuc, Cahors (Tel 010 33 65 36 58 63); Chateau de Malitourne (Tel 0440 730263); Chinon Loire Valley Cottages (Tel 0524 823777); Classic Wine Tours (Tel 0803 299292; Fax 0803 292008); Ian Dickson Travel (Tel 031 556 6777); Facet Travel (Tel 0825 732266; Fax 0825 733330); Francophiles (Tel 0272 621975); Friendship Travel (Tel 0483 273355); French Alps (081 670 6885); Gourmet Espionage (Tel 0379 71234); Knights of Languedoc (Tel 071-704 0589); Moswin Tours Ltd (Tel 0533 714982; Fax 0533 716016); Tanglewood Wine Tours (Tel 0932 348720; Fax 0932 350861); Travel Club of Upminster (Tel 0708 227260); Walking with Wines (Tel 0432 840649); Vacances Cuisine (Tel 010 33 94 04 49 77); Vinescapes (Tel 0903 744279); Vinidoc (Tel 010 33 67 93 84 65); Vintage Wine Tours (Tel 0225 315834; Fax 0225 446093); Walking With Wine (Tel 0432 840649); Wessex Continental Travel (Tel 0752 846880); Wine Trails (Tel 081-463 0012; Fax 081-463 0011) .

Hotels running wine weekends include Chewton Glen Hotel (Tel 0425 275341); Gleneagles, with Jancis Robinson (Tel 0764 62231; fax 0764 62134); Hollington House Hotel (Tel 0635 255100); Imperial Hotel (Tel 0493 851113); Millers House Hotel (Tel 0969 22630); Mynd House Hotel (Tel 0694 722212); Norton House Hotel (Tel 031 333 1275; Fax 031 333 5305); Porth Avallen Hotel (Tel 0726 812183); Studley Priory Hotel (Tel 0865 351203; Fax 0865 351613).

STARTING A CELLAR

A few simple rules: avoid areas in which the temperature varies – constant warmth is better than the variations in, say, a kitchen. Avoid areas that are too dry; well-insulated cupboards and attics can make ideal cellars, but be sure to keep the humidity up with a sponge left in a bowl of water. Try to find a space where there is at least some air movement; cut air holes in cupboards if necessary. If the area you have chosen is damp, remember not to store wine in cardboard boxes. It sounds obvious, but even experienced wine buffs have lost wine by letting it fall from soggy boxes.

Spiral Cellars sell (and also install, if you like) a purpose-built cellar kit that can be sunk into the floor of your kitchen, garage or garden. Wine racks, custom-built to fit into awkward shaped areas, are available from Majestic Wine Warehouses and from most helpful wine merchants.

To buy direct, contact RTA Wine Racks (Tel 0328 78666; Fax 0328 78667); The Wine Rack Co. (Tel 0243 552710); A & W Moore (Tel 0602 607012; Fax 0602 491308); Spiral Cellars Ltd (Tel 0372 842692; Fax 0372 360142).

A simple exercise book can make a perfect cellar-book. Simply rule it up to allow space for you to indicate where and when you bought each wine; the price you paid; its position in your racks; when you opened each bottle and the guests to whom you served it, together with tasting notes. Most home computers will enable you to log the same information electronically.

If you would prefer not to store your wine at home, there is always the option of cellaring it with the merchants from whom you bought it (see our Merchants' Services chart), provided you ensure your stock is clearly marked. Or you can rent space at the following cellars, all of whom are steadily broadening the range of services they offer very effectively.

Prime Wine Cellars (Tel 071-613 0763; Fax 071-613 0765); Smith & Taylor (Tel 071-627 5070; Fax 071-622 8235); Abacus (Tel 081-991 9717; Fax 081-991 9611); or Octavian (Tel 081-853 5551; Fax 081-858 4402).

GLASSES AND VINOUS GIFTS

There is so much nonsense talked about the 'right' glasses for the 'right' wine that I am tempted not to discuss the subject at all. My advice is simply to use any kind of clear glass whose rim has a smaller circumference than its bowl, and which is large enough to hold more than a few mouthfuls.

For real luxury, however, there are no better glasses than those produced by Riedel. They're available from the Conran Shop (071-589 7401) or Bibendum (see The Stockists) but unfortunately cost an arm and a leg. More affordable are Cristal d'Arques' wine taster-designed glasses (from Roberson, see The Stockists). As an inveterate glass-breaker, though, I buy Royal Leerdam's bargain Bouquet range. Very happily used by tasters at the 1994 WINE International Wine Challenge, they can be bought from The Wine Glass Company (Tel 0234 721300; Fax 0234 720759).

> For gifts try Hugh Johnson's ultra-smart St James's shop (Tel 071-491 4912; Fax 071-493 0602), Harrods, The Wine Society(see The Stockists) or Birchgrove Accessories (0483 285369; Fax 0483 285360). Richard Stanford (Tel 071-836 1321) stocks old wine books; Richard Kihl (Tel 071-586 3838) is a good source of antiques and curiosities.

CORKSCREWS

Every year I test at least half a dozen 'new' corkscrews, almost every one of which ends up gathering dust at the back of a drawer. The best corkscrew is still made by Screwpull (Tel 0264 358036; Fax 0264 356777) in a variety of styles from the simple 'Spin-handle' (our favourite) to the ultra-sophisticated (and ultra-pricy) lever model. Widely available.

WINE PRESERVATION DEVICES

The Vacuvin vacuum pump (Tel 0264 332821; Fax 0264 358036), though economical, seems to suck fruit out of some wines. I prefer the 'Winesaver' from Drylaw House (Tel 031 558 3666), which keeps wine fresh in the same way as most modern wineries, by creating a layer of harmless, heavier-than-air inert gas which sits on the wine surface and prevents oxidation. It was once again used to great effect in the 1994 International Wine Challenge.

CHILL OUT

Ten minutes in a bucket full of water and ice will chill down most bottles very efficiently. As an alternative, there is the widely available 'Rapid Ice' a £5.99 foil jacket which lives in the freezer and which will cool bottles in six minutes and keep them that way for up to three hours. It works better on table wines than fizz, but is a handy means of keeping the chill on a wine you are taking with you to a dinner or for a picnic. (Rapid Ice (Tel 0264 332821; Fax 0264 356777). Professionals for whom it may be worth spending £700 to chill bottles in two minutes, should also consider the Chilla (0850 264582).

WINE IN PUBS

I've always admired people with the courage to order a glass of wine in a pub and risk being given a deep golden 'Blancs de Blancs' only distinguishable from sherry by the size of the measure. Pubs don't have to serve bad wine; after all, they have come round to real beer, a choice of malt whiskies and even edible food; which is why, with this edition, we are launching a search for Britain's best wine pubs. Our list includes the cream of the crop so far, but we'd be grateful to hear from readers and publicans about pubs we should include in the 1995 Guide.

> Beetle & Wedge, Moulsford, Oxfordshire; The Cornish Arms, Pendoggett, Cornwall; The Crown, Southwold, Suffolk; La Galoche, Tunbridge Wells, Dorset; The Green Man, Toot Hill, Essex; The New Inn, Cerne Abbas, Dorset; The Nobody Inn, Doddiscombsleigh, Devon; The Plough, Blackbrook, Surrey; The Red Lion, Steeple Aston, Oxfordshire; The Royal Oak, Yattendon, Cornwall; The Wykeham Arms, Winchester, Hampshire.

BUYING ABROAD

While one of the main *raison d'êtres* of the Guide has always been as a source of information on where to buy wine in Britain, given the ludicrous attitude of the UK government, it would be journalistically unethical for me not to point out that anyone buying a few cases of wine in Britain rather than France is missing the opportunity to save a considerable amount of money.

With excise duty at £1-2 (it's higher on fizz), it is worthwhile taking one of those cheap tickets over or under the water. But why stop in Calais, one of France's unloveliest towns? Why not increase the savings and have fun driving to the vineyards, thus denying at least one middle-man his cut? British duty-free rules allow you to bring in as much wine as you like (none of that nonsense about 10 cases per person) provided it is all for your and your friends' consumption (a stick-on red nose may help convince customs officers) and that local taxes have been paid in France.

If you have no alternative to shopping on the French coast, tread carefully. To play really safe, head for Marco's, Sainsbury's, Tesco, Richard Harvey or the Wine Society, all of whom will sell you wines you could have seen and bought in Britain. Buying in French supermarkets is more foolhardy – unless they are having a special 'wine fairs' in which big name Bordeaux and Champagnes are often sold off at huge discounts. Otherwise make it a rule to taste before you splash out.

> To dial from the UK use pre-fix 010 33. **Boulogne:** The Grape Shop *85-87 Rue Victor Hugo, (Tel 21-33 92 30);* **Calais:** Le Chais, *40 Rue de Phalfbourg, Centre Fradère,* Champagne Charlie's *14 Rue de Condstadt (Tel 21 97 96 49),* East Enders *Rue des Garennes, ZI des Dunes (Tel 21-34 53 33),* Marco's Calais Beer & Wine Co *Rue de Judée, Zone Marcel Doret (Tel 21-97 63 00; Fax 21-97 88 56)* PG *Ave Roger Salengro (Tel 21-34 17 34)/Rte St Honoré (Tel 21-34 65 98)* Royal Champagne *9 Rue Andre Gerschell (Tel 21-96 51 62),* Le Terroir *29 Rue des Fontinettes (Tel 21-36 34 66);* **Cherbourg:** La Maison du Vin *71 Avenue Carnot (Tel 33-43 39 79);* **Hesdin** The Wine Society *Rue Fressin (Tel 21-81 61 70).*

WINE WITH FOOD

Who needs rules? Isn't all that stuff outdated? Surely all you have to do is introduce your favourite food to a bottle of wine you know and like? Well, yes and no. Just as the notion of marrying off your best friends can frequently end in tears, there are some combinations of wines and foods which will always clash violently – on the other hand some dishes and bottles were positively made to make music together. Here 's what you should know before you start matchmaking...

SMOKED FISH AND MEAT

Smoked salmon and Champagne might be a cliché – but it is a partnership hard to beat! Light, lemony wines can't handle the distinctive tastes and textures of smoked fish and meat. They need something more robust, like fat oaky Chardonnays or good fino sherries. Smoked meats are well matched with light fruity reds or warm spicy rosés.

LIGHT STARTERS

Delicately flavoured dishes such as vegetable terrines need the gentle touch of a soft white, such as a St Veran, while patés are well suited to fruity reds. Wild Californian concoctions of citrus fruits and leaves are difficult to pair with wine so go for something with good acidity such as the lighter style of Chardonnay or Muscadet; play safe with sherry, or go a little frivolous with a glass of fizz.

EGG DISHES

If your dish contains an assertive ingredient such as strong cheese, you'll need something fairly full bodied. Straight eggs like something crisp, such as a Sauvignon, Muscadet, a good English wine, or even a light north Italian number.

WHITE MEAT WITHOUT SAUCE

Grilled or roasted chicken, pork or veal will happily partner a range of wines from White Burgundy to Cabernet Sauvignon, but to bring out the best in a plainly cooked duck or goose, choose something fleshy, ripe and fruity.

FISH WITHOUT SAUCE

Delicate dishes are happiest with a light Chardonnay or a Soave with gentle acidity. Oily fish, such as sardines, need the refreshing bite of a good Muscadet or Vinho Verde.

WHITE MEAT OR FISH IN CREAMY SAUCE

Subtle dishes such as salmon in a cream sauce like a fairly soft wine such as an unoaked Chardonnay. Chicken can take on something firmer, perhaps a fresh gooseberryish Sauvignon, or a dry Vouvray.

SHELLFISH

There's no finer match for oysters than a steely Sancerre or Chablis. Richer shellfish enjoys the company of something fruitier. If you like to spice things up with a little aioli or garlic butter on the side, you might fancy a fino sherry or retsina.

WHITE FISH OR FISH IN A PROVENCALE-TYPE SAUCE

New World Chardonnays with strong acidity and freshness are the natural partners for forceful, tangy sauces – or choose a red with strong fruit and some tannin.

RED MEAT

Good, plain roast lamb or beef are often safer with fine light clarets, but rich, saucy numbers cry out for something more powerful. Hearty regional dishes are often happier in the company of familiar local rustic reds.

GAME

The assertiveness of well hung game and venison needs the gutsiness of big Italian and Portuguese reds, Rhônes, Zinfandels or Shirazes; lighter game is better with a fruity red without too much wood: a cru Beaujolais or Merlot-based Bordeaux perhaps?

SPICY FOOD

The intriguing, spicy allure of the classiest Gewürztraminers go arm in arm with Chinese food – or try a demi-sec Loire-style white. Champagne can be interesting with Indian food but, if you really want to play safe, go for ice-cold lager!

CHEESE

The world of cheese and wine is full of excitement and discovery ... so go ahead and experiment. Reds might be more reliable, but white wines are often often more adaptable, especially with fatty and creamy cheeses. For sheer indulgence, introduce a honeyed, late-harvest dessert wine with blue cheese!

PUDDING

Good old-fashioned stodgy puddings are delicious with Sauternes or the stickier German wines - and positively sinful with Madeira or Rutherglen Muscat. Creamy desserts are trickier to partner. Try a sweet wine made from the Chenin Blanc or Sémillon grape, or go for a good-quality sparkling wine or Champagne.

FRESH FRUIT AND FRUIT PUDDINGS

Fresh and fruity dishes meet their match with Muscat (not Australian fortified) or German Riesling of Spätlese quality. Fruity tarts and puddings can handle slightly sweeter German or New World Rieslings.

CHOCOLATE

Surely the ultimate hedonistic dream: chocolate and wine. However, to make this partnership work, there is nothing for it but to throw caution to the winds and go way over the top. Forget soft, subtly flavoured wines, and revel in the strength and assertiveness of Brown Brothers Orange Muscat and Flora, or a Christmas pudding-style fortified Muscat from Australia, Portugal, Spain or France. Utterly decadent!

A PERSONAL SELECTION

In the next six pages, I've indulged myself by listing a few personal favourites – and a few bêtes noirs. To kick off, there are 12 regions whose wines are specially worth looking out for over the next year:

THE RISING STARS

Austria. Back in the news – with the anouncement that Kracher has been named White Winemaker of the Year. Watch out for luscious sweeties and some great dry whites from a growing band of producers.

Casablanca. Not the town in North Africa, but an up-and-coming region in Chile. Look out particularly for wines from the Casablanca winery.

Douro. Port producers like drinking good red wine. The spicy Quinta de la Rosa shows what can be done with good winemaking and local grapes.

Limoux. Grapes from this coolish southern area have reportedly been used by Burgundy producers. Try them under the region's own name.

Lenswood. A brand new cool-climate red and white region in the hills above Adelaide. All of the producers are first class – most notably Henschke, Knappstein and Stafford Ridge.

Navarra. Fast rivalling Rioja, with whom, though it is seldom mentioned in Spain, this region shares a chunk of land. If Spain is going to make Super-Reds to rival the Super-Tuscans, this is where it will happen.

Nelson. A little-known region of the South Island of New Zealand. So far there are only two wineries of any note, Neudorf and Weingut Siefried, but others are bound to follow in their impressive wake.

Other parts of California. aka non-Napa. Look for wines from Amador, Sonoma, Mendocino, Santa Barbara, Monterey and Santa Cruz, all of which offer more value for money than the over-hyped Napa Valley.

Southern Italy and Islands. Forget the over-priced Tuscans. Puglia, Sardinia and Sicily are surprising everyone with their new wave wines.

Tokay. Thanks to people like Jean-Michel Cazes (of Lynch Bages), this historic region is just beginning to exploit its long-vaunted potential.

Vin de Pays d'Oc. The success story of this and last year, but you ain't seen nothing yet. The only part of Europe to worry the Aussies – partly because it's full of Antipodean winemakers.

White Burgundy. Back on form in 1992 with a stunning vintage and greatly improved winemaking. Who needs £20 New World Chardonnay when the lads in the Côte d'Or can make better stuff – at a lower price?

THE UNDERPERFORMERS

Ten regions and countries which have yet to live up to the potential expected of them:

Alto Adige. 10 years ago wine writers were ecstatic about this north-eastern region of Italy where the producers like to wear lederhosen and pretend to be Austrian. Today, there are a few good producers but there is no reason to get excited.

Beaujolais. I know that they've had a set of poor vintages recently, but there's no excuse for the price we have been asked to pay for some very basic wine, little of which has any recogniseable fruity Beaujolais character.

(Basic) Bordeaux. Again, those rainy years have had their effect – but maybe we're just harder to please nowadays. Why drink toughly tannic dilute red wines which need a hunk of cheddar to obscure their flavour? Go for Vin de Pays d'Oc Cabernet or Merlot instead.

Cheap Chardonnay. It is almost impossible profitably to make Chardonnay that tastes identifiably of the variety and sells in Britain for much under £4. All too often other varieties or water will have been added. Either pay more or try a different style.

Dry German Wines The winemakers of the Rhine and Mosel are still trying to persuade us that they can make wine to compete with the Loire and Burgundy. Most are flying in the face of their climate. Avoid anything labelled Mosel Kabinett Trocken – it will have been made from unripe grapes.

Sancerre (and Pouilly Fumé). Despite the competition from New Zealand, the producers here still make far too much dull wine which is ordered and drunk unthinkingly in restaurants by people who, a few years ago, would have asked for Chablis.

Napa Valley. A meaningless marketing-aid-cum-appellation. Often its only role is to raise prices. Look out instead for worthwhile desginations within Napa such as Mount Veeder, Carneros, Stags Leap and Howell Mountain – or trust individual producers.

Penedès. The Alto Adige of Spain. Always on the brink of being really exciting. Even Torres, of whom much was expected, is setting off few fireworks now. As for Cava, the region's fizz, we're still waiting for a Spanish wine to rival the best of the New World, let alone Champagne.

Oregon. Apart from a few exceptions such as the great Domaine Drouhin, this is steadily proving to be the ideal place to pay Premier Cru prices for a basic Bourgogne Rouge style wine with smart New World packaging.

Rioja. Martinez Bujanda and Remelleuri show what can be done, but too much uninspiring wine is being made. I love the new wave styles like Albor, but Rioja needs more than these to maintain its prestige.

REDS

This varied bunch represents some of the most exciting winemaking:

Chateau Léoville Barton, St-Julien 1989, £19.19 (L&W) A classic and very fairly priced Bordeaux from a ripely seductive vintage. This one's not for drinking yet, but give it five years and it will be stunning.

Henschke Abbotts Prayer Merlot/Cabernet, Lenswood 1990, £11.65 (L&W) Proof that the Merlot *can* work in Australia and that Lenswood is as good a place for red grapes as white. A delicious, plummy, blackcurranty new-style Aussie red with far more subtlety than you might expect.

Neudorf Vineyard Moutere Pinot Noir 1992, £11.95 Neudorf is a name to watch in New Zealand, as this impeccably made, raspberryish Pinot Noir proves. A first class New World version of this grape variety.

Pinot Noir, Domaine Drouhin Oregon 1990, £19.99 (OD) The wine which helps to disprove the often disappointing Oregon rule. Very classy stuff with decidedly Burgundian characteristics.

Madiran Bouscassé, Alain Brumont 1991, £6.25 (BU) Bringing the ultra-traditional appellation of Madiran into the late 20th century: a fascinating example of indigenous grapes making lovely gamey-fruity wine.

Leziria Tinto, Vega Co-operativa Almeirim £2.49 Still an extraordinary bargain, this is a really easy-going fruit-juicy red offering much of what I'd like to be getting from Beaujolais.

Pago de Carraovejas Ribera del Duero 1992, £5.99 (LEA) A new wave wine from this – so far – little-known region of Spain. Intensely flavoursome wine with strawberry fruit and rich oak.

Ridge Geyserville 1992, £15.75 (OD) Paul Draper once again demonstrates to his peers and neighbours that his long-life wines can be seductively easy to drink when they are young. Intense fruit and spice with ripe tannin and sweet oak. Classy.

Esk Valley Reserve Merlot/Malbec/Cabernet Franc 1991, £13.99 (TH) The Kiwis' success at mastering red wine becomes more evident with every vintage. This classic Bordeaux blend has a very claret-like style.

Cono Sur Cabernet Sauvignon Selection Reserve 1992, £4.99 (OD) From one of the most exciting new names in Chile, this is a wonderful pure-tasting Cabernet, with lots of crunchy blackcurrant flavour.

Fetzer Valley Oaks Bonterra Red 1991, £7.99 (SAF) An organic blend from Mendocino, this is apparently handicapped in the States by lacking the words 'Napa' and 'Cabernet' or 'Merlot' on its label. Well, that's no handicap in my book and this is a great mouthful of spicy, oaky red.

Kanonkop Pinotage 1991, £8.99 (TO) One of the few really successful examples of South Africa's traditional red wine grape. Richly concentrated, spicy and berryish.

WHITES

A set of wines which inevitably includes a few Chardonnays, but there also several other grape varieties for those days when you feel, as one Australian put it: 'Chardonnayed Out'.

Puligny Montrachet 1er Cru 'Les Champs Gains', Henri Clerc 1992, £23.00 (ABY) A great white Burgundy from a really great vintage. Complex, leafy-oaky, with flavours that linger beautifully.

Ca Del Solo Malvasia Bianca, Bonny Doon 1992, £7.50 (M&V) Randall Grahm's American version of an Italian classic is spicy, grapey and dry – all at once.

Pewsey Vale Vineyard Riesling, S. Smith & Son 1993, £4.99 (TO) Appley young Riesling with lemon-jelly-cube fruit and a touch of petrolly spice. One of the best bargains around, and a lesson for the Germans.

Chardonnay, Petaluma 1992, £9.99 (TH, FUL, OD) The best Petaluma Chardonnay so far: a brilliant blend of ripe pineappley fruit, richness and subtle oak. An Australian classic. Worth keeping for a couple of years.

Rully 1er Cru Les Clous, Olivier Leflaive 1992, £9.19 (L&W) Lovely ripe, quite complex wine. A great, affordable opportunity from Southern Burgundy to taste just how good a vintage this is for the region's whites.

Swanson Vineyards Carneros Chardonnay 1991, £10.25 (AV) From California's best-known cool climate region, this is a very Burgundian wine, with a classy blend of creamy-melony fruit and sweet oak.

La Serre Sauvignon Blanc, Vin de Pays d'Oc 1993, £4.25 (BI, VW) Watch out Sancerre, here comes Mr Ryman with a great value, gooseberryish Sauvignon from Languedoc Roussillon. Unashamedly fruity, but not overstated.

Cullens Sauvignon Blanc 1993, £10.45 (ADN) A blend of Sauvignon and Semillon which leaves most Bordeaux Blancs standing. A subtle wine with complex fruit and oak flavours.

Chablis Vieilles Vignes, La Chablisienne 1990 £7.89 (TH) The reliable La Chablisienne cooperative strikes again, with a benchmark Chablis. Clean, dry-yet-rich, with delicious buttery appley flavours.

Chardonnay Vin de Pays d'Oc, Hugh Ryman 1993 £4.95(JS) Burgundy-class wine at a Vin de Pays d'Oc price. Hugh Ryman at his best.

Hermanos Lurton Rueda Sauvignon, J & F Lurton 1993 £3.99 (JS, OD) Brothers – 'hermanos' – Jacques and Francois Lurton have produced one of the most successful white wines to come out of Spain. Lovely, reliable, grassily attractive Sauvignon.

Hardy's Moondah Brook Estate Verdelho, BRL Hardy Wine Co 1993 £4.99 (VW, TO) From Western Australia, this is the limeyest, most tangily refreshing dry wine I tasted all year.

FIZZ

A selection of sparkling wines from several continents, ranging in price from well under a tenner to around £40. They have three things in common: bubbles, delicious flavour and great value for money.

Pongracz, Bergkelder £6.49 (SAF) Even it this didn't come in a fancy Krug-like bottle, this honeyed Wine of the Year from the Cape would put you in mind of classy Champagne.

Daniel le Brun 1990 Vintage, Cellier Le Brun, £19.95 (HW) Daniel le Brun came to Marlborough, New Zealand with the ambition of making a wine to equal his father's Champagne. Today, he has gone way beyond that, making one of the richest, nuttiest fizzes in the world.

J Schram, Schramsberg 1988, £28.66 (WIN) The first Schramsberg fizz I've ever been convinced by. This 'prestige cuvée', isn't cheap, but it has a complex enough flavour to compete with far pricier Champagne.

Cuvée Prestige Pinot Noir Chardonnay, Yalumba £7.99 (VW, OD etc) A worthy wine of the year, and a great bargain fizz. I love the way the Pinot Noir raspberry fruit is allowed to show through unashamedly.

Mountadam Eden Valley Sparkling Wine 1990, £16.95 (ADN, H&D) Adam Wynn's first commercial effort with bubbles is a great success – full of richly intense Pinot flavour.

Champagne Drappier Blanc de Blancs £15.91 (ABY) From a cult producer, this is a great value opportunity to taste pure Chardonnay fizz: pineappley, creamy and yeasty.

Victoria Wine Vintage Champagne, Marne et Champagne 1986, £18.59 At its peak; a bargain for anyone who enjoys nutty-biscuity mature Champagne. Proof that a well-chosen own-label can beat a big name.

Champagne Philipponnat Grand Blanc 1986, £29.99 (RAV) From a relatively little-known Grande-Marque, this is a really classy taste of mature, complex, nutty fizz.

Champagne Charles Heidsieck, Blanc Des Millenaires Brut 1983 £39.00
Worth every penny. Impeccable fizz with wonderfully complex flavours. A great flagship for the most improved major Champagne house.

Billecart Salmon Brut £18.95 (OD, TH) Quite simply the best, most reliable fizz of them all at the moment. Subtle creamy and fruity.

Champagne Le Mesnil Blanc De Blancs Brut £14.35 (TH, BU) A bargain from one of the best Chardonnay villages in Champagne. Appley, yeasty fizz at its best.

Champagne Pommery Brut Rosé £24.00 (BI) Pink fizz can be so disappointing; this one, however, gets it right, packed with plenty of fruit and not too much sweetness. Classy stuff.

SWEET AND FORTIFIED

One in the eye for the health fascists who'd have us live on margarine and mineral water, the following wines are all about hedonism:

Denbies Wine Estate Noble Harvest 1992,17.50 (SEL) English stickies have been a pretty hit-or-miss bunch until now, but this intense, grapey and curranty wine shows what can be done.

Ch. De Berbec, Premières Côtes de Bordeaux 1990 £5.95 From an often underrated region, this is a reliable Sauternes-like wine at a ludicrously low price. Honeyed and beautifully balanced.

Les Cypres de Climens, Sauternes, Ch. Climens 1984,10.29 (VW) The second label of a top class Sauternes; an unusually affordable example of sweet white Bordeaux at its apricotty-peachy-oaky best.

Primo Estate Botrytis Riesling 1993 (£6.99 half AUC) Celebrate the legally sanctioned return of Australian late harvest to Britain with this intense, spicy, grapey wine from a revolutionary estate near Adelaide.

Domaine Du Haut Rauly Monbazillac 1990 (£3.49, half CWS) A bargain alternative to Sauternes, this is beautifully balanced and has lovely peachy-ripe flavours.

Blauberger Red Trockenbeerenauslese, Willi Opitz 1991 (£35.30 T&W) Only Willi Opitz would have thought of making a red-grape ultra-late-harvest wine. But thank heavens he did, otherwise we'd never have tasted this glorious mouthful of berry and spice.

Chardonnay/Welschriesling Beerenauslese 'Nouvelle Vague', Kracher 1992 £18.99 (NY) Late-harvest Chardonnay is a pretty eccentric idea, but in this Austrian blend, it really works, adding a creaminess to the raisiny flavour of the Welschriesling.

Yalumba Museum Show Reserve Rutherglen Muscat £6.99 half (OD, TH, VW etc) Liqueur Muscats remain one of my desert island drinks: christmas puddingy and extremely indulgent.

Niepoort Colheita 1983 £17.50 (BTH etc) Dirk Niepoort is the master of Colheita – dated – tawnies. This 10-year old is a very classy, plummy glass of wine.

Dow's 20 Year Old Tawny Port £20.99 (TH, OD etc) As one who still fears the vintage hangovers you get from vintage port, I love this safer alternative. It is packed with plummy marmaladey fruit and is as delicious chilled as chambré.

Matusalem Oloroso Muy Viejo, Gonzalez Byass £18.95 (OD etc) Still crazily wonderful after all these years, this nutty, richly intense wine is what old fashioned sherry is all about.

Pedro Ximenez Solera Superior, Valdespino £9.75 (LEA) Unashamedly, intensely, luxuriously rich and sweet wine with the flavour of dried fruit.

A-Z

HOW TO READ THE ENTRIES

Tim Adams[1] (CLARE VALLEY, Australia) Highly successful producer of rich, peachy SEMILLON[2] and deep-flavoured SHIRAZ 88 90 91 92.[3] *****[4] Semillon 1993 £8[5] (AUC)[6] **** Shiraz 1990 £10.75 (BWS, MG, SEL).

1 Names of producers, wines and regions which feature on labels appear in red (grape varieties are in boxes; wine terms appear in SMALL CAPITALS).
2 Words that have their own entry elsewhere in the A-Z appear in SMALL BOLD CAPITALS.
3 Only those vintages that are good have been listed.
4 Where specific wines are mentioned they are rated in the context of their style: from * (poor value for money) to ***** (exceptional value) All were in stock as we went to print, but availability will inevitably vary.
5 Prices given represent those quoted as we go to print in July 1994. Prices from other merchants may vary. Prices marked with an * refer to the average cost at auction.
6 Stockists. See page 12 for an explanation of merchants' codes. (Note: representative stockists have been chosen. Many of the wines may also be found in supermarkets and high street merchants.)

Abbocato (Italy) SEMI-DRY. Tesco Orvieto Classico Abbocato, Barbi £3.49 (TO).
Abfüller/Abfüllung (Germany) BOTTLER/BOTTLED BY.
Abocado (Spain) SEMI-DRY.
Abruzzi (Italy) Region on the east coast. Often dull TREBBIANO whites. Finer MONTEPULCIANO reds. *** Montepulciano d'Abruzzo 1992 Contenova £3 (MRN).
AC (France) See APPELLATION CONTROLEE.
Acacia (CARNEROS, California) One of California's best, if sometimes uneven, producers of CHARDONNAY and PINOT NOIR. *** Marina Chardonnay 1989 £18 (MWW) *** Pinot Noir 1989 £11 (MWW, WR).
Acetic acid THIS VOLATILE ACID (CH_3COOH) FEATURES IN TINY PROPORTIONS IN ALL WINES. CARELESS WINEMAKING CAN RESULT IN WINE BEING TURNED INTO ACETIC ACID - A SUBSTANCE BETTER KNOWN AS VINEGAR.
Acidity ESSENTIAL NATURAL BALANCING COMPONENT (USUALLY TARTARIC) THAT GIVES FRESHNESS. IN HOTTER COUNTRIES (AND SOMETIMES COOLER ONES) IT MAY BE ADDED.
Aconcagua Valley (CHILE) CENTRAL VALLEY region noted for its CABERNET SAUVIGNON. *** Don Maximiano Cabernet Sauvignon Special Reserva, Errazuriz Estate 1991 £9.99 (OD).
Tim Adams (CLARE VALLEY, Australia) Highly successful producer of rich, peachy SEMILLON and deep-flavoured SHIRAZ 88 90 91 92. **** Semillon 1993 £8 (AUC) **** Shiraz 1990 £10.75 (BWS, MG, SEL).
Adega (Portugal) WINERY – EQUIVALENT TO SPANISH BODEGA.
Adelaide Hills (SOUTH AUSTRALIA) Cool, high-altitude vineyard region, producing top-class RIESLING; now also growing more fashionable varieties such as SAUVIGNON BLANC, CHARDONNAY and PINOT NOIR 82 88 90 91 92. ***** Petaluma Chardonnay 1992 £7 (OD) ***** Cyril Henschke Cabernet Sauvignon 1990 £11 (L&W).
Graf Adelmann (WÜRTTEMBERG, Germany) One of the best producers in the region, making good *** red wines from such grapes as the TROLLINGER, Lemberger and Urban. Look for Brüssele'r Spitze wines.

Adelsheim Vineyard (WILLAMETTE VALLEY, OREGON) Good PINOT NOIR producer, notable for the portraits of women on its labels. Look out for the PINOT GRIS, too. *** Pinot Gris 1993 £9 (WDW).

Aglianico Thick-skinned grape grown by the Ancient Greeks but now more or less restricted to Southern Italy, where it produces dark, hefty TAURASI and AGLIANICO DEL VULTURE.

Aglianico del Vulture (BASILICATA, Italy) Tannic, licoricey-chocolatey blockbusters made on the hills of an extinct volcano. Give them a decade – and a plateful of tasty food 85 86 87 88 90. **** Aglianico del Vulture Riserva, D'Angelo 1988 £8.65 (RBS, V&C) *** Aglianico del Vulture, Le Vigne Basse 1990 £6 (WSO, WCE).

Agricola vitivinicola (Italy) WINE ESTATE.

Aguja (LEON, Spain) So-called 'needle' wines which owe their slight SPRITZ to the addition of ripe grapes to the fermented wine.

Ahr (Germany) Northernmost ANBAUGEBIET, producing light red wines little seen in the UK. ***Walporzheimer Klosterberg, QbA 1990 £5.29 (WSC).

Airén (Spain) The most widely planted variety in the world – and one of the very dullest. With modern winemaking methods it can produce commercial stuff, which explains why flying winemakers are so often to be found in Spanish plains. *** Marius, Bodegas Piqueras £5.50 (AV).

Coteaux d'Aix-en-Provence (France) Pleasant floral whites, up-and-coming reds and dry rosés using BORDEAUX and RHONE varieties. A recent AC 89 90 91 92 93 ***Ch de Fonscolombe 1992 £5 (AV).

Ajaccio (CORSICA, France) This would-be independent island has far too many appellations – there's politics for you – but the tangily intense reds and the oaked whites made by Comte Peraldi are better than mere holiday fare.

Albana di Romagna (Italy) Improving but traditionally dull white wine which, for political reasons, was made Italy's first white DOCG, thus making a mockery of the whole Italian system of denominations. ***'I CROPPI' 1993 £6 (WCE).

Albariño (Spain) The Spanish name for the Portuguese ALVARINHO. Is used to produce peachy-spicily attractive wine in Galicia. *** Lagar De Cervera, Rias Baixas, Lagar De Fornelos SA 1992 £8.49 (TH, TAN, L&W, WTR, SOM).

Aleatico (Italy) Red grape producing sweet, MUSCAT-style, often fortified wines. Gives name to DOCs: A. di Puglia and A. di Gradoli. **** Aleatico di Sovana Avignonese 1988 £13 (half) (V&C).

Alella (Spain) DO district of Catalonia, producing better whites (from grapes including the XAREL-LO) than reds. **** Marques de Alella Classico, Parxet 1993 £6 (ADN, MOR, WSO, PTR).

Alenquer (OESTE, Portugal) Coolish region producing good reds from the PERIQUITA, MUSCATY whites from the FERNAO PIRES & increasingly successful efforts with more familiar varietals from France. *** Quinta da Panças Cabernet Sauvignon 1991 £5 (D&F) *** Casa de Panças Chardonnay 1991 £5 (D&F).

Alentejo (Portugal) Up-and-coming province north of the Algarve in which good red BORBA is made, Australian-born David Baverstock produces his juicy red ESPERAO, JM DA FONSECA makes Morgado de Reguengo and Peter BRIGHT, another Aussie, has long produced Tinto da Anfora, former Red Wine of the Year. **** Tinto da Anfora, JP Vinhos 1990 £5 (SAF) **** Esporão, Finagra 1993 £5 (TH) **** Borba, Co-op de Borba 1993 £3 (TO) **** Tinto Velho, JM da Fonseca 1993 £6 (MWW).

Alexander Valley (SONOMA, California) Appellation in which SIMI, JORDAN, Murphy Goode and GEYSER PEAK are based. Good for approachable reds and classy (especially in the case of ***** SIMI) CHARDONNAYS.

Algarve (Portugal) Denominated for political reasons. If there were no beaches and tourists to hand, the wines here would be well-nigh unsaleable.

Algeria Hearty, old-fashioned mostly red wines produced by state-run cooperatives.

Caves Aliança (Portugal) Reliable producer of **** modern BAIRRADA, DOURO and better-than-average DAO. **** Foral Douro Reserva 1991 £3.99 (BTH, DBY).

Alicante (VALENCIA, Spain) Hot region producing generally dull stuff apart from the sweetly honeyed Moscatels that appreciate the heat. *** Tesco Moscatel De Valencia, Gandia £3 (TO).

Alicante-Bouschet Unusual dark-skinned and dark-fleshed grapes traditionally popular as a (usually illegal) means of dyeing pallid reds made from nobler fare. In Australia, ROCKFORD use it to make tiny quantities of good rosé that is sadly only available at the winery. *** Topolos 1992 £10 (BI).

Aligoté (BURGUNDY, France) The region's lesser white grape, making dry, sometimes sharp, white wine that is traditionally mixed with cassis to make KIR. Also grown in Eastern Europe, where they think a lot of it 89 90 91 92 93 **** Domaine Daniel Rion 1992 £6 (M&V) ***Dufouleur 1992 £5.29 (WM).

Allegrini (VENETO, Italy) Go-ahead producer of VALPOLICELLA and SOAVE. **** Amarone Recioto Classico della Valpolicella, Allegrini 1985 £17.19 (WCE) *** La Grola Valpolicella, Allegrini 1990 £8.99 (WCE) ****Recioto Classico 1990 £13 (half) (L&W).

Allier (France) SPICY OAK MUCH FAVOURED BY MAKERS OF WHITE WINE.

Almacenista (JEREZ, Spain) FINE, OLD, UNBLENDED SHERRY FROM A SINGLE SOLERA – THE SHERRY EQUIVALENT OF A SINGLE MALT WHISKY. LUSTAU ARE SPECIALISTS. ****Oloroso Añada 1918 Solera (Pilar Aranda y Latorre), Emilio Lustau £12 (L&W).

Almansa (Spain) Warm region noted for softish reds which can be almost black, thanks to the red juice of the grapes used here.

Aloxe-Corton (BURGUNDY, France) COTE DE BEAUNE commune producing slow-maturing, majestic but at times uninspiring reds (including the GRAND CRU CORTON) and potentially sublime whites (including Corton Charlemagne). Invariably pricy; variably great 78 85 88 89 90 (red) 88 89 90 92 (white). **** Corton-Pougets Grand Cru, Domaine des Héritiers, Louis Jadot 1990 £30 (TH) **** Aloxe Corton Tollot-Beaut 1989 £18.90 (ADN) ***** Corton Charlemagne, Bonneau de Martray 1990 £38.95 (L&W).

Alsace (France) Northerly region enjoying a warm micro-climate that enables producers to make riper-tasting wines than their counterparts across the Rhine, despite often huge yields per acre and the most generous CHAPTALISATION allowances in France. The wines are named after the grapes – PINOT NOIR, GEWURZTRAMINER, RIESLING, TOKAY/PINOT GRIS, PINOT BLANC (known as Pinot d'Alsace) and (rarely) MUSCAT. In the right hands, the GRAND CRU vineyards, of which there are about 50, yield better wines, though their name on a label offers no guarantee of quality. Late harvest, off-dry wines are labelled VENDANGE TARDIVE and SELECTION DES GRAINS NOBLES. References to Reserve and Sélection Personnelle often mean nothing 83 85 86 88 89 90 91. See individual grape varieties for recommendations.

Elio Altare (PIEDMONT, Italy) The Svengali-like leader of the BAROLO revolution. Some say his followers like CLERICO and ROBERTO VOERZIO have overtaken him, but it's a very close race. **** Nebbiolo 1991 £8 (V&C).

Alto-Adige (Italy) Aka Italian Tyrol and Sudtirol. **DOC** for a range of mainly white wines, often from Germanic grape varieties. Also light and fruity reds made from the **LAGREIN** and Vernatsch. Not living up to its promise of the early 1980s when it was considered to be one of the most exciting regions in Europe. 90 91. *** Sainsbury's Chardonnay Alto-Adige Tiefenbrunner £4.00 (JS) *** Chardonnay 'Lowengang' 1991 £16.50 (PON)

> **Alvarinho** (Portugal) White grape aka (in Portugal) **ALBARINO**; at its fresh, lemony best in **VINHO VERDE** and in the **DO** Alvarinho de Monção. *** Quinta da Aveleda £6 (AV) *** Dão Grão Vasco, Branco 1993 £6 (AV).

Amabile (Italy) SEMI-SWEET.

Amador County (California) Region noted for intense-flavoured, old-fashioned **ZINFANDEL**. Depressingly, the obsessional mania to promote the **NAPA** region has helped to ensure that few examples of these often far more interesting wines reach UK shores. In the US, look out for Amador Foothills Winery's old-vine **ZINFANDELS**. ****Monteviña Cabernet Sauvignon 1990 £6 (VW).

Amaro (Italy) BITTER

Amarone (VENETO, Italy) ALSO 'BITTER', USED PARTICULARLY TO DESCRIBE RECIOTO. BEST KNOWN AS AMARONE DELLA VALPOLICELLA. **** Amarone Recioto Classico della Valpolicella, Allegrini 1986 £13 (V&C) ***** Amarone Capitel Monte Olmi, Azienda Agricola Tedeschi £15.93 (ADN, HAR, WCE).

Amberley Estate (WESTERN AUSTRALIA) Young estate with a particularly impressive **SEMILLON & CABERNET-MERLOT** blend. **Semillon 1993 £10 (NI).

Amézola de la Mora (RIOJA, Spain) Young (eight-year-old) estate promising classy red **RIOJA** in which **GRENACHE** plays no part.

Amity (OREGON, US) High quality producer of **PINOT NOIR**.

Amiral de Beychevelle See **CHATEAU BEYCHEVELLE**.

Amontillado (JEREZ, Spain) Literally 'like Montilla'. In Britain, medium-sweet **SHERRY**; in Spain, dry, nutty wine. ***** Fortnum & Mason Amontillado, Lustau £6.45 (F&M) *** Waitrose Amontillado Sherry, Antonio Romero £4.35 (W) ***** Amontillado Del Duque, Gonzalez Byass £18.95 (OD, TDS).

Amoroso (JEREZ, Spain) SWEET **SHERRY** STYLE DEVISED FOR THE BRITISH.

Robert Ampeau (BURGUNDY, France) **MEURSAULT** specialist who also produces fine traditional reds, including first class **POMMARD**. **** Savigny les Beaune, 1er Cru Les Lavières 1984 £14 (HR).

Ampurdan-Costa Brava (CATALONIA, Spain) A great place for a holiday. Ignore the wines – but if you do trip over a dull white, remember that this is one of the main sources of juice for the sparkling winemakers of the **PENEDES**. So now you know why those **CAVAS** taste the way they do.

Amtliche Prüfüngsnummer (Germany) OFFICIAL IDENTIFICATION NUMBER SUPPOSEDLY RELATING TO QUALITY. (IN FACT, TO GET ONE, WINES HAVE TO HAVE SCORED 1.5 OUT OF 5 IN A BLIND TASTING). APPEARS ON ALL QBA/QMP WINES.

Anbaugebiet (Germany) TERM FOR 11 LARGE WINE REGIONS (EG **RHEINGAU**). QBA AND QMP WINES MUST INCLUDE THE NAME OF THEIR ANBAUGEBIET ON THEIR LABELS, A STIPULATION THAT DOESN'T HELP SIMPLIFY GERMAN WINE LABELLING.

Coteaux d'Ancenis (LOIRE, France) Light reds and deep pinks from the **CABERNET FRANC** and **GAMAY**, and **MUSCADET**-style whites 89 90 92. *** Coteaux Ancenis 1992 Pierre Guidon £5 (YAP).

Andalucia (Spain) The hot southern part of the country in which the fortified wines of **JEREZ**, **MONTILLA** and **MALAGA** are made.

Anderson Valley (California, US) Small cool area within **MENDOCINO**, good for white and sparkling wines. Do not confuse with the less impressive Anderson Valley in New Mexico. *** Gewürztraminer, Husch 1992 £7.50 (J&B).

Ch. l'Angélus (BORDEAUX, France) Flying high since the late 1980s, this is a **ST EMILION** to watch; classy, plummy and skilfully oaked. The **SECOND LABEL**, Carillon d'Angelus, is also well worth seeking out 82 83 84 86 88 89 90 91. *** 1983 £28 (SEL) **** 1988 £25 (C&B).

The Angelus See WIRRA WIRRA.

Anghelu Ruju (SARDINIA, Italy) Intensely nutty-raisiny wine made from dried Cannonau grapes. *** Sella & Mosca 1981 £10 (V&C).

Ch. d'Angludet (BORDEAUX, France) CRU BOURGEOIS made by Peter Sichel (the merchant responsible for CHATEAU PALMER). Classy cassis-flavoured MARGAUX-like wine that can be drunk young but is worth waiting for. *****1983 £15 (EV).

Angoves (SOUTH AUSTRALIA) MURRAY RIVER producer with improving, good-value CHARDONNAY and CABERNET. ***Classic Reserve Chardonnay 1993 £3.79 (KS).

Paul Anheuser (NAHE, Germany) One of the most stalwart supporters of the TROCKEN movement, this excellent estate is particularly successful with its RULANDER and PINOT NOIR.

Anjou (LOIRE, France) The source of many dry and DEMI-SEC whites, mostly from the CHENIN BLANC grape. The rosé is almost always awful but there are good, light, claretly, CABERNET SAUVIGNON reds, too. For the best, look out for Anjou-Villages in which the GAMAY is not permitted 85 86 90 92. *** Anjou Villages, Domaine du Closel 1992 Madame de Jessey £6 (YAP).

Annata (Italy) VINTAGE.

Año (Spain) YEAR, PRECEDED BY A FIGURE – eg 5 – WHICH INDICATES THE WINE'S AGE AT THE TIME OF BOTTLING. BANNED BY THE EC SINCE 1986.

Anselmi (VENETO, Italy) Source of SOAVE CLASSICO good enough to disprove the generally dismal rule. *** Soave Classico Superiore 1993 £7 (UBC, BIN, V&C, PON).

Antinori (TUSCANY, Italy) A pioneer merchant-producer who has improved the quality of CHIANTI while also spearheading the SUPER-TUSCAN revolution with superb wines like TIGNANELLO and SOLAIA. ***** Tignanello 1990 £22 (SV, V&C, C&B, HAR, WR, L&W) ***** Solaia 1990 £46 (SV, HAR, BAL, V&C, C&B) *** Chianti Classico Riserva 1989 £6.49 (TH, WR, BU) *** Chianti Classico Peppoli 1990 £9 (L&W).

AOC (France) See APPELLATION CONTROLEE.

AP (Germany) See AMTLICHE PRUFUNGSNUMMER.

Appellation Contrôlée (AC/AOC) (France) INCREASINGLY QUESTIONED DESIGNATION FOR 'TOP QUALITY' WINE: GUARANTEES ORIGIN, GRAPE VARIETIES AND METHOD OF PRODUCTION – BUT NOT QUALITY.

Aprémont (Eastern France) Floral, slightly PETILLANT dry white from skiing region 90 92 93. ** Les Rocailles 1990 £5.50 (THP).

Apulia (Italy) See PUGLIA.

Aquileia (FRIULI-VENEZIA-GIULIA, Italy) DOC for easy-going, single-variety reds, rosés and whites made from a wide range of grapes. The REFOSCO can be plummily refreshing.

Ararimu (AUCKLAND, NEW ZEALAND) See MATUA VALLEY.

Arbin (SAVOIE, France) Red wine from Mondeuse grapes. A wine that tastes best in its usual context (after skiing rather than after work).

Arbois (Eastern France) AC region. Light reds from Trousseau and PINOT NOIR, dry whites from the JURA, most notably VIN JAUNE and fizz.

Viña Ardanza (RIOJA, Spain) Fairly full-bodied red made with a high proportion (40 per cent) of GRENACHE; good oaky white, too. *** Reserva, La Rioja Alta 1986 £10 (L&W, ADN).

Coteaux de l'Ardèche (RHONE, France) Light country reds & whites, mainly from the SYRAH and CHARDONNAY grapes by certain Burgundians 88 89 90 91 92 . *** Les Terrasse Blanc 1993, Cave de St Désirat-Champagne £4 (DIR, YAP). *** Syrah de l'Ardèche 1992, Cave de St. Désirat-Champagne £5 (YAP).

Argentina Slowly beginning to compete with its Andean neighbour in quality, Argentina produces soft, easy-going CABERNET and MERLOT reds and improving CHARDONNAY whites. It stands apart, though, with its grapey Torrontes and spicy red MALBEC 84 85 86 88 90 91 93. **** Cafayate Torrontes, Arnaldo Etchart £4 (JS) ****Gauchos Lurton Cabernet Sauvignon £3 (TH) ***Torrontes, La Agricola SA £4 (WTR).

Argyll Oregon fizz from Brian Croser (of **PETALUMA**). One of the classiest offerings from the New World. **** Argyll Brut, The Dundee Wine Company £12 (OD).

Ch. d'Arlay (JURA, France) Reliable producer of **VIN JAUNE** and **PINOT NOIR**. *** Vin Jaune 1986 £47 (LV).

Domaine de l'Arlot (BURGUNDY, France) ***** recently constituted **NUITS ST GEORGES** estate with a rare, top-class, **COTE DE NUITS** white. Superlative. ***** Nuits St Georges 1er cru 1991, Clos l'Arlot £21 (L&W, ABY, WR).

Arneis (PIEMONTE, Italy) Spicy white variety, used to make good, unoaked wines. **** Cru San Michele, Deltetto 1993 £8 (WCE).

Ch. l'Arrosée (BORDEAUX , France) Small, well-sited **ST EMILION** property whose fruitily intense wines rise above the dull herd of the appellation 82 83 85 86 88 89 90 91. **** 1989 £22 (J&B).

Arrowfield (HUNTER VALLEY, Australia) Producer of ripe, full-flavoured **CHARDONNAY**. *** Show Reserve Chardonnay 1993 £8 (W) *** Show Reserve Shiraz 1991 £8 (W).

Arrowood (SONOMA, California) Producer of excellent **CHARDONNAY** and good **CABERNET** made by the former winemaker of **CHATEAU ST JEAN**.

Arroyo (RIBERA DEL DUERO, Spain) A name to watch for well-made, intensely flavoursome reds.

Arruda (OESTE, Portugal) Fresh, inexpensive **BEAUJOLAIS**-style reds which help to win friends for Portugal. **** Sainsbury's Arruda £3 (JS).

Ascheri (PIEDMONT, Italy) New-wave producer with impressive single-vineyard wines. *** Bric Milieu 1992 £7 (WCE) *** Barolo 1990 £9 (OD).

Asciutto (Italy) DRY.

Asenovgrad (BULGARIA) Demarcated northern wine region. Reds from **CABERNET SAUVIGNON**, **MERLOT** and **MAVRUD** 85 87 88 89 90 91. *** Asenovgrad Cabernet Sauvignon, Vinzavod 1990 £3 (WOW).

Ashton Hills (ADELAIDE HILLS, SOUTH AUSTRALIA) Small up-and-coming winery whose winemaker, Stephen George, is producing subtle, increasingly credible **CHARDONNAY**. *** Chardonnay 1991 £8 (AUC).

Assemblage (France) THE ART OF BLENDING WINE FROM DIFFERENT GRAPE VARIETIES IN A **CUVEE**. ASSOCIATED WITH **BORDEAUX** AND **CHAMPAGNE**.

Assmanhausen (RHEINGAU, Germany) If you like sweet **PINOT NOIR**, this is the place to come. Even the light dry versions are rarely worth a detour.

Asti (PIEDMONT, Italy) Town famous for sparkling **SPUMANTE**, lighter **MOSCATO D'ASTI** and red **BARBERA** d'Asti. *** Fontanafredda Spumante NV £6 (widely available).

Astringent MOUTH-PUCKERING. MOSTLY ASSOCIATED WITH YOUNG RED WINE. SEE **TANNIN**.

Aszu (HUNGARY) THE SWEET 'SYRUP' MADE FROM DRIED AND (ABOUT 10-15 PER CENT) 'NOBLY ROTTEN' GRAPES (SEE **BOTRYTIS**) USED TO SWEETEN **TOKAY**.

Ata Rangi (MARTINBOROUGH, NEW ZEALAND) Inspiring small estate with high quality **PINOT NOIR** and **NEW ZEALAND**'s only successful **SHIRAZ**. **** Pinot Noir 1991 £17 (J&B).

Coteaux de l'Aubance (LOIRE, France) Light wines (often semi-sweet) grown on the banks of a **LOIRE** tributary 83 85 88 89 90 92 93 *** Domaine de Bablut Moelleux, C Daviau £14.70 (ADN).

Au Bon Climat (SANTA BARBARA, California) Despite his Fabulous Furry Freak Brothers looks, Jim Clendenen is a serious, top quality producer of characterfully flavoursome, if sometimes slightly horseradishy, **PINOT NOIR** and classy **CHARDONNAY**. A great example of what **SANTA BARBARA** can do – and yet another blow to **NAPA** hype. ***** Pinot Noir 'La Bauge Au-dessus' 1991 £18 (M&V, SAN, HAR) *** Chardonnay 1992 £12.50 (HAR, HN, NY).

Domaine des Aubuisiers (LOIRE, France) Superb **VOUVRAY DOMAINE** producing impeccable wines, ranging from richly dry to lusciously sweet. ***** Vouvray Sec/Demi-sec £7 (OD).

Auckland (NEW ZEALAND) All-embracing designation which once comprised over 25 per cent of the country's vineyards. Good for a wide range of wines, especially reds which do well on Waiheke Island. ★★★★ Goldwater Chardonnay 1993 £9 (POR, FUL, MWW)

Aude (South-West France) Prolific département traditionally producing much ordinary red, white and rosé. Now CORBIERES and FITOU are improving as are the VINS DE PAYS, thanks to plantings of new grapes (such as the VIOGNIER) and the efforts of go-ahead firms like Skalli (FORTANT DE FRANCE) 83 85 86 88 89 90 91 92 93. ★★★ Campagnard Vin de Pays de L'Aude, Les Vignerons £3 (TH).

Ausbruch (AUSTRIA) TERM FOR WINES SWEETER THAN BEERENAUSLESEN BUT LESS SWEET THAN TROCKENBEERENAUSLESEN.

Auslese (Germany) MOSTLY SWEET WINE FROM SELECTED RIPE GRAPES USUALLY AFFECTED BY BOTRYTIS. THIRD RUNG ON THE QMP LADDER.

Ch. Ausone (BORDEAUX, France) Pretender to the crown of top ST EMILION, this estate which owes its name to the Roman occupation can produce some of the tastiest, most complex wine to be found in the area. ★★★★★ 1990 £54 (ADN).

Austria Now fully recovered from the anti-freeze scandal, this has become the home of all sorts of whites, ranging from dry SAUVIGNON BLANCS, greengagey GRUNER-VELTLINERS and ripe RIESLINGS to luscious late-harvest wines. Reds are less successful, but the lightly fruity St Laurents are worth seeking out 81 83 85 87 88 89 90 91 93. See WILLI OPITZ & LENZ MOSER. ★★★Grüner-Veltliner, Lenz Moser 1993 £4 (W).

Auxerrois Named after the main town in northern BURGUNDY, this is the term Alsatians use to describe a fairly dull local variety that may be related to the SYLVANER, MELON DE BOURGOGNE or CHARDONNAY. In Luxembourg this is the name used for the PINOT GRIS. It is also grown, with little success, in Luxembourg, and with rather more in Britain. ★★★ Wooton Auxerrois 1992 £5 (WSO).

Auxey-Duresses (BURGUNDY, France) Best known for its buttery whites but produces greater quantities of raspberryish reds. A slow developer 83 85 87 88 89 90 92. ★★★ Olivier Leflaive 1992 £10 (JAR) ★★★ Louis Jadot 1989 £11 (TH).

Quinta da Aveleda (Penafiel, Portugal) Estate producing serious dry VINHO VERDE. ★★★ Aveleda Vinho Verde £6 (AV).

Avelsbach (MOSEL-SAAR-RUWER, Germany) RUWER village producing delicate, light-bodied wines 83 85 86 87 88 89 90 92

Avignonesi (TUSCANY, Italy) Classy producer of VINO NOBILE DI MONTALCINO, SUPER-TUSCANS such as Grifi, a pure MERLOT and a great VIN SANTO. ★★★★ Avignonesi Bianco 1993 £7 (RD).

Avize (CHAMPAGNE, France) Village known for fine white grapes.

Ay (CHAMPAGNE, France) Ancient regional capital growing mainly black grapes 79 82 83 85 88 89 ★★★★ Bollinger NV £22 (widely available).

Ayala (CHAMPAGNE, France) Underrated producer which takes its name from the village of Ay. ★★★★★ Champagne Ayala, Château d'Ay Brut NV £14.95 (LAV)

Ayl (MOSEL-SAAR-RUWER, Germany) Distinguished SAAR village producing steely wines 85 86 87 88 89 90 92 ★★★ Ayler Kupp Riesling Spätlese 1990 Bischöfliches Konvikt £8 (ADN).

Azienda (Italy) ESTATE. ★★★★★ Barbaresco, Azienda Agricola Guiseppe Cortese 1988 £12 (GI, LAY) ★★★★★ Amarone Capitel Monte Olmi, Azienda Agricola Tedeschi 1988 £16 (ADN).

Babich (Henderson, New Zealand) The rich 'Irongate' CHARDONNAY is the prize wine here, but the SAUVIGNON BLANC is good, too, and the reds improve with every vintage. ★★★★ Chardonnay 1992 £7.80 (ABY, CNL) ★★★★ Hawkes Bay Sauvignon Blanc 1993 £6.80 (ABY, CNL).

> **Bacchus** White grape, a **Muller-Thurgau x Riesling** cross, making light, flowery wine. Grown in Germany and also England. See **Denbies**.

Domaine Denis Bachelet (**Burgundy**, France) Classy small **Gevrey Chambertin** estate making cherryish wines that are as good young as with five or six years of age. **** Cuvée Vieilles Vignes 1991 £15 (HR).

Backsberg (**Paarl**, **South Africa**) A **Chardonnay** pioneer, making a richly Burgundian version, also notable for its blackcurranty **Cabernet Sauvignon**. **** Backsberg Chardonnay 1992 £5 (G&M, CAP, A&A).

Bad Durkheim (**Rheinpfalz**, Germany) Chief **Rheinpfalz** town, producing some of the region's finest whites, plus some reds 83 85 88 89 90 91 92.

Bad Kreuznach (**Nahe**, Germany) Chief and finest wine town of the region, giving its name to the entire lower **Nahe**. 83 85 88 89 90 91 92.
*** Kahlenberg Riesling Spätlese, Staatsweingut 1988 £6 (VW).

Badacsony (**Hungary**) Wine region renowned for full-flavoured whites.

Baden (Germany) Warm (well, relatively) southern region in which it is possible to use ripe grapes to make dry (**trocken**) wines, usually from grapes other than the Riesling. Some good **Pinot Noirs** are produced, too, by Karl-Heinz Johner, former winemaker at **Lamberhurst**, but there is little to set the world alight. ** Baden Dry 1993 £3.35 (W).

Baden Winzerkeller (ZBW) (Germany) Huge cooperative whose reliability has done much to set **Baden** apart from the rest of Germany – and to produce the vast proportion of the region's wines. If you must have dry German wines, this is a good place to find them 83 85 86 88 89 90 91 92.
***Co-op Baden £3.50 (CWS).

> **Baga** (Portugal) High-quality, spicily fruity red grape varieties – used in **Bairrada** *** Bairrada, Luis Pato 1988 £5 (OD, TH).

Bailey's (North-East **Victoria**, Australia) Traditional producer of good Liqueur **Muscat** and hefty, old-fashioned **Shiraz**. Current wines are lighter and less impressive. **** Founders Reserve Muscat £11 (AUC) *** Shiraz 1992 £5 (OD).

Bairrada (Portugal) DO wine region south of Oporto, traditionally producing dull whites and tough reds, often from the **Baga**. Revolutionaries like **Sogrape**, **Luis Pato** and **Alianca** are proving what can be done. Look for spicy, blackberryish reds and clean, creamy whites 85 88 89 90 92. See **Baga**.

Balance Harmony of fruitiness, acidity, alcohol and tannin. Balance can develop with age but should be evident in youth, even when, through acidity or tannin for example, wines may appear difficult to taste.

Balaton (**Hungary**) Wine region producing fair-quality reds and whites.
** Co-op Hungarian Country Red 1993 £3 (WOW, CWS).

Anton Balbach (Erben Rheinhessen, Germany) Potentially one of the best producers in the region – especially for its late-harvest wines.
**** Niersteiner Klostergarten Riesling Kabinett 1990 £7 (ADN).

Balbás (**Ribera del Duero**, Spain) Small producer of juicy **Tempranillo** reds and rosé.

Ch. Balestard-la-Tonnelle (**Bordeaux**, France) Good, quite traditional **St Emilion**, built to last.

Balgownie (**Victoria**, Australia) One of **Victoria**'s most reliable producers of lovely intense blackcurranty **Cabernet** in **Geelong**. **Chardonnays** are big and old-fashioned and **Pinot Noirs** are improving. ***** Balgownie Estate Cabernet Sauvignon 1988 £9.49 (PHI) *** Balgownie Estate Pinot Noir 1989 £11.50 (PHI).

Balthasar Ress (**Hattenheim**, Germany) Classy producer who blends delicacy with concentration. **** Hattenheimer Riesling QbA 1992 £6.50 (WDW).

Ban de Vendange (France) OFFICIALLY SANCTIONED HARVEST DATE.

Bandol (PROVENCE, France) AOC red and rosé. MOURVEDRE reds are particularly good and spicy. Worth keeping. Whites, though improving, are uninspiring 79 83 85 86 89 90 91 92. **** Château Pibarnon, Bandol 1990 £11.50 (ABY) **** Mas de la Rouvière 1990, Paul & Pierre Bunan £7.75 (YAP).

Bannockburn (GEELONG, Australia) Gary Farr uses his experience making wines at DOMAINE DUJAC in BURGUNDY to produce concentrated, toughish **** PINOT NOIR at home. The CHARDONNAY is good, too, if slightly big for its boots 85 86 88 90.**** Chardonnay, Geelong 1992 £10 (ADN, LEA, BEN). **** Pinot Noir 1990 £12 (ADN, LEA, BEN).

Banyuls (PROVENCE, France) France's answer to TAWNY PORT. Fortified, GRENACHE-based VIN DOUX NATUREL, ranging from off-dry to lusciously sweet. The RANCIO style is rather more like MADEIRA. 82 85 86 88 89 90 91 92. *** Banyuls Tradition, Domaine De Baillaury 1985 £9.25 (HR, RD).

Barancourt (CHAMPAGNE, France) BOUZY-based grower of full-bodied CHAMPAGNES.

Barbadillo (JEREZ, Spain) Great producer of FINO and MANZANILLA. **** Fino £12 (MG, GMV).

Barbaresco (PIEDMONT, Italy) DOCG red from the NEBBIOLO grape, with spicy fruit plus depth and complexity. Traditionally approachable earlier (three to five years) than neighbouring BAROLO but, in the hands of men like ANGELO GAJA and in the best vineyards, potentially of almost as high a quality – and even higher prices! 82 83 84 85 86 87 88 89 90 92. ****Azienda Agricola Guiseppe Cortese 1988 £12.06 (GI, LAY).

> **Barbera** (PIEDMONT, Italy) Grape making fruity, spicy, characterful wine (eg B. d'Alba and B. d'Asti), usually with a flavour reminiscent of cheese-cake with raisins. Now in California and (at BROWN BROS) Australia 86 87 88 89 90 92. **** Barbera D'Asti, Viticoltori dell'Acquese 1992 £4.50 (ADN) **** Barbera D'Alba Vignota, Conterno Fantino 1992 £7.50 (OD, WIN).

Barca Velha (DOURO, Portugal) Portugal's most famous red, made from port varieties by FEIRREIRA. It's quite tough stuff, but has enough plummy fruit to make it worth keeping – and paying for. **** Barca Velha 1985 £25 (OD).

Bardolino (VENETO, Italy) Light and unusually approachable for a traditional DOC Italian red. Commercial versions are often dull as ditchwater but at best are Italy's answer to BEAUJOLAIS – refreshing with a hint of bitter cherries. Best drunk young unless from an exceptional producer. See MASI. 88 89 90 91 92. *** Bardolino Classico Tacchetto, Guerrieri-Rizzardi 1993 £6 (BAR, F&M) ***Tesco Bardolino £3 (TO) *** Safeway Bardolino £3 (SAF)

Barolo (PIEDMONT, Italy) Noblest of DOCG reds, made from NEBBIOLO. Old-fashioned versions are undrinkably dry and tannic when young but, from a good producer (like BORGOGNO) and year, can last and develop extraordinary complexity. Look out also for examples from MASCARELLO, ALDO CONTERNO, CLERICO, ROBERTO VOERZIO, ELIO ALTARE and FONTANAFREDDA. Modern versions are ready earlier, but still last 83 85 86 87 88 89 90 92.*** Barolo Riserva, Giacomo Borgogno & Figli 1988 £9 (A, RIB, RBS).

Baron de Ley (RIOJA, Spain) Small RIOJA estate whose wines, partly aged in French oak, take several years to 'come round'. Less dazzling than it would like to be. *** Baron De Ley Rioja Reserva 1987 £7 (TH, BU, WR, HAR, SEL).

Barossa Valley (SOUTH AUSTRALIA, Australia) Big, warm region north-east of Adelaide, famous for traditional SHIRAZ, 'ports' and RIESLING which age to oily richness. CHARDONNAY and CABERNET have moved in more recently and the former makes subtler, classier wines in the increasingly popular higher altitude vineyards of the ADELAIDE HILLS overlooking the Valley. See KRONDORF, ROCKFORD, MELTON, PENFOLDS, PETER LEHMANN 80 84 86 87 90 91. **** Saltram Pickwick Barossa Valley Fortified Wine £10 (OD) **** Basedows Barossa Valley Semillon £5 (BI) *** Grant Burge Old Vine Semillon 1993 £7 (OD, VW).

Barrique FRENCH BARREL, PARTICULARLY IN BORDEAUX, HOLDING 225 LITRES. TERM USED IN ITALY TO DENOTE BARREL AGEING.

Jim Barry (CLARE VALLEY, Australia) Producer of the dazzling, spicy, mulberryish Armagh SHIRAZ, not yet available in this country.

Barsac (BORDEAUX, France) AC neighbour of SAUTERNES, with similar, though not quite so rich, SAUVIGNON/SEMILLON dessert wines 75 76 83 86 88 89 90 91. ***** Château Climens, Barsac 1991 £21.50 (TH, WR, BU).

Barton & Guestier (BORDEAUX, France) Increasingly commercial BORDEAUX shipper. Now Seagram-owned and unsurprisingly available in Oddbins. *** Château La Foret, Barton & Guestier 1993 £3.50 (SAF).

Basedows (SOUTH AUSTRALIA) Producer of big, concentrated SHIRAZ and CABERNET and ultra-rich SEMILLON and CHARDONNAYS. Unashamedly Australian. **** Semillon 1993 £5 (VW, BI) **** Chardonnay 1990 £6.50 (VW, BI) **** Shiraz 1992 £5.50 (BI).

Basilicata (Italy) Southern wine region chiefly known for AGLIANICO DEL VULTURE and some improving VINI DA TAVOLA 85 86 87 88 90 91 92. **** Aglianico del Vulture Riserva, D'Angelo 1988 £8.65 (RBS, V&C).

Von Bassermann-Jordan (RHEINPFALZ, Germany) Traditional producer often using the fruit of its brilliant vineyards to produce TROCKEN RIESLINGS with more ripeness than is often to be found in this style. **** Forster Jesuitgarten Riesling Spätlese 1988 £10 (VW) **** Forster Pechstein Riesling Spätlese 1989 £11 (BI).

> **Bastardo** (Portugal) Red grape used widely in PORT and previously in MADEIRA, where there are a few wonderful bottles left. Shakespeare refers to a wine called 'Brown Bastard'.

Ch. Bastor-Lamontagne (SAUTERNES, France) Remarkably reliable, classy and surprisingly inexpensive alternative to the big name properties among which it is situated. **** 1989 £8 (half) (JS).

Ch. Batailley (BORDEAUX, France) Approachable, quite modern PAUILLAC with more class than its price might lead one to expect. *** 1983 £19 (D).

Bâtard-Montrachet (BURGUNDY, France) Biscuity-rich white GRAND CRU shared between CHASSAGNE and PULIGNY MONTRACHET. Very fine, very expensive 78 79 81 82 83 85 86 87 88 89 90 92. ***** Domaine Jean-Marc Boillot, 1992 £50 (HR).

Coteaux des Baux-en-Provence (Provence, France) Inexpensive fruity reds, whites and rosé of improving quality, plus the cult DOMAINE DE TREVALLON, which shows what can be done round here 85 86 88 89 90 91 92. ***** Domaine de Trévallon Eloi Dürrbach 1992 £12.75 (YAP).

Bava (PIEDMONT, Italy) Innovative producer making good MOSCATO, BARBERA and a rare source of the traditional, but now rarely grown, raspberryish Rucche. **** Moscato D'Asti, Bava 1992 £8 (T&W).

Ch. de Beaucastel (RHONE, France) The top estate in CHATEAUNEUF-DU-PAPE, using organic methods to produce richly gamey-spicy reds. **** 1991 £13.50 (FAR, L&W).

Beaujolais (BURGUNDY, France) Light, fruity red from the GAMAY, good chilled and for early drinking; BEAUJOLAIS-VILLAGES is better, and the 10 CRUS better still. With age, these can taste like (fairly middle-of-the-road) BURGUNDY, though I can't see why this is a prized quality when it means sacrificing the boiled sweet and banana flavour of them when they are young. See BEAUJOLAIS-VILLAGES, MORGON, CHENAS, BROUILLY, COTE DE BROUILLY, JULIENAS, MOULIN A VENT, FLEURIE, REGNIE, ST AMOUR, CHIROUBLES 88 89 91. *** Beaujolais-Boutinot 1993 £4 (OD) ***Beaujolais Georges Duboeuf 1993 £5 (widely available).

Beaujolais Blanc (BURGUNDY, France) From the CHARDONNAY, rarely seen under this name. Commonly sold as ST VERAN 87 88 90 91 92. ****St Véran, Domaine des Valanges 1992 £8 (BI) *** Somerfield Beaujolais Blanc 1990 £5 (SMF).

Beaujolais-Villages (BURGUNDY, France) From the north of the region, fuller-flavoured and more alcoholic than plain BEAUJOLAIS, though not necessarily from one of the named CRU villages. Good plain BEAUJOLAIS from a quality-conscious producer can outclass many a 'Villages' 85 88 89 91. ***Beaujolais-Villages, Georges Duboeuf 1992 £5 (Widely available) *** Beaujolais Villages, Les Roches Grillées 1992 £4.50 (JS).

Beaulieu Vineyard (NAPA, California) Historic winery, famous from the turn of the century and now owned by UK giant Grand Metropolitan. The Georges de Latour Private Reserve Cabernet can be impressive and keeps well and recent vintages of Beautour show great improvement, possibly thanks to the efforts of the late, great Andre Tchelistcheff. Others are memorably and unworthily ordinary. Pronounced 'Bow-Ly-ew' or, more confidently, 'Bee-Vee' in the US. **** Beautour Cabernet Sauvignon 1991 £6.95 (JS)

Beaumes de Venise (RHONE, France) COTES DU RHONE village producing spicy dry reds and better-known sweet, grapey fortified VIN DOUX NATUREL from the MUSCAT (white) 88 89 90 91 (red) 86 88 89 90 91 *** Muscat des Beaumes de Venise 1992 J Vidal-Fleury £16 (WWT)

Beaune (BURGUNDY, France) Large, reliable commune for soft, raspberry-and-rose-petal PINOT NOIR with plenty of PREMIERS but,strangely no GRANDS CRUS. The walled city is the site of the famous HOSPICES charity auction. Also (very rare) whites made with great success by JOSEPH DROUHIN 78 80 82 83 85 87 88 89 90 92. **** 1er Cru Beaune 'Les Vignes Franches'1988 £14 (M&V).

JB Becker (RHEINGAU, Germany) One of Germany's only successful producers of ripe, classy PINOT NOIR (here known as SPATBURGUNDER).

Beerenauslese (Germany) LUSCIOUS SWEET WINES FROM SELECTED RIPE GRAPES (BEEREN), HOPEFULLY AFFECTED BY BOTRYTIS. ***** Kiedricher Grapenberg Riesling Beerenauslese, Robert Weil 1992 £70 **** Chardonnay/Welschriesling Beerenauslese 'Nouvelle Vague' Kracher 1992 £19 (BAR, NY).

Bekaa Valley (LEBANON) War-torn region in which Serge Hochar grows the grapes for his red and (very uninspiring) white CHATEAU MUSAR wines. ***Château Musar (red) 1987 £8 (widely available).

Ch. Belair (BORDEAUX, France) CHATEAU AUSONE's stablemate. Lighter in style and not always up to the mark, but still a classy, long-lived ST EMILION. **** 1985 £21 (ADN).

Bellet (PROVENCE, France) Tiny AC behind Nice producing fairly good red, white and rosé from local grapes including the Rolle, the Braquet and the Folle Noir. (Excessively) pricey and rarely seen in the UK 83 85 87 88 89 90 91 92. ***Château de Crémat, Charles Bagnis 1988 £16 (YAP).

Bendigo (VICTORIA, Australia) Great warm region for big-boned, long-lasting reds with intense berry fruit. See BALGOWNIE, JASPER HILL and PASSING CLOUDS. **** Water Wheel Bendigo Shiraz 1992 £8 (AUC).

Bentonite TYPE OF CLAY USED AS A CLARIFYING AGENT TO REMOVE IMPURITIES BEFORE BOTTLING. POPULAR AS A NON-ANIMAL-DERIVED FINING MATERIAL.

Berberana (RIOJA, Spain) Producer of the attractive but often unexceptional Carta de Plata and Carta de Oro wines. Introducing juicier, fruitier young-drinking styles. *** Rioja Berberana Oak Aged Tempranillo 1992 £4 (SAF).

Bereich (Germany) VINEYARD AREA, SUBDIVISION OF AN ANBAUGEBIET. ON ITS OWN INDICATES SIMPLE QbA WINE, eg NIERSTEINER. FINER WINES ARE FOLLOWED BY THE NAME OF A GROSSLAGE SUBSECTION; EVEN BETTER ONES BY THE NAMES OF INDIVIDUAL VINEYARDS.

Bergerac (BORDEAUX, France) Lighter, often good-value alternative to everyday CLARET or dry white BORDEAUX, revolutionised in the 1980s by CH. DE LA JAUBERTIE, former stationery magnate Henry Ryman's property and the place where his son, the ubiquitous Hugh, first cut the vinous teeth which he would use to such good effect as a FLYING WINEMAKER. Fine, sweet MONBAZILLAC is produced here, too 85 86 88 89 90. **** Château de la Jaubertie Bergerac Sec, Henry Ryman 1993 £5 (MWW).

Bergkelder (Cape, SOUTH AFRICA) Huge winery that still matures and bottles wines for such top-class Cape estates as MEERLUST, which, like its counterparts in BORDEAUX and California, really ought to bottle their own. Even so, the Bergkelder's own Stellenryck wines are worth watching out for, and the cheaper Fleur du Cap range is likeable enough and the Pongrasz fizz is first class. **** Stellenryck Cabernet Sauvignon, The Bergkelder 1987 £9 (NGF)

Beringer Vineyards (NAPA, California) Big, Swiss-owned producer notable for two CABERNETS, the **** Knights Valley and the even better **** Private Reserve. **** Beringer Private Reserve Cabernet Sauvignon 1989 £21 (BWC).

Bernkastel (MOSEL-SAAR-RUWER, Germany) Town and vineyard area on the MITTELMOSEL making some of the finest RIESLING (including the famous Bernkasteler Doktor) and a lake of (poor-quality wine 83 85 86 88 89 90 91 92 93. *** Lay Riesling 1989 SA Prum £9 (D).

Berri Remano (RIVERLAND, Australia) Big producer now associated with THOMAS HARDY. Reliable, inexpensive reds and whites including a recently released unoaked CHARDONNAY. *** Berri Estates Unwooded Chardonnay, Berri Remano 1993 (SMF).

Best's Great Western (VICTORIA, Australia) Under-appreciated winery in GREAT WESTERN making concentrated SHIRAZ from old vines, attractive CABERNET, DOLCETTO and rich CHARDONNAY. **** Dolcetto 1993 £7 (AUC).

Ch. Beychevelle (BORDEAUX, France) An over-performing Second Growth which belongs to an insurance company. Very typical ST JULIEN with lots of cigar-box character. The SECOND LABEL, AMIRAL DE BEYCHEVELLE can be a good buy 88 89 90 91 92. **** Château Beychevelle 1989 £25 (J&B, VW, TP).

Léon Beyer (ALSACE, France) Serious producer of lean, long-lived wines. *** Gewürztraminer 1991 £8 (WSO).

Bianco di Custoza (VENETO, Italy) Widely exported DOC, a reliable, crisp, light white from a blend of grapes. A better value alternative to most basic SOAVE. 88 89 90 91 92. **** Sainsbury Bianco di Custoza, Geoff Merrill GIV 1993 £3.50 (JS)

Maison Albert Bichot (BEAUNE, France) Big NEGOCIANT with excellent CHABLIS and VOSNE ROMANEE, plus a range of perfectly adequate wines sold under a plethora of other labels. ***Pinot Noir Bichot £5.50 (U).

Biddenden (Kent, England) Maker of the usual range of Germanic grape wines but supreme master in this country of the peachy Ortega.

Billecart-Salmon (CHAMPAGNE, France) Possibly the region's best all-rounder. Superlative non-vintage, vintage and rosé. ***** Billecart-Salmon £18 (OD).

Bingen (RHEINHESSEN, Germany) Village giving its name to a RHEINHESSEN BEREICH that includes a number of well-known GROSSLAGEN 76 83 85 88 89 90 91 92. *** Binger St Rochuskapelle Kabinett 1993 £3.10 (WSC).

Binissalem (Mallorca, Spain) The holiday island is proud of its demarcated region, though why it's hard to say. Jose Ferrer's and Jaime Mesquida's wines are attractive enough. *** Ferrer Reserva 1985 £7 (L&S).

Biondi-Santi (TUSCANY, Italy) Big-name property; supreme underperformer. *** Brunello di Montalcino 1985 £38 (V&C) *** 1971 £125 (V&C).

Biscuity FLAVOUR OF BISCUITS (eg DIGESTIVE OR RICH TEA) OFTEN ASSOCIATED WITH THE CHARDONNAY GRAPE, PARTICULARLY IN CHAMPAGNE AND TOP-CLASS MATURE BURGUNDY, OR WITH THE YEAST THAT FERMENTED THE WINE.

Black Muscat Grown chiefly as a table grape, also produces very mediocre wine – except that made at the QUADY winery in California. **** Elysium, Quady Winery 1993 £6 (VW, MWW, BBR, JS, THP).

Blagny (BURGUNDY, France) Tiny source of good unsubtle red (sold as Blagny) and potentially top-class white (sold as MEURSAULT, PULIGNY MONTRACHET, Blagny, Hameau or Piece sous le Bois). **** Blagny 1er Cru La Piece sous le Bois (rouge), Rene Lamy 1992 £10 (ABY).

Blain-Gagnard (BURGUNDY, France), Excellent producer of creamy, modern CHASSAGNE MONTRACHET. ***** Chassagne-Montrachet 1er cru, Caillerets 1988 £20 (DD) ***** Chassagne-Montrachet 1990 £15 (ADB)

Blanc de Blancs WHITE WINE, USUALLY SPARKLING, MADE SOLELY FROM WHITE GRAPES. IN CHAMPAGNE, DENOTES 100 PER CENT CHARDONNAY. ***** Taittinger Comtes de Champagne, Blanc de Blancs 1985 £60 (HAR, SEL, F&M) **** Le Mesnil Blanc de Blancs Brut N V £14.35 (TH, WR, BU, J&B) **** Champagne Drappier Blanc de Blancs NV £16 (ABY).

Blanc de Noirs WHITE (OR PINK) WINE MADE FROM BLACK GRAPES. **** 1990 Mountadam Eden Valley Sparkling Wine £16.50 (ADN) *** Boschendal Blanc de Noirs 1993 £5.50 (MYS).

Blandy's (MADEIRA, Portugal) Historic brand belonging to the Madeira Wine Company and named after the sailor who began the production of fortified wine here. Brilliant old wines. ***** Blandy's Sercial Madeira 1940 £70 (TH) **** Blandys 5 Year Old Malmsey Madeira £13.50 (TO, W, WR, OD).

Blanquette de Limoux (MIDI, France) METHODE CHAMPENOISE sparkler, which, when good, is appley and clean. Best when made with a generous dose of CHARDONNAY, as the local MAUZAC tends to give it an earthy flavour with age.The local Aimery cooperative is one of the most modern in France and quality is improving. *** Blanquette de Limoux 1991 Vurgres £7.00 (U)

Wolf Blass (BAROSSA VALLEY, Australia) German immigrant who prides himself on making immediately attractive 'sexy' (his term) reds and whites by blending wines from different regions and allowing them plentiful contact with new oak. Varying label colours indicate expense and expertise, with black signifying the peak of the range. **** President's Selection Cabernet Sauvignon 1989 £10 (BKW, SAF) **** President's Selection Shiraz 1990 £9 (BKW, SAF).

Blauburgunder (AUSTRIA) The Austrian term for PINOT NOIR, making light, often sharp reds. *** Georg Steigelmar 1988 £14 (SEL).

Blauer Portugieser (Germany) Red grape used in Germany and Austria to make light, pale wine.

Côtes de/Premières Côtes de Blaye (BORDEAUX, France) Reasonable Blayais whites and sturdy AC reds. PREMIERES COTES are better 82 83 85 86 88 89 90. *** 1er Côtes de Blaye Château Peyonhomme les Tours 1990 £5 (MWW) *** Château Capville 1990 £5.55 (TAN).

Schloss Böckelheim Southern region of the Nahe producing varied fare. Wines from the Kupfergrube vineyard and the State Wine Domaine are worth buying. *** Schloss Böckelheimer Kupfergrube Riesling Auslese 1990 £16 (OWL).

Bodega (Spain) WINERY OR WINE CELLAR; PRODUCER.

Body USUALLY USED AS 'FULL-BODIED', MEANING A WINE WITH MOUTH-FILLING FLAVOURS AND PROBABLY A FAIRLY HIGH ALCOHOL CONTENT.

Jean-Claude Boisset (BURGUNDY, France) Fast-growing NEGOCIANT which has recently bought the impressive JAFFELIN negociant, plus BOUCHARD AINE. Its own wines and those of the latter firm are improving and they are usefully exploring new regions further south. But they need to improve their Burgundies. *** Sainsburys Gamay Vin de Pays des Coteaux de Barronnies 1993 £3.35 (JS) *** Mercurey Blanc Tastevinage £7.75 (W, FDL).

Bolla (VENETO, Italy) Producer of plentiful, adequate VALPOLICELLA and SOAVE and smaller quantities of impressive single vineyard wines like Jago and Creso. One of the Italian companies to have popularised its wines in the States. *** Amarone della Valpolicella Classico 1986 £10.50 (HAR).

Bollinger (CHAMPAGNE, France) Great, family-owned firm at AY, whose wines need age. The luscious & rare VIEILLES VIGNES is made from pre-PHYLLOXERA vines, while the nutty RD was the first late-disgorged CHAMPAGNE to hit the market. Best buy: the vintage. **** 1985 £31 (VW, TH, TDS).

Bommes (BORDEAUX, France) SAUTERNES Commune and village containing several PREMIERS CRUS. 75 76 79 80 81 83 86 88 89 90. ★★★★ Château Rabaud Promis, Premier Cru 1990 £15 (BI).

Ch. le Bon-Pasteur (BORDEAUX, France) The impressive private estate of Michel Rolland, the winemaker more often to be found acting as consultant for half his neighbours as well as producers in ARGENTINA, California, Spain, and almost every other winegrowing region in the universe 81 82 83 85 88 89 90 91. ★★★★ 1989 £19 (C&B, F&M, OD).

Domaine Bonneau du Martray (BURGUNDY, France) Largest grower of Corton-Charlemagne and a reliable producer thereof. Also produces a classy red GRAND CRU CORTON. ★★★★ Corton-Charlemagne 1992 £37 (OD) ★★★★ 1989 £39 (L&W).

Bonnezeaux (LOIRE, France) Delicious sweet whites produced from the CHENIN BLANC which last for ever 71 76 83 85 88 89 90 92. Château des Gauliers 1964 Madame Fourlinnie £40 (YAP).

Bonny Doon Vineyard (SANTA CRUZ MOUNTAINS, California) The wonderfully eccentric dude, Randall Grahm, one of the dozen or so Californian winemakers with a proven sense of humour, has been dubbed the 'Rhône Ranger' for his love of that region's grapes. But his affection for Italian varieties is increasingly evident in a range of characterful red, dry and late harvest whites. ★★★★★ The Catalyst £6 (OD) ★★★ Cinsault 1992 £13.20 (ADN) ★★★★ Ca Del Solo Malvasia Bianca 1992 £7.50 (SAN, POR, HN, NY, M&V).

Borba (ALENTEJO, Portugal) See ALENTEJO

Bordeaux (France) Largest quality wine region in France, producing reds from CABERNET SAUVIGNON, CABERNET FRANC, PETIT VERDOT, and MERLOT, and dry and sweet whites from (principally) blends of SEMILLON and SAUVIGNON. Bordeaux Supérieur denotes slightly riper grapes. Bordeaux Sec is the name used for dry wines from SAUTERNES 81 82 83 85 86 88 89 90. See GRAVES, MEDOC, POMEROL, ST.EMILION, etc.

Borgogno (PIEDMONT, Italy) Resolutely old-fashioned BAROLO producer whose wines develop a sweet, tobaccoey richness with age. In their youth though, they're often not a lot of fun. ★★★ Barolo Riserva 1988 £9 (A, RIB, RBS) ★★★ Barbaresco Riserva 1988 £11 (V&C).

Boschendal (Cape South Africa) Modern winery belongng to the owners of Rothmans, producing some of the Cape's best fizz and fast-improving whites. ★★★ Boschendal Brut NV £10 (SUM) ★★★ Chardonnay 1993 £7 (JS) ★★★ Grand Cuvée Sauvignon Blanc 1993 £6 (MYS, JS, TO).

Botrytis BOTRYTIS CINEREA, A FUNGAL INFECTION THAT ATTACKS AND SHRIVELS GRAPES, EVAPORATING THEIR WATER AND CONCENTRATING THEIR SWEETNESS. VITAL TO SAUTERNES AND THE FINER GERMAN AND AUSTRIAN SWEET WINES. SEE SAUTERNES, TROCKENBEERENAUSLESE.

Bottle-fermented COMMONLY FOUND ON THE LABELS OF US SPARKLING WINES TO INDICATE THE METHODE CHAMPENOISE, GAINING WIDER CURRENCY. BEWARE, THOUGH – IT CAN INDICATE INFERIOR 'TRANSFER METHOD' WINES.

Bouchard Aîné (BURGUNDY, France) For a long-time, an unimpressive merchant, recently taken over by BOISSET and now under the winemaking control of the excellent Bernard Repolt of JAFFELIN. Watch this space. ★★★ Beaune 1er Cru 'Les Sceaux' 1988 £14 (WWT, CAC) ★★★ Mâcon Rouge Supérieur 1992 £4 (MWW).

Bouchard Père et Fils (BURGUNDY, France) Traditional merchant with some great vineyards. Wines – apart from the Beaune de l'Enfant Jesus and LA ROMANEE are generally less impressive. ★★★ Fine Red Burgundy 1990 £6 (CWW) ★★★ Fine White Burgundy 1990 £7 (CWW).

Bouquet OVERALL SMELL, OFTEN MADE UP OF SEVERAL SEPARATE AROMAS.

Côtes de Bourg (BORDEAUX, France) (Relatively) inexpensive, fast-maturing, AC reds with solid MERLOT-dominant fruit. Whites are less impressive 85 86 88 89 90 92. ★★★ Château Plaisance Côtes de Bourg, Pelissac 1992 £4 (A) ★★★ Château Rousset 1990 £5 (ADN).

Bourgogne (France) See BURGUNDY.

Bourgueil (LOIRE, France) Red AC in the TOURAINE area, producing crisp, grassy-blackcurranty 100 per cent CABERNET FRANC wines that can age well in good years 83 85 86 88 89 90 92. **** Dom. Grand Clos. Audebert 1990 £8 (L&W) **** Les Barrois Couly-Dutheil 1993 £6 (U).

Bouvet-Ladubay (LOIRE, France) Producer of good LOIRE fizz and better SAUMUR CHAMPIGNY reds. *** Saumur Brut, Bouvet Ladubay NV £8 (SEL).

Bouvier (Austria) Characterless variety used to produce tasty but simple late-harvest wines. *** Kracher Trockenbeerenauslese 1984 £20 (NY).

Bouzeron (BURGUNDY, France) Village in the COTE CHALONNAISE, principally known for ALIGOTE which is supposedly at its best here 88 89 90 92. ***Aligoté de Bouzeron, A. de Villaine 1992 £7.20 (ADN).

Bouzy Rouge (CHAMPAGNE, France) Sideline of a black grape village: an often thin-bodied, rare and overpriced red wine which, despite what they say, rarely ages 88 89 90 92. *** André Clouet 1988 £15.30 (T&W).

Bowen Estate (COONAWARRA, Australia) Good producer who proves that COONAWARRA can be good for SHIRAZ as well as CABERNET. **** Cabernet Sauvignon, Merlot, Cabernet Franc 1991 £8 (AUC).

Domaines Boyar (BULGARIA) Privatised producers especially in the SUHINDOL region – selling wines under the LOVICO label, which has yet to live up to its promise *** Bulgarian Reserve Merlot 1989 £2.99 (JS).

Brachetto d'Acqui (PIEDMONT, Italy) Eccentric MUSCATY red grape. Often frizzante. *** Araldica 1993 £5 (V&C).

Ch. Branaire-Ducru (BORDEAUX, France) Revival in the 1980s for this fourth-growth ST JULIEN Estate 82 83 85 86 88 89 90. **** 1982 £29 (J&B).

Brand's Laira (COONAWARRA, Australia) Underperforming, traditional producer.

Ch. Brane-Cantenac (BORDEAUX, France) Perennial under achieving MARGAUX, though the second label, the discouragingly named Château Notton can be a worthwhile buy 85 86 88 89 90 91. *** 1988 £15 (VW).

Braquet (MIDI, France) Grape variety used in Bellet. *** Ch. de Crémat 1988 Charles Bagnis £5.75 (YAP).

Brauneberg (MOSEL-SAAR-RUWER, Germany) Village best known in UK for the Juffer vineyard. *** Brauneberger Juffer-Sonnenuhr Auslese 1989 Haag £17 (LV) **** Brauneberger Juffer-Sonnenuhr Riesling Spätlese, Max-Ferd Richter 1990 £20 (SUM).

Brazil Country in which large quantities of fairly light-bodied wines are produced in a region close to Puerto Allegre, where it tends to rain at harvest time. Progress is being made, however, and, as we go to press, there are rumours that Tesco are about to startle a blasé world with their first offering – in answer presumably to Sainsbury's first Uruguayan. The Palomas vineyard on the Uruguayan border has a state-of-the-art winery and a good climate. The wines have yet to reflect those advantages, however. ** Diamantina Brut 1988 £7.95 (W).

Breaky Bottom (Sussex, England) One of Britain's best, making SEYVAL to rival dry wines from the LOIRE. *** Seyval Blanc 1990 £7.50 (SEL).

Georg Breuer (RHEINGAU, Germany) Innovative producer with classy RIESLINGs and high quality RULANDER. **** Trockenbeerenauslese 1989 £79 (half) (OD).

Bricco Manzoni (PIEDMONT, Italy) Non-DOC oaky red blend of NEBBIOLO and BARBERA grapes grown on vines which could produce BAROLO. Drinkable young 83 85 86 87 88 89 90 92. **** Valentino Migliorini 1988 £13 (V&C).

Bridgehampton (LONG ISLAND, New York State) Producer of first class MERLOT and CHARDONNAY to worry a Californian.

Bridgewater Mill (ADELAIDE HILLS, SOUTH AUSTRALIA) Second label of
PETALUMA. Also a wonderful restaurant in which to stop for lunch.
**** Bridgewater Mill Riesling 1993 £5 (VW,OD,TH).

Bright Australian-born Peter Bright of the JOAO PIRES winery makes top-class
Portuguese wines, including Tinto da Anfora and QUINTA DA BACALHOA,
plus a growing range made under the Bright Brothers label for Sainsbury's.
**** Sainsbury's do Campo Tinto, Peter Bright £3 **** Sainsbury's do Campo
Rosado, Peter Bright £3 *** Sainsbury's do Campo Branco, Peter Bright £3 (JS).

British Wine 'MADE' WINE FROM DILUTED GRAPE CONCENTRATE BOUGHT IN FROM
A NUMBER OF COUNTRIES. AVOID IT. ENGLISH WINE IS THE REAL STUFF, PRODUCED
FROM GRAPES GROWN IN ENGLAND.

Jean-Marc Brocard (BURGUNDY, France) Classy CHABLIS producer with well-
defined individual vineyard wines and quite typical lean style. **** Chablis
Premier Cru 'Montmains', Domaine des Manants 1992 £9.50 (SHJ, ADN)
***Chablis 1992 £7 (LAV, OD).

Brokenwood (HUNTER VALLEY, Australia) Starry source of great SEMILLON,
SHIRAZ and even (unusually for the HUNTER VALLEY) CABERNET. *****
Shiraz 1991 £7 (NY, LV, RES, H&H) ***Cricket Pitch Sauvignon Blanc/Semillon
1993 £6.50 (NY, LV, RES, H&H).

Brouilly (BURGUNDY, France) Largest of the ten BEAUJOLAIS CRUS. Pure, fruity
GAMAY 85 88 89 91. *** Brouilly, Georges Duboeuf 1992 £5.65 (SMF).

Ch. Broustet (BORDEAUX, France) Rich, quite old-fashioned, well-oaked
BARSAC 2ème CRU. ***1989 £20 (OWL).

Brown Brothers (North-East VICTORIA, Australia) Family-owned winery
and intrepid explorer of new wine regions and grapes Wines are good but
rarely outstanding, apart from the first class SHIRAZ andthe liqueur
MUSCAT. The ORANGE MUSCAT and Flora also remains a delicious mouthful
of liquid marmalade. *** Tarrango 1993 £5 (W, VW, CWS) ***King Valley
Chardonnay 1992 £7.50 (OD, MWW, TAN, CPW) ****King Valley Shiraz 1991 £6
(OD, THP, GRO, CPW).

Bruder, Dr Becker (RHEINHESSEN, Germany) Known in Germany for
TROCKEN RIESLINGS, but a good source of late-harvest wines and well-made
SCHEUREBE **** Scheurebe Dienheimer Tafelstein Kabinett 1993 £5 (SAF, WMK)
*** Riesling Spätlese Dienheimer Kreuz 1991 £8 (SAF, WMK).

Daniel le Brun (MARLBOROUGH, NEW ZEALAND) The Antipodes' leading
French-style fizz-maker. Probably not for keeping (they mature quickly)
these wines are classy by any standards. ***** Vintage, Cellier Le Brun 1990
£20 (SV, HW) ****Brut NV, Cellier Le Brun £12 (HAR, VW, F&M, CWS).

Brunello di Montalcino (TUSCANY, Italy) Prestigious DOCG red from a
SANGIOVESE clone. Needs at least five years to develop complex and intense
fruit and flavour 83 85 87 88 89 90 91. ***** Brunello di Montalcino, Banfi
1989 £16 (PST, HLV) *** Brunello di Montalcino Riserva, Poggio all'Oro, Banfi
1986 £25 (PST) *** Mandrielle Merlot, Banfi 1991 £10 (PST).

Brut DRY, PARTICULARLY OF CHAMPAGNE AND SPARKLING WINES. BRUT
NATURE/SAUVAGE/ZERO ARE EVEN DRIER, WHILE 'EXTRA-SEC' IS PERVERSELY
APPLIED TO (SLIGHTLY) SWEETER FIZZ.

Bual (MADEIRA) Grape producing a soft, nutty wine that is wonderful
with cheese. *** Cossart & Gordon 5 Year Old Bual £11 (BU).

Buçaco Palace Hotel (Portugal) Red and white wines made from grapes
grown in BAIRRADA and DAO which last forever but cannot be bought
outside the Walt Disneyesque Buçaco Palace Hotel.

Bucelas (Portugal) DO area near Lisbon, known for its intensely coloured,
aromatic, bone-dry white wines which are very hard to find in Britain.

Buena Vista (CARNEROS, California) One of the biggest estates in CARNEROS,
this ought to be one of the best producers of Californian CHARDONNAY and
PINOT NOIR – but it isn't. The CABERNET is worth looking out for when it
reaches UK shores, though.

Bugey (East France) SAVOIE district producing a variety of wines, including white Roussette de Bugey from the grape of that name. *** Vin de Bugey, Crussy Blanc de Blanc (Sparkling) £7.50 (WSO).

Von Buhl (RHEINPFALZ, Germany) One of the area's best estates, due partly to vineyards like the Forster Jesuitengarten See FORST. ****Forster Jesuitengarten Riesling Spätlese 1985 £12 (OWL).

Buitenverwachting (CONSTANTIA, SOUTH AFRICA) Enjoying a revival since the early 1980s, this organic CONSTANTIA winery can sell far more than it produces. Whites are very impressive. **** Chardonnay 1991 £8 (L&W).

Bulgaria Developing quickly since the advent of privatisation and the arrival of flying winemakers. Even so, we have yet to see proof that the good-value, but less than brilliant, country wines, CABERNET SAUVIGNON and MERLOT, with which it has made its reputation, can be bettered. Ironically, the old state-run wineries are now outpacing the supposedly more go-ahead DOMAINES BOYAR privatised ones. Progress is being made with CHARDONNAY at last. MAVRUD is the traditional red variety 81 83 84 85 86 87. *** Sliven Bulgarian Cabernet Sauvignon, Vini Sliven 1989 £3 (TDS, VW, BUD) *** Sainsbury's Bulgarian Chardonnay £3 (JS).

Bull's Blood (EGER, HUNGARY) Red wine, aka EGER BIKAVER, which, according to legend, gave defenders the strength to fight off Turkish invaders. Today it is mostly feeble, poorly made stuff but privatisation promises better things. ** Bull's Blood, St Ursula 1992 £3.50 (SMF).

Burdon (JEREZ, Spain) The brand used by Luis Caballero for his top-class range of sherries.

Burgenland (AUSTRIA) Wine region bordering HUNGARY, climatically ideal for fine, sweet AUSLESEN and BEERENAUSLESEN. *** Eiswein Neusielersee, Weinkellerei Burgenland 1992 £7 (A&N, OD, RBS, BWS) *** Bouvier Trockenbeerenauslese, Weinkellerei Burgenland 1991 £6 (JS).

Alain Burguet (BURGUNDY, France) Good, one-man DOMAINE which proves how good plain GEVREY CHAMBERTIN can be without the help of new oak. Look for his VIEILLES VIGNES. **** Gevrey Chambertin 1989 £20 (D).

Burgundy (France) Home to PINOT NOIR and CHARDONNAY; wines ranging from banal to sublime, but never cheap (Red) 78 83 85 88 89 90 91 92 (White) 85 86 88 89 90 92.

Leo Buring (BAROSSA VALLEY, Australia) Yet another of the PENFOLDS stable – noted for RIESLINGS.

Bürklin-Wolf (RHEINPFALZ, Germany) Impressive estate with great organic RIESLING vineyards. **** Wackenheimer Rechbachel Kabinett 1985 £9 (THP).

Buttery RICH FAT SMELL OFTEN FOUND IN GOOD CHARDONNAY (OFTEN AS A RESULT OF MALOLACTIC FERMENTATION) OR IN WINE THAT HAS BEEN LEFT ON ITS LEES.

Cave des Vignerons de Buxy (BURGUNDY, France) Reliable cooperative with good value oaked Bourgogne Rouge and MONTAGNY PREMIER CRU. *** Montagny 1er Cru, Cave des Vignerons de Buxy 1992 £7 (M&S) ***Somerfield Red Burgundy, Caves de Buxy 1991 £5 (SMF).

Buzbag (TURKEY) Rich, dry, red wine. Sadly, it's rarely well made and often oxidised.

Côtes de Buzet (BORDEAUX, France) AC region adjoining BORDEAUX, producing light claret reds, and whites from SAUVIGNON 88 89 90 92. *** Domaine de la Croix, Vignerons de Buzet 1989 £4 (TO).

Ca' dei Frati (LOMBARDY, Italy) One of Italy's finest white wine producers, both of LUGANA and CHARDONNAY-based fizz. **** Dal Cero 1993 £6.50 (V&C).

Ca' del Bosco (LOMBARDY, Italy) Classic, BARRIQUE-aged CABERNET/MERLOT blend, fine CHARDONNAY and good METHODE CHAMPENOISE FRANCIACORTA from perfectionist producer Maurizio Zanella, who has single-handedly – if pricily – helped put this PINOT BIANCO/PINOT NOIR/CHARDONNAY blend on the international map. ***Franciacorta Brut £25 (V&C). **** Rosso 1983 £24 (V&C) **** Rosso 1988 £25 (V&C).

Ca' del Pazzo (TUSCANY, Italy) Ultra-classy oaky SUPER-TUSCAN from Caparzo with loads of ripe fruit and oak **** 1990 £14 (LAV, WIN).

Cabardès (MIDI, France) Up-and-coming region north of Carcassonne using traditional Southern and BORDEAUX varieties to produce good, if rustic reds. Château Ventenac is good. Also *** Cabardès Domaine de Caunettes Hautes, G & A Rouquet 1992 £4 (DIR, U).

Cabernet d'Anjou/de Saumur (LOIRE, France) Light, fresh, grassy, blackcurranty rosés, typical of their grape, the CABERNET FRANC 85 86 87 88 89 90 92. *** Safeway Cabernet d'Anjou, Rémy Pannier £4 (SAF).

Cabernet Franc Kid brother of CABERNET SAUVIGNON; blackcurranty, but more leafy. Best in the LOIRE, Italy, and partnering CABERNET SAUVIGNON and particularly MERLOT in ST. EMILION. See CHINON and TRENTINO.

Cabernet Sauvignon The great red grape of BORDEAUX, where it is blended with MERLOT and other varieties. The most successful red varietal, grown in every reasonably warm winemaking country. See BORDEAUX, COONAWARRA, CHILE, NAPA. etc.

Cadillac (BORDEAUX, France) Sweet but rarely luscious (non-BOTRYTIS) old-fashioned SEMILLON AND SAUVIGNON whites for drinking young and well chilled. *** Château du Juge Cadillac AC £7 (WR).

Cafayate (ARGENTINA) See ETCHART.

Cahors (South-West France) 'Rustic' BORDEAUX-like reds produced mainly from the local TANNAT and the COT (MALBEC). Some examples are frankly BEAUJOLAIS-like in style while others are tannic, and quite full-bodied, though far lighter than they were in the days when people spoke of 'the black wines of Cahors' 83 85 88 89 90 91. *** Cahors, Clos La Coutale 1990 £7 (NIC) ***Sainsbury's Cahors £3 (JS).

Cairanne (RHONE, France) Named COTES DU RHONE village for good, peppery reds 82 83 85 88 89 90 91. **** Côtes du Rhone Villages, Domaine de la Presidente, Max Aubert, 1990 £5.50 (MWW).

Calabria (Italy) The 'toe' of the boot, making little-seen CIRO from the local Gaglioppo reds and GRECO whites. CABERNET and CHARDONNAY are showing promise, especially those made by LIBRANDI. *** Librandi Cirò 1991 £5 (V&C).

Calem (DOURO, Portugal) Quality-conscious Portuguese-owned producer with a British winemaker. The speciality COLHEITA tawnies are among the best of their kind. **** Colheita 1986 £11.50 (AMA, AV, CNL) **** Quinta da Foz 1982 £14 (F&M) **** 20 Year Old Tawny Port £18 (ABY).

Calera (Santa Benito, California) Maker of some of California's best PINOT NOIR from individual vineyards such as Jensen, Mills, Reed and Selleck. The CHARDONNAY and VIOGNIER are pretty special, too. **** Jensen Pinot Noir 1990 £21 (LAV) ****Central Coast Chardonnay 1991 £11 (MWW).

Caliterra (CURICO, CHILE) Go-ahead winery, making particular progress with its whites, thanks to the efforts of winemaking superstar Ignacio Requabaran. ***Cabernet Sauvignon Reserva, Viña Caliterra 1991 £6 (OD) *** Casablanca Chardonnay 1993 £5 (OD).

Ch. Calon-Ségur (BORDEAUX, France) Traditional ST ESTEPHE that doesn't always live up to its 3rd Growth status and can be dauntingly tough. Lasts well though 82 83 85 86 88 89 90. *** 1989 £19 (AV, JAR).

Cameron (OREGON, US) One of a handful of high-quality PINOT-makers here. CHARDONNAYS are improving too. ****Pinot Noir Reserve 1989 £13 (BI).

Camille-Giroud (BURGUNDY, France) Little-known, laudably old-fashioned merchant with no great love of new oak and small stocks of great mature wine which prove that good BURGUNDY doesn't need it.

Campania (Italy) Region surrounding Naples, best known for TAURASI, LACRYMA CHRISTI and GRECO DI TUFO 85 86 87 88 90 91 92.

Campillo (RIOJA, Spain) A rare example of RIOJA made purely from TEMPRANILLO, showing what this grape can do. The white is less impressive. *** Rioja Gran Reserva 1982 £10 (TO) **** Rioja Crianza 1988 £5 (OD, A).

Campo Viejo (RIOJA, Spain) A go-ahead, often underrated BODEGA whose RESERVA and GRAN RESERVA are full of rich fruit. Albor, the unoaked red (pure TEMPRANILLO) and white (VIURA) are first-class examples of modern Spanish winemaking, while the Reserva 1988 is a good example of why it is often worth not spending the extra on a GRAN RESERVA. **** Albor Rioja 1992 £3.50 (TH, BU, TDS) *** Rioja Gran Reserva 1981 £7.50 (OD, SMF) **** Rioja Reserva 1988 £5 (OD).

Canada Surprising friends and foes alike, the winemakers of British Columbia and, more specifically, ONTARIO are producing good CHARDONNAY, RIESLING, improving PINOT NOIRS and more regularly, intense Ice Wines, usually from the Vidal grape. *** Château des Charmes Chardonnay 1990 £4.50 (SEL) *** Château des Charmes Pinot Noir 1988 £6 (SEL). *** Inniskillin, Pinot Noir Reserve 1991 £10 (AV).

Cannonau di Sardegna (SARDINIA, Italy) Heady, robust, dry-to-sweet, DOC red made from the Cannonau, a clone of the GRENACHE 82 83 84 85 86 88 89 90 91 92. *** Sella & Mosca 1988 £6 (V&C).

Ch. Canon (BORDEAUX, France) First rate property whose subtle wines are wonderful examples of the ST EMILION at their best.Worth seeking out in difficult vintages 82 83 85 86 88 89 90 91. ***** 1989 £39 (AV).

Canon Fronsac (BORDEAUX, France) Small AC bordering on POMEROL for attractive reds from some goodvalue if slightly rustic PETITS CHATEAUX 78 79 82 85 86 88 89 90. *** Château Moulin Pey Labrie 1989 £13 (C&B).

Ch. Cantemerle (BORDEAUX, France) A (5ème) CRU CLASSE situated outside the main villages of the MEDOC. Classy, perfumed wine with bags of blackcurrant fruit 83 85 86 87 88 89 90. **** 1989 £20 (BBR, F&M).

Cantenac (BORDEAUX, France) HAUT-MEDOC commune within MARGAUX whose CHATEAUX include PALMER 82 83 85 86 88 89 90. *** Château Brane-Cantenac 1988 £15 (VW, TP) **** Château Cantenac Brown 1990 £14 (TP).

Canterbury (NEW ZEALAND) Despite early success with PINOT NOIR by St Helena, this cool area of the South Island is best suited to highly aromatic RIESLING and CHABLIS-like CHARDONNAY. Look for wines from GIESEN Amberly Estate, Larcomb, St Helena and Waipara Springs.

Cantina (Sociale) (Italy) WINERY COOPERATIVE.

Cape Mentelle (MARGARET RIVER, Australia) One of the best wineries in Western Australia, with impressive SEMILLON-SAUVIGNON, SHIRAZ, CABERNET and, most remarkably, a wild, berryish ZINFANDEL to shame many a Californian. **** Semillon Sauvignon 1993 £8 (THP, EUR, HHC, MMW, TO) **** Shiraz 1991 £8.50 (JAR, J&B, HN, BAB, N&P), **** Cabernet Merlot 1991 £8 (THP, HHC).

Capel Vale (MARGARET RIVER, Australia) Just outside the borders of MARGARET RIVER (demonstrating the dubious value of New World appellations), a good souce of RIESLINGS and GEWURZTRAMINERS as well as improving reds such as the Baudin blend. **** Shiraz 1989 £8 (AUC).

Villa di Capezzana (TUSCANY, Italy) Conte Ugo Contini Bonacossi not only deserves credit for getting CARMIGNANO its DOCG, he also helped to promote the once unthinkable notion of CABERNET and SANGIOVESE as compatible bedfellows, thus helping to kick open the door for all those priceless – and pricy – SUPER-TUSCANS. *** Carmignano Riserva, Tenuta di Capezzana 1988 £9 (WCE).

Capsule THE SHEATH COVERING THE CORK ON A WINE BOTTLE WHICH, SINCE THE BANNING OF LEAD, IS USUALLY MADE OF PLASTIC OR A TYPE OF TIN.

Caramany (PYRENEES, France) New AC for an old section of the COTES DU ROUSSILLON-VILLAGES. VIGNERONS CATALANS produce a good example.

Carbonic Maceration SEE MACERATION CARBONIQUE.

Ch. Carbonnieux (BORDEAUX, France) Until recently, the whites here aged well but lacked fresh appeal in their youth. Since 1991, however, they are beginning to compete with CHATEAUX FIEUZAL and LA LOUVIERE and the raspberryish reds are becoming some of the most reliable in the region 85 86 88 89 90 91. *** 1988 (red) £13 (C&B).

Carcavelos (Portugal) Sweet, usually disappointing fortified wines from a DO region close to Lisbon. Rare in Britain.

Carema (PIEDMONT, Italy) Wonderful, perfumed NEBBIOLO produced in limited quantities. Look out for Ferrando which V&C are planning to stock.

Carignan Prolific red grape making usually dull, coarse wine for blending, but classier fare in CORBIERES and FITOU. In Spain it is known as CARINENA and Mazuelo, while Italians call it Carignano. **** Minervois, Carignanissime de Centeilles, Boyer-Domergue 1992 £6 (ADN, SOM).

Louis Carillon & Fils (BURGUNDY, France) Superlative modern PULIGNY estate producing impeccable wines ***** Puligny-Montrachet 1er Cru, Champs Canet 1992 £23 (L&W).

Cariñena (Spain) Important DO of Aragon for rustic reds, high in alcohol and confusingly made, not from the Cariñena (or CARIGNAN) grape but mostly from the Garnacha Tinta. Also some whites 88 89 90 91 92. ***Cariñena, Co-op San Valero 1988 £4 (SAF).

Carmenet Vineyard (SONOMA, California) Excellent and unusual winery tucked away in the hills and producing long-lived, very BORDEAUX-like but (unusually for California) very approachable reds, and (even more unusually for California) good SEMILLON-SAUVIGNON whites. ***** Carmenet Cabernet Sauvignon 1988 £12.95 (LAV) **** Sauvignon Blanc/Semillon 1987 £9 (MWW).

Carmignano (TUSCANY, Italy) Exciting alternative to CHIANTI, in the same style but with the addition of CABERNET grapes 82 83 85 86 87 88 89 90 91. *** Carmignano Capezzana 1990 £10 (WCE).

Carneros (California) Small, cool, high-quality region shared between the NAPA and SONOMA Valleys, and producing top-class CHARDONNAY and PINOT NOIR 85 86 87 88 89 90 91. ***** Saintsbury Carneros Reserve Chardonnay 1991 £14 (ADN, HHC, WSO) **** Swanson Vineyards Carneros Chardonnay 1991 £10 (AV).

Carneros Creek (California) Producer of ambitious but toughly disappointing wine under this name and the far better (and cheaper) Fleur de Carneros. ** Carneros Creek Pinot Noir, Signature Reserve 1991 £22 (WWT) **** Fleur de Carneros Pinot Noir 1992 £7 (MWW, WL, RTW).

Carr Taylor (Sussex, England) One of England's more businesslike and reliable estates which has been particularly successful with its fizz . ** Carr Taylor Medium Dry, David Carr Taylor 1992 £5 (EWC, SAS) *** Carr Taylor NV Sparkling Wine 9.50 (EWC, SAS).

Ch. Carras (MACEDONIA, Greece) Until recently the only internationally visible Hellenic effort at modern winemaking. Disappointing when compared with HATZIMICHALIS. ** Château Carras, Côtes de Meliton 1987 £6 (SEL).

Casa (Italy, Spain, Portugal) FIRM OR COMPANY.

Casa vinicola (Italy) FIRM BUYING AND VINIFYING GRAPES.

Casablanca (CHILE) New region in ACONCAGUA acting as a magnet for quality conscious winemakers and producing especially impressive SAUVIGNONS, CHARDONNAYS and GEWURZTRAMINERS, especially from producers like CALITERRA, Santa Carolina, Santa Emiliana, Villard and Casablanca. *** Caliterra Casablanca Estate Chardonnay 1993 £4.99 (OD).

Caslot-Galbrun (LOIRE, France) Top-class producer of serious, long-lived red Loires. ****Bourgueil 1986 £7.25 (WSO).

Castellare (TUSCANY, Italy) Innovative small CHIANTI CLASSICO estate whose SANGIOVESE/MALVASIA NERA I Sodi di San Niccoló VINO DA TAVOLA is worth seeking out. ****I Sodi di San Niccoló 1988 £14.95 (LAV).

Castell'in Villa (TUSCANY, Italy) Producer of powerful CHIANTI CLASSICO RISERVA and a VINO DA TAVOLA called Santa Croche.

Furstlich Castell'sches Domanenamt (FRANKEN, Germany) Prestigious producer of typically full-bodied FRANKEN dry whites. *** Casteller Kirschberg, Müller-Thurgau 1988 £10 (F&M).

Castellblanch (CATALONIA, Spain) Producer of better-than-most CAVA, provided you catch it very young. *** Cava £4.99 (BU)

Casteller (TRENTINO, Italy) Pale red, creamy-fruity wines for early drinking.

Castelli Romani (LATIUM, Italy) FRASCATI-like whites produced close to Rome. Reds are dull.

Castello dei Rampolla (TUSCANY, Italy) Good CHIANTI producer whose wines require patience.

Castello della Sala (UMBRIA, Italy) ANTINORI's rather over-priced but sound CHARDONNAY and good SAUVIGNON and Procanico blend. *** Borro della Sala 1993 £8 (V&C).

Castello di Volpaia (TUSCANY, Italy) High quality CHIANTI estate with SUPER-TUSCAN Coltassala making its mark. **** Coltassala, Castello di Volpaia 1988 £14 (ADN, V&C).

Castellogiocondo (TUSCANY, Italy) High-quality BRUNELLO estate. **** Brunello di Montalcino Castellogiocondo Riserva, Marchesi de Frescobaldi 1986 £19 (ADN, W, WIN) ****1988 £13 (LAV).

Vignerons Catalans (ROUSSILLON, France) Dynamic cooperative producing decent, inexpensive wines. **** Château de Belesta Côtes du Roussillon Villages 1992 £3.50 (SAF) ***Corbières Rouge 1992 £2.50 (MRN).

Catalonia (Spain) The semi-autonomous region in which is found the PENEDES, PRIORATO and the little-known CONCA DE BARBERA, TERRA ALTA and COSTERS DEL SEGRE.

Cat's pee DESCRIBES THE TANGY SMELL OFTEN FOUND IN TYPICAL – AND FREQUENTLY DELICIOUS – MULLER-THURGAU AND SAUVIGNON.

Domaine Cauhapé (South-West France) Extraordinary JURANCON producer of excellent VENDANGE TARDIVE and dry wines from the MANSENG grape. **** Vendange Tardive 1991 £13.00 (M&V)

Cava (Spain) SPARKLING WINE PRODUCED BY THE MÉTHODE CHAMPENOISE BUT WOEFULLY HANDICAPPED BY INNATELY DULL LOCAL GRAPES AND THE TENDENCY TO ALLOW AGE TO DEPRIVE IT OF ANY TRACE OF FRESHNESS AND FRUIT. AVOID VINTAGE VERSIONS AND LOOK INSTEAD FOR ANA DE CODORNIU AND RAIMAT CAVA WHICH (TO LOCAL REACTIONARY HORROR) ARE MADE FROM CHARDONNAY, OR SUCH WELL-MADE EXCEPTIONS TO THE EARTHY RULE AS JUVE I CAMPS AND CONDE DE CARALT (TRADITIONALLY 'EARTHY' BUT NOW MUCH IMPROVED), AND THE FOLLOWING EXAMPLES: *** Torre Del Gall, Gran Reserva Brut, Cava Chandon 1990 £8 (VW) ***Segura Viudas Cava Brut Reserva £6 (WR, OD, ES, WRW).

Cave (France) CELLAR.

Cave Co-operative (France) COOPERATIVE WINERY

Caymus Vineyards (NAPA, California) Traditional producer of concentrated, sometimes rather Italianate reds (including a forceful ZINFANDEL) and a characterful CABERNET FRANC.

Domaine Cazes (ROUSSILLON, France) Maker of great MUSCAT DE RIVESALTES, rich marmaladey stuff which makes most BEAUMES DE VENISE taste dull. **** Muscat de Rivesaltes, Domaine Cazes 1992 £10.50 (HN, PON, LV).

Cellier des Samsons (BURGUNDY, France) Source of better-than-average BEAUJOLAIS. *** Fleurie, Cellier Des Samsons 1993 £6.69 (TH, WR, BU).

Cencibel The name for TEMPRANILLO in VALDEPENAS.

Central Valley (California) Huge, irrigated region controlled by winemaking giants who annually make nearly three quarters of the state's wines without, so far, producing anything to compete with the fruit of very similar regions Down Under. HUGH RYMAN is on his way there, so we'll see what Aussie-style winemaking can achieve. For the moment, QUADY's fortified and sweet wines are the honorable exceptions to the regional rule. ****Starboard (Batch 88) Quady Winery £9 (half) (MWW, WRW, VW).

Central Valley (CHILE) The main region in which most of CHILE's wines were made until producers began to explore further afield in the late 1980s. See UNDURRAGA.

Cépage (France) GRAPE VARIETY.

Cepparello (TUSCANY, Italy) Brilliant, pure SANGIOVESE VINO DA TAVOLA made by Paolo de Marchi of ISOLE E OLENA. ***** Cepparello 1990 £17.25 (WCE, V&C).

Ceretto (PIEDMONT, Italy) Big producer of mid-quality BAROLOS and more impressive single-vineyard offerings. *** Piana 1991 £10 (V&C) *** Bricco Rocche Brunate 1988 £20 (V&C).

Cérons (BORDEAUX, France) Bordering on SAUTERNES with similar, less fine, but cheaper wines 82 85 86 88 89 90. *** Château de Cérons 1989 £17 (NIC).

Ch. Certan de May (BORDEAUX, France) Top-class POMEROL estate with subtly plummy wine. ***** 1989 £47 (C&B).

L. A. Cetto (Baja California, Mexico) With wines like L. A. Cetto's tasty CABERNET and spicy-soft PETITE SIRAH, it's hardly surprising that Baja California is featuring on merchants' lists rather more often than many big names from that slightly more northerly region across the US frontier. **** Petite Sirah 1991 £5 (MRN,CEL,THP) *** Cabernet Sauvignon 1990 £5 (MRN,CEL,THP) *** Nebbiolo 1986 £9 (MRN,CEL,THP).

Chablais (VAUD, Switzerland) A good place to find PINOT NOIR rosé and young CHASSELAS (sold as Dorin).

Chablis (BURGUNDY, France) Often overpriced and overrated white, but fine examples still offer a steely European finesse that New World CHARDONNAYS have trouble capturing. GRANDS CRUS from good producers are worth seeking out for their extra complexity 78 79 81 85 86 87 88 89 90 92. **** Co-op Chablis, La Chablisienne 1990 £7 (CWS) ****Chablis Vieilles Vignes, La Chablisienne 1990 £8 (TH) ****Chablis, Etienne & Daniel Defaix 1990 £10.65 (L&W).

La Chablisienne (BURGUNDY, France) Huge cooperative selling everything from PETIT CHABLIS to GRANDS CRUS under a raft of different labels. Can rival the best estates in the appellation. See CHABLIS.

Chai (France) CELLAR/WINERY.

Chalone (MONTEREY, California) Under the same ownership as ACACIA, EDNA VALLEY and CARMENET, this 25-year-old winery is one of the big California names for PINOT NOIR and CHARDONNAY and even PINOT BLANC. After a rocky period during the late 1980s – when wines displayed some dodgy wood flavours – and the arrival of heavy investment from the Château Lafite Rothschilds, it's right back on form with long-life, very Burgundian wines. *** Chardonnay 1989 £19 (LAV).

Chalonnais/Côte Chalonnaise (BURGUNDY, France) Increasingly sought-after source of lesser-known, less complex Burgundies – GIVRY, MONTAGNY, RULLY and MERCUREY. Potentially (rather than always actually) good-value 85 86 87 88 89 90 92. **** Rully 1er Cru Les Clous, Olivier Leflaive 1992 £10 (L&W).

Chambers Rosewood (RUTHERGLEN, Australia) Competes with Morris for the crown of best Liqueur MUSCAT maker. The Rosewood is worth seeking out. **** Chambers-Rosewood Rutherglen Liqueur Muscat £6 (half) (AUC, ADN, TAN, NY).

Chambertin (BURGUNDY, France) Ultra-cherryish and damsony GRAND CRU whose name was adopted by the village of GEVREY. Already famous in the 14th century, later it was Napoleon's favourite – though he drank it with water. Chambertin Clos-de-Bèze, Charmes-Chambertin, Griottes-Chambertin, Latricières-Chambertin, Mazis-Chambertin and Ruchottes Chambertin are all neighbouring GRANDS CRUS. **** Charmes Chambertin G Roumier 1989 £30 (DD) ***** Chambertin Rossignol-Trapet 1988 £40 (C&B).

Chambolle Musigny (BURGUNDY, France) COTE DE NUITS village whose wines sometimes are more like perfumed examples from the COTE DE BEAUNE. Criticism of quality in recent years drove producers to tighten up the appellation tastings in 1993. Watch this space 78 83 84 85 88 89 90 92. ***** 'La Combe D'Orveau', Domaine Henri Perrot-Minot 1990 £20 (WTR) *** Chambolle-Musigny Masy-Perrier 1991 £12 (SAF).

Champagne (France) Situated in the north-east of France, source of the finest and greatest (and most jealously guarded) sparkling wines, from the PINOT NOIR, PINOT MEUNIER and CHARDONNAY grapes. See individual listings.

Champigny (LOIRE, France) See SAUMUR.

Domaine Chandon de Briailles (Burgundy, France) Good SAVIGNY-LES-BEAUNE estate whose owner is related to the original Chandon of the Champagne house. **** Clos du Roi 1989 £27 (HR).

Chanson (BURGUNDY, France) Long-established but undistinguished merchant. ** Chablis 1er Cru Montmains, Chanson et Fils 1992 £8.49 (MRN).

Chapel Hill (MCLAREN VALE, South Australia) Pam Dunsford's impressively rich – some say too rich – reds and whites have recently been joined by an equally noteworthy but leaner unoaked CHARDONNAY. **** Cabernet Sauvignon 1992 £8 (AUC) *** Reserve Chardonnay 1992 £9 (AUC).

Chapel Hill (Balatonboglar, HUNGARY) Label used for adequate rather than inspiring wines made in Hungary by FLYING WINEMAKER Kym Milne. ** Sainsbury's Hungarian Country White Wine £2.69 (JS).

Chapoutier (RHONE, France) Family-owned merchant which, until recently, was resting on its faded laurels. Now, however, a new generation of Chapoutiers is making some of the best wines in the region, and using more or less organic methods to do so. ***** Crozes Hermitage La Petite Ruche 1992 £8 (VW) ****Châteauneuf-du-Pape La Bernadine 1990 £10 (OD).

Chaptalisation THE LEGAL (IN SOME REGIONS) ADDITION OF SUGAR DURING FERMENTATION TO BOOST A WINE'S ALCOHOL CONTENT.

Charbono Obscure grape variety grown in CALIFORNIA but thought to come from France. Makesvery spicy, full-bodied reds at INGLENOOK VINEYARDS and DUXOUP WINEWORKS. **** Duxoup 1991 £10 (BI).

Chardonnay The great white grape of BURGUNDY, CHAMPAGNE and now the New World. As capable of fresh simple charm in BULGARIA as of buttery, hazelnutty richness in MEURSAULT. See under various producer headings.

Charmat THE INVENTOR OF THE CUVE CLOSE METHOD OF PRODUCING CHEAP SPARKLING WINES. SEE CUVE CLOSE.

Charta (RHEINGAU, GERMANY) SYNDICATE OF RHEINGAU PRODUCERS USING AN ARCH AS A SYMBOL TO INDICATE THEIR NEW DRY (TROCKEN) STYLES MANY OF WHICH SEEM ACIDIC ENOUGH TO REMOVE THE TARTAR – AND ENAMEL – FROM THE TOUGHEST TEETH. SPÄTLESE AND PREFERABLY AUSLESE VERSIONS WILL HAVE BEEN MADE FROM RIPER GRAPES. KABINETTS ARE FOR KEEN LEMON-SUCKERS.

Chartron & Trébuchet (BURGUNDY, France) Good, recently founded, small merchant specialising in white BURGUNDY. **** Rully, La Chaume £9 (LAY) *** Burgundian Chardonnay £6 (LAV).

Chassagne-Montrachet (BURGUNDY, France) COTE DE BEAUNE Commune making grassy, biscuity, fresh yet rich whites and mid-weight, wild fruit reds. Pricy but less so than neighbouring PULIGNY and just as recommendable 85 86 88 89 90 92. ***** 1er Cru 'Les Grandes Ruchottes', Olivier Leflaive 1992 £17 (JAR) **** Chassagne Montrachet, Joseph Drouhin 1990 £20 (VW) *** Chassagne Montrachet Blanc 1991 Louis Latour £14 (MWW).

Ch. Chasse-Spleen (BORDEAUX, France) CRU BOURGEOIS CHATEAU whose wines can, in good years, rival those of many a CRU CLASSE 82 83 86 89 90 91 92. **** 1983 £18 (ADN) **** 1990 £14 (BI).

Chasselas Widely grown, prolific white grape making light, often dull fruity wine principally in Switzerland, eastern France and Germany. ** Fendant du Valais, Caves St Pierre 1992 £10 (SEL) ** Pouilly, Cépage Chasselas, Guyot 1992 £6.50 (YAP).

Domaine du Chasseloir (LOIRE, France) Makers of good domaine MUSCADET
*** Muscadet de Sèvre-et-Maine 1992 £4 (WSO).

Château (usually BORDEAUX) LITERALLY 'CASTLE'; PRACTICALLY, VINEYARD OR
WINE ESTATE.

Château-Chalon (JURA, France) Speciality JURA AC for a VIN JAUNE of good
keeping quality.*** Château Chalon, Bourdy 1986 £25 (62cl) (WSO).

Château-Grillet (RHONE, France) Tiny appellation consisting of a single estate
and producer of once great, now disappointing VIOGNIER white 88 89 90 91
92.** 1990 £27 (YAP).

Châteauneuf-du-Pape (RHONE, France) Traditionally the best reds (rich and
spicy) and whites (rich and floral) of the SOUTHERN RHONE. Thirteen
varieties can be used for the red, though purists still favour GRENACHE
(reds) 78 81 83 85 86 88 89 90 91. Recommended: CHATEAU DE BEAUCASTEL,
CHAPOUTIER (Barbe Rac vineyard), FONT DE MICHELLE, GUIGAL, Rayas.

Gerard Chave (RHONE, France) The best estate in HERMITAGE? Certainly but
the wines demand patience. NB: earlier labels read JL Chave; the eldest son
in alternate generation is thus named, so it is thought to be unnecessary to
bother about printing anything other in between times 82 83 85 88 89 90.
***** Hermitage 1985 £36 (ADN) ***** 1982 £30 (YAP).

Chavignol (LOIRE, France) Village within the commune of SANCERRE.
**** F Cotat 1990 £13 (ADN).

Chef de culture (France) VINEYARD MANAGER.

Chénas (BURGUNDY, France) Least well-known of the BEAUJOLAIS CRUS, but
well worth seeking out 88 89 90 91 92 93. *** Château Desvignes, Paul
Beaudet 1993 £6 (ABY), **** Cave du Château de Chénas 1992 £7 (ROG).

Chêne (France) OAK, AS IN FUTS DE CHENE (OAK BARRELS).

Chenin Blanc The white grape of the LOIRE, making wines with high
acidity varying from bone-dry to very sweet and long-lived, with a
characteristic honeyed taste. Grown successfully in SOUTH AFRICA, NEW
ZEALAND and AUSTRALIA, it makes dull semi-sweet stuff in California. See
VOUVRAY, QUARTS DE CHAUMES, BONNEZEAUX, SAUMUR. **** Millton
Chenin Blanc 1993 £7 (SAF) **** Vouvray Sec Domaine des Aubuisières £7
(OD).

Ch. Cheval Blanc (BORDEAUX, France) Supreme ST EMILION property,
unusual in using a lot more CABERNET FRANC than MERLOT. Great, complex
stuff 81 82 85 86 89 90. ***** 1986 £30 (L&W).

Domaine de Chevalier (BORDEAUX, France) Great PESSAC-LEOGNAN estate
which proves itself in difficult years. The rich, SAUVIGNON-influenced white
is a match for the best BURGUNDY while the restrained, raspberryish red is
one of the most subtle, classy wines in BORDEAUX 83 85 86 87 88 89 90.
***** 1990 (red) £22 (ADN, TP).

Cheverny (LOIRE, France) Light, floral whites from SAUVIGNON and CHENIN
BLANC 76 83 85 86 88 89. *** Dom Le Portail, Michel Cadoux 1992 £4.49 (GWI).

Chianti (Classico, Putto, Rufina) (TUSCANY, Italy) Famous red DOCG
made principally of Sangiovese and of decidedly variable quality. To be
fair, most of it is better than it was pre-1984, when it was customary to add
wine from further south and mandatory to put large amounts of dull white
grapes into the vat with the black ones. The cockerel or cherub, respectively
the insignia of the Classico or Putto growers, is supposed to indicate a finer
wine than the basic Chianti, which is sold in straw-covered *fiasco* bottles,
and the producers in the Rufina area claim that their region makes better
stuff, too. Well, maybe; trusting good producers is a far safer bet. Look for
ANTINORI, ISOLE E OLENA, Castello di Ama, CASTELL'IN VILLA, CASTELLARE,
RUFFINO, CASTELLO DEI RAMPOLLA, CASTELLO DI VOLPAIA, FRESCOBALDI,
SELVAPIANA 82 83 85 86 87 88 89 90 91. **** Chianti Classico, Conti Serristori
1990 £4.85 (SMF) **** Tesco Chianti Classico, Ampelos, San Casciano 1991 £4
(TO) *** Chianti Classico Riserva Ducale Oro, Ruffino 1988 £10.75 (V&C).

Chiaretto di Bardolino (LOMBARDY, Italy) Sadly rare in the UK: refreshing, berryish light reds and rosés from around Lake Garda. ***Chiaretto Classico Bardolino, Rizardi 1992 £10 (BAR).

Chile Rising source of juicy blackcurranty CABERNET and (potentially even better) MERLOT, SEMILLON, CHARDONNAY and SAUVIGNON. See SANTA RITA, CASABLANCA, CONCHA Y TORO, ERRAZUREZ, CALITERRA, MONTES and COUSINO MACUL 81 82 83 84 85 86 88 89 90 91. *** Asda Chilean Cabernet Merlot, Vinicola Lastaguas 1993 £3.50 (A) *** Co-op Chilean Cabernet Sauvignon, Vinhos de Chile £3.50 (CWS).

Chinon (LOIRE, France) CABERNET FRANC-based reds, rosés and whites that are light and grassy when young. Reds from a hot summer can age for up to 10 years 83 85 86 88 89 90. See OLGA RAFFAULT and COULY-DUTHEIL. *** Chinon, Château de la Grille, Antoine Gosset 1992 £8.90 (WIN) *** Chinon Les Violettes, Jacques Morin 1993 £4.25 (AV).

Chiroubles (BURGUNDY, France) One of the BEAUJOLAIS CRUS, drinks best when young and full of almost nouveau-style fruit 88 89 90 91 92. **** Alain Passot 1992 £8 (ROG).

Julian Chivite (NAVARRA, Spain) Innovative producer whose reds and rosés easily outclass many of those from big name RIOJA BODEGAS. **** Reserva 1989 £4.49 (BU).

Chorey-lès-Beaune (BURGUNDY, France) Modest warm reds once sold as COTE DE BEAUNE VILLAGES and now beginning to be appreciated in their own right. Look for TOLLOT BEAUT and the Château de Chorey 78 83 85 86 88 89 90 92. **** Chorey lès Beaune, Edmond Cornu 1990 £11.45 (CAR, GI).

Churchill Graham (DOURO, Portugal) Small **** dynamic young PORT producer, founded by Johnny Graham, whose family once owned a rather larger PORT house. One of the most successful new ventures in the DOURO *** Churchill's Finest Vintage Character Port £9 (HW) .

Chusclan (RHONE, France) Named village of COTES DU RHONE with maybe the best rosé of the area ***Co-op Côtes du Rhone, Co-op Chusclan £3 (CWS).

Cinsaut/Cinsault Prolific, hot climate, fruity red grape with high acidity, often blended with GRENACHE. One of the 13 permitted varieties of CHATEAUNEUF-DU-PAPE, and also in the blend of CHATEAU MUSAR in the Lebanon. **** Bonny Doon Vineyard Cinsault 1992 £13.20 (ADN) *** Spar Cabernet Sauvignon & Cinsault Country Wine Russe Winery £3 (SPR).

Cirò (CALABRIA, Italy) Well-known hefty southern red made from the Gaglioppo, dull white and rosé.*** Ciro Rosso Classico, Librandi 1990 £4.35 (SMF)

Ch. Cissac (BORDEAUX, France) Traditional CRU BOURGEOIS, close to ST ESTEPHE, making tough wines that last. Non TANNIN-freaks should stick to ripe vintages. Very popular among the pinstriped customers of El Vino. 78 79 82 83 85 86 88 89 90. *** 1989/1990 £11 (J&B, OD).

Ch. Citran (BORDEAUX, France) Fast-improving CRU BOURGEOIS thanks to major investment by the Japanese.

Bruno Clair (BURGUNDY, France) Based in MARSANNAY, good wines from FIXIN, GEVREY-CHAMBERTIN, MOREY-ST-DENIS and SAVIGNY. *** Marsannay Vaudenelles £10 (WSO).

Clairet The derivation of 'claret' – very light red wine, almost rosé. *** Château Bonnet Bordeaux Clairet 1993 £5 (TH).

Clairette Dull, white, workhorse grape of southern France used to make CLAIRETTE DE DIE. ** Clairette de Die, Jean-Claude Vincent £5 (SPG).

Clairette de Die (RHONE, France) Pleasant, if rather dull, sparkling wine. The Cuvée Tradition made with MUSCAT is invariably far better; grapey and fresh – like a top-class French ASTI SPUMANTE. *** Georges Aubert Clairette de Die Tradition, Cave Cooperative de Die £6.99 (U).

Auguste Clape (RHONE, France) One of the masters of CORNAS. Great, intense, long-lived wines. ***** Cornas 1990 £17 (YAP).

Clare Valley (Australia) Well-established, slatey soil region enjoying a renaissance with high-quality RIESLINGS that age well and deep-flavoured SHIRAZ, CABERNET and MALBEC. (Look for PETALUMA, PENFOLDS, MITCHELLS, Leasingham, TIM ADAMS, TIM KNAPPSTEIN, Pikes, LINDEMANS) 80 84 86 88 89 90 91. **** Tim Knappstein Clare Valley Riesling 1992 £4.99 (OD) ****Penfolds Clare Estate Chardonnay 1992 £6.99 (OD)

Claret ENGLISH TERM FOR RED BORDEAUX. SEE UNDER SEPARATE BORDEAUX CHATEAU HEADINGS.

Clarete (Spain) TERM FOR LIGHT RED WINE – FROWNED ON BY THE EC.

Ch. Clarke (BORDEAUX, France) A good CRU BOURGEOIS estate recently founded by a Rothschild connected with neither Lafite nor Mouton.*** 1982 £45 (mag) (NIC) *** 1985 £15 (THP).

Classico (Italy) MAY ONLY BE USED ON A CENTRAL, HISTORIC AREA OF A DOC, EG CHIANTI CLASSICO, VALPOLICELLA CLASSICO.

Raoul Clerget (BURGUNDY, France) Traditional, old-fashioned BURGUNDY NEGOCIANT.

Clerico (PIEDMONT, Italy) Superb new wave BAROLO and DOLCETTO producer, with Arte, a terrific NEBBIOLO/BARBERA blend.

Climat (BURGUNDY, France) AN INDIVIDUAL VINEYARD.

Ch. Climens (BORDEAUX, France) Gorgeous, quite delicate BARSAC which easily outlasts many heftier SAUTERNES 83 86 88 89 90 91. ***** 1986 £35 (J&B) ***** 1983 £30 (Bl).

Clone SPECIFIC STRAIN OF A GIVEN GRAPE VARIETY. FOR EXAMPLE, MORE THAN 300 CLONES OF PINOT NOIR HAVE BEEN IDENTIFIED.

Clos (France) LITERALLY, A WALLED VINEYARD – AND OFTEN A FINER WINE.

Clos de la Roche (BURGUNDY, France) One of the most reliable GRAND CRUS in the COTE D'OR. ***** Domaine Armand Rousseau 1990 £31 (ADN).

Clos de Tart (BURGUNDY, France) GRAND CRU vineyard in MOREY ST DENIS exclusively made by Mommessin. Others might do more with it. **** Domaine Mommessin 1988 £44 (F&M).

Clos de Vougeot (BURGUNDY, France) GRAND CRU vineyard divided among more than 70 owners, some of whom are decidedly uncommitted to quality. But who cares when the world is full of fools ready to buy the label? Sensible wine drinkers will seek out names like DOM RION, JOSEPH DROUHIN, JEAN GROS, LEROY, MEO CAMUZET, FAIVELEY, Arnoux and Confuron. **** Grand Cru, Jean Grivot 1989 £30 (L&W).

Clos des Papes (RHONE, France) Once top class CHATEAUNEUF-DU-PAPE estate. *** Clos des Papes 1989 £13 (Bl).

Clos du Bois (SONOMA, California) Top flight producer whose 'Calcaire' CHARDONNAY (named, like Chalk Hill, after the chalky soil of BURGUNDY of which there is none in California) and Marlstone CABERNET-MERLOT are particularly impressive. ***** Chardonnay, Calcaire Vineyard 1992 £15.75 (WIN) ****Briarcrest Cabernet Sauvignon 1990 £16.58 (WIN).

Clos du Roi (BURGUNDY, France) BEAUNE PREMIER CRU that is also part of CORTON GRAND CRU. *** Grand Cru Domaine Comte Senard 1991 £26 (HR).

Clos du Val (NAPA, California) Bernard Portet, brother of Dominique, who runs TALTARNI in Australia, makes good STAGS LEAP CABERNET and MERLOT that develop well with time. **** Cabernet Sauvignon 1989 £13 (WSO, RD, BEN) **** Merlot 1990 £14 (RD, BEN, LEA, CEB).

Clos Floridène (BORDEAUX, France) Great value oaky white GRAVES made by BORDEAUX Blanc superstar Denis Dubourdieu. The inspirationally-titled SECOND LABEL – 'Le Second de Clos Floridène'– is worth buying, too 86 88 89 90. ****Clos Floridène 1992 £12 (OD).

Clos René (BORDEAUX, France) POMEROL estate making intensely concentrated, spicy wines. ****1988 £13.80 (J&B).

Clos St-Georges (BORDEAUX, France) SAUTERNES-like wine produced just outside that appellation 85 86 88 90. *** 1990 £7 (JS).

Cloudy Bay (MARLBOROUGH, NEW ZEALAND) Under the same (now largely French) ownership as CAPE MENTELLE, this is the ten-year-old cult winery that proved how classily the SAUVIGNON can perform in MARLBOROUGH. The CHARDONNAY is equally impressive and the leanish reds improving. The PELORUS fizz is a buttery mouthful. ***** SAUVIGNON BLANC is widely but briefly available to those who have joined merchants' waiting lists. ***** Chardonnay 1992 £12 (J&B) *** Pelorus (Sparkling) 1989 £13 (VW).

J-F Coche-Dury (BURGUNDY, France) A superstar MEURSAULT producer whose basic reds and whites outclass his neighbours' supposedly classier fare. **** Bourgogne Rouge 1991 £12 (L&W) *** Bourgogne Aligoté 1991 £10 (L&W).

Cockburn-Smithes (DOURO, Portugal) Well known for the unexceptional Special Reserve but producer of great vintage and up-market TAWNY PORT. **** 1985 Vintage Port £25 (THP).

Codorniu (CATALONIA, Spain) Humungous fizz maker whose Ana de CODORNIU is a reasonable CAVA from CHARDONNAY. The dull prestige cuvée is popular in Spain. Unsurprisingly perhaps, the new Californian effort tastes… well, CAVA-ish, despite using CHAMPAGNE varieties (widely available).

Colares (Portugal) DO region near Lisbon for heavy, tannic red wines. The vines are grown in deep sand. Almost impossible to find in the UK. **Colares 1983 Chitas £11 (SEL).

Colchagua Valley (CHILE) CENTRAL VALLEY region in which LOS VASCOS and UNDURRAGA are located.

Coldstream Hills (YARRA VALLEY, Australia) Former lawyer turned winemaker and wine writer James Halliday makes stunning PINOT, great (Reserve) CHARDONNAY and increasingly impressive CABERNET-MERLOT. Proof that some critics can make as well as break. **** Cabernet Merlot 1992 £8.50 (W) *** Cabernet Sauvignon 1990 £10 (M&S) ***** Pinot Noir 1993 £8 (OD, M&S).

Colheita (Portugal) HARVEST OR VINTAGE – PARTICULARLY USED TO DESCRIBE TAWNY PORT OF A SPECIFIC YEAR.

Marc Colin (BURGUNDY, France) Large family estate with vineyards in ST-AUBIN, SANTENAY CHASSAGNE and a small chunk of LE MONTRACHET. A class act. **** Santenay 1988 £13 (WSO) **** Chassagne-Montrachet 1992 £15 (OD).

Collards (AUCKLAND, NEW ZEALAND) Small producer of lovely pineappley CHARDONNAY and appley CHENIN BLANC. **** Rothesay Vineyard Chardonnay 1991 £7 (BI, WL).

Colle/colli (Italy) HILL/HILLS.

Colli Berici (VENETO, Italy) DOC for red and white – promising CABERNET ***Colli Berici Cabernet, Vinicola Iseldo Maule £4.35 (GAR).

Colli Orientali del Friuli (FRIULI-VENEZIA GIULIA, Italy) Lively single-variety whites and reds from near the Yugoslav border. Subtle, honeyed and very pricy Picolit, too 88 89 90 91 92. **** La Viarte Pinot Grigio 1993 £9 (BI).

Collio (FRIULI-VENEZIA GIULIA, Italy) High altitude region with a basketful of white varieties, plus those of BORDEAUX and red BURGUNDY. Refreshing and often unshowy. Recommended producers: JERMANN, Puiatti.

Collioure (LANGUEDOC-ROUSSILLON, France) Intense RHONE-style red, often marked by the MOURVEDRE in the blend. *** Domaine Du Mas Blanc, Collioure Jeunes Vignes £7 (WDW).

Colombard White grape grown in South-West France principally for distillation into Armagnac and more recently for good, light modern whites by YVES GRASSA and PLAIMONT. Also planted in AUSTRALIA (see PRIMO ESTATE) and the US, where it is known as FRENCH COLOMBARD and used by E&J GALLO to make their only reasonably priced recommendable wine. *** Deakin Estate Colombard/Chardonnay, Katnook 1993 £4 (VW) *** E&J Gallo French Colombard 1993 £4 (widely available) ****Primo Estate 1993 £6 (AUC)

Columbia Crest (WASHINGTON STATE, US) Affordable producer of MERLOT and second label of CHATEAU SAINTE MICHELLE. *** Merlot 1991 £8 (U).

Columbia Winery (WASHINGTON STATE, US) Producer of good, CHABLIS-style CHARDONNAY and GRAVES-like SEMILLON; subtle single-vineyard CABERNET, MERLOT and SYRAH and Burgundian PINOT NOIR. *** Merlot 1988 £8 (BAR) *** Pinot Noir Woodburne Cuvée 1992 £10 (BAR).

Commandaria (CYPRUS) Traditional dessert wine with rich raisiny fruit *** St John, Keo £5 (U, SEL).

Commune (France) SMALL DEMARCATED PLOT OF LAND NAMED AFTER ITS PRINCIPAL TOWN OR VILLAGE. EQUIVALENT TO AN ENGLISH PARISH.

Conca de Barberà (CATALONIA, Spain) Newish, cool region where Torres makes its (quite) impressive but (very) pricy Milmanda CHARDONNAY and large amounts of bulk wine are produced. Little else to report. *** Milmanda 1990 £21.99 (SEL).

Concha y Toro (MAIPO, CHILE) Fast improving, thanks to the efforts of winemaker Gaetana Carron. Greatest successes so far have been the CABERNETS. Best wines are sold under Don Melchior, Marques de Casa Concha and Casillero del Diablo labels. *** Don Melchior Cabernet Sauvignon 1991 £8 (OD).

Conde de Caralt (CATALONIA, Spain) One of the best names in CAVA. Catch it young though. *** Somerfield Cava £5 (SMF) *** Tanners Cava Brut £6.50 (TAN).

Conde de Valdemar (RIOJA, Spain) See MARTINEZ BUJANDA.

Condrieu (RHONE, France) Potentially fabulous pricy pure VIOGNIER. A cross between dry white wine and perfume. Far better than the ludicrously hyped and high-priced CHATEAU-GRILLET next door, but under pressure from all those VIN DE PAYS VIOGNIERS which are coming onto the market 86 87 88 89 90 91 92. **** Coteau de Vernon, George Vernay 1992 £25 (YAP) *** Guigal 1992 £20 (OD).

Consejo Regulador (Spain) SPAIN'S ADMINISTRATIVE BODY FOR THE ENFORCEMENT OF THE DO LAWS.

Consorzio (Italy) SYNDICATE OF PRODUCERS, OFTEN USING THEIR OWN SEAL OF QUALITY.

Constantia (SOUTH AFRICA) The first wine region in the first New World country. Until recently, inexplicably, the big name here was the government-run and undistinguished ** Groot Constantia. Now KLEIN CONSTANTIA produces wines which go much further to explain this region's enduring reputation. See KLEIN CONSTANTIA. ****Vin de Constance 1988 £13.59 (50cl) (WTR).

Aldo Conterno (PIEDMONT, Italy) A truly top class BAROLO estate from individual vineyards as well as top class BARBERA. Nobody does it better. *ç* Vigna Cicala 1990 £20 (WCE) **** Granbussia 1985 £27 (WCE).

Contino (RIOJA, Spain) Good, reliable RIOJA ALAVESA estate whose wines have more fruit and structure than most. Reserva is estate-bottled. *** ***Reserva 1987 £10 (L&W).

Coonawarra (SOUTH AUSTRALIA) Extraordinary cool(ish) red-soil region in the middle of nowhere. Produces great blackcurranty-minty CABERNET as well as big CHARDONNAYS and full-bodied RIESLING. Still Australia's only internationally acknowledged top-class mini-region. (red) 82 84 85 86 87 88 90 91 92 (white) 86 87 88 90 91 92. See PETALUMA, WYNNS, ROUGE HOMME, PARKER ESTATE, LINDEMANS, KATNOOK.

Coopers Creek (AUCKLAND, NEW ZEALAND) Good, individualistic whites including Coopers Dry, a CHENIN-SEMILLON blend, CHARDONNAY, SAUVIGNON and RIESLING. ****Chardonnay 1993 £6 (MWW).

Cope Williams (VICTORIA, Australia) Small but superb producer of possibly the best fizz in Oz. As yet unavailable in the UK.

Copertino (Italy) Richly fascinating, intensely berryish wine made from the NEGROAMARO. ****Sainsbury's Copertino Riserva, Cantina Sociale Co-op Copertino 1991 £4 (JS).

Corbans (Henderson, NEW ZEALAND) Big winery (encompassing Cooks). Good rich MERLOT reds. **** Private Bin Merlot 1992 £9 (VW)
**** Private Bin Cabernet Sauvignon/Merlot 1991 £7 (JS).

Corbières (MIDI, France) Fast-improving red wines, moving from rustic to RHONE in style. Whites and rosés have further to go 85 86 88 89 90 91 92.
**** Château de Lastours Corbières, Fûts de Chêne 1989 £7 (TH, WR).

Corked UNPLEASANT MUSTY SMELL AND FLAVOUR, CAUSED BY FUNGUS ATTACKING CORK. ALMOST ALWAYS GETS WORSE ON CONTACT WITH OXYGEN.

Cornas (RHONE, France) Dark red from the SYRAH grape, hugely tannic when young but worth keeping 76 78 79 82 83 85 88 89 90 91. Recommended: CLAPE, Tain Cooperative, JUGE, DE BARJAC, Colombo. ***** Cuvée 'SC', Marcel Juge 1991 £14 (WTR) **** Les Coteaux, Robert Michel 1989 £11 (YAP)

Corsica (France) Mediterranean island making robust reds, whites and rosés under a raft of appellations (doled out with the kind of generosity to be expected of governments who need to keep rebellious islanders happy). VINS DE PAYS are often more interesting. *** Pinot Noir 'L' 1992 Vin de Pays de L'Ile de Beauté £5 (TP).

Cortese (Italy) Grape used in PIEMONTE and to make GAVI.

Corton (BURGUNDY, France) GRAND CRU hill potentially making great, intense, long-lived reds and – as Corton Charlemagne – whites. Disappointments can be attributed to the fact that the supposedly uniformly great vineyards run a suspiciously long way round the hill. Some are far less well sited than others. Reds can be very difficult to taste young; many never develop.
**** Corton Grand Cru, Domaine Tollot-Beaut 1986 £24 (J&B).

Corvo (SICILY, Italy) Ubiquitous producer of pleasant reds and whites.
*** Corvo Rosso, Vinicola Duca di Salaparuta 1991 £6 (TAN).

Ch. Cos d'Estournel (BORDEAUX, France) In ST ESTEPHE, but making wines with PAUILLAC richness and fruit, this SUPER SECOND is one of the best CHATEAUX in BORDEAUX. Spice is the hallmark 82 83 85 86 88 89. ***** 1985 £23 (AV, C&B, BBR, F&M).

Cosecha (Spain) HARVEST OR VINTAGE.

Cossart Gordon (MADEIRA, Portugal) High quality brand used by the Madeira Wine Co. **** 5 Year Old Malmsey Madeira £11 (J&B).

Costers del Segre (CATALONIA, Spain) Denomination more or less created for RAIMAT.

Costières de Nimes (MIDI, France) Up-and-coming region which can make reds of the class of the northern Rhône. ***Ch Paul Blanc Rouge 1992 £4.50 (OD) ***Viognier, Jacques Frelin 1993 £5.99 (VER).

Costières du Gard (South-West France) Fruity reds, rarer whites and rosés. Surprisingly hard to find in the UK.

Cot The red grape of CAHORS and the Loire, aka MALBEC.

Côte de Beaune (Villages) (BURGUNDY, France) Geographical distinction for the southern half of the COTE D'OR. With the suffix 'Villages', indicates red wines from one or more of the villages in the Côte de Beaune. Confusingly, wine labelled simply 'Côte de Beaune' comes from a small area around BEAUNE itself and often tastes like wines of that appellation. These wines (red and white) are rare 79 80 82 83 85 87 88 89 90 92.

Côte de Brouilly (BURGUNDY, France) One of the BEAUJOLAIS CRUS; distinct from BROUILLY and often finer. Floral and ripely fruity; will keep for a few years 88 89 90 91 92 93. *** Domaine De Chavannes, Duboeuf 1992 £7 (AV).

Côte de Nuits (BURGUNDY, France) Northern and principally 'red' end of the COTE D'OR. The suffix 'Villages' indicates wine from one or more of the communes in the area 78 80 82 83 84 85 86 87 88 89 90 92.

Côte des Blancs (CHAMPAGNE, France) Principal CHARDONNAY-growing area 78 83 85 86 88 90. ***Champagne Le Mesnil Blanc de Blancs £14.35 (TH).

Côte d'Or (BURGUNDY, France) Geographical designation for the central, finest slopes running down the region, encompassing the COTE DE NUITS and COTE DE BEAUNE. See under various BURGUNDY entries.

Côte Rôtie (RHONE, France) Powerful, smoky yet refined SYRAH (possibly with a touch of white VIOGNIER) reds from the northern RHONE, divided into two principal hillsides, the 'Brune' and 'Blonde'. Need at least six (better 10) years. Best producers: GUIGAL, GERIN, ROSTAING, Champet, JAMET, JASMIN, Burgaud, Dervieux-Thaizé 76 78 79 82 83 85 88 89 90 91.
***** Côte Rôtie Champin Le Seigneur, Jean-Michel Gerin 1991 £16 (WTR)
**** Côte Rôtie, Côtes Brune et Blonde, E Guigal 1989 £17 (BU).

Côte(s), Coteaux (France) HILLSIDES – PREFIXED TO, eg BEAUNE, INDICATES FINER WINE.

Coteaux Champenois (CHAMPAGNE, France) Appellation for the madly over-priced still wine of the area. Mostly thin, light and acidic; justification for putting bubbles into this region's wines. LAURENT-PERRIER is better than most, but it's still only worth buying in the ripest vintages – if you can find it 88 89 90 92.

Côtes du Rhône (Villages) (France) Large APPELLATION for both medium and full-bodied spicy reds produced throughout, but mostly in the southern part of the RHONE Valley. The best supposedly come from a set of better villages (and are sold as C d R Villages) though some single domaine 'simple' COTES DU RHONES outclass many Villages wines. GRENACHE is the key red wine grape but the SYRAH is gaining ground. Whites can include new wave VIOGNIERS but most are flabby and dull 83 85 86 87 88 89 90 91 92. *** Cairanne Domaine de la Presidente, Max Aubert 1990 £5.49. (MWW) *** Château La Diffre, Séguret 1992 £4 (VW)

Cotesti (ROMANIA) Easterly vineyards growing some French varieties.

Cotnari (ROMANIA) Traditional white dessert wine.

El Coto (RIOJA, Spain) Small Estate producing good, medium-bodied El Coto and Coto Imaz reds. **** Rioja Crianza 1991 £5 (EOO).

Coulure VINE DISORDER CAUSED BY ADVERSE CLIMATIC CONDITIONS WHICH RESULTS IN GRAPES SHRIVELLING AND FALLING. THE REMAINING GRAPES CAN MAKE HIGHER QUALITY WINES THANKS TO REDUCED YIELDS.

Couly-Dutheil (LOIRE, France) High-quality CHINON estate with vines growing to just behind the château in which Henry II imprisoned Eleanor of Aquitaine, his scheming wife. **** Chinon Rosé 1992 £5 (MWW).

Pierre Coursodon (RHONE, France) One of the best producers in ST JOSEPH.
***** Saint Joseph L'Olivaie 1991 £11.30 (BU).

Cousiño Macul (MAIPO, CHILE) Arguably the only producer in CHILE to master traditional methods. Reds are more successful than whites.
**** Antiguas Reserva Cabernet Sauvignon 1989 £5.99 (ADN, CWN) *** Limited Release Merlot 1989 £4.80 (TO).

Ch. Coutet (BORDEAUX, France) Delicate neighbour to CHATEAU CLIMENS, often making comparable wines: Cuvée Madame is top flight 82 83 85 86 88 89 90 **** 1989 £20 (AV, BBR, C&B).

Cowra (NEW SOUTH WALES, Australia) Up-and-coming region, making a name for itself with CHARDONNAY. May well eclipse its better known but less viticulturally ideal neighbour, the HUNTER VALLEY. **** Rothbury Estate Cowra Vineyards Chardonnay £6 (JS) *** Triple Eagle, Cowra Estate 1990 £6.99 (SK).

Cranswick Estate (South-East Australia) Successful RIVERLAND producer making reliable inexpensive wines widely available under the Barramundi label. *** Chardonnay 1993 £4 (MWW)

Cream sherry POPULAR STYLE (THOUGH NOT IN SPAIN) PRODUCED BY SWEETENING AN OLOROSO. THE NAME IS ATTRIBUTED TO A VISITOR TO THE HARVEYS CELLARS WHO REMARKED HOW MUCH SHE PREFERRED ONE OF THE COMPANY'S SHERRIES TO THE ONE THEN BEING SOLD AS 'BRISTOL MILK'. "IF THAT IS THE MILK", SHE IS SAID TO HAVE JOKED, " THIS MUST BE THE CREAM". **** Waitrose Cream Sherry, Antonio Romero £4.35 (W) **** Don Zoilo Cream £8 (GHS, LV).

Crémant (France) IN CHAMPAGNE, LIGHTLY SPARKLING. ELSEWHERE, eg CREMANT
DE BOURGOGNE, DE LOIRE AND D'ALSACE, **MÉTHODE CHAMPENOISE** FIZZ
*** Mayerling Crémant d'Alsace, Cave Vinicole de Turckheim £9 (TH)
*** Domaine de Martinolles, Crémant de Limoux 1990 £7.30 (ET, ABV).

Criado y Embotellado (por) (Spain) GROWN AND BOTTLED (BY).

Crianza (Spain) LITERALLY 'KEEPING' – 'CON CRIANZA' MEANS AGED IN WOOD –
OFTEN PREFERABLE TO THE **RESERVA** AND **GRAN RESERVA** WHICH ARE HIGHLY
PRIZED BY SPANIARDS BUT TO US BRITONS CAN TASTE DULL AND DRIED-OUT.
**** Rioja Berberana Tempranillo Crianza 1990 £3.49 (WL,WCE,TPW), ***
Señorio de Nava Ribera del Duero Crianza 1989 £6 (A, SPR, SAF, CWS, FUL).

Crisp FRESH, WITH GOOD ACIDITY.

Croft (Spain/Portugal) PORT and SHERRY producer making highly commercial
but rarely memorable wines in either style **** Sainsbury's Late Bottled
Vintage Port, Croft 1987 £6.60 (JS) *** Croft Vintage Port 1982 £18.20 (VW).

Croser Made by Brian Croser of **PETALUMA** in the **PICCADILLY VALLEY**, this is
one of the New World's most **CHAMPAGNE**-like fizzes. Once a little lean;
improving as the proportion of **PINOT NOIR** in the blend increases.
**** Croser Petaluma 1991 £11 (VW, OD, ROB, BEN, BH).

Crouchen (France) Obscure grape capable of producing agreeable whites.
Known as Clare Riesling in Australia and **PAARL** Riesling in **SOUTH AFRICA**.
***White Clare, Wakefield Wines 1991 £5.00 (BTH, U, HAR, RAE, W).

Crozes-Hermitage (RHÔNE, France) Up-and-coming appellation on the hills
behind supposedly greater **HERMITAGE**. Smoky, blackberryish reds are pure
SYRAH. Whites (made from **MARSANNE** and **ROUSSANNE**) are creamy but less
impressive. And they rarely keep. Recommended: **CHAPOUTIER** (including
White), DELAS, GRAILLOT, Pochon, Tain cooperative, TARDY & ANGE 78 79
82 83 85 88 89 90 91. ***** La Petite Ruche, M Chapoutier 1992 £8 (VW) ***
Rouge, Domaine des Entrefaux 1990 £6.30 (ABY) *** Domaine Pochon 1992 £7
(J&B).

Cru Artisan (France) OBSOLETE CLASSIFICATION FOR SUB-**CRU BOURGEOIS** WINES.

Cru Bourgeois (BORDEAUX) WINES BENEATH THE **CRUS CLASSES**, SATISFYING
CERTAIN REQUIREMENTS, WHICH CAN BE GOOD VALUE FOR MONEY AND, IN CERTAIN
CASES, BETTER THAN SUPPOSEDLY CLASSIER CLASSED GROWTHS. *** Château Tour
Haut Caussan, Médoc 1991 £8.20 (ADN).

Cru Classé (BORDEAUX) THE BEST WINES OF THE **MEDOC** ARE CRUS CLASSES, SPLIT
INTO FIVE CATEGORIES FROM FIRST (TOP) TO FIFTH GROWTH (OR CRU) IN 1855. THE
GRAVES, ST EMILION AND SAUTERNES HAVE THEIR OWN CLASSIFICATIONS.

Cru Grand Bourgeois /Exceptionnel (France) AN ESTATE-BOTTLED HAUT-
MEDOC CRU BOURGEOIS, WHICH IS SUPPOSEDLY AGED IN OAK BARRELS. TERM IS
THE SAME AS CRU BOURGEOIS SUPERIEUR, THOUGH EXCEPTIONNEL WINES MUST
COME FROM THE AREA ENCOMPASSING THE **CRUS CLASSES**. FUTURE VINTAGES WILL
NOT BEAR THIS DESIGNATION AS IT HAS FALLEN FOUL OF THE EC.

Hans Crusius (NAHE, Germany) One of the most famous estates in Germany
run by Hans and his son Dr Peter Crusius. Famous for a clarity and depth
of flavour, strongly marked by the soil and preserved by careful, traditional
winemaking. Big old oak casks are the norm with many of the wines. Better
TROCKEN wines than most, thanks to the use of riper grapes.85 86 88 89 90
92 93. **** Traiser Rotenfels Riesling Spätlese Trocken 1990 £10 (L&W).

Crusted port AFFORDABLE ALTERNATIVE TO **VINTAGE PORT**, A BLEND OF
DIFFERENT YEARS BOTTLED YOUNG AND ALLOWED TO THROW A DEPOSIT **** Dows
Crusted Port 1987 £10.45 (SAF) **** Grahams Crusted Port £11.99 (TO, MWW,
CNL) *** Booths Crusted Port Martinez £9.95 (BTH).

Cullen (MARGARET RIVER, Australia) Brilliant estate run by mother and
daughter team of Di and Vanya Cullen. Source of stunning SAUVIGNON-
SEMILLLON blends, CLARET-like reds and Burgundian CHARDONNAY.
***** Cullens Sauvignon Blanc 1993 £10.45 (ADN) **** Cullens Cabernet
Sauvignon/ Merlot Reserve 1991 £11.60 (DIR).

Curico (CHILE) Wine region in which TORRES, SAN PEDRO and CALITERRA have vineyards. Rapidly being eclipsed by CASABLANCA. *** Co-op Chilean Cabernet Sauvignon, Vinhos de Chile £3.50 (CWS).

Cuvaison (NAPA, California) Swiss-owned winery which produces high-quality CARNEROS CHARDONNAY, increasingly approachable MERLOT and now, good PINOT NOIR. Calistoga Vineyards is a new second label. *** Chardonnay 1991 £13 (MWW).

Cuve close THE THIRD-BEST WAY OF MAKING SPARKLING WINE, WHERE THE WINE UNDERGOES SECONDARY FERMENTATION IN A TANK AND IS THEN BOTTLED. ALSO CALLED THE CHARMAT OR TANK METHOD.

Cuvée (de Prestige) MOST FREQUENTLY A BLEND PUT TOGETHER IN A PROCESS CALLED ASSEMBLAGE. PRESTIGE CUVEES ARE (PARTICULARLY IN CHAMPAGNE) SUPPOSED TO BE THE CREAM OF A PRODUCER'S PRODUCTION.

CVNE (RIOJA, Spain) COMPANIA VINICOLA DEL NORTE DE ESPANA IN FULL, 'COO-NAY' IN SHORT: A LARGE OPERATION BY THE OWNERS OF CONTINO, PRODUCING THE EXCELLENT VINA REAL IN CRIANZA, RESERVA; IMPERIAL OR GRAN RESERVA IN THE BEST YEARS, AND A LIGHT CVNE TINTO. UNTIL RECENTLY, CONSISTENT, HIGH-QUALITY WINES, THOUGH SOME RECENT RELEASES HAVE BEEN SLIGHTLY LESS DAZZLING. **** Viña Real Rioja Reserva CVNE 1986 £8.99 (WSO).

Didier Dagueneau (LOIRE, France) The iconoclastic producer of some of the best, steeliest POUILLY FUME. Prices are high but his super SILEX is worth seeking out **** Pouilly Fumé Pur Sang, 1992 £16.90 (ABY). ****Pouilly Fumé Domaine Buisson Ménard, 1992 £15 (TH,WR, BU).

Dão (Portugal) Once Portugal's best known wine region – despite the dullness of most of what was produced. Today, thanks to a few pioneering producers like SOGRAPE, both reds and whites are improving. Even so, BAIRRADA is intrinsically more interesting 88 89 90 92 *** Co-op Dão, Sogrape 1990 £2.99 (CWS).

Kurt Darting (RHEINPFALZ, Germany) One of Germany's all too small band of new wave producers who care more about ripe flavour than making excessive quantities of tooth-scouringly dry wine. Men like Darting deserve every true German wine lover's support. ***** Forster Schnepfenflug Huxelrebe Trockenbeerenauslese 1992 £13.99 (OD) **** Ungsteiner Herrenberg Riesling Spätlese 1992 £5.99 (OD).

Réné Dauvissat (BURGUNDY, France) One of the best estates in CHABLIS. Watch out for other Dauvissats – the name is one of the many used by the LA CHABLISIENNE Cooperative. **** Les Forêts 1992 £13 (TVW) **** Les Preuses 1992 £20 (TVW).

Guy de Barjac (RHONE, France) A master of the SYRAH grape, producing some of the best, smokiest examples around. ***** Cornas 1990 £16.25 (L&W).

De Bartoli (SICILY, Italy) If you want to drink MARSALA rather than use it in cooking, this is the name to remember. The raisiny Bukkuram, made from PASSITO Muscat grapes is an alternative delight **** Josephine Doré £8 (WCE) **** Bukkuram Moscato Passito Di Pantelleria £18 (half) (WCE).

De Bortoli (RIVERINA, Australia) Fast-developing firm (following its move into the YARRA VALLEY) which startled the world by making a Botrycised peachy, honeyed SEMILLON which beat CHATEAU D'YQUEM in blind tastings – and by making it in the unfashionable RIVERINA. That wine, like other Aussie stickies, is still hard to find in Europe, thanks to the EC's attempts over the past few years to protect us from the pleasure of drinking them. Now, however, new agreements which, in return for a ban on the Aussies making and selling their own "CHABLIS" (in Australia), will allow us to see just how well winemakers there can outperform the Old World *** Windy Peak Cabernet Merlot 1992 £5.69 (SAF) ***Windy Peak Chardonnay 1992 £5.29 (JS) ***St Michael Australian Brut Sparkling Wine £5 (M&S).

Ch. de Francs (BORDEAUX, France) Good-value property making crunchy, blackcurranty wine and proving the worth of the little-known region of the Côtes de Francs. **** 1990 £8 (TH, WR, BU).

Ch. de Pez (BORDEAUX, France) Well-made, late-developing CRU BOURGEOIS in ST ESTEPHE which, with time, can rival the CRUS CLASSES. 82 83 85 86 88 90. *** 1990 £12 (J&B).

Ch. de Puygueraud (BORDEAUX, France) The Côtes de Francs red wine made by the Belgian Thienpont family and treated with the same care as their Labégorce Zédé and VIEUX CHATEAU CERTAN. *** 1988 £10 (DIR).

Comte de Vogüe (BURGUNDY, France) Old COTE DE NUITS estate famous for its Vieilles Vignes MUSIGNY, rare white from that vineyard and its BONNES MARES. Went through a dodgy phase during the 1980's but has been back on form of late. *** Musigny Blanc 1988 £130 (T&W) *** Musigny Vieilles Vignes 1988 £60 (T&W).

Danie De Wet (ROBERTSON, SOUTH AFRICA) Starry producer of top class Burgundian style CHARDONNAY. **** Grey Label Chardonnay 1993 £5 (JS) ***Chardonnay Sur Lie 1993 £4.30 (OD, SAF).

Dealul Mare (ROMANIA) Carpathian region once known for whites, now producing pleasant if unexceptional reds from 'noble' varieties. ** Cabernet Sauvignon Special Reserve, Rovit SA 1985 £2.99 (MRN).

Etienne & Daniel Defaix (BURGUNDY, France) Classy, traditional CHABLIS producer, making long-lived wines with a steely bite. **** Chablis 1990 £10.65 (L&W) ***Chablis Premier Cru 'Les Lys' 1988 £14.65 (L&W).

Dégorgée (dégorgement) THE REMOVAL OF THE DEPOSIT OF INERT YEASTS FROM CHAMPAGNE AFTER MATURATION. SEE RD.

Deidesheim (RHEINPFALZ, Germany) Distinguished wine town noted for flavoursome RIESLINGS. *** Deinhard Collection, Deidesheim 1988 £6.75 (CNL).

Delas Frères (RHONE, France) Often underrated NEGOCIANT whose red individual vineyard wines can rival those of GUIGAL and the reconstructed CHAPOUTIER. ***** Hermitage Cuvée Marquise de la Tourette 1990 £18 (LAY, PST) ***** 1987 £11.95 (EV) ****Crozes-Hermitage Les Launes 1990 £6.50 (LAY).

Delatite (Central VICTORIA, Australia) Producer of lean-structured, long-lived wines. *** Merlot 1992 £6.99 (AUC) ****Devil's River 1991 £8 (AUC, TO).

Delegats (AUCKLAND, NEW ZEALAND) Family firm which has hit its stride recently with impressively ripe reds, especially plummy MERLOTS. Export wines are often labelled 'Oyster Bay'. **** Merlot 1991 £6 (WR) **** Oyster Bay Chardonnay 1993 £8 (MWW) **** Proprietor's Reserve Cabernet Sauvignon 1991 £9 (MWW).

Demi-sec (France) MEDIUM-DRY.

Denbies (Surrey, England) Dynamic co-production between a UK landowner and a South African winery owner (of La Bri). Part tourist attraction part winery, it has so far produced good dry wines and far better sweet ones, but the arrival of an Australian colleague is expected to improve the German winemaker's game. It may even lead to the production and release of the sparkling wines for which the chalky hillsides seem ideal. **** Noble Harvest 1992 £17.50 (RWW, SEL, HAR).

Deutches Weinsiegel (Germany) SEALS OF VARIOUS COLOURS AWARDED FOR MERIT TO GERMAN WINES, USUALLY PRESENT AS NECK LABELS. TO BE TREATED WITH CIRCUMSPECTION.

Deutscher Tafelwein (Germany) TABLE WINE, GUARANTEED GERMAN AS OPPOSED TO GERMANIC-STYLE EC TAFELWEIN.

Deutz (CHAMPAGNE, France; Spain, New Zealand, California) Good, traditional producer which was one of the first of the Champenois to try to make better than adequate wine overseas. The New Zealand Deutz MARLBOROUGH Cuvée, made with MONTANA, is back on form after a rocky patch, the Deutz-influenced Yalumba 'D' is first-class and the Californian Maison Deutz is a rich winner too. **** Deutz Marlborough Cuvée Brut, Montana Wines Ltd £10 (OD).

Diabetiker Wein (Germany) INDICATES A VERY DRY WINE WITH MOST OF THE SUGAR FERMENTED OUT (AS IN A DIAT LAGER), THUS SUITABLE FOR DIABETICS.

Disznókó (TOKAY, Hungary) Newly consituted estate owned by the giant AXA Insurance Co. and run by Jean Michel Cazes of CHATEAU LYNCH BAGES. Wines have yet to be released in the UK but they will be worth watching out for. (Contact TH).

Diamond Creek (NAPA, California) Big name producer with good vineyards (Gravelly Meadow, Red Rock Terrace and Volcanic Hill) but tough wine.

DLG (Deutsche Landwirtschaft Gesellschaft) BODY AWARDING MEDALS FOR EXCELLENCE TO GERMAN WINES. FAR TOO GENEROUSLY.

DO Denominaci/on/ão d'Origen (Spain, Portugal) DEMARCATED QUALITY AREA, GUARANTEEING ORIGIN, GRAPE VARIETIES AND PRODUCTION STANDARDS.

DOC(G) Denominazione di Origine Controllata (é Garantita) (Italy) QUALITY CONTROL DESIGNATION BASED ON GRAPE VARIETY AND/OR ORIGIN. 'GARANTITA' IS SUPPOSED TO IMPLY A HIGHER QUALITY LEVEL BUT IT IS NOT A RELIABLE GUIDE.

Ch. Doisy-Daëne (BORDEAUX, France) Fine BARSAC property whose wines can be more restrained than those of some of its neighbours 82 85 86 88 89 90. **** 1989 £20 (BBR, ADN).

Ch. Doisy-Dubroca (BORDEAUX, France) Little-known, underrated four-star SAUTERNES estate producing ultra-rich wines at often attractively low prices. Sadly hard to find in the UK 82 85 86 88 89 90.

Ch. Doisy-Védrines (BORDEAUX, France) A generally reliable BARSAC property which made a stunningly concentrated 1989 (and a less impressive 1990) 82 85 85 88 89 90. *** 1989 £19 (WDW, BBR).

Dolcetto (d'Alba, di Ovada) (PIEDMONT, Italy) Red grape making anything from soft, everyday wine to more robust, long-lasting DOCs. In all but the best hands, worth catching young 83 85 86 88 89 90 92. **** Dolcetto d'Alba Pianromualdo, Mascarello 1993 £8 (WCE) **** Dolcetto d'Alba, Conterno 1992 £9.50 (V&C).

Dôle (Switzerland) Appellation of VALAIS producing attractive, rather than stunning reds from the PINOT NOIR and/or GAMAY. Best bought by people who have plenty of Swiss currency and who like very light wines to knock back after a day on the piste. **Caves St. Pierre 1991 £9.49 (SEL).

Dom Pérignon (CHAMPAGNE, France) Top-end of MOET ET CHANDON's CHAMPAGNE, named after the Abbey cellarmaster who is erroneously said to have invented the CHAMPAGNE method. One of the few instances where Rock Stars who buy by the label actually end up with worthwhile goods. (Incidentally, Moët will disgorge older vintages to order for customers' birthdays and anniversaries. Write and ask.) ***** £60 (OD).

Domaine (France) WINE ESTATE, CAN ENCOMPASS A NUMBER OF VINEYARDS.

Domaine Carneros (NAPA, California) ROEDERER's US fizz – produced in a perfect and thus ludicrously incongruous replica of the CHAMPAGNE house's HQ in France. One of the best New World efforts by the Champenois. **** Not, as yet, available in the U.K.

Domaine Chandon (NAPA, California) MOET & CHANDON's long-established but so far under-performing Californian winery with a first class winemaker who ought to be given the chance to compete with her counterpart at DOMAINE CHANDON in Australia. Not, as yet, available in the U.K, though MWW's unimpressive Shadow Creek is made by DOMAINE CHANDON and gives a fair idea of the disappointing stuff being sold by them in the US.

Domaine Chandon (YARRA VALLEY, Australia) Sold as Green Point in the UK, this is the winery whose winemaker Tony Jordan proved to its owners MOET & CHANDON (though they hate to admit it) that Aussie grapes grown in a variety of cool climates can make wine that's every bit as good as all but the best CHAMPAGNE. Improving with every vintage – and now joined by a creditable, CHABLIS-like still CHARDONNAY. **** Green Point, Domaine Chandon 1991 £10.50 (W, FUL, MWW, JS, VW).

Domaine Drouhin (OREGON, US) BURGUNDY producer's highly expensive investment in the US that's finally producing world-beating reds, thanks to Veronique Drouhin's skill and personal commitment and some of OREGON's best vineyards. The 1990 beat a top class array of Burgundies – including several of Drouhin père's company's wines – to take the International Wine Challenge Trophy in 1994. ***** Pinot Noir 1990 £20 (OD).

Dominus (NAPA, California) Christian MOUEIX of CHATEAU PETRUS's modestly named competitor to OPUS ONE has always been a heftily tannic CABERNET. Since 1989 that TANNIN has been matched by more attractive fruit, making for wine in which it is (somewhat) easier to believe. Even so wines like the 1987 need to be left to their own devices for several years. Unless you need a 1987 red you know will still be alive and kicking for a 21st birthday in 2008, why not save money and buy one of M. MOUEIX's cheaper and far more approachable BORDEAUX? 87 88 89 90 91 *** 1987 £27 (L&W).

Dopff 'Au Moulin' (ALSACE, France) Underrated NEGOCIANT whose GRAND CRU wines are among the most concentrated around. **** Riesling Schoenenburg Grand Cru de Riquewihr 1990 £13 (VW) ***Sylvaner D'Alsace 1990 £6 (MWW).

Dopff & Irion (ALSACE, France) Not to be confused with its namesake. Definitely second division. *** Riesling 1992 £5.50 (EP) **Gewürztraminer 1992 £6 (EP).

Dosage THE ADDITION OF SWEETENING SYRUP TO CHAMPAGNE, THAT IS NATURALLY DRY.

Douro (Portugal) The great PORT region and river, producing much demarcated and increasingly good table wine thanks partly to the efforts of SOGRAPE and Australians David Baverstock (at QUINTA DE LA ROSA) and PETER BRIGHT. SEE BARCA VELHA 85 88 89. *** Foral Douro Reserva, Caves Alianca 1991 £4 (BTH, DBY) **** Quinta de la Rosa, Douro 1992 £5 (M&V, POR) ***Bright Brothers 1992 £5 (TH).

Doux (France) SWEET.

Dow (DOURO, Portugal) One of the big two (with TAYLORS) and under the same family ownership as WARRES, SMITH WOODHOUSE and GRAHAMS. Great vintage port and similarly impressive tawny 63 66 70 77 80 83 85 91. ***** Dow's 20 Year Old Tawny Port £20.99 (GRT, LAY) *****Dow's Vintage Port 1966 £30* ****Dow's Crusted Port 1987 £10.45 (SAF).

Jean-Paul Droin (BURGUNDY, France) Small, good CHABLIS producer with approachable, 'modern' wines. *** Grand Cru Vaudesir 1991 £25 (F&M).

Dromana Estate (MORNINGTON PENINSULA, Australia) Ace viticulturalist Gary Crittenden has pioneered this region, with leanish CHARDONNAY and raspberryish PINOT NOIR. *** Chardonnay 1991 £12 (BBR).

Joseph Drouhin (BURGUNDY, France) One of the very best NEGOCIANTS in BURGUNDY with a range of first class reds and whites including a rare white BEAUNE from its own Clos des Mouches, top class CLOS DE VOUGEOT and unusually (for a NEGOCIANT) CHABLIS. **** Savigny les Beaune 1990 £12 (OD) **** Chassagne Montrachet 1990 £20 (VW).

Pierre-Jacques Druet (LOIRE, France) Reliable BOURGUEIL producer making characterful individual cuvées. **** Cuvée Beauvais 1990 £11.40 (ADN).

Dry River (MARTINBOROUGH, NEW ZEALAND) Small estate with a particularly impressive PINOT GRIS.

Château du Tertre (BORDEAUX, France) MARGAUX château in the village of Arsac making good if often lightish wines 82 83 85 86 87 88 89 90 91 92.

Georges Duboeuf (BURGUNDY, France) The 'king of BEAUJOLAIS' who introduced the world to the boiled sweet flavour of young GAMAY at a time when most commercial versions tasted like CHATEAUNEUF-DU-PAPE. A wide range of good examples from individual growers, vineyards and villages. Reliable NOUVEAU and good straightforward MACONNAIS white and now the biggest plantation of VIOGNIER in the world. *** Fleurie 1992 £7 (MRN). *** St. Michael Duboeuf Selection Rouge £3.29 (M&S) ***Viognier, Vin de Pays de l'Ardèche 1993 £5 (BWC).

Duc de Magenta (BURGUNDY, France) Classy estate now managed by JADOT

Duckhorn (NAPA, California) Vaunted (by some wine buffs) producer of intentionally inpenetrable and highly priced MERLOT which seems to delight some collectors and wine snobs, who presumably derive similar pleasure from cold showers and being beaten with birch twigs. Life, as they say, is too short. *** Merlot 1991 £17 (L&W) ***Cabernet Sauvignon 1990 £17 (L&W).

Ch. Ducru-Beaucaillou (BORDEAUX, France) SUPER SECOND ST JULIEN with less obvious style than peers such as LEOVILLE-LAS-CASES and PICHON LALANDE. Second wine is Croix-Beaucaillou. 85 86 88 89 90 91 92. **** 1989 £27 (SEL, BBR, C&B).

Domaine Dujac (BURGUNDY, France) Cult BURGUNDY producer with fine, long-lived, if sometimes rather pallid wines including CLOS DE LA ROCHE. Now busily investing time and effort into vineyards in Southern France **** Morey St Denis 1989 £18 (ADN, JAR) **** Chambolle-Musigny £19 (HR).

Dumazet (RHONE, France) Top flight Northern RHONE producer making fewer than 200 cases of perfumed CONDRIEU per year from his one-acre plot of steeply sloping vineyards. *****Condrieu 1990 'La Viniphile' £17 (THP).

Dumb AS IN DUMB NOSE, MEANING WITHOUT SMELL.

Dunn Vineyards (NAPA, California) Tough, forbidding CABERNETS from HOWELL MOUNTAIN for patient masochists who've run out of DUCKHORN MERLOT and DOMINUS.

Côtes de Duras (BORDEAUX, France) Inexpensive whites from the SAUVIGNON, often better value than basic BORDEAUX Blanc 88 89 90 92. ***Croix du Beurrier 1993 £3 (W)

Durbach (BADEN, Germany) Top vineyard area of this ANBAUGEBIET.

Durif See PETITE SIRAH. *** Morris Durif 1990 £10 (CDE, WTR, DBW).

Jean Durup (Burgundy, France) Modern estate whose owner believes in extending vineyards of CHABLIS into what ,many claim to be less distinguished soil. The best wines are sold under the Château de Maligny label. *** Chablis, 1990, £6.50, (EP) **** Chablis, Vigne de la Reine, Château de Maligny 1991 £8 (WR).

Duxoup Wine Works (SONOMA, California) Inspired winery-in-a-shed, producing very good PINOT NOIR, CHARBONO and fine SYRAH from bought-in grapes. Not a name to drop among US collectors; they prefer tougher fare from more château-like edifices. **** Charbono 1991 £10 (BI) **** Carneros Pinot Noir, Hudson Vineyard 1991 £12 (BI).

Echézeaux (BURGUNDY, France) GRAND CRU vineyard between CLOS DE VOUGEOT and VOSNE ROMANEE andmore or less an extension of the latter commune. The village of Flagey Echézeaux on the wrong – relatively vineless - side of the *Route Nationale* apparently takes its name from the 'flagellation' used by the peasants to gather corn in the 6th century .The famous producers of what ought to be wonderfully spicy, rich wines are the DOMAINE DE LA ROMANEE-CONTI and HENRI JAYER. GRANDS-ECHEZEAUX should be finer. 76 78 80 83 85 86 88 89 90 92. ****Echézeaux Grand Cru, Thierry Vigot 1989 £25 (HR)

Edelfäule (Germany) BOTRYTIS CINEREA, OR 'NOBLE ROT'.

Edelzwicker (ALSACE, France) Generic name for a blend of grape varieties. The idea of blends is coming back– but not the name (see HUGEL).

Eden Ridge (SOUTH AUSTRALIA) Organic wines made by MOUNTADAM. **** Shiraz 1992 £7.30 (CHF, DBY, CWI, JAR) ****Cabernet Sauvignon 1992 £7.30 (ADN, CHF, BOO, VER, HPD).

Eger Bikaver (Eger, **Hungary**) The source – and now the preferred Hungarian name for BULLS BLOOD, named after its revitalising effect on the defenders of a besieged town. Now generally one of the most ordinary red wines in the world, though privatisation is now performing a transfusion. ** Bulls Blood, St Ursula 1992 £3.50 (SMF)

Einzellage (Germany) SINGLE VINEYARD; MOST PRECISE AND OFTEN THE LAST PART OF A WINE NAME, FINER BY DEFINITION THAN A **GROSSLAGE.**

Eiswein (Germany) THE ULTIMATE, UTRA-CONCENTRATED LATE-HARVEST WINE, MADE FROM GRAPES NATURALLY FROZEN ON THE VINE. RARE AND HARD TO MAKE (AND CONSEQUENTLY VERY PRICY) IN GERMANY BUT NOT INFREQUENTLY PRODUCED IN **AUSTRIA** AND - INCREASINGLY - **CANADA**. CONCENTRATED AND DELICIOUS BUT OFTEN WITH WORRYINGLY HIGH LEVELS OF ACIDITY ***** Kiedricher Wasseros Riesling Eiswein, Robert Weil 1992 £70 (BAR) ****Welschriesling Eiswein, Kracher 1990 £18 (NY).

Eitelsbach (**MOSEL-SAAR-RUWER**, Germany) One of the top two **RUWER** wine towns, site of the famed Karthäuserhofberg vineyard. *** Eitelsbacher Karthäuserhofberg Riesling Auslese 1990 £20 (OWL).

Elaborado y Anejado por (Spain) 'MADE AND AGED FOR'.

Elba (Italy) Island off the Tuscan coast making full dry reds and whites.

Elbling Inferior Germanic white grape.

Eléver/éléveur TO MATURE OR 'NURTURE' WINE, ESPECIALLY IN THE CELLARS OF THE **BURGUNDY NEGOCIANTS**, WHO ACT AS ELEVEURS.

Neil Ellis (**STELLENBOSCH, SOUTH AFRICA**) One of the Cape's best new wave winemakers. *** St Michael Merlot/Cabernet Sauvignon, Jan Coetzee/Neil Ellis 1993 £5 (M&S).

Eltville (**RHEINGAU**, Germany) Town housing the **RHEINGAU** state cellars and the German Wine Academy, producing good **RIESLING** with backbone 83 85 88 89 90 91 92. **** Sonnenberg Riesling Spätlese Hirt Gebhardt 1990 £8.50 (FDL).

Emerald Riesling (California) Bottom of the range white grape cross (**RIESLING** x **MUSCADELLE**), at best fresh, fruity but undistinguished. Popular in the **CENTRAL VALLEY** in California.

Emilia-Romagna (Italy) Region surrounding Bologna best known for **LAMBRUSCO**, but also the source of **ALBANA** and **SANGIOVESE DI ROMAGNA** and **PAGADEBIT**. ***Lambrusco Grasparossa di Modena Secco, Tenuta Generale Cialdini, Chiarli 1993 £3 (SAF).

En primeur SPECIALIST MERCHANTS BUY AND OFFER WINE (USUALLY **BORDEAUX**) 'EN PRIMEUR' I.E. BEFORE IT HAS BEEN RELEASED; CUSTOMERS RELY ON THEIR MERCHANT'S JUDGEMENT TO MAKE A GOOD BUY - OR WAIT UNTIL ODDBINS, CHRISTIES OR SOTHEBYS SELL PRECISELY THE SAME WINE FOR THE SAME PRICE A YEAR OR SO AFTER EVERYBODY ELSE HAS TIED UP THEIR CASH BUYING IT EN PRIMEUR.

English wine Produced from grapes grown in England (or Wales), as opposed to **BRITISH WINE**, which is made from imported concentrate. Quality has improved in recent years, as winemakers have developed their own vinous personality, changing from semi-sweet, mock-Germanic to mock-dry-**LOIRE** and now, increasingly to aromatic-but-dry 88 89 90 91. *** Warden Vineyard, English White Wine 1992 £5.90 (TO) ***English Table Wine, High Weald Winery £2.99 (TO).

Enoteca (Italy) LITERALLY, WINE LIBRARY OR, NOWADAYS, WINE SHOP.

Entre-Deux-Mers (**BORDEAUX**, France) Once a region of appalling medium dry wine from vineyards between the cities of **BORDEAUX** and **LIBOURNE**. Now an up-and-coming source of basic **BORDEAUX** Blanc, principally dry **SAUVIGNON** 88 89 90 92. Reds are sold as **BORDEAUX** Rouge. **** Château Bonnet, A Lurton 1992 £5 (TH, WR) *** Château Thieuley 1993 £4.99 (MWW).

Epernay (**CHAMPAGNE**, France) Centre of **CHAMPAGNE** production, where famous houses such as **MERCIER, MOET & CHANDON, PERRIER JOUET** and **POL ROGER** are based.

Erbach (**RHEINGAU**, Germany) Town noted for fine, full **RIESLING**, notably from the Marcobrunn vineyard 85 86 88 89 90 91 92. **** Erbacher Marcobrunn Riesling Kabinett, Staatsweinguter Eltville 1989 £9 (AV).

Erden (MOSEL-SAAR-RUWER, Germany) Northerly village producing full, crisp, dry RIESLING. In the BERNKASTEL BEREICH, includes the famous Treppchen vineyard 83 85 86 88 89 90 91 92. **** Erdener Treppchen, Riesling Kabinett, Dr Loosen 1989 £9 (ADN).

Errazuriz Panquehue (ACONCAGUA Valley, CHILE) One of CHILE's big name producers and owner of CALITERRA; good but could do better.
*** Sauvignon Blanc Reserva 1994 £4.50 (BU) *** Don Maximiano Cabernet Sauvignon 1990 £7 (VW) *** Cabernet Sauvignon 1992 £5 (SEL).

Erzeugerabfüllung (Germany) BOTTLED BY THE GROWER/ESTATE.

Esk Valley (HAWKES BAY, NEW ZEALAND) Under the same ownership as VIDAL and VILLA MARIA,; increasingly successful with BORDEAUX-style reds and juicy rosé.****Esk Valley Reserve Merlot/Malbec/Cabernet Franc 1992 £14 (WR)

Esperão (ALENTEJO, Portugal) Revolutionary wines made by Australian winemaker David Baverstock. See ALENTEJO.

Espum-oso/ante (Spain/Portugal) SPARKLING.

Esters VOLATILE CHEMICAL COMPONENTS IN WINE RESPONSIBLE FOR A VARIETY OF ODOURS, MAINLY FRUITY (THE SIMPLEST ESTER SMELLS OF PEAR DROPS).

Estufa THE VATS IN WHICH MADEIRA IS HEATED, SPEEDING MATURITY AND IMPARTING ITS FAMILIAR 'COOKED' FLAVOUR.

Eszencia (HUNGARY) ESSENCE OF TOKAY, LOW-ALCOHOL (3%) MADE FROM INDIVIDUALLY PICKED, RAISINY AND (PARTLY) NOBLY ROTTEN GRAPES. ONCE PRIZED FOR ITS LIFE-SAVING PROPERTIES AND IMPROBABLE EFFECTS ON THE MALE LIBIDO. NOW VIRTUALLY UNOBTAINABLE, EVEN BY THOSE WHO CAN SEE THE POINT IN DOING ANYTHING WITH THE OUTRAGIOUSLY EXPENSIVE SYRUP APART FROM POURING IT OVER ICE CREAM. NOT TO BE CONFUSED WITH THE EASIER-TO-FIND ASZU ESZENCIA (THE SWEETEST LEVEL OF TOKAY) WHICH IS A MORE SENSIBLE BUY.

Arnaldo Etchart (ARGENTINA) Dynamic producer, benefiting from advice by Michel Rolland, of POMEROL fame. The key wine here though is the grapey TORRONTES. **** Cafayate Torrontes 1993 £4 (WTR).

Etna (Italy) From the Sicilian volcanic slopes, hot-climate, soft, fruity DOC reds, whites and rosés. Can be flabby.

Ch. l' Evangile (BORDEAUX, France) A classy POMEROL which can, in great vintages like 1982 and 1988, sometimes rival its neighbour PETRUS, but in a more tannic style. Back on form after patchy years in the 1980s. 82 83 85 86 88 89 90 *** 1982 £70 (TVW).

Evans Family (HUNTER VALLEY, Australia) Len Evans of ROTHBURY VINEYARDS' own estate using grapes from the vines surrounding his house in the Upper HUNTER VALLEY. Good rich CHARDONNAY and SEMILLON as characterful and generous as their maker. Not yet available in the UK.

Evans & Tate (WESTERN AUSTRALIA,) Once old-fashioned, now, following its move from the SWAN VALLEY into the MARGARET RIVER, a source of good, modern wines. **** Two Vineyards Chardonnay 1992 £10 (WCE).

Eventail de Vignerons Producteurs (BURGUNDY, France) Reliable source of BEAUJOLAIS. **** Juliénas Les Fouillouses, Domaine M Pelletier £5.90 (EP)

Eyrie Vineyards (WILLAMETTE VALLEY, OREGON, US) Pioneering PINOT NOIR producer whose success in a blind tasting alongside top Burgundies helped to attract JOSEPH DROUHIN to invest his francs on the DOMAINE DROUHIN vineyard in Oregon. Wines last well. **** Pinot Noir Reserve 1989 £16.50 (WDW).

Fairview Estate (PAARL, SOUTH AFRICA) Go-ahead estate associated with BACKSBERG, making modern CHARDONNAY and CABERNET. ****Shiraz 1992 £5 (A, THP) **** Cabernet Sauvignon 1993 £6.50 (CAP).

Joseph Faiveley (BURGUNDY, France) Modern, reliable negociant with particular strength in his backyard, NUITS-ST-GEORGES. **** Mercurey 'Les Mauvarennes' 1991 £7.95 (MWW) **** Nuits St Georges 1er Cru Clos de la Maréchale 1989 £23 (GRO, DBY, BEN).

Ch. de Fargues (BORDEAUX, France) Elegant wines made by the winemaker at CHATEAU D'YQUEM. 82 83 85 86 88 89 90. ****1983 £50 (SEL).

Fat HAS A SILKY TEXTURE WHICH FILLS THE MOUTH. MORE FLESHY THAN MEATY.

Fattoria (Italy) ESTATE, PARTICULARLY IN TUSCANY.

Faugères (MIDI, France) Good, full-bodied AC reds, some whites and rosés, a major cut above the surrounding COTEAUX DU LANGUEDOC 88 89 90 91.
**** Cuvée Syrah, Château des Estanilles, Michel Louison 1992 £9.75 (ADN) Sainsbury's Faugères £3 (JS).

Faustino Martinez (RIOJA, Spain) Dependable RIOJA producer with excellent (GRAN) RESERVAS, fair whites and a decent CAVA 81 82 85 87. **** Faustino I Gran Reserva 1987 £9.50 (OD, TO) *** Faustino V Reserva 1989 £6 (OD, TO).

Favorita (PIEDMONT, Italy) Traditional variety from PIEDMONT. Transformed by modern oenological practice. Crisp delicate floral whites. ***Cru San Michele, Deltetto 1993 £7.55 (WCE).

Felsina Berardenga (TUSCANY, Italy) High quality CHIANTI estate, known for its Fontalloro Vino da Tavola. **** Chianti Classico, Felsina Berardenga 1991 £7.69 (OD, WCE).

Fendant (Switzerland) Both an Appellation of VALAIS and another name for CHASSELAS .

Fermentazione naturale (Italy) 'NATURALLY SPARKLING' BUT, IN FACT, INDICATES THE CUVE CLOSE METHOD.

Fernão Pires (ALENTEJO, Portugal) MUSCAT-like white grape, used to greatest effect by PETER BRIGHT of JP Vinhos – See ALENTEJO.

Ferreira (DOURO, Portugal) Traditional Portuguese port producer, equally famous for its excellent tawnies as for its BARCA VELHA, Portugal's best traditional unfortified red. **** Ferreira Duque de Bragança 20 Year Old Tawny Port £23.99 (CWS, NI, LEA) Barca Velha, Ferreira 1985 £24.99 (OD, GI).

Sylvain Fessy (BEAUJOLAIS, France) Reliable small producer with wide range of crus. ****Juliénas 1993 £7.49 (LAV, WIN) St Amour 1993 £8.54 (LAV, WIN).

Fetzer (MENDOCINO, California) The best of the bigger Californian wineries, one of the few which really tries to make good wine at (relatively) lower prices and a laudable pioneering producer of organic wines. Recently taken over but still run by the family. ***** Valley Oaks Cabernet Sauvignon 1991 £6.99 (OD, W, WL, VW) **** Eagle Peak Merlot 1992 £8.37 (LAV, WIN) ***** Bonterra Chardonnay and Red (both organic) £7.95 (SAF).

William Fèvre (BURGUNDY, France) Quality CHABLIS producer who has been a reactionary in his resistance to expanding the region and a revolutionary in his use of new oak. **** Chablis 1991 £10.50 (F&M) **** 1er cru Montée de Tonnerre 1991 £14 (F&M).

Ch. de Fieuzal (BORDEAUX, France) PESSAC-LEOGNAN property regularly making great whites and lovely raspberryish reds. Abeille de Fieuzal is the (excellent) SECOND LABEL 82 85 86 88 89 90. *** 1988 (red) £14* ***1990 (red) £12 (THP, OD, BBR).

Ch. Figeac (BORDEAUX, France) Forever in the shadow of its neighbour, CHEVAL BLANC, but still one of the most characterful and best-made ST EMILIONS 82 83 85 88 89 90. *** 1988 £22 (LAY, OWL).

Finger Lakes (NEW YORK STATE, US) Cold region whose producers struggle (sometimes effectively) to produce good Vinifera, including late harvest RIESLING. Hybrids such as SEYVAL BLANC are more reliable, though late-harvest RIESLINGS can be good.

Fining THE CLARIFYING OF YOUNG WINE BEFORE BOTTLING TO REMOVE IMPURITIES, USING A NUMBER OF AGENTS INCLUDING ISINGLASS AND BENTONITE.

Finish WHAT YOU CAN STILL TASTE AFTER SWALLOWING.

Fino (Spain) Dry, delicate SHERRY, the finest to aficionados. Drink chilled and drink up once opened. See LUSTAU, BARBADILLO, HIDALGO and GONZALEZ BYASS. ***Carta Blanca, Agustin Blazquez £3 (MRN) ***Somerfield Fino Sherry, Luis Caballero £4 (SMF) ***Waitrose Fino Sherry, Luis Caballero £4.35 (W).

Firestone (SANTA YNEZ, California) Good producer – particularly of good value MERLOT and SAUVIGNON and late harvest RIESLING – in Southern California. ****Cabernet Sauvignon 1991 £9.52 (TH, MWW, CWS).

Fitou (MIDI, France) Long considered to be an up-market CORBIERES and still a quite reliable southern AC, making reds largely from the CARIGNAN grape. Formerly dark and stubborn, the wines have become more refined, with a woody warmth, though they never quite shake off their rustic air 88 89 90 91. *** St Michael Fitou, Caves du Mont Tauch 1991 £3.49 (M&S) ***Spar Fitou, Val D'Orbieu £3.49 (SPR) ****Fitou Terroir De Tuchan, Tuchan 1991 £7.55 (TH, WR, BU).

Fixin (BURGUNDY, France) Northerly village of the COTE DE NUITS, producing lean, tough, uncommercial reds which can mature well 85 87 88 89 90 92. **** Fixin, Domaine Fougeray de Beauclair 1992 £9 (BBR) ***Fixin, La Mazière £17 1985 (EV).

Flabby LACKING BALANCING ACIDITY. NOT TO BE CONFUSED WITH FAT.

Fleurie (BURGUNDY, France) One of the 10 BEAUJOLAIS CRUS, ideally fresh and fragrant, as its name suggests. Best vineyards within it include La Madonne and Pointe du Jour 85 87 88 89 90 91 93. **** Domaine des Quatre Vents, Georges Duboeuf 1993 £6 (BWC, D, WAC, JN).

Flor YEAST WHICH GROWS NATURALLY ON THE SURFACE OF SOME MATURING SHERRIES, MAKING THEM POTENTIAL FINOS.

Flora White grape, a cross between SEMILLON and GEWURZTRAMINER best known in BROWN BROTHERS ORANGE MUSCAT and Flora.*** Late Harvest Orange Muscat & Flora, Brown Brothers 1993 £5.50 (OD, MWW, TH, U, FUL).

Flora Springs (NAPA Valley, California) Good, unusual SAUVIGNON BLANC (Soliloquy) and MERLOT, CABERNET SAUVIGNON & CABERNET FRANC blend (Trilogy). **** Trilogy 1984 £16 (T&W).

Emile Florentin (RHONE, France) Ultra-traditional, ultra-tannic ST. JOSEPH, *** Clos de L'Arbalestrier 1988 £12 (ADN).

Flying Winemakers YOUNG (USUALLY) ANTIPODEANS WHO ARE ANNUALLY AND INCREASINGLY DESPATCHED TO WINERIES (ESPECIALLY COOPERATIVES) WORLDWIDE TO MAKE BETTER AND MORE RELIABLE WINE THAN THE HOME TEAM. OFTEN, MERELY KEEPING TANKS AND PIPES CLEAN IS A MAJOR PART OF THE JOB – AS IS THE AVOIDANCE OF LEAVING TRUCKLOADS OF GRAPES TO COOK IN THE SUN WHILE WINERY WORKERS ENJOY THEIR TRADITIONAL TWO-HOUR LUNCH.

Folle Noir (MIDI, France) Traditional grape used to make BELLET. *** Ch. de Crêmat Charles Bagnis 1988 £15.75 (YAP).

Fonseca (DOURO, Portugal) Now a subsidiary of TAYLORS but still independently making great port; during the late 1980s, in blind tastings, the 1976 regularly beat supposedly classier houses' supposedly finer vintages. See also GUIMARAENS. **** Fonseca Vintage Port 1985 £21.15 (VW) **** Fonseca Vintage Port 1980 £21 (TH, VW).

JM da Fonseca Internacional (Est, Portugal) Big, highly commercial offshoot of the even bigger and more commercial Grand Metropolitan. Principal wines are Lancers, the MATEUS-lookalike semi-fizzy, semi-sweet pinks, and whites sold in mock-crocks and fairly basic commercial fizz produced by a process known as the RUSSIAN CONTINUOUS.

J M da Fonseca Successores (Est, Portugal) Unrelated to the port house of the same name and no longer connected to JM DA FONSECA INTERNACIONAL. A family-run firm which, with ALIANCA and SOGRAPE, is one of Portugal's big three dynamic wine companies. Top red wines include Pasmados, PERIQUITA (made from the grape of the same name), Quinta da Camarate, Terras Altas Dao and the CABERNET-influenced 'TE' GARRAFEIRAS. Dry whites are less impressive, but the sweet old MOSCATEL DE SETUBAL are luscious classics. **** Garrafeira TE, Jose Maria da Fonseca Succs 1988 £6.50 (RWC, BAB).

Font de Michelle (RHONE, France) Reliable producer of a lightish-bodied red CHATEAUNEUF-DU-PAPE and tiny quantities of an almost unobtainable, brilliant white. **** Domaine Font de Michelle Châteauneuf-du-Pape Rouge 1990 £10.39 (TH).

Fontana Candida (LAZIO, Italy) Good producer, especially for FRASCATI; their top wine being Colle Gaio which is good enough to prove the disappointing nature of most other wines from this area. *** Frascati Superiore 1992 £4.50 (MWW) **** Colle Gaio Frascati £12 (WCE).

Fontanafredda (PIEDMONT, Italy) Big producer with impressive Asti Spumante and very approachable (especially single-vineyard) BAROLO. **** Barolo 1989 £8 (PTR, CEL, MRN, JN, TH) *** Asti Spumante £7.50 (F&M, HAR, LV, V&C).

Forst (RHEINPFALZ, Germany) Wine town producing great, concentrated RIESLING. Famous for the JESUITENGARTEN vineyard 75 76 79 83 85 86 88 89 90 91 92. *** Stift Auslese 1989 £7 (WSC).

Fortant de France (MIDI, France) Good quality, revolutionary varietal producer from this region. Will improve still further when its own winemakers take over every aspect of production. Often has "Skalli" on the label. **** Fortant de France Collection Viognier, Skalli Fortant de France 1993 6.50 (TDS, WR, SAF, CEL, BKW) ***Syrah, Vin de Pays d'Oc 1992 £4 (MWW).

Les Forts de Latour (PAUILLAC, France) Second label of CHATEAU LATOUR, bottle-aged for 3 years prior to release. Not, as is often suggested, made exclusively from the juice of young vines and wine which might otherwise have ended up in bottles labelled CHATEAU LATOUR – there are vineyards whose grapes are grown specially for Les Forts – but still often better than other classed growth CHATEAUX. *** 1987 £17 (JS).

Ch. Fourcas-Hosten (BORDEAUX, France) CRU BOURGEOIS estate in LISTRAC producing firm old-fashioned wine with plenty of 'grip' for TANNIN fans. *** 1982 £19 (AV).

Franciacorta (LOMBARDY, Italy) DOC for good, light, French-influenced reds but better noted for sparklers made to compete with – and sell at the same price as – CHAMPAGNE 85 86 88 89 90 92. *** Franciacorta Brut, Ca' del Bosco £25 (V&C).

Franciscan Vineyards (NAPA Valley, California) Reliable NAPA winery whose Chilean owner, Agustin Huneeus, has not only pioneered wines using their own yeast with his great, BURGUNDY-like 'Cuvée Sauvage' CHARDONNAY but has also creditably tried to puncture the pretentious balloons of some of his neighbours – including those who tried to create a 'RUTHERFORD BENCH' appellation. ***** Chardonnay Sauvage 1991 £10 (OD).

Franken (Germany) ANBAUGEBIET making characterful, sometimes earthy, dry whites, traditionally presented in the squat flagon-shaped 'bocksbeutel' on which the Mateus bottle was modelled. One of the key varieties is the SYLVANER which helps explain the earthiness of many of the wines. The weather here does make it easier to make dry wine than in many other regions 83 85 86 87 88 89 90 91 92. ***Alte Vogtei, Kabinett 1990 £4 (WSC).

Frascati (Italy) Clichéd dry or semi-dry white from LATIUM, with few exceptions (those made by GEOFF MERRILL, a visiting Australian, and FONTANA CANDIDA), at best soft and clean, more usually dull. Drink within 12 months of vintage. *** Sainsburys Frascati Secco Superiore, Geoff Merrill/GIV 1993 £4 (JS) ***Frascati Superiore 'Tullio' San Marco 1993 £4 (U).

Freie Weingartner (WACHAU, AUSTRIA) A multitude of crus from this co-operative, thanks to the dynamic young winemaker Fritz Darthvader, winning 15 Smaragd awards (the top WACHAU classification) in 1991. **** Riesling Smaragd Durnsteiner Kellerberg 1993 £9 (OD).

Freixenet (Catalonia, Spain) Giant in the CAVA field and strong supporters of the campaign to preserve the role of traditional Catalonian grapes in fizz. Its dull but big-selling Cordon Negro is as good a justification for adding CHARDONNAY to the blend as anyone who likes refreshing wine could ever require. ** Cordon Negro £6 (widely available)

Frescobaldi (TUSCANY, Italy) Top-class family estate with wines including CASTELGIOCONDO, the CABERNET SAUVIGNON Mormoreto and the rich white Chardonnay Pomino Il Benefizio. **** Mormoreto Capitolare Di Biturica 1990 £16. (ADN, BH). *** Chianti Rufina, Castello Di Nipozzano Riserva 1990 £7 (OD) *** Pomino Il Benefizio 1989 £10 (LAV).

Friuli-Venezia Giulia (Italy) Northerly region containing a number of DOCs which focus on single-variety wines like MERLOT, CABERNET (mostly FRANC) PINOT BIANCO, PINOT GRIGIO and TOCAI 85 88 89 90 91 92 93. *** Pinot Grigio, Villa del Borgo 1993 £5 (WCE) *** Merlot Collio Enofriulia 1991 £8 (WCE).

Frizzante (Italy) SEMI-SPARKLING, ESPECIALLY LAMBRUSCO.

Frog's Leap (NAPA Valley, California) Winery whose owners combine winemaking skill with the kind of humour that is all too rarely encountered in the NAPA Valley (their slogan is 'Time's fun when you're having flies'). Tasty ZINFANDEL and unusually good SAUVIGNON. **** Frog's Leap Zinfandel 1991 £10.65 (L&W, BOO, M&V).

Fronsac/Canon Fronsac (Bordeaux, France) ST EMILION neighbour, producing potentially better value if often robust reds. Canon Fronsac is usually better 81 82 83 85 86 88 89 90. *** Château Moulin Pey-Labrie, Canon Fronsac, G Hubau 1989 £9 (WL).

Frontignan (Muscat de) (PROVENCE, France) Grape making rich, sweet, grapey fortified wine in the BANDOL area in PROVENCE. More forceful (and cheaper) than BEAUMES DE VENISE. Also a synonym for Muscat à Petits Grains. *** Chateau de la Peyrade Tradition, Muscat de Frontignan £8 (ADN).

Côtes du Frontonnais (South-West France) Up-and-coming inexpensive red (and some rosé), full and fruitily characterful 85 86 88 89 90. *** Carte Blanche Côtes du Frontonnais, Cave de Fronton 1991 £4 (LES).

Ch. Fuissé (BURGUNDY, France) By far the best producer in this commune, making wines comparable to some of the best of the COTE D'OR. The Vielles Vignes has the distinction of lasting as long as a good Chassagne-Montrachet *** 1987 £16 (T&W) *** 1989 £20 (ADN).

Fumé Blanc Name adapted from POUILLY FUME by ROBERT MONDAVI to describe his oaked SAUVIGNON. Now widely used for this style. *** Beringer Fumé Blanc 1992 £6 (PAG, SEL) ***Corbans Private Bin Marlborough Fumé Blanc 1991 £7 (WTR).

Fürmint Lemony Eastern European white grape, used in Hungary for TOKAY and, though examples are rare, good dry wines. Watch out for those from the Royal Tokay Wine Co and DISZNOKO 1993 when they reach the UK. (There are plans for Threshers to stock the latter).

Fûts de Chêne (élévé en) (France) OAK BARRELS (MATURED IN).

Jean-Noel Gagnard (BURGUNDY, France) Thanks to the French inheritance laws which dish out estates equally between all heirs, and to the Burgundian winemakers' habit of marrying the sons and daughters of neighbouring vignerons, this is a domaine with vineyards spread far and wide across CHASSAGNE-MONTRACHET. Best of all is the BATARD-MONTRACHET, of which he has nearly an acre, but all are impeccably made – as is his red SANTENAY. ***** Chassagne-Montrachet, Les Masures 1992 £17 (J&B).

Jacques Gagnard-Delagrange (BURGUNDY, France) A top class producer in Chassagne-Montrachet with vines in both the BATARD-MONTRACHET and MONTRACHET. A do maine to follow for those who like their wines delicately oaked. **** Chassagne-Montrachet 1992 £20 (OD) ***** Bâtard-Montrachet Grand Cru 1992 £50 (OD).

Gaillac (South-west, France) Light, fresh, good-value reds and whites, produced using GAMAY and SAUVIGNON grapes. Reds can rival BEAUJOLAIS 88 89 90 91. *** Gaillac Blanc, Cave de Labastide de Levis 1993 £3.49 (VW,BUD, SAF, OD).

Gaja (PIEDMONT, Italy) The man who proved that the previously modest region of BARBARECO could make wines which were saleable at prices higher than those asked for first-growth clarets, let alone the supposedly classier neighbouring region of BAROLO. Individual vineyard reds are of great quality and the CHARDONNAY is the best in Italy. Whether they're worth these prices, though, is another question. ***** Barbaresco Sorì San Lorenzo 1988 £69 (V&C) ***** Chardonnay, Gaia & Rey 1988 £31 (V&C, T&W).

Galestro (TUSCANY, Italy) There is no such thing as CHIANTI Bianco – the light, grapey stuff that is made in the CHIANTI region is sold as Galestro. *** Antinori 1993 £5 (V&C).

E & J Gallo (CENTRAL VALLEY, California) The world's biggest wine producer; annual production is around 60 per cent of the total Californian harvest and more than the whole of Australia or CHAMPAGNE. At the top end, there is now some pretty good CABERNET and CHARDONNAY from SONOMA. Unfortunately, quantities of both are laughably small (the UK only received a few hundred cases of each), and prices ludicrously high. With the exception of the French COLOMBARD, the rest of the range, though widely stocked, is unrecommendable by any standards. Sales are attributable to heavy marketing – to the tune of several million pounds a year, which has helped these wines break into the market as effectively as a slingshot missile through a window. **** E & J Gallo Reserve Chardonnay, Northern Sonoma 1991 £20 (VW).

Gamay The BEAUJOLAIS grape, making wine with youthful, fresh, cherry/plummy fruit. Also successful in the LOIRE and GAILLAC. Beware of Californian 'Gamay Beaujolais' which is usually dull wine made from PINOT NOIR. *** Sainsbury's Gamay Vin de Pays des Coteaux de Barronnies, Jean Claude Boisset 1993 £3 (JS).

Gamey SMELL OR TASTE REMINISCENT OF HUNG GAME. PARTICULARLY ASSOCIATED WITH OLD PINOT NOIRS AND SYRAHS. POSSIBLY AT LEAST PARTLY ATTRIBUTABLE TO THE COMBINATION OF THOSE GRAPES' NATURAL CHARACTERISTICS WITH OVERLY GENEROUS DOSES OF SULPHUR DIOXIDE BY WINEMAKERS. MODERN EXAMPLES OF BOTH STYLES SEEM TO BE DISTINCTLY LESS GAMEY THAN IN THE PAST.

Gancia (PIEDMONT, Italy) Reliable producer of ASTI SPUMANTE and good, dry PINOT BLANC fizz. *** Gancia Pinot Di Pinot £5.99 (V&C, WAV).

Vin de pays du Gard (MIDI, France) Huge VIN DE TABLE producing area with one fair VDQS, COSTIERES DU GARD 89 90 91 92. *** Domaine de Barjac 1992 £3 (A).

Garrafeira (Portugal) INDICATES A PRODUCER'S 'RESERVE' WINE, SELECTED AND GIVEN EXTRA TIME IN CASK (MINIMUM 2 YEARS) AND BOTTLE (MINIMUM 1 YEAR. ***** Garrafeira TE, Jose Maria da Fonseca Succs 1988 £7 (RWC, BAB).

Vin de Pays des Côtes de Gascogne (South-West, France) This region was once only known for d'Artagnan of the Three Musketeers, a town called Condom and ARMAGNAC. Today, thanks largely to the efforts of YVES GRASSA, the PLAIMONT cooperative and HUGH RYMAN, it is further known for the production of good-value, fresh, floral whites and increasingly good light reds. *** Co-op Vin De Pays des Côtes de Gascogne, Grassa £3 (CWS).

Rolly Gassmann (ALSACE, France) Fine producer of subtle, long-lasting wines which are sometimes slightly marred by an excess of SULPHUR DIOXIDE. **** Riesling Reserve 1991 £8 (TH, WR, BU).

Gattinara (PIEDMONT, Italy) Red DOC from the NEBBIOLO – varying in quality but reliably full-flavoured and dry 82 85 88 89 90 92. *** Nervi 1986 £8 (V&C).

Gavi (TUSCANY, Italy) Full, dry white from the CORTESE grape. Often compared by Italians to white BURGUNDY (although I can't see why) except that Gavi and Gavi di Gavi tend to be creamily pleasant and overpriced 88 90 91 92. *** Gavi Granduca, Michele Chiarlo 1992 £5. (WL) **** Gavi di Gavi 1993, La Minaia, Bergaglio £9 (WCE).

Ch. Gazin (BORDEAUX, France) POMEROL property that has become far more polished since the mid 80s. 82 85 86 88 89 90 91. *** 1989 £15 (JAR, WSO, SEL).

Geelong (VICTORIA, Australia) Cool region pioneered by Idyll Vineyards (makers of old-fashioned reds) and rapidly attracting notice with BANNOCKBURN's and Scotchman Hill's PINOT NOIRS 85 86 88 89 90 91 92 93.

Geisenheim (RHEINGAU, Germany) Town and the home of the German Wine Institute wine school, once one of the best in the world but long overtaken by more go-ahead seats of learning in France, California and Australia 83 85 88 89 90 91 92 93. *** Schlossgarten Riesling Spätlese von Schönborn 1990 £11 (WSO).

Generoso (Spain) FORTIFIED OR DESSERT WINE.

Gentilini (Cephalonia, Greece) Nick Cosmetatos's modern white wines, made using classic Greek grapes and French varieties should be an example to all his countrymen who are still happily making and drinking stuff which tastes as fresh as an old election manifesto. *** Gentilini Fumé 1992 £10 (ADN).

Gevrey Chambertin (BURGUNDY, France) Best-known big red COTE DE NUITS commune; very variable, but still capable of superb, plummy cherryish wine. The top GRAND CRU is LE CHAMBERTIN but, in the right hands, PREMIERS CRUS like Les Cazetiers can beat this and the other GRANDS CRUS. Best producers include VALLET FRERES, ALAIN BURGUET, DENIS BACHELET, Roty, ROSSIGNOL-TRAPET, ARMAND ROUSSEAU, DUJAC, Philippe Leclerc Dugat, Esmonin, and LEROY, Magnien, Maume 78 80 82 83 85 88 89 90 92. ***** Gevrey-Chambertin 'Les Cazetiers', Vallet Frères 1990 £23 (POR) *** Gevrey Chambertin, Antonin Rodet 1983 £13 (JS).

Gewürztraminer White (well, slightly pink) grape, making dry-to-sweet, full, oily-textured, spicy wine, best in ALSACE but also grown in Australasia, Italy, the US and Eastern Europe. ***** Gewürztraminer Heimbourg, Zind Humbrecht 1992 £12 (ABY) **** Gewürztraminer Grand Cru Kessler, Domaines Schlumberger 1989 £15 (JN) ***** Gewürztraminer Kritt Sélection Des Grains Nobles, Marc Kreydenweiss 1990 £37 (LV).

Geyser Peak (ALEXANDER VALLEY, California) Australian winemaker Darryl Groom revolutionised Californian thinking in this once Australian-owned winery with his SEMILLON-CHARDONNAY blend ('You mean Chardonnay's *not* the only white grape in the world?'), and decent reds which show an Aussie attitude towards ripe TANNIN. *** Premium Red 1990 £6 (AV) *** Premium White 1992 (AV)

Ghiaie della Furba (TUSCANY, Italy) Great CABERNET-based **Super-Tuscan** from VILLA DI CAPEZZANA. *** 1988 15 (V&C).

Giaconda (North East VICTORIA, Australia) Small producer hidden away in the hills, making impressive PINOT NOIR and CHARDONNAY. Not exported.

Bruno Giacosa (PIEDMONT, Italy) One of Italy's best winemakers in the region, with a large range, including BAROLOS (Vigna Rionda in best years) and BARBARESCOS (Santo Stefano, again in best years). Recent success with whites, including a SPUMANTE (a range to be stocked by V&C from August).

Giesen (CANTERBURY, NEW ZEALAND) Small estate, with particularly appley RIESLING from CANTERBURY and SAUVIGNON from MARLBOROUGH. **** Sauvignon Blanc 1993 £7 (OD) **** School Road Marlborough, Chardonnay 1993 £7 (OD).

Gigondas (RHONE, France) COTES DU RHONE commune, producing good-value, reliable, full-bodied, spicy/peppery, blackcurranty reds which show the GRENACHE at its best. A good competitor for nearby CHATEAUNEUF-DU-PAPE 79 82 83 85 86 88 89 90 91. *** Domaine Raspail Ay, Dominique Ay 1990 £8 (HVW).

Ch. Gilette (BORDEAUX, France) Wonderful, eccentric, unclassified but classed-growth quality SAUTERNES kept in tank (rather than cask) for 20 or 30 years. Rare and expensive. ***** Château Gilette, Crème de Tête 1970 £76 (C&B).

Giropalette MACHINES WHICH, IN **METHODE CHAMPENOISE**, AUTOMATICALLY PERFORM THE TASK OF **REMUAGE**. USED BY ALL BUT A VERY FEW PRODUCERS, DESPITE THE EFFORTS OF THE BIG HOUSES TO CONCEAL THE FACT FROM THE TOURISTS WHO TROOP THROUGH THEIR CELLARS.

Gisborne (NEW ZEALAND) North Island vine-growing area since 1920s. Cool, wettish climate, mainly used for (good) **CHARDONNAY** 89 90 91 93. Recommended: **COOPERS CREEK**, **MATAWHERO** (variable), **MILLTON** (organic). **** Coopers Creek Gisborne Chardonnay 1992 £6 (MWW) ***Millton Vineyard Chardonnay 1992 £7 (SAF).

Ch. Giscours (BORDEAUX, France) **MARGAUX** property which, despite the lovely blackcurranty wines it produced in the late 1970s and early 1980s remains on the threshold of competition with the best. A great place to watch polo though – thanks to the owner's enthusiasm for the sport 82 83 85 86 87 88 89 90. *** 1988 £15 (VW).

Givry (BURGUNDY, France) **COTE CHALONNAISE** commune, making typical and affordable, if generally unexciting, reds and creamy whites. French wine snobs point out that this was one of King Henri IV's favourite wines, forgetting the fact that a) he had quite a few such favourites and b) his mistress happened to live here. Look for wines from Steinmaier, Joblot, Thénard and Mouton 83 85 87 88 89 90 92. *** La Grande Berge, Gérard Mouton 1992 £10.45 (TAN) *** Dom. Thénard, Remoissenet 1990 £10 (WSO).

Glen Ellen (SONOMA VALLEY, California) Recently-purchased dynamic family firm producing large amounts of good commercial **CHARDONNAY** under its 'Proprietor's Reserve' label for Californiaphiles who like tropical fruit juice – and who dislike **E & J GALLO**'s dull offerings. Reds are approachable and good value. The Benziger range, although more expensive, is perhaps better value. *** Cabernet Sauvignon 1991 £4 (WL, U) Proprietor's Reserve Merlot 1991 £4.50 (SMF, SAF, HAR).

Ch. Gloria (ST JULIEN, BORDEAUX, France) One of the first of the super **CRU BOURGEOIS**, looking less stunning nowadays 82 83 85 86 88 89 90 91. *** 1989 £14 (AV, MWW, BBR).

Golan Heights (Israel) Until recently almost the only non-sacramental wines in Israel were made by Carmel, whose dire range included one of the least palatable **SAUVIGNONS** I have ever encountered. Today, Carmel wines are greatly improved, thanks to competition from this enterprise at which Californian expertise is used to produce **KOSHER** wines, **CABERNET** and **MUSCAT**. *** Yarden Muscat, Golan Heights Winery Galilee 1990 £5 (SEL).

Goldwater Estate (AUCKLAND, NEW ZEALAND) **BORDEAUX**-like red wine specialist on Waiheke Island whose wines are expensive but every bit as good as many similarly-priced French offerings. **** Cabernet Sauvignon /Merlot 1990 £19 (POR) **** Chardonnay 1993 £9 (POR, FUL, MWW).

Gonzalez Byass (JEREZ, Spain) Producer of the world's best-selling **Fino** (**** Tio Pepe), this winery produces some of the finest, most complex, traditional sherries available to mankind. ***** Matusalem Oloroso Muy Viejo, Gonzalez Byass £19 (TO, SAF, TDS, OD) ***** Amontillado Del Duque, Gonzalez Byass £19 (TDS).

Goulburn Valley (VICTORIA, Australia) Small, long-established region reigned over by the respectively ancient and modern **CHATEAU TAHBILK** and **MITCHELTON** both of whom make great **MARSANNE**. *** Mitchelton Goulburn Valley Reserve Marsanne 1991 £7 (W, JS, OD).

Goundrey (WESTERN AUSTRALIA) Young winery in the up-and-coming region of **MOUNT BARKER**, making fruity but not overstated **CHARDONNAY** and **CABERNET**. ***** Windy Hill Cabernet Sauvignon 1989 £9 (A, GRT, RWW) Langton Chardonnay 1993 £7 (A, RWW, GRT, RBS).

Graach (MOSEL-SAAR-RUWER, Germany) **MITTELMOSEL** village producing fine wines. Best known for Himmelreich vineyard. **DEINHARD**, **JJ PRUM**, **FRIEDRICH-WILHELM-GYMNASIUM** and **VON KESSELSTADT** are names to look out for 83 85 86 88 89 90 91 92 93. **** Graacher Himmelreich Riesling Kabinett, Reichsgraf von Kesselstatt 1993 £6 (A).

Graham (DOURO, Portugal) Sweetly delicate wines, sometimes outclassing the same stable's supposedly classier and heftier DOWS. Malvedos is the SINGLE QUINTA. ***** Graham's Malvedos Vintage Port 1979 £17 (OD, WR, BU, SAF, MRN) ***** Graham's Vintage Port 1966 £35 (WSO) *** Grahams 10 Year Old Tawny Port £15 (SEL).

Alain Graillot (RHONE, France) Producer who should be toasted for shaking up the sleepy, largely undistinguished appellation of CROZES HERMITAGE using grapes from rented vineyards. All the reds are excellent, and La Guiraude is the wine from the top vineyard. **** Crozes Hermitage 1992 £8 (YAP, OD, L&W).

Gran Reserva (Spain) A QUALITY WINE AGED FOR A DESIGNATED NUMBER OF YEARS IN WOOD AND, IN THEORY, ONLY PRODUCED IN THE BEST VINTAGES. **** Montecillo Viña Monty Rioja Gran Reserva 1986 £7 (OD, BAR).

Grand Cru (France) THE FINEST VINEYARDS. OFFICIAL DESIGNATION IN BORDEAUX, BURGUNDY AND ALSACE. VAGUE IN BORDEAUX AND SOMEWHAT UNRELIABLE ALSACE. IN BURGUNDY DENOTES A SINGLE VINEYARD WITH ITS OWN AC, eg MONTRACHET.

Ch. du Grand Moulas (RHONE, France) Very classy COTES DU RHONE property with unusually complex flavours. **** 1993 £5 (TAN).

Grand Vin (BORDEAUX, France) THE FIRST (QUALITY) WINE OF AN ESTATE – AS OPPOSED TO ITS SECOND LABEL.

Ch. Grand-Puy-Ducasse (BORDEAUX, France) Excellent wines from fifth-growth PAUILLAC property 82 83 85 86 88 89 90. **** 1986 £13 (EV).

Ch. Grand-Puy-Lacoste (BORDEAUX, France) Top class fifth growth owned by the Borie family of DUCRU-BEAUCAILLOU and busily chasing the super seconds. Great value 82 83 85 86 88 89 90. *** 1990 £18 (L&W, THP).

Grande Rue (BURGUNDY, France) Recently promoted GRAND CRU in VOSNE-ROMANEE, across the track from ROMANEE-CONTI (hence the promotion). However the Domaine Lamarche to whom this MONOPOLE belongs is a long-term under-performer which is only beginning to improve. *** Vosne-Romanée, Domaine Lamarche 1983 £42 (T&W).

Grandes marques SUPPOSEDLY SIGNIFICANT SYNDICATE OF THE MAJOR CHAMPAGNE MERCHANTS CAST IN ASPIC AND INCLUDING FIRMS WHICH EXIST IN NO MORE THAN NAME. ITS RECENTLY LAUNCHED QUALITY CHARTER INADVERTENTLY REVEALED HOW CONSERVATIVE AND – IN REAL TERMS – QUALITY UNCONSCIOUS IT IS.

Grands-Echézeaux (BURGUNDY, France) One of the best GRAND CRUs in BURGUNDY, see ECHEZEAUX. *** DRC 1983 £70 (T&W).

Yves Grassa (South-West France) Pioneering producer of VIN DE PAYS DES COTES DE GASÇOGNE. *** Co-op Vin De Pays des Côtes de Gasçogne £3 (CWS).

Grant Burge (SOUTH AUSTRALIA) Former winemaker of KRONDORF, now producing well-regarded commercial BAROSSA SHIRAZ and CHARDONNAY. *** Shiraz 1992 £6 (AUC).

Alfred Gratien (CHAMPAGNE, France) Good CHAMPAGNE house, using traditional methods. Also owner of less impressive LOIRE fizz-maker, Gratien et Meyer, based in Saumur. *** Champagne Alfred Gratien Brut 1985 £20 (WSO).

Domaine la Grave (BORDEAUX, France) New-wave white and red GRAVES made by Danish-born innovator, Peter Vinding-Diers. *** Domaine La Grave, Bordeaux Rouge 1990 £6 (GH).

Grave del Friuli (Friuli-Venezia Giulia, Italy) DOC for young-drinking reds and whites. CABERNET and MERLOT are increasingly successful 85 86 87 88 90 91 92. *** Merlot, Ladino 1992 £4 (ADN).

Graves (BORDEAUX, France) Large, southern region producing vast quantities of white, from good to indifferent. Reds have a better reputation for quality, particularly since most of the best whites come from the northern part of the Graves and are sold as PESSAC-LEOGNAN. (red) 78 79 81 82 83 85 86 88 89 90. (white) 78 79 81 82 83 85 86 88 89 90 92, 93. ****Château Coucheroy, Graves, A Lurton 1992 £6 (TH, WR, BU, TDS) ***Château Saint Robert, Graves, Credit Foncier 1988 £5 (SMF) ***Graves Blanc, Collection Anniversaire, Yvon Mau 1993 £5 (U).

Great Western (VICTORIA, Australia) Region noted for SEPPELT's fizzes including the astonishing 'Sparkling Burgundy' SHIRAZes for Best's, (an example of the 1963 refreshed us while preparing this year's *Guide*), and for the wines of MOUNT LANGI GHIRAN. **** Seppelt Great Western Brut £5 (OD, MWW, TH, W, VW).

Greco di Tufo (Italy) From CAMPANIA, best-known white from the ancient GRECO grape; dry, characterful southern wine. **** Antonio Mastroberardino Nova Serra 1992 £13 (V&C).

Green Point (Yarra, Australia) See DOMAINE CHANDON.

Grenache Red grape of the RHÔNE (the Garnacha in Spain) making spicy, peppery, full-bodied wine provided yields are kept low. Also increasingly used to make rosés across Southern France and California. *** Mount Hurtle Grenache Rosé, Geoff Merrill 1993 £5 (JS, OD) ***Peter Lehmann Barossa Valley Grenache 1989 £4 (OD) ****The Catalyst 1992 £6 (OD) *** Fortant De France Grenache Rouge, Vin de Pays d'Oc, Skalli 1993 £3.50 (FUL).

Marchesi de Gresy Good producer of single vineyard BARBARESCO. *** Camp Gros Martinenga £13 (LAV).

Grgich Hills (NAPA VALLEY, California) Pioneering producer of CABERNET SAUVIGNON, CHARDONNAY AND FUMÉ BLANC. The name is a concatenation of the two founders – Mike Grgich (who made the French-beating 1972 CHÂTEAU MONTELENA CHARDONNAY) and Austin Hills – rather than a topographical feature of the area. **** Cabernet Sauvignon 1988 £17 (EP) *** Zinfandel 1989 £11 (EP).

Grignolino (PIEDMONT, Italy) Red grape and its modest, but refreshing, wine, eg the DOC Grignolino d'Asti. Drink young 90 91 92 93. *** Aldo Conterno 1993 £8 (V&C).

Jean-Louis Grippat (RHÔNE, France) An unusually great white RHÔNE producer in HERMITAGE and ST JOSEPH. His reds in both APPELLATIONS are less stunning, but still worth buying in their subtler-than-most way. Look out too for his ultra-rare Cuvée des Hospices St Joseph Rouge. **** Hermitage Blanc 1992 £16 (YAP).

Jean Grivot (BURGUNDY, France) Top class VOSNE ROMANÉE estate whose winemaker Etienne has recently come under the spell of Lebanese guru OENOLOGIST Guy Accad. His influence and the introduction of new techniques has made for wines which appear to need longer to develop. *** Vosne-Romanée 1988 £16 (L&W).

Schloss Groenesteyn (RHEINGAU, Germany) Now underperforming, this RHEINGAU estate was once highly-rated. *** Kiedricher Sandgrub Kabinett Riesling, 1988 £6. (VW).

Jean Gros (BURGUNDY, France) Great VOSNE ROMANÉE producer, with unusually reliable CLOS VOUGEOTs. ***** Vosne Romanée, Domaine Jean Gros 1989 £21 (TH, WR, BU).

Gros Lot/Grolleau Workhorse grape of the LOIRE, particularly ANJOU, used for white, rosé and base wines for sparkling SAUMUR *** Azay le Rideau Rosé, Gaston Pavy 1992 £6 (YAP).

Gros Plant (du Pays Nantais) (LOIRE, France) Light, sharp white VDQS wine from the same region as MUSCADET, named after the grape elsewhere known as the FOLLE BLANCHE. In all but the best hands, serves to make even a poor MUSCADET look good. 89 90 92 93. *** La Maisdonnière, Bernard Baffreau 1992 £5 (YAP).

Grosslage (Germany) WINE DISTRICT, THE THIRD SUBDIVISION AFTER ANBAUGEBIET (EG RHEINGAU) AND BEREICH (EG NIERSTEIN). FOR EXAMPLE, MICHELSBERG IS A GROSSLAGE OF THE BEREICH PIESPORT.

Ch. Gruaud-Larose (BORDEAUX, France) One of the stars of the Cordier stable. Rich but potentially slightly unsubtle. Buy in good years 82 83 85 86 88 89 90. *** 1988 £23 (AV, SEL).

Grüner Veltliner Spicy white grape of Austria and Eastern Europe, producing light, fresh, aromatic wine – and for WILLI OPITZ an extraordinary late harvest version 87 88 89 90. **** Gruner Veltliner Trockenbeerenauslese, Willi Opitz 1993 £27.50 (T&W). *** Lenz Moser 1993 £4 (W)

Guerrieri-Rizzardi (Veneto, Italy) Solid organic producer, with good 1985 AMARONE and single vineyard SOAVE Classico Costeggiola. *** Bardolino Classico Tacchetto 1993 £6 (BAR, F&M) *** Soave Classico Costeggiola 1993 £6 (BAR, SEL).

Guigal (RHONE, France) Still the yardstick for RHONE Reds, despite increased competition from CHAPOUTIER. His extraordinarily pricey single vineyard La Mouline, La Landonne and La Turque wines are still ahead of the young turks. The basic COTES DU RHONE is also well worth looking out for. 81 82 83 85 88 89 90. ***** Hermitage Rouge 1990 £20 (OD, L&W) ****Côte Rôtie, Côtes Brune Et Blonde 1989 £17 (TH, WR, BU) ****Côte Rôtie 1990 £19 (WR, OD, L&W) *****Côte Rôtie La Turque 1986 £100 (F&M) ****Côte Rôtie La Landonne 1976 £350 (F&M)

Guimaraens (DOURO, Portugal) Associated with FONSECA; under-rated port-house producing good wines. **** Fonseca Guimaraens Vintage Port 1967 £26 (VW).

Ch. Guiraud (BORDEAUX, France) SAUTERNES classed-growth, recently restored to original quality and now back in the pack which trail s closely in the wake of YQUEM. 82 83 85 86 88 89 90. *** 1986 £30 (AV, LEA, J&B).

Gundlach-Bundschu (SONOMA VALLEY, California) A good source of well-made, juicy MERLOT and spicy ZINFANDEL. *** Rhinefarm Vineyards Zinfandel 1991 £11 (EP) ***Rhinefarm Vineyards Merlot 1989 £13 (EP).

Louis Guntrum (RHEINHESSEN, Germany) Family-run estate with a penchant for SYLVANER.

Gutedel (Germany) GERMAN NAME FOR THE CHASSELAS GRAPE.

Gyongyos Estate (HUNGARY) The ground-breaking winery in which HUGH RYMAN first proved that Eastern Europe could make drinkable SAUVIGNON and CHARDONNAY. The PINOT NOIR shows promise too. *** Chardonnay, Hugh Ryman 1993 £3. (SMF, JS, SAF, TH, MWW) *** Sauvignon 1992 £3 (Widely available).

Fritz Haag (MOSEL-SAAR-RUWER, Germany) Top class, small estate with classic RIESLINGS. **** Riesling Kabinett 1990 £11 (HN).

Franz Haas (ALTO-ADIGE, Italy) One of the few producers to live up to the promise we all saw in this region a decade ago. A soulmate for Sylvio JERMANN in the purity of his single-variety whites. *** Pinot Grigio 1993 £7 (WCE).

Halbtrocken (Germany) OFF-DRY. RISING STYLE INTENDED TO ACCOMPANY FOOD. USUALLY A SAFER BUY THAN TROCKEN IN REGIONS LIKE THE MOSEL, RHEINGAU AND RHEINHESSEN, BUT STILL OFTEN AGGRESSIVELY ACIDIC STUFF. LOOK FOR QBA OR AUSLESE VERSIONS. *** Binger Scharlachberg Riesling Kabinett Halbtrocken, Villa Sachsen 1992 £4.99 (TO).

Hallgarten (RHEINGAU, Germany) Important town near Hattenheim producing robust wines including the – in Germany – well-regarded produce from SCHLOSS VOLLRADS. *** Hallgartener Hendelberg Riesling Green Gold QbA £6 (EP).

Hamilton Russell Vineyards (Walker Bay, South Africa) Pioneer of impressive PINOT NOIR and CHARDONNAY at a winery in Hermanus at the southernmost tip of the Cape. **** Pinot Noir 1992 £8 (AV) *** Chardonnay 1993 £8 (AV).

Hardy (Australia) Or more properly BRL Hardy, as the merged Berri-Renmano/Hardys is now known, is the second biggest wine producer in Australia, encompassing HOUGHTON and MOONDAH BROOK in WESTERN AUSTRALIA, Leasingham in the CLARE, the improved but still underperforming Redman in COONAWARRA, HARDY's itself and Chateau Reynella. HARDY's range is reliable throughout, including the commercial Nottage Hill and Stamp Series multi-regional blends wines. though the wines to look for are the top-of-the-range Eileen and Thomas Hardy. The Chateau Reynella wines made at the company's 150-year old headquarters exclusively from McLAREN VALE fruit, are good, quite lean examples of the region. ****Chateau Reynella Cabernet Merlot 1992 £7 (CWS, OD, WHC) ****Eileen Hardy Reserve Shiraz 1991 £9.99 (OD, SAF, WHC) ****Moondah Brook Estate Verdelho 1993 £5 (OD, TO, VW).

Haro (RIOJA, Spain) Town at the heart of the RIOJA region, home of many BODEGAS, eg CVNE and La Rioja Alta. *** La Rioja Alta Viña Ardanza 'Reserva' 1987 £9 (L&S) ***CVNE Reserva 1986 £7 (L&W).

Harveys (JEREZ, Spain) Maker of the ubiquitous ***Bristol Cream £6 (widely available).

Hattenheim (RHEINGAU, Germany) One of the greatest JOHANNISBERG villages, producing some of the best German RIESLINGS 76 79 83 85 88 89 90. *** Nussbrunner Riesling Auslese, Von Simmern 1990 £30 (ADN).

Hatzimichalis (Atalanti, Greece,) The face of Greek winemaking in the late 1990s? Hopefully. This small estate produces nop-notch CABERNET SAUVIGNON, MERLOT and fresh, dry Atalanti white. ***Merlot 1992 £13 (GWC)

Haut Poitou (LOIRE, France) Often boring yet (quite) good value SAUVIGNON and CHARDONNAY whites and even less exciting reds 89 90 92 93. *** Sauvignon Blanc de Haut Poitou, Caves de Haut Poitou £4 (SMF).

Ch. Haut-Bages-Averous (BORDEAUX, France) SECOND LABEL of Ch Lynch Bages. Good value blackcurrant PAUILLAC. **** 1988 £15 (VW).

Ch. Haut-Bages-Liberal (BORDEAUX, France) Top class small PAUILLAC property in the same stable as CHASSE SPLEEN 82 83 85 86 88 89 90. **** 1988 £14 (TAN).

Ch. Haut-Bailly (BORDEAUX, France) Little known PESSAC-LEOGNAN property consistently making reliable, long-lived wines 82 85 86 88 89 90. **** 1989 £19 (AV, ADN, THP, VW).

Ch. Haut-Batailley (BORDEAUX, France) Subtly-styled fifth-growth PAUILLAC from the same stable as DUCRU BEAUCAILLOU and GRAND PUY LACOSTE. 85 86 88 89 90. *** 1989 £14 (M&V).

Ch. Haut-Brion (BORDEAUX, France) Pepys' favourite and still a supreme GRAVES First Growth (the only non MEDOC) on the outskirts of BORDEAUX (with a great view of the gasworks). Wines can be tough and hard to judge young but, at their best they develop a rich, fruity perfumed character which sets them apart from their peers. 1989 was especially good; 1983 currently tastes disappointing. The white is rare and can be sublime 78 82 85 86 88 89 90. ***** 1989 £60 (BBR, J&B).

Ch. Haut-Marbuzet (BORDEAUX, France) A CRU BOURGEOIS which thinks it's a CRU CLASSE. Well made immediately imposing wine with bags of oak. Decidedly new-wave ST ESTEPHE 82 83 85 86 88 89 90. *** 1986 £17 (EV).

Haut-Médoc (BORDEAUX, France) Large APPELLATION which includes nearly all of the well-known CRUS CLASSES. Basic HAUT-MEDOC should be better than plain MEDOC 78 81 82 83 85 86 88 89 90 91. ***Château Le Bourdieu Vertheuil, Haut Médoc £8 (CPW) ***Société Richard 1990 £7.95 (CPW) ***Château Cissac, Haut Médoc, 1985 £13 (FDL, EP, CWS).

Hautes Côtes de Beaune (BURGUNDY, France) Sound, soft, strawberry PINOT NOIR hailing from a group of villages situated in the hills above the big-name communes. Worth buying in good vintages; in poorer ones the grapes have problems ripening. Most of the wine seen outside the region is made by one of Burgundy's improving cooperatives. 85 86 87 88 89 90 92. *** Hautes Côtes de Beaune Rouge, Labouré Roi 1991 £5 (SMF) *** Hautes Côtes de Beaune, Les Caves des Hautes Côtes 1991 £5 (ABY, WL).

Hautes Côtes de Nuits (BURGUNDY, France) Slightly tougher than HAUTES COTES DE BEAUNE, particularly when young. White wines are very rare. 85 86 87 88 89 90 92. *** Bourgogne Hautes-Côtes De Nuits, Domaine A-F Gros 1989 £6 (CAC) *** Hautes Côtes De Nuits, Cave Des Hautes Côtes 1990 £7 (TH, WR, BU).

Hawkes Bay (NEW ZEALAND) Major North Island vineyard area which is finally beginning to live up to the promise of producing top-class reds. Whites can be fine too, though rarely achieving the bite of MARLBOROUGH. Top producers include TE MATA, ESK VALLEY, VIDAL, NGATARAWA, and BABICH 87 89 90 91. **** Vidal Hawkes Bay Reserve Cabernet Sauvignon/ Merlot 1992 £19 ****Vidal Private Bin Hawkes Bay Merlot Rosé 1993 £6 (TH) ***Ngatarawa Hawkes Bay Chardonnay 1991 £8 (NY, LEA). ***Babich Hawkes Bay Sauvignon Blanc 1993 £7 (BAB, ABY).

Heemskerk (Tasmania, Australia) Until recently associated with ROEDERER in the making of Jansz, this is a producer of (good) Aussie fizz and also the source of some good, sturdy reds. *** Heemskerk Jansz Brut 1990 £14 (ADN, OD, JN) ***Heemskerk Cabernet Sauvignon 1990 £8 (ADN, OD, MRT).

Charles Heidsieck (CHAMPAGNE, France) A rare example of a CHAMPAGNE house which managed to match a rise in price with a corresponding rise in quality. Today the non-vintage is amongst the best value around **** NV £20 (widely available).

Heitz Cellars (NAPA Valley, California) One of the great names of California and the source of stunning reds in the 1970s, some of this emperor's new clothes look decidedly transparent. Current releases of the flagship Martha's Vineyard Cabernet taste unacceptably musty, as do the traditionally almost-as-good Bella Oaks. In the US, such criticisms are treated as lèse-majesté (Robert Parker is circumspect in his comments), so collectors queue up every year to buy these wines as they are allowed on to the market. The late Geoffrey Roberts, Heitz's last importer into the UK, had no doubts that there was a problem. Current vintages are almost unfindable here.

Henschke (Adelaide Hills, Australia) One of the world's best. From the long-established Hill of Grace and (slightly less intense) Mount Edelstone Shirazes to the new Abbott's Prayer MERLOT-CABERNET from Lenswood, the RIESLING and Tilly's Vineyard white blend, there's not a duff wine in the cellar, and the reds last forever. Compare and contrast with HEITZ. ***** Abbotts Prayer Merlot/Cabernet, Lenswood 1990 £12 (L&W) ****Mount Edelstone Shiraz 1990 £11 (L&W, AUC, BOO) *****Hill of Grace Shiraz 1990 £21 (L&W, AUC).

Vin de pays de l' Hérault (MIDI, France) Largest vine growing *département*, producing some 20 per cent of France's wine, nearly all VIN DE PAYS or VDQS, of which COTEAUX DU LANGUEDOC is the best known. Also the home of the extraordinary MAS DE DAUMAS GASSAC, where no expense is spared to produce wines which so far surpass 'country wines' so as to compete with the best from supposedly far greater regions. The potential in this area is enormous. Watch this space 82 83 85 86 88 89 90 91. **** Mas de Daumas Gassac, Vin de Pays de l'Herault 1992 £11 (ADN, OD) ****Mas de Daumas Gassac Blanc, Vin de Pays de l'Herault 1993 £16 (ADN, OD) ***Vin de Pays des Cevennes, Vin de Pays de l'Herault, Caves Coop De L'Uzège £3 (VW).

Hermitage (RHONE, France) Top-class, long-lived northern RHONE wines; superb, complex (SYRAH) reds and sumptuous, nutty (MARSANNE and ROUSSANE) whites. Also, the old Australian name for SYRAH and, confusingly, the South African term for CINSAULT. Best producers: CHAPOUTIER (since 1990), JABOULET AINE, CHAVE, DELAS (individual vineyard wines), SORREL, GRIPPAT, GUIGAL, VIDAL-FLEURY 76 78 79 82 83 85 88 89 90 91. **** Hermitage Cuvée Marquise de la Tourette, Delas 1990 £18 (LAY, PST, EV) ****Hermitage Rouge, E Guigal 1990 £20 (OD, IRV, L&W, S&J).

The Hess Collection (NAPA VALLEY, California) High class CABERNET producer, high in the Mount Veeder hills. The lower-priced MONTEREY wines are worth buying too. **** Chardonnay, Hess Winery 1991 £11 (JAR). ****Cabernet Sauvignon 1990 £14 (JAR).

Hessische Bergstrasse (Germany) Smallest ANBAUGEBIET, rarely seen in the UK, but capable of fine EISWEINS and dry SYLVANERS which can surpass those of nearby Franken.

Hidalgo (MANZANILLA/JEREZ, Spain) Specialist producer of impeccable dry 'La Gitana' sherry and a great many own-label offerings. **** Booths Manzanilla £4 (BTH) ***Tanners Mariscal Fino and Manzanilla £6 (TAN).

Hochfeinste (Germany) 'VERY FINEST'.

Hochgewächs QbA (Germany) RECENT OFFICIAL DESIGNATION FOR RIESLINGS WHICH ARE AS RIPE AS A QMP BUT CAN STILL ONLY CALL THEMSELVES QBA. THIS FROM A NATION SUPPOSEDLY DEDICATED TO SIMPLIFYING WHAT ARE ACKNOWLEDGED TO BE THE MOST COMPLICATED LABELS IN THE WORLD.

Hochheim (RHEINGAU, Germany) Village whose fine RIESLINGS gave the English the word 'HOCK'. **** Hochheim, Deinhard Heritage Collection 1988 £7 (TDS, CNL) ***Hochheimer Holle Riesling Kabinett, Geheimrat Aschrott Erben 1992 £5 (A).

Hock ENGLISH NAME FOR RHINE WINES, DERIVED FROM HOCHHEIM IN THE RHEINGAU. *** Safeway Hock 1993 £3 (SAF).

Hogue Cellars (WASHINGTON STATE, US) Dynamic YAKIMA VALLEY producer of good CHARDONNAY, RIESLING, MERLOT and CABERNET.

Hollick (SOUTH AUSTRALIA) A good, traditional COONAWARRA, producer; the Ravenswood has a cult following Down Under and is well worth seeking out. **** Coonawarra Red 1991 £8 (F&M, WWI, R) **** Ravenswood Cabernet Sauvignon 1990 £15 (NY, SK, WWI, R).

Hospices de Beaune (BURGUNDY, France) Charity hospital, whose wines (often CUVEES or blends of different vineyards), are sold at an annual charity auction, the prices supposedly – though less and less often – setting the tone for the COTE D'OR year. Beware that although price lists often merely indicate 'Hospices de Beaune' as a producer, all of the wines bought at the auction are matured and bottled by local merchants, some of whom are more scrupulous than others. Quality of the winemaking over recent years has, in any case, been very questionable. A new winemaker is expected to raise standards 78 85 88 90.

Houghton (SWAN VALLEY, Australia) Long-established subsidiary of HARDYS. Best known for its CHENIN-based rich white blend, sold Down Under as 'White Burgundy' (not for much longer). The wines to watch though are the ones from the MOONDAH BROOK vineyard. **** Gold Reserve Verdelho, 1993 £5. (AR) ***Gold Reserve Cabernet Sauvignon 1988 £5 (AR).

Von Hövel (SAAR, Germany) 200-year-old estate with fine RIESLINGS from great vineyards. These repay the patience they demand. *** Scharzhofberger Riesling Kabinett 1989, von Hövel £7 (TH, WR).

Howell Mountains (NAPA, California) Hillside region to the north of NAPA, capable of fine whites and reds from La Jota and pricey mouth-puckering reds from DUNN.

Alain Hudelot-Noellat (BURGUNDY, France) A great winemaker whose generosity with oak is matched, especially in his GRAND CRU RICHEBOURG and ROMANEE ST VIVANT by intense fruit flavours. **** Chambolle-Musigny 1990 £19 (HR).

Huelva (Spain) **DO** of the Extremadura region, producing rather heavy whites and fortified wines.

Gaston Huet (LOIRE, France) Long-time mayor of **VOUVRAY** and one of the very few producers who has consistently produced top quality individual vineyard examples of **SEC**, **DEMI-SEC** and **MOELLEUX** wines. His non-vintage fizz, though only made occasionally, is top class too. ***** Clos de Bourg, 1969 £49 (ADN) ***Le Haut Lieu 1988, £8.50. (ADN).

Hugel et Fils (ALSACE, France) Reliable **NEGOCIANT** whose wines rarely reach great heights. Look out for the Jubilee wines and – hard-to-find – late harvest offerings. Gentil is a recommendable revival of the tradition of blending different grape varieties. **** Hugel Gentil 1992 £5 (JS) *** Gewürztraminer 1991 £11 (AV).

Hungary Country previously known for its famous **TOKAY**, infamous **BULL'S BLOOD**, and **OLASZ RIZLING**. Now a popular destination for **FLYING WINEMAKERS** – a country to watch . ** Egri Bikavér 1991 £4 (WOW) *** Gyongyos Estate Chardonnay, Hugh Ryman 1993 £3 (SMF, G, JS) **** Tokaji Aszu 6 Puttonyos, Hetszolo 1981 £20 (GRO, SOB, RWW).

Hunter Valley (Australia) For many, the best-known region in Australia is ironically one of the least suitable parts in which to make wine. When the vines are not dying of heat and thirst they are drowning beneath the torrential rains which like to fall at precisely the same time as the harvest. Even so, the **SHIRAZES** and **SEMILLONS** – traditionally sold as 'Hermitage', 'Claret', 'Burgundy', 'Chablis' and 'Hunter Valley Riesling' – can develop remarkably. Best producers: **LAKE'S FOLLY**, **BROKENWOOD**, **ROTHBURY ESTATE**, **ROSEMOUNT**, **TYRRELLS**, **MCWILLLIAMS**, **LINDEMANS**, Reynolds, **EVANS FAMILY**, Petersons.(red): 83 86 87 88 90 91 92. (white) 83 86 87 88 90 91 92 93. ***** Rosemount Cabernet Sauvignon/Shiraz 1993 £5 (JS) ***McWilliams Mount Pleasant Chardonnay 1992 £5 (OD, AUC).

Hunter's (MARLBOROUGH, NEW ZEALAND) One of **MARLBOROUGH**'s most consistent producers of ripe fruity **SAUVIGNON BLANCS**. **** Sauvignon Blanc 1993 £9 (WR).

Huxelrebe Minor white grape, often grown in England but proving what it can do when harvested late in Germany. *****Forster Schnepfenflug Trockenbeerenauslese, Kurt Darting 1992 £14 (half) (OD).

Hybrid CROSS-BRED GRAPE VITIS VINIFERA (EUROPEAN) X VITIS LABRUSCA (NORTH AMERICAN) – AN EXAMPLE IS **SEYVAL BLANC**.

Hydrogen sulphide NATURALLY OCCURRING GAS GIVEN OFF BY ESPECIALLY YOUNG RED WINE, RESULTING IN SMELL OF ROTTEN EGGS. OFTEN CAUSED BY INSUFFICIENT RACKING. IF YOU SUSPECT A WINE OF HAVING THIS SMELL, YOU MAY BE ABLE TO REMOVE IT BY ADDING A PENNY (OR ANY OTHER COPPER COIN).

Vin de Pays de l' Ile de Beauté (CORSICA, France) Picturesque name for improving wines thanks to the involvement of such outsiders as **LAROCHE**. Often a better bet than this island's **APPELLATION** wines. ***Pinot Noir 'L', Laroche 1992 £4 (EP).

Imbottigliato nel'origine (Italy) Estate-bottled.

Imperiale (BORDEAUX, France) LARGE BOTTLE CONTAINING ALMOST SIX AND A HALF LITRES OF WINE (EIGHT AND A HALF BOTTLES). CHERISHED BY COLLECTORS PARTLY THROUGH RARITY, PARTLY THROUGH THE GREATER LONGEVITY THAT LARGE BOTTLES ARE SUPPOSED TO GIVE THEIR CONTENTS. MIND YOU, IT HELPS IF YOU CAN EMPLOY ARNOLD SCHWARZENEGGER TO DO THE POURING RATHER THAN TAKING IT IN TURNS WITH A LONG STRAW.

Inferno (Italy) Lombardy **DOC**, chiefly red from **NEBBIOLO**, which needs to be aged for at least five years.*** Nino Negri 1990 £6 (V&C).

Inglenook Vineyards (NAPA, California) Once-great winery which has, like **BEAULIEU**, hardly benefitted in quality terms from being owned by a division of UK giant Grand Metropolitan. The Cask reds are still good, while the **CHARBONO** is a good buy. ***Charbono 1985 £5 (PF).

Inniskillin (ONTARIO, CANADA) Long-established winery with good Ice Wines (made from the Vidal), a successful CHARDONNAY and a rare example of a wine made from the Maréchal Foch. *** Chardonnay 1992 £7 (AV)

Institut National des Appellations d'Origine (INAO) FRENCH ADMINISTRATIVE BODY WHICH DESIGNATES AND POLICES QUALITY. UNDER INCREASING FIRE FROM CRITICS OUTSIDE (AND TO A LESSER EXTENT WITHIN) FRANCE WHO WANT TO KNOW WHY APPELLATION CONTROLEE WINES ARE SO OFTEN INFERIOR TO THE NEW WAVE OF VINS DE TABLE OVER WHICH THIS BODY HAS NO AUTHORITY.

Irancy (BURGUNDY, France) Little-known, light reds and rosés made near CHABLIS from a blend of grapes including the PINOT NOIR and the little-known César. Curiously, Irancy has AC status whereas SAUVIGNON DE ST BRIS a nearby source of superior whites is merely a VDQS region ** Andre Sorin 1992 £9 (ABY).

Iron Horse Vineyards (SONOMA, California) One of the best sparkling wine producers in the NEW WORLD, thanks to cool climate vineyards. Reds are increasingly impressive too. **** Cabernet Sauvignon 1984 £15 (RD, WIN).

Irouléguy (South-West France) Earthy, spicy reds and ROSÉS, duller whites *** Irouléguy rouge, Domaine Mignaberry 1992 £7.40 (ABY) **Dom. de Mendisoka 1990 £6 (WSO).

Irsay Oliver (SLOVAKIA, HUNGARY) Native white varietal giving aromatic, spicy but dry wines which are quite reminicent of GEWURZTRAMINER. Excellent value for money. *** Chapel Hill, Irsai Oliver 1993 £3 (JS, VW).

Isinglass FINING AGENT DERIVED FROM THE STURGEON

Isole e Olena (TUSCANY, Italy) Brilliant, small CHIANTI estate with a pure SANGIOVESE SUPER-TUSCAN, CEPPARELLO and Italy's first (technically illegal) SYRAH. 83 86 88 89 90 91.**** Chianti Classico 1990 £17 (WCE). *****Cepparello 1990 £17 (WCE).

Israel Once the source of appalling stuff, but the new-style Varietal wines are improving. See GOLAN HEIGHTS. ***Yarden Chardonnay 1991 £8 (SEL) ***Gamla Cabernet Sauvignon 1988 £7 (SEL).

Ch. d' Issan (BORDEAUX, France) Recently revived MARGAUX Third Growth with recogniseable blackcurrany CABERNET SAUVIGNON intensity 82 83 85 86 89 90. *** 1989, £18 (BBR, J&B)

Italian Riesling/Riesling Italico Not the great RHINE RIESLING, but another name for the unrelated WELSCHRIESLING, LUTOMER AND LASKI RIZLING, going under many names, and widely grown in Northern and Eastern Europe.

Paul Jaboulet Aîné (RHONE, France) NEGOCIANT-owner of the illustrious HERMITAGE LA CHAPELLE. and producer of good COTES DU RHONE and CHATEAUNEUF-DU-PAPE. Reliable but now overshadowed by GUIGAL and the reconstructed CHAPOUTIER ****Hermitage La Chapelle, P Jaboulet 1987 £14 (TH) *****Hermitage La Chapelle 1978 £73 (EV) .

Jackson Estate (MARLBOROUGH, NEW ZEALAND) Next-door neighbour to CLOUDY BAY and producer of SAUVIGNON which is giving that superstar producer a run for its money. **** Marlborough Sauvignon Blanc 1993 £7.95 (JS) ****Marlborough Chardonnay 1992 £8 (TAN, HN, W, WR).

Louis Jadot (BURGUNDY, France) Good, sometimes great BEAUNE NEGOCIANT . **** Meursault-Blagny 1er Cru 1989 £28 (VW, TH) ****Corton Pougets 1989 £30 (BU).

Jaffelin (BURGUNDY, France) Small NEGOCIANT recently bought from DROUHIN by BOISSET. Particularly good at supposedly 'lesser' appellations. ****Monthelie, Jaffelin 1991 £10 (OD) ***Saint Romain, Jaffelin 1992 £9 (OD).

Joseph Jamet (RHONE, France) Top-class COTE ROTIE estate. *** Côte Rôtie 1991 £19 (BI).

Vin de Pays du Jardin de la France (LOIRE, France) Marketing device to describe LOIRE VINS DE PAYS. ***Chardonnay, Auguste Couillaud 1991 £7 (FUL)

Robert Jasmin (RHONE, France) Traditionalist COTE ROTIE estate, eschewing new oak **** Côte Rôtie 1992 £16 (YAP).

Jasnières (LOIRE, France) Rare, bone-dry and – even rarer – MOELLEUX sweet CHENIN BLANC wines from TOURAINE. Buy carefully; poorly made wines offer an expensive chance to taste the CHENIN at its worst 88 89 90 92. **** Jasnières, Les Truffières 1986 Jean-Baptiste Pinon £8 (YAP).

Jasper Hill (VICTORIA, Australia) Winery in Heathcote, BENDIGO, with a deserved cult following for both reds and whites. **** Georgia's Paddock Riesling 1992 £8 **** Georgia's Paddock Shiraz 1992 £12 (ADN).

Domaine de la Jaubertie (South-West France) Pioneering BERGERAC property established by Henry Ryman and now under his son, HUGH RYMAN's winemaking control. Reliable alternative to SANCERRE. **** Château de la Jaubertie Bergerac Sec, Henry Ryman 1993 £5 (VW, JS).

Henri Jayer (BURGUNDY, France) Cult winemaker whose top COTE DE NUITS reds are more than a match for the DOMAINE DE LA ROMANEE CONTI. Now retired but still represented on labels referring to Georges et Henri, and as an influence on the wines of MEO CAMUZET. ***** Echézeaux 1989 Georges et Henri Jayer £43 (J&B).

Robert Jayer-Gilles (BURGUNDY, France) Henri Jayer's cousin, whose top wines – including a NUITS ST GEORGES les Damodes and an ECHEZEAUX – bear comparison with those of his more famous relative. (His whites are worth following, too).**** Côtes de Nuits Villages 1991 £12 (OD).

Jekel Vineyards (Arroyo Seco, California) Founded by Southern Californian pioneer, Bill Jekel, a famous critic of TERROIR, but since sold to the new owners of FETZER. RIESLING is the real success story here but CABERNETS and CHARDONNAYS are increasingly worth following if you accept their slightly herbaceous style *** Sanctuary Estate Cabernet Sauvignon 1991 £9 (WIN). *** Gravelstone Chardonnay 1992 £8 (WIN).

Jerez (de la Frontera) (Spain) Centre of the SHERRY trade, and thus naming the entire DO SHERRY-producing area. See GONZALEZ BYASS, LUSTAU, HIDALGO, BARBADILLO.

Jermann (FRIULI-VENEZIA GIULIA, Italy) Brilliant, innovative, white winemaker with a knack of getting the best out of every variety he touches. Look out for Silvio's Vintage Tunina, a blend of Tocai, Picolit & MALVASIA, and the 'Where the Dreams have no End' white blend (he is a U2 fan) plus Capo Martino, a single-vineyard blend of PINOTS. **** Where The Dreams Have No End 1991 £30 (PON, SEL, V&C) *** Vinnae 1992 £11 (BWS, V&C, LV).

Jeroboam LARGE BOTTLE – IN CHAMPAGNE CONTAINING THREE LITRES (FOUR BOTTLES); IN BORDEAUX, IT CAN BE FOUR AND ONE HALF LITRES (SIX BOTTLES). DO CHECK BEFORE WRITING YOUR CHEQUE.

Jesuitengarten (RHEINGAU, Germany) One of Germany's top vineyards – well-handled by BASSERMANN-JORDAN **** Forster Jesuitgarten Riesling Spätlese 1988, Bassermann-Jordan £8 (VW).

Jeunes Vignes denotes vines too young for their crop to be sold as an APPELLATION CONTROLEE wine, eg the CHABLIS sold under this label by LA CHABLISIENNE cooperative. *** Jeunes Vignes 1992 £6 (M&S).

Jobard (BURGUNDY, France) Small in size alone, this white wine estate makes great wines. **** Meursault 'Genevrières' 1991 £23 (ADN).

Charles Joguet (LOIRE, France) One of the top names for red LOIRE, making wines that can last. ***Chinon, Les Varennes du Grand Clos 1992 £11 (HHC).

Johannisberg (RHEINGAU, Germany) Village making superb RIESLING, which has lent its name to a BEREICH covering all the RHEINGAU. 75 76 79 83 85 88 89 90 91 92 ****Deinhard Johannisberg QbA 1989 £8 (WR) Johannisberger Ernteberger Reisling Kabinett QmP R Muller 1992 £5 (TAN).

Johannisberg Riesling CALIFORNIAN NAME FOR RHINE RIESLING.

Karl-Heinz Johner (BADEN, Germany) The former winemaker at LAMBERHURST, now making good wine in southern Germany.

Jordan (SONOMA, California) A SONOMA winery surrounded by the kind of hype more usually associated with NAPA. Table wines – from the ALEXANDER VALLEY – would not warrant a long letter home from an open-minded wine lover, but they're decent enough and the 'J' fizz, though inevitably pricy, is of CHAMPAGNE quality. *** Chardonnay 1990 £15 (L&W) *** Cabernet Sauvignon 1988 £17 (L&W).

Toni Jost (MITTELRHEIN, Germany) A new-wave producer with (well-sited) vines in Bacharach and a penchant for experimenting (successfully) with new oak barrels. ***Bacharacher Schloss Stahleck Riesling Kabinett 1992 £6 (OD).

Jug wine AMERICAN TERM FOR QUAFFABLE VIN ORDINAIRE, ESPECIALLY FROM THE CENTRAL VALLEY IN CALIFORNIA.

Marcel Juge (RHONE, France) Producer of one of the subtlest, classiest examples of CORNAS. 1990 £10 (EP).

Juliénas (BURGUNDY, France) One of the 10 BEAUJOLAIS CRUS, producing classic, vigorous wine which often benefits from a few years in bottle 88 89 90 91. **** Juliénas, Sylvain Fessy 1993 £7 (LAV ,WIN) ***Château des Capitans 1992 £7 (JS).

Juliusspital Weingut (FRANKEN, Germany) Top-class estate whose profits go to care for the poor and sick. **** Iphoefer Julius-Echter Silvanner Spätlese 1985 £14 (OWL).

Jumilla (Spain) Improving DO region, traditionally known for heavy, high-alcohol wines but increasingly making lighter ones. *** Jumilla, Carchelo 1990 £4 (VW).

Côtes de Jura (Eastern France) Region containing ARBOIS and SAVOIE, home of the SAVAGNIN grape and best known for specialities such as VIN GRIS, VIN JAUNE and VIN DE PAILLE. ***Côtes de Jura Blanc 1990 £7 (WSO) **Arbois, Type Savagnin 1988 £7 (TP).

Jurançon (South-west, France) Rich, dry apricotty white and excellent long-living sweet wines made from the GROS and PETIT MANSENG, traditional grapes grown almost nowhere else 86 87 88 89 90 91. **** Dom Cauhapé Vendange Tardive 1991 £13 (M&V) *** Dom. Cauhapé sec 1991 £8 (M&V, WSO, WDW)

Juve y Camps (CATALONIA, Spain) The exception which proves the rule – by making and maturing decent CAVA from traditional grapes. *** Reserva de Familia Brut 1989 £9 (L&S).

Kabinett FIRST STEP IN GERMAN QUALITY LADDER, FOR WINES WHICH FULFIL A CERTAIN NATURAL SWEETNESS. ***** Haardter Mandelring Scheurebe Kabinett, Muller Cattoir 1991 £9 (OD). *** Wiltinger Klosterberg Riesling Kabinett, Van Volxem 1989 £5 (WL).

Kaiserstuhl (BADEN, Germany) Finest BADEN BEREICH with top villages producing rich, spicy RIESLING and SYLVANER from volcanic slopes. *** Boetzinger Silvaner (Organic) Weingut Zimmerlin 1991 £4 (WSC).

Kallstadt (RHEINPFALZ, Germany) Village containing the best-known and finest vineyard of Annaberg, making luscious, full RIESLING. *** Kallstadter Steinacker Beerenauslese 1971 £35.00 (LV)

Kalterersee (Italy) Germanic name for the Lago di Caldaro in the SUDTIROL /ALTO ADIGE.

Kanonkop (STELLENBOSCH, SOUTH AFRICA) Modern estate reponsible for one of the few Pinotages which shows real class. The BORDEAUX-blend Kadette is good too. **** Pinotage 1991 £7 (TO).

Katnook Estate (COONAWARRA, Australia) Small estate belonging to large (non-vinous) corporation which allows it the freedom to make such innovative wines as a late harvest CHARDONNAY (VW) as well as top-class COONAWARRA MERLOT, CABERNET and **** Riddoch Cabernet-Shiraz 1991 £7 (TH, WR, BU, VW) ****Botrytised Chardonnay 1992 £6.50 (half) (VW)

Kellerei/kellerabfüllung (Germany) CELLAR/PRODUCER/ESTATE-BOTTLED.

Kendall-Jackson (Clear Lake, California) High profile producer which has made a fortune by making supposedly classy CHARDONNAY and SAUVIGNON which are actually decidedly off-dry. *** Chardonnay Vintners Reserve 1992 £8 (MWW) *** Cabernet Sauvignon Vintners Reserve 1991 £8 (MWW).

Kenwood Vineyards (SONOMA VALLEY, California) A classy SONOMA winery with good single vineyard CHARDONNAYS, impressive, if tough, CABERNETS (including wine made from the author Jack London's vineyard) and brilliant ZINFANDEL. Sadly, it's unavailable in the UK.

> **Kerner** White grape, a RIESLING-cross, grown in Germany and now England. *** Barkham Manor Kerner Dry, Barkham Manor Vineyard 1992 £7 (BAK).

Von Kesselstatt (MOSEL-SAAR-RUWER, Germany) Fine, though large, improving collection of four estates spread between the MOSEL-SAAR-RUWER **** Piesporter Goldtröpfchen Riesling Auslese 1990 £10 (MWW) **** Graacher Himmelreich Riesling Kabinett 1993 £6 (A).

Kiedrich (RHEINGAU, Germany) Top village high in the hills with some renowned vineyards 75 76 79 83 85 88 89 90 91 92. ***** Kiedricher Grapenberg Riesling Beerenauslese, Robert Weil 1992 £70 (BAR). **** Kiedricher Sandgrub Kabinett Riesling, Schloss E Groenestyn 1988 £6.29 (VW).

Kientzheim (ALSACE, France) Village noted for the quality of its RIESLING. **** Riesling Paul Blank 1989 £6 (ADN).

Kiona (WASHINGTON STATE, US) Small producer in the middle of nowhere with a penchant for intensely flavoured late harvest wines. *** Chardonnay 1990 £7 (OD) **** Late-Harvest Gewürztraminer 1993 £6 (OD).

Kir A BLEND OF WHITE WINE WITH A DASH OF CASSIS SYRUP INVENTED BY CANON KIR, THE THEN MAYOR OF DIJON, AS A MEANS OF DISGUISING THE OFTEN OTHERWISE UNPALATABLY ACIDIC LOCAL ALIGOTE. WITH SPARKLING WINE (PROPERLY CHAMPAGNE), A KIR ROYALE.

Kistler (SONOMA, California) Probably California's top CHARDONNAY producer, with a range of individual vineyard wines and improving PINOTS. BURGUNDY quality at BURGUNDY prices. **** Chardonnay 'Dutton Ranch' 1992 £20 (ADN, WTR).

Klein Constantia (CONSTANTIA, South Africa) Small go-ahead estate on the site of the great 17th-century CONSTANTIA vineyard. Wines, especially the SAUVIGNON, are thankfully good enough to justify the hype surrounding that name, which is more than can be said for Groot Constantia, the state-owned domain next-door. **** Vin De Constance 1989 £12 (AV, D, GON WTR). ***Sauvignon Blanc 1994 £6 (AV).

Klusserath (MOSEL-SAAR-RUWER, Germany) Small village best known in UK for Sonnenuhr and Konigsberg vineyards 76 79 83 85 88 89 90 91 92. *** Klusserather St Michael Riesling Kabinett Muller £5 (L&W).

Tim Knappstein (CLARE VALLEY, Australia) Long-time master of CLARE RIESLING whose name lost a little lustre during a period of ownership by MILDARA-BLASS. Now in the PETALUMA stable. Apart from CLARE wines, look out for the brilliant SAUVIGNON and promising PINOT NOIRS from LENSWOOD. ***** Lenswood Vineyard Sauvignon Blanc 1993 £7 (LAV) *** Cabernet/Merlot 1991 £7 (OD).

Knudsen-Erath (OREGON, US) One of the better pioneers of this region but still far from earth-shattering.

Kracher (Neusiedlersee, Austria) Source of great (very) late-harvest wines including a very unusual effort with CHARDONNAY. ***** Beerenauslese, Kracher 1987 £15 (NY) **** Chardonnay/Welschriesling Beerenauslese 'Nouvelle Vague' Kracher 1992 £19 (NY).

Krems (WACHAU, AUSTRIA) Town and WACHAU vineyard area producing AUSTRIA's most stylish RIESLING from terraced vineyards. *** Kremser Wachtberg Traminer, Weingut Undhof 1990 £7 (HAR, WTR).

Kreuznach (NAHE, Germany) Northern BEREICH, with fine vineyards around the town of BAD KREUZNACH. ****Kreuznacher Bruckes Riesling Auslese, Schloss Von Plettenburg 1989 £9 (TH, WR, BU).

Domaine Kreydenweiss (ALSACE, France) Top-class organic producer with particularly good PINOT GRIS and RIESLING. **** Gewürztraminer Kritt Sélection Des Grains Nobles 1992 (half) £29 (LV) ***Kritt Klevner 1992 £10 (LV).

Krondorf (BAROSSA VALLEY, Australia) Well-regarded winery specialising in unashamedly traditional, big, BAROSSA styles. **** Limited Release Cabernet Sauvignon 1989 £7.50 (VW) Show Reserve Chardonnay 1992 £9 (JS, D, OD).

Krug (CHAMPAGNE, France) At its best, the CHATEAU LATOUR of CHAMPAGNE. Great vintage wine, extraordinary rosé and pure CHARDONNAY from the Clos de Mesnil vineyard. Theoretically the best non-vintage on the market, thanks to the inclusion of greater proportions of aged reserve wine. But some examples on the market at the moment, especially the half bottles, are looking past their sell-by date.Ask Lord Archer where he gets his. *** NV £55 (widely available)

Kuentz-Bas (ALSACE, France) Reliable producer, especially of PINOT GRIS and GEWURZTRAMINER. *** Pinot Blanc, Kuentz Bas 1992 £8 (F&M).

Kumeu River (AUCKLAND, NEW ZEALAND) Innovative young winemaker (one of the few Antipodeans to have worked a harvest at CHATEAU PETRUS), Michael Brajkovich is successful with a wide range of wines, including a very unusual dry BOTRYTIS SAUVIGNON BLANC which easily outclasses many a dry wine from SAUTERNES. **** Kumeu River Chardonnay 1991 £11 (NI) *** Sauvignon Blanc 1992 £10 (BEN) *** Merlot Cabernet 1990 £12 (BEN)

KWV (South Africa) Huge cooperative formed by the South African government at a time when surplus wine seemed set to flood the industry and maintained by the National Party when it needed to keep the members of the big wine cooperatives, well, cooperative. Still controls the industry, though, post-election, who knows what role it will play in the future. Produces wine for export including a respectable CHENIN BLANC and red Roodeberg blend as well as the worthwhile Cathedral Cellars range. **** Roodeberg 1990 £4 (VW) *** Cabernet Sauvignon, Coastal Region 1990 £4 (MWW).

Labouré-Roi (BURGUNDY, France) Highly successful and very commercial NEGOCIANT, responsible for some quite impressive wines. Quality is rarely less than respectable – which explains why so many British retailers sell these wines under their own names (a NUITS ST GEORGES address at the foot of the label is often the tell-tale sign) 85 88 89 90 91 92. **** Gevrey Chambertin 1991 £13 (BAR) *** Burgundy Pinot Noir 1991 £5 (BKW) *** Chardonnay de Bourgogne 1992 £5 (MWW).

Labrusca (ITALY) VITIS LABRUSCA, THE NORTH AMERICAN SPECIES OF VINE, MAKING WINE WHICH IS OFTEN REFERRED TO AS 'FOXY'. ALL VINIFERA VINE STOCKS ARE GRAFTED ON TO PHYLLOXERA-RESISTANT LABRUSCA ROOTS, THOUGH THE VINE ITSELF IS BANNED IN EUROPE AND ITS WINES, THANKFULLY, ARE ALMOST UNFINDABLE.

Lacryma Christi (Campania, Italy) Literally, 'tears of Christ', the melancholy name for some amiable, light, rather rustic reds and whites. Those from Vesuvio are DOC. 86 87 88 89 90 92 *** Antonio Mastroberardino 1988 £13 (V&C).

Michel Lafarge (BURGUNDY, France) One of the very best producers in VOLNAY – if not BURGUNDY. Fine, long-lived modern wine. ***** Volnay 1er Cru 1990 £26 (HR).

Henri Lafarge (BURGUNDY, France) Small producer in southern BURGUNDY, producing rich, buttery MACONS to compete with supposedly classier fare from the COTE D'OR. **** Mâcon-Bray, Domaine De La Combe, Henri Lafarge 1992 £6 (TH, WR, BU).

Ch. Lafaurie-Peyraguey (BORDEAUX, France) Much-improved SAUTERNES estate that has produced creamy, long-lived wines in the 80s and in 1990 82 85 86 88 89 90. **** 1986 £11 (half) (WSO).

Ch. Lafite-Rothschild (BORDEAUX, France) Often almost impossible to taste young, this PAUILLAC FIRST GROWTH is still one of the monuments of the wine world – especially since the early 80s. Earlier vintages such as 1970, though, were disappointing and the 1962 – though faded now – was a far more enjoyable wine than the more vaunted 1961, which still sells for a fortune. Save your money and buy the brilliant 1990 instead 81 82 85 86 88 89 90 ***** 1990 £50 (C&B, L&W).

Ch. Lafleur (BORDEAUX, France) Christian MOUEIX's pet POMEROL. A tiny property with very old vines making traditional ultra-concentrated wine which, since 1981, has often been on a level with the wine Moueix makes down the road at PETRUS 83 85 89 90. ***** 1989 £80 (FAR).

Ch. La Fleur-Petrus (BORDEAUX, France) For those who find PETRUS a touch too hefty, not to mention rather a touch unaffordable, this next-door neighbour offers gorgeously accessible POMEROL flavour for (in PETRUS terms) a bargain price 82 83 85 86 87 88 89 90. ***** 1990 £35 (THP C&B).

Dom. des Comtes Lafon (BURGUNDY, France) The best domaine in MEURSAULT, with great vineyards in VOLNAY and a small slice of MONTRACHET. Wines last forever. ***** Volnay Santenots 1991 £23 (M&V) **** Meursault 1991 £22 (M&V).

Ch. Lafon-Rochet (BORDEAUX, France) A long-lived traditional ST ESTEPHE fourth growth which tends to be pretty tough in all but the ripest vintages – surprising for a close neighbour of the more come-hitherish Cos d'Estournel 82 83 85 86 88 89 90. ***1988 £30 (THP).

Alois Lageder (Alto-Adige, Italy) New-wave producer of high quality, if pricy, examples of the kind of wine the Alto Adige ought to be producing *** Chardonnay 1993 £5.00 (OD, VW) *** Chardonnay 'Lowengang', 1991 £17 (PON).

Lago di Caldaro (TRENTINO-ALTO ADIGE, Italy) Also known as the Kalterersee, using the local Schiava grape to make cool, light reds with slightly unripe, though pleasant fruit 88 89 90 91.

Ch. Lagrange (BORDEAUX, France) Once under-performing second growth St Julien which now shows what an injection of Japanese cash and local know-how (from Michel Delon of Leoville-Lascases) can do. Look out for Les Fiefs de Lagrange, the impressive SECOND LABEL 82 85 86 88 89 80. ****1989 £19 (AV, EV, J&B).

> **Lagrein** (Italy) Red grape grown in the TRENTINO-ALTO ADIGE region making dry, light, fruity DOC reds and rosés under the picturesque name of Lagrein Dunkel. ***Lagrein, Viticoltorialto Adige 1989 £6 (V&C).

Ch. La Lagune (BORDEAUX, France) A Third Growth without a famous village? La Lagune is a bit of an oddity, almost as close to the north of BORDEAUX as HAUT BRION is to the south. Lovely, accessible wines that last well and are worth buying even in poorer years 82 83 85 86 88 89 90. ***** 1989 £18 (L&W, Bl).

Lake County (California) Vineyard district salvaged by improved irrigation techniques and now capable of some fine wines 86 87 88 89 90 92. *** Cabernet Sauvignon Kah-Nock-Tie, Konocti Winery 1992 £5 (Bl).

Lake's Folly (HUNTER VALLEY, Australia) Meet Stephen Lake, surgeon-turned-winemaker-cum writer/researcher (he has wonderful theories about the sexual effects of sniffing various kinds of wine). Pioneer of CHARDONNAY and still a rare success with CABERNET SAUVIGNON. ***Lakes Folly, Chardonnay 1991 £11 (L&W) **** Cabernet Sauvignon 1991 £11 (L&W).

Lalande de Pomerol (BORDEAUX, France) Bordering on POMEROL with similar, but less fine wines. Still generally better than similarly priced ST EMILIONS. Some good-value PETITS-CHATEAUX 81 83 85 86 88 89 90. ****Ch. Bertineau St-Vincent 1990 £9 (OD).

Lamberhurst (Kent, England) One of the first English vineyards and still one of the more reliable, though rarely the most innovative. ***Priory NV £3 (W).

Lambrusco (Emilia-Romagna, Italy) Famous/infamous low-strength (7.5 per cent) sweet, fizzy UK and North American version of the fizzy dry red wine favoured in Italy. The real thing – fascinating with its unripe cherry flavour – is easily spotted thanks to its cork (the sweet stuff comes with a screwcap). ***Lambrusco Secco Grasparossa Chiarli £3.89 (V&C)

Landwein (Germany) A RELATIVELY RECENT QUALITY DESIGNATION – THE EQUIVALENT OF A FRENCH VIN DE PAYS FROM ONE OF 11 NAMED REGIONS (ANBAUGEBIET). OFTEN DRY

Ch. Lanessan (BORDEAUX, France) Old-fashioned CRU BOURGEOIS made by people who hate the flavour of new oak. A surprisingly long-lived argument for doing things the way they used to be done. ***1987 £7 (EP).

Langhe (PIEDMONT, Italy) A range of hills; when preceded by 'Nebbiolo delle', indicates declassified BAROLO and BARBARESCO. ****Nebbiolo delle Langhe G Mascarello 1991 £7 (WCE).

Ch. Langoa-Barton (BORDEAUX, France) LEOVILLE BARTON's (slightly) less complex kid brother. Often one of the best bargain classed growths in BORDEAUX. Well made in poor years 88 89 90 91 92. *** 1991 £11 (L&W).

Coteaux du Languedoc (MIDI, France) A big appellation which has become a popular source of fast-improving everyday reds from RHONE and southern grapes 85 86 88 89 90 91. ***** Mas Jullien Les Vignes Oubliees, Blanc, Olivier Jullien 1992 £9 (LV) ***Monastère de Trignan 1992 £4 (MWW).

Languedoc-Roussillon (MIDI, France) One of the world's largest wine regions and, until recently, a major source of the wine lake. But a combination of government-sponsored up-rooting and keen activity by FLYING WINEMAKERS and (a few) dynamic producers has turned this into the world's most worrying competitor for the NEW WORLD. The region includes appellations like CORBIERES and MINERVOIS but the stuff you're most likely to encounter is VIN DE PAYS D'OC.

Lanson (CHAMPAGNE, France) Producer of average-to-okay non vintage 'Black Label' and sublime vintage fizz. *** Black Label £19 (widely available).

Laroche (BURGUNDY, France) Good CHABLIS NEGOCIANT with some enviable vineyards of its own including PREMIERS and GRANDS CRUS. Reliable southern French CHARDONNAY VIN DE PAYS D'OC and innovative wines from CORSICA. **** Chablis, Fourchaume 1969 £35 (LV).

Laski Riesling/Rizling (Yugoslavia) Yugoslav name for poor-quality white grape, unrelated to the RHINE RIESLING, aka WELSCH, OLASZ and Italico. **Lutomer Laski Riesling £3 (A).

Ch. de Lastours (LANGUEDOC, France) Combined winery and home for the mentally handcapped, and proof that CORBIERES can produce wine to rival BORDEAUX. Look out for the Cuvée Simone Descamps. **** Corbières, Château de Lastours, Cuvée Simone Descamps 1991 £6 (TH, WR).

Late Harvest MADE FROM GRAPES THAT ARE PICKED AFTER THE MAIN VINTAGE, GIVING A HIGHER SUGAR LEVEL. ***** Stellenzicht Weisser Riesling Noble Late Harvest 1992 £4 (VW) ***Wente Brothers Late Harvest Riesling 1989 £11 (BAR).

Late-bottled vintage (port) (LBV) (DOURO, Portugal) OFFICIALLY, PORT WHICH HAS BEEN BOTTLED FOR FOUR OR SIX YEARS AFTER A SPECIFIC (USUALLY NON-DECLARED) VINTAGE. THE MOST WIDELY AVAILABLE, COMMERCIAL 'MODERN' STYLE, PIONEERED BY TAYLORS IS TREATED PRETTY MUCH LIKE RUBY AND VINTAGE CHARACTER AND FILTERED BEFORE BOTTLING SO IT NEEDS NO DECANTING. HOWEVER IT BEARS VERY LITTLE RESEMBLANCE TO REAL VINTAGE OR EVEN CRUSTED PORT. FORTUNATELY WARRES AND SMITH WOODHOUSE MAKE 'TRADITIONAL' – UNFILTERED – LBV WHICH CAN BE A GREAT ALTERNATIVE TO VINTAGE, NOT JUST IN TERMS OF PRICE . *** Sainsbury's Late Bottled Vintage Port, Croft 1987 £7 (JS) ***** Warres Traditional Late Bottled Vintage Port 1981 £12 (JS, OD, HHC, W, ADN).

Latium/Lazio (Italy) The vineyard area surrounding Rome. Avoid most of its FRASCATI, although there are some exciting BORDEAUX-style reds. 88 89 90 92 **** Lazio Merlot/Sangiovese, Casale del Giglio 1993 £3 (SMF).

Louis Latour (BURGUNDY, France) Underperforming NEGOCIANT who still pasteurises his – consequently muddy-tasting – reds, treating them in a way no quality-conscious New World producer would dream of. Whites, however, including CORTON CHARLEMAGNE, can be sublime. **** Meursault-Blagny 1er Cru 1989 £28 (TH) ** Nuits-St-Georges 1987 £19 (VW).

Ch. Latour (BORDEAUX, France) First Growth PAUILLAC which can be very tricky to judge when young. Recently bought (by a Frenchman) from its British owners, Allied Breweries. LES FORTS DE LATOUR is the – often worthwhile – SECOND LABEL 82 85 86 88 89 90. **** 1990 £60 (BI, C&B).

Ch. Latour-a-Pomerol (BORDEAUX, France) A great value tiny (3,500-case) POMEROL under the same ownership as Ch Petrus and the same MOUEIX winemaking. It is a little less concentrated than its big brother but around a quarter of the price 82 83 85 86 87 88 89 90 91. **** 1986 £27 (C&B).

Laudun (RHONE, France) Named village of COTES DU RHONE, with some atypical fresh, light wines and attractive rosés. *** Blanc, Pelaquie £6 (L&W).

Laurel Glen (SONOMA Mountain, California) Small hillside estate wines made by Patrick Campbell. A winery to watch for its ripe-flavoured, BORDEAUX-like reds that are well respected by true Californian wine lovers though, inevitably, not by the wretched collectors. Terra Rosa is the accessible SECOND LABEL. ****Terra Rosa 1990 £9 (WDW).

Laurent-Perrier CHAMPAGNE, France) For many years now, one of the more reliable larger houses with particularly recommendable rosé. Owns SALON. *** N.V. £19 (widely available).

Ch. Laville-Haut-Brion (BORDEAUX, France) Exquisite white Graves that is delightful young but will last for 20 years or more. 82 83 85 86 88 89 90 **** 1983 £54 (BBR).

Coteaux du Layon (LOIRE, France) Whites from the CHENIN BLANC grape which are slow to develop and long lived. Lots of lean dry wine but the sweet BONNEZEAUX and QUARTS DE CHAUME are superior. *** Château de la Roulerie 1990 Dominique Jaudeau £7 (YAP) ****'Fay', Ravouin-Ceseron 1971 £17 (ADN).

Lazio See LATIUM.

Lean LACKING BODY (CONSIDERED A FEATURE OF CERTAIN WINES).

Lebanon Chiefly represented in the UK by the remarkable CHATEAU MUSAR, made in BORDEAUX style but from CABERNET SAUVIGNON, CINSAULT and SYRAH 78 79 80 81 82 86 87 89 90. ****Château Musar, Serge Hochar 1987 £8 (SMF).

Lees or lie(s) THE SEDIMENT OF DEAD YEASTS LET FALL AS A WHITE WINE DEVELOPS. SEE SUR LIE. *** Muscadet de Sèvre et Maine Sur Lie, Domaine de l'Ecu, Guy Bossard 1993 £5 (SAF) ***'Muscadet de Sèvre et Maine sur Lie 'Première', Domaine Jean Douillard 1992 £5 (JS).

Leeuwin Estate (MARGARET RIVER, Australia) Showcase winery (and concert venue) and producer of one of Australia's, most influential, priciest and longest-lived *****CHARDONNAYs. Other wines are less dazzling. **** Leeuwin Estate Art Series Chardonnay 1989 £15 (DD). Leeuwin Prelude Cabernet Sauvignon 1990 £10 (DD).

Domaine Leflaive (PULIGNY MONTRACHET, BURGUNDY, France) One of the great characters of BURGUNDY, the late Vincent Leflaive was the uncriticable superstar of white BURGUNDY – despite the fact that wines ranged from dilutely disappointing to richly sublime. Will the next generation provide greater consistency? ***Puligny Montrachet 1991 £19 (ADN) ***Puligny Montrachet 'Clavoillon' 1991 £25 (ADN).

Olivier Leflaive (BURGUNDY, France) The NEGOCIANT business launched by Vincent LEFLAIVE's nephew. High class white wines with greater reliability than those of the domaine. ****Rully 1er Cru Les Clous 1992 £9. (L&W) **** Chassagne Montrachet 1er Cru 'Les Grandes Ruchottes' 1992 £17 (JAR).

Peter Lehmann (BAROSSA VALLEY, Australia) Locally respected as the grand (not so) old man of the BAROSSA VALLEY, Peter Lehmann and his son Doug make the kind of intensely concentrated SHIRAZES, CABERNETS, SEMILLONS and CHARDONNAYS which amply make up in character what they lack in subtlety. **** Cabernet Sauvignon/Malbec 1990 £13 (OD) ***Shiraz 1990 £5 (OD, GNW) ****Stonewell Shiraz, Cellar Collection 1988 £13 (OD).

Length HOW LONG THE TASTE LINGERS IN THE MOUTH.

Lenswood (SOUTH AUSTRALIA, Australia) Newly developed high-altitude region close to Adelaide, proving its potential with SAUVIGNON, CHARDONNAY, PINOT NOIR and even (in the case of HENSCHKE's Abbott's Prayer), MERLOT and CABERNET SAUVIGON) 90 91 92 93 SAUVIGNONS from STAFFORD RIDGE and KNAPPSTEIN who also makes good PINOT NOIR. ***** Henschke Abbotts Prayer Merlot/Cabernet, Lenswood 1990 £12 (L&W) ***Tim Knappstein Lenswood Vineyard Sauvignon Blanc 1993 £7 (LAV).

Léognan (BORDEAUX, France) Leading village of GRAVES with its own AC, PESSAC-LEOGNAN **** L'Esprit de Chevalier, Pessac-Léognan 1990 £12 (ADN).

Léon (Spain) North-western region producing acceptable dry, fruity reds and whites. *** Palacio de Léon 1989 £4 (VW).

Jean Leon (CATALONIA, Spain) American pioneer of CHARDONNAY and CABERNET and still – thanks to Hispanic conservatism – one of the few to succeed with these varieties. *** Jean Leon Cabernet Sauvignon 1987 £7 (L&S).

Ch. Léoville-Barton (BORDEAUX, France) Anthony Barton makes one of the classiest bargains in BORDEAUX. An unusually fairly priced, reliably stylish ST JULIEN second growth whose wines are among the best in the MEDOC. LANGOA BARTON is the sister property 82 83 86 88 89 90. ***** 1989 £17 (ADN).

Ch. Léoville-Las-Cases (BORDEAUX, France) Impeccably made ST JULIEN Super-Second which often matches its neighbour CH LATOUR. The SECOND LABEL, Clos du Marquis, is worth buying too, as is the CRU BOURGEOIS, Château Potensac 83 84 85 86 88 89 90. **** 1983 £30 (ADN) *****1990 £30 (C&B).

Ch. Léoville-Poyferré (BORDEAUX, France) Improving toughly traditional ST JULIEN property but still not of the class of LEOVILLE LAS-CASES. The SECOND LABEL, Moulin Riche, is a more approachable wine and is a worthwhile buy 82 83 85 86 87 88 89 90 91. **** 1985 £20 (L&W) ***1983 £25 (EV).

Dom Leroy (BURGUNDY, France) Organic domaine in VOSNE-ROMANEE recently founded by the former co-owner of the DOMAINE DE LA ROMANEE-CONTI making red wines which compete with those of that illustrious estate. *****Nuits St. Georges, Lavières 1991 £35 (HR) *****Vosne-Romanée 1er Cru, Les Beaux Monts 1991 £55 (HR).

Lie(s) SEE LEES/SUR LIE.

Liebfraumilch (Germany) The most seditious exploitation of the German QbA system – a good example is perfectly pleasant but the vast majority, though cheap, is money down the drain. Responsible for the ruination of the German wine market in the UK 90 91 92. *** Liebfraumilch Rheingau, Langenbach 1993 £3.(TH).

Ch Lilian Ladouys (BORDEAUX, France) A rare phenomenon: a recently constituted ST ESTEPHE CRU BOURGEOIS. Classily made, modern wine with ripe fruit and just enough oak. ****1990 £15 (SUM).

Limestone Ridge see LINDEMANS

Limousin (FRANCE) OAK FOREST THAT PROVIDES BARRELS THAT IMPART A LOT OF WOOD TANNIN TO THE WINE. BETTER, THEREFORE, FOR RED WINE THAN FOR FOR WHITE.

Limoux (MIDI, France) New APPELLATION for CHARDONNAYS which were previously sold as VIN DE PAYS d'Oc . See BLANQUETTE.

Lindauer (MARLBOROUGH, NEW ZEALAND) See MONTANA. *** Montana Lindauer Brut £7 (MRN, TH, TO, SAF).

Lindemans (Australia) Once PENFOLDS' greatest rival, now its subsidiary (aren't they all?) Noted for long-lived HUNTER VALLEY SEMILLON and SHIRAZ, COONAWARRA reds and good-value multi-region blends such as the internationally successful Bin 65 CHARDONNAY and Bin 45 CABERNET. **** St George Cabernet Sauvignon 1991 £10 (OD, BU, TH, WR, AUC) ****Pyrus 1990 £10 (OD, JS, TH, WR, BU) *****Botrytis Semillon 1987 £6 (OD) ****Limestone Ridge 1989 £10 (MWW).

Karl Lingenfelder (RHEINPFALZ, Germany) Great new wave RHEINPFALZ producer of a special RIESLING and unusually succesful PINOT NOIR.
*** Riesling, Lingenfelder 1992 £5 (WL).

Jean Lionnet (RHONE, France) Classy CORNAS producer whose Rochepertuis is a worthwhile buy. **** Cornas, Domaine de Rochepertius 1991 £14 (J&B).

Liqueur de Tirage (CHAMPAGNE, France) THE YEAST AND SUGAR ADDED TO BASE WINE TO INDUCE SECONDARY FERMENTATION (AND HENCE THE BUBBLES) IN BOTTLE.

Liqueur d'Expedition (CHAMPAGNE, France) SWEETENING SYRUP USED FOR DOSAGE

Liquoreux (France) RICH AND SWEET.

Liquoroso (Italy) RICH AND SWEET.

Lirac (RHONE, France) Peppery, TAVEL-like roses, and – increasingly impressive – deep, berry-fruit reds 80 81 85 89 90 91. ***Lirac Cuvée Prestige La Fermade, Domaine Maby 1989 £9 (RES, SAC) ***Lirac Rouge, Château D'Aqueria 1990 £7 (MWW).

Listel (LANGUEDOC, France) Big producer belonging to a salt refinery and based on partially organic vineyards grown on sandy beaches close to Sète. Best wines are the rose ('Grain de Gris') and low alcohol sparkling MUSCAT (Petillant de Raisin). *** Pierres Blanches Cabernet Sauvignon, Domaines Viticoles Listel 1993 £3 (WMK, GI) ***Rosé, Grain de Gris £4 (TH).

Listrac (BORDEAUX, France) Small commune in the HAUT-MEDOC, next to MOULIS. Look out for CHATEAUX CLARKE, FOURCAS-HOSTEN & Fourcas-Dupré 82 83 85 86 88 89 90. *** Château Fourcas-Loubaney, Listrac 1989 £9 (J&B)

Livermore (Valley) (California) A warm climate vineyard area with fertile soil producing full, rounded whites, including increasingly fine CHARDONNAY *** Wente Brothers Estate Reserve Chardonnay, Livermore Valley 1991 £11 (BBR, BAR, JAR).

Coteaux du Loir (LOIRE, France) Clean vigorous whites from a LOIRE tributary; JASNIERES is little seen but worth looking out for 85 89 90 92. **** Jasnières, Les Tuffières, Jean-Baptiste Pinon 1986 £8 (YAP).

Loire (France) An extraordinary variety of wines come from this area – dry whites such as MUSCADET and the classier SAVENNIERES, SANCERRE and POUILLY FUME; grassy, summery reds; buckets of rosé – some good, most dreadful; glorious sweet whites and very acceptable sparkling wines. Refer to sub-categories for recommended wines. See under various APPELLATIONS.

Lombardy (Italy) The region (and vineyards) around Milan, known mostly for sparkling wine but also for increasingly interesting reds, and the whites of LUGANA *** Mompiano Rosso, Pasolini 1992 £6 (WCE).

Long Island (New York, USA) A unique micro-climate where fields once full of potatoes are now yielding classy MERLOT and CHARDONNAY. Unfortunately, even in Manhattan across the bridge, snobs prefer overpriced Californian fare . All of which doesn't help reputation-building internationally and is of little encouragement to importers in the U.K. Mme de Lenquesaing of Ch PICHON LONGUEVILLE LALANDE is a believer

Dr Loosen (MOSEL-SAAR-RUWER, Germany) New Wave RIESLING producer.
**** Dr Loosen Wehlener Sonnenuhr Riesling Spätlese 1992 £11 (HAM)
**** Dr Loosen Riesling 1992 £6 (TH, BAL, HAM).

Lopez de Heredia (RIOJA, Spain) Ultra traditional winery producing old fashioned Viña Tondonia white and GRAN RESERVA reds. *** Viña Tondonia 1985 £10 (L&S).

Los Llanos (VALDEPENAS, Spain) Commendable modern exception to the tradition of dull VALDEPENAS. *** Señorio de los Llanos Reserva 1990 £4 (L&S).

Ch. Loudenne (BORDEAUX, France) Great wine school. Ordinary wine.
** 1989 £8 (SEL, TH).

Loupiac (BORDEAUX, France) Bordering on SAUTERNES, with similar but less fine
wines 83 85 86 87 88 89 90. *** Château Segur du Gros 1992 £8.50 (AV).

Ch. La Louvière (BORDEAUX, France) The LURTON family's best known
GRAVES property. Reliable, rich, modern whites and reds 82 85 86 88 89
90. **** Blanc 1990 £13 (OD, MWW) ****'L' de la Louvière 1990 £7 (MWW).

Luberon (Côtes du) (RHONE, France) Reds, like light COTES DU RHONE, pink
and sparkling wines; the whites CHARDONNAY-influenced. A new
APPELLATION and still good value 88 89 90 91 92. **** Château La Verrerie,
Blanc de Blancs 1992 £9 (RTW) **** Château La Verrerie 1989 £7 (RTW).

Ludon (BORDEAUX, France) HAUT-MEDOC village and Commune 81 83 85 86 88
89 90. **** Le Moulin de Ludon, Haut-Médoc, Château La Lagune 1990 £8 (MWW).

Lugana (LOMBARDY, Italy) Grown on the shores of Lake Garda, smooth,
pungent white wine, a match for food. LOMBARDY's best wine 90 91 92.
*** Santi Lugana, Santi 1992 £4 (SAF).

Lugny (BURGUNDY, France) See MACON.

Pierre Luneau (LOIRE, France) A rare beast: a top class MUSCADET producer.
Wines are sadly hard to find outside France.

Lungarotti (Umbria, Italy) Innovative producer who more or less created the
TORGIANO denomination.*** San Giorgio, Rosso Dell'Umbria 1985 £18 (V&C).

Lurton (Jacques) Young son of the owner of CHATEAU LA LOUVIERE and
Château Bonnet in ENTRE DEUX MERS who, having made a success there
(especially with white wines), now makes wine under contract all over the
world. Look for Hermanos Lurton wines from Spain. *** Domaine des Salices
Merlot, Vin de Pays d'Oc 1993 £4 (TH, WR, BU) **** Hermanos Lurton Rueda
Sauvignon Blanc 1993 £4 (OD, JS) *** Hermanos Lurton Rosado 1993 £4 (VW).

Lussac-St-Emilion (BORDEAUX, France) A satellite of ST EMILION 78 79 81 82
83 85 86 88 89 90. *** Château Lyonnat 1988 £11 (ABY) ** Lussac-St-Emilion
ACP Sichel (NV) £5 (TAN).

Emilio Lustau (JEREZ, Spain) Great sherry producer, particularly noted for
individual ALMACENISTA wines. ***** Fortnum & Mason Amontillado, Lustau
£6 (F&M) *** Anada Oloroso (Pilar Aranda y latorre), Lustau £6 (L&W, LV, RTW)
Old Dry Oloroso, Lustau £3 (SAF).

Lutomer (Slovenia) Wine producing area still known mostly for its (very
basic) LUTOMER RIESLING, but now doing better things with CHARDONNAY.
** Tiger Milk, Slovenijavino 1992 £3 (MRN).

Luxembourg Source of fairly basic white wines from ALSACE grape varieties.
** Sparkling Brut, Bernard Massard £7 (EP).

Ch. Lynch-Bages (BORDEAUX, France) Reliably over-performing Fourth
Growth PAUILLAC which belongs to Jean-Michel Cazes, the man responsible
for the success of CHATEAU PICHON BARON. The (very rare) white is worth
seeking out 82 83 85 86 88 89 90. **** 1981 £23 (BI).

Coteaux du Lyonnais (RHONE, France) Just to the south of BEAUJOLAIS,
making some very acceptable good-value wines from the same grapes. Best
producers: Descottes, DUBOEUF, Fayolle 89 90 91.

Macedonia (Greece) Considered, by Greeks, to be the quality region of the
north. ** Naoussa, Boutari 1990 £4 (SAF, AMA).

Macération carbonique TECHNIQUE IN WHICH UNCRUSHED GRAPES FERMENT
UNDER PRESSURE OF A BLANKET OF CARBON DIOXIDE GAS TO PRODUCE FRESH,
FRUITY WINE. USED IN BEAUJOLAIS, SOUTH OF FRANCE AND BECOMING
INCREASINGLY POPULAR IN THE NEW WORLD. *** Garnacha Veganueva 1993
Vinicoal Navarra £4 (OD).

Mâcon/Mâconnais (BURGUNDY, France) Avoid unidentified 'rouge' or 'blanc'
on restaurant wine lists. MACONS with the suffix VILLAGES, SUPERIEUR or
PRISSE, VIRE, LUGNY or CLESSE should be better and can afford some
pleasant, good-value CHARDONNAY 89 90 91 92. *** Mâcon Villages Drouhin
1992 £6.50 (OD). *** Mâcon Chardonnay P&P Talmard 1992 £6 (TAN, ADN,
HOT).

Maculan (Veneto, Italy) A superstar producer of blackcurranty CABERNET BREGANZE, an oaked PINOT BIANCO-PINOT GRIGIO-CHARDONNAY blend called Prato di Canzio and the lusciously sweet TORCOLATO. **** Torcolato Vino Dolce Naturale 1991 £23 (GAR).

Madeira (Portugal) Atlantic island producing famed fortified wines, usually identified by style: BUAL, SERCIAL, VERDELHO or MALMSEY. Also home to the Madeira Wine Company, owners of the Rutherford & Miles, BLANDY, Leacock and COSSART GORDON labels. This well-run quasi-monopolistic company now belongs to the Symingtons who, with DOWS, GRAHAMS, WARRES etc, have long had a similar role in the DOURO. ***** Rutherford & Miles Jubilee Selection Verdelho 1952 £69 (TH) **** Henriques & Henriques, Finest Full Rich 5 Year Old Madeira £9 (HAR) **** Tesco Finest Madeira, Madeira Wine Co £7 (TO).

Maderisation DELIBERATE PROCEDURE IN MADEIRA, PRODUCED BY THE WARMING OF WINE IN ESTUFAS. OTHERWISE UNDESIRED EFFECT, COMMONLY PRODUCED BY HIGH TEMPERATURES DURING STORAGE, RESULTING IN A DULL, FLAT FLAVOUR TINGED WITH A SHERRY TASTE AND COLOUR.

Madiran (South-West France) Heavy, robust country reds made from the TANNAT grape, tannic when young but age extremely well. With CAHORS, potentially one of the best old-fashioned French Country reds and to be found in knowledgeable Wine Bars 82 85 86 88 89 90. ***** Bouscassé, Alain Brumont 1991 £6 (BU, LV, NY, HN, H&H) **** Château Laroche Madiran, Vignoble de Gascogne, 1988 £7 (SAF).

Ch. Magdelaine (BORDEAUX, France) ST EMILION estate owned by JP MOUEIX and neighbour to CHATEAU AUSONE, producing reliable, rich wines 82 83 85 86 89 90. *** 1988 £23 (THP, NIC, C&B, TAN).

Magnum LARGE BOTTLE CONTAINING THE EQUIVALENT OF TWO BOTTLES OF WINE (ONE AND ONE-HALF LITRES IN CAPACITY).

Maipo (CHILE) One of four viticultural regions identified by the Chilean Ministry of Agriculture. Contains many good producers, including Canepa, COUSINO MACUL, Peteroa, SANTA CAROLINA, SANTA RITA, UNDURRAGA, VINA CARMEN. **** Santa Carolina Cabernet Sauvignon Gran Reserva 1989 £8 (OD, G&M) *** Santa Rita Medalla Real Chardonnay 1993 £7 (JS, BI, CWW, MAR).

Maître de chai (France) CELLAR MASTER.

Malaga (Spain) Andalusian DO producing dessert wines of varying degrees of sweetness, immensely popular in the 19th century. **** Solera 1885, Scholtz Hermanos £9 (W, WSO, L&W, SEL, DBW) **** Moscatel Palido, Scholtz Hermanos £8 (CNL, GWI, L&S).

Ch. Malartic-Lagravière (BORDEAUX, France) PESSAC-LEOGNAN estate, bought a few years ago by LAURENT PERRIER, improving new-wave whites; reds still need time. (red) 70 75 78 82 83 85 86 88 89 90. (white) 82 83 85 86 87 88 89 90 91 92. **** 1982 Red £88 (mag) (NIC).

Malbec Red grape, now rare in BORDEAUX but widespread in ARGENTINA and CAHORS, where it is known as the COT or AUXERROIS. ** Santa Julia Malbec Oak 1992 £5 (T&T) **** Malbech del Veneto Orientale, Santa Margherita 1987 £9 (LU, RBS, V&C).

Malmsey Traditional, rich MADEIRA made from the MALVASIA grape – the sweetest style, but with a dry finish. **** Cossart Gordon Reserve 10 Year Old Malmsey Madeira £14 (BU, WR, BBR, AV, GMV).

Malolactic Fermentation SECONDARY FERMENTATION IN WHICH APPLEY MALIC ACID IS CONVERTED INTO THE 'SOFTER', CREAMIER LACTIC ACID. COMMON IN BURGUNDY; VARYINGLY USED IN THE NEW WORLD WHERE NATURAL ACID LEVELS ARE OFTEN LOW. RECOGNISABLE IN EXCESS AS A BUTTERMILKY FLAVOUR. ****Rosemount Roxburgh Chardonnay £16 (VW).

Ch. de la Maltroye (BURGUNDY, France) Classy modern CHASSAGNE-based estate with fingers in 14 AC pies around BURGUNDY, all of whose wines are made by JL PARENT. ***Santenay La Comme 1er Cru 1992 £14 (OD).

Malvasia Muscatty white grape vinified dry in Italy (as a component in FRASCATI for example), but far more successfully as good, sweet traditional MADEIRA, where it is known as MALMSEY. It is not the same grape as MALVOISIE (see below). **** Ca Del Solo Malvasia Bianca, Bonny Doon 1992 £8 (SAN, POR, HN, NY, M&V).

Malvoisie (LOIRE, France) Local name for the PINOT GRIS 89 90 92. ** Malvoisie Pierre Guindon 1992 £5 (YAP).

La Mancha (Spain) Big region producing mostly dull and old-fashioned but in recent times increasingly modern (mostly red) wine. *** Viña Del Castillo, Vinicola De Castilla 1993 £3 (TO) *** Castillo de Alhambra Tinto 1993 £3 (JS).

Manseng, Gros & Petit (JURANCON, France) Gros is particularly used for dry whites; Petit for sweet VENDANGE TARDIVES, though many wines traditionally involve a blend of both. **** Moelleux 'Vendange Tardives', Domaine Cauhapé 1992 £12 (WS,M&V) *** Domaine Cauhapé Sec 1992 £7 (M&V, WS).

Manzanilla Dry, tangy SHERRY – a FINO-style wine widely (though possibly mistakenly) thought to take on a salty tang from the coastal BODEGAS of Sanlucar de Barrameda. **** Booths Manzanilla, Emilio Hidalgo £4 (BTH) *** Tesco Superior Manzanilla Sanchez Romate £3 (TO).

Maranges (BURGUNDY, France) New hillside APPELLATION promising potentially affordable COTE D'OR wines. **** Maranges Premier Cru, Joseph Drouhin 1990 £11.60 (VW).

Marc RESIDUE OF PIPS, STALKS AND SKINS AFTER GRAPES ARE PRESSED – OFTEN DISTILLED INTO A FIERY UNWOODED BRANDY OF THE SAME NAME, eg MARC DE BOURGOGNE.

Marches (Italy) Central region on the Adriatic coast best known for ROSSO CONERO and good, dry, fruity VERDICCHIO whites. (red) 85 86 87 88 89 90 92. (white) 89 90 91 92. **** Verdicchio 'Casal Di Serra' Umani Ronchi 1993 £6 (BIN, PON, OD, V&C, VW) **** Cumaro Umani Ronchi 1990 £10 (MG, PON, V&C, UBC, TAN).

Marcillac (South-West France) Full-flavoured country reds principally from the Fer grape – may also contain CABERNET and GAMAY. *** Marcillac Cave des Vignerons du Vazlon 1992 £6 (NIC).

Margaret River (Australia) Cool(ish) vineyard area on the coast of WESTERN AUSTRALIA, gaining notice for CABERNET SAUVIGNON and CHARDONNAY. Also Australia's only ZINFANDEL from CAPE MENTELLE The region's best-known wineries are MOSS WOOD, CAPE MENTELLE, LEEUWIN, CULLEN, PIERRO, VASSE FELIX and Château Xanadu 86 87 88 89 90 93. **** Moss Wood Cabernet Sauvignon 1992 £11 (ADN, F&M, DBY, LV) ***** Cullen Sauvignon Blanc 1993 £10 (ADN).

Margaux (BORDEAUX, France) Large commune with a concentration of CRUS CLASSES including CHATEAU MARGAUX. Sadly, wines which should be deliciously blackberryish are variable, partly thanks to the diverse nature of the soil and partly through producers' readiness to sacrifice quality for the sake of yields. Curiously, though, if you want a good 1983, this vintage succeeded better here than elsewhere in the MEDOC 78 79 81 82 83 85 86 88 89 91. *** Château Palmer 1989 £28 (TAN) *****1983 £35 (EV).

Ch. Margaux (BORDEAUX, France) Peerless First Growth back on form since the dull 1970s and now frequently producing intense wines with cedary perfume and velvet softness when mature. The SECOND WINE, Pavillon Rouge is worth buying, as is the matching SAUVIGNON white, one of the best whites in the MEDOC 81 82 83 85 86 88 89 90 *****1990 £16 (OD)***** 1983 £60 (BI).

Marino (LATIUM, Italy) Creamy alternative to FRASCATI.

Marlborough (NEW ZEALAND) Important wine area with cool climate in the South Island making excellent SAUVIGNON, CHARDONNAY and improving MERLOT and PINOT NOIR. Made famous by the emergence of CLOUDY BAY as a contender for the best SAUVIGNON in the world; other good names include HUNTER'S, VAVASOUR, JACKSON ESTATE, Cellier LE BRUN and MONTANA 90 91 92 93. **** Vavasour Reserve Chardonnay 1993 £11 (DBY, OD, FUL) **** Dashwood Sauvignon Blanc 1993 £8 (OD, HHC) ***** Daniel le Brun Vintage Cellier Le Brun 1990 £20 (SV, HW).

Côtes du Marmandais (South-West France) Uses the BORDEAUX red grapes plus GAMAY, SYRAH and others to make pleasant, inexpensive, if rather rustic wines. **** Château Beaulieu Saint-Sauveur, Univitis en Bordeaux 1990 £3.30 (TO).

Marne et Champagne (CHAMPAGNE, France) Huge unglamorous producer which, for some reason, is almost always omitted from books on CHAMPAGNE. which prefer to focus on companies with more active public relations departments. Owns Besserat de Bellefon, LANSON and ALFRED ROTHSCHILD labels and seems to be able to provide really good own-label wines (eg Victoria Wine 1986 Champagne) for buyers prepared to pay the price. ***** Victoria Wine Vintage Champagne 1986 £19 (VW) **** André Simon Champagne Brut NV £10 (LAY).

Marqués de Cáceres (RIOJA, Spain) Modern French-influenced BODEGA making fresher-tasting wines than many of its neighbours. A good, if anonymous, new-style white has now been joined by a promising oak fermented version and a pleasant rosé (Rosado). **** Marques de Caceres Crianza Tinto 1990 £4 (L&W).

Marqués de Griñon (LA MANCHA, Spain) Dynamic exception to the dull LA MANCHA rule, making wines which often outclass RIOJA. High quality juicy CABERNET-MERLOT and fresh white RUEDA . *** Rueda Blanco 1993 £5 (MOR)

Marqués de Monistrol (CATALONIA, Spain) Single-estate CAVA. Better than most. *** Tesco Vintage Cava £7 (TO).

Marqués de Murrieta (RIOJA, Spain) Still the best old-style oaky white RIOJA (sold as Castilllo Ygay) and a rich, classy, carefully-made red. *** Marqués de Murrieta Reserva Tinto 1987 £8 (TH, WR, BU).

Marqués de Riscal (RIOJA, Spain) Famous, but for a long time flawed, property that seems to be getting its act together at last, though a muddy taste persists. Whites, including the SAUVIGNON, are reliably fresh. *** Marqués de Riscal Rioja Reserva 1989 £7 (VW).

Marsala (SICILY) Dark, rich, fortified wine from SICILY essential in a number of recipes, such as zabaglione. DE BARTOLI make stuff worth drinking. **** Marsala 'Vigna La Miccia' De Bartoli £14 (WCE) *** Marsala Superiore Garibaldi Dolce Carlo Pellegrino £6 (JS).

Marsannay (BURGUNDY, France) Pale red and rosé from the PINOT NOIR plus elegant affordable CHARDONNAY 85 87 88 89 90 92. *** Marsannay Blanc, Maison Louis Jadot 1991 £10 (TH).

***

Marsanne The grape usually responsible (in blends with ROUSSANNE) for most of the northern RHONE white wines. Also successful in the GOULBURN VALLEY in Victoria for CHATEAU TAHBILK and MITCHELTON and in California for BONNY DOON 85 86 88 89 90 91 92. **** Guigal Hermitage Blanc 1991 £17 (WR,IRV) **** Mitchelton Goulburn Valley Reserve 1991 £8 (W, JS, JMC, OD, BWL). ***** Château Tahbilk 1992 £6 (TO, OD).

***

Martinborough (NEW ZEALAND) Up-and-coming North Island region for PINOT NOIR and CHARDONNAY. Recommended: ATA RANGI, Dry River, MARTINBOROUGH VINEYARD, PALLISER ESTATE. **** Palliser Estate Pinot Noir 1991 £10 (TH, WR, BU, OD).

Martinborough Vineyard (NEW ZEALAND) Producer of the best Kiwi PINOT NOIR and one of the best CHARDONNAYs. Wines can be extraordinarily Burgundian in style. **** Pinot Noir 1992 £11 (TDS, OD, ADN, SOM) *** Chardonnay 1992 £11 (TDS, OD, WL, ADN, SOM).

Martinez Bujanda (RIOJA, Spain) New-wave producer of fruit-driven wines sold as Conde de Valdemar. **** Rioja Reserva Excepcionel 1987 £12 (TH, WR, BU) **** Conde de Valdemar Rioja Gran Reserva 1982 £12 (TH, WR, BU).

Martini (PIEDMONT, Italy) Good ASTI SPUMANTE from the producer of the vermouth house which invented 'lifestyle' advertising. *** Asti Spumante £5.80 (JS, TO, SAF, SMF).

Louis Martini (NAPA, California) A grand old name with superlative long-lived CABERNET from the Monte Rosso vineyard. Sadly hard to find in Britain.

Marzemino (Italy) Spicy red grape. *** de Tarcel 1992 £8 (WTR).

Mas de Daumas Gassac (LANGUEDOC-ROUSSILLON, France) Ground-breaking VIN DE PAYS with an eccentric, complex red blend of half a dozen varieties (including PINOT NOIR and CABERNET) and white made from a blend that includes VIOGNIER. ***** Mas de Daumas Gassac Blanc Vin de Pays de l'Hérault 1993 £16 (ADN, OD) **** Mas de Daumas Gassac Vin de Pays de l'Hérault 1992 £11 (ADN, OD).

Masi (ITALY) VALPOLICELLA producer with reliable, affordable reds and whites and single-vineyard wines which serve as justification for the existence of the Valpolicella as a denominated region. **** Campo Fiorin 1990 £9 (L&W).

Massandra (CRIMEA, CIS) Producer of good but not great CABERNET and source of great, historic, dessert wines which were sold at a memorable Sothebys auction. **** Massandra White Muscat 1938 £70 (THP).

Master of Wine (MW) ONE OF A SMALL NUMBER OF PEOPLE (FEWER THAN 200) WHO HAVE PASSED A GRUELLING SET OF TRADE EXAMS.

Matanzas Creek (SONOMA, California) Top-class complex CHARDONNAY, good SAUVIGNON and high-quality accessible MERLOT. **** Sauvignon, Sonoma County 1990 £12 (HHC).

Mataro See MOURVEDRE.**** Ridge Vineyards Mataro 1991 £13 (ADN) *** Tesco Australian Mataro, Kingston Estate £6 (TO).

Matawhero (GISBOURNE, NEW ZEALAND) Unpredictable, often great GEWURZTRAMINER specialist.

Mateus (Portugal) Highly commercial pink and white off-dry, FRIZZANTE wine made by SOGRAPE, sold in bottles traditional in FRANKEN, Germany, and with a label depicting a palace with which the wine has no connection. A 50-year-old marketing masterpiece (widely available).

Thierry Matrot (BURGUNDY, France) Top-class white producer with great white and recommendable red BLAGNY. **** Blagny Rouge la Pièce sous le Bois 1986 £16 (C&B).

Matua Valley (AUCKLAND, NEW ZEALAND) Reliable maker of great (MARLBOROUGH) SAUVIGNON, (Judd Estate) CHARDONNAY and MERLOT. Also producer of the even better ARARIMU red and white. *** Marlborough Sauvignon Blanc 1993 £8 (JS) Judd Estate Chardonnay £8.99 (TH, BU) **** Ararimu Cabernet Sauvignon 1992 £17 (VW) **** Ararimu Chardonnay 1992 £17 (VW).

Mauzac (France) Characterful, wild, floral, white grape used in southern France for VINS DE PAYS and GAILLAC. *** Gaillac Blanc Cépage Mauzac Cave de Labastide 1992 £4 (EP).

Mavrodaphne Greek red grape and the wine made from it. Dark and strong, it needs ageing to be truly worth drinking. **Mavrodaphne Tsantali 1992 £5 (GWC).

Mavrud (BULGARIA) Traditional red grape and the characterful, if rustic, wine made from it. *** Reserve Mavrud Vinzavod Asenovgrad 1990 £3 (JS).

Maximin Grünhaus (MOSEL-SAAR-RUWER, Germany) 1,000-year-old estate with great, intense RIESLINGS. **** Herrenberg Riesling Kabinett Von Schubert 1991 £12 (L&W).

Mayacamas (NAPA, California) Long-established winery on MOUNT VEEDER with tannic but good CABERNET and long-lived, rich CHARDONNAY. **** Cabernet Sauvignon 1985 £23 (LAV).

McLaren Vale (SOUTH AUSTRALIA) Region close to Adelaide renowned for European-style wines, but too varied in topography, soil and climate to create a recogniseable identity for itself. **** Hardy's Château Reynella Cabernet Merlot 1992 £7 (CWS, OD, WHC) **** Mount Hurtle Shiraz, Geoff Merrill 1991 £6 (OD) **** Chapel Hill Reserve Chardonnay 1992 £8 (AUC) **** The Angelus Cabernet Sauvignon, Wirra Wirra Vineyards 1992 £9 (OD, BBR, WSO, WOI, SOM).

McWilliams (NEW SOUTH WALES, Australia) HUNTER VALLEY-based evidently non-republican firm with great, traditional ('Elisabeth') SEMILLON and ('Philip') SHIRAZ which need time. Fortified wines can be good, too. *** St Michael Pheasant Gully Shiraz McWilliams £3.50 (M&S) *** McWilliams Mount Pleasant Chardonnay 1992 £5 (OD, AUC).

Médoc (BORDEAUX, France) As a generic term, implies soundly made, everyday CLARET to be drunk young. As an area, it encompasses that region of BORDEAUX south of the GIRONDE and north of the town of BORDEAUX 78 79 82 83 85 86 88 89 90. *** Médoc AC La Mouline Anthony Sarjeant 1989 £5 (TAN).

Meerlust (STELLENBOSCH, SOUTH AFRICA) One of the Cape's very best estates. Classy MERLOTS and a BORDEAUX-blend called 'Rubicon' both of which will hopefully one day benefit from being bottled on the estate rather than by the BERGKELDER. **** Merlot, Meerlust Estate 1986/87 £12 (F&M) **** Rubicon 1987 £12 (F&M).

Gabriel Meffre (RHONE, France) Sound commercial RHONE producer. *** Château de Vaudieu Châteauneuf-du-Pape 1992 £9 (VW) *** Crozes Hermitage 1991 £6 (VW).

Melon de Bourgogne (LOIRE, France) White grape producing mostly dry, not very exciting wine that can nevertheless be good in MUSCADET and in California where it is sold as PINOT BLANC. **** Muscadet de Sèvre et Maine Clos de Beauregard, Pierre Laroux 1990 £6 (JAR).

Charles Melton (BAROSSA VALLEY, Australia) Small-scale producer of lovely still and sparkling SHIRAZ and world-class rosé called 'Rosé of Virginia', as well as Nine Popes, a wine based on, and mistakenly named after, Châteauneuf-du-Pape. ***** Shiraz 1992 £9 (AUC, ADN) ****Nine Popes 1993 £9 (ADN) **** Sparkling Shiraz £13 (AUC).

Mendocino (California, US) Northern, coastal wine county successfully exploiting cool microclimates to make 'European-style' wines, thanks, especially to the efforts of FETZER and Scharffenberger 83 84 85 86 87 88 90 91 92. **** Bonterra Chardonnay Fetzer Vineyards 1992 £8 (SAF) *** Scharffenberger Brut NV £9 (A, JAR).

Mendoza (ARGENTINA) Capital of principal wine region. Source of good rich reds from firms including TRAPICHE, Catena, St Felicien. Finca Flichman and San Telmo. *** Trapiche Cabernet Sauvignon 'Oak Cask' 1990 £5 (JS).

Ménétou-Salon (LOIRE, France) Bordering on SANCERRE making similar if earthier, less pricy SAUVIGNON as well as some decent PINOT NOIR. (red) 87 88 89 90 92. **** Blanc Morogues, Henry Pelle 1993 £8 (BP, TH) ***Blanc, B Clement 1993 £7 (ABY)

Méo-Camuzet (BURGUNDY, France) Brilliant COTE DE NUITS estate with top-class vineyards and intense, oaky wines, which were for a long time, until his retirement, made by the great HENRI JAYER. ***** Nuits St Georges, 1er Cru Boudots 1990 £40 (GH) ***** Richebourg £100 (GH).

Mercaptans SEE HYDROGEN SULPHIDE.

Mercier (CHAMPAGNE, France) Subsidiary/sister company of MOET & CHANDON and producer of improving but pretty ordinary fizz.

Mercurey (BURGUNDY, France) Good-value if rustic wine from the COTE CHALONNAISE. Reds are tough but can be POMMARD-like and worth waiting for, while the nutty, buttery whites can be similar to basic MEURSAULT 85 87 88 89 90 92. **** Mercurey Rouge Juillot 1990 £10 (DD) **** 'Les Mauvarennes', Mercurey Blanc, Faiveley 1991 £8 (MWW).

Merlot Red grape making soft, honeyed, even toffee-ish wine with plummy fruit, especially when planted in clay soil. Used to balance the tannic CABERNET SAUVIGNON throughout the MEDOC, where it is actually the most widely planted grape, as it is in POMEROL and ST EMILION, where clay also prevails. Also increasingly successful in California (especially for NEWTON), WASHINGTON STATE, VENETO, HUNGARY and Australia. **** Corbans Private Bin Merlot 1992 £9 (VW) ** Asda Merlot Vin de Pays d'Oc £3 (A) **** Domaine de l'Eglise 1991 £12 (OD).

Geoff Merrill (MCLAREN VALE, Australia) The ebullient mustachioed winemaker who has been nicknamed 'The Wizard of Oz'. Impressive if restrained (arguably too much so) SEMILLON-CHARDONNAY and CABERNET in MCLAREN VALE and, in 1993, a range of Italian wines for Sainsbury. Botham and Gower's favourite (vinous) tipple. ****Mount Hurtle Grenache Rosé 1993 £5 (JS) ***Semillon-Chardonnay 1989 £8 (OD) ***Sainsbury Bianco di Custoza 1993 £4 (JS).

Méthode Champenoise AS A TERM, NOW RESTRICTED BY LAW TO WINES FROM CHAMPAGNE, BUT IN EFFECT A METHOD USED FOR ALL QUALITY SPARKLING WINES; LABOUR-INTENSIVE, BECAUSE BUBBLES ARE PRODUCED BY SECONDARY FERMENTATION IN BOTTLE, RATHER THAN IN A VAT OR BY THE INTRODUCTION OF GAS. THUS BOTTLES MUST BE INDIVIDUALLY 'DEGORGED', TOPPED UP AND THEN RECORKED.

Methuselah SAME SIZE BOTTLE AS AN IMPERIALE (SIX LITRES). USUALLY APPLIED TO CHAMPAGNE.

Meursault (BURGUNDY, France) Superb white BURGUNDY; the CHARDONNAY showing off its nutty, buttery richness in mellow, full-bodied dry wine. Like NUITS ST GEORGES and BEAUNE it has no GRANDS CRUS but great PREMIERS CRUS such as Charmes, Perrières and Génévrières. There is a little red wine here too, some of which is sold as VOLNAY. 81 82 85 86 88 89 90 92. ***Meursault-Blagny 1er Cru Maison Louis Jadot 1989 £28 (TH) **** Meursault 'Les Narvaux', Olivier Leflaive 1992 £14 (JAR).

Ch. de Meursault (BURGUNDY, France) See PATRIARCHE.

Ch. Meyney (BORDEAUX, France) Improving ST ESTEPHE property, richer in flavour than some of its neighbours 82 85 86 88 89 90 91. *** 1989 £12 (THP).

Domaine Michel Niellon (BURGUNDY, France) An estate which ranks consistently among the top five white BURGUNDY producers. Elegant and amazingly concentrated wines. **** Chassagne Montrachet 1er Cru Les Champgains 1992 £20 (OD).

Domaine Michelot-Buisson (BURGUNDY, France) One of the great old MEURSAULT properties. A pioneer of estate bottling – and of the use of new oak. Wines are rarely subtle, but then they never lack typical MEURSAULT flavour either. **** Meursault 1992 £12 (OD).

Millésime (France) YEAR OR VINTAGE.

Millton Estate (NEW ZEALAND) James Millton is an obsessive, not to say masochist. He loves the hard-to-make CHENIN BLANC and uses it to make first class organic wine near AUCKLAND. Sadly, in Britain, we'd rather buy his CHARDONNAY. ****Barrel Fermented Chardonnay 1993 £7 (SAF).

Minervois (South-West France) Firm, fruity and improving suppertime reds – CORBIERES' (slightly) classier cousin 88 89 90 91. ***Dom. Villerambert 1993 £4.50 (OD). *****Carignanissime de Centeilles, Boyer-Domergue 1992 £6 (ADN, SOM, OD) *** Domaine Sainte Eulalie M Blanc 1991 £4 (TH, BU, WR) ***Château Villerambert Julien, Cuvée Trianon 1990 £8 (TAN).

Mis en Bouteille au Château/Domaine (France) BOTTLED AT THE ESTATE.

Ch. la Mission-Haut-Brion (BORDEAUX, France) Tough but rich reds which can rival its supposedly classier neighbour HAUT BRION 82 85 86 88 89 90. **** 1989 £45 (BBR, C&B, J&B).

Mitchell (CLARE VALLEY, Australia) Good producer of RIESLING and of the Peppertree SHIRAZ, one of the CLARE VALLEY's best reds. **** Mitchell Peppertree Shiraz 1992 and **** Cabernet Sauvignon 1991 £7 (L&W, LS, SHJ, G&M, HOT) **** Semillon 1992 £7 (ADN).

Mitchelton (GOULBURN VALLEY, VICTORIA, Australia) Modern producer of MARSANNE and SEMILLON. Late harvest RIESLINGS are also good, as is a BEAUJOLAIS-style red, known as Cab Mac. The Preece range – so named after the former winemaker – is also worth seeking out. **** Marsanne 1993 £6 (OD, A, PHI) **** Reserve Cabernet Sauvignon 1991 £7 (BWL, RAM, DBY, COK).

Mittelhaardt (RHEINPFALZ, Germany) Central and best BEREICH of the RHEINPFALZ 86 87 88 89 90 91 92.

Mittelmosel (MOSEL-SAAR-RUWER, Germany) Middle and best section of the MOSEL, including the BERNKASTEL BEREICH 85 86 87 88 89 90 91 92. *** Bereich Bernkastel 1992 £3 (W).

Mittelrhein (Germany) Small, northern section of the RHINE. Good RIESLINGS that are sadly rarely seen in the UK 83 85 86 88 89 90 91 92. *** Bacharacher Schloss Stahleck Riesling Kabinett, Toni Jost 1992 £6 (OD).

Mme. Theo Faller (ALSACE, France) Aka the Weinbach Estate, under which name MME FALLER produces stunning late harvest wines as well as creditable dry styles. **** Gewürztraminer, Reserve Particulière, Dom. Weinbach 1990 £16 (L&W).

Moelleux (France) SWEET. TO BE FOUND ON FRENCH WINES OTHER THAN THOSE FROM SAUTERNES. ***** Vouvray Moelleux Clos du Bourg, Gaston Huët 1990 £22 (TH) **** Jurançon Moelleux 'Vendange Tardives', Domaine Cauhapé 1992 £12 (M&V).

Moët & Chandon (CHAMPAGNE, France) The biggest though not always the best. DOM PERIGNON, the top wine, and Vintage Moët are reliably good and new CUVEES of Non-Vintage show a welcome reaction to recent criticism of inconsistency. See TORRE DE GALL, DOMAINE CHANDON, GREEN POINT. *** NV £19 (widely available).

Moillard (BURGUNDY, France) Middle-of-the-road NEGOCIANT whose best, really quite decent wines are sold under the 'Domaine Thomas Moillard' label. **** Chambertin Clos de Bèze, Domaine Thomas Moillard 1988 £45 (BBR).

Moldova Young republic next to ROMANIA and with exciting vinous potential. *** Moldova Chardonnay Hincesti Hugh Ryman 1993 £3 (SMF).

Monbazillac (South-West France) BERGERAC AC which is using the grapes of sweet BORDEAUX to make improving inexpensive alternatives to SAUTERNES 76 83 85 86 88 89 90. **** Domaine du Haut Rauly 1990 £4 (CWS) **** Château La Gironie 1990 £8 (ADN)

Robert Mondavi (NAPA, California) Pioneering producer of great Reserve CABERNET and PINOT NOIR and back-on-form CHARDONNAY, and inventor of oaky "Blanc Fumé" SAUVIGNON. Wines sold under the Woodbridge label are less interesting. ***** Pinot Noir Reserve 1991 £17 (F&M, JN) ***** Reserve Cabernet 1987 £25 (J&B).

Mongeard-Mugneret (BURGUNDY, France) A source of invariably excellent and sometimes stunningly exotic red BURGUNDY. *****Clos Vougeot 1989 £37 (ADN) **** Bourgogne Rouge 1991 £6 (MWW).

Monica (di Cagliari/Sardegna) (Italy) Red grape and wine of SARDINIA producing drily tasty and fortified spicy wine. *** Tesco Monica di Sardegna, Dolianova £5 (TO).

Monopole (France) LITERALLY, EXCLUSIVE – IN BURGUNDY DENOTES SINGLE OWNERSHIP OF AN ENTIRE VINEYARD.

Montagne St Emilion (BORDEAUX, France) A 'satellite' of ST EMILION. Often good-value reds which can outclass supposedly classier fare from ST EMILION itself. 82 83 85 86 88 89 90 92 ***Comte de Perjan £5 (OD).

Montagny (BURGUNDY, France) Tiny COTE CHALONNAISE commune producing good, lean CHARDONNAY that is a match for many POUILLY FUISSES. PREMIER CRUS are not from better vineyards; they're just made from riper grapes 83 85 87 88 89 90 92. ***Montagny 1er Cru, Cave des Vignerons de Buxy 1992 £7 (M&S).

Montalcino (TUSCANY, Italy) Village near Sienna known for BRUNELLO DI MONTALCINO, CHIANTI's big brother, whose reputation was largely created by the BIONDI SANTI estate which no longer deserves the prices it commands. Altesino, FRESCOBALDI and Banfi offer better value, as does the lighter ROSSO DI MONTALCINO **** Brunello di Montalcino Castellogiocondo Riserva, Frescobaldi 1986 £19 (W, LAV, WIN)

Montana (MARLBOROUGH, NEW ZEALAND) Huge firm with tremendous SAUVIGNONS and GEWURZTRAMINERS (sadly unavailable in the UK), improving CHARDONNAYS and good-value LINDAUER fizz. Reds are getting there, too, but still tend to be on the lean and green side. **** Lindauer Brut £7 (CD, TO, BKW, MRN, TH, SAF) **** Sauvignon Blanc 1993 £5 (TH, VW, TO, OD, BKW).

Monte Real Made by Bodegas Riojanos, generally decent, richly flavoured and tannic RIOJA. *** Monte Real Rioja Gran Reserva, Bodegas Riojanas 1982, £5 (ABY) *** Monte Real Rioja Gran Reserva, Bodegas Riojanas 1975 £12 (ABY).

Montecillo (RIOJA, Spain) Classy wines including the oddly named – to Anglophones at least – Viña Monty. The Cumbrero Blanco white is good, too. **** Montecillo Viña Monty Rioja Gran Reserva 1986 £7 (BAR, OD, WG).

Montée de Tonnerre (BURGUNDY, France) Excellent CHABLIS PREMIER CRU. ****Domaine de Vauroux 1992 £10 (L&W).

Montefalco Sagrantino (UMBRIA, Italy) Intense cherryish red made from the local Sagrantino grape. **** Sagrantino Montefalco, Caprai 1988 £9 (WCE).

Château Montelena (NAPA, California) Its two long-lived CHARDONNAYS (from NAPA and, rather better, ALEXANDER VALLEY) make this one of the more impressive producers in the state. The vanilla-and-blackcurrant CABERNET is too impenetrable, however. ****Chardonnay 1978 £25 (LV).

Montepulciano (Italy) Confusingly, both a red grape making red wines in central and South-East Italy (Montepulciano d'ABRUZZI etc) and the name of a town in TUSCANY (see VINO NOBILE DI MONTEPULCIANO).

Monterey (California, US) Underrated region south of San Francisco, producing tangier, 'grassier' wines. **** Monterey Vineyard Chardonnay 1990 £5 (OD).

Montes (Curico, CHILE) Go-ahead winery with improving reds (including the flagship Alpha) and improved SAUVIGNON. Nogales is another label. *** Merlot 1991 £5 (ADN) *** Villa Montes Sauvignon Blanc, Discover Wines 1994 £4 (EOR, L&W, PLA) *** Nogales Estate Cabernet Sauvignon 1990 £6 (L&W, HW) ***Montes Alpha Cabernet Sauvignon 1989 £9 (MWW, ADN).

Monteviña (California, US) Good ZINFANDEL from AMADOR COUNTY, reliable CABERNET and a FUME BLANC to make ROBERT MONDAVI weep. **** Fumé Blanc £5 (WMK).

Monthélie (BURGUNDY, France) Often overlooked COTE DE BEAUNE village producing potentially stylish reds and whites 83 85 87 88 89 90.
**** Monthélie, Jaffelin 1989 £9 (JAV).

Montilla-Moriles (Spain) DO region producing SHERRY-type wines in SOLERA systems, often so high in alcohol that fortification is unnecessary. *** Tesco Montilla Vinicola del Sud £3 (TO) *** Waitrose Montilla Cream, Perez Barquero £3 (W).

Montlouis (LOIRE, France) Neighbour of VOUVRAY making similar, lighter-bodied, wines 85 88 89 90. **** Domaine des Liards Moelleux Vendange Tardive, Berger Frères 1990 £12 (ADN) **** Montlouis Mousseux, Brut NV £8 (YAP).

Le Montrachet (BURGUNDY, France) With its neighbours (BATARD-M, CRIOTS-BATARD-M, BIENVENUE- BATARD-M AND CHEVALIER-M) vineyards shared between PULIGNY and CHASSAGNE which can make the greatest and the priciest dry white in the world. Big, biscuity, brilliant. **** Domaine Leflaive 1992 £172 (ADN).

Côtes de Montravel (South-West France) Source of dry and sweet whites and reds which are comparable to neighbouring BERGERAC. *** Château Le Bondieu 1992 £4 (EP).

Ch. Montrose (BORDEAUX, France) Back-on-form ST ESTEPHE renowned for its intensity and longevity. More typical of the appellation than COS D'ESTOURNEL but often less approachable in its youth 82 83 85 86 88 89 90 91. **** 1989 £25 (J&B).

Moondah Brook (SWAN VALLEY, WESTERN AUSTRALIA) An untypically (for the baking Swan) cool vineyard belonging to HOUGHTONS (and thus HARDYS). The star wines are the wonderful, tangy VERDELHO and richly oaky CHENIN BLANC which are brilliant. The CHARDONNAY and reds are less impressive. *** Show Reserve Chenin Blanc 1987 £13 (WHC) *** Chenin Blanc 1993 £5 (R, WL, JS, TDS, VW) **** Verdelho 1993 £5 (OD, VW, TO).

Mór (HUNGARY) Hungarian town making clean, aromatic white wines from a blend including the TRAMINER. *** Safeway Hungarian Country Wine, A'gos 1993 £3 (SAF).

Morellino di Scansano (TUSCANY, France) Amazing cherry 'n' raspberry, young-drinking red made from a clone of SANGIOVESE. **** Morellino di Scansano Riserva Le Pupitre 1987 £7 (OD).

Pierre Morey (BURGUNDY, France) Top-class MEURSAULT producer known for the power and concentration of his wines. **** Meursault 1er Cru Les Charmes 1990 £30 (HR).

Morey St Denis (BURGUNDY, France) COTES DE NUITS village which produces deeply fruity, richly smooth reds, especially the GRAND CRU CLOS DE LA ROCHE vineyard 78 82 83 85 86 88 89 90 92. **** Domaine Dujac 1992 £14 (HR) **** Morey-St-Denis 'En la Rue de Vergy', Domaine Henri Perrot-Minot 1990 £14 (WTR).

Morgon (BURGUNDY, France) One of the 10 BEAUJOLAIS CRUS. Worth maturing, as it can take on a delightful chocolate/cherry character 88 89 90 91. **** Morgon Jean Descombes, Georges Duboeuf 1993 £6 (BWC, TDS) Marcel Jonchet 1991 £7 (WMK).

Morio Muskat White grape grown in Germany and Eastern Europe and making simple, grapey wine. *** Kwik Save Morio Muskat, St Ursula 1993 £2 (KS).

Mornington Peninsula (VICTORIA, Australia) Some of Australia's newest and most southerly vineyards, close to Melbourne and under continuous threat from housing developers. Good for PINOT NOIR, minty CABERNET and juicy CHARDONNAY, though the innovative (but as yet unavailable in the UK) T'Gallant is leading the way in experimenting with other varieties and achieving encouraging results. See DROMANA 85 86 87 88 90 91 92 ***** Stoniers Pinot Noir 1992 £8 (WAW).

Morris of Rutherglen (VICTORIA, Australia) Extraordinarily successful producer of Liqueur MUSCAT and TOKAY (seek out the Show Reserve) and intense DURIF, both still and, along with SHIRAZ, weirdly sparkling. *** Morris Liqueur Muscat £8.49 (AUC, OD, HHC, L&W, WTR) *** Morris Durif 1990 £10 (WTR, DBW).

Morton Estate (Waikato, NEW ZEALAND) Top-class producer of SAUVIGNON, CHARDONNAY and LOIRE/BORDEAUX-style reds. **** Black Label Chardonnay 1992 £8 (BWC, PAG, ROB) *** Black Label Cabernet/Merlot 1991 £9 (BWC, PAG, ROB).

Moscatel de Setubal see SETUBAL.

Mosel-Saar-Ruwer (MSR) (Germany) Major region surrounding the three rivers that make up its name, capable of superbly elegant RIESLINGS which differ noticeably in each of the three regions 76 78 82 83 85 88 89 90 91 92. **** Trittenheimer Apotheke Riesling Kabinett Frederic Wilhelm-Gymnasium 1991 £6 (TO) **** Brauneberger Juffer-Sonnenuhr Riesling Spätlese Max-Ferd Richter 1990 £10 (SUM).

Mosel/Moselle (Germany) River and loose term for MOSEL-SAAR-RUWER wines, equivalent to the 'HOCK' of the RHINE. Not to be confused with the usually uninspiring Vins de Moselle produced on the other side of the river in France.

Moselblumchen (Germany) MOSEL-SAAR-RUWER equivalent to the RHINE's LIEBFRAUMILCH.

Lenz Moser (Austria) Big producer with a broad range, including particularly crisp dry whites and luscious sweet dessert wines. *** Pinot Blanc, Lenz Moser 1993 1992 £4 (SAF).

Moss Wood (MARGARET RIVER, WESTERN AUSTRALIA) Pioneer producer of PINOT NOIR and CABERNET; only the CABERNET has lived up to early promise. The **** SEMILLON, though, is reliably good. **** Cabernet Sauvignon 1992 £11 (ADN, DBY, F&M, LV) **** Chardonnay 1993 £11 (ADN, F&M, DBY) **** Semillon 1991 £9 (HHC).

JP Moueix (BORDEAUX, France) Top-class NEGOCIANT/PRODUCER, Christian MOUEIX specialises in POMEROL and ST EMILION and is responsible for PETRUS, La Fleur-Pétrus, Bel Air, Richotey and DOMINUS in California). ***** Château Petrus 1983 £194 (C&B) **** Château Bel Air 1988 £5 (C&B).

Moulin-à-Vent (BURGUNDY, France) One of the 10 BEAUJOLAIS CRUS – big and rich at its best and, like MORGON, benefits from ageing a few years 88 89 90 91. ***E Loron 1991 £7 (U) **** Paul Janin 1991 £9 (CPW).

Moulis (BORDEAUX, France) Red wine village of the HAUT-MEDOC; like LISTRAC, with good-value CRUS BOURGEOIS 81 82 83 85 86 88 89 90. See CHATEAU CHASSE-SPLEEN. **** Château Duplessis 1988 £8 (BI).

Mount Barker (WESTERN AUSTRALIA, Australia) Cooler-climate southern region with great RIESLING, VERDELHO, IMPRESSIVE CHARDONNAY and restrained SHIRAZ. **** Goundrey Windy Hill Mount Barker Chardonnay 1991 £9 (ADN, GRT, RWW) **** Plantagenet Shiraz 1990 £8 (GI).

Mount Langhi Ghiran (GREAT WESTERN, Australia) A maker of excellent cool-climate RIESLING, peppery SHIRAZ and very good CABERNET, though the latter two can be a touch lean. **** Shiraz 1991 £8 (AUC).

Mount Mary (YARRA, Australia) Dr Middleton makes PINOT NOIR and CHARDONNAY that are unpredictably BURGUNDY-like in the best and worst sense of the term. The clarety Quintet blend is more reliable. ***Quintet 1991 £25 (AUC)

Mountadam (EDEN VALLEY, SOUTH AUSTRALIA) Son of DAVID WYNN (the 'saviour' of COONAWARRA, by popular acclaim), Adam makes classy Burgundian CHARDONNAY and PINOT NOIR (both still and sparkling) and an impressive blend called 'The Red'. Also worth seeking out are the EDEN RIDGE organic wines and the fruity DAVID WYNN range, especially the unoaked CHARDONNAY. **** Mountadam Chardonnay 1992 £12 (TDS, ADN, BOO) **** Mountadam Pinot Noir 1992 £12 (TDS, DBY, BOO) **** Mountadam 'The Red' 1991 £16 (CHF, ADN).

Mount Veeder (NAPA, California) Convincing hillside appellation where MOUNT VEEDER Winery, Château Potelle, HESS COLLECTION and MAYACAMAS all produce impressive reds.

> **Mourvèdre** Floral-spicy RHONE grape usually found in blends. Increasingly popular in France and California where, as in Australia, it is called MATARO. See PENFOLDS and RIDGE. **** Ch. de la Rouvière 1989 £10 (YAP).

Mousse THE BUBBLES IN CHAMPAGNE AND SPARKLING WINES.

Mousseux (France) SPARKLING. VIN MOUSSEUX TENDS TO BE CHEAP AND UNREMARKABLE. ** GF Cavalier Brut, Caves De Wissembourg NV £4 (Widely Available).

Mouton Cadet (BORDEAUX, France) Dull but acceptable red, which, despite widespread misconceptions and the flourish with which it is often served, has absolutely no tasteable connection with CHATEAU MOUTON ROTHSCHILD (see below). A brilliant commercial invention by Philippe de Rothschild who used it to profit handsomely from the name of his first growth. The white, though better than in the past, has even less of a *raison d'être*..

Ch. Mouton Rothschild (BORDEAUX, France) Brilliant First Growth PAUILLAC with gloriously complex flavours of roast coffee and blackcurrant. Since the early 1980s equal to the very best in the MEDOC. 61 66 70 75 81 82 85 88 89 90. ****1981 £52 (BI).

Mudgee (NEW SOUTH WALES, Australia) Australia's first APPELLATION region, though heaven knows why. This high-altitude, isolated area is making far better wines than the robust, often clumsy stuff it used to turn out, but it's still not a name to look out for 82 84 88 89 90 91 92. **** Marsanne, Botobolar Vineyard 1992 £7 (VR) *** Montrose Cabernet Merlot 1990 £6.50 (WTR).

Muga (RIOJA, Spain) Old-fashioned **** producer of good old fashioned RIOJA wines, of which Prado Enea is the best. **** Prado Enea Rioja Gran Reserva 1985 £12 (A&A) *** Rioja Reserva 1988 £8 (ES, A&A).

Müller-Catoir (RHEINPFALZ, Germany) Great new-wave producer using new-wave grapes, such as Rieslaner and Scheurebe to great effect. Wines of all styles are impeccable and packed with flavour. Just what Germany needs to remind the world of what it can do. ***** Mussbacher Eselshaut Rieslaner Trockenbeerenauslese, Müller-Catoir 1992 £29 (OD) ***** Haardter Mandelring Scheurebe Spätlese 1992 £9 (OD).

Egon Müller-Scharzhof (MOSEL-SAAR-RUWER, Germany) Top-class SAAR producer. **** Scharzhofberger Riesling Spätlese 1990 £14 (L&W).

> **Müller-Thurgau** Workhorse white grape, a RIESLING x SYLVANER cross - also known as RIVANER – making much unremarkable wine in Germany, but yielding some gems for producers like MULLER-CATOIR. Very successful in England. *** Langenlonsheimer Müller-Thurgau Kabinett, Willi Schweinhardt 1990 £7 (OD).

Mumm (CHAMPAGNE, France/NAPA, California) Maker of decidedly disappointing Cordon Rouge CHAMPAGNE and far better CUVEE NAPA out west. The rosé is better than the white and the WINERY LAKE is best. **** Cuvée Napa, Mumm, Napa Valley £9 (Widely available) *** Mumm Cuvée Napa Rosé £9 (Widely available).

Muré (ALSACE, France) Producer of full-bodied wines, especially from the Clos St Landelin vineyard. **** Gewürztraminer Clos St Landelin Grand Cru Vorbourg 1992 £8 (BWC) *** Tokay Pinot Gris Clos St Landelin Grand Cru Vorbourg 1992 £9.50 (BWC).

Murfatlar (ROMANIA) Major vineyard and research area having increasing success with CHARDONNAY *** Romanian Cellars Chardonnay 1993 £3 (MRN).

Murphy-Goode (ALEXANDER VALLEY, California) CHARDONNAYs Classy producer of quite Burgundian style whites which sell at – in Californian terms – affordable prices. ****Chardonnay 1990 £10 ADN).

Murray River Valley (Australia) The vineyard area ranging between VICTORIA and NEW SOUTH WALES which produces much of the Antipodes' cheapest wine – a great deal of which is to be found in UK retailers' own-label bottles.

Murrumbidgee (NEW SOUTH WALES, Australia) Area formerly known for bulk dessert wines, now improving irrigation and vinification techniques to make good table wines and some stunning BOTRYTIS-affected sweet wines for DE BORTOLI and LINDEMANS.

Château Musar (Ghazir, LEBANON) Serge Hochar makes a different red every year, varying the blend of CABERNET, CINSAULT and SYRAH. The style veers wildly between BORDEAUX, the RHONE and Italy, but there's never a risk of becoming bored. Good vintages easily keep for a decade. The CHARDONNAY-based whites are less than dazzling, though. *** Château Musar, Serge Hochar 1987 £8 (MWW, SMF).

Muscadelle Spicy ingredient in white BORDEAUX, aka TOKAY in Australia **** Bailey's Founder Liqueur Tokay £10 (WWT, AUC, DBY).

Muscadet (LOIRE, France) Area at the mouth of the LOIRE making dry, appley white from the MELON DE BOURGOGNE. Clean and refreshing when good, which, sadly, is a rare thing. SUR LIE is best. May be barrel-fermented. See SEVRE-ET-MAINE. **** Muscadet Clos de Beauregard 1990 £6 (JAR).

Muscat à Petits Grains Aka FRONTIGNAN, the best variety of MUSCAT and the grape responsible for MUSCAT DE BEAUMES DE VENISE, Muscat de Rivesaltes, ASTI SPUMANTE, Muscat of SAMOS, RUTHERGLEN Muscats and dry ALSACE Muscats. ***Muscat de Beaumes de Venise, J Vidal-Fleury 1992 £16 (WWT) *** Domaine Brial Muscat de Rivesaltes, Vignerons De Baixas 1993 £4 (SAF).

Muscat of Alexandria Grape responsible for MOSCATEL DE SETUBAL, MOSCATEL DE VALENCIA and some sweet SOUTH AUSTRALIAN offerings. Also known as Lexia. **** Setubal Superior Moscatel, Jose Maria da Fonseca Succs 1966 £10 (TAN, F&M).

Muscat Ottonel MUSCAT variety grown in Middle and Eastern Europe. **** Muskat Ottonel Eiswein Kracher 1992 (37.5cl) £16 (NY) **** Kracher Muskat Ottonel Trockenbeerenauslese 1981 £28 (NY).

Musigny (BURGUNDY, France) Potentially wonderful but more often disappointing GRAND CRU from which CHAMBOLLE MUSIGNY takes its name. **** Chambolle-Musigny, Faively 1987 £55 (T&W) **** Musigny blanc, De Vogüe 1988 £111 (T&W).

Domaine Mussy (BURGUNDY, France) Top-class, tiny POMMARD estate with very concentrated wines. **** Pommard 1er cru 1988 £19 (HR).

Must UNFERMENTED GRAPE JUICE.

MW SEE MASTER OF WINE.

Nackenheim (RHEINHESSEN, Germany) Village in the NIERSTEIN BEREICH, producing good wines but better known for its debased GROSSLAGE, Gutes Domtal. *** Rothenberg Scheurebe Kabinett, Gunderloch 1992 £6 (WSO).

Nahe (Germany) ANBAUGEBIET producing wines which can combine delicate flavour with full body 87 88 89 90 91 92. **** Kreuznacher Bruckes Riesling Auslese, Schloss Von Plettenburg 1989 £9 (TH, WR, BU) **** Bretzenheimer Vogelsang Riesling Spätlese, Schloss Plettenberg 1992 £6 (G).

Naoussa (Greece) Region producing dry red wines, often from the XYNOMAVRO grape. *** Boutari Xinomavro Naoussis 1991 £4 (SAF) *** Naoussa, Boutari 1990 £4 (SAF, AMA).

Napa (California) Named after the American-Indian word for 'plenty', this is a region with plentiful wines ranging from ordinary to sublime. Too many are hyped; none is cheap. In the future, APPELLATIONS within NAPA, such as CARNEROS, STAGS LEAP and MT VEEDER, and other nearby regions (like SONOMA) will take greater prominence when it is realised that parts of the county never make spectacular wine. (red) 85 86 87 88 90 91 92 (white) 85 86 87 88 90 91 92. ***** Saintsbury Carneros Pinot Noir 'Reserve' 1991 £18 (BI, ADN) **** Stag's Leap Wine Cellars Chardonnay Reserve 1991 £18 (WTR).

Navajas (RIOJA, Spain) Small producer making reds and oaky whites worth keeping. **** Navajas Rioja Sin Crianza 1992 £4 (WL, WCE).

Navarra (Spain) Northern DO, traditionally for rosés and heavy reds but now producing better value, exciting wines, easily rivalling and often surpassing those from neighbouring RIOJA, where prices are often higher. Look out too for innovative CABERNETS and CABERNET blends 85 86 87 88 89 90 91. **** Señorio de Sarria Navarra Cabernet Sauvignon Crianza, Bodega de Sarria 1987 £7 (TH, BU, WR) *** Chivite Reserva, Chivite 1989 £5.50 (VW, OD).

Nebbiolo Great red grape of Italy, producing wines which are slow to mature but become richly complex and fruity, epitomised by BAROLO and BARBARESCO aka SPANNA. Resembles the PINOT NOIR in making wines whose flavour varies enormously depending on the soil in which it is grown. **** Nebbiolo, L. A. Cetto 1986 £9 (THP, ALV, TAN, ECK, R) **** Barbaresco, Azienda Agricola Guiseppe Cortese 1988 £12 (GI, LAY).

Nederburg (PAARL, SOUTH AFRICA) Huge producer with plentiful commercial wines including an improving CHARDONNAY. Edelrood is a fair red blend; but the Edelkeur late harvest wines are the gems of the cellar. **** Noble Late Harvest 1990 £4 (CAP, DBW, WTR) *** Chardonnay 1992 £6 (LWL, CAP, LWE).

Négociant (-Eléveur) (France) A MERCHANT WHO BUYS (MATURES) AND BOTTLES WINE.

Négociant-manipulant (NM) (CHAMPAGNE, France) BUYER AND BLENDER OF WINES FOR CHAMPAGNE, IDENTIFIABLE BY NM NUMBER MANDATORY ON LABEL.

Negroamaro (Italy) A Puglian grape that produces warm, gamey reds. Found in SALICE SALENTINO and COPERTINO. *** Salice Salentino Riserva 1989 Candido £5 (WSO, WCE, V&C).

Nelson (South Island, NEW ZEALAND) Small region, a glorious bus-ride to the north-west of MARLBOROUGH, in which NEUDORF and REDWOOD VALLEY make increasingly impressive wines.

Nemea (Peloponnese, Greece) Improving cool(ish) climate region for reds made from the Agiorgitiko grape. *** Nemea Kouros, D Kourtakis SA 1988 £4 (U) *** Nemea, Boutari 1991 £4 (WL, AMA, OD, TO).

Neuchâtel (Switzerland) Lakeside region, which together with Les Trois Lacs, is a good source of CHASSELAS and CHARDONNAY whites and PINOT NOIR. reds and rosés. Good producers include Château d'Auvernier and Porret.

Neudorf (NELSON, NEW ZEALAND) Pioneering small-scale producer of beautifully made CHARDONNAY, SEMILLON, RIESLING and even better PINOT NOIR. ***** Moutere Pinot Noir 1992 £12 (ADN, HN) *** Moutere Chardonnay 1992 £15 (ADN, TDS) ** Neudorf Vineyard Riesling 1993 £8 (ADN, TDS, JN).

Neusiedlersee (Austria) BURGENLAND region on the Hungarian border, source of great late harvest wines and increasingly good whites and reds. See WILLI OPITZ . *** Blaufrankisch & Zweigelt 'Blend II' Kracher 1992 £8 (NY).

Nevers (France) SUBTLEST OAK – FROM A FOREST IN BURGUNDY.

New South Wales (Australia) Major wine-producing state which is home to the famous HUNTER VALLEY, along with the COWRA, MUDGEE and MURRUMBIDGEE regions.

New York State (US) See FINGER LAKES and LONG ISLAND.

New Zealand Superstar nation with proven SAUVIGNON BLANC and CHARDONNAY and increasingly successful reds. After two difficult vintages 92 & 93, now having an easier time but still finding it difficult to meet home & international demand

Newton Vineyards (NAPA, California) High altitude vineyards with top-class CHARDONNAY, MERLOT and CABERNET which are now being made with help from MICHEL ROLLAND (look for the moreimpressive unfiltered examples). *** Chardonnay, Napa Valley 1991 £11 (ADN, NI, TDS, ECK, CAF) **** Cabernet Sauvignon 1990 £11 (ADN, UBC, CHF, SOM) ***** Unfiltered Merlot 1991 £15 (CHF, BOO, RAM).

Nicholson River (Gippsland, Australia) The temperamental Gippsland climate ensures that this estate has a frustratingly small production, however its efforts have been repaid over and over by stunning CHARDONNAYS.

Niebaum Coppola (NAPA, California) You've read the book and seen the movie. Now taste the wine. The *Dracula* and *Godfather* director's own estate includes some of the oldest vines in the state and makes intensely concentrated CABERNETS to suit those of a patient disposition. **** Cabernet Franc 1990 £10 (LEA, HOL, RD, PON) **** Rubicon 1982 £20 (RD, LEA, SAN, PON, CEB).

Niederhausen Schlossböckelheim (NAHE, Germany) State-owned estate producing highly concentrated RIESLING from great vineyards. **** Niederhauser Hermannshöhle Riesling Halbtrocken Staatlichen Weinbaudomanen 1992 £7 (L&W).

Niepoort (DOURO, Portugal) Small independent PORT house making subtle vintage and particularly impressive COLHEITA tawnies. A name to watch. **** Niepoort LBV Port 1987 £10.50 (BTH, BI,) ***** Niepoort Colheita 1978 £25 (BOO, BI).

Nierstein (RHEINHESSEN, Germany) Village and (with PIESPORT) BEREICH best known in the UK. Some very fine wines, obscured by the notoriety of the reliably dull GUTES DOMTAL 83 85 88 89 90 91 92. *** Niersteiner Pettenthal Riesling Spätlese, Balbach 1988 £7 (VW) *** Niersteiner Pettenthal Riesling Auslese, Graf Wolff Metternich 1992 £7 (A).

Nikolaihof (Niederösterreich, AUSTRIA) Producer of some of the best GRUNER VELTLINERS and RIESLINGS in AUSTRIA.

Nitra (SLOVAKIA) Promising hilly region, especially for PINOTS BLANC, GRIS and NOIR. *** Irsay Oliver 1992 £4 (WR).

Nobilo (Huapai, NEW ZEALAND) Family-owned firm making good OAKY CHARDONNAY from GISBOURNE (to be found on British Airways) and a pleasant commercial off-dry White Cloud blend. *** White Cloud 1993 £5 (AV, JS, TH, CWS, MWW) **** Dixon Vineyard Chardonnay 1991 £9 (AV).

Noble rot POPULAR TERM FOR BOTRYTIS CINEREA.

North-East Victoria (Australia) The region to find the liqueur-MUSCAT producers of RUTHERGLEN and GLENROWAN, including MORRIS, CHAMBERS and BAILEYS, as well as BROWN BROTHERS and their pioneering cooler climate vineyards. ***** Yalumba Museum Show Reserve Rutherglen Muscat £7 (TH, BEN, TO, VW, SOM) **** Brown Brothers Liqueur Muscat £9 (AUC, WWT).

Nose SMELL.

Nouveau NEW WINE, MOST POPULARLY USED OF BEAUJOLAIS.

Nuits St Georges (BURGUNDY, France) Commune producing the most CLARET-like of red Burgundies, properly tough and lean when young but glorious in age. Whites are good but ultra-rare 82 83 85 88 89 90. ***** 1er Cru Clos des Forêts St Georges, Domaine de l'Arlot 1991 £28 (ABY) **** Nuits St Georges, Georges Désiré 1991 £10 (SMF, G) **** 1er Cru Clos de la Maréchale, Faiveley £18 (MWW).

Nuragus di Cagliari (SARDINIA, Italy) Good-value, tangy, distinctively floral white wine from the Nuragus grape. *** Nuragus, Dolianova 1993 £3 (TO, W, C&B).

NV Non-vintage, meaning a blend of wines from different years.

Oaky Flavour imparted by oak casks which will vary depending on the source of the oak (American is more obviously sweet than French). Woody is usually less complimentary.

Ochoa (Navarra, Spain) New-wave producer of fruitily fresh Cabernet, Tempranillo and Viura. *** Navarra Reserva 1982 £7 (TAN) *** Cabernet Sauvignon, Navarra 1987 £7 (MWW, TPW) **** Tempranillo 1990 £6 (MWW, TH, HAR, RTW).

Ockfen (Mosel-Saar-Ruwer, Germany) Village producing some of the best wines of the Saar-Ruwer Bereich, especially from the Bockstein vineyard. *** Ockfener Bockstein Riesling Kabinett, Rheinart 1993 £5 (RTW).

Oechsle (Germany) Sweetness scale used to indicate the sugar levels in grapes or wine.

Oenology/ist The study of the science of wine / one who advises winemakers.

Oeste (Portugal) Western region in which are being made a growing number of fresh, light, commercial wines, of which the most successful has undoubtedly been Arruda. *** Uva do Monte Rosé £4 (D&F) *** Arruda £3 (JS).

Oesterich (Rheingau, Germany) Source of good Riesling. **** Hochheim, Deinhard Heritage Collection 1988 £7 (TDS, CNL) *** Oestricher Doosberg Riesling Kabinett, Schloss Schonborn Hattenheim 1983 £5 (G).

Oidium Insidious fungal infection of grapes, causing them to turn grey and shrivel.

Olarra (Rioja, Spain) Unexceptional producer whose whites are pleasantly adequate. *** Sainsbury's Rioja Blanco, Bodegas Olarra £3 (JS).

> **Olasz Rizling** (Hungary) Term for the inferior Welschriesling.
> ** Olasz Rizling, Szoloskert Co-operative 1993 £3 (CWS).

Oloroso (Jerez, Spain) Style of full-bodied sherry, dry or semi-sweet. *** Sainsbury's Oloroso £4 (JS) ***** Matusalem Oloroso Muy Viejo, Gonzalez Byass £19 (TO, OD, SAF, TDS).

Oltrepó Pavese (Italy) Lombardy DOC made from grapes including the characterfully spicy-fruity red Gutturnio and the local white Ortrugo. Fugazza is the most famous producer.

Omar Khayyam (Maharashtra, India) Champagne-method wine that has more than mere novelty value – but drink it young. *** Omar Khayyam 1987 £7 (CWS, MRN, FUL, GRO).

Ontario (Canada) The best wine region in Canada, especially for Ice Wines Look out for bottles with VQA stickers which guarantee quality and provenance. *** Inniskillin, Chardonnay 1992 £7 (AV) *** Inniskillin, Pinot Noir Reserve 1991 £10 (AV).

Willi Opitz (Austria) Odd-ball producer of a magical mystery tour of late harvest wines, including an extraordinary botrytis red. ***** Weisser Schilfmandl, Schilfwein Vin Paille 1992 £31 (T&W) ***** Blauberger Red Trockenbeerenauslese 1991 £35 (T&W).

Oppenheim (Rheinhessen, Germany) Village in Nierstein Bereich best known, though often unfairly, for unexciting wines from the Krottenbrunnen. Elsewhere produces soft wines with concentrated flavour 76 83 85 86 88 89 90 91 92. *** Oppenheimer Louis Guntrum 1989 £7.50 (U)

Opus One (Napa, California) Claret-like co-production between Mouton Rothschild and Robert Mondavi. Decidedly more successful so far than Dominus – but it will have to be. The latter wine is still produced in rented space in another producer's winery, while the recently completed Opus One winery, excavated into land to the side of the main road through Napa, has been described as the world's most expensive hole in the ground. Mind you, they never suspected they'd hit water down there. ***** 1990 £45 (BU, ABY).

Orange Muscat Yet another member of the MUSCAT family, this is the one which is best known for dessert wines in California and VICTORIA, including the delicious BROWN BROTHERS Late Harvest Orange Muscat & Flora. *** Late Harvest Orange Muscat & Flora, Brown Brothers 1993 £6 (OD, U, MWW, TH, FUL) *** Essensia, Quady Winery 1992 £6 (MWW, GNW, CPW, HAR, THP).

Oregon (US) Fashionable cool-climate wine-producing state which is best known for its PINOT NOIRS, though few yet surpass a good producer's basic BOURGOGNE Rouge, despite their high price. The CHARDONNAYS are even less successful, thanks to the planting of a late-ripening CLONE as recommended by experts from California. A conspiracy theorist might suspect some inter-state sabotage under foot 83 85 86 87 88 90 91 92. ***** Pinot Noir, Domaine Drouhin Oregon 1990 £20 (OD) *** Argyle Brut, The Dundee Wine Company 1989 £11.75 (WIN) **** Pinot Noir, Cameron Winery £8 (BI).

Oriachovitza (BULGARIA) Major source of (fairly) reliable CABERNET SAUVIGNON and MERLOT 87 88 89 90 91. *** Oriachovitza Vintage Blend Reserve Merlot/Cabernet Sauvignon, Menada Stara Zagora 1990 £3 (JS, WOW).

Orlando (SOUTH AUSTRALIA) Huge, French (Pernod-Ricard) owned producer of the world-beating and surprisingly reliable Jacob's Creek wines. The RF range is good, but the Gramps, Flaxmans, Lawsons and Jacaranda Ridge wines are undoubtedly the ones to look for. ***** Jacaranda Ridge Cabernet Sauvignon 1989 £18 (WTR) **** Flaxmans Traminer 1990 £8 (AUC, CUM, WTR) **** Lawsons Padthaway Shiraz 1989 £10 (WTR, OD). **** Gramps Cabernet Sauvignon/Merlot/Cabernet Franc 1989 £7 (WTR)

Orléanais (LOIRE France) A vineyard area around Orleans in the Central Vineyards region of the LOIRE, specialising in unusual white blends of CHARDONNAY and PINOT GRIS, and reds of PINOT NOIR and CABERNET FRANC. **** Vin d'Orléanais Blanc, Covifruit 1992 £5 *** Rouge £5 (YAP).

Ornellaia (TUSCANY, Italy) BORDEAUX-style blend SUPER-TUSCAN from the brother of Pierro ANTINORI. Serious wine worth maturing for another few years. The estate also produces a good VINO DA TAVOLA Le Volte, which, at about £8, is a fair alternative if your budget is not upto Ornellaia. ***** Ornellaia 1991 £23 (WCE).

Orvieto (UMBRIA, Italy) White Umbrian DOC responsible for a quantity of dull wine. Orvieto CLASSICO is better. Look out for SECCO if you like your white wine dry; AMABILE if you have a sweet tooth 89 90 91 92.** Vigneto Torricella Bigi 1991 £7 (F&M) *** Cardeto Orvieto Classico Secco, COVIO 1993 £4 (W, OD, A, VW).

Osborne (JEREZ, Spain) Producer of a good range of sherries including a brilliant Pedro Ximenez. **** Oloroso Solera BC 200 £22 (BAR) **** Alonso el Sabio £22 (BAR).

Domaine Ostertag (ALSACE, France) Poet and philosopher Andre Ostertag presides over this superb Alsace Domaine. **** Gewürztraminer Fronholz 1992 £11 (M&V).

Overgaauw (STELLENBOSCH, South Africa) MERLOT pioneer who also makes Overtinto 'port', one of the best fortified wines in the Cape. **** Merlot 1989 £9 (NGF).

Oxidation THE EFFECT (USUALLY DETRIMENTAL, OCCASIONALLY – AS IN SHERRY – INTENTIONAL) OF OXYGEN ON WINE.

Oyster Bay (MARLBOROUGH, NEW ZEALAND) See DELEGATS.

Paarl (SOUTH AFRICA) Warm region in which BACKSBERG and the larger BOSCHENDAL make a more modern style of wine. Hotter and drier than neighbouring STELLENBOSCH but a particularly good area for CHARDONNAY. **** Fairview Estate Cabernet £7 (CAP).

Pacherenc-du-Vic-Bilh (South-West France) Dry or fairly sweet white wine made from the PETIT and GROS MANSENG. A speciality of MADIRAN growers. Very rarely seen, worth trying. **** St Albert, Plaimont 1990 £8 (WSO) **** Pacherenc-du-Vic-Bilh, Collection Plaimont 1988 £5 (EP).

Padthaway (SOUTH AUSTRALIA) Vineyard area just north of COONAWARRA specialising in CHARDONNAY and SAUVIGNON, though reds work well here too 84 85 86 87 88 90 91 92. **** St Hilary Padthaway Chardonnay, Orlando Wines 1992 £8 (WTR, A) **** Lindemans Padthaway Chardonnay 1992 £8 (TH, TO, WR, BU, AUC).

Pagadebit di Romagna (EMILIA-ROMAGNA, Italy) Dry, sweet and fizzy whites made from the plummy Pagadebit grape. **** Celli 1993 £5 (WSC).

Pais Very basic Chilean red grape and its wine. Rarely exported.

Bodegas Palacio (RIOJA, Spain) Stylish fruit-driven reds and distinctively oaky whites. ****Cosme Palacio y Hermanus 1990 £5 (OD, T&W, W).

Palate THE TASTE OF A WINE.

Palatinate (Germany) Obsolete term for the RHEINPFALZ.

Palazzo Altesi (TUSCANY, Italy) Oaky SUPER-TUSCAN made from pure SANGIOVESE by Altesino. **** Palazzo Altesi Rosso 1990 £15 (POR).

Pale Cream (Spain) A HEAVILY SWEETENED PALE SHERRY WHICH ALLOWS PEOPLE WHO'D RATHER BE DRINKING BRISTOL CREAM TO LOOK AS THOUGH THEY'RE SIPPING TIO PEPE. *** Wisdom & Warter Pale Cream £4 (HOT, MYS, MRN, LWL) *** Don Cavala Pale Cream, Blazquez £4 (TH, TDS, WR, BU).

Palette (PROVENCE, France) AC rosé and light white, well liked by holidaymakers in Nice, St Tropez and Cannes who are so used to paying a fiver for a coffee that they don't notice paying more for a pink wine than a serious CLARET. *** Ch Simone Rosé 1992 £13 (YAP).

Palliser Estate (MARTINBOROUGH, NEW ZEALAND) Source of classy SAUVIGNON BLANC and CHARDONNAY from the up-and-coming region of MARTINBOROUGH. **** Sauvignon Blanc 1993 £9 (J&B, HOU, WR, BU, DBY) **** Chardonnay, Martinborough 1992 £10 (WR, HHC, OD, BU, J&B, PON).

Ch. Palmer (BORDEAUX, France) Superbly perfumed Third Growth MARGAUX which stands alongside the best of the MEDOC and often outclasses its more highly ranked neighbours. The 1983s are a good buy – more than can be said for most MEDOCS of that vintage 82 83 85 86 88 89 90. ***** 1983 £35 (EV).

Palo Cortado (Spain) A rare SHERRY wine pitched between an AMONTILLADO and an OLOROSO in style and flavour. **** Sainsbury's Palo Cortado, Francisco Gonzalez Fernandez, (half) £3 (JS) *** Tesco Superior Palo Cortado, Sanchez Romate (half) £4 (TO).

Palomino (Spain/SOUTH AFRICA) White grape responsible for virtually all fine SHERRY, when fortified– and almost invariably dull white wine, when unfortified.

Parellada (Spain) Dullish grape used for CAVA. At its best in TORRES' Viña Sol, but even then more the beneficiary of skilled winemaking than a star in its own right. ***Torres Gran Vina Sol 1993 £5 (GRT, WR, TO, OD, CC).

Dom Parent (BURGUNDY, France) POMMARD-based grower/NEGOCIANT with claims to be the oldest in the world to have remained in the hands of the same family – and certainly the only one to include Thomas Jefferson among its former clients. Wines are quite old-fashioned too, but attractively so in their fruit-packed way. *** Pommard Premier Cru, Domaine Parent 1989 £18 (CAC, F&M) *** Pinot Noir, Domaine Parent 1990 £7 (OD, TAN, F&M, TH, WSO).

Pasado/Pasada (Spain) TERM APPLIED TO OLD OR FINE FINO AND AMONTILLADO SHERRY. WORTH SEEKING OUT.**** Sainsburys Manzanilla Pasada, Vinicola Hidalgo £3 (half) (JS).

C J Pask (HAWKES BAY, NEW ZEALAND) CABERNET pioneer with good SAUVIGNON too. **** C J Pask Cabernet/Merlot 1992 £8 (L&W, HOT) *** C J Pask Chardonnay 1992 £8 (L&W) *** C J Pask Cabernet Sauvignon 1991 £9 (L&W).

Paso Robles (SAN LUIS OBISPO, California) Warmish, long-established region, good for ZINFANDEL, RHONE and Italian varieties. And then there are the increasingly successful CHARDONNAY and PINOT. Watch this space. *** Wild Horse Chardonnay 1992 £8 (OD).*** Wild Horse Pinot Noir 1990 £8 (OD)

Pasqua (VENETO, Italy) VENETO producer whose wines are fairly priced and among the most reliable in the region. *** Chardonnay del Veneto, 1993 £3 (MWW).

Passetoutgrains (BURGUNDY, France) Wine supposedly made of two-thirds GAMAY, one-third PINOT NOIR – though few producers respect these proportions. Once the Burgundians' daily red – until they decided to sell it and drink cheaper wine from other regions 86 87 88 90 92. **** Daniel Rion 1990 £6.40 (M&V).

Passing Clouds (BENDIGO, Australia) 'We get clouds here, but it never rains...' Despite what some may find a fairly hideous label, this is one of Australia's most serious red blends. A wine worth keeping. *** Shiraz/ Cabernet 1990 £11 (ADN).

Passito (Italy) SWEET RAISINY WINE, USUALLY MADE FROM SUN-DRIED GRAPES. NOW BEING USED IN AUSTRALIA BY PRIMO ESTATE. **** Passito Di Pantelleria, Carlo Pellegrino & C. Spa 1993 £9 (LAV).

Frederico Paternina (RIOJA, Spain) Ernest Hemingway's favourite BODEGA – which is just about the only reason to buy its wine nowadays. Virtually unfindable in Britain.

Luis Pato (BAIRRADA, Portugal) One of Portugal's rare superstar winemakers, proving, among other things, that the BAGA grape can make first class spicy, berryish reds. **** Bairrada 1988 £7 (TH, BU).

Patriarche Huge merchant whose name is not a watchword for great BURGUNDY. The CHATEAU DE MEURSAULT domaine which it owns, however, produces good MEURSAULT, Bourgogne Blanc, VOLNAY and BEAUNE. ***** Volnay Clos des Chênes, Domaine du Château de Meursault 1992 £15 (HAR, BTH) *** Beaune 1er Cru, Domaine du Château de Meursault 1992 £12 (HAR, BTH).

Pauillac (BORDEAUX, France) One of the four famous 'Communes' of the MEDOC, Pauillac is the home of CHATEAUX LATOUR , LAFITE and MOUTON-ROTHSCHILD. The epitome of full-flavoured, blackcurranty BORDEAUX; very classy (and expensive) wine 78 79 81 82 83 85 86 88 89 90. See PICHON-LALANDE.

Pauly-Bergweiler (MOSEL-SAAR-RUWER, Germany) Ultra-modern winery with good, modern RIESLING.

Ch. Pavie (BORDEAUX, France) Classy, impeccably made, plummily rich ST. EMILION wines. The neighbouringPavie Decesse is similar, as one might expect from common ownership to Château Pavie, but a shade less impressive 82 83 85 86 88 89 90 91. ***** 1989 £22 (AV).

Pécharmant (South-West France) In the BERGERAC area, producing light, BORDEAUX-like reds. Worth trying 85 86 88 89 90 91. **** Ch Tiregand 1992 £6 (JS).

Pedro Ximénez (PX) White grape, dried in the sun for sweet, curranty wine and used in the production of the sweeter SHERRY styles favoured by Britain's diminishing band of sherry drinkers. Also produces a very unusual wine at DE BORTOLI in Australia ***** Cream of Cream Sherry, Pedro Ximénez, Argueso Valdespino £9. (SAF)

Pelorus (Australia) See CLOUDY BAY.

Pelure d'Oignon (France)'ONION SKIN'; ORANGEY-BROWN TINT OF SOME ROSE.

Penedés (Spain) Largest **DOC** of **CATALONIA** with varying altitudes, climates and styles. Table wines are improving disappointingly slowly, however, despite the early example of **TORRES**. More importantly, this is the centre of the **CAVA** industry 86 87 88 89 90 91. **** Torres Gran Sangredetoro 1989 £6.(WR, LWL, OD, U, BU) *** Somerfield Cava, Conde de Caralt £5 (G, SMF).

Penfolds (South Australia) Huge company with a high quality range at every price level from bag-in-box to Bins 389, 707 and Grange. Previously a red wine specialist but rapidly proving to be equally skilful with whites. ***** Grange Bin 95 1988 £35 (ADN, MWW, L&W, WR, TH) ***** Bin 707 Cabernet Sauvignon 1990 £15 (TO, TH, U, MWW, BU) ***** Coonawarra Cabernet Sauvignon 1991 £8 (SAF, JS, VW, TH, WR) **** Chardonnay 1993 £7 (TH, MWW, OD, FUL, WR).

le Pergole Torte (Tuscany, Italy) Long-established pure **SANGIOVESE**, oaky **SUPER-TUSCAN**. **** Montevertine 1986 £24 (V&C).

Periquita (Portugal) Spicy, tobaccoey grape – and the wine **J M DA FONSECA** makes. **** Jose Maria da Fonseca Succs 1991 £4 (TO, OD, WR, W, MWW) **** Periquita Reserva, Jose Maria Da Fonseca Succs 1985 £8 (ES)

Perlé/Perlant (France) LIGHTLY SPARKLING.

Perlwein (Germany) SPARKLING WINE

Pernand-Vergelesses (BURGUNDY, France) Commune producing rather jammy reds but fine whites, including some of the best buys on the COTE D'OR 82 83 85 88 89 90 92. **** Pernand-Vergelesses Blanc, Olivier Leflaive 1992 £8 (ADN) *** Pernand 1er Cru Rouge Ile des Vergelesses, Domaine Chandon des Briailles £11 (HR).

Andre Perret (RHONE, France) Producer of notable **CONDRIEU** and decent **ST JOSEPH**. **** Condrieu Coteaux de Chéry 1992 £17 (ADN).

Pesquera (RIBERA DEL DUERO, Spain) US guru Robert Parker dubbed this the **CHATEAU PETRUS** of Spain. Well, maybe. Others might just say that it's a top class **TEMPRANILLO** often equal to **VEGA SICILIA** and the best of **RIOJA**. **** Pesquera Ribera del Duero Tinto, Alejandro Fernandez 1990 £11 (JAR).

Pessac-Léognan (BORDEAUX, France) **GRAVES** Commune containing most of the finest **CHATEAUX** 82 83 85 86 88 89 90. See (& try) **CHATEAU FIEUZAL, DOMAINE DE CHEVALIER, LA LOUVIERE** or **HAUT-BAILLY**.

Petaluma (ADELAIDE HILLS, SOUTH AUSTRALIA) High-tech creation of **BRIAN CROSER**, Australia's top winemaker. Top class **CHARDONNAY**, Clare **RIESLING** and **COONAWARRA CABERNET**. **** Petaluma Coonawarra Red 1990 £10 (OD, AUC, TH, ADN, ROB) **** Petaluma Chardonnay 1992 £10 (OD, ADN, TH, FUL).

Pétillant LIGHTLY SPARKLING.

Petit Chablis (BURGUNDY, France) Less fine than plain **CHABLIS** 85 86 87 88 89 90 91 92. *** Petit Chablis, Etienne Boileau 1992 £6 (WTR, HLV) *** Petit Chablis, Domaine Jean Goulley 1992 £7 (TH, WR, BU,WR, G).

Petit château (BORDEAUX, France) LOOSE TERM FOR MINOR PROPERTY, SUPPOSEDLY BENEATH **CRU BOURGEOIS**.

Petit Verdot (France) Spicy, tannic, hard-to-ripen variety used in minute proportions in red **BORDEAUX** and (rarely) California.

Ch. Petit Village (BORDEAUX, France) Classy, intense blackcurranty-plummy **POMEROL**. Worth keeping 82 85 86 87 89 90. **** 1989 £30 (J&B).

Petite Sirah Red grape, aka **DURIF** in the **MIDI** and grown in California. Nothing to do with the **SYRAH** but can produce very good, spicy red (neat or in blends by good producers like **RIDGE** and **FETZER**). See also **MORRIS** in Australia. **** L. A. Cetto Petite Sirah 1991 £5 (CEL, TAN, CWS, EP, THP).

Petrolly A NOT UNPLEASANT OVERTONE OFTEN FOUND IN MATURE **RIESLING**.

Ch. Pétrus (BORDEAUX, France) Priciest (but best?) of all clarets. Ultra-concentrated voluptuous **JP MOUEIX POMEROL** which hits the target especially well in the USA and Belgium, though sometimes fails to dazzle U.K. critics who seek more complexity 82 83 85 88 89 90. ******** 1988 £100 (C&B, GH).

Pfaffenheim (ALSACE, France) Fast improving **ALSACE** Co-op which is already hitting the big time. ******** Gewürztraminer Grand Reserve Cuvée Bacchus 1992 £6 (ADN), ******** Steinert Riesling 1992 £5 (ADN).

Pfalz (Germany) See **RHEINPFALZ**.

Pfeffingen (RHEINPFALZ, Germany) Good source of impeccably made **RIESLING** and **SCHEUREBE**.

Joseph Phelps (NAPA, California) Innovative winery – one of the first to introduce **RHONE** varieties (**SYRAH** and **VIOGNIER**) and a rare producer of late harvest **RIESLING**. The Insignia and Eisele **CABERNETS** are good, if tough. ********* Cabernet Sauvignon, Backus Vineyard 1991 £17 (LAV, WIN) ******** Insignia 1990 £28 (SK).

Philipponnat (CHAMPAGNE, France) Small producer famous for Clos des Goisses but notable for Vintage and rosé. ********* Grand Blanc 1986 £30 (RAV) ******** Le Reflet Brut £25 (SEL).

Phylloxera Vastatrix DASTARDLY LOUSE THAT WIPED OUT EUROPE'S VINES IN THE 19TH CENTURY. FOILED BY THE PRACTICE OF GRAFTING VINIFERA VINES ON TO RESISTANT AMERICAN ROOTSTOCK. ISOLATED POCKETS OF PRE-PHYLLOXERA AND/OR UNGRAFTED VINES STILL EXIST IN FRANCE (IN A VINEYARD BELONGING TO BOLLINGER AND ON THE SOUTH COAST – THE LOUSE HATES SANDY SOIL), PORTUGAL (IN **QUINTA DA NOVAL'S** 'NACIONAL'), AUSTRALIA AND CHILE. ELSEWHERE, A NEW BREED - 'PHYLLOXERA B' - IS SO DEVASTATING AREAS OF CALIFORNIA THAT **NAPA** VALLEY GROWERS WHO (MOSTLY) PLANTED ON INSUFFICIENTLY RESISTANT ROOTSTOCK WILL HAVE TO REPLANT UP TO 90% OF THEIR VINES. WHICH, THOUGH TRAGIC FOR A GREAT MANY QUALITY-CONSCIOUS PRODUCERS, OUGHT TO TEACH THE OVER-CONFIDENT SCIENTISTS AT THE UNIVERSITY OF CALIFORNIA A LESSON IN HUMILITY. MAYBE NEXT TIME THEY WON'T DISREGARD WARNINGS FROM THE FRENCH.

Piave (VENETO, Italy) **DOC** in **VENETO** region, including reds made from a **BORDEAUX**-like mix of grapes 88 89 90 91 92 93

Ch. Pichon Longueville (BORDEAUX, France) An underperforming Second Growth **PAUILLAC** until 1988. A.k.a. Pichon Baron. Following purchase by the giant AXA insurance company (which now owns **CH SUDUIRAUT, CLOS DE L'ARLOT, CANTENAC BROWN, PETIT VILLAGE** and **QUINTA DA NOVAL**) and the arrival of Jean-Michel Cazes and winemaker Daniel Lioze, it has moved right into the front line, alongside and sometimes ahead of **CHATEAU PICHON-LALANDE**, once the other half of the estate. Wines are intense and complex. **LYNCH BAGES** tastes great – and remains great value – until you see what the same winemaker achieves here with better-sited vines. Les Tourelles, the SECOND LABEL, is often a good value alternative 85 86 88 89 90. ********* 1989 £31 (BI).

Ch Pichon-Lalande (BORDEAUX, France) Famed 'Super Second' still often referred to as Pichon Longueville (Comtesse de) Lalande. A tremendous success story, thanks to the unswerving efforts of its owner, Mme de Lencquesaing, top class winemaking and the immediate appeal of its unusually high **MERLOT** content. Classy, long-lived wine. Are current vintages as great, following the departure of the winemaker? We will see. ********* 1990 £30 (BI).

Piedmont/Piemonte (Italy) Increasingly ancient-and-modern north-western region producing old-fashioned, tough, tannic **BAROLO** and **BARBARESCO** and increasing amounts of brilliant new-style, fruit-packed wines. Also the source of **OLTREPO PAVESE, ASTI SPUMANTE** and **DOLCETTO D'ALBA**. ******** St Michael Chardonnay del Piemonte Vino da Tavola, Giordano 1993 £4 (M&S) ******** Morrisons Asti Spumante, Gianni £5 (MRN) ******* Barolo, Terre del Barolo 1989 £7 (VW, SAF, CWS).

Pieropan (Italy) SOAVE's top producer who more or less invented single vineyard wines here. **** Soave Classico Superiore, Vigneto Calvarino 1992 £8 (L&W) **** Recioto di Soave, Le Colombare 1990 (half) £11 (L&W).

Pierro (MARGARET RIVER, Australia) Small estate with superlative, MEURSAULT-like CHARDONNAY. **** Semillon- Chardonnay 1992 £6.50 (AF).

Piesport (MOSEL-SAAR-RUWER, Germany) With its GROSSLAGE Michelsberg, a region infamous for dull German wine bought by people who think themselves above LIEBFRAUMILCH. Try a single vineyards – Gunterslay or Goldtröpfchen – for something more memorable 85 86 87 88 89 90 91 92. **** Piesporter Goldtröpfchen Riesling Auslese, Reichsgraf von Kesselstatt 1990 £10 (MWW) **** Piesporter Goldtröpfchen Riesling QbA, Grans-Fassian 1992 £6 (OD).

Pikes (SOUTH AUSTRALIA) Top class estate in CLARE with especially good RIESLING and SHIRAZ. and unusually successful SAUVIGNON. A name to follow. **** Pikes Sauvignon Blanc 1992 £7 (JAR).

Pineau de la Loire (LOIRE, France) Local name for the CHENIN BLANC grape.*** Pineau de la Loire, Oisly at Thésée 1993 £5 (WS).

Pinot Blanc / Bianco Never quite as classy or complex as PINOT GRIS or CHARDONNAY, but fresh, creamy and adaptable: a bit like CHARDONNAY without all that fruit flavour. Widely grown, at its best in ALSACE (PINOT D'ALSACE), the ALTO-ADIGE, elsewhere in Italy (as Pinot Bianco) and in Germany and AUSTRIA (as WEISSBURGUNDER). In California, though not universally admitted, a synonym for MELON DE BOURGOGNE. Quite widely planted in Eastern Europe. **** Pinot Blanc, Zind Humbrecht 1992 £7 (LV, TH, ABY)

Pinot Chardonnay Misleading name for CHARDONNAY. Still used by TYRRELLS in Australia.

Pinot Grigio / Gris White grape of uncertain origins, making full, rather heady, spicy wine. Best in ALSACE (also known as TOKAY D'ALSACE), Italy (as Pinot Grigio) and Germany (as Rulander or Grauburgunder). **** Sainsburys Pinot Grigio, Atesino, GIV 1993 £3 (JS) **** Tokay Pinot Gris Reserve Particulière, Kuehn 1992 £7 (LV,EVI).

Pinot Meunier Dark pink-skinned grape that plays an unsung but major role in CHAMPAGNE, where it is the most widely planted variety. Grown in England as the Wrotham Pinot or Dusty Miller. BESTS in VICTORIA produce a Varietal wine from it, as, inevitably, does the wondrous Mr Grahm at BONNY DOON. **** Pinot Meunier, Bonny Doon 1993 £6 (OD).

Pinot Noir Black grape responsible for all of the world's greatest red BURGUNDY and in part for sparkling white CHAMPAGNE. Also grown in the New World with varying success. Getting it right depends largely on finding sites in which the climate is neither too warm (heat gives stewed plum flavours) nor too cold; and winemakers with the patient dedication which might otherwise have destined them for a career in the church or psychiatric nursing. Buying Pinot Noir is always like Russian Roulette, but once you've got a taste for that complex, raspberryish flavour, you'll go on pulling that expensive trigger. See OREGON, CARNEROS, YARRA, SANTA BARBARA, BURGUNDY. ***** Sanford Pinot Noir 1992 £14 (VW, BEN, CAC, BH)

Pinotage Spicy **PINOT NOIR** x **CINSAULT** cross used in **SOUTH AFRICA** and (now very rarely) **NEW ZEALAND**. Good old examples are rare; most taste muddy and rubbery. ****Simonsig Pinotage 1991 £6 (W) **** Kanonkop Pinotage 1991 £5.50 (TO).

Pipers Brook Vineyards (**TASMANIA**, Australia) Dr Andrew Pirie is a top class pioneering producer of **CHARDONNAY**, **PINOT NOIR AND PINOT GRIS** and a great publicist for an island that mainland Aussies like to leave off maps. Tasmania Wine Co, the **SECOND LABEL**, includes an excellent unoaked **CHABLIS**-like **CHARDONNAY**. **** Pinot Noir 1992 £14 (AUC, DBY, ADN, BEN) **** Chardonnay 1992 £13 (AUC, ADN, BEN) **** Tasmanian Wine Company Chardonnay 1992 £8 (JS).

Fernão Pires (Portugal) Muscatty grape, used to great effect by **PETER BRIGHT** of the **JOAO PIRES** winery.

João Pires (Portugal) Winemaker Peter **BRIGHT** shows that it is possible to make distinctive local styles using clean modern technology. Sadly, too few Portuguese producers have followed the example set by such internationally successful wines as **BRIGHT**'s Tinto da Anfora. *** João Pires 1990 £5 (MWW).

Plantagenet (**MOUNT BARKER**, Australia) Good producer of **CHARDONNAY**, **RIESLING**, **CABERNET** and lean **SHIRAZ** in this newish region in the south-west corner of Australia. **** Omrah Vineyard Chardonnay 1993 £7 (GI) **** Shiraz 1990 £8 (GI).

Plovdiv (**BULGARIA**) Region for – so far – unexceptional **MAVRUD**, **CABERNET** and **MERLOT**.*** Cabernet Sauvignon, Vinzavod Assenovgra 1990 £4 (TH).

Podravski (**SLOVENIA**) Source of dread **LJUTOMER RIZLING** and far better **MUSCAT** and **PINOT GRIS**.

Pol Roger (**CHAMPAGNE**, France) One of the most reliable producers, with subtle Non Vintage, spectacular Cuvée Winston Churchill, reliable rosé and an unusually good **DEMI-SEC**. **** 'White Foil' Non-Vintage £19 (TO, OD, WR) **** Rosé 1986 £26 (CWW).

Pomerol (**BORDEAUX**, France) With **ST EMILION**, the **BORDEAUX** for lovers of the **MERLOT** grape, which predominates in its rich, soft, plummy wines. **CHATEAU PETRUS** is the big name but wines like **PETIT VILLAGE** and **CLOS RENE** abound. None is cheap because production here is often limited to a few thousand cases a year (in the **MEDOC**, 20-40,000 is a common figure even among the big names). However, quality is far more consistent than in **ST EMILION** and the flavours far richer, spicier and plummier than all but the best of that larger, more disparate commune. See **PETRUS** and **MOUEIX**. 78 81 82 83 85 86 88 89 90.

Pomino (**TUSCANY**, Italy) A small **DOC** within the **CHIANTI RUFINA** region and virtually a monopoly for **FRESCOBALDI** who make a buttery unwooded white **PINOT BIANCO-CHARDONNAY**, the oaky-rich Il Benefizio and a tasty **SANGIOVESE-CABERNET** red. **** Il Benefizio 1990 £11 (ADN).

Pommard (**BURGUNDY**, France) Variable quality commune, theoretically blessed with a higher proportion of old vines, making slow-to-mature, then solid and complex reds There is a rumoured tradition of using grapes from the less well-sited vineyards on the other side of the *route nationale* 83 85 88 89 90 92. **** 1er Cru, Domaine Parent 1989 £18 (CAC, F&M) **** 1er Cru Rugiens de Courcel 1989 £19 (HR) **** 1er Cru Les Jarollières, Jean Marc Boillot 1991 £21 (GH)

Pommery (**CHAMPAGNE**, France) Returned-to-form big-name with rich, full-flavoured style. The top label, Louise Pommery white and rosé are both tremendous. Prices can be fair in comparison to other **GRAND MARQUES**. ***** Champagne Louise Pommery Vintage Brut 1985 £35 (BI) **** Brut Vintage 1988 £24 (BI) **** Brut Royal £18 (BI).

Ponsot (BURGUNDY, France) Top class estate particularly for CLOS DE LA
ROCHE and (rare) white MOREY ST DENIS. **** Cuvée William Ponsot 1989
£40 (L&W) ***** Latricières-Chambertin 1991 £50 (L&W).

Ch. Pontet-Canet (BORDEAUX, France) Rich, concentrated Fifth Growth
PAUILLAC 82 83 85 86 88 89 90. ****1986 £15 (OD).

Ponzi (OREGON, US) For some, the ideal combination: a producer of good
PINOT NOIR and even better beer. Sadly, only the former can be bought in
the UK. *** Pinot Noir 1991 £13 (WDW).

Port (Portugal) FORTIFIED, USUALLY RED WINE MADE IN THE UPPER DOURO VALLEY.
COMES IN SEVERAL STYLES; SEE TAWNY, RUBY, LBV, VINTAGE, CRUSTED AND
WHITE. SUPERMARKET PORTS, OFTEN LARGE PRODUCERS' PORT UNDER OWN
LABEL, HAVE BEEN IMPROVING ***** Dow's 20 Year Old Tawny Port £21 (GRT,
LAY).

Pouilly Fuissé (BURGUNDY, France) White beloved by the Americans, and so
sold at vastly inflated prices. POUILLY VINZELLES, POUILLY LOCHE and other
MACONNAIS wines are more affordable and often just as good, though top
class POUILLY FUISSE from producers like CHATEAU FUISSE, Dom Noblet, or
Domaine Ferret can compete with the best of the COTE D'OR 85 86 87 88 89
90 92. ***** 'Fûts de Chêne', Domaine des Gerbeaux 1992 £10 (WTR, HLV) ***
Winemark, Paul Boutinot 1992 £7 (WMK).

Pouilly Fumé (LOIRE, France) Potentially ultra-elegant SAUVIGNON BLANC
with classic gooseberry fruit and 'smoky' overtones derived from flint
('SILEX') sub-soil. Like SANCERRE, rarely repays cellaring. Ladoucette is the
big name here, though his widely-available example of the APPELLATION is
unremarkable. If you want to see what he and the appellation can do,
splash out instead on his Baron de 'L' – or buy one of our recommendations
86 87 88 89 90 92. ***** Pur Sang, Didier Dagueneau 1992 £17 (ABY) ****
Domaine Jean Claude Chatelain 1993 £7 (CT, HV, WCE).

Ch Poujeaux (BORDEAUX, France) Sumptuous, up-and-coming plummy-
blackcurranty wine from MOULIS 82 85 86 88 89 90. *** 1989 £10 (FDL).

Pourriture noble (France) BOTRYTIS CINEREA OR NOBLE ROT, THE STUFF WHICH
GIVES GREAT DESSERT WINES THEIR FLAVOUR.

Prädikat (Germany) AS IN QUALITATSWEIN MIT PRADIKAT (QMP), THE HIGHER
QUALITY LEVEL FOR GERMAN WINES INDICATING A GREATER DEGREE OF RIPENESS.

Precipitation THE CREATION OF A HARMLESS DEPOSIT, USUALLY OF TARTRATE
CRYSTALS, IN WHITE WINE WHICH THE GERMANS ROMANTICALLY CALL DIAMONDS.

Premier Cru PRINCIPALLY A BURGUNDY RANKING, INDICATES WINES THAT ARE
BETTER THAN PLAIN VILLAGE LEVEL AND SECOND ONLY TO A GRAND CRU. IN
COMMUNES LIKE MEURSAULT, BEAUNE AND NUITS ST GEORGES WHICH HAVE NO
GRAND CRU, THE TOP PREMIERS CRU (LIKE BEAUNE GREVES AND THEURONS,
VOLNAY SANTENOTS, NUITS ST GEORGES LES ST GEORGES, AND MEURSAULTS
PERRIERES, GENEVRIERES AND CHARMES) CAN BE GOOD ENOUGH TO LEAVE YOU
WONDERING ABOUT THE SYSTEM.

Premières Côtes de Bordeaux (France) Up-and-coming riverside
APPELLATION for reds and (often less interestingly) sweet whites.
**** Château De Berbec, Premières Côtes de Bordeaux Blanc, M Camille Brun
1990 £6 (TDS, SAF) *** Château Lamothe de Haux, Premières Côtes de
Bordeaux Rouge, Fabrice Neel 1990 £7 (CAR, FSW).

Ch. Prieuré-Lichine (BORDEAUX, France) Improving Fourth Growth
MARGAUX with good blackcurrant fruit. The consultant here is the great
Michel Rolland, but cynics still wonder about an estate which can afford a
new helicopter landing pad but which has yet to line some of its concrete
tanks 82 85 86 88 89 90 91. **** 1989 £20 (THP, AV).

Primeur (France) NEW WINE, eg BEAUJOLAIS PRIMEUR.

Primitivo di Mandura (Puglia, Italy) Spicy, plummy red made from the
Primitivo, supposedly another name for the ZINFANDEL. *** Primitivo del
Salento Le Trulle, Centele/Kym Milne 1993 £4 (TO, TH, VW, SAF, OD).

Primo Estate (SOUTH AUSTRALIA) Second generation Italian immigrant Joe Grilli has created an extraordinarily imaginative venture among the fruit farms of the Adelaide Plains. His passionfruity yet dry COLOMBARD may be the best example of this unloved grape in the world, his (tiny production) sparkling SHIRAZ, made with large doses of reserve wine produced by longer-established wineries, is top class, as are the BORDEAUX-style blends he makes as if he were in the VENETO, using grapes partially dried in the sun. We need more Joe Grillis, men and women who cause headaches for the big company bean-counters and official legislators who'd prefer a neat and tidily predictable world. *** Colombard 1993 £6 (AUC) *** Shiraz 1990 £7 (AUC).

Priorato (CATALONIA, Spain) Heftily alcoholic reds and (rare) whites from CARINENA and GARNACHA grapes grown in a very warm region. New wave producers are bringing a touch of class. *** Priorato Negre Scala Dei, Cellers de Scala Dei 1991 £6 (WCE, HAR, WIN).

Producteurs Plaimont (South-West France) Extremely reliable cooperative from the Côtes de St Mont region in Armagnac producing an excellent and affordable range of BORDEAUX-lookalike reds and whites with some use of local grapes. Côtes de Saint Mont rouge, Les Haut de Bergelle 1992 £5.(L&W).

Propriétaire (-Récoltant) (France) VINEYARD OWNER-MANAGER.

Prosecco (VENETO, Italy) Soft, sometimes slightly earthy dry and sweet sparkling wines made from the Prosecco grape and often served from bottles containing the yeast which has made them fizz. Less boisterous than ASTI SPUMANTE and often less fizzy. An interesting taste of the past. **** Prosecco di Coneglione Carpenè Malvoti £8 (WCE).

Côtes de Provence Improving, good value fruity rosés and whites, and ripe spicy reds. And, for some reason, a region with as much appeal to organic winemakers (like the producers of our two recommendations) as to fans of Mr Mayle's rural tales. Go figure. 85 86 87 88 89 90 91. **** Terres Blanches Aurelia, Noel Michelin 1990 £7 (ABY) **** Domaine Richeaume Cabernet Sauvignon 1992 £8 (SAF).

Provence (France) Southern region producing a quantity of honest country wine with a number of minor ACs. Rosé de Provence should be dry and fruity with a hint of peppery spice. **** Château Pibarnon, Bandol 1990 £12 (ABY). **** Mas de Gourgonnier Reserve du Mas 1990 £8 (ADN, SAN, UBC,) *** Tesco's Sparkling Chardonnay, Les Vins Breban £5 (TO).

J J Prüm (MOSEL-SAAR-RUWER, Germany) Top RIESLING producer with fine Wehlener vineyards. **** Wehlener Sonnenuhr Riesling Spätlese Studert 1992 £9 (AV).

S A Prüm (MOSEL-SAAR-RUWER, Germany) Separate MOSEL estate with very respectable wines though none of the class of JJ's best. **** Graacher Himmelreich Riesling Kabinett 1989 £7 (CCL).

Prunotto (PIEDMONT, Italy) Improving, ANTINORI-owned, BAROLO producer. **** Barolo 1990 £7 (V&C) **** Barbera d'Alba, Filot 1993 £6 (L&W).

Puglia (Italy) Hot region which is beginning to make some pretty cool wines thanks partly to the efforts of FLYING WINEMAKERS like Kym Milne. **** Chardonnay del Salento, Centele/Kym Milne 1993 £4 (TO, TH, VW, SAF, OD) **** Squinzano, Mottura £3 (VW) **** Salice Salentino, Candido 1989 £5 (WCE) Le Trulle £5 (VW).

Puisseguin St Emilion (BORDEAUX, France) Satellite of ST EMILION making similar, MERLOT-dominant wines which are often far better value 82 83 85 86 88 89 90. **** Château Durand Laplagne 1989 £7 (ADN).

Puligny-Montrachet Aristocratic white COTE D'OR Commune that shares the MONTRACHET vineyard with CHASSAGNE. At its best, wonderfully complex buttery CHARDONNAY with a touch more elegance than MEURSAULT. 78 79 81 83 85 86 88 89 90 92. ***** Puligny-Montrachet, 1er Cru Les Truffières 1992 £27 (HR) **** Domaine Jean-Marc Boillot 1er Cru 1989 £17(OD) **** Puligny-Montrachet, Maroslavac-Leger 1991 £15 (M&S).

Putto (Italy) As in CHIANTI Putto: wine from a consortium of growers who use the cherub (putto) as their symbol. Taken very seriously in Italy but interestingly, neither Winecellars nor Valvona & Crolla (Britain's two keenest Italophile importers) seem to have found an example worth buying, despite Philip Contini of the latter merchant's steadfast efforts so to do.

Puttonyos (HUNGARY) THE MEASURE OF SWEETNESS (FROM 1 TO 6) OF TOKAY.
***** Tokaji Aszu 6 Puttonyos, Hetszolo 1981 £20 (GRO, RWW) **** Tokaji Aszu 5 Puttonyos, Tokaji Hegyalja 1981 £12 (J&B) **** Tokaji Aszu 6 Puttonyos 1957 £52 (ADN).

PX See PEDRO XIMENEZ

Pyrenees (VICTORIA, Australia) One of the classiest regions in VICTORIA, thanks to the efforts of TALTARNI and DALWHINNIE. **** Taltarni Shiraz 1990 £7 (RD, LAY, TP) **** Dalwhinnie Chardonnay 1992 £13 (WTR).

Pyrénées Orientales (LANGUEDOC-ROUSSILLON, France) Big region including ROUSSILLON and RIVESALTES. Source of increasingly interesting VINS DE PAYS. **** Côtes de Roussillon, Domaine Gauby 1992 £6 (WR).

Pyrus see LINDEMANS

QbA (Germany) QUALITATSWEIN BESTIMMTER ANBAUGEBIET: BASIC QUALITY GERMAN WINE MEETING CERTAIN STANDARDS FROM ONE OF THE 11 ANBAUGEBIET, EG RHEINHESSEN.

QmP (Germany) QUALITATSWEIN MIT PRADIKAT: QbA WINE WITH 'SPECIAL QUALITIES' SUBJECT TO RIGOROUS TESTING. THE QmP BLANKET DESIGNATION IS BROKEN INTO FIVE SWEETNESS RUNGS, FROM KABINETT TO TROCKENBEERENAUSLESEN PLUS EISWEIN.

Quady (CENTRAL VALLEY, California) Quirky producer of 'port' (labelled 'Starboard'), the ORANGE MUSCAT Essencia (one of the only wines to drink with chocolate), BLACK MUSCAT Elysium and an innovative, low alcohol white, Electra. Quady is also notable for being the only quality wine producer in a hot region otherwise devoted to basic JUG WINE.
**** Starboard (Batch 88) 1988 £9 (MWW, WRW, VW) **** Elysium 1993 £6. (VW, JS, MWW, BBR, THP) **** Essencia 1992 £6 (MWW, GNW, CPW, HAR, THP).

Qualitätswein (Germany) LOOSE 'QUALITY' DEFINITION TO COVER QbA AND QmP WINES, WHOSE LABELS WILL CARRY MORE INFORMATIVE IDENTIFICATION OF THEIR EXACT STATUS.

Quarts de Chaume (LOIRE, France) Luscious but light sweet wines, uncloying, ageing beautifully, from the COTEAUX DU LAYON 76 83 85 88 89 90 92. **** Château de L'Écharderie 1989 £17 (YAP).

Queensland (Australia) The Granite Belt produces HUNTER VALLEY-style SHIRAZ and SEMILLON from (relatively) cool vineyards. Not exported.

Côtes de Quenelle (South-West France) Suzanne Brochet and Colin Morue, respectively of the Dom Lotte and Château Hareng-Rouge, are the sole producers of this little-known APPELLATION perched above the river Merlan. Using such rare varieties as the Ouallope-du-Codde, Anguille and Truiteau-Xamandes, they make a lovely salmon-pink rosé, most of which is sold over the bar of the local cafe, the Poisson d'Avril. Look out for their top cuvée, 'Carpé-Diem'.**** Raie du Soleil 1969 £38 (EEL).

Quincy (LOIRE, France) Dry SAUVIGNON, lesser-known and often good-value alternative to SANCERRE or POUILLY FUME 89 90 92. **** Quincy, Denis Jaumier 1993 £7 (YAP).

Quinta (Portugal) VINEYARD OR ESTATE, PARTICULARLY IN THE DOURO WHERE 'SINGLE QUINTA' VINTAGE PORTS ARE INCREASINGLY BEING TAKEN AS SERIOUSLY AS THE BLENDS TRADITIONALLY SOLD BY THE BIGGER PRODUCERS. FOR A COMPARATIVE TASTING OF SINGLE-QUINTA PORTS, LAY & WHEELER OFFER A RANGE OF HALF A DOZEN. ***** Quinta de Eira Velha, Single Quinta Vintage Port 1987 £16 (HC) ***** Quinta da Agua Alta, Churchill 1990 £14 (L&W).

Quinta da Bacalhôa (Portugal) the innovative CABERNET made by Peter BRIGHT at JOAO PIRES.

Quinta da Camarate (Portugal) Attractive CABERNET SAUVIGNON-based red from JM DA FONSECA.

Quinta do Côtto (DOURO, Portugal) Small estate producing so-so PORT and flavoursome table reds. ** Grande Escolha 1990 £11 (ADN).

Quinta de la Rosa (DOURO, Portugal) Recently established PORT estate producing (under guidance from David Baverstock, Australian-born former winemaker at DOWS) a dazzling berryish, unfortified red. Quinta de la Rosa, Douro 1992 £5 (HAM, SAN, POR, M&V) *** Quinta de la Rosa Port, Douro 1988 £12 (M&V, HC, OLS).

Quinta do Noval (DOURO, Portugal) Fine and potentially finer PORT estate recently bought by AXA, the insurance company which owns CH PICHON BARON, The ultra-rare and highly-praised/prized Nacional vintage ports are the jewel, made from ungrafted vines. **** Quinta Do Noval Colheita 1976 (half) £10 (F&M, SEL, SB) **** Quinta do Noval Port 1982 £20 (VW, SEL, TH, THP, F&M).

Quintarelli (VENETO, Italy) Wonderful old fashioned RECIOTO-maker producing some of the quirkiest, most sublime (and unfortunately most expensive) VALPOLICELLA. ***** Recioto 1985 £30 (V&C) **** Valpolicella Classico Superiore Monte Ca Paletta 'Ripasso' 1988 £10 (ADN)

Qupé (CENTRAL COAST, California) Run by Bob Lundqvist (with Jim Clendenen, one of the founders of AU BON CLIMAT) this SANTA BARBARA winery is one of the places to find truly brilliant New World SYRAH. **** Syrah 1992 £10 (M&V).

Racking THE DRAWING OFF OF WINE FROM ITS LEES INTO A CLEAN CASK OR VAT

Olga Raffault (LOIRE, France) There are several Raffaults in CHINON; Olga's is the best estate – and it follows, the best source of some of the richest, ripest examples of this often underrated APPELLATION. **** Chinon Rouge 1989 £7.95 (WSO).

Raïmat (CATALONIA, Spain) Sometime superstar innovative winery founded by fizz giant CODORNIU in the newly recognised COSTERS DEL SEGRE region, and notable for being unusual in being allowed to use the irrigation, without which it would be impossible to grow grapes in this parched region. Now recovering from a period at the end of the 1980s when it sold very inconsistent wines. MERLOT, a CABERNET-MERLOT blend called Abadia and TEMPRANILLO are interesting and CHARDONNAY – both still and sparkling – has been good. *** Tempranillo 1990 £6 (BVL) *** Merlot 1990 £6 (VW).

Rainwater (MADEIRA) LIGHT, DRY STYLE OF MADEIRA POPULAR IN THE US.

Ramitello (Molise, Italy) An intensely spicy-fruity red and a creamy, citric white produced by di Majo Norante in Biferno on the Adriatic coast.

Dom Ramonet (BURGUNDY, France) This CHASSAGNE-MONTRACHET grower's cellar is a Mecca for white BURGUNDY lovers the world over who queue to buy wines like the Bienvenue-Bâtard-Montrachet. Pure class; worth waiting for too. ***** Chassagne Montrachet 1992 £16 (OD).

Ramos Pinto (DOURO, Portugal) Family-run winery recently taken over by ROEDERER CHAMPAGNE. Vintage-dated COLHEITA tawnies are a speciality, but the Vintage can be good too. **** Quinta da Urtiga Vintage Character £8.50 (L&W).

Rancio TERM FOR THE PECULIAR YET PRIZED OXIDISED FLAVOUR OF CERTAIN FORTIFIED WINES, PARTICULARLY IN FRANCE (eg BANYULS) AND SPAIN. **** Banyuls Tradition, Domaine de Baillaury 1985 £9 (RD).

Rapitalà (SICILY, Italy) Estate producing a fresh, peary white wine from a blend of local grapes. **** Rapitalà Gran-Cru Alcano, Tenuta di Rapitalà £10 (CC).

Rasteau (RHONE, France) Southern COTES DU RHONE village producing sound, peppery reds with rich berry fruit. The fortified MUSCAT can be good too 86 88 89 90 91. **** Côtes du Rhône Villages, Château du Trignon 1989 £5.50 (WL).

Ch. Rausan Segla (BORDEAUX, France) For a long time an under-performing MARGAUX 2nd Growth, this property was brought back to life in 1983 when Jacques Théo took over, rejected half the crop and made one of the best Margaux of that vintage. The commitment and investment, not to mention the advice of the great Prof Emile Peynaud have continued to pay off - despite the financial problems suffered by Brent Walker, for a while Rausan Segla's ultimate owner. The 1990 is full of blackberry fruit and oak; one of the best buys in BORDEAUX. 82 83 85 86 88 89 90. *** 1990 £18 (OD).

Raventos i Blanc (CATALONIA, Spain) Josep Raventos's ambition is to produce the best fizz in Spain, adding a small dose of CHARDONNAY to the traditional varieties of the region.

Ch de Rayne-Vigneau Sauternes estate, located at BOMMES, producing a rich, complex wine 76 86 90. **** 1970 £23 (TP).

RD (CHAMPAGNE, FRANCE) RÉCEMMENT DÉGORGÉE — A TERM INVENTED BY BOLLINGER TO DESCRIBE THEIR DELICIOUS VINTAGE CHAMPAGNE, WHICH HAS BEEN ALLOWED A LONGER THAN USUAL PERIOD ON ITS LEES. OTHER PRODUCERS MAKE THEIR OWN VERSIONS BUT MAY NOT CALL THEM 'RD'. Bollinger 1982 RD £45 (widely available).

Recioto (Italy) SWEET OR DRY ALCOHOLIC WINE MADE FROM SEMI-DRIED, RIPE GRAPES. MOST USUALLY ASSOCIATED WITH VALPOLICELLA AND SOAVE. **** Amarone Recioto Classico della Valpolicella, Allegrini 1985 £17.19 (WCE) *** Recioto Della Valpolicella, Flli Tedeschi 1988 £5.99 (MWW).

Récoltant-manipulant (RM) (CHAMPAGNE, FRANCE) INDIVIDUAL WINEGROWER AND BLENDER, IDENTIFIED BY MANDATORY RM NUMBER ON LABEL.

Récolte (France) VINTAGE, LITERALLY 'HARVEST'.

Refosco (FRIULI-VENEZIA GIULIA, Italy) Red grape and its DOC wine, dry and full-bodied, benefits from ageing. **** Refosco Giovanni 91, Collavini £6 (V&C, LAV).

Regaleali (SICILY, Italy) Big aristocratic estate, using traditional local varieties to produce Sicily's most serious wines **** Conte Tasca D'Almerita 1993 £6 (V&C).

Régisseur IN BORDEAUX, THE MANAGER OF A CHATEAU AND ITS WINE PRODUCTION.

Régnié (BURGUNDY, France) Recently created tenth BEAUJOLAIS CRU - and a vinous exemplar of the Peter Principal which suggests that employees tend to be promoted beyond their level of competence. The wines of Regnié were perfectly respectable BEAUJOLAIS VILLAGES, now they have to compete with CHIROUBLES, CHENAS and the other Crus, they're generally like decent amateur sportsmen who suddenly have to play with the pros. Fortunately for Regnié, those pros aren't on great form 88 89 9192 **** Regnié, Domaine des Buyats, Marc Dudet 1992 £5.99 (C&B).

Reguengos (ALENTEJO, Portugal) One of the most important wine regions of ALENTEJO, just south of Redondo, next to the Spanish border. *** Adega Co-op de Reguengos de Monsaraz 1991 £4 (D&F).

Reichensteiner Recently developed white grape popular in England (and Wales). *** East Sutton Vine Garden, Reichensteiner 1992 £4.95 (BGV, ESG).

Reims (CHAMPAGNE, France) Capital town of the area and HQ of many GRANDES MARQUES, eg KRUG, ROEDERER.

Schloss Reinhartshausen (RHEINGAU, Germany) An innovative estate which has proven unusually successful with PINOT BLANC and CHARDONNAY (the latter having been introduced following a suggestion by ROBERT MONDAVI). The RIESLINGS are good too. **** Hattenheimer Hassel Riesling Kabinett 1989 £8 (JN).

Rémélluri (RIOJA, Spain) For most modernists, this is the nearest RIOJA has to a top class, small-scale estate. Wines are more serious (& tannic) than most, but they're fuller of flavour too and they're built to last. Telmo Rodriguez is a young winemaker to watch and should be cloned for the benefit of the rest of the Spanish wine industry. ✶✶✶✶ Reserva 1989 £9 (ADN).

Remuage (CHAMPAGNE, France) PART OF THE METHODE CHAMPENOISE, THE GRADUAL TURNING AND TILTING OF BOTTLES SO THAT THE YEAST DEPOSIT COLLECTS IN THE NECK READY FOR DEGORGEMENT.

Reserva (Spain) INDICATES THE WINE HAS BEEN AGED FOR A NUMBER OF YEARS SPECIFIED BY THE RELEVANT DO.

Réserve (France) LEGALLY MEANINGLESS, AS IN 'RESERVE PERSONELLE', BUT IMPLYING A WINE SELECTED AND GIVEN MORE AGE.

Residual sugar TASTING TERM FOR WINES WHICH HAVE RETAINED NATURAL GRAPE SUGAR NOT CONVERTED TO ALCOHOL BY YEASTS DURING FERMENTATION. IN FRANCE, ANYTHING BEYOND 4 GRAMMES PER LITRE IS RECKONED TO BE SWEET. IN THE US, THE FIGURE IS 5 AND MANY SO-CALLED 'DRY' WHITE WINES MADE THERE CONTAIN AS MUCH AS 10. NEW ZEALAND SAUVIGNONS ARE RARELY BONE DRY, BUT THE ACIDITY IS EVIDENT ENOUGH TO DISGUISE ANY RESIDUAL SUGAR, I.E. THEY ARE NOT DISCERNABLY SWEET.

Balthasar Ress (RHEINGAU, Germany) Classy producer who blends delicacy with concentration and understands that dry wines need to be made from ripe grapes. Other CHARTA winemakers please copy. ✶✶✶✶ Johannisberger Erntebringer Riesling Kabinett 1992 £7.69 (WDW).

Retsina (Greece) Dry white wine made the way the ancient Greeks used to – resinating it with pine to keep it from going off. Today, it's an acquired taste for non-holidaying non-Greeks, but, if you can suppress the association with pine-fresh cleansing products, give the stuff a chance by finding the freshest examples you can (yes, I know it's not easy when there's no vintage indicated, but do try all the same). ✶✶✶ Retsina of Attica, D Kourtakis £3 (MRN, VW, W, TH, OD).

Reuilly (LOIRE, France) (Mostly) white AC for dry SAUVIGNONS, good-value alternatives to nearby SANCERRE. Some spicy PINOT rosé 89 90 91 92 93. ✶✶✶ Reuilly, Gérard Cordier 1993 £6.95 (YAP).

Rheingau (Germany) Should produce the finest RIESLINGS of the 11 ANBAUGEBIETE, but has sadly been hijacked by producers who prefer quantity to quality and the CHARTA campaign for dry wine. There are still great things to be found, however 83 85 88 89 90 91 92 93. ✶✶✶✶✶ Kiedricher Wasseros Riesling Eiswein, Robert Weil 1992 £70 (BAR) ✶✶✶✶ Niersteiner Rehbach Riesling Auslese 1989 £10 (OWL).

Rheinhessen (Germany) Largest of the 11 ANBAUGEBIETE, producing fine wines but better known in Britain for huge amounts of uninspiring LIEBFRAUMILCH and NIERSTEINER. Fewer than one vine in 20 is now RIESLING; throughout the region, easier-to-grow varieties and lazy cooperative wineries prevail 83 85 88 89 90 91 92 93 ✶✶✶✶ Niersteiner Gütes Domtal Kabinett, St. Ursula 1993 £4 (OD) ✶✶ Liebfraumilch St Dominicus, Weinkellerei GmbH 1993 £2.79 (BKW).

Rheinpfalz/Pfalz (Gemany) Formerly known as the PALATINATE, warm, southerly ANBAUGEBIET noted for riper, spicier RIESLING 83 85 88 89 90 91 92 93. ✶✶✶ Co-op Spätlese Pfalz, GWG Rietburg 1990 £3.49 (CWS).

Rhine Riesling/Rheinriesling Widely used – though frowned-on by the EC — name for the noble RIESLING grape. ✶✶✶✶ Rothbury Estate Rhine Riesling 1993 £5.50 (LAV).

Rhône (France) Up-and-coming region, packed with the newly sexy GRENACHE, SYRAH and VIOGNIER. See ST JOSEPH, CROZES HERMITAGE, HERMITAGE, CONDRIEU, COTES DU RHONE, CHATEAUNEUF-DU-PAPE, TAVEL, LIRAC, GIGONDAS, CHATEAU-GRILLET, BEAUMES DE VENISE.

Rias Baixas (Galicia, Spain) The place to find Spain's best examples of spicy, apricotty ALBERINO. Drink young 90 91 92. ✶✶✶✶ Lagar de Cervera 1992 £7.50 (WTR).

Ribatejo (Portugal) **DO** area north of Lisbon whose cooperatives have recently begun to discover the art of making highly commercial white and red wine. Traditional **GARRAFEIRAS** are worth watching out for too, however 85 86 87 88 89 90 **** Bright Brothers Chardonnay, Peter Bright 1993 £3.65 (JS) **** 'Beira Mar' Garrafeira Reserva, Antonio Bernadino 1980 £5.99 (U).

Ribera del Duero (Spain) Watch out **RIOJA**; here's a region which will give you a major headache over the next few years. Traditionally known as the source of wines such as **VEGA SICILIA** and, more recently, **PESQUERA,** this is increasingly inventive country in which small estates are beginning to flourish using the **TEMPRANILLO** and **BORDEAUX** varieties Look out also for **BALBAS**, Pedrosa and Mauro, a high quality red **VINO DE LA TIERRA** produced just outside this **DO** 82 83 85 86 89 90.   ***** Pago de Carraovejas 1992 £6 (BWC, LEA, PTR) *** Tinto Callejo Ribera del Duero Crianza, Bodegas Felix Callejo 1989 £7.40 (WSO).

Domaine Richeaume (**PROVENCE**, France) One of the leading lights in the new wave of quality conscious Southern French estates, and a dynamic producer of good, earthy, organic **CABERNET** and **SYRAH**. Sadly, as with many smaller organic wineries, quality can be distinctly variable from bottle.to bottle. Recommendable, nonetheless. *** Domaine Richeaume Syrah 1992 £7 (SAF).

Richebourg (**BURGUNDY**, France) Top class red **GRAND CRU** just outside **VOSNE ROMANEE** with an extraordinary floral-spicy-plummy style. **GROS** and **JAYER** reliably offer first class examples, as do the following: **** Domaine Hudelot-Noellat 1992 £55 (HR) **** Domaine Romanée-Conti 1990 £100 (C&B).

Max Ferd Richter (**MOSEL-SAAR-RUWER**, Germany) An excellent producer of fine, elegant **MOSEL RIESLINGS** sourced from extremely high quality vineyards. **** Brauneberger Juffer-Sonnenuhr Riesling Spätlese, Max-Ferd Richter 1990 £10 (SUM) *** Cuvée Constantin, Max Ferd Richter 1992 £5 (MWW).

Ridge Vineyards (**SANTA CRUZ**, California) The longest-established, most consistent, and generally best winery in California, thanks to Paul Draper's skill at making reds using **CABERNET, MATARO, ZINFANDEL** and **PETITE SIRAH** which age elegantly but are deliciously drinkable young. These wines are to those of **DOMINUS** and **DUCKHORN** what Mozart is to Stockhausen. In recent years, his **CHARDONNAY**, though underrated, has become a stunner. Perhaps most importantly, Draper, and Ridge's hilltop **SANTA CRUZ** vineyards are living proof that, despite the hype, the **NAPA** Valley does not even begin to have a monopoly on top-quality California wine-making. ***** Geyserville 1992 £15.75 (OD, HAR, F&M, ADN) ***** Santa Cruz Mountains Cabernet 1991 £15.50 (ADN) ***** Santa Cruz Mountains Chardonnay 1991 £17.20 (OD, LEA, MWW, BEN).

Riesling The hard-to-grow, noble and woefully misunderstood grape variety which produces most of the finest wines in Germany and **ALSACE** and some brilliant traditional offerings in Australia. Sadly, in Britain, the word has become synonymous with cheap Germanic fare, little of which has even shared a winery with a Riesling grape. Styles range from light, floral everyday wines to the delights of the **BOTRYTIS**-affected sweet wines, which still retain their freshness after several years. Also performs well in California, **SOUTH AFRICA** and Australia.
***** Stellenzicht Weisser Riesling Noble Late Harvest 1992 £3.99 (VW) **** Rothbury Estate Rhine Riesling 1993 £5.50 (LAV) **** Riesling Gueberschwihr, Zind Humbrecht 1990 £8.44 (ABY)

Riesling Italico See **ITALIAN RIESLING**.

Rioja (Alavesa/Alta/Baja, Spain) Spain's best-known (though not necessarily finest) wine region, split into three parts. The Alta produces the best wines, followed by the Alavesa while the Baja is by far the largest. Most Riojas are blends from two or three of the regions – and of local grapes (TEMPRANILLO and the lesser quality GARNACHA for reds) and are made by large BODEGAS. BORDEAUX and BURGUNDY-style estates are rare, though REMELLURI, CONTINO and BARON DE LEY show what could be done. Sadly though, apart from the great MARTINEZ BUJANDA and the innovative new-wave unoaked wines like Albor, this once top region stands at risk of being eclipsed by the greater dynamism and quality-consciousness evident in neighbouring NAVARRA and in RIBERA DEL DUERO 81 82 85 86 87 88 89.

Dom. Daniel Rion (BURGUNDY, France) Patrice Rion, head of this family-run estate, produces impeccably made NUITS ST GEORGES and VOSNE ROMANEES. **** Bourgogne Rouge Bons Batons 1992 £7.50 (M&V, SAN) ***** Vosne Romanée Premier Cru Les Beaux-Monts 1989 £24 (M&V).

Ripasso (Italy) VALPOLICELLA WHICH, HAVING FINISHED ITS FERMENTATION, IS PUMPED INTO FERMENTING VESSELS RECENTLY VACATED BY RECIOTO AND AMARONE, CAUSING A SLIGHT REFERMENTATION. THIS INCREASES THE ALCOHOL AND BODY OF THE WINE. **** Capitel San Rocco Rosso, Vino di Ripasso, Flli Tedeschi 1990 £7 (LAV, WIN).

Riquewihr (ALSACE, France) Town and commune noted for RIESLING. **** Riesling d'Alsace, Marcel Deiss £9 (BD) **** Hugel, Riesling, Cuvée des Evêques 1989 £7 (J&B).

Riserva (Italy) DOC WINES AGED FOR A SPECIFIED NUMBER OF YEARS – OFTEN AN UNWELCOME TERM ON LABELS OF WINES LIKE BARDOLINO WHICH ARE USUALLY BEST DRUNK YOUNG. **** Parrina Rosso Riserva, La Parrina 1990 £6.99 (WCE).

Rivaner aka the MULLER-THURGAU grape with reference to its RIESLING/SYLVANER parents. *** St. Ursula Rivaner Scheurebe, Hugh Ryman 1993 £3.50 (SAF).

Riverina (NEW SOUTH WALES, Australia) Irrigated NEW SOUTH WALES region which produces basic-to-good wine, much of which ends up in 'SOUTH-EAST AUSTRALIAN' blends. Late harvest SEMILLONS can, however, be spectacular. *** Australian Dry White, Riverina £2.95 (SAF, BWC, TDS).

Riverland (Australia) GENERIC NAME FOR IRRIGATED WINEGROWING REGIONS. *** Kingston Reserve Riverland Chardonnay 1991 £10 (TO).

Rivesaltes (MIDI, France) Fortified dessert wine of both colours; the white made from MUSCAT is lighter and more lemony than that of BEAUMES DE VENISE, the red, made from GRENACHE is almost like liquid Christmas pudding and ages wonderfully. Domaine Cazes is the name to look for. **** Domaine Cazes Rivesaltes Vieux 1980 £12.45 (BWS) **** Domaine Brial Muscat de Rivesaltes, Vignerons de Baixas 1993 £3.49 (SAF)

Château de la Rivière (BORDEAUX, France) Picture-book FRONSAC property producing instantly accessible, MERLOT-dominant red wines. They aren't the classiest of fare, but they give a lot more pleasure than many a duller ST EMILION or more 'serious' (and pricier) wine from the MEDOC 82 85 86 88 89 90. *** 1990 £8 (THP).

Robertson (SOUTH AFRICA) Up-and-coming area where the Cape's new wave of CHARDONNAYS and SAUVIGNONS are grabbing the spotlight from the MUSCATS previously the region's pride. **** Danie de Wet Grey Label 1993 £4.99 (JS) **** Weltevrede Chardonnay 1992 £8 (NY, LWE).

Rocca delle Macie (TUSCANY, Italy) Reliable if unspectacular CHIANTI producer. *** Chianti Classico 1991 £6 (LV).

Rockford (SOUTH AUSTRALIA, Australia) Robert 'Rocky' O'Calaghan makes great, intense BAROSSA SHIRAZ using 100-year-old vines and 50-year-old equipment. There's a mouthfilling SEMILLON, a fruity RIESLING, a wonderful Black SHIRAZ fizz and a magical ALICANTE BOUSCHET rosé, sadly only to be found at the winery. ***** Rockford Basket Press Shiraz 1990 £9.95 (ADN).

Louis Roederer (CHAMPAGNE, France/MENDOCINO, California) Family-owned, and still one of the most reliable CHAMPAGNE houses. No longer involved with the Jansz sparkling wine in TASMANIA but making good fizz at the Roederer Estate in MENDOCINO, California. **** Brut Première N.V. £20 (TH) **** 'Cristal' Brut 1986 £61 (OD).

Domaine de la Romanée-Conti (BURGUNDY, France) Small, exclusively GRAND CRU estate, familiarly known as the DRC by BURGUNDY buffs and others who can afford to buy some of the world's priciest red wines. The jewel in the crown is the MONOPOLE Romanée-Conti vineyard itself, though the LA TACHE runs it a close second. Both can be extraordinary, ultra-concentrated spicy wine beyond compare, as can the Romanée-St-Vivant. The RICHEBOURG, ECHEZEAUX and GRANDS ECHEZEAUX and MONTRACHET are comparable to those produced by other estates – and sold for less kingly ransoms. **** Romanée-Conti DRC 1990 £400 (C&B).

Romania Traditional source of sweet reds and whites, but trying to develop drier styles from classic European varieties. FLYING WINEMAKERS are moving in, but progress is still quite slow. *** Safeway Romanian Special Reserve Pinot Noir 1989 £3 (SAF) *** Merlot, Prahova SA 1987 £3.50 (MRN).

Rongopai (Te Kauwhata, NEW ZEALAND) Estate in a region of the North Island which has fallen out of favour with other producers. The speciality here is BOTRYTIS wines, but the dry SAUVIGNONs are good too. **** Sauvignon Blanc 1993 £7 (CCL)

Ch. Roquefort (BORDEAUX, France) Good value, modern white BORDEAUX, produced in small quantities. *** 1990 £5 (OD).

Rosato (Italy) ROSE.

Rosé de Riceys (CHAMPAGNE, France) Rare and occasionally delicious still rosé from the PINOT NOIR made only in the ripest years by adding whole bunches to a small amount (10%) of trodden grapes and then subjecting it to MACERATION CARBONIQUE. Pricy stuff. **** Bonnet 1992 £13 (FDL).

Rosé d'Anjou (LOIRE, France) Widely exported, usually dull semi-sweet pink from the MALBEC, GROSLOT and CABERNET FRANC.

Rosemount Estate (NEW SOUTH WALES, Australia) The ultra-dynamic company which, 20 years ago, both established the northern Upper HUNTER VALLEY (previously disdained by winemakers in the Lower Hunter) and introduced the outside world to plentiful doses of oaky Hunter CHARDONNAY, including the benchmark Show Reserve. Since then, there have arrived a showpiece Roxburgh Chardonnay and reliably good value blends of grapes from other regions. Not the Rolls Royce of Aussie wines; more the BMW. **** Cabernet Sauvignon/Shiraz 1993 £5 (JS) ***** Show Reserve Syrah 1991 £9 (WR, BU) *** Chardonnay 1993 £5 (SAF).

Rossignol-Trapet (BURGUNDY, France) Once old-fashioned, now recommendable, more up-to-the-minute estate in GEVREY-CHAMBERTIN. **** Chapelle-Chambertin 1991 £23 (OD).

Rosso Conero (MARCHES, Italy) Big DOC MONTEPULCIANO and SANGIOVESE red, with a hint of bitter, herby flavour. Good value characterful stuff. **** Rosso Conero, Umani Ronchi 1992 £4 (W, WL, V&C).

Rosso di Montalcino (TUSCANY, Italy) Recently created DO for lighter, earlier-drinking versions of the more famous BRUNELLO DI MONTALCINO, and often better – and better value – than that wine. Good producers include Altesino, Caparzo and Fattoria dei Barbi. **** Rosso di Montalcino La Caduta, Tenuta Caparzo 1991 £8 (ROB) **** Rosso di Montalcino, Col d'Orcia 1991 £5.75 (LU).

Rosso di Montepulciano (TUSCANY, Italy) Younger, lighter version of VINO NOBILE DI MONTEPULCIANO. Well made SANGIOVESE from producers like Poliziano, AVIGNONESI, Boscarelli and Tenuta Trerose. **** Le Casalte 1992 £5 (WCE).

Rene Rostaing (RHONE, France) High quality producer of serious Northern RHONE reds. *** Côte Rôtie 1991 £17 (L&W).

Rothbury Estate (NEW SOUTH WALES, Australia) Founded by Len Evans, *éminence grise*, coach, Svengali, or what you will, of the Australian wine industry, this is an exemplary source of SHIRAZ, SEMILLON and improving CHARDONNAY from the HUNTER VALLEY as well as wines from nearby COWRA and even a little SAUVIGNON from NEW ZEALAND. ***** Shiraz 1993 £6 (L&W) **** Rhine Riesling 1993 £5.50 (LAV).

Alfred Rothschild (CHAMPAGNE, France) Brand name used (exclusively) in France by MARNE & CHAMPAGNE and nothing to do with the family of the same name. Despite low prices, wines can be surprisingly good.

Joseph Roty (BURGUNDY, France) Superstar producer of intensely concentrated but unsubtle GEVREY-CHAMBERTIN.**** Gevrey-Chambertin Les Fontenys 1988 £25 (TVW).

Rouge Homme (SOUTH AUSTRALIA) Founded by the evidently linguistically talented Mr Redman, this PENFOLDS subsidiary is one of the most reliable producers in COONAWARRA. Reds are more successful than whites. ***** Shiraz/Cabernet 1991 £5 (FUL) **** Chardonnay 1992 £7 (AV).

Georges Roumier (BURGUNDY, France) Blue chip winery with great quality at every level, from village CHAMBOLLE-MUSIGNY to the GRAND CRU, BONNES MARES and (more rarely seen) white CORTON CHARLEMAGNE **** Chambolle-Musigny 1992 £13 (HR) **** Bonnes Mares Grand Cru 1991 £33 (HR).

Roussanne (RHONE, France) With the Marsanne, one of the key white grapes of the northern Rhone. Producers argue over their relative merits. *** St Péray, Marcel Juge 1992 £10 (WTR) **** Crozes Hermitage Blanc, Cave de Tain l'Hermitage 1991 £5.80 (BP).

Armand Rousseau (BURGUNDY, France) Long-established GEVREY CHAMBERTIN estate with a range of PREMIERS and GRANDS CRUS. Well-made, long-lasting wines. **** Gevrey-Chambertin, Clos St Jacques 1987 £25 (GH) **** Chambertin Clos de Bèze 1986 £30 (OWL).***** Charmes Chambertin 1988 £27 (OD) ****Clos de la Roche 1990 £25 (WTR).

Côtes du Roussillon (MIDI, France) Up and coming for red, white and rosé, though not always worthy of its AC. Côtes du Roussillon Villages is usually better fare without greater outlay 85 86 88 89 90 91. **** Château de Belesta, Les Vignerons Catalans 1992 £3.49 (SAF) *** Domaine Gauby 1990 £8.49 (THP).

Rubesco di Torgiano (UMBRIA, Italy) Well made modern red DOCG; more or less the exclusive creation of LUNGAROTTI 82 83 85 86 87 88 89 90 91. *** Lungarotti 1990 £7 (V&C).

Ruby CHEAPEST, BASIC PORT; YOUNG, BLENDED, SWEETLY FRUITY WINE. *** Safeway Fine Ruby Port, Calem £5.50 (SAF).

Ruby Cabernet (California) A cross between CABERNET SAUVIGNON and CARIGNAN producing big, unsubtly fruity wines. ** Ruby Cabernet, The California Wine Company 1992 £3.50 (W).

Rudesheim (RHEINGAU, Germany) Tourist town producing, at their best, rich and powerful RIESLINGS *** Rudesheimer Kirchenpfad Riesling Spätlese, Josef Leitz 1992 £11.50 (LWE).

Rueda (Spain) DO for clean dry pinks, whites made from the local VERDEJO and a traditional, FLOR-growing, sherry-style wine. Progress is being led by the LURTONS and MARQUES DE RISCAL 82 83 84 85 86. *** Lurton Rueda Sauvignon 1993 £4 (OD, JS, VW, CWS) *** Rueda Rosado 1993 £4 (VW).

Rufina (TUSCANY, Italy) Subregion of the CHIANTI DOCG.

Rully (BURGUNDY, France) COTE CHALONNAISE commune producing a red which has been called the 'poor man's VOLNAY'. The white used to end up as CREMANT DE BOURGOGNE but today, merchants like JADOT and OLIVIER LEFLAIVE use it to great effect. **** Château de Rully, Rodet 1990 £9 (JS) *** Rully Rouge, Les Villeranges, Faiveley 1992 £8 (MWW).

Ruppertsberg (RHEINPFALZ, Germany) Top-ranking village with a number of excellent vineyards making vigorous, fruity RIESLING 83 85 88 89 90 91 92 93. *** Hoheburg Riesling Kabinett Winzerverein 1990 £5 (WSO).

Russe (BULGARIA) Danube town best known in Britain for its reliable red blends but vaunted – in BULGARIA - as a place to go looking for modern whites. *** Sainsbury's Bulgarian Country Red Russe, Cabernet Sauvignon and Cinsault (1.5l) £5.35 (JS).

Russian Continuous SYSTEM USED BY JM DA FONSECA INTERNACIONAL WHICH INVOLVES PUMPING STILL WINE, YEAST AND SYRUP THROUGH A SERIES OF TANKS SLOWLY ENOUGH FOR THE YEAST BOTH TO CREATE BUBBLES IN THE WINE AND TO SETTLE ON WOODEN RACKS, ALLOWING THE LIQUID WHICH EMERGES FROM THE FINAL TANK TO BE PERFECTLY CLEAR AND FIZZY. AN APPARENTLY ELEGANT ALTERNATIVE TO CUVE CLOSE BUT NOT ONE BY WHICH MOST OTHER FIZZ-MAKERS HAVE BEEN CONVINCED.

Russian River Valley (California) Cool vineyard area north of SONOMA and west of NAPA. Ideal for apples and good fizz, as is proven by the excellent Iron Horse who also make increasingly impressive table wines. **** Iron Horse Sonoma Brut 1986 £16 (CEB) **** Geyser Peak Chardonnay, Geyserville 1992 £9 (WIN).

Rust (AUSTRIA) Wine centre of BURGENLAND, famous for Ruster AUSBRUCH, sweet white wine. *** Ruster Beerenauslese, Weinkellerei Burgenland 1981 £6 (half) (SEL).

Rust-en-Vrede (SOUTH AFRICA) One of the Cape's most successful red wine producers and one of the very few to make recommendable SHIRAZ. **** Rust-en-Vrede Estate Wine 1989 £13 (L&W).

Rustenberg (STELLENBOSCH, SOUTH AFRICA) Once a star producer of PINOT NOIR (by South African standards) this old estate is now best known for its CLARET-style 'Gold', its straight CABERNET and richly Burgundian CHARDONNAY. **** Rustenberg Cabernet Sauvignon 1991 £8 (AV) **** Rustenberg Gold 1990 £10 (AV).

Rutherglen (North East VICTORIA, Australia) Hot area on the MURRAY RIVER pioneered by gold miners. Today noted for rich MUSCAT and TOKAY dessert and port-style wines, incredibly tough reds and attempts at CHARDONNAY which are used by cool-region winemakers to demonstrate why port and light dry whites cannot be successful in the same climate. ***** Campbells Bobbie Burns Shiraz 1992 £7 (PHI, CPW, GNW) **** Mick Morris Cabernet Sauvignon 1989 £9 (WTR, DBW) ***** Yalumba Museum Show Reserve Rutherglen Muscat £7 (TH, BEN, TO, VW, SOM).

Ruwer (MOSEL-SAAR-RUWER, Germany) Tributary of the MOSEL river which includes Kasel, Eitelsbach and the great MAXIMIN GRUNHAUS estate and the the Romerlay GROSSLAGE.

Hugh Ryman (The world) Peripatetic FLYING WINEMAKER whose team annually and extraordinarily reliably turn grapes into wine under contract (usually for UK retailers) in BORDEAUX, BURGUNDY, Southern France, Spain, Germany, CHILE, California and HUNGARY. Further Eastern European and South American destinations are already in the pipeline. The give-away sign of a Ryman wine is the initials HDR at the foot of the label.

Saar (MOSEL-SAAR-RUWER, Germany) The other tributary of the MOSEL river associated with lean, slatey RIESLING. Villages include Ayl Ockfen, Saarburg, Serrig and WILTINGEN 83 84 85 86 88 89 90 91 92. *** Von Hövel, Oberemmel Huette Riesling 1991 £7 (OWL).

Sablet (RHONE, France) Good COTES DU RHONE village. **** Sablet La Ramillade, Château du Trignon 1991 £6 (TH, WR, BU).

St Amour (BURGUNDY, France) One of the 10 BEAUJOLAIS CRUS – usually light and delicately fruity 83 85 88 89 91 92. *** Loron 1991 £7.19 (AV).

St Aubin (BURGUNDY, France) Underrated COTE D'OR village for (jammily rustic) reds and rich, nutty white; affordable alternatives to MEURSAULT 85 86 88 89 90 92. **** St Aubin 1er Cru, 'La Chatenière', Olivier Leflaive 1992 £10 (JAR).

St Chinian (South-West France) Neighbour of FAUGERES and a fellow AC in the COTEAUX DU LANGUEDOC so far producing mid-weight, good-value wines principally using the CARIGNAN. Greater things may come of the RHONE grapes now being planted here 88 89 90 91 93. *** St. Chinian, Jean d'Almon, RMDI 1992 £3 (SMF) *** Berloup Prestige St Chinian, Co-op de Berloup 1992 £4 (TH, WR, BU).

St Emilion (BORDEAUX, France) Large commune with very varied soils and wines. At best, sublime MERLOT-dominated CLARET; at worst dull, earthy and fruitless. Supposedly 'lesser' satellite neighbours – LUSSAC, Puisseguin, ST GEORGES etc – often make better value wine. See PAVIE, AUSONE, CANON, FIGEAC, CHEVAL BLANC 81 82 83 85 86 88 89 90.

St Estèphe (BORDEAUX, France) Northernmost MEDOC Commune with clay soil and wines which are often a shade more rustic than those of neighbouring PAUILLAC and ST JULIEN. Tough when young but potentially very long-lived. See CALON SEGUR, COS D'ESTOURNEL, MONTROSE 82 83 85 86 88 89 90.

St Georges St Emilion (BORDEAUX, France) Satellite of ST EMILION with good, MERLOT-dominant reds 82 83 85 86 88 89 90. **** Ch Macquin-St-Georges (ADN).

St Hallet (SOUTH AUSTRALIA) Superstar BAROSSA winery whose name has been made on its century-old vines. Rich, spicily intense SHIRAZ. Big, buttery CHARDONNAY. ***** Old Block Shiraz 1991 £10 (WR, L&W, TO, F&M, RD) **** Cabernet Sauvignon/Cabernet Franc/Merlot 1992 £7 (JS, AUC, RD) **** Chardonnay 1993 £7.50 (WR, AUC, RD).

St Hubert's (VICTORIA, Australia) Improving (since its purchase by ROTHBURY) pioneering YARRA winery with ultra-fruity CABERNET and mouthfilling CHARDONNAY. **** Cabernet Sauvignon 1992 £10 (LAV).

Chateau St Jean (SONOMA, California) Named after the founder's wife, this now Japanese-owned showpiece has long been a source of good single-vineyard CHARDONNAYs and late-harvest RIESLINGs. ***Chardonnay 1990 £17 (WWT).

St Joseph (RHONE, France) Variable but potentially vigorous, fruity SYRAH from the northern RHONE. Whites are more variable still, ranging from flabby to fabulously fragrant MARSANNES. Look for wines from GRIPPAT and TROLLOT 85 86 88 89 90 91. ***** Clos de L'Arbalestrier, Dr. Florentin 1988 £12 (ADN) *** A. Ogier et Fils 1990 £7 (LAV, WIN, MWW).

St Julien (BORDEAUX, France) Aristocratic MEDOC Commune producing classic rich wines, full of cedar and deep, ripe fruit. See LEOVILLE BARTON, LEOVILLE LASCASES, DUCRU-BEAUCAILLOU, BEYCHEVELLE. 82 83 85 86 88 89 90

St Nicolas de Bourgueil (LOIRE, France) Lightly fruity CABERNET FRANC, needs a warm year to ripen its raspberry fruit. Good producers include Jamet, Mabileau and Vallée 85 86 87 88 89 90 92. **** Clos de la Contrie, Claude Ammeux 1993 £7 (YAP).

St Péray (RHONE, France) AC near Lyon for full-bodied, still white and METHODE CHAMPENOISE sparkling wine, at risk from encroaching housing development. Often dull; never cheap 88 89 90 91. *** St Péray nature £8.25 (YAP).

Ch. St Pierre (BORDEAUX, France) Reliable ST. JULIEN fourth growth under the same ownership as GLORIA. *** 1989 £17 (ADN).

St-Pourçain-sur-Sioule (LOIRE, France) Red and rosé from GAMAY and PINOT NOIR, and the white from a blend of SAUVIGNON, CHARDONNAY and the local Trésallier. *** Saint Pourçain sur Sioule 1992 £5 (YAP).

St Romain (BURGUNDY, France) High in the hills of the HAUTES COTES DE BEAUNE, a village producing undervalued fine whites and rustic reds 83 85 87 88 89 90 92. *** St Romain Clos Sous Le Château, Jean Germain 1991 £11 (D).

St-Véran (BURGUNDY, France) Once sold as BEAUJOLAIS BLANC; affordable alternative to POUILLY FUISSE, often as good – and better than most MACONNAIS whites 90 91 92 93. *** Domaine de la Batie, Georges Duboeuf 1993 £6 (BWC, AV) *** Domaine de Roche 1993 £9 (BWS).

Ch. Sainte Michelle (WASHINGTON STATE, US) Big winery producing reliable MERLOT, RIESLING AND SAUVIGNON. **** Chardonnay 1989 £10 (TAN).

Sakar (BULGARIA) Long-time source of much of the best CABERNET SAUVIGNON from BULGARIA 86 88 89 90 *** Sakar Mountain Cabernet 1986 £3 (WOW)

Sainte Croix-du-Mont (BORDEAUX, France) Neighbour of SAUTERNES with comparable though less fine wines 83 85 86 87 88 89 90. **** Château des Tours 1990 £8 (ADN).

Saintsbury (California, US) Superstar CARNEROS producer of CHARDONNAY and - more specially – PINOT NOIR. (hence the slogan: 'BEAUNE in the USA'). The Reserve Pinot is a world-beater. Garnet is the good value SECOND LABEL. **** Carneros Reserve Chardonnay 1991 £14 (ADN, BI, J&B, GEL, HHC, WSO) ***** Pinot Noir Reserve 1991 £20 (BI, HHC, ADN, GEL, J&B).

Salice Salentino (PUGLIA, Italy) Spicily intense red made from the Negroamaro. Great value when mature. **** Candido 1989 £5 (WCE).

Salon le Mesnil (CHAMPAGNE France) Small traditional subsidiary of LAURENT PERRIER with cult following for its pure, long-lived CHARDONNAY fizz from LE MESNIL, one of the region's best white grape villages. ***** 1982 £62 (C&B).

> **Samling 88** (AUSTRIA) Unromantic Austrian name for SCHEUREBE. Great for late harvest. ***** Beerenauslese, Kracher 1987 £15 (half) (NY)

Samos (Greece) Aegean island producing sweet, fragrant, golden MUSCAT once called 'the wine of the Gods'. *** Nectar, 10 year old Muscat, Vins Côtes de Samos £5 (WCE).

San Luis Obispo (California, US) Californian region gaining a reputation for CHARDONNAY and PINOT NOIR. *** Wild Horse Pinot Noir 1990 £8 (OD).

San Pedro (CHILE) Well-established CURICO winery whose wines have often fallen short of the standards of their competitors. The arrival of Jacques LURTON in 1994 as consultant-winemaker is expected to improve matters. *** Cabernet Sauvignon 1992 £3.39 (SAF), *** Gato Negro Cabernet Sauvignon 1992 £3.49 (MRN).

Sancerre (LOIRE, France) Much exploited AC, but at its best the epitome of elegant, steely dry SAUVIGNON. Quaffable, overpriced pale reds and rosés from the PINOT NOIR Good producers include, Jean-Max Roger, Bourgeois, Pierre Dézat, Crochet, VACHERON, Natter and Vatan. 89 90 91 92 93. ****Sancerre Rosé 'Les Romains', Domaine Vacheron £9 (ADB) ***Sancerre Les Roches, Jean Louis Vacheron 1993 £9 (ADB, MWW, ABV, U, JAV).

Sanford Winery (Southern California) SANTA BARBARA superstar producer of CHARDONNAY and, especially, distinctive, slightly horseradishy PINOT . NOIR. ***** Pinot Noir 1992 £14.50 (VW, BEN, CAC, BH) **** Barrel Select Chardonnay 1991 £11 (LAV, WIN) **** Pinot Noir 1992 £14.50 (VW, BEN, CAC BH).

> **Sangiovese** The tobaccoey- herby-flavoured red grape of CHIANTI and MONTEPULCIANO, (and, under various names, all over Italy) is now being used increasingly in VINO DA TAVOLA and in CALIFORNIA where it is seen as a lucrative alternative to CABERNET SAUVIGNON. See ANTINORI, ISOLE E OLENA, BONNY DOON. **** Atlas Peak Reserve Napa Sangiovese 1992 £13.58 (LAV, WIN) *** Riva Sangiovese Di Romagna, Ronco/Gaetana Carron 1993 £2.79 (OD, CEL, SAF, A).

Sanlúcar de Barrameda (Spain) Coastal town neighbouring JEREZ, and the centre of production for MANZANILLA sherry.

Santa Barbara (California) Increasingly succesful cool-climate region to the north of Los Angeles which is making a name for itself, particularly with PINOT NOIR and CHARDONNAY. It is no accident that ROBERT MONDAVI and KENDALL JACKSON have invested here, but so far, the greatest excitement has come from SANFORD and from the wild boys at AU BON CLIMAT, QUPE and OJAI

Santa Cruz Mountains (California) Region to the south of San Francisco in which RIDGE and BONNY DOON produce some of the most exciting wines in California. ***** Ridge Santa Cruz Mountains Cabernet 1991 £15.50 (ADN).

Santa Helena (CHILE) Improving SECOND LABEL of SAN PEDRO. *** Seleccion del Directorio 1991 £6 (THP).

Santa Maddalena (ALTO-ADIGE, Italy) Eccentric high-altitude region whose often lederhosen-clad winemakers use grapes including the local Schiava to make refreshingly tangy red wine. *** Viticoltori 1992 £6 (V&C).

Santa Rita (MAIPO, CHILE) Once the only big success story in CHILE; now overtaken by some of its competitors, including, ironically, CALITERRA and SANTA CAROLINA, two wineries at which Ignacio Requabaren, Santa Rita's former winemaker, now holds sway. **** Medalla Real Chardonnay 1993 £7 (JS, MAR, BI, CWW) *** Merlot Reserva 1992 £5 (BI, MAR, ABY) *** Reserva Cabernet Sauvignon 1989 £5 (SMF).

Santenay (BURGUNDY, France) Village situated at the southern tip of the COTE D'OR, producing pretty whites and good, though occasionally rather rustic reds 83 85 87 88 89 90 92. ***** Santenay Rouge Clos de la Confrérie, Vincent Girardin 1992 £12.50 (TAN, HW).

Caves São João (Portugal) Small company which produces high quality BAIRRADA.

Sardinia (Italy) Traditionally the source of good, hearty, powerful reds, robust whites and a number of interesting DOC fortified wines including **** Marchese di Villamarina, Sella & Mosca 1989 £17 (LU) *** Carignano del Sulcis, C S Santadi 1991 £5 (WCE).

Sassicaia (TUSCANY, Italy) World-class CABERNET-blend SUPER-TUSCAN. ***** Sassicaia, Incisa Della Rochetta 1990 £40 (TH, RBS, HAR, F&M, V&C).

Saumur (LOIRE, France) White and rosé METHODE CHAMPENOISE sparklers mostly from the CHENIN BLANC. Often dull enough to compete with CAVA. Langlois-Château and BOUVET-LADUBAY make reliably clean and appley versions. Reds and pinks made from CABERNET FRANC can be pleasantly light. *** Saumur, Vignerons de Saumur, £6.50 (CWS) *** Tesco Cabernet de Saumur 1993 £3.50 (TO) *** Saumur Blanc, Domaine Langlois-Château 1993 £6 (MWW).

Saumur Champigny (LOIRE, France) Crisp, refreshing CABERNET FRANC red; like BEAUJOLAIS, serve slightly chilled 85 86 88 89 90 92. **** La Grande Vignolle 1992 Filliatreau, £7.25 (YAP).

Sauternes (BORDEAUX, France) Rich, honeyed dessert wines from SAUVIGNON and SEMILLON (and possibly MUSCADELLE) blends. Should be affected by BOTRYTIS but the climate does not always allow this. That's one explanation for disappointing Sauternes; the other: poor winemaking. See BARSAC, YQUEM, RIEUSSEC, CLIMENS, SUDUIRAUT 80 83 85 86 88 89 90.

Sauvignon Blanc White variety grown the world over, but rarely really loved: people find its innate 'grassy', 'catty', 'asparagussy', 'gooseberryish' character too much to handle. In France it has moved beyond its heartland of the LOIRE and BORDEAUX, and proven successful for SKALLI and HUGH RYMAN in VIN DE PAYS D'OC. NEW ZEALAND gets it tremendously right – especially in MARLBOROUGH, though the French hate the tropical fruit style it achieves there. In Australia, despite feeble early efforts by others, producers like KNAPPSTEIN, CULLEN, STAFFORD RIDGE and SHAW & SMITH are also right on target. California has been a relative disaster, as wineries have either banged the Sauvignon on the head with oak (as in the MONDAVI FUME BLANC) or made it sweet (as in KENDALL JACKSON). Ironically, E&J GALLO used to make a better version than most (theirs is sweet too now) and the flag is only being flown by wineries like MONTEVINA, Quivira, SIMI, MATANZAS CREEK, Adler Fels and Dry Creek and – in SEMILLON blends – Guenoc and CARMENET. CHILE is making better versions every year, despite starting out with Sauvignon vines which proved to be a lesser variety.

Sauvignon de St Bris (BURGUNDY, France) Burgundy's only VDQS, an affordable alternative to SANCERRE from the CHABLIS region 89 90 91 92. *** Domaine des Remparts, A Sorin 1992 £6 (TAN).

Etienne Sauzet (BURGUNDY, France) Absolutely first rank white wine estate whose wines are almost unfindable outside collectors' cellars and the kind of Michelin-starred restaurants whose wine-loving guests take as much notice of prices as British royalty does of the cost of dogfood. ***** Puligny-Montrachet £20 (BI).

Savagnin (France) White JURA variety used for VIN JAUNE and blended with CHARDONNAY for ARBOIS. Also, confusingly, the Swiss name for the GEWÜRZTRAMINER. *** Château Chalon 1979 £35 (WSO).

Savennières (LOIRE, France) Fine, rarely seen, vigorous and characterful CHENIN BLANC whites which are very long-lived. Coulée de Serrant and La Roche aux Moines are the top names in this small AC 82 83 84 85 86 88 89 90 92. *** La Roche aux Moines 1990 £12 (YAP) **** Coulée de Serrant 1990 £28 (YAP).

Savigny-lès-Beaune (BURGUNDY, France) Rarely seen whites and delicious plummy/raspberry reds. When at their best they can compare with the wines of neighbouring BEAUNE 83 85 87 88 89 90 92. *** Drouhin 1990 £12 (OD).

Savoie (Eastern France) Mountainous region best known for crisp, floral whites such as Abymes, APREMONT, SEYSSEL and Crépy. *** Abymes Cuvée Prestige 1993 £5 (EP) *** La Taconnière Seyssel 1992 £6.50 (WSO).

Scharffenberger (MENDOCINO, California) POMMERY-owned, independently-run producer of top class fizz. **** Scharffenberger Brut £9 (A).

Scharzhofberg (MOSEL-SAAR-RUWER, Germany) Top-class SAAR vineyard, producing quintessential RIESLING. **** Scharzhofberger Riesling Kabinett von Hövel 1989 £7 (TH, WR).

Schaumwein (Germany) LOW-PRICED SPARKLING WINE.

Scheurebe White RIESLING x SYLVANER cross, grown in Germany and in England, where it imparts a grapefruity tang. Far more interesting than its cousin, the Müller Thurgau. *** Scheurebe Dienheimer Tafelstein Kabinett, Bruder Dr. Becker 1993 £5 (SAF) ***** Haardter Mandelring Scheurebe Kabinett, Müller Catoir 1991 £9 (WMK).

Schilfwein (Austria) LUSCIOUS 'REED WINE' — AUSTRIAN VIN DE PAILLE PIONEERED BY WILLI OPITZ. ***** Weisser Schilfmandl, Schilfwein Vin Paille, Willi Opitz 1992 £31 (T&W)

Schloss (Germany) LITERALLY 'CASTLE', OFTEN (AS IN CHATEAU) DESIGNATING A VINEYARD OR ESTATE.

Schlossböckelheim (NAHE, Germany) Village which gives its name to a large NAHE BEREICH, and produces elegant, balanced RIESLING. Best vineyard: Kupfergrube. **** Schlossböckelheimer Kupfergrube Riesling Kabinett 1989 £10 (WSC).

Schloss Saarstein (MOSEL-SAAR-RUWER, Germany) High quality RIESLING specialist in Serrig. **** Riesling 1991 £7 (BI).

Schlumberger (ALSACE, France) Great estate owner whose wines can rival those of the somewhat more showy ZIND HUMBRECHT. ***** Gewürztraminer Grand Cru Kessler, Domaines Schlumberger 1989 £14.70 (JN).

Scholl & Hillebrand (RHEINGAU, Germany) Reliable merchant belonging to Bernhard Breuer who markets his estate wines under the Georg Breuer label. A sensible CHARTA producer.

Scholz Hermanos (MALAGA, Spain) Pretty well the only serious producer of MALAGA still in operation. Top class wines. ***** Malaga Solera 1885 £8.50 (W,SEL,WSO, L&W, DBY) **** Malaga, Moscatel Palido £8 (WDW, CNL, L&S).

Schramsberg (NAPA, California) Winery responsible for putting Californian sparkling wine back on the quality trail, reviving classic grape varieties and techniques culled from France. Until recently, wines tended to be over-ripe and too big for their boots, possibly because too many of the grapes were from warm vineyards in NAPA. The recently launched J Schram is aimed at DOM PERIGNON and gets pretty close. *** J Schram 1988 £29 (F&M).

Sciacarello (CORSICA, French) Red grape variety, making smooth, aromatic, RHONE-style wine 88 89 90 91.

Seaview (SOUTH AUSTRALIA) In the UK, a sparkling wine brand belonging to PENFOLDS; in Australia a name to follow for well made reds. Generally excellent value for money. **** Seaview Pinot Noir-Chardonnay Penfolds 1990/91 £7.50 (OD).

Sebastiani (SONOMA, California) Despite the SONOMA address, the main activity here lies in producing inexpensive, unexceptional wine from CENTRAL VALLEY grapes. The ZINFANDEL is the strongest suit. ** Chardonnay £4.50 (A, MRN, TO, D) ** Somerfield Californian Dry Red £3.50 (SMF) *** Zinfandel 1988 £5.50 (SMF).

Sec/secco/seco (France/Italy/Spain) DRY.

Second Label (BORDEAUX, FRANCE) WINE MADE FROM A BORDEAUX CHATEAU'S LESSER VINEYARDS AND/OR YOUNGER VINES AND/OR LESSER CUVEES OF WINE. ESPECIALLY WORTH BUYING IN GOOD VINTAGES. See LES FORTS DE LATOUR.

Seifried Estate (South Island, NEW ZEALAND) Sold as Seifried Estate in NZ, the export label is REDWOOD VALLEY ESTATE. Hermann Seifried makes superb RIESLING especially LATE HARVEST style, and creditable SAUVIGNON and CHARDONNAY. With NEUDORF, demonstrates the potential of NELSON as one of New Zealand's best regions. **** Redwood Valley Estate Late Harvest Rhein Riesling 1991 (half) £8 (C&B).

Sekt (Germany) Very basic sparkling wine best won in rifle booths at carnivals. Watch out for anything that does not state that it is made from RIESLING – other grape varieties almost invariably make highly unpleasant wines. Only the prefix 'Deutscher' guarantees German origin. *** Deutscher Sekt Privat £7 (WSC).

Selaks (AUCKLAND, NEW ZEALAND) A large (by NEW ZEALAND standards) and successful company based in Kumeu near AUCKLAND, best known for the excellent, piercingly fruity SAUVIGNON which was first made a decade ago by a young Aussie-trained Brit called Kevin Judd who went on to produce a little-known wine called CLOUDY BAY. **** Marlborough Sauvignon Blanc 1993 £8 (THP).

Selbach-Oster (MOSEL-SAAR-RUWER, Germany) Archetypal MOSEL RIESLING *** Zeltinger Sonnenuhr Riesling Spätlese 1991 £10 (L&W).

Séléction de Grains Nobles (ALSACE, France) EQUIVALENT TO GERMAN BEERENAUSLESEN: RICH, SWEET BOTRYTISED WINE FROM SELECTED GRAPES. **** Tokay Grand Cru Rotenburg Selection de Grain Nobles, Zind Humbrecht 1991 £50 (ABY)

Selvapiana (TUSCANY, Italy) Estate with 35 ha of vines in the CHIANTI RUFINA which has gradually been modernised. A benchmark CHIANTI, an excellent VIN SANTO, and a terrific olive oil. **** Chianti Rufina 1991 £7 (L&W).

Sémillon Peachy grape blended with SAUVIGNON in BORDEAUX to give fullness in both dry and sweet wines, notably SAUTERNES and, vinified separately, to great effect, in Australia, though rarely as successful in other New World countries where many versions taste more like SAUVIGNON. See ROTHBURY, MCWILLIAMS, MOSS WOOD, CARMENET and GEYSER PEAK **** Cranswick Estate Botrytis Semillon 1993 £7 (GAR) ***** Tim Adams Semillon 1993 £8 (AUC, OD) **** Penfolds South Australian Semillon-Chardonnay 1993 £5 (TO, U, OD, TH, MWW).

Ch. Sénéjac (BORDEAUX, France) Agreeable modern MEDOCS made – until 1994 – by young NEW ZEALAND-born Jenny Dobson. More notable still is the excellent Blanc de Sénéjac dry white – one of the very few to be made in the MEDOC 82 85 86 88 89 90 91. *** 1991 £8 (BBR).

Seppelt (SOUTH AUSTRALIA) Old Australian firm now under the control of PENFOLDS. Pioneers of the GREAT WESTERN region of VICTORIA where they have made huge quantities of generally excellent sparkling wine including the CHAMPAGNE-like Sallinger. Other specialities include wonderful sparkling SHIRAZ (look for old 'Show Reserve' bottlings) and the rich Drumborg bubble-free version. **** Seppelt Show Sparkling Shiraz 1985 £12.49 (OD) **** Seppelt Salinger, Seppelt 1990 £10.50 (TO, OD, BU, TH, WR).

> **Sercial** Grape used for MADEIRA, making the driest and some say the finest wines. **** Henriques & Henriques, 10 Year Old Sercial Sec Madeira £15 (HAR).

Servir frais (France) SERVE CHILLED.

Setúbal (Portugal) Source of MOSCATEL DE SETUBAL, most notably the one made by J M DA FONSECA , but now equally notable for the rise of two new wine regions, Arrabida and Palmela, where J M FONSECA and J P VINHOS are making some excellent new wave wines from local and international grape types.. **** Moscatel de Setúbal, Co-op 1981 £5.20 (CEB) *** João Pires, J P Vinhos SA 1993 £4 (SAF).

Sèvre et Maine (MUSCADET de) (LOIRE, France) Demarcated area supposedly producing a cut above plain MUSCADET. (Note that this 'higher quality' region produces the vast majority of each MUSCADET harvest.) *** Muscadet de Sèvre et Maine sur Lie 'Première', Domaine Jean Douillard 1992 £5.45 (JS).

Seyssel (SAVOIE, France) AC region near Geneva producing light white wines that are usually enjoyed on the spot and in *après-ski* mood when no one is overly concerned about value for money. *** La Taconnière 1992 £6.50 (WSO).

> **Seyval blanc** Hybrid grape, a cross between French VINIFERA and US LABRUSCA vines. Unpopular with EC authorities but successful in eastern US and England, especially at BREAKY BOTTOM.

Shaw & Smith (ADELAIDE HILLS, Australia) Recently founded winery producing one of Australia's best SAUVIGNONs and an increasingly Burgundian CHARDONNAY. **** Shaw & Smith Sauvignon Blanc 1993 £8 (OD, WCE) ***** Shaw & Smith Reserve Chardonnay 1992 £10 (OD, WCE).

Sherry (Spain) The fortified wine made around JEREZ. Similar-style wines made elsewhere should not use this name. See LUSTAU, GONZALEZ BYASS, HIDALGO, BARBADILLO, ALMECENISTA, FINO, ALMONTILLADO, MANZANILLA, CREAM SHERRY and SOLERA.

> **Shiraz** Taking its name from the Iranian town where it is presumably no longer grown for wine, this is pseudonym for the SYRAH grape in Australia and SOUTH AFRICA. See WOLF BLASS, PENFOLDS, ROTHBURY, ST HALLETT, ROCKFORD, PLANTAGENET etc.

Sicily (Italy) Best known for MARSALA, but produces a variety of unusual fortified wines, also much sturdy 'southern' table wine. See CORVO, DE BARTOLI, REGALEALI. **** Morsi Di Luce, Moscato De Pantelleria, Florio 1990 £12.50 (JN, V&C, BWS, TAN).

Siglo (RIOJA, Spain) Good brand of modern red and old-fashioned whites. **** Siglo Rioja Reserva 1985 £5.79 (A&A CTL, MHC, MCC).

Silex (France) TERM DESCRIBING FLINTY SOIL, USED BY DIDIER DAGUENEAU FOR HIS OAK-FERMENTED POUILLY FUME. ***** Pouilly Fumé Silex, Didier Dagueneau 1992 £23.50 (ABY).

Silver Oaks Cellars (NAPA, California) Specialist CABERNET producers favouring fruitily accessible wines which benefit from long ageing in (American oak) barrels and bottle before release. **** Alexander Valley Cabernet Sauvignon 1989 £18 (T&W) **** Napa Valley Cabernet Sauvignon 1989 £20 (T&W).

Simi Winery (SONOMA, California) MOET & CHANDON subsidiary whose (ex MONDAVI) boss Zelma Long is deservedly respected for her complex, long-lived Burgundian CHARDONNAY, archetypical SAUVIGNON and lovely blackcurranty ALEXANDER VALLEY CABERNET. In a properly ordered world, Simi would be one of the best-known wineries in California. **** Sauvignon Blanc 1991 £8.50 (L&W).

Bert Simon (MOSEL-SAAR-RUWER, Germany) Newish Estate in the SAAR river valley with super-soft RIESLINGS and elegant WEISSBURGUNDER. **** Serringer Herrenberg Riesling Spätlese 1985 £6 (VW).

Simon Whitlam (HUNTER VALLEY, Australia) One of ARROWFIELD's labels, used for their top of the range wines. Classy CHARDONNAYS. **** Show Reserve Chardonnay 1993 £8 (TLC).

Sin crianza (Spain) NOT AGED IN WOOD. **** Navajas Rioja Sin Crianza 1992 £4 (WL, WCE)).

Skin contact THE LONGER THE SKINS ARE LEFT IN WITH THE JUICE AFTER THE GRAPES HAVE BEEN CRUSHED, THE GREATER THE TANNINS AND THE DEEPER THE COLOUR. SOME WHITE VARIETIES (CHARDONNAY AND SEMILLON IN PARTICULAR) TOO CAN BENEFIT FROM EXTENDED SKIN CONTACT (USUALLY BETWEEN SIX AND TWENTY-FOUR HOURS) WHICH INCREASES FLAVOUR EXTRACTION AND HELPS REDUCE MUST ACIDITY.

Slovakia Up-and-coming source of wines made from grapes little seen elsewhere such as the Muscatty IRSAY OLIVER.*** Irsay Oliver 1992 £3.50 (VW).

Soave (VENETO, Italy) For the most part, dull white wine; Soave CLASSICO is better; single vineyard versions are best. Sweet RECIOTO di Soave is delicious. PIEROPAN and ANSELMI are almost uniformly excellent 86 87 88 89 90 91. *** Rocca Suena, Amarone Recioto Della Valpolicella, Produttori Associati Soave 1986 £8.50 (U) *** Montegrande Soave Classico, Pasqua 1993 £3.55 (SMF).

Ch. Sociando-Mallet (BORDEAUX, France) A CRU BOURGEOIS which consistently produces carefully oaked, fruity red wines way above its status. 82 85 88 89 90 91. **** 1989 £15 (J&B).

Sogrape (Portugal) Big producer of Mateus Rosé and (relatively) modern DAO, DOURO and BAIRRADA. **** Vinha do Monte, Sogrape 1991 £5.29 (GI, NI) *** Bairrada Branco, Quinta de Pedralvites, Sogrape 1993 £5 (OD, GI) *** Co-op Dão, Sogrape 1990 £3 (CWS).

Solaia (TUSCANY, Italy) Piero ANTINORI family has been instrumental in creating the SUPER TUSCAN phenomenon. The blackcurranty, herby, well-oaked Solaia, a blend of CABERNET SAUVIGNON and FRANC, with a little SANGIOVESE, is acknowledged to be one of the world's truly great reds..***** Vino de Tavola, Antinori 1988 £47 (L&W).

Solera AGEING SYSTEM WHICH INVOLVES A SERIES OF BUTTS CONTAINING WINE OF ASCENDING AGE, THE OLDER WINE BEING CONTINUALLY 'REFRESHED' BY THE YOUNGER.***** Malaga Solera 1885, Scholtz Hermanos S.A. £8.49 (W, SEL, WSO, L&W, DBY) ***** Pedro Ximenez Solera Superior, Valdespino £9.75 (LEA).

Felix Solís (VALDEPENAS, Spain) By far the biggest winery in VALDEPENAS, the most go-ahead, and, at the top of the range, perhaps also the best. *** Safeway Oak Aged Valdepeñas 1987 £4 (SAF) ***

Somlo (HUNGARY) Ancient wine district, now source of top-class whites. See FURMINT.

Somontano (Spain) DO Region in the foothills of the Pyrenées near Aragon now experimenting with international grape varieties. *** Señorio de Lazan Reserva, Bodega Cooperativa Comarcal 1988 £6 (BOD).

Sonoma Valley (California) Despite the NAPA hype, this lesser known region not only contains some of the state's top wineries; it is also home to E&J GALLO's super-premium vineyard. The region is subdivided into the SONOMA, ALEXANDER and RUSSIAN RIVER Valleys and Dry Creek. Visibly very different to the NAPA – like the GRAVES and ST EMILION this is a very easy place in which to get lost, looking for wineries like SIMI, CLOS DU BOIS, IRON HORSE, MATANZAS CREEK, SONOMA-CUTRER, JORDAN, LAUREL GLEN, KISTLER, DUXOUP, Ravenswood, KENWOOD, QUIVIRA, Dry Creek, GUNDLACH BUNDSCHU, Adler Fels, ARROWOOD and CARMENET. ***** Clos du Bois Chardonnay, Calcaire Vineyard 1992 £15.75 (LAV, WIN) **** Quivira Sauvignon Blanc Dry Creek Valley 1991 £7 (ADN).

Sonoma-Cutrer (SONOMA, California) Single-vineyard CHARDONNAY producer of the highest order. The Les Pierres Vineyard frequently turns out wines that rank among the best in the world. ***** Les Pierres Vineyard Chardonnay 1990 £18 (AV) **** Russian River Ranches Chardonnay 1991 £12 (AV).

Marc Sorrel (RHONE, France) Long-established DOMAINE with two good red HERMITAGES (Le Gréal is the top cuvée) and an attractively floral white, **** Hermitage Blanc "Les Rocoules" 1990 £18 (ADN).

South Africa Oldest winemaking country in the New World (300 years), and increasingly the focus of interest today as it emerges from a period when a repressive government-sponsored organisation often stopped winegrowers from developing new styles. First class simple dry CHENINS and surprisingly good PINOTAGES; otherwise still very patchy in quality. **** Simonsig Pinotage 1991 £5.50 (W) *** Chenin Blanc, Klippenkop 1993 £4 (LEF).

South Australia Home of almost all the biggest wine companies and still producing over 50% of Australia's wine. The BAROSSA VALLEY is one of the country's oldest wine producing regions, but it increasingly faces competition from cooler areas like the ADELAIDE HILLS, PADTHAWAY and COONAWARRA.

South East Australia A relatively meaningless regional description increasingly to be found on labels of (usually) lower price wines. Technically, it comprises NEW SOUTH WALES, VICTORIA and SOUTH AUSTRALIA and only omits TASMANIA and WESTERN AUSTRALIA.

Spanna (Italy) The Piedmontese name for the NEBBIOLO grape and the more humble wines made from it. *** Spanna del Piemonte, Agostino Brugo & Co. 1991 £3 (OD).

Spätlese (Germany) SECOND STEP IN THE QMP SCALE, LATE-HARVESTED GRAPES MAKING WINE A NOTCH DRIER THAN AUSLESE.

Spritz/ig SLIGHT SPARKLE OR FIZZ. ALSO PETILLANCE.

Spumante (Italy) SPARKLING.

Staatsweingut (Germany) A State wine estate or domaine e.g. Staatsweingut ELTVILLE (RHEINGAU), a major cellar in the town of ELTVILLE.

Stafford Ridge (ADELAIDE HILLS, Australia) Fine CHARDONNAY and especially SAUVIGNON from LENSWOOD by the former chief winemaker of HARDYS. **** Lenswood Chardonnay 1991 £8 (AUC).

Stag's Leap District (NAPA, California) A long-established district of the NAPA Valley specialising in toughish CABERNET SAUVIGNON. Good wineries include Stag's Leap, Shafer and CLOS DU VAL.

Stalky or stemmy FLAVOUR OF THE STEM RATHER THAN OF THE JUICE.

Steely REFERS TO YOUNG WINE WITH EVIDENT ACIDITY. A COMPLIMENT WHEN PAID TO CHABLIS AND DRY SAUVIGNONS.

Steen (South Africa) Local name for (and possibly clone of) CHENIN BLANC Widely planted (over 30% of the vineyard area) but producing few wines of distinction. *** Swartland Co-operative Winery 1993 £3.50 (SAF).

Steiermark (AUSTRIA) An Austrian wine region more commonly known in England as Styria. Generally expensive dry whites in a lean austere style.

Georg Steigelmar (AUSTRIA) Producer of extremely expensive but highly acclaimed dry whites from CHARDONNAY and PINOT BLANC and reds from PINOT NOIR and St Laurent. **** Chardonnay 1989 £14 (SEL) *** Pinot Blanc 1989 £10 (SEL).

Stellenbosch (SOUTH AFRICA) Very much the centre of the Cape wine industry; a beautiful university town full of delightful Cape Dutch architecture and flanked by craggy mountains. Many of the most famous traditional estates are to be found within fifteen miles of the centre of town and the bigger companies are sited here *** Tesco Stellenbosch Merlot, Vinfruco £3.99 (TO).

Sterling Vineyards (NAPA, California) Founded by British-born Peter Newton (now at NEWTON) and once the plaything of Coca Cola, this showcase NAPA estate today belongs to Canadian liquor giant, Seagram, owners of MUMM and Oddbins. PINOT NOIR shows promise, there are some good CABERNETS but quality could generally improve. At least prices are more realistic than is usual for NAPA. *** Sterling Vineyards Chardonnay, Napa Valley £6 (OD).

Stoneleigh (MARLBOROUGH, NEW ZEALAND) Reliable label owned by Cooks-CORBANS though less impressive than in the past, possibly since competition for MARLBOROUGH grapes has grown more fierce. *** Stoneleigh Cabernet Sauvignon 1992 £7 (TH, BU, WR, TO, VW) *** Stoneleigh Chardonnay, Marlborough 1993 £7 (TH, BU, WR, J&B).

Stoniers (VICTORIA, Australia) Small MORNINGTON winery proving remarkably successful with PINOT NOIR and MERLOT. (Previously known as Stoniers-Merrick.) **** Stoniers Pinot Noir 1992 £7.50 (WAW,).

Structure THE 'STRUCTURAL' COMPONENTS OF A WINE INCLUDE TANNIN ACIDITY AND ALCOHOL. THEY PROVIDE THE SKELETON OR BACKBONE THAT SUPPORTS THE 'FLESH' OF THE FRUIT. A YOUNG WINE WITH STRUCTURE SHOULD AGE WELL

Ch. de Suduiraut (BORDEAUX, France) SAUTERNES, consistently good, occasionally exceptional and promising greater things since its purchase by insurance-to-wine giant AXA 85 86 88 90. ***** 1985 £19 (L&W).

Suhindol (BULGARIA) One of BULGARIA's best-known regions, the source of reasonable reds, particularly CABERNET SAUVIGNON 85 87 88 89 90 91. *** Bulgarian Country Red, Merlot and Gamza £3 (JS).

Sulfites AMERICAN TERM NOW FEATURING AS A LABELLING REQUIREMENT ALERTING THOSE SUFFERING FROM AN (EXTREMELY RARE) ALLERGY TO THE PRESENCE OF SULPHUR DIOXIDE. CURIOUSLY, NO SUCH REQUIREMENT IS MADE OF CANS OF BAKED BEANS, BOTTLES OF KETCHUP OR JUST ABOUT EVERYTHING ELSE IN THE LARDER.

Sulphur Dioxide/SO2 ANTISEPTIC ROUTINELY USED BY FOOD PACKAGERS AND WINEMAKERS TO PROTECT THEIR PRODUCE FROM BACTERIA AND OXIDATION. NEW WORLD WINEMAKERS HAVE INCREASINGLY REDUCED THE DOSES; SUPPOSEDLY TOP CLASS WHITE WINE PRODUCERS IN EUROPE, ESPECIALLY IN GERMANY, THE LOIRE AND BORDEAUX, FREQUENTLY – AND UNFORGIVABLY – USE OBSCENE AMOUNTS, OFTEN SPOILING WHAT MIGHT OTHERWISE BE GREAT WINE.

Suntory (Japan) Japanese drinks conglomerate with substantial interests in various wineries around the world, e.g. FIRESTONE in California; Château LAGRANGE in ST JULIEN and DR WEIL in Germany.

Supérieur/Superiore (France/Italy) OFTEN MEANINGLESS IN TERMS OF QUALITY, BUT DENOTES WINE THAT HAS BEEN MADE FROM RIPER GRAPES.

Super Second ONE OF A LOOSELY-KNIT GANG OF MEDOC SECOND GROWTHS: PICHON LALANDE, LEOVILLE LASCASES, DUCRU BEAUCAILLOU, COS D'ESTOURNEL WHOSE WINES RIVAL – IN QUALITY AND PRICE – THE FIRST GROWTHS. LIKE ANY CLIQUE, THE ORIGINAL MEMBERSHIP LIST LOOKS RATHER DATED NOW THAT CHATEAUX LIKE PICHON LONGUEVILLE AND RAUSAN SEGLA HAVE TIDIED UP THEIR ACT. LEOVILLE BARTON ISN'T GREEDY ENOUGH IN ITS PRICING TO BE A SUPER SECOND, BUT THE WINE DESERVES TO BE CONSIDERED AS ONE – AS DO LYNCH BAGES, PALMER, LA LAGUNE, MONTROSE AND BRANAIRE DUCRU.

Super Tuscan NEW WAVE VINO DA TAVOLA WINES PIONEERED BY PRODUCERS LIKE ANTINORI WHICH STAND OUTSIDE WHAT ARE OFTEN CONSIDERED TO BE UNNECESSARILY RESTRICTIVE DOC RULES. GENERALLY BORDEAUX-STYLE BLENDS OR SANGIOVESE OR A MIXTURE OF BOTH.

Sur lie THE AGEING 'ON ITS LEES' - OR DEAD YEASTS - MOST COMMONLY ASSOCIATED WITH MUSCADET, BUT NOW BEING INTRODUCED TO OTHER STYLES IN SOUTHERN FRANCE AND IN THE NEW WORLD. THE EFFECT IS TO MAKE WINE FRESHER AND RICHER AND POSSIBLY SLIGHTLY SPARKLING. *** Muscadet de Sèvre et Maine sur Lie 'Première', Domaine Jean Douillard 1992 £5 (JS).

Süssreserve (Germany) UNFERMENTED GRAPE JUICE USED TO BOLSTER SWEETNESS AND FRUITINESS IN GERMAN AND ENGLISH WINES, IN A PROCESS KNOWN AS BACK-BLENDING.

Sutter Home Winery (NAPA, California) Home of robust red ZINFANDEL in the 1970s, and responsible for the invention of sweet 'white' (or as the non colour blind might say, pink) ZINFANDEL which has become such a phenomenal success in California and has incidentally helped to save this variety from the extinction it seemed to face a few years ago. *** Sutter Home Zinfandel 1991 £5 (TAN).

Swan Valley (WESTERN AUSTRALIA, Australia) Well-established, hot and generally unexciting vineyard area in which ports, sherries and port-like wines used to be made. MOONDAH BROOK is an exception to the rule 85 86 89 90 92 93.

Switzerland Produces, in general, enjoyable but expensive light, floral wines for early drinking. See DOLE, FENDANT, CHABLAIS.

Sylvaner/Silvaner White, relatively non-aromatic grape, originally from Austria but adopted by other European areas, particularly ALSACE and FRANKEN, as a prolific yielder of young, dry wine which can taste unrefreshingly earthy. **** Sylvaner, Zind Humbrecht 1992 £5 (ABY).

Syrah The red RHONE grape, an exotic mix of ripe fruit and spicy, smoky, gamey, leathery flavours. Skilfully adopted by Australia where it is called SHIRAZ or HERMITAGE and in southern France for VIN DE PAYS D'OC.

La Tâche (BURGUNDY, France) Wine from the La Tâche vineyard, exclusively owned by the DOMAINE DE LA ROMANEE CONTI. Frequently as good as the rarer and more expensive 'La Romanée Conti' **** La Tâche 1990 Domaine de la Romanée Conti, Burgundy £100 (EP, C&B).

Tafelwein (Germany) TABLE WINE. ONLY PREFIX 'DEUTSCHER' GUARANTEES GERMAN ORIGIN.

Ch. Tahbilk (VICTORIA, Australia) Defender of old-fashioned winemaking and wines in the GOULBOURN VALLEY. Great long-lived SHIRAZ from 100-year-old vines and lemony MARSANNE which needs a decade. Look out for the bargain second wine, Dalfarras Marsanne from Sainsbury's. **** Chateau Tahbilk Marsanne 1992 £5.99 (OD).

Taittinger (CHAMPAGNE, France) GRAND MARQUE CHAMPAGNE house producing elegant wines. The Comtes de Champagne remains one of the region's best prestige cuvées **** Taittinger Brut Reserve £20 (VW).

Ch. Talbot (BORDEAUX, France) Richly reliable fourth growth ST. JULIEN, like GRUAUD LAROSE, under patronage of the Cordier group. The second wine, Connetable Talbot, is a worthwhile buy. ***** 1985 £21, 1989 £19 (THP).

Taltarni (VICTORIA, Australia) Run by Dominique Portet whose brother Bernard runs CLOS DU VAL in California. Rich and spicy, though by Australian standards, understated SHIRAZ and – unsurprisingly – European-style CABERNETS. The sparkling wines are impressive too. ***** Shiraz 1990 £6.99 (RD, LAY, TP) **** Merlot 1991 £8.99 (RD, CAC) **** Cabernet Sauvignon 1988 £8.99 (TP, T&W, LAY).

> **Tannat** Rustic French grape variety traditionally widely used in the
> blend of **CAHORS** and in South America, principally Uruguay.
> *** Chateau Pichard 1988 Madiran £6 (WS) *** Castel Pujol Tannat,
> Canelones Uruguay 1988 £5 (JS).

Tannin ASTRINGENT COMPONENT OF RED WINE WHICH COMES FROM THE SKINS, PIPS AND STALKS AND HELPS THE WINE TO AGE.

Tardy & Ange (RHONE, France) Partnership of Charles Tardy and Mrs Bernard Ange producing top class wine in CROZES HERMITAGE at the Domaine des Entrefaux. **** Crozes Hermitage, Domaine des Entrefaux 1992 £8 (ABY).

Tarragona (CATALONIA, Spain) DO region of Spain south of PENEDES and home to many co-operatives. Contains the rather better quality separate DO region of TERRA ALTA.

Tarrawarra (YARRA VALLEY, VICTORIA, Australia) Pioneer of PINOT NOIR in the cool climate regions of the YARRA VALLEY. Well regarded but could do better. SECOND LABEL is Tunnel Hill. *** Tunnel Hill Pinot Noir, Tarrawarra Vineyards 1993 £8 (AUC, PHI).

Tarry RED WINES FROM HOT COUNTRIES OFTEN HAVE AN AROMA AND FLAVOUR REMINISCENT OF TAR. THE SYRAH GRAPE IN PARTICULAR EXHIBITS THIS CHARACTERISTIC, THOUGH OLD CLARET CAN GO QUITE TARRY TOO - IN A VERY ATTRACTIVE WAY.

Tartrates HARMLESS WHITE CRYSTALS OFTEN DEPOSITED BY WHITE WINES IN THE BOTTLE. OFTEN A RELIABLE INDICATION OF A WINE WHICH HAS NOT BEEN SUBJECTED TO THE FULL PANOPLY OF MODERN COMMERCIAL WINEMAKING TECHNIQUES. (MOST BIG PRODUCERS CHILL THE WINE IN VAT TO PRECIPITATE THESE CRYSTALS BEFORE BOTTLING). IN GERMANY, THESE ARE CALLED 'DIAMONDS'.

Tasmania (Australia) Up-and-coming island vineyards (which are similar in climate to NEW ZEALAND), showing great potential, and producing increasingly impressive sparkling wine, CHARDONNAY, PINOT NOIR and even CABERNET SAUVIGNON. Questions remain, however, over which are the best parts of the island for growing vines. (Look out for HEEMSKERK, Moorilla, PIPER'S BROOK and Freycinet.) **** Heemskerk Jansz Brut 1990 £13 (ADN)

Tasmania Wine Co (TASMANIA, Australia) SECOND LABEL of PIPER'S BROOK VINEYARD and recommendable for its unoaked, CHABLIS-like CHARDONNAY. **** Chardonnay 1993 £8.25 (POL, HN, JS, LEA).

Tastevin THE SILVER BURGUNDY TASTING CUP. ADOPTED AS AN INSIGNIA BY VINOUS BROTHERHOODS (CONFRERIES), AS A MEANS OF INTIMIDATION BY (OFTEN IGNORANT) WINE WAITERS, AND AS AN ASHTRAY BY LESS REVERENT WINE MERCHANTS AND WRITERS. THE CHEVALIERS DE TASTEVIN ORGANISE AN REASONABLY RELAIBLE ANNUAL TASTING OF BURGUNDIES, THE SUCCESSFUL WINES FROM WHICH ARE RECOGNISABLE BY AN UGLY TASTEVINAGE LABEL. CHEVALIERS DE TASTEVIN ARE MEMBERS OF A 'CONFRERIE' WHO ATTEND BANQUETS, OFTEN IN MOCK-MEDIAEVAL CLOTHES. MEMBERSHIP DOES NOT NECESSARILY INDICATE VINOUS EXPERTISE; MERELY THAT A BURGUNDY MERCHANT THOUGHT IT WORTH SHELLING OUT FOR AN INVITATION TO AN INITIATION BANQUET.

Taurasi (CAMPANIA, Italy) Big, old fashioned red from the AGLIANICO grape, needs years to soften and develop a characteristic cherryish taste 83 85 88 89 90. **** Antonio Masteroberadino 1985 £13 (V&C).

Tavel (RHONE, France) Dry rosé, usually (wrongly) said to age well. Often very disappointing. Seek out young versions and avoid the bronze colour revered by traditionalists. 90 91 92 93. *** Château d'Aqueria Rosé 1992 £8 (LAV).

Tawny (Port) EITHER RUBY PORT THAT HAS BEEN BARREL-MATURED TO MELLOW AND FADE OR A CHEAP BLEND OF RUBY AND WHITE PORT. EXAMPLES WITH AN INDICATION OF THEIR AGE (eg 10-YEAR-OLD) ARE THE REAL THING. SEE DOWS, NIEPOORT, RAMOS PINTO, CALEM. *** Sainsbury's 10 Year Old Tawny £10 (JS).

Taylor, Fladgate & Yeatman (Oporto, Portugal) With **Dows,** one of the two great 'First Growths' of the **Douro.** Outstanding **Vintage Port** for the last 40 years and – less creditably – creators of 'modern' **Late Bottled Vintage.** They also own **Fonseca** and **Guimaraens** and produce the excellent Quinta de Vargellas **Single-Quinta** port. **** Sainsbury's Vintage Character Port £6 (JS) ****Taylors Vintage Port 1977 £40 (L&W).

Te Mata (Hawkes Bay, New Zealand) Pioneer John Buck was not only one of the first to prove what **New Zealand** could do with **Chardonnay** (in the Elston Vineyard); but also how good its reds could be (his Coleraine). **** Te Mata Coleraine Cabernet/Merlot 1991 £14.99 (WR, BU, TH, OD) **** Castle Hill, Sauvignon Blanc 1993 £9 (LV).

Tedeschi (Veneto, Italy) Two brothers based in **Valpolicella,** crafting some rich and concentrated **Valpolicellas.** Their **Amarones** are particularly impressive. ***** Amarone Capitel Monte Olmi, Azienda Agricola Tedeschi 1988 £15.93 (ADN, WIN) **** Recioto della Valpolicella, Flli Tedeschi 1988 £6 (MWW, WIN) *** Soave Classico 1993 £3 (MWW).

Tempranillo (Spain) The red grape of **Rioja,** whose sturdy fruit is a match for the vanilla/oak flavours of barrel-ageing. *** Rioja Oak Aged Tempranillo 1992 £4.29 (SAF).

Tenuta (Italy) Estate or vineyard.

Terlano/Terlaner (Trentino-Alto-Adige, Italy) Northern Italian village and its wine: usually fresh, crisp and carrying the name of the grape from which it was made 90 91 92 93. *** Cabernet Riserva 1985 Lageder £10 (WCE).

Teroldego (Trentino-Alto-Adige, Italy) Dry reds, quite full-bodied with lean, slightly bitter berry flavours 85 86 87 88 89 90 91. *** Teroldego Rotaliano Ca'Donini 1992 £4 (V&C).

Terra Alta (Catalonia, Spain) Small **DO** within the larger **Tarragona DO,** but generally producing wines of higher quality due to the difficult climate and resulting low yields.

Terre di Ginestra (Sicily, Italy) New wave Sicilian wine with plenty of easy-going fruit. *** Bianco 1993 £5 (V&C).

Terret (France) Suddenly fashionable white grape which, like **Malbec,** used to be used in blends. *** Domaine de Lenthéric 1992 £4 (MWW) *** Domaine la Fadèze 1992 £5 (L&W).

Tête de Cuvée (France) An old expression still used by traditionalists to describe their finest wine. *** Muscat de Beaumes de Venise, 'Tete de Cuvée' (EV)

Ch. du Tertre (Bordeaux, France) **Margaux** Fifth Growth recently restored to former glory by the owners of **Calon-Segur.** **** 1983 £16 (THP).

Thames Valley Vineyard (Reading, England) Home winery of roving *enfant terrible* John Worontschak, Australian winemaking consultant to The Harvest Group which is consistently at the cutting edge of **English Wine** production. *** Valley Vineyard Fumé, Thames Valley Vineyard 1992 £7.99 (SAF).

Dr H Thanisch (Mosel-Saar-Ruwer, Germany) With **Wegeler-Deinhard,** part-owner of the great Bernkasteler Doctor vineyard, the wines from which are sadly almost impossible to find. As an alternative, try the **** Bernkasteler Badstube Riesling Spätlese, Dr Thanisch 1989 £9.80 (J&B).

Ch. Thieuley (Bordeaux, France) Reliable **Entre-deux-Mers** producing quite concentrated **Sauvignon**-based, well-oaked whites, and a rather silky red. *** Château Thieuley Bordeaux Blanc, Cuvée Barrique 1992 £7.89 (MWW).

Vin de Thouarsais (Loire, France) VDQS for a soft, light red from the **Cabernet Franc;** whites from the **Chenin Blanc.** *** M. Gigon 1992 £6 (YAP).

Three Choirs (Gloucestershire, England) Named for the three cathedrals of Gloucester, Hereford and Worcester, Tom Day's is one of England's leading estates. *** English House Medium Dry, Three Choirs Vineyards Ltd £2.99 (MRN, WL).

Tiefenbrunner (ALTO-ADIGE, Italy) Consistent producer of good VARIETAL whites, most particularly CHARDONNAY and GEWURZTRAMINER. One of a small band of ALTO-ADIGE producers who are living up to some of the early promise shown by this region. **** Gewürztraminer 1992 £7 (ADN).

Tignanello (TUSCANY, Italy) ANTINORI's Sangiovese-based SUPER-TUSCAN, the partner to the BORDEAUX-lookalike SOLAIA, and a consistently good example of how happily the SANGIOVESE grape can work with new oak and CABERNET SAUVIGNON. Unlike most CHIANTI, well worth keeping – it should last for at last a decade. **** Tignanello, Antinori 1990 £21 (C&B, HAR, WR, V&C).

Tinta Negra Mole Versatile and widely used MADEIRA grape traditionally found in cheaper blends instead of one of the four 'noble' varieties. Said to be a distant cousin of the PINOT NOIR.

Tocai (Italy) Lightly herby Venetian white grape, confusingly unrelated to others of similar name. Drink young 90 91 92 93. *** Tocai Friulano, Collio 1993 £6 (WCE).

Tokay d'Alsace See PINOT GRIS.

Tokay/Tokaji (HUNGARY) Not to be confused with Australian Liqueur Tokay, TOCAI Friulano or TOKAY D'ALSACE, Tokay Aszu is a dessert wine made in a specific region of Eastern Hungary (and a tiny corner of Slovakia) since the 17th century by adding measured amounts (PUTTONYOS) of ESZENCIA (a paste made from individually picked, over-ripe and/or nobly rotten grapes) to dry wine made from the local FURMINT and Harslevelu grapes. Sweetness levels, which depend on the amount of Eszencia added, range from 1-6 puttonyos, anything beyond which is labelled Aszu Eszencia. Not surprisingly, this last is often confused with the pure syrup which is sold – at vast prices – as Eszencia, though why anyone should want to write a large cheque for a thick, grapey syrup which is best used as a sauce for ice cream remains unclear. The heavy investment (principally by French companies such as AXA and by VEGA SICILIA of Spain) has raised quality, international interest, and local controversy over the way Tokay is supposed to taste. Traditionalists like it OXIDISED like sherry. The newcomers and some locals disagree. Names to look for include the Royal Tokay Wine Co and DISZNOKO. **** Tokaji Aszu 6 Puttonyos, Hetszolo 1981 £20 (GRO, RWW).

Tollot-Beaut (BURGUNDY, France) Wonderful BURGUNDY domaine matching modern techniques and plenty of new wood with lots of rich fruit flavour. **** Chorey-lès-Beaune 1991 £11 (HR) **** Beaune 1er Cru, Clos du Roi 1988 £22 (OD).

Torcolato see MACULAN.

Torgiano (UMBRIA, Italy) Zone in UMBRIA and modern red wine made famous by LUNGAROTTI. See RUBESCO. *** Lungarotti 1990 £7 (V&C).

Toro (Spain) Region on the Portuguese border lying on the DOURO, producing up-and-coming wines from the TEMPRANILLO *** Tesco Toro 90, Bodegas Farina £4 (TO) *** Vega de Toro Tinto Reserva 1985 £8 (MOR).

Torre de Gall (PENEDES, Spain) MOET & CHANDON's Spanish fizz. About as good as you can get using traditional CAVA varieties. But why use traditional CAVA varieties? Watch out for innovations, as MOET & CHANDON are determined to get it right. **** Brut 1990 £8 (FUL, VW).

Torres Acclaimed, family-owned bodega based in PENEDES which, under Miguel Torres Junior, revolutionised Spain's table-wine production with reliable commercial labels like Viña Sol, Gran Viña Sol, Gran Sangre De Toro, Esmeralda and Gran Coronas, before attempting to perform the same trick in CHILE. Sadly, while Torres is still at the forefront in Spain, this is partly because too few of its peers have shown similar dynamism. In CHILE, they are far from the front of the grid. The best wine bearing the family name is probably Miguel's sister Marimar's effort in California.
***** Marimar Torres Chardonnay, Don Miguel Vineyard 1991 £11.49 (BTH, FSW,) **** Torres Gran Sangredetoro 1989 £5.99 (WR, LWL, OD, U, BU) *** Viña Sol 1993 £5 (MWW).

Toscana (Italy) See TUSCANY.

Ch. la Tour Haut-Caussan (BORDEAUX, France) Semi-organic MEDOC producer making intense reds from a 50/50 blend of CABERNET and MERLOT. Replaces one third of oak barrels annually. A winery to watch 88 89 90 91. **** 1991 £8 (ADN).

Touraine (LOIRE, France) Area encompassing the ACs CHINON, VOUVRAY and BOURGUEIL. Also an increasing source of quaffable VARIETAL wines – SAUVIGNON, GAMAY DE TOURAINE etc. *** Sauvignon de Touraine, Domaine Gibault 1993 £4 (W) *** Touraine 'Les Granges', J. M. Monmousseau 1992 £5 (AV).

Touraine-Mesland (LOIRE, France) AC within TOURAINE producing reds that can occasionally rival CHINON and BOURGUEIL. *** Gamay, Girault Artois 1991 £5 (MWW).

Touriga (Nacional/Francesa) (Portugal) Red port grape, also (though rarely) seen in the New World.

Traminer Alternative name for the GEWURZTRAMINER grape, particularly in Italy and Australia. **** Orlando Flaxmans Traminer, Orlando Wines 1990 £8.49 (CAX, AUC, CDE, CUM, PEA, WTR).

Trapet (BURGUNDY, France) See ROSSIGNOL TRAPET.

Trapiche (MENDOZA, ARGENTINA) Big, go-ahead producer with noteworthy barrel-fermented CHARDONNAY and CABERNET-MALBEC. **** Chardonnay 'Oak Cask' Reserve, Trapiche 1993 £5.50 (TRA, JS, GI) *** Trapiche Cabernet Sauvignon Reserve 1990 £4 (A, GI, SMF).

Tras-os-Montes (Portugal) Wine region of the Upper DOURO, right up by the Spanish border, source of BARCA VELHA.

Trebbiano (Italy) Much appreciated and widely planted white grape in Italy, though less vaunted in France, where it is known as the UGNI BLANC. *** La Zerbina Trebbiano Dalbiere 1993 £5 (V&C) *** Riva Trebbiano di Romagna, Ronco/Gaetana Carron 1993 £3 (OD, SSM, SAF, CEL, WL).

Trebbiano d'Abruzzo (Italy) DOC region within Italy where they grow a clone of TREBBIANO, confusingly called Trebbiano di Toscana, and use it to make generally unexceptional dry whites. *** Cantina Miglianico 1993 £6 (WCE).

Trentino-Alto-Adige (Italy) Northern wine region combining the two DOC areas TRENTINO and ALTO-ADIGE. TRENTINO specialities include crunchy red MARZEMINO, nutty white Nosiola and excellent VIN SANTO. *** Pinot Grigio 1993 £8 (WCE).

Coteaux du Tricastin (RHONE, France) Southern RHONE APPELLATION, emerging as a source of good value, soft, peppery/blackcurranty reds. Domaine de Montine 1991 £4 (TH) **** Coteaux du Tricastin, Domaine de St Luc 1991 £8 (THP).

F E Trimbach (ALSACE, France) Distinguished grower and merchant; can be one of the best in Alsace. **** Riesling Cuvée Frederic Emile, F E Trimbach 1988 £16 (OD, DBY, JEH, HAR).

Trittenheim (MOSEL-SAAR-RUWER, Germany) Village whose vineyards are said to have been the first in Germany planted with RIESLING, making soft, honeyed wine 76 79 83 85 86 88 89 90 91 92. *** Trittenheimer Altarchen Riesling Kabinett Grans-Fassian 1991 £8 (MWW) *** Trittenheimer Apotheke Riesling Auslese, Grans-Fassian 1983 £10 (MWW).

Trocken (Germany) DRY, OFTEN AGGRESSIVELY SO. AVOID TROCKEN KABINETT FROM SUCH NORTHERN AREAS AS THE MOSEL, RHEINGAU AND RHEINHESSEN. QBA (CHAPTALISED) AND SPATLESE TROCKEN WINES (MADE, BY DEFINITION, FROM RIPER GRAPES) ARE BETTER, SEE ALSO HALBTROCKEN. **** Traiser Rotenfels, Reisling Spätlese, Crusius 1992 £10 (L&W).

Trockenbeerenauslese (AUSTRIA/Germany) FIFTH RUNG OF THE QMP LADDER, WINE FROM SELECTED DRIED GRAPES WHICH ARE USUALLY BOTRYTIS-AFFECTED AND FULL OF CONCENTRATED NATURAL SUGAR. ONLY MADE IN THE BEST YEARS, RARE AND EXPENSIVE, THOUGH LESS SO IN AUSTRIA THAN GERMANY. *****Blauberger Red Trockenbeerenauslese, Willi Opitz 1991 £35 (T&W) **** Forster Schnepfenflug Huxelrebe, Kurt Darting 1992 £14 (OD).

Trollinger (Germany) The German name for the Black Hamburg grape, used in WURTTEMBURG to make light red wines.

Tronçais (France) FOREST PRODUCING SOME OF THE VERY BEST OAK FOR WINE BARRELS.

Tunisia Best known for dessert MUSCAT wines.

Cave Vinicole de Turckheim (ALSACE, France) First class cooperative whose top wines rival those of the best estates. ***Muscat, Cuvée Tradition 1993 £5 (VW)

Turkey Producer of big, red, often oxidised table wine, rarely seen in the UK. * Diren Dortnal Dry 1990 £5 (SEL) * Diren Karmen Red 1987 £5 (SEL).

Vin de Tursan (South-West France) MADIRAN VDQS whose big, country reds are now beginning to be seen in the UK. *** Château de Bachen 1991 £9 (C&B).

Tuscany (Italy) Major wine region, the famous home of CHIANTI and some of the more intractable reds, BRUNELLO DI MONTALCINO and the New Wave of SUPER TUSCAN VINI DA TAVOLA. **** Ornellaia, Vino da Tavola, Tenuta dell'Ornellaia 1991 £17 (WCE).

Tyrrell's (NEW SOUTH WALES, Australia) CHARDONNAY (or, as the label calls it, PINOT CHARDONNAY) pioneer in the HUNTER VALLEY, and producer of old-fashioned SHIRAZ and SEMILLON and even older-fashioned PINOT NOIR which tastes just the way that BURGUNDY used to in the days when France still owned ALGERIA. **** Tyrrell's Vat 47 Chardonnay 1993 £13 (AV).

Ugni Blanc Undistinguished white grape of southern France which needs modern winemaking to produce anything better than very basic fare. Curiously, in Italy, where it is known as the TREBBIANO, it takes on a mantle of (spurious) nobility. For reasonable French examples try VIN DE PAYS DES COTES DE GASCOGNE.

Ull de Llebre (Spain) Literally 'hare's eye' — a pink TEMPRANILLO in Catalonia.

Ullage SPACE BETWEEN SURFACE OF WINE AND TOP OF CASK OR, IN BOTTLE, CORK. THE WIDER THE GAP, THE GREATER THE DANGER OF OXIDATION. OLDER WINES ALMOST ALWAYS HAVE SOME DEGREE OF ULLAGE, THE LESS THE BETTER.

Umbria (Italy) Central wine region, best known for white ORVIETO AND TORGIANO 86 87 88 89 90 91. *** Cardeto Orvieto Classico Secco, COVIO 1993 £4 (W, OD, VW).

Undurraga (CENTRAL VALLEY, CHILE) Founded in 1882, greatly improved, independent family-owned estate.******** Sauvignon Blanc 1993 £5 (AV, SUM) Reserve Selection Cabernet Sauvignon 1988 £6 (AV, SUM).

Urzig (MOSEL-SAAR-RUWER, Germany) Village on the MOSEL with steeply sloping vineyards and some of the very best producers, including Mönchof and DR LOOSEN. *** Urziger Wurzgarten Riesling Kabinett, Mönchhof 1991 £8 (L&W).

Utiel-Requeña (Spain) DO of VALENCIA, producing heavy red and good fresh rosé from the Bobal grape. *** Viña Carmina 1992 £4 (GI).

Vacheron (LOIRE, France) Good, if unspectacular, producer of SANCERRE. *** Sancerre les Roches 1993 £8 (MWW).

Vacqueyras (RHONE, France) COTES DU RHONE Village producing fine, full-bodied, peppery reds which can compete with (pricier) GIGONDAS 85 86 87 88 89 90 91. *** Cuvée les Templiers 1990 £7 (ADN) *** Vacqueyras, Vieux Clocher, Arnoux et Fils 1991 £5 (SMF).

Vajra (PIEDMONT, Italy) Producer of serious reds, including rich, complex BAROLO. ******** Barbera d'Alba, Bricco delle Viole, Aldo Vajra 1989 £8 (WCE).

Valençay (LOIRE, France) AC within TOURAINE, near CHEVERNY, making comparable whites: light, clean if rather sharp.

Vignerons du Val d'Orbieu (France) The face of the future. An association of over 200 co-ops and growers in Southern France which competes with SKALLI for the prize of most innovative source in LANGUEDOC-ROUSSILLON. Not a name to seek out in large print on labels, but one which may appear on those of many retailers' better own-label wines. *** Rosé D'Syrah, Vin de Pays d'Oc £3 (SPR) *** Asda Corbières, Val d'Orbieu £3 (A).

Val d'Aosta (Italy) Small, spectacularly beautiful area between PIEDMONT and the French/Swiss border. Great for tourism; less so for wine-lovers.

Valais (Switzerland) Vineyard area on the upper RHONE, making good FENDANT (CHASSELAS) and some reasonable – in all but price — light reds. *** Fendant du Valais 1992 £10 (SEL).

Valdeorras (Spain) a barren and mountainous DO in Galicia beginning to replant with high quality native grapes. *** Montenovo Tinto, Bodegas Senorio 1992 £5 (ADN).

Valdepeñas (Spain) LA MANCHA DO striving to refine its rather hefty, alcoholic reds and whites. Progress is being made, however, with producers like LOS LLANOS and FELIX SOLIS particularly with reds; white wine lovers will have to await the replacement of the locally widespread AIREN 88 89 90 91. ** Señorio de los Llanos Reserva 1989 £4 (L&S).

Valdespino (JEREZ, Spain) Old-fashioned SHERRY company that still uses wooden casks to ferment most of their wines. Makes a classic FINO Innocente and an excellent PEDRO XIMENEZ. ********* Cream of Cream Sherry, Pedro Ximenez, Argueso Valdespino £9 (SAF).

Valencia (Spain) DO producing quite alcoholic red wines and also deliciously sweet, grapey Moscatel de Valencia. *** Tesco Moscatel de Valencia £3 (TO).

Valpolicella (VENETO, Italy) Over commercialised light red wine which should – with rare exceptions – be drunk young to catch its interestingly bitter-cherryish flavour. Bottles labelled CLASSICO are better; best are RIPASSO versions, made by refermenting the wine on the LEES of an earlier vat. MASI make serious versions, as do ALLEGRINI, Boscaini, TEDESCHI, Le Ragose, Serego Alighieri, GUERRIERI-RIZZARDI and QUINTARELLI. BOLLA'S run-of-the-mill Valpolicella is well, run-of-the-mill, but their JAGO is good. For a different experience though it really is worth paying more for a bottle of AMARONE or RECIOTO 78 79 81 83 85 86 88 89 90. ********* Amarone Capitel Monte Olmi, Azienda Agricola Tedeschi 1988 £16 (ADN).

Valréas (RHONE, France) Peppery and inexpensive red COTES DU RHONE village 85 86 88 89 90 91. *** Côtes du Rhône Villages, Bouchard 1991 £6 (WSO).

Valtellina (LOMBARDY, Italy) Red DOC from the NEBBIOLO grape, of variable quality. Improves with age. *** Valtellina Nino Negro 1990 £6 (V&C) *** Valtellina Sfursat, Nino Negri 1989 £13 (V&C, LV).

Varietal A WINE MADE FROM AND NAMED AFTER A SINGLE GRAPE VARIETY, eg CALIFORNIA CHARDONNAY. THE FRENCH AUTHORITIES WOULD LIKE TO OUTLAW SUCH REFERENCES FROM THE LABELS OF MOST OF THEIR APPELLATION CONTROLEE WINES. HOWEVER THE WORLD HAS LEFT THEM LITTLE ALTERNATIVE BUT TO COMPLY.

Los Vascos (COLCHAGUA VALLEY, CHILE) 50% ownership by Lafite-Rothschild since 1988 has vastly improved the quality of the BORDEAUX-style reds here, but by not enough to rank with the best in CHILE. The whites remain unrecommendable. *** Los Vascos Cabernet Sauvignon 1992 £5 (L&W, ADN).

Vasse Felix (WESTERN AUSTRALIA) Classy MARGARET RIVER winery belonging to the widow of millionaire Rupert Holmes à Court and specialising in high quality reds. ***** Vasse Felix Cabernet Sauvignon 1991 £12 (LAV, ADN, OD, BEN, MWW).

Vaucluse (RHONE, France) COTES DU RHONE region producing good VIN DE PAYS and peppery reds and rosés from villages such as VACQUEYRAS. *** Coteau des Garances, Vin de Pays de Vaucluse Rouge 1993 £4.20 (ADN).

Vaud (Switzerland) Swiss wine area on the shoes of Lake Geneva, famous for tangy CHASSELAS.

Vaudésir (BURGUNDY, France) Possibly the best of the seven CHABLIS GRAND CRUS. **** Chablis Grand Cru Vaudesir, Domaine des Malandes 1992 £16 (WSO).

Vavasour (MARLBOROUGH, NEW ZEALAND) Pioneers of the Awatere Valley sub-region of MARLBOROUGH hitting high standards with BORDEAUX-style reds, powerful SAUVIGNONS and impressive CHARDONNAYS. Dashwood is the SECOND LABEL. *** Vavasour Reserve Chardonnay, Marlborough 1993 £11 (DBY, OD, FUL).

VDQS (France) VIN DELIMITEE DE QUALITE SUPERIEUR; OFFICIAL DESIGNATION FOR WINES BETTER THAN VIN DE PAYS BUT NOT FINE ENOUGH FOR AN AC. ENJOYING A STRANGE HALF-LIFE (AMID CONSTANT RUMOURS OF ITS IMMINENT ABOLITION) THIS NEITHER-FISH-NOR-FOWL CAN BE A SOURCE OF MUCH GOOD VALUE WINE – INCLUDING SUCH ODDITIES AS SAUVIGNON DE ST BRIS.

Vecchio (Italy) OLD.

Vecchio Samperi (Italy) Best MARSALA estate, belonging to DE BARTOLI, although not DOC; a dry aperitif not too dissimilar to an AMONTILLADO sherry. *** Marco de Bartoli, 20 Year Old £19 (V&C).

Vega Sicilia (RIBERA DEL DUERO, Spain) Great reputation as Spain's top wine with prices to match. Wines are improving as the period of time spent in barrel is being reduced from what was often as long as a decade (excessive OXIDATION was often a problem for non-Spaniards) and it is easier to appreciate the intense flavour of the TEMPRANILLO-BORDEAUX blend. Even so, for a cheaper, slightly fresher taste of the Vega Sicilia style try the supposedly lesser Valbuena. **** Vega Sicilia Unico 1980 £41 (L&S, TAN) **** Valbuena 5th year 1985 £33 (MWW).

Vegetal OFTEN USED OF SAUVIGNON BLANC AND CABERNET FRANC: LIKE 'GRASSY'. CAN BE COMPLIMENTARY – THOUGH RARELY IN CALIFORNIA OR AUSTRALIA WHERE IT IS USED AS A SYNONYM FOR 'UNRIPE'.

Caves Velhas (Portugal) Large, traditional merchants who buy and bottle wine from all over the country to sell under their own label. Almost single-handedly saved the BUCELAS DO from extinction. *** Garrafeira 1980 £3 (SMF, G) *** Dão 1990 £3 (D&F).

Velho/velhas (Portugal) OLD, AS OF RED WINE.

Velletri (Lazio, Italy) One of the many towns in the Alban hills (Colli Albani), producing mainly TREBBIANO and MALVASIA-based whites, similar to FRASCATI.

Veltliner See GRUNER VELTLINER.

Vendange (France) HARVEST OR VINTAGE.

Vendange Tardive (France) PARTICULARLY IN ALSACE, WINE FROM LATE HARVESTED GRAPES, USUALLY LUSCIOUSLY SWEET. ***** Gewürztraminer Grand Cru Hengst Vendange Tardive, Zind Humbrecht 1990 £28 (ABY).

Vendemmia (Italy) HARVEST OR VINTAGE.

Vendimia (Spain) HARVEST OR VINTAGE.

Venegazzú (VENETO, Italy) Remarkably good claret-like VINO DA TAVOLA from the CABERNET SAUVIGNON. Needs five years. **** Venegazzu della Casa, Loredan Gasparini 1989 £9 (WCE, F&M, VW, PTR, V&C).

Veneto (Italy) North-eastern wine region, the home of SOAVE, VALPOLICELLA and BARDOLINO. *** Bardolino Classico Tacchetto, Guerrieri-Rizzardi 1993 £6 (BAR, F&M) *** Soave, Via Nova 1993 £4 (WCE).

Côtes du Ventoux (RHONE, France) Improving source of everyday, country reds 88 89 90 91 92 93. *** Côtes du Ventoux La Ciboise, M Chapoutier 1993 £5 (MWW).

Verdejo (Spain) White grape grown in the central region of Spain; confusingly not the VERDELHO of **Madeira** and Australia, but the variety used for RUEDA.

Verdelho White grape used for MADEIRA and White PORT and for tastily limey table wine in Australia. *** Rutherford & Miles Jubilee Selection Verdelho 1952 £69.00 (TH, BU) *** Hardy's Moondah Brook Estate Verdelho, 1993 £5 (WHC, OD, VW, JMC, TO, GMN).

Verdicchio (MARCHES, Italy) Spicy white grape seen as a number of DOCs in its own right, the best of which – when made by Bucci – is VERDICCHIO DEI CASTELLI DI JESI. In UMBRIA, a major component of ORVIETO 88 89 90 91. *** Verdicchio Classico dei Castelli di Jesi, Azienda Agricola Fratelli Bucci 1992 £8 (LAV, WIN) *** Cardeto Orvieto Classico Secco, COVIO 1993 £4 (W, OD, A, VW, CEL).

Verdicchio dei Castelli di Jesi (MARCHES, Italy) One of the DOCs concentrating on the VERDICCHIO grape and aiming to make light, clean and crisp wines to drink with seafood. *** San Nicolo 1993 £6.50 (BI).

Verdicchio di Matelica (MARCHES, Italy) More obscure than VERDICCHIO DEI CASTELLI DI JESI, but bigger in taste. Almost impossible to find in the U.K.

Verduzzo (FRIULI-VENEZIA GIULIA, Italy) White grape making a dry and a fine AMABILE style wine in the Colli Orientali. *** Verduzzo di Ramandolo 1990 £9 (V&C).

Vermentino (Liguria, Italy) The dry white wine of the Adriatic. Best drunk in situ with seafood. *** 1994 £7 (V&C).

Vernaccia White grape making the Tuscan DOC VERNACCIA DI SAN GIMIGNANO and Sardinian Vernaccia di Oristano, at best with a distinctive, characterful flavour 88 89 90 91. *** Castello di Montauto, Cecchi 1993 £4 (VW).

Vernaccia di San Gimignano (TUSCANY, Italy) One of the few tourist hot spots whose wine producers have resisted the temptation to cash in. Still producing some very characterful creamy, nutty wines with a buttery richness reminiscent of CHARDONNAY. *** Vernaccia di San Gimignano, Teruzzi e Puthod 1993 £7 (WCE).

Georges Vernay (RHONE, France) The great master of CONDRIEU who can do things with VIOGNIER that no one else seems able to match **** Condrieu 1991 £21 (YAP).

Veuve Cliquot (CHAMPAGNE, France) The distinctive orange label is often seen in the classiest of establishments, so it is fortunate that the wine is back on form after a few years of producing a rather green non-vintage brut. The much more reliable prestige cuvée is called Grande Dame after the famous Widow Cliquot. ***** Vintage Reserve 1988 £26 (TH, OD, THP, FUL) *** Yellow Label Brut £20 (OD).

Victoria (Australia) Huge variety of wines from the liqueur MUSCATS of RUTHERGLEN to the peppery SHIRAZES of BENDIGO and the elegant CHARDONNAYS and PINOT NOIRS of the YARRA VALLEY. See these, plus MURRAY RIVER, MORNINGTON PENINSULA, GOULBURN VALLEY, GEELONG and PYRENEES.

Vidal (HAWKES BAY, NEW ZEALAND) One of NEW ZEALAND's top four red wine producers. ***** Vidal Hawkes Bay Reserve Cabernet Sauvignon/Merlot 1992 £9.50 **** Sauvignon Blanc £7 (VW).

Vidal-Fleury (RHONE, France) RHONE grower and shipper, bought recently by GUIGAL. **** Côte Rôtie 1990 £26 (WWT) *** Côtes de Ventoux 1990 £5 (MWW).

VIDE (Italy) A MARKETING SYNDICATE SUPPOSEDLY DENOTING FINER ESTATE WINES.

Vieilles Vignes (France) WINE MADE FROM A PRODUCER'S OLDEST AND BEST VINES. **** Chablis 'Vieilles Vignes', Gilbert Picq et Ses Fils 1992 £11 (LAV, WIN).

Domaine du Vieux-Télégraphe (RHONE, France) Modern CHATEAUNEUF-DU-PAPE domaine. Slightly underperforming. Domaine du Vieux-Télégraphe, Châteauneuf-du-Pape, H. Brunier £11 (ADN).

Vigneto (Italy) VINEYARD.

Vignoble (France) VINEYARD; VINEYARD AREA.

Villa Maria (AUCKLAND, NEW ZEALAND) Beginning to produce some really world class reds under the guidance of KYM MILNE. ***** Villa Maria Cabernet Sauvignon/Merlot Reserve 1991 £17.

Villa Sachsen (RHEINHESSEN, Germany) Great freshness and elegance from low yielding vineyards in BINGEN. *** Binger Scharlachberg Riesling Kabinett Halbtrocken, Villa Sachsen 1992 £6 (TO).

Villages (France) THE SUFFIX 'VILLAGES' e.g. COTES DU RHONE OR MACON GENERALLY INDICATES A SLIGHTLY SUPERIOR WINE (IN THE WAY THAT CLASSICO DOES IN ITALY) FROM A SMALLER DELIMITED AREA ENCOMPASSING CERTAIN VILLAGE VINEYARDS. St Michael Beaujolais Villages, Georges Duboeuf 1992 £5 (M&S).

Villany (HUNGARY) Sunny area of HUNGARY with a promising future for soft young drinking reds, though UK marketing men might recommend a name-change. *** Cabernet Sauvignon Villany Hills Estate 1992 £3 (TH).

Vin de Corse (CORSICA, France) APPELLATION within CORSICA where strange local grapes and arcane wine making practices hinder a wider acceptance. However, French producers like Skalli are beginning to take an interest and things are looking up. See FORTANT DE FRANCE.

Vin de garde (France) WINE TO KEEP.

Vin de l'Orléanais (LOIRE, France) Small AC in the CENTRAL VINEYARDS of the LOIRE. See ORLEANNAIS. *** Vin d'Orléanais, Covifruit 1992 £5 (rouge & blanc) (YAP).

Vin de paille (JURA, France) SPECIALITY OF THE REGION; RICH AND SWEET GOLDEN WINE FROM GRAPES LAID OUT AND DRIED ON STRAW MATS. *** Vin de Paille, Bourdy 1989 £17 (WSO).

Vin de Pays (France) LOWEST/BROADEST GEOGRAPHICAL DESIGNATION; SIMPLE COUNTRY WINES WITH CERTAIN REGIONAL CHARACTERISTICS. ESPECIALLY SUCCESSFUL AS WHITES IN VIN DE PAYS DES COTES DE GASCOGNE AND IN VARIOUS STYLES IN VIN DE PAYS D'OC. ***** Cuvée du Cépage Cabernet Sauvignon, Vin de Pays d'Oc, Domaine St Hilaire 1992 £4.65 (BEN) **** La Serre Sauvignon Blanc, Vin de Pays d'Oc 1993 £4.25 Bl (VW).

Vin de Savoie See SAVOIE.

Vin de table (France) TABLE WINE FROM NO PARTICULAR AREA.

Vin doux naturel (France) FORTIFIED DESSERT WINES, BEST KNOWN AS THE SWEET, LIQUOROUS MUSCATS OF THE SOUTH, eg **BEAUMES DE VENISE**. ****Domaine de Coyeux Muscat de Beaumes de Venise 1991 £5.70 (TH) *** Muscat Beaumes de Venise, J Vidal-Fleury 1992 £16 (MWW).

Vin du Bugey (SAVOIE, France) Formerly thin astringent whites of little merit, but becoming rather trendy in France as a source of fresh crisp **CHARDONNAY**. *** Chardonnay, Vin de Bugey, VDQS 1992 £6 (WSO).

Vin gris (France) CHIEFLY FROM **ALSACE** AND THE **JURA**, PALE ROSE FROM RED GRAPES PRESSED BEFORE, NOT AFTER, FERMENTATION.

Vin jaune (JURA, France) A speciality of **ARBOIS**, golden yellow, slightly oxidised wine, like a dry **SHERRY**. ***Château d'Arlay 1987£47 (SEL) *** Côte de Jura, Bourdy 1985 £24 (ADN) **** Château Chalon, Bourdy 1986 £25 (WSO).

Vin Santo (Italy) Powerful white dessert wine from grapes dried after picking by hanging the bunches in airy barns especially in **TUSCANY** and **TRENTINO**. Fermented and matured for up to six years in small 11 gallon barrels called *caratelli* . Best drunk with sweet almond biscuits 82 84 85 87 88 89 90 91. **** Val d'Arbia, Badia à Coltibrono 1985 £10 (half) (ADN).

Vin vert (France) Light, refreshing, acidic white wine, found in **ROUSSILLON**.

Viña de Meso (Spain) Spanish for table wine. *** Yllera Tinto 1990 £7 (WR).

Viña Pedrosa (RIBERA DEL DUERO, Spain) Modern wine showing what the **TEMPRANILLO** can do when blended with **BORDEAUX** varieties. The Spanish equivalent of a **SUPER-TUSCAN**.

Viña Pomal (RIOJA, Spain) Dull, unexceptionable **RIOJA**.

Vinho Verde (Portugal) Commercial versions are generally quite sweet. Aveleda is bone dry- and better. *** Asda Vinho Verde £3 (A) *** Trajadura 1992 £4 (TO) *** Aveleda N.V. £6 (AV).

J.P. Vinhos (Portugal) Excellent modern wine company that employs **PETER BRIGHT** as winemaker and makes an impressively wide range of wines from all over Portugal. **** Tinto da Anfora, J.P. Vinhos 1990 £5 (WR, OD, MWW, W, SAF).

Vinícola Navarra (NAVARRA, Spain) Ultra modern winemaking facilities and newly planted vineyards beginning to come on stream. Owned by the **BODEGAS Y BEBIDAS** group. *** Las Campañas Navarra Crianza, Vinicola Navarra 1990 £4 (OD) *** Las Campañas Navarra Cabernet Sauvignon, Vinicola Navarra 1990 £5 (OD).

Vinifera PROPERLY VITIS VINIFERA, THE SPECIES NAME FOR ALL EUROPEAN VINES.

Vino da tavola (Italy) TABLE WINE, BUT THE **DOC** DESIGNATION HAS AN ALICE IN WONDERLAND-LIKE REASONING SUCH THAT WHILST SOME 'BAD' **DOC** WINE IS MADE BY FOLLOWING THE RULES, PRODUCERS OF MANY SUPERB – AND PRICEY – WINES CONTENT THEMSELVES WITH THIS 'MODEST' **APPELLATION**. **** I Grifi, Avignonesi 1988 £15 (V&C) *** Le Volte, Tenuta Dell'Ornellaia 1992 £8 (TH, WCE).

Vino Nobile di Montepulciano (TUSCANY, Italy) **CHIANT**i in long trousers; potentially truly noble (though often far from it), and made from the same grapes. Can age well to produce a traditional full red. **ROSSO DI MONTEPULCIANO** is the lighter more accessible version. The Montepulciano of the title is the Tuscan town, not the grape variety 83 85 86 88 89 90 91. **** Le Casalte 1989 £9 (TH,WR) **** Vino Nobile di Montepulciano, Avignonesi 1986 £10.50 (V&C) **** Lodola Nuova Vino Nobile di Montepulciano, Ruffino 1989 £7.10 (M&S).

Vino novello (Italy) NEW WINE FROM THIS YEAR'S HARVEST, EQUIVALENT TO FRENCH NOUVEAU. *** Novello Sangiovese, Antinori 1994 £10 (V&C).

Vinos de Madrid (Spain) Wine area that gained **DO** status in 1990. *** Vega Madroño, Bodegas Aigaco 1992 £4 (L&S).

Vintage Champagne A WINE FROM A SINGLE, GOOD, 'DECLARED' YEAR.

Vintage character (Port) (DOURO, Portugal) SUPPOSEDLY INEXPENSIVE ALTERNATIVE TO VINTAGE, BUT REALLY AN UP-MARKET RUBY MADE BY BLENDING VARIOUS YEARS' WINES. **** Sainsbury's Vintage Character Port, Taylor Fladgate & Yeatman £6 (JS) **** Churchill's Finest Vintage Character Port £9 (CPW).

Vintage (Port) (DOURO, Portugal) ONLY PRODUCED IN 'DECLARED' YEARS, AGED IN WOOD THEN IN BOTTLE FOR MANY YEARS. IN 'OFF' YEARS, PORT HOUSES RELEASE WINES FROM THEIR TOP ESTATES AS SINGLE **QUINTA** PORTS. MUST BE DECANTED. 1991 LOOKS PROMISING 70 75 77 80 83 85 91. See **WARRES**, **DOWS TAYLORS** etc for examples.

Viré (BURGUNDY, France) Village of **MACON** famous for whites. **JADOT** produces a typical wine that is widely available. *** Mâcon Viré Co-op, Cave De Vire 1992 £5 (TO). *** Mâcon Viré, Domaine de Roally, Henri Goyard 1991 £10 (THP).

Viticulteur (-Propriétaire) (France) VINE GROWER/VINEYARD OWNER.

Viura (Spain) White grape of the **RIOJA** region. *** D'Avalos Viura, Rioja 1993 £4 (WSO).

Côtes du Vivarais (PROVENCE, France) Light southern **RHONE**-like reds, a great deal of fruity rosé and occasional fragrant, light whites. *** Dom. du Belvezet, VDQS 1992 £4 (L&W).

Dom Michel Voarick (BURGUNDY, France) Slow maturing old fashioned wines that avoid the use of new oak. The **CORTON CHARLEMAGNE** is particularly spectacular and hard to find. *** Corton Charlemagne 1992 £33 (TVW).

Domaine Robert Vocoret (BURGUNDY, France) Classy producer of **CHABLIS** that is known for its ageability. *** Chablis 1er Cru Vaillon, Domaine Vocoret & Fils 1992 £9 (MWW) **** Chablis Grand Cru Blanchot, Vocoret 1991 £15 (MWW).

Volatile Acidity (VA) THE OBVIOUSLY VINEGARY CHARACTER ENCOUNTERED IN WINES WHICH HAVE BEEN SPOILED BY BACTERIA – AND ALSO FOUND IN SUBTLER AND MORE ACCEPTABLE MEASURE IN MANY ITALIAN REDS, **PENFOLDS** GRANGE, **PINOT NOIRS** AND **EISWEINS**. ANYONE WHO HAS TASTED THE DIFFERENCE BETWEEN REALLY GOOD BALSAMIC VINEGAR AND THE STUFF MOST OF US PUT ON OUR CHIPS WILL APPRECIATE THE DISTINCTION.

Schloss Vollrads (RHEINGAU, Germany) Important **RHEINGAU** estate producing lean, dry **RIESLINGS** which are generally said to go with food and to age well. In other words, they're like those friends and relatives we all seem to have who can only be invited to precisely the right dinner party. *** Schloss Vollrads, Blue Capsule 1988 £10 (AV).

Volnay (BURGUNDY, France) Arguably the finest red wine village to be found in the **COTE DE BEAUNE** (the Caillerets vineyard was once ranked equal to le **CHAMBERTIN**), this is the home of fascinating plummy-violetty reds 78 79 82 83 85 86 87 88 89 90. ***** Robert Ampeau 1985 £30 (HR) ***** Volnay Clos des Chênes, Domaine du Château de Meursault 1992 £15 (HAR, BTH).

Volnay-Santenots (BURGUNDY, France) Once the equivalent of a **GRAND CRU**, now first among its peers as a **PREMIER**. A great vineyard under whose name can be sold some red wine from **MEURSAULT**. **** Volnay Santenots, Domaine des Comtes Lafon 1991 £20 (M&V).

Vosges (France) FOREST WHICH IS THE SOURCE OF FINE OAK; LESS AROMATIC THAN **ALLIER**. GOOD FOR WHITE WINE.

Vosne Romanée (BURGUNDY, France) The red wine village which numbers **ROMANEE-CONTI** among its many grand names and the home of potentially gorgeous plummy-rich wines 78 80 82 83 85 86 87 88 89 90. **** Domaine Grivot 1988 £26 (L&W, D) ***** Vosne-Romanée, Mongeard-Mugneret 1990 £16 (MWW) ***** Vosne Romanée, Domaine Jean Gros 1989 £21 (TH, WR, BU).

Vougeot (BURGUNDY, France) COTE DE NUITS Commune comprising the famous **GRAND CRU CLOS DE VOUGEOT** and a great number of growers of varying skill 78 80 82 83 85 87 88 89 90 92. **** Clos Vougeot 'Musigni' 1987 Gros Frères £28 (J&B). **** Vougeot 1er Cru, Petite Vougeot, Dom. Hudelot-Noellat 1990 £20 (HR).

Vouvray (LOIRE, France) White wines from the CHENIN BLANC, ranging from clean, dry whites and refreshing sparklers to DEMI SECS and astonishingly honeyed, long-lived, sweet – MOELLEUX – wines. What a pity so many producers spoil it all with massive doses of SULPHUR DIOXIDE 69 71 75 76 83 85 88 89 90 92. **** Viticulteurs du Vouvray 1976 £10 (U) **** Marc Brédif Vouvray 1989 £8 (MWW, PTR, N&P).

Wachau (Austria) Major wine region producing some superlative RIESLING from steep, terraced vineyards. **** Riesling Smaragd Durnsteiner Kellerberg, Freie Weingartner Wachau 1993 £8.21 (OD) *** Riesling Smaragd Burgerspitalstiftung Spitz, Freie Weingartner Wachau 1990 £9 (OD).

Wachenheim (RHEINPFALZ, Germany) Superior MITTELHAARDT village which should produce full, rich, unctuous RIESLING 75 76 79 83 85 86 88 89 90 91 92. *** Bohlig Riesling Auslese Dr Bürklin-Wolf 1990 £17 (BBR).

Wairau River (MARLBOROUGH, NEW ZEALAND) Classic Kiwi white wines with piercing fruit character. *** Wairau River Chardonnay, Marlborough 1992 £10 (WR, SOM) *** Wairau River Sauvignon, Wairau River 1993 £7.50 (SAF).

Walker Bay (SOUTH AFRICA) Now emerging as a genuine region as more new wineries (like Wildekrans) begin to spring up. Established vineyards include HAMILTON RUSSELL and Bouchard Finlayson. **** Hamilton Russell Pinot Noir 1992 £7.50 (AV).

Warre (Oporto, Portugal) One of the big seven PORT houses and the oldest of them all; this stablemate to DOWS, GRAHAMS and SMITH WOODHOUSE makes traditional PORT which is both rather sweeter and more tannic than most. The old fashioned LATE BOTTLED VINTAGE is worth seeking out too. ***** Warre's Vintage Port 1983 £19 (widely available).

Warwick (SOUTH AFRICA) Norma Ratcliffe manages to cram an amazing amount of fruit flavour and concentration into her exclusively red wines – making one each from CABERNET SAUVIGNON, MERLOT and CABERNET FRANC, and a blend of all three which is called Trilogy. **** Trilogy 1989 £11 (WTR).

Washington State (US) Underrated (especially in the US) state in which dusty, irrigated vineyards produce RIESLING, SAUVIGNON and MERLOT to make a NAPA VALLEY winemaker wince. **** Columbia Merlot, Columbia Winery 1988 £7.50 (BAR, SEL, F&M) *** Kiona, Late-Picked Reisling 1993 £6 (OD).

Wegeler Deinhard (RHEINGAU, Germany) One of the largest producers with estates all over Germany; they have taken the innovative step of leaving out the vineyard name from most of their labels. A large range of acceptable dry RIESLINGS and some of the best German sparkling wine. *** Wegeler Deinhard Forster Ungeheuer, Deinhard 1990 £11.40 (TAN) **** Wegeler-Deinhard Riesling Kabinett, Deinhard 1990 £9 (DN).

Wehlen (MOSEL-SAAR-RUWER, Germany) MITTELMOSEL village making fresh, sweet, honeyed wines; look for the Sonnenuhr vineyard and wines from the great DR LOOSEN, PRUM or WEGELER DEINHARD 75 76 79 83 85 86 88 89 90 91 92. **** Dr Loosen Wehlener Sonnenuhr Riesling Spätlese 1992 £10.79 (WSG) **** Wehlener Sonnenuhr Riesling Auslese, Dr F. Weins-Prum Erben 1988 £10 (ADN, THP).

Dr R Weil (Kiedrich, Germany) Property now owned by SUNTORY whose investment is allowing it to produce stunning late harvest wines selling at prices more easily afforded by Japanese than British wine drinkers. ***** Kiedricher Grapenberg Riesling Beerenauslese 1992 £70 (BAR).

Weingut Germany) WINE ESTATE.

Weinkellerei (Germany) CELLAR OR WINERY.

Weissburgunder The PINOT BLANC in Germany and AUSTRIA Relatively rare, so often made with more care than RIESLING or the newer varieties. ***Deinhard Pinot Blanc Dry 1991 £4 (TH).

Welschriesling Aka Riesling Italico, Ljutomer, Olasz, Lazki Rizling. A dull grape unrelated to the Rhine RIESLING, this variety comes into its own when Austrians have allowed it to be affected by BOTRYTIS. ***** Kracher Welschriesling Trockenbeerenauslese 1981 £28 (NY).

Domdechant Werner'sches Weingut (RHEINGAU, Germany) Excellent vineyard sites at HOCHHEIM and RIESLING produce a number of traditional wines that age beautifully. *** Hocheimer Domdechaney Riesling Spätlese 1985 £8 (VW).

Western Australia (Australia) Varied state whose climates range from the baking SWAN VALLEY to the far cooler MOUNT BARKER and MARGARET RIVER. ***** Tesco Western Australian Chenin Blanc, Moondah Brook 1993 £5 (TO) **** Western Australian Red, Plantagenet £8 (GI).

White port (DOURO, Portugal) Made from white grapes, an increasingly popular dry or semi-dry aperitif, though it's hard to say why, when vermouth's fresher and cheaper. PORT producers tend to drink it with tonic water and ice. *** Delaforce Special White Port £7.60 (SEL, MRN, TH)

Willamette Valley (OREGON, US) The heart of OREGON's PINOT NOIR vineyards. *** Willamette Valley Vineyards Oregon Müller-Thurgau 1992 £6.49 (LWE) *** Willamette Valley Vineyards Dry Riesling 1992 £6.99 (LWE, WOC).

Wiltingen (MOSEL-SAAR-RUWER, Germany) Distinguished SAAR village, making elegant, slatey wines. Well-known for the SCHARZHOFBERG vineyard 76 79 83 85 86 88 89 90 91 92. ***** Wiltinger Klosterberg Riesling Kabinett, Van Volxem 1989 £4.99 (WL) **** Wiltinger Braunfels Riesling Kabinett, Van Volxem 1992 £4.99 (A).

Winkel (RHEINGAU, Germany) Village with an established reputation for complex, delicious wine, housing the famous SCHLOSS VOLLRADS estate 82 83 85 86 88 89 90 91 92.

Winzerverein/Winzergenossenschaft (Germany) COOPERATIVE.

Wirra Wirra High flying MCLAREN Vale winery making first class RIESLING, SHIRAZ and CABERNET which at best vintages is sold as the ANGELUS. *** Church Block Red 1991 £7.50 (AUC) **** RSW Shiraz 1991 £9 (WOI) *** Angelus 1991 £10 (WOI).

Wolff-Metternich (Germany) Good rich RIESLING from the granite slopes of BADEN. *** Niersteiner Rosenberg Riesling Kabinett 1991 £5 (A).

Wootton (England) Successful vineyard, noted for its SCHONBERGER but recently entering the commercial arena in a very un-English way with the highly marketable 'Trinity'. *** Trinity English Wine, Wootton Vineyard £3.95 (JS).

Wurttemburg (Germany) ANBAUGEBIET surrounding the Neckar region, producing more red than any other. Little seen in the UK. ** Unteruerkheimer Herzogenberg 1990 £6 (WSC).

Wyndham Estate (HUNTER VALLEY, Australia) Ultra-commercial winery which now belongs to Pernod Ricard. Quite what that firm's French customers would think of these blockbusters is anybody's guess. *** Wyndham Estate Bin 444 Cabernet Sauvignon 1992 £5.50 (MWW, MRN, HAL, A&A, WCO) *** Wyndham Estate Oak Cask Chardonnay 1992 £6.49 (MWW, MRN).

David Wynn (South Australia) See MOUNTADAM.

Wynns (SOUTH AUSTRALIA) Top class producer of COONAWARRA CABERNETS (especially the John Riddoch) and buttery CHARDONNAY. The Ovens Valley SHIRAZ is another rich, spicy gem. ***** Wynns Coonawarra Estate John Riddoch Cabernet Sauvignon 1991 £15 (VW, OD) **** Wynns Coonawarra Estate Cabernet Sauvignon 1991 £7.50 (VW, OD).

Xarel-Lo A low quality grape exclusive to Catalonia. Usually employed in the manufacture of CAVA. *** Xarel-lo Blanco, Jaume Serra 1993 £4 (BI).

"Y" d' Yquem (BORDEAUX, France) Hideously expensive dry wine of CHATEAU D'YQUEM which, like other such efforts by SAUTERNES CHATEAUX is of accademic rather than hedonistic interest 85 88 90. *** 1988 £45 (J&B).

Yakima Valley (WASHINGTON STATE, US) Principal region of WASHINGTON STATE. Good for MERLOT, RIESLING and SAUVIGNON. COLUMBIA CREST, COLUMBIA WINERY, CHATEAU SAINTE MICHELLE, Château Sainte Chapelle. **** Columbia Merlot, Columbia Winery 1988 £7.50 (BAR, F&M, SEL).

Yalumba (SOUTH AUSTRALIA) Associated with HILL-SMITH, and producer of good dry and sweet whites, serious reds and some of Australia's most appealing fizz, including Angas Brut and the CHAMPAGNE-like Yalumba D. ***** The Menzies Cabernet Sauvignon, Yalumba 1991 £6.99 (LAV, WIN, JN, OD) JS. Yalumba Family Reserve Botrytis Semillon 1991 £7.50 (LAV, WIN, JN) Yalumba Museum Show Reserve Rutherglen Muscat £6.99 (TH, TO, VW, BEN, SOM).

Yarra Valley (VICTORIA, Australia) The fact that this historic wine district is the focus for 'boutiques' making top class BURGUNDY-like PINOT NOIR and CHARDONNAY for COLDSTREAM HILLS and TARRAWARRA shouldn't overshadow the fact that it has also produced some first class BORDEAUX-style reds and, at YARRA YERING, a brilliant SHIRAZ. *** Mount Mary Quintet 1991 £24.95 (AUC).

Yarra Yerring (YARRA VALLEY, VICTORIA, Australia) Proving that this is not just a region for BURGUNDY varieties (though he does make an off-beat Pinot), Dr Bailey Carrodus produces an ultra-rich, complex CABERNET blend including a little PETIT VERDOT ('Dry Red No 1) and a SHIRAZ (Dry Red No 2) in which he puts a bit of VIOGNIER and MARSANNE. Underhill is the SECOND LABEL. *** Underhill Shiraz 1992 £12.50 (OD).

Yeasts NATURALLY PRESENT IN THE 'BLOOM' ON GRAPES, OR ADDED BY (USUALLY NEW WORLD) WINEMAKERS, THEY CONVERT SUGAR TO ALCOHOL, OR, IN SPARKLING WINES, CREATE CARBON DIOXIDE. SOME WINES, eg CHAMPAGNE AND MUSCADET — BENEFIT FROM AGEING IN CONTACT WITH THEIR YEASTS — OR SUR LIE. CHARDONNAY PRODUCERS INCREASINGLY LIKE TO INCREASE THE BISCUITY EFFECT OF THE YEAST ON THEIR WINES BY STIRRING THEIR BARRELS.

Yecla (Spain) DO region of Spain near VALENCIA producing mostly rough alcoholic reds. ** Viña Las Gruesas, Bodegas Castáno 1993 £4 (ADN).

Yonne (BURGUNDY, France) Wine department, home of CHABLIS. See under various CHABLIS growers' entries.

Ch. d' Yquem (BORDEAUX, France) Sublime SAUTERNES, not produced every year 85 86 88 90. ***** 1986 £155 (C&B).

Zell (MOSEL-SAAR-RUWER, Germany) Bereich of lower MOSEL and village, making pleasant, flowery RIESLING. Famous for the Schwarze Katz (black cat) Grosslage 76 79 83 85 86 88 89 90 91 92. *** Merler Konigslay-Terrassen Riesling Auslese Halbtrocken, Schneider'sch Weinguterverwaltung, Zell 1990 £2.53.

Zentralkellerei (Germany) Massive, central cellars for groups of cooperatives in six of the ANBAUGEBIET — the MOSEL-SAAR-RUWER Zentralkelleri is Europe's largest Co-operative.

Zimbabwe Winemaking – in ex-tobacco fields – started during the days of UDI. Quality is climbing towards adequacy, though producers still complain that Mr Mugabe even favoured South African whites when sanction fever was at its peak** Mukuyu Flirt Rosé 1993 £3.79 (VER)

Zind-Humbrecht (ALSACE, France) Producer of great single-vineyard wines. ***** Gewürztraminer Heimbourg, Zind Humbrecht 1992 £12 (ABY) **** Tokay Rotenburg Selection de Grain Nobles, Zind Humbrecht 1991 £50 (ABY).

Zinfandel (California) Versatile red grape producing everything from dark, jammy, leathery reds to pale pink, spicy 'BLUSH' wines. Also grown by CAPE MENTELLE in MARGARET RIVER, Australia. **** Fetzer Barrel Select Zinfandel 1991 £7.90 (LAV, WIN) **** Frog's Leap Zinfandel 1991 £10.65 (L&W, M&V, BOO) *** Tesco Californian White Zinfandel, Stratford Winery £4.29 (TO) ***** Ridge Vineyards 'Lytton Springs' Sonoma 1991 £15 (ADN).

THE MERCHANTS

After the description of each merchant we give a selection of some of
the most interesting wines to appear on their lists. The codes which
precede these wines indicate the following styles:

1 Sparkling wine	8 Drier Germanic whites	15 Burgundy/Pinot Noirs
2 Richer dry whites	9 Medium Germanic	16 Italian reds
3 Oaked whites	whites	17 Iberian reds
4 Dry Loire-style/ country	10 Rosé	18 Muscats
whites	11 Country reds	19 Botrytis and all that rot
5 Medium-dry whites	12 Cabernet/claret style	20 Sherry
6 Aromatic whites	13 Rhônes/spicy reds	21 Port/fortified
7 Grapey whites	14 Beaujolais	22 Low/non alcohol

While every effort has been made to verify the availability and prices
of these wines, naturally both may vary during the months following
publication.

ADB   Addison-Bagot Vintners Ltd (Eaton Elliot) ★★★

13 London Road, Alderley Edge, Cheshire SK9 7JT (Tel 0625 582354). **Opening
Hours:** Mon–Fri 9am-830pm, Sat 9am-7pm. **Delivery:** free locally, nationally at cost.
Tastings: occasional in-store, tutored sessions on request. **Services:** mail order,
gift mailing, glass hire, ice.

Eaton Elliot is such a familiar name among wine lovers in the 'golden triangle' of
Cheshire, that it comes as a surprise to learn that it is no more. But purchase by John
Bagot, and a rechristening to Addison Bagot has done nothing to diminish the range
of classics established by Christopher Tatham MW and Nick Elliot. The Castello di
Volpaia Tuscans are still there, and the Vacheron Sancerres. Some may regret the
absence of the Jura wines of which Eaton Elliot was a rare source, but we'd sacrifice a
prematurely aged Eastern French wine for a fresh one from Neudorf in New Zealand.
And in a Napa-obsessed world, it's good to see a Sangiovese from the Shenandoah
Valley made by the appropriately named Jim and Suzy Gullett.

3	Coopers Creek Chardonnay, 1992, Hawkes Bay, New Zealand £10.95
4	Mauzac, L'Aude, Dom. Lamoure, 1993, Midi, France £4.65
4	Vinho Verde, Quinta da Franqeira, 1992, Minho, Portugal £6.50
5	High Weald Winery, English Vineyard, Kent, England £5.40
12	Ngatarawa, Cabernet-Merlot, 1991, Hawkes Bay, New Zealand £7.85
16	Locorotondo, Puglia, Francesco Candido, 1993, Puglia, Italy £4.80
16	Barbera, "Ceppi Storici", Nizza Monferrato, 1991, Piedmont, Italy £4.90
17	Gran Caus, Can Ràfols del Caus, 1987, Penedès, Spain £9.75

ADN   Adnams Wine Merchants   ★★★★★

The Crown, High Street, Southwold, Suffolk IP18 6DP (Tel 0502 724222). **Opening
Hours:** Mon–Fri 9am-5pm, Sat 9am-12pm. **Delivery:** free for 2 cases or more.
Tastings: regular in-store plus Autumn season of 'Meet the Winemaker' evenings.
Services: cellarage, en primeur, mail order (cases only), gift mailing, glass hire, ice.

**Wine Merchant of the Year; East of England Merchant of the Year;
New World Specialist Merchant**

When the judges handed in their secret votes for the Wine Merchant of the Year, the
agreement between them was extraordinary. Over the last few years, Simon Loftus

and his team have found a winning formula and they're not about to lose it. As one customer described this firm: 'dealing with Adnams is like watching Eric Cantona at play. You know he'll play well, but you can never predict precisely what he'll do'. Which helps to explain how Adnams ended up carrying away quite so many of this year's prizes.

The wines are extraordinarily good across the range, showing the buying team's refusal to stock wine for the sake of it. The Italians, southern French, Californians and Australians include an astonishing set of superstars – and omit the producers whom other merchants feel they ought to include. As for the list, it is simply the very best combination of form and content offered by any merchant.

1	Adnams Fizz, Chardonnay Brut. France £6.20
1	Heemskerk Jansz, Tasmania, Australia £12.95
1	Champagne Le Mesnil, Blanc de Blancs, France £13.50
1	Billecart Salmon Brut Champagne, France £17.20
2	St Véran, Domaine Corsin, 1992, Burgundy, France £8.95
2	Mas de Daumas Gassac, Vin de Pays de l'Hérault, 1992, France £16.50
2	Château Chalon, Jean Bourdy, 1985, Jura, France £26.40
3	Pernand-Vergelesses, Olivier Leflaive, 1992 Burgundy, France £8.20
3	Mountadam Chardonnay, 1990, High Eden, South Australia £8.70
3	Rockford Semillon, 1989, Barossa Valley, South Australia £8.65
4	Ozidoc Sauvignon, Domaine Virginie, 1993, Languedoc-Roussillon, France £4.75
4	Quivira Sauvignon Blanc, 1991, Sonoma, California £7.20
4	Cullen Sauvignon Blanc, 1993, Margaret River, Western Australia £10.75
6	Condrieu, Coteaux de Chéry, Andre Perret, 1992, Rhône, France £16.95
8	Jasper Hill, Georgia's Paddock Riesling, 1992, Australia £8.15
9	Maximiner Grunhauser 'Abtsberg' Riesling Kabinett, Von Schubert, 1992, Mosel, Germany £12.75
10	Ch. Thieuly, 1993, Bordeaux Clairet, France £5.40
11	Corbières Domaine du Grand Crès, 1991, Languedoc-Roussillon, France £6.45
11	Ch. Pech–Céleyran, 1992, Coteaux de Languedoc, La Clape, France £4.50
12	Lady Langoa, St Julien, Anthony Barton, 1990, Bordeaux, France £9.75
12	L'Esprit de Chevalier, Pessac-Leognan, Domaine de Chevalier, 1990, Bordeaux, France £11.75
12	Ridge Santa Cruz Mountains Cabernet, 1991, California £15.50
13	Rockford Dry Country Grenache, 1992, South Australia £7.20
13	Charles Melton Shiraz, 1992, South Australia £8.75
13	Jasper Hill Georgia's Paddock Shiraz, 1992, Australia £12.20
13	Ridge Vineyards Mataro, 1991, California £12.95
13	Bonny Doon Vineyard Cinsault, 1992, California £13.20
14	Juliénas, Domaine Joubert, 1992, Beaujolais, France £6.20
15	Chassagne Montrachet, 1991, Henri Germain, Burgundy, France £9.95
15	Saintsbury Pinot Noir, 1991, Carneros, California £11.95
15	Nuits St. Georges, Cuvée des Sires de Vergy, G.Faiveley 1985 Burgundy, France £37.10
16	Coltassala, Castello Di Volpaia, 1988, Tuscany, Italy £13.75
17	Remelluri Rioja Reserva, 1989, Rioja, Spain £8.75
19	Ch. La Gironie, Monbazillac, 1990, South West France £7.75
19	Ch. Coutet 1983, Barsac, Bordeaux, France £26.95
20	Inocente El Fino Sherry, Valespino, Jerez, Spain £7.95
20	Matusalem, Oloroso Muy Viejo, Gonzalez Byass £20.20
21	Adnams Vintage Character Port, Portugal £8.20
21	Guimaraens-Fonseca 1976 Port, Portugal £18.95

AMA   Amathus Wines Ltd   ★★★

377 Green Lanes, Palmers Green, London N13 4JG (Tel 081 886 3787/1864).
Opening hours: Mon-Sat 9.30am-9.30pm, Sun 12-2.30pm. **Delivery:** free locally.
Tastings: occasional in-store. **Services:** glass hire, ice.

Harry Georgiou's North London establishment may not be the most chic of wine
merchants. However, who's bothered, when you can buy Chardonnays from
Louisvale and Te Mata, Joseph Mellot's Loire Sauvignons, some very classy Italian
reds and a long list of tasty Aussies?

3	Backsberg Chardonnay, 1992, Paarl, South Africa £5.99
3	Te Mata Estate, Elston Chardonnay, 1992, Hawkes Bay, New Zealand £11.99
4	Ch. Coucheroy 1991, Blanc Graves, Bordeaux, France £5.99
4	Sauvignon de St. Bris, 1990, J. Brocard 1990 Burgundy France £6.19
4	Wairau River, Sauvignon Blanc, 1992, Marlborough, New Zealand £7.49
12	Ch. Lanessan, Haut-Médoc, Bordeaux, France 1986 £11.89
21	Fonseca Guimaraen's 1976 Douro, Portugal £17.99

AMW   Amey's Wines   ★★★

83 Melford Road, Sudbury, Suffolk CO10 6JT (Tel: 0787 377144). **Opening Hours:**
Mon-Sat 10am-7pm, half day closing Monday. **Delivery:** free locally. **Tastings:**
regular in-store **Services:** glass hire.

This small and entirely reliable Suffolk merchant shows a heavy bias towards
Australia - but who doesn't these days? We are pleased, though, to see a fine, if less
fashionable, range of sherries including all the best names (Barbadillo, Lustau and
don Zoilo) a worthy haul of Italians culminating in Mascarello's Barolo Monprivato,
and one of Allegrini's Valpolicella Amarones.

3	Hickbotham Mornington Peninsular Chardonnay, 1992, Victoria, Australia £7.99
11	Les Chemins de Bassac, Vin de Pays d'Oc, 1992, France £5.50
12	Agramont, Tinto 'Black Stripe', 1990, Navarra, Spain £4.51
12	Ch. Ramage la Batisse, 1989, Bordeaux France £9.45
12	Hogue Cellars Merlot, 1989, Washington State, USA £9.45
15	Beaune 1er Cru Les Epenottes, Vallet Frères, 1989, Burgundy, France £16.86
16	Le Volte, Tenuta Dell' Ornellaia, 1992, Tuscany, Italy £7.59
16	Carignano Del Sulcis, Reserva Rocca Rubia 1990, Sardinia, Italy £7.95
16	Barolo Monprivato, Guiseppe Mascarello, 1988, Piedmont, Italy £16.00
21	Old Trafford Tawny, Seppelts, Australia £7.65

LAV   Les Amis du Vin

See The Winery

JAV   John Arkell Vintners   ★★★

Arkells Brewery Ltd, Hyde Road, Stratton St. Margaret, Swindon SN2 6RU (Tel 0793
823026). **Opening Hours:** Mon-Fri 9am-5.30pm. **Delivery:** free locally, nationally
at cost. **Tastings:** occasional in-store and tutored. **Services:** cellarage, en primeur,
mail order, gift mailing, glass hire, ice.

Tradition is still very much the order of the day at this brewery-based merchant in
Wiltshire, with clarets dating back to 1970 forming the core of the list. The rest of the
selection is full of safe, if rather unadventurous wines such as Louis Latour

Burgundies, Torres Spaniards and Lindemans Aussies, although the Cuvaison Californians , Jaffelin Burgundies, Chapoutier Rhônes and Jackson Estate Kiwis add a little more spice.

1	Boschendal, Le Grand Pavillon, Paarl, South Africa £6.87
3	Saint Romain, Jaffelin, 1992, Burgundy, France £8.70
3	Cuvasion Chardonnay, 1987, Napa, California £14.86
4	Sancerre, 'Les Roches', Vacheron, 1993 Loire France £9.05
12	Los Vascos, Cabernet Sauvignon, 1991, Colchagua Province, Chile £5.93
12	Babich, Irongate Cabernet-Merlot, 1987, Hawke's Bay, New Zealand £12.22
12	Ch. de Fieuzal 1990, Pessac-Léognan, Bordeaux. France £15.69
12	Ch. Grand Puy Lacoste, Pauillac, 1985, Bordeaux, France £19.27
12	Gran Coronas, Black Label, 1971, Torres, Catalonia, Spain £30.32
13	Best's Shiraz, 1993, Victoria Australia £5.99
15	Rully Rouge, 1991, Jaffelin, Burgundy, France £7.40
15	Monthelie, Jaffelin, 1989, Burgundy, France £9.46
17	Cune Monopole, 1990, Rioja, Spain £6.23
17	Ochoa Tempranillo, 1990, Navarra, Spain £6.76
21	John Arkell LBV 1987, Smith Woodhouse, Douro, Portugal. £7.34
21	Graham's Malvedos, 1979 Douro, Portugal £17.57

JAR   John Armit Wines   ★★★★

5 Royalty Studios, 105 Lancaster Road, London W11 1QF (Tel 071 727 6846). Wines by the case only. **Opening Hours:** Mon–Fri 10am-5pm. **Delivery:** free for three cases or more. **Tastings:** twice yearly tastings, plus tutored programme and private sessions on request. **Services:** cellarage, en primeur, mail order, gift mailing,

Having stunned everyone with – and won a prize for – his beautifully illustrated lists, John Armit has really rung the changes this time; bold and graphic black text and Mondrian-esque blocks of colour serve to highlight a fine selection of carefully chosen wines. As ever, Burgundy leads the field in strength as well as depth; Domaine de l'Arlot, Domaine Dujac and Olivier Leflaive are all first class and Mr Armit is one of the few people to receive an allocation of Domaine Ponsot's Clos de la Roche Vielles Vignes. Outside France most of the major countries are represented by one or maybe two of their top estates; Mr A was one of the first non Spaniards to notice the now-celebrated Pesquera and his firm remains one of rare places to find it. The New World selection is short but exciting, with Californians from Hess, Ravenswood and Groth, Weinert from Argentina and Mulderbosch from South Africa, to name but a few.

2	Pierre Vidal Chardonnay, James Herrick, 1992, Vin de Pays d'Oc, France £5.83
3	Rully 1er Cru Mont Palais, Olivier Leflaive, 1992, Burgundy, France £9.83
3	Bourgogne Chardonnay, Domaine Roulot 1991, France £10.00
3	Hess Collection Chardonnay, Hess Winery, 1991, California £11.25
3	Piano della Capella, Fattoria Terrabianca, 1991, Italy £11.25
3	Chassagne Montrachet 1er Cru 'Les Grandes Ruchottes', Olivier Leflaive 1992, Burgundy, France £17.08
3	Meursault Les Vireuils, Domaine Guy Roulot, 1991, Burgundy, France £22.50
4	Château Bel Air Bordeaux Blanc, Vignobles Despagne, 1993, France £5.58
4	Muscadet de Sèvre et Maine, Clos de Beauregard, Pierre Leroux, 1990, Loire, France £5.67

4	Steenberg Sauvignon Blanc, 1993, South Africa £6.83
4	Mulderbosch Barrel Fermented Sauvignon Blanc, 1993, South Africa, £7.17
4	Groth Vineyards Sauvignon Blanc, 1992, California £7.92
6	Tokay Pinot Gris, Andre Kientzler, 1991, Alsace, France £8.60
11	Domaine de Triennes, Les Aureliens, Vin de Pays du Var, 1991, France £6.83
12	Hess Collection Cabernet Sauvignon, 1990, Napa, California £14.16
12	Dominus, 1988, Napa, California £31.67
13	Blewitt Springs Shiraz, 1990, Australia £6.00
13	Ravenswood Vintners Blend Zinfandel, 1992, Sonoma, California £8.50
15	Bourgogne Mont Avril, Michel Goubard, 1990, France £7.08
15	Domaine de l'Arlot Nuits St Georges Clos des Forêts, 1990, Burgundy, France £28.75
16	Scassino Chianti Classico, Fattoria Terrabianca, 1991, Tuscany, Italy £9.16
17	Pesquera Ribera del Duero Tinto, Alejandro Fernandez, 1990, Spain £11.00

A — Asda Stores Ltd ★★★

Asda House, Southbank, Great Wilson Street, Leeds LS11 5AD (0532 435435).
Opening Hours: most stores: Mon–Sat 9am-8pm, Sun 10am-4pm. **Tastings:**
regular in-store. **Services:** glass hire.

In a year when its supposedly smarter competitors have been wrestling in the gutter with rock-bottom prices, Philip Clive has quietly continued to grow his range. Depending on the status of your nearest store, you might be offered a Dom Mellil red from Morocco, a Fairview Gewürztraminer from South Africa, a Goundrey Langton Chardonnay from Western Australia and even a Louis Carillon Puligny Montrachet 1988 (a bargain at £12). There are, of course, some much more ordinary wines to hack through before you get to these, but the overall standard is rising with every year, giving Asda very much the look of a young Tesco...

1	Asda Champagne Brut, Marne et Champagne, Champagne, France £11.75
2	Asda Chablis, G Mothe, 1992, Chablis, France £6.69
3	Rowanbrook Chardonnay Reserve, Canepa, 1993, Chile £4.49
4	Asda Chardonnay, Vin de Pays d'Oc Midi France £3.75
9	Graacher Himmelreich Riesling Kabinett, Reichsgraf von Kesselstatt, 1993, Mosel, Germany £5.99
11	Asda Hungarian Kekfrankos, 1993, Szolo-Bor, Hungary £2.69
11	Asda Corbières, 1992, Val d'Orbieu , Midi, France £2.75
11	Asda St Chinian, 1992 Val d'Orbieu, Midi, France £2.85
11	Asda Merlot Vin de Pays D'Oc, Skalli, Midi, France £2.89
11	Asda Cape Red, Simonsvlei South Africa £2.89
12	Asda Hungarian Cabernet Sauvignon, 1993, Szolo-Bor Hungary £2.69
12	Asda South Australian Cabernet Sauvignon, 1991, Angoves, South Australia £3.69
12	Asda Chilean Cabernet Merlot, 1993, Vinicola Lastaguas, Chile £4.99
12	Ch. de Parenchère, Bordeaux Supérieur, 1990, France £5.25
13	Asda South Eastern Australia Shiraz-Cabernet, 1992 Yaldara, South Eastern Australia £3.29
13	Asda South Australian Shiraz, 1991, Angoves, South Australia £3.61
13	Côteaux-du-Tricastin, Domaine De Grangeneuve, 1992, Rhône France £4.15
13	Ch. Val Joanis, Côtes du Luberon, 1992, Rhône, France £4.45
15	Santenay Foulot, Château Perruchot 1991 Burgundy, France £8.59
16	Montepulciano d'Abruzzo, Cantina Tollo, 1992, Italy £2.79

16	Barbera d'Asti, Gemma, 1990, Italy £4.49	
16	Montescudaio, 'Rosso Delle Miniere' Sorbaiano, 1990, Italy £6.99	
16	Barolo 'Bricco Boschis', Cavalotto 1988 Piedmont Italy £8.59	
17	Asda Douro, Viso 1991, Douro, Portugal £2.99	
17	Asda Bairrada, Cavas Alianca, 1990, Bairrada, Portugal £3.25	
21	Asda Amontillado, Bodega La Caridad, Jerez, Spain £3.85	
21	Asda Fino, Barbadillo, Jerez, Spain £3.85	
21	Asda Vintage Character Port, Smith-Woodhouse, Douro, Portugal £5.99	
21	Asda LBV Port, Smith-Woodhouse, Douro, Portugal £6.75	

AUC   The Australian Wine Club   ★★★★★

50 The Strand, London WC2N 5LW (Tel 0800 716893). Wines by the case only.
Opening Hours: Mon–Fri 9am-7pm, Sat 10am-4pm. **Delivery:** free over £75.
Tastings: The Great Australian Wine Tasting 13 May 1995. Phone for details.
Services: mail order.

The Strand has another trio of homeless folk. The only difference is that this time, the cardboard boxes are full of top class Aussie wine. The decision of the South Australian Government not to renew the lease on on its Strand headquarters at the end of 1994 has forced The Australian Wine Centre to reincarnate as a mail order wine club with free membership for twelve months and free delivery anywhere on the UK mainland for orders over £75. The real joy of this operation is their ability to source wine from the rising stars of the Aussie wine scene like Turkey Flat and RBJ and ship them to the UK before anyone else has latched on. Eight newsletters a year and an invitation to The Great Australian Wine Tasting every May should keep all Ockerphiles as happy as a koala in an eucalyptus bush.

1	Sparkling Pinot Chardonnay, Penley Estate, 1990, South Australia £10.00
3	Primo Estate Chardonnay, 1991, South Australia £6.99
3	The Willows Vineyard Semillon, W.H. Scholz, 1992, Australia £6.99
3	Tim Adams Semillon, 1993, Clare, South Australia £7.99
3	Stafford Ridge Lenswood Chardonnay, 1991, South Australia £7.99
3	Chapel Hill Reserve Chardonnay, 1993, South Australia £8.99
4	St Hallet's Poachers Blend, 1993, £4.99
4	Château Tahbilk, Marsanne, 1992, Goulburn Valley Australia £5.49
4	St Hallett Semillon-Sauvignon Blanc, 1993, £5.49
6	Delatite Dead Man's Hill, Gewürztraminer, 1992, Australia £6.70
8	Quelltaler Estate Riesling, 1993, Clare, South Australia £4.75
11	Heritage Cabernet Franc, 1993, Australia £6.99
12	St Hallett's Cabernet Sauvignon-Cabernet Franc-Merlot, 1992, South Australia £6.99
12	Delatite Merlot, 1992, Australia £6.99
12	Buckley's Clare Valley Cabernet Sauvignon, 1992, Australia £7.00
12	Cassegrain Cabernet Sauvignon, 1991, Hunter Valley, Australia £7.99
12	Capel Vale Cabernet Sauvignon, 1989 Western Australia £7.99
12	Chapel Hill Cabernet Sauvignon, 1992, Australia £7.99
12	Water Wheel Cabernet Sauvignon, 1992, Australia £7.99
12	Penley Estate Cabernet Sauvignon, 1991, Australia £11.00
13	St Hallett's Gamekeeper's Reserve, 1993, Australia £6.49
13	Buckleys Barossa Valley Grenache, 1992, Australia £6.50
13	Primo Estate Shiraz, 1991, Australia £6.99
13	R B J Theologicum, Grenache-Mouvèdre, 1993, Australia £7.00
13	St Hallett's Barossa Shiraz, 1992, Australia £7.49
13	Penley Estate Hyland Shiraz, 1992, Australia £7.50
13	Water Wheel Bendigo Shiraz, 1992, Australia £7.99
13	Chapel Hill Shiraz, 1991, Australia £7.99
13	Tim Adams Grenache 'The Fergus', 1993, Australia £7.99

13	Charles Melton Shiraz, 1992, Australia £8.49
13	Penley Estate Shiraz-Cabernet, 1991, Australia £8.50
13	Rockford Basket Press Shiraz, 1990, Barossa, Australia £9.99
13	Henschke Mt. Edelstone Shiraz, 1991, Eden Valley, Australia £9.99
13	Zema Estate Shiraz, 1992, Australia £9.99
15	Wignalls Pinot Noir, 1992, Albany, Western Australia £10.99
15	Coldstream Hills Reserve, Pinot Noir, 1992, Yarra Valley, Australia £12.99
16	Best's Dolcetto, 1993, Great Western, Victoria, Australia £6.99
19	Primo Estate Botrytis Riesling, 1993, Australia £6.99

AV   Avery's   ★★★★

7 Park street, Bristol BS1 5NG (Tel 0272 214141) **Opening Hours:** Mon-Sat 9am-7pm, Sunday, Bank Holidays 12-3pm. **Delivery:** Free nationally for 2 cases or more. **Tastings:** in-store and tutored events. **Services:** En primeur, mail-order, gift mailing, export, glass, hire, and ice.

'There is hardly anything in the world that some man cannot make a little worse and sell a little cheaper, and the people who consider price only, are that man's lawful prey.' This quotation from Ruskin appears on the back of Avery's list and goes some way toward explaining the presence of a large range of top Californian wines and quite a sprinkling of Super-Tuscans, none of which could be accused of being 'a little cheaper'. John Avery was a New World pioneer when most British wine merchants thought Rioja a trifle adventurous; today, a substantial chunk of the firm belongs to a Californian banker who also conveniently happens to own the Swanson winery, producer of a stunning - and by Californian standards, very fairly priced - Chardonnay. Watch out also for the special cuvée of Champagne, produced in conjunction with Andrew Lloyd-Webber and entitled 'The Phantom of the Opera Brut NV'. Perfect when you are feeling misérable or if you miss Saigon. It may also enhance certain aspects of love.

2	Poverty Bay Chardonnay, House of Nobilo, 1993, New Zealand £5.99
3	Klein Constantia Estate Chardonnay, 1993, South Africa £6.99
3	Hamilton Russell Vineyards Chardonnay, 1993, South Africa £7.75
3	Swanson Vineyards Carneros Chardonnay, 1991, California £10.25
3	Tyrrell's Vat 47 Chardonnay, 1993, Australia £13.00
4	Touraine 'Les Granges', J. M. Monmousseau, 1992, Loire, France £4.69
4	Château de la Tuilerie, Carte Blanche, 1992, France £5.40
4	Klein Constantia Sauvignon Blanc, 1994, South Africa £6.25
4	Sancerre Cuvée Edmond, Domaine La Moussière, Alphonse Mellot, 1992, Loire, France £13.00
5	Long Flat White – Chardonnay-Semillon – Tyrrells Vineyards, 1993, Australia £5.50
5	Stevens Semillon, Tyrrells Vineyards, 1993, Australia £7.75
9	White Cloud, House of Nobilo, 1993, New Zealand £4.50
11	Chinon Les Violettes, Jacques Morin 1993, Loire, France £4.25
12	Vina Undurraga Cabernet Sauvignon Reserva 1990, Chile £5.75
12	Rustenberg Merlot-Cabernet, 1991, Stellenbosch, South Australia £5.99
12	Rutherford Hill Merlot, 1989, Napa Valley, California £12.00
12	Swanson Vineyards Cabernet Sauvignon, 1988, Napa Valley, California £14.50
12	Far Niente Cabernet Sauvignon, 1989, California £27.25
15	Hamilton Russell Pinot Noir, 1992, South Africa £7.50
15	Nuits St Georges Premier Cru, Château Gris, Lupe-Cholet 1992, £16.40
19	Vin De Constance, Klein Constantia Estate 1989, £11.50

BH   B H Wines   ★★★★★

Bousted Hill House, Boustead Hill, Burgh-by-Sands, Carlisle CA5 6AA (Tel 0228 576711). Wines by the case only. No credit cards. **Opening Hours:** Mon, Tues, Wed Fri, Sat 9am-5pm, Sundays and evenings by appointment. **Delivery:** free locally, nationally at cost. **Tastings:** occasional in-store, plus wine tasting society. **Services:** mail order glass hire.

North of England Wine Merchant of the Year

A Cumbrian tea shop was the setting for the scene in the cult film 'Withnail and I' in which Richard E Grant drunkenly demanded 'the finest wines known to humanity...and cake'. Rather than calling the police and having their inebriated customers thrown out, the owners could well have popped along to B. H. Wines in nearby Carlisle. Here they would have found six vintages of Cos d'Estournel, Crozes Hermitage from Alain Graillot and Mosels from Max Ferd Richter alongside such oddities as Willi Opitz's Blauberger Trockenbeerenauslese and Recioto di Soave from Guerrieri-Rizzardi. Bring your own cake.

1	Daniel le Brun Brut, New Zealand £10.60
2	Dom. Servin Chablis 1er Cru Vaillons Chablis, 1988, Burgundy France £10.70
3	Pikes, Chardonnay, 1990, Clare Valley, Australia £6.15
3	Clos du Blois Calcaire Vineyard, 1988, Alexander Valley, California £13.00
3	Vidal Gimblett Road Reserve Chardonnay, 1989, Hawkes Bay, New Zealand £13.40
3	Newton Unfiltered Chardonnay, 1990, Napa, California £13.65
4	Bianco di Custoza Ceresa, Rizza-Pastrengo, 1992, Veneto, Italy £3.90
4	Tim Adams Semillon, 1993, Australia £8.75
4	Te Mata, Elston Chardonnay, 1991, Hawkes Bay, New Zealand £12.50
9	Willi Opitz, Pinot Blanc Spätlese, 1992, Austria £10.50
11	Ch. La Canorgue, 1990, Côtes du Lubéron, France £6.95
11	Mas de la Rouviere 1986 Bandol, France £8.30
11	Dom. de Trèvallon, 1989, Côteaux de Baux, France £12.95
12	Johnston Reserve Claret, Bordeaux, France £4.45
12	Ch. de Prade, 1986, Côtes de Castillon, Bordeaux, France £5.50
12	Glen Carlou Les Trois, 1991, Paarl, South Africa £8.45
12	Simon Whitlam Cabernet Sauvignon, 1986, Hunter Valley, Australia £10.00
12	Carmenet Cabernet Sauvignon-Merlot-Cabernet Franc, 1988, Sonoma, California £14.00
12	Ch. Pape Clement, 1988, Graves, Bordeaux, France £17.50
12	Vieux-Château-Certan, 1983, Pomerol, Bordeaux, France £27.50
13	Peter Lehman Clancy's Shiraz-Cabernet, 1989, Barossa, South Australia £7.00
13	Brézème, Cuvée du Grand Chène, 1985, Côtes du Rhône, France £7.90
13	Ridge Geyserville Vineyard, 1990, Santa Cruz, California £10.00
13	Fetzer Reserve, Petite Sirah, 1985, Mendocino, California £13.75
15	Hauts-Côtes de Nuits, Alain Verdet, 1986, Burgundy, France £12.85
16	Ca' del Pazzo-Caparzo, 1988, Lombardy, Italy £13.80
16	Mon Pra'-Conterno e Fantino, 1988, Piedmont, Italy £14.00
19	Redwood Valley Estate, Late-Harvest Rhine Riesling, 1992, Nelson, New Zealand £6.65 (half)
19	Noble Bacchus, Chiltern Valley, Oxon, England £11.00 (half)
19	Recioto della Valpolicella, Monte Fontana, 1981, Veneto, Italy £14.50
19	Ch. Romer du Hayot, 1983, Sauternes France £15.00
21	Marsala Terre Arse, Vergine-Cantine, Florio, Sicily, Italy £9.75

DBW   David Baker Wines   ★★★

4 Derwen Road, Bridgend CF31 1LE (Tel 0656-650732). **Opening Hours:** Tues-Sat 9.30am-5.30pm, Closed Monday **Delivery:** free locally, nationally at cost. **Tastings:** every Saturday, tutored tastings given free of charge to organisations and groups. **Services:** mail order, gift mailing, glass hire.

Now with Richard Watkins at the helm, David Baker is the place to go if you're after Mick Morris or other Aussies from Cape Mentelle and Coldstream Hills, Argentinians from Norton and a fine set of Italians from the likes of Vajra, Santadi and La Parrina. Francophiles won't be disappointed by the many affordable clarets, and traditionalists will enjoy the Louis Latour red Burgundies.

1	Champagne Veuve Clicquot White Label Demi Sec, France £19.99
12	Montrose Cabernet Sauvignon, 1989, Australia £6.49
13	Mick Morris Shiraz, 1989, Australia £8.99
13	Morris Durif 1990 £9.99, Australia
19	Nederburg Noble Late Harvest, 1990, South Africa £4.19

BAL   Ballantynes of Cowbridge   ★★★★

3 Westgate, Cowbridge, South Glamorgen CF7 7YW (Tel 0446 774840 Fax 0446 775253). **Opening Hours:** Mon-Sat 9am-6pm. **Delivery:** free locally, nationally at cost. **Tastings:** regular themed.**Services:** cellarage, en primeur, mail order, gift mailing, glass hire.

Some classy fare is to be found in the Ballantyne family shop, which has just celebrated its first birthday (although the mail order side has been running for much longer). Whether your preference is for top Burgundy from Ponsot, Ramonet and Leflaive, Marcel Deiss Alsace, a set of toothsome country wines, some fine Italians or the New World offerings from Neil Ellis, Kumeu River and Cullens, the Ballantynes can slake your thirst, and provide much else besides.

2	Viognier, Côteaux des Baronnies, Dom. la Rosière, 1993, Rhône France £6.98
2	Pouilly Fuissé 'Tête de Cru', Dom. Ferret, 1986, Burgundy, France £18.40
3	Meursault 1er Cru Charmes, 1992, Chartron et Trebuchet, Burgundy, France £16.46
3	Chassagne Montrachet, 1990, Dom. Ramonet, Burgundy, France £22.75
4	Moscato d'Asti, Araldica, 1992, Piedmont, Italy £3.49
4	Marcel Deiss, Pinot Blanc 'Bergheim', 1991, Alsace, France £6.99
4	Dashwood Sauvignon Blanc, 1993, Marlborough, New Zealand £8.49
6	Gewürztraminer 'Cuvée Anne', M. Deiss, 1989, Alsace, France £42.00
9	Ruppertsberger Gaisböhle, Riesling Kabinett, Burklin-Wolf, 1990, Pfalz, Germany £10.75
11	Minervois 'Cuvée Tradition', Ch. de Blomac, 1991, Languedoc-Roussillon, France £4.73
12	Ch. Tour Haut Caussan, 1989 Médoc, France £7.48
12	Cape Mentelle Zinfandel, 1991, Margaret River, Western Australia £9.35
12	Ch. Grand Puy Lacoste, 1988, Pauillac, France £15.75
12	Castello di Ama, Vigna L'Apparita (Merlot), 1988, Tuscany, Italy £29.95
12	Ch. Vieux Château Certan, 1970, Pomerol, France £44.50
13	Cornas Les Ruchets, 1989, Jean-Luc Colombo, Rhône, France £12.98
14	Beaujolais, 1992 Dom. Terres Dorées, Burgundy, France £5.98
15	Pommard 1er Cru Les Cazetières, Philippe Naddef, Burgundy France £23.70

16	Barbera d'Asti, Ceppi Storici, 1990, Piedmont, Italy £4.98
16	Parrina, Tenuta la Parrina, 1990, Tuscany, Italy £4.98
17	Masia Barril Tipico, 1991, Priorato, Spain £7.34
19	Ch. Coutet, 1989, Barsac, France £20.00

BWS   The Barnes Wine Shop   ★★★★

51 Barnes High Street, London SW13 9LN(Tel 081 8788643). **Opening Hours:**
Mon-Sat 9.30am-8.30pm, Sun 12-2pm. **Delivery:** free locally, nationally at cost.
Tastings: in-store tastings regularly. **Services:** cellarage, en primeur, mail order,
gift mailing, glass hire, ice.

The Barnes Wine Shop emerges from a difficult year which has seen financial
problems and the death of James Rogers, the vinous guru who helped to establish
this merchant and the Fulham Road Wine Centre. Unlike the latter firm which closed
its doors between the publication of the 1994 and 1995 Guides, the Barnes villagers'
favourite Saturday gathering-place survives in a leaner and fitter form. Former
policeman Francis Murray has plodded on resolutely with an arresting selection of
wines. His list of Australians, South Africans and Italians of all hues should be taken
down as evidence of skilled winebuying.

1	Scharffenberger Brut, Rosé, Mendocino, California £13.50
3	Mantanzas Creek, Chardonnay, 1990, Sonoma, California £15.95
4	Dom. Osterag, Pinot Gris 'Barriques', 1992, Alsace, France £12.75
9	Dr. Loosen Riesling Qba, 1992, Germany £6.45
11	Cuvée Jean Paul, France £3.49
13	Quivira Zinfandel, 1989, Sonoma, California £9.95
13	St. Joseph, Pierre Gaillard, 1991, Rhône, France £10.95
14	Fleurie Dom. Berrod, 1992, Burgundy, France £7.99
15	Bourgogne Rouge 'Les Bons Batons' 1991, Patrice Rion, Burgundy France £8.95
16	Valpolicella Riserva, 1988, Le Ragose, Veneto, Italy £7.99
17	Rioja, Baron de Ley, 1987, Rioja, Spain £7.95
18	Dom. Cazes 1980, Rivesaltes Vieux, Languedoc, France £9.95
20	Don Zoilo, Very Old Fino, Jerez, Spain £9.95

BAR   Barwell & Jones

Barwell House, 24 Foer Street, Ipswich, Suffolk IP4 1JU (Tel 0473 280381). **Opening
Hours:** Mon-Fri 9am-12:30p.m.;2p.m.-6pm, Sat 9a.m.-1p.m. **Delivery:** free locally,
nationally at cost. **Tastings:** in-store tastings occasionally. **Services:** en primeur,
gift mailing, free glass loan.

Barwell & Jones continues with its organisational changes, splitting retail sales and
trade sales. If the retail list emulates the trade list, then one can expect a dependable,
albeit restaurant-directed selection world wines, especially French wines (with notable
second - fifth growth clarets), and organic Italians from Guerrieri-Rizzardi. Tokay
freaks will relish the chance to sample the 'Museum Wines' of the 1950s and 60s.

3	Chardonnay Woodburne Cuvée, Columbia Winery, 1992, Washington State, USA £12.50
4	Blanche de Bosredon Bergerac Sec, Tête de Cuvée, 1992, South West France £6.99
5	Soave Classico Costeggiola, Guerrieri-Rizzardi, 1993, Veneto, Italy £6.00
8	Riesling Mambourg, Pierre Sparr, 1991, Alsace, France £13.50
9	Rheingau Riesling Spätlese, Robert Weil, 1992, Germany £14.60
12	Columbia Merlot, Columbia Winery 1988, Washington State, USA £7.50
13	Woodstock Shiraz, 1992, Australia £7.99

15	Pinot Noir Woodburne Cuvée, 1992, Columbia Winery, Washington State, USA £12.50
15	Gevrey Chambertin, Labouré Roi, 1991, Burgundy, France £13.00
17	Montecillo Viña Monty, Rioja Gran Reserva, 1986, Spain £7.00
19	Wente Brothers Late Harvest Riesling 1989, California £10.60
19	Tokaji Aszu 5 Puttonyos, 1981, Tokaji, Hegyalja, Hungary £12.00
19	Kiedricher Wasseros Riesling Eiswein, Robert Weil 1992, Germany £70.00
20	Oloroso Solera BC 200, Osborne, Jerez, Spain £22.00

BEN Bennetts ★★★★★

High Street, Chipping Camden, Glos. GL55 6AG (Tel 0386 840392). **Opening Hours:** Mon–Fri 9am-1pm, 2-5.30pm, Sat 9am-5.30pm. **Delivery:** free locally, nationally at cost, free for 2 cases or more. **Tastings:** twice yearly, plus tutored wine dinners. **Services:** mail order, glass hire.

Charlie and Vickie Bennett's opening comments on their wine list bemoan the lakes of 'dull and disgusting' wines that so many producers and merchants still respectively insist on making and shipping. Fortunately they have bravely 'sifted through copious samples at home' to eradicate all of the dubious bottles and have come up with a list that is both quality-driven and good value. This year sees a substantial expansion of the Californian selection adding the admirable Newton, Ojai, Phelps and Sandford to a list that already includes Ridge and Calera but wisely and unapologetically sidesteps the wasteland of west-coasters at under a tenner.

1	Seppelts, Salinger, 1990, Australia £11.99
1	Champagne Francois Billion 'Le Mesnil' Blanc de Blancs, France £18.99
2	Olivier Merlin, Mâcon La Roche Vineuse, 1992, Burgundy, France £9.45
2	'Y' d'Yquem (sec) 1985, Bordeaux, France £35.95
3	Edna Vale Chardonnay 1990, California, £9.95
3	Felsina Berardenga, Chardonnay 'I Sistri', 1992, Tuscany, Italy £12.85
3	Bâtard Montrachet, Leflaive, 1986, Burgundy, France £59.50
4	Araldica, Chardonnay del Piedmont, 1993, Italy £4.95
4	Pewsey Vale Rhine Riesling, 1993, Adelaide Hills, Australia £6.75
4	Soave Classico, Pieropan, 1993, Veneto, Italy £6.95
6	Hugel, Gewürztraminer 'Jubilee', 1983, Alsace, France £16.40
12	Penfolds Bin 407 Cabernet Sauvignon, 1990, South Australia £9.95
12	La Reserve Du Général, 1988, Margaux, France £15.95
12	Clos Du Marquis, St. Julien, France £22.80
13	Cornas, Caves de Tain L' Hermitage, 1990, Rhône, France £10.65
13	Faugères, Château des Estanilles 'Cuvée Syrah, 1992, Languedoc France £11.30
13	Ojai Syrah, 1991, Santa Barbara, California, £12.20
14	Morgon, Côte de Py, 1992, Trenel, Burgundy, France £8.40
15	Joseph Drouhin, La Forêt Bourgogne Rouge, 1992, Burgundy, France £8.50
15	Bannockburn Pinot Noir, 1990, Geelong, Australia £11.95
15	Beaune,1er Cru, 'Les Epenottes', Vallet Frères, 1992 Burgundy, France £17.95
15	Yarra Yering Pinot Noir, 1990, Yarra Valley, Australia £24.90
17	Viña Ardanza, 1985, La Rioja Alta Rioja, Spain £10.35
19	Matua Valley Late Harvest Muscat, 1992, Auckland, New Zealand £5.50 (half)
19	Côteaux du Layon, Chaume, 1990, Petit Metris, Loire, France £9.85
19	Ch. Gilette, 1947, Sauternes, France £99.50
21	Ramos Pinto, 10 year old Tawny, Quinta da Ervamoira, Douro, Portugal £12.95

BKW   Berkeleys Wines   ★★

(Head Office:) China Lane, Warrington, Cheshire WA4 6RT (Tel 0925 444555).
Opening Hours: Mon-Sat 9am-10pm, Sun 12-3pm 7-10pm. **Delivery:** free locally
Services: gift mailing, glass hire.

This, the 'up-market' part of the Cellar 5 empire is expected to benefit from some upgrading this year and has already seen a decided improvement in its wine range. Watch this space.

1	Lindauer Rosé, Montana, New Zealand £6.99
1	Cuvée Napa, Mumm, California £8.99
3	Wolf Blass Chardonnay, 1993, Australia £6.99
4	Montana Sauvignon Blanc, 1993, New Zealand £4.99
12	Fortant De France Merlot, Skalli, 1993, Southern France £3.99
12	Ch. Monbousquet, Daniel Querre, 1990, St Emilion, Bordeaux £9.99
17	Marquès de Villamagna Rioja Gran Reserva, Bodegas Campo Viejo, 1982, Rioja, Spain £11.29

BWC   Berkmann Wine Cellar/Le Nez Rouge ★★★★

12 Brewery Road, London N7 9NH (Tel 071-609 4711). **Opening hours:** Mon-Fri 9am-5.30pm. **Delivery:** free locally, nationally at cost. **Tastings:** occasional in-store
Services: cellarage, mail order, gift mailing, glass hire.

Restaurateur Joseph Berkmann started his wine business in 1971, importing the then little-known wines of a certain Georges Duboeuf. Still understandably strong on the latter's Beaujolais, Mâconnais and Rhônes, Mr B who has returned to the helm from his beloved southern France, is also relishing the chance to offer Burgundies from the likes of Bernard Morey and Jean-Marc Boillot, James Halliday's Coldstream Hills wines from Australia and the Morton Estates from New Zealand. The Beringers from California are a mixed bag, but that winery's efforts to match food and wine must help endear them to Berkmann's faithful band of restaurateur customers.

2	St Véran Domaine de la Batie, Georges Duboeuf, 1993, France, £5.75
3	Morton Estate Reserve Black Label Chardonnay, 1991, Hawkes Bay, New Zealand £8.20
3	Coldstream Hills Chardonnay, 1993, Yarra Valley, Victoria, Australia £8.50
3	Coldstream Hills Reserve Chardonnay, 1992, Yarra Valley, Victoria, Australia £11.99
4	Muscadet de Sèvre et Maine sur Lie, Château du Cleray, Sauvion et Fils 1993, France £5.90
6	Viognier, Vin de Pays de l'Ardèche, Georges Duboeuf, 1993, France £5.00
12	Coldstream Hills Cabernet Merlot, 1992, Victoria, Australia £8.50
12	Morton Estate Black Label Cabernet-Merlot, 1991, New Zealand £8.60
12	Beringer Private Reserve Cabernet Sauvignon, 1989, California £21.50
13	Syrah Rouge, Vin de Pays d'Oc, Georges Duboeuf, 1993, France £3.50
14	Beaujolais Villages, Georges Duboeuf 1993, France £4.99
14	Morgon Jean Descombes, Georges Duboeuf 1993, France £6.00
14	Fleurie Domaine des Quatre Vents, Georges Duboeuf, 1993, France £6.00
15	Coldstream Hills Pinot Noir, 1993, Yarra Valley, Victoria, Australia £8.50
19	Gewürztraminer Côtes St Landelin, Grand Cru Vorbourg, Rene Muré, 1991, Alsace, France £21.25
21	Château de Beaulon, 10 Year Old Pineau des Charentes, South-West France £14.30

BBR   Berry Bros & Rudd   ★★★★

3 St. James's Street, London SW1A 1EG (Tel 071-396 9600). **Opening Hours:** Mon–Fri 9am-5.30pm. **Delivery:** free locally, nationally for one case or more. **Tastings:** regular in-store, tutored on request. **Services:** cellarage, en primeur, mail order, gift mailing, glass hire.

Leaping from 18th to 20th century without the aid of a time-machine, Berry Bros has opened a new branch, But you'll need to have your passport with you to get into the Duty Free Fine Wine Shop in Terminal 3 Heathrow Airport. It's a clever wheeze, especially given the quality of wine still served by quite a few airlines. Despite the welcome arrival of a few New World interlopers, the range, as ever, is reliably conservative, concentrating on top notch claret, Burgundy, port and serious German wines which these days rarely interest the younger customers of younger firms. Remember to bring a corkscrew and only to use it when in international airspace.

2	Hamilton Russell Chardonnay, 1992, Walker Bay, South Africa £8.78
6	Gewürztraminer Fronholz, Grand Cru, Domaine Ostertag, 1992, Alsace, France £12.95
8	Forster Kirchenstück, Riesling Kabinett, Bassermann-Jordan, 1990 Rheinpfalz, Germany £8.65
12	Berry's Good Ordinary Claret, France £4.50
12	Chateau Cheval Blanc, 1982, St Emilion, Bordeaux, France £98.00
13	Ch. Beaucastel 1990, Châteauneuf du Pape, Rhône, France £13.75
13	Qupe Syrah, Bien Nacido Vineyard, 1990 California £18.90
15	Beaune, Clos des Mouches, Joseph Drouhin 1988, Burgundy, France £26.00
19	Ch. Filhot 1989, Sauternes, France £23.00

BI   Bibendum Wine Ltd   ★★★★★

113 Regents Park Road, London NW1 8UR (071-722 5577). Wine by the case only. **Opening Hours:** Mon-Thurs 10am-6.30pm, Fri 10am-8pm, Sat 9.30-6.30pm. **Delivery:** free locally, nationally at cost. **Tastings:** regular in-store and informal tutored sessions, including fine wine. **Services:** cellarage, en primeur, mail order, gift mailing, glass hire, ice.

Like naughty schoolboys after too much sherbet, the Bibendum team continue to peddle wine with more enthusiasm than your average wine merchant. The ranges from regional France, Italy, California, the Rhône, Burgundy and Bordeaux in particular demand attention, although Aussies from Yeringberg and Seville Estate, Rolly Gassmann's Alsace and Germans from Mönchhof and Schloss Saarstein also merit more than just a passing glance. Keep a look out for the regular festivals and tutored tastings – a chance to try some great wines and to see an unbeatable range of bow ties. All in all a selection fit (for anyone luxuriously wanting) to be drunk.

2	La Serre Chardonnay, 1993, Vin de Pays d'Oc, France £4.25
2	Puligny Montrachet 'La Truffière', J M Boillot, 1991, Burgundy, France £27.75
3	Basedows Semillon, 1991, Barossa, South Australia £5.40
3	Rothesay Vineyard Chardonnay, Collard Brothers, 1991, New Zealand £7.00
3	Saintsbury Carneros Chardonnay, 1992, California £11.00
3	Morgan Chardonnay, 1992, California, £12.00
3	Saintsbury Carneros Reserve Chardonnay, 1991, California £14.00
4	La Serre Sauvignon Blanc, 1993, Vin de Pays d'Oc, France £4.25
4	Chenin Blanc, Hawkes Bay, Collard Brothers, 1993, New Zealand £5.75
4	Sauvignon Blanc Rothesay Vineyard, Collard Brothers, 1993, New Zealand £6.75

10	La Serre Rosé de Syrah, 1993, Vin de Pays d'Oc, France, £4.00
11	Fitou, Château L'Espigne, 'Fûts de Chêne', 1991, France £6.50
12	La Serre Cabernet Sauvignon, 1993, Vin de Pays d'Oc, France £4.00
12	Cabernet Sauvignon Kah-Nock-Tie, Konocti Winery, 1992, California, £5.00
12	Morgan Cabernet Sauvignon, 1990, Carmel Valley, California £12.00
12	Château Le Pin, 1982, Pomerol, France £345
13	La Serre Syrah, 1993, Vin de Pays d'Oc, France £4.00
13	Basedows Shiraz, 1992, Barossa, South Australia £5.50
13	Duxoup Charbono, 1991, California, £9.98
15	Saintsbury Pinot Noir, 1992, California, £11.00
15	Duxoup Carneros Pinot Noir, Hudson Vineyard, 1991, California £11.75
15	Morgan Pinot Noir, 1992, California, £12.00
15	Saintsbury Pinot Noir Reserve, 1991, California, £18.00
15	Clos St Denis, Domaine Dujac, 1980, Burgundy, France, £25.00
15	Clos de Vougeot Grand Cru, Domaine Méo-Camuzet, 1991, Burgundy, France £42.00
16	Uvello Rosso, Emme Effe Emme, 1993, Italy, £3.25
19	Vouvray 'Le Mont' Moelleux, Gaston Huët, 1961, France £65
19	Ch. d'Yquem 1939, Sauternes, France, £495
21	Niepoort Colheita Tawny Port, 1962, Douro, Portugal £45.00

BIN Bin '89 Wine Warehouse

89 Trippet Lane, Sheffield, South Yorkshire S1 4EL (Tel 0742 755889). **Opening Hours:** Sat 10.30-2pm. Closed every other day. **Delivery:** free in Sheffield and North Derbyshire (min. 3 cases), elsewhere at cost. **Tastings:** two in-store tastings per year. **Services:** glass hire.

Not so much early-closing as hardly-open; Saturday is the only day to catch this emporium trading, and even then the hours are 10.30 am. to 2 p.m. – ideal for those between recovering from Friday night and kick-off on Saturday. Prices are keen - most around £5 and rarely over £10 - and the selection of wines reflects this - strong on French regionals, Spanish, Italian, Australian and South American. If you want North American, look elsewhere, but you should discover some treats amongst the Crus Classés from the early 1980s. With a list that is vintage-lite, you may find it convenient - not to say enjoyable to discuss details and sample a few glasses with the owner, Jonathan Park, in his wine bar, Trippet's.

2	Dom. de la Batteuse, Chardonnay, Bernard Delmas, 1993, France £4.95
11	Ch. Roubia, Minervois, SCEA Mestre Grotti, 1991, France £4.25
14	Morgon, Gerard Belaid, 1991, Burgundy, France £7.25
15	Bourgogne Côte Chalonnaise, D'Heilly-Hubereau, 1991, Burgundy, France £7.30
17	Rioja Vega Crianza, Bodegas Muerza, 1989, Spain £3.46

BN Bin Ends (Rotherham)

83-85 Badsley Moor Lane, Rotherham, S. Yorks S65 2PH (Tel 0709 367771). **Opening Hours:** Mon-Fri 9.30am-5.30pm. **Delivery:** free locally, nationally at cost. **Tastings:** occasional in-store, plus tutored sessions for groups on request **Services:** gift mailing.

Showing enormous fortitude, Patrick Toone continues his quest for wines and spirits that, as he says, have yet to arrive on the shelves of even the most adventurous duty-free peddlers across the Channel. Just try asking the staff of such Calais *hypermarchés* as Auchan or Carrefour for the kind of venerable Madeiras, vintage Brandies and 30-year-old Borgogno Barolos Mr Toone has on offer.

BTH   Booths (Supermarkets)   ★★★★

4-6 Fishergate, Preston, Lancs PR1 3LJ (Tel 0772 251701). **Opening Hours:** vary from branch to branch. **Tastings:** occasional in-store. **Services:** occasional en primeur, glass hire.

Latour, Domaine de la Romanée Conti, Beaucastel, Mas de Daumas and Opus 1 in a supermarket? Congratulations! – you have just stumbled across one of the best kept secrets of the North; the small but perfectly formed chain of around 20 shops that has the guts to list a bewildering array of the world's brightest and best wines for extremely reasonable prices. Not many families spend £142.00 on their weekly shop, but if you can fast for seven days, you might wish to blow the budget on a bottle of Petrus 1981! Of course there is a range of much more sensibly priced own label wines too as well as some thumpingly good Australians.

3	Rosemount Chardonnay 1993, Hunter Valley, Australia £5.99	
4	Wairau River Sauvignon Blanc, 1993, Malborough, New Zealand £7.29	
13	Booths Côtes du Rhône 1990, France £3.39	
13	Ch. Grand Pontet St Emilion, 1990, Bordeaux, France £11.99	
16	Barolo Riserva Aldo Conterno, 1970, Piedmont, Italy £22.49	

BOO   Booths of Stockport   ★★★★

62 Heaton Moor Road, Heaton Moor, Stockport SK4 4NZ (Tel and Fax 061 432 3309). **Opening Hours:** Mon-Fri 9am-7pm, Sat/Sun 9am-5.30pm **Delivery:** free locally, nationally at cost. **Tastings:** occasional saturday in-store, plus monthly tutored sessions. **Services:** glass hire.

It may be symptomatic of wine consumption in the nineties, but Booth's are far from the only wine merchants to list more Australian wines than French. The reds from down-under catch the eye, made as they are by such producers as Henschke, Chapel Hill, Mountadam and Yarra Yering. With more than 50 to chose from (and over 30 whites), there is plenty to keep you busy without turning the page to glance through the impressive Spanish selection or the small but well formed list of Italians. The nod to France is more than cursory, including such gems as Vallet-Frères Burgundies to satisfy even the most ardent Francophile.

3	Henschke Eden Valley Chardonnay, 1991, South Australia £9.65
3	Henschke Lenswood Vineyard Croft Chardonnay, 1991, South Australia £10.65
3	Mountadam Chardonnay, 1992, South Australia £11.95
3	Tucks Ridge Chardonnay, 1992, Australia £7.50
12	Cousiño Macul Antiguas Reservas Cabernet Sauvignon, 1989, Chile, £5.99
12	Eden Ridge Cabernet Sauvignon, 1992, Australia £7.30
12	Cyril Henschke Cabernet Sauvignon, 1988, Australia £9.65
12	Newton Unfiltered Merlot, 1991, California £15.05
13	Peel Estate Shiraz, 1988, Western Australia £7.95
13	David Wynn Patriach Shiraz, 1992, South Australia £9.25
13	Frog's Leap Zinfandel, 1991, California £10.65
13	Henschke Mount Edelstone Shiraz, 1990, South Australia £10.65
15	Mountadam Pinot Noir, 1992, South Australia £11.95
17	Moralinos Toro, Bodega Cooperativa Nuestra Senora de las Viñas, 1992, Spain £4.00
12	Cismeira Reserva, Quinta da Cismeira, 1990, Portugal £5.50
12	Artadi Viñas de Gain Rioja Crianza, Cosecheros Alaveses, 1991, Rioja, Spain £5.50
21	Niepoort Colheita Port, 1978, Douro, Portugal £25.00

BD   Bordeaux Direct   ★★★

New Aquitaine House, Paddock Road, Reading, Berks. RG4 0JY (Tel 0734 4817).
Opening Hours: Office: Mon–Fri 10am-7pm, Sat 9am-6pm; Shops: Mon-Fri 9am-7pm, Sat/Sun 10am-4pm plus 24-hour answerphone. **Delivery:** free over £50.
Tastings: regular in-store, including tutored. **Services:** mail order, glass hire.

A group of five shops selling the same range as the Sunday Times Wine Club (qv).

BGC   Borg Castel Wines   ★★★

Samlesbury Mill, Goosefoot Lane, Samlesbury Bottoms, Preston PR5 0RN (Tel 0254 852128). No credit cards. **Opening Hours:** Mon-Fri 10am-5pm, Sat by appointment, first Sunday in the month 12-4pm **Delivery:** free locally, nationally at cost.
Tastings: regular in-store, plus tutored tastings for groups (minimum 30). **Services:** cellarage, mail order, gift mailing, glass hire, ice.

Hidden amongst some fairly ordinary minor clarets and a patchy range of New World wines are some real rarities, albeit in limited quantities. What about a bottle of 'Y' d'Yquem from 1960 for £51.09? (Why? You may well ask.) The Burgundy section features the excellent wines of Vallet Frères and Chablis from William Fèvre and J.M. Bonnet. Alsace is represented by the reliable Turkheim range and there's quite a find in Wildekrans, a highly rated newcomer to the South African scene.

2	Pinot Blanc Turkheim, 1993, Alsace, France	£5.10
4	Wildekrans Sauvignon Blanc 1993, South Africa	£5.26
15	Gevrey Chambertin Vallet Frères, 1989, Burgundy, France	£16.45

BU   Bottoms Up   ★★★★★

Sefton House, 42 Church Road, Welwyn Garden City, Herts AL8 6RJ (Tel 0707 328244). **Opening Hours:** Mon-Sat 10a.m.-10p.m., Sun various. **Delivery:** free locally (within 48 hours); nationally at cost. **Tastings:** occasionally in-store **Services:** gift vouchers, free glass loan (with order).

For some reason, this, the most exciting part of the Threshers/Drink Stores/Wine Rack empire has not attracted as much attention as it deserves. The atmosphere is pitched midway between Majestic and Oddbins (both qv) and the staff often look and sound as though they might easily find alternative employment at either of those chains. The range is wider than that of Wine Rack (qv), in our experience the chances of finding the bottle you want is far greater than in those shops and, if you join the ranks of what the company has (to our mind, rather worryingly) named 'Bottoms Up Imbibers', you get to save 15% on every case you buy. But it's still worth doing your sums; some of the prices could do without that discount. But, if you haven't wandered into one of these shops, do give one a try: if only to pick up a free copy of the brilliant, *Independent Magazine* -like black-and-white price list-cum-magazine.

1	Seppelt Salinger, 1991, Australia	£10.50
1	Champagne Piper Heidsieck Brut, France,	£14.99
2	Red Cliffs Estate Colombard-Chardonnay, 1993, Australia	£3.99
2	Chablis 1er Cru Beauroy, Alain Geoffroy, 1992, Burgundy, France	£9.99
2	Hermitage Blanc Guigal, 1991, Rhône, France	£14.99
3	Penfolds Bin 21 Semillon-Chardonnay, 1993, Australia	£3.99
4	Le Cordon, Lot 39, Vin de Pays d'Oc Blanc, Meffre, 1993, France	£3.99
4	Vernaccia, Falchini, 1992, Tuscany, Italy	£4.99
5	Vouvray Demi-Sec, Domaine de la Mabillière, 1992, Loire, France	£4.55
6	Viognier, Vin De Pays D'Oc, Fortant de France, 1992, France	£6.95
7	Tollana Dry White, Penfolds, 1993, Australia	£3.49
8	Riesling Reserve, Rolly-Gassmann, 1991, Alsace, France	£8.29

11	Domaine des Salices Merlot, Vin de Pays d'Oc, J & F Lurton, 1993, South-West France £3.99
11	Ch. Montus fûts de chêne, Madiran, Brumont, 1990, France £9.99
12	Lindemans Pyrus, 1991, Australia £9.99
12	Ch. D'Angludet, Margaux, 1987, France £11.99
13	Saint Joseph L'Olivaie, P Coursodon, 1992, Rhône, France £11.29
14	Fleurie, Cellier Des Samsons, 1993, Beaujolais, France £6.69
15	Savigny Les Beaune, Domaine Maillard, 1990, Burgundy, France £9.99
15	Nuits St Georges Premier Cru, Clos de l'Arlot, Dom. de l'Arlot, 1990, Burgundy, France £25.99
16	Le Volte, Tenuta dell'Ornellaia, 1992, Tuscany, Italy £7.99
16	Recioto Amarone della Valpolicella Classico, Zenato, 1986, Veneto, Italy £9.99
17	Albor Rioja, Campo Viejo, 1992, Rioja, Spain £3.49
17	Bairrada, Luis Pato, 1990, Portugal £6.99
21	Dow's 10 Year Old Tawny Port, Douro, Portugal £14.49
21	Rutherford & Miles Jubilee Selection Verdelho, 1952, Madeira, Portugal £69.00

BWI   Bute Wines   ★★★★

Mount Stuart, Rothesay, Isle of Bute, Argyll & Bute PA20 9LP (Tel 0700 502730). Wine by the case only. No credit cards. **Opening Hours:** Mon–Fri 9am-5pm. **Delivery:** free locally. **Tastings:** occasional. **Services:** cellarage, en primeur, mail order, gift mailing, glass hire, ice.

The Island of Bute may seem a curious place to find one of the country's best wine merchants, but Jennifer, Marchioness of Bute, continues to direct operations from the ancestral Isle. Of course most of the wine is stored in warehouses in London and Scotland and delivery can be arranged anywhere in the country, which is lucky because the range and depth of wines available is astonishing. Lady Bute's policy from the start has been to concentrate on the top names in the top vintages and to buy lots of them – which explains the presence of over 90 Classed Growth Clarets from 1989 alone. Indeed, it was a revelation for her to find that wine could be bought by the bottle from some merchants.

Burgundy and the Rhône have rarely been better served with names like Dujac, Ampeau, Mongeard Mugneret, Domaine de l'Arlot, Jean Noel Gagnard, Jaboulet, Guigal and Chave catching the eye. Recent developments have seen a diversification into more affordable everyday wines like the Weinert range from Argentina and a red and white from Ryecroft Flame Tree in Australia, which are now taking care of the bread and butter business.

| 6 | Tokay Pinot Gris Grand Cru Gloeckelberg, Vendange Tardive, Charles Koehly, 1989, Alsace, France £17.82 |
| 17 | Collection Privada, Bodega J E Navarro Correas, 1988 Argentina £9.75 |

BUT   The Butlers Wine Cellar   ★★★

247 Queens Park Road, Brighton, E. Sussex BN2 2X3 (Tel 0273 698724/622761). **Opening Hours:** Tues, Wed 10am-6pm, Thurs, Fri 10am-7pm, Sat 9am-7pm. **Delivery:** free locally, nationally at cost. **Tastings:** regular in-store, starting up new short wine courses. **Services:** mail order, glass hire.

1954 Chianti, 1916 Branaire Ducru, 1952 Clos de Vougeot, 1975 Zonnebloem Shiraz... Vinous antiques of the most interesting sort abound in Geoffrey Butler's establishment, but they also share the shelves with more modern fare, such as Californians from Goosecross, d'Arenberg Aussies and some great Italians. Despite the endearingly-Woodstockian appearances of young Mr Butler, the golden thread that runs through this merchant's offerings is tradition.

ABY   Anthony Byrne Fine Wines Ltd   ★★★★★

88 High Street, Ramsey, Huntingdon, Cambs. PE17 1BS (Tel 0487 814555).
Opening Hours: Mon–Fri 9am-5.30pm. **Delivery:** free for five cases or more (or orders over £250). **Tastings:** throughout the year at various venues. **Services:** cellarage.

Anthony Byrne's range is pretty familiar – to people who are lucky enough to be on more of a nodding acqaintance with Britain's starrier restaurants. Mr Byrne's popularity with chefs and sommeliers is understandable. Like a cook who has discovered fresh ways of preparing a traditional dish, he has put together a team of great new-wave, old-world producers, including such names as Domaine de l'Arlot, Zind Humbrecht, Didier Dagueneau, Alain Graillot and Pierre-Jacques Druet of Bourgueil. The new world is not neglected, with welcome but little-known producers as Esk Valley, Bannockburn and Delatite. Indeed, it all seems so well chosen that one can almost believe it is worth having another try of the Gallo Sauvignon and Jaboulet Vercherre Burgundy which somehow slipped in amongst the vinous aristocracy.

1	Champagne Drappier Blanc de Blancs, France £15.91
1	Seppelt Sparkling Shiraz, 1991, Australia £8.99
2	Chablis 1er Cru Fourchaume, Ch. de Maligny, 1992, France £11.20
2	Santa Rita 120 Chardonnay, 1993, Chile £4.49
4	Pouilly Fumé Silex, Didier Dagueneau 1992, France £23.50
7	Muscat, Zind Humbrecht 1992, Alsace, France £8.92
8	Riesling Clos St. Urbain, Zind Humbrecht, 1992, Alsace, France £14.20
12	Opus One, Rothschild/Mondavi, 1990, California £45.00
13	Crozes Hermitage, Dom. des Entrefaux, 1992, Rhône, France £6.30
13	Château Pibarnon, Bandol, 1991, Midi, £11.34
14	Fleurie Classique, Cellier des Samsons, 1993, Beaujolais, France £6.83
15	Nuits-Saint-Georges, Dom. de L'Arlot, 1991, Burgundy, France £14.60
19	Tokay Rotenburg Selection de Grain Nobles, Zind Humbrecht, 1991, Alsace, France £49.28
19	Ch. Haut Caplane, 1990, Sauternes, France £13.99
21	Calem Fine Ruby Port, Douro, Portugal £6.99
21	Calem 20 Year Old Tawny Port, Douro, Portugal £17.99

DBY   David Byrne & Co   ★★★★

Victoria Buildings, 12 King Street, Clitheroe, Lancs BB7 2EP (Tel 0200 23152). No credit cards. **Opening Hours:** Mon, Tues,Weds, Sat 8.30am-6pm, Thurs, Fri 8.30am-8pm. **Delivery:** free locally, nationally at cost. **Tastings:** in-store most weekends and on request to groups. **Services:** en primeur depending on quality, glass hire.

David Byrne remains in (the lime)light. This must be the place for anyone looking to stock up on 1994 International Wine Challenge medal winners. Andrew & Philip Byrne - the merchant's present talking heads - have put together a wide-ranging list, taking particular care over Australasia and Spain. The ongoing rivalry between the Byrnes and their neighbours Whitesides must make Clitheroe a city of dreams for any wine buff looking to spend a lifetime piling up such delights as St Halletts, Tim Adams, Chapoutier and Coopers Creek. Not bad for a town on the road to nowhere.

2	Chablis Premier Cru Fourchaume, Paul Boutinot, 1992, France £7.99
3	Mitchelton Reserve Chardonnay, 1992, Australia £7.49
3	Moss Wood Chardonnay, Margaret River, 1993, Australia £11.00
3	Pipers Brook Vineyard Chardonnay, 1992, Tasmania £12.99
4	Dashwood Sauvignon Blanc, 1993, New Zealand £7.99
8	Jackson Estate Marlborough Dry Riesling, 1993, New Zealand £6.49

Merchants 177

8	Riesling Cuvée Frederic Emile, Trimbach, 1988, Alsace £15.99
10	Miguel Torres Cabernet Sauvignon Rosé, 1993, Chile £4.49
12	Rouge Homme Cabernet Sauvignon, 1991, Australia £6.99
12	Yalumba Signature Reserve Cabernet Sauvignon-Shiraz, 1990, South Australia £8.99
12	Amiral de Beychevelle, St Julien, 1989, Bordeaux, France £12.99
13	David Wynn Shiraz, 1992, South Australia £6.10
15	Mountadam Pinot Noir, 1992, South Australia £11.95
17	Vina Arana Rioja Reserva, La Rioja Alta, 1986, Spain £8.75
20	Alegria Manzanilla, Perez Megia, Jerez, Spain £6.50
21	Gould Campbell Late Bottled Vintage Port, 1987, Douro, Portugal £8.99
21	Bailey's Founder Liqueur Tokay, Victoria, Australia £9.95
21	Churchill's 10 Year Old Tawny Port, Douro, Portugal £12.99

CPS CPA's Wine Ltd

44 Queens Road, Mumbles, Swansea SA3 4AN (Tel 0792 360707). **Opening Hours:** Mon, Wed, Thurs, 2-6.30pm, Sat 10am-6pm **Delivery:** free locally, nationally at cost. **Tastings:** regular in-store, plus tutored tastings with guest speaker and gourmet dinners at a country-house hotel. **Services:** mail order, glass hire.

It may not surprise you to learn that you can pop in to CPA's in Swansea and walk out with a bottle of Welsh white or rosé. There are, after all, not many other places where you can find the stuff. Less adventurous - or locally patriotic - wine lovers might prefer to stick to the Seppi Landmann Alsace wines or Henschke's stunners from South Australia.

2	Pouilly Fuissé, Gilles Noblet, 1992, Burgundy, France £9.10
4	Sancerre, André Dézat, 1992, Loire, France £10.05
5	Seyval/Reichensteiner 1992, Cariad Wines, Wales, £6.60
6	Tokay d'Alsace Vallée Noble 1992, S. Landmann, Alsace, France £7.95
12	Ch. Tour du Haut Moulin, 1985, Haut Médoc, France £10.45
12	Penley Estate Cabernet Sauvignon, 1990, South Australia, £12.55
13	Ch. de Grand Moulas 1991, Côtes du Rhône Villages, France £6.40
13	Mount Edelstone Shiraz, 1990, Henschke, South Australia £10.60
19	Vouvray Clos du Bourg 1989, Huët, Loire, France £11.70 (half)

CAC Cachet Wines

Lysander Close, Clifton Moor, York, YO3 4XB (Tel 0904 690090). **Opening Hours:** Mon–Fri 8.30am-5pm, Sat 9am-12.30pm. Wine by the case only. **Delivery:** free locally. **Tastings:** regular in-store. **Services:** cellarage, en primeur, mail order, gift mailing, glass hire, ice.

The particular cachet here lies in wines like Georges Gardet Champagne, Materne Haegelin Alsace, Château Tour de Pez, Daniel Defaix Chablis, Capezzana Carmignano, Sanford Californians, Vavasour Kiwis, Simon Hackett Aussies, and Simonsig South Africans.

1	Champagne Georges Gardet Rosé Brut, France £17.50
3	Nautilus Chardonnay, Marlborough, 1993, New Zealand £7.99
4	Ch. Elget, Muscadet de Sevre et Maine, G. Luneau, 1992, France £5.25
6	Fetzer Gewürztraminer, 1993, California £5.94
12	Oxford Landing Cabernet-Shiraz, Yalumba, 1992, South Australia £4.99
13	Yalumba Family Reserve Shiraz 1990, South Australia £6.99
15	Sanford Pinot Noir 1992, California, U.S. 14.31
15	Bourgogne Hautes-Cotes De Nuits, Dom. A-F Gros 1989, France £6.00
15	Beaune 1er Cru, Domaine Parent 1990, Burgundy, France £15.00

CAP Cape Province Wines ★★★

1 The Broadway, Kingston Road, Staines, Middlesex TW18 1AT (Tel 0784 451860).
Opening Hours: Mon–Sat 9am-9pm. **Delivery:** free in immediate neighbourhood.
Tastings: lectures at local societies. **Services:** mail order, gift mailing.

The deal here is pretty simple: mail order South African wines by the mixed case.
You would be well advised to invest in John Platter's South African wine guide as
there is little descriptive text on the single A4 sheet to help you make your selection,
and after all most Cape Wines have yet to be tried and tested by the UK palate.
Prices are much the same as you might find in a regular shop, but there is a superb
range including many of the best estates, although there are quite a few of the merely
ordinary. Look out for anything from Fairview, Kanonkop, Meerlust or Boschendal.

1	Pongràcz Brut, Bergkelder, South Africa £9.70
4	Le Bonheur Sauvignon Blanc, 1993, South Africa £6.99
12	Meerlust Rubicon, 1986, South Africa £10.83
13	Fairview Shiraz, 1990, South Africa £4.72
19	Neethlingshof Weisser Reisling, Noble Late Harvest, 1991, South Africa £8.22 (half)

CWI A Case of Wine ★★★

Harford, Pumpsaint, Ilanwrda, Dyfed SA19 8DT (Tel 0558 650671). **Opening Hours:**
Mon-Fri 8am till late, Sat 9am till late, Sun 9am-5pm. **Delivery:** free locally, nationally
at cost. **Tastings:** regularly in-store and tutored for private occasions and colleges.
Services: cellarage, glass hire, ice.

Wales used to be a disaster zone for wine lovers, but over the last few years, there
has been a sudden explosion of small merchants, many of which would be the envy
of people living in the supposedly spoiled areas of South-East England. A Case of
Wine is a good example, offering a decent set of French country wines, Californians
from Newton and some fine Aussies from Mount Langi Ghiran and Shaw & Smith.
However, Aldo Steccanella's real passion is Italy, and his range sweeps impressively
over the country from hip to toe. We'd particularly point out the Allegrini
Valpolicella, Puiatti whites, Vajra Piemontese and the Chianti Classico from Isole e
Olena.

CEL Cellar 5 Ltd ★★

China Lane, Warrington, Cheshire WA4 6RT (Tel 0925 444555). **Opening Hours:**
10am-10pm, Sunday and public holidays 12-2pm 7-10pm. **Delivery:** free locally.
Tastings: upon application **Services:** glass hire free with order.

Why include Cellar 5 here? Only because we've heard a whisper that it may be worth
keeping an eye on these shops over the next few months. The rumours say that the
sleepy, fag-'n-beer besotted giant of wine-buying (close on 500 shops) may be
developing a better taste for wine. (qv Berkeley Wines).

1	Ackerman '1811' Brut, Saumur, France £7.29
1	Seppelt Great Western Rosé, Australia £4.99
2	Fortant De France Chardonnay, 1993, South West France £3.99
3	Mitchelton Chardonnay 1992, Victoria, Australia £5.99
4	Santa Rita 120 Sauvignon Blanc, 1994, Chile £3.99
4	Riva Trebbiano di Romagna, Ronco/Gaetana Carron, 1993, Italy £2.79
12	Penfold's Bin 389 Cabernet-Shiraz, 1991, Australia £7.99
12	Cabernet Sauvignon, L A Cetto, 1990, Mexico £4.75
16	Barolo, Fontanafredda, 1989, Piedmont, Italy £7.99
17	Campo Viejo Rioja Reserva, 1988, Spain £4.99

CHF — Chippendale Fine Wines ★★★

15 Manor Square, Otley, West Yorks. LS21 3AP (Tel 0943 850633). **Opening Hours:** Mon, Tues, Thurs, Fri 10am-5.45pm, Sat 9.30am-5pm. **Delivery:** negotiable rate for three cases or more. **Tastings:** regular in-store. **Services:** gift mailing, glass hire, ice.

Mention 'Chippendales' in Otley and there is a good chance that instead of raising a salacious smirk you will be directed instead to Manor Square where you should find the well-oiled Michael Pollard flexing his taste buds. Muscular Australian reds like Yarra Yering and Tim Adams Shiraz pose languidly next to strapping Rhônes from Marc Sorrel and the beefy Château Musar from as far back as 1979. If you can't make it to South Yorkshire, 'phone up and ask for a list and expose yourself to Mr Pollard's hilariously scathing prose, while you decide which of the excellent line up of Aussies, Kiwis, Italians and Californians you would most like to take home for the evening.

1	David Wynn Brut, South Australia £8.30	
4	Babich Semillon-Chardonnay, 1993, New Zealand £6.80	
12	Newton Unfiltered Merlot, 1991, California, £15.05	
21	Niepoort LBV Port 1987, Douro, Portugal £10.50	

CC — Chiswick Cellar ★★★

84 Chiswick High Road, Chiswick W4 WSY (Tel 081 9947989). **Opening Hours:** Mon-Fri 10am-10pm, Sat 10am-11pm, Sun 12-3pm 7-10pm. **Delivery:** free locally. **Tastings:** regular in-store. **Services:** glass hire, ice.

With the external appearance of a local off-licence that might do at 9.50 p.m. for a packet of fags and a Ginsters cheese slice a week or two past its sell-by- date, Chiswick Cellar is not likely to lure in many wine enthusiasts. Those who do venture inside, however, are guaranteed to find that they have stumbled across one of the most impressive independent wine shops in London. If you live anywhere near, do yourself a favour and investigate; you could well bump into a few familiar faces from the nearby BBC.

3	Goldwater Chardonnay, 1993, Auckland, New Zealand £8.99	
3	Torres Gran Vina Sol, 1993, Spain £5.40	
12	Miguel Torres Cabernet Sauvignon, 1991, Chile £4.99	
19	Torcolato Vino Dolce Naturale, Maculan, 1991, Italy, £22.85	

CWW — Classic Wines & Spirits Ltd ★★★

Unit A2, Stadium Industrial Estate Stendal Road, Chester CH1 4LU (Tel 0244 390444 Fax 0244 378980). **Opening Hours:** Mon-Fri 7.30am-6pm, Sat 9am-5pm. **Delivery:** Free nationally. **Tastings:** occasional in-store. **Services:** mail order, gift mailing, ice.

Primarily operating as wholesale merchants to the trade, Classic has grown large in the ten years of its existence. Private customers can take advantage of the extremely competitive prices offered, provided they are prepared to buy twelve bottles. Of note is "The Champagne Exchange", their nationwide mail-order company, which offers some extremely tempting prices on an excellent range of Grandes Marques (but do remember to add on the dreaded VAT before flexing the old plastic).

1	Champagne Lanson Brut Rosé, France £22.99	
1	Champagne 'R' de Ruinart Brut, France £22.00	
4	Foundation 1725 Bordeaux Blanc, Barton & Guestier, 1992, France £4.99	

180 Merchants

CWS   The Co-operative Wholesale Society   ★★★

New Century House, P.O. Box 53, Manchester M60 4ES (Tel 061 8341212).
Opening Hours: normal trade hours. **Delivery:** not available. **Tastings:**
occasionally. **Services:** ice in selected stores.

As we have said before, it isn't easy being the Co-op – or not if you want to sell good
wine. But Arabella Woodrow seems to relish a challenge. So, she's steadily improved
the quality of the own-label wines which make up a major proportion of her range,
to the point at which they stand comparison with 'domaine' wines sold by 'smarter'
chains. Much of the rest of the selection comprises a reliable but unexciting range of
branded (and T.V. advertised) products indistinguishable from those offered
elsewhere, but there is a growing number of agreeable and adventurous surprises
such as Château Cissac, Brown Bros Tarrango or Hamilton Russell Pinot Noir. Take
the trouble to find a bigger store and you could well pick up a few bargain bottles
while having a very serendipitous time.

1	Omar Khayyam, Indian Sparkling Wine, 1987, £6.99
1	Daniel Le Brun Brut, Cellier Le Brun, New Zealand £11.99
2	Co-op Chablis, La Chablisienne, 1990, Burgundy, France £6.79
3	Sanford Chardonnay, 1992, California £13.82
3	Houghton Swan Valley Dry White, 1991, Australia £4.79
4	Hermanos Lurton Rueda, J & F Lurton, 1993, Spain, £3.89
4	Vina Alfali Valdepeñas Blanco, Bodegas Felix Solis, 1993, Spain £2.99
4	Co-op Vin De Pays des Côtes de Gascogne, Grassa, France £2.99
8	White Cloud, House of Nobilo, 1993, Australia £4.50
9	Co-Op Spätlese Pfalz, GWG Rietburg, 1990, Germany £3.49
9	Hastings Medium Dry, Carr Taylor Vineyards, England £3.95
9	Graacher Himmelreich Riesling Spätlese, Adolph Huesgen, 1992, Germany £4.35
11	Co-op Cape Red, Simonsvlei Coop, South Africa £2.99
12	Chateau Reynella Cabernet Merlot, 1992, Hardy's, Australia £6.75
12	Firestone Cabernet Sauvignon, 1991, California £9.52
12	Caliterra Estate Cabernet Sauvignon, Viña Caliterra, 1992, Chile, £3.99
12	La Serre Cabernet Sauvignon, Vin de Pays d'Oc, 1993, France £4.00
12	Brown Brothers King Valley Cabernet Sauvignon, 1991, Australia £6.50
12	St Emilion, Baron Philippe De Rothschild, 1991, Bordeaux, France £8.79
12	Ch. Cissac, Haut Médoc, 1985, Bordeaux, France £12.60
13	Vacqueyras Cuvée Du Marquis de Fonséguille, Caves de Vacqueyras, 1991, Rhône, France £5.49
13	Co-op Côtes du Rhône, Co-op Chusclan, France £2.99
13	L.A.Cetto Petite Sirah, 1991, Mexico £4.75
13	Co-op Jacaranda Hill Shiraz-Cabernet, Australia £3.39
14	Rosemount Shiraz/Cabernet Sauvignon, 1993, Australia £4.69
14	Brown Brothers Tarrango, 1993, Victoria, Australia £4.99
16	Co-op Montepulciano D'Abruzzo, Girelli, Italy £2.99
17	Señorio de Nava Ribera del Duero Crianza, 1989, Spain £5.99
17	Monte-Vannos Ribero del Duero Reserva, 1987, Spain £10.36
17	Co-op Dão, Sogrape, 1990, Portugal £2.99
17	Co-op Santos, Caves Aliança, Portugal £2.99
17	Co-op Navarra Tinto, Julian Chivite, Spain £2.59
19	Domaine Du Haut Rauly Monbazillac, 1990, France, £3.49
20	Co-op Pale Dry, Luis Caballero, Jerez, Spain £3.99
21	Niepoort Senior Port, Douro, Portugal £10.00
21	Co-op Vintage Character, Smith Woodhouse, Douro, Portugal £6.25
21	Late Bottled Vintage Port, Sandeman 1989, Douro, Portugal £9.99
21	Dow's 10 Year Old Tawny Port, Douro, Portugal £14.49
22	Piemontello Light, Santero, Italy £1.99

CCL Cockburns of Leith/The Wine Emporium ★★★

7 Devon Place, Edinburgh EH12 5HJ (Tel 031 346 1113 Fax 031 313 2607). **Opening Hours:** Mon-Fri 9am-6pm, Sat 10-6pm; Sun 11-5pm **Delivery:** free nationally. **Tastings:** regularly in store, plus regular tutored tastings. **Services:** cellarage, mail order, glass loan, ice.

'Scotland's oldest Wine Merchants' (we presume they mean the business and not the staff) are shortly about to celebrate their bicentenary (in 1996) and are in pretty good shape for the next couple of hundred years. Earlier this year they added the Broad Street Wine Company (who brought with them the agency for Rongopai Estate and a very tempting range of Cognacs and Armagnacs) to their Emporium and further expanded a range which now includes all of the Lustau sherries, as well as a selection of wines from Jean-Pierre Perrin of Chateau Beaucastel's La Vielle Ferme estate

1	Champagne Charbaut N.V. France £20.00
2	Chablis, La Chablisienne, 1990, Burgundy, France £9.00
4	La Vielle Ferme Blanc, Côtes du Lubéron, 1992, Southern France £6.00
9	Wehlener Sonnenuhr Riesling Kabinett, 1989, Mosel, Germany £10.50
10	Château de Sours, Bordeaux Rosé, 1992, France £8.50
11	Taltarni Fiddleback Terrace Red, 1991, Victoria, Australia £8.00
12	Ch. de Cardaillon, Graves , 1990, Bordeaux, France £12.00
12	Clos du Marquis, St. Julien, 1989, Bordeaux, France £24.00
17	Contino Reserva, 1988, Rioja, Spain £10.50
19	Rongopai Botrytised Chardonnay 1992, New Zealand £19.50 (half)
20	'Los Arcos', Lustau Dry Amontillado, Jerez, Spain £8.00

CNL Connolly's (Wine Merchants) Ltd ★★★

Arch 13, 220 Livery Street, Birmingham B3 1EU (Tel 021 236 9269). **Opening Hours:** Mon-Fri 9am-5.30pm, Sat 10am-2pm. **Delivery:** free locally. **Tastings:** regular in-store, plus monthly tutored sessions. **Services:** mail order, gift mailing, glass hire, ice.

Chris Connolly is as good a wine merchant as he is a rotten poet, which is praise indeed. We readily forgive the execrable McGonnegallesque verse with which he introduces his wine list; indeed, after a glass or three of any of the wines we've listed below, we might even be persuaded to request an encore.

1	Champagne Georges Gardet Rosé Brut, France £17.50
4	Babich Hawkes Bay Sauvignon Blanc, 1993, New Zealand £6.80
8	Hochheim, Deinhard Heritage Collection, 1988, Germany £6.99
8	Deinhard Collection, Deidesheim, 1988, Germany £6.75
13	Houghton Wildflower Ridge Shiraz, 1992, Western Australia £4.79
17	Rioja Alavesa Artadi, Cosecheros Alaveses, 1993, Spain £3.99
21	Calem Colheita, 1986, Portugal £11.50

COK Corkscrew Wines ★★★

Arch no 5, Viaduct Estate, Carlisle CA2 5BN (Tel: 0228 43033). **Opening Hours:** Mon-Sat 10am-6pm. **Delivery:** free locally. **Tastings:** regular in-store, plus new wine club. **Services:** en primeur, gift mailing, glass hire.

How is it that there are so many superb wine merchants in Cumbria? Here is another one, tucked away in a railway arch in a corner of Carlisle and offering a laudable selection of good Cru Bourgeois Bordeaux and Australian reds and white. The stock of inexpensively priced, well-kept old wines has also recently been further improved by the acquisition of the private cellar of a leading member of the wine trade.

1	'J' Brut 1988, Jordan Winery, Sonoma, California £17.99	
2	Chablis, Dom. Voceret et Fils, 1993, Burgundy, France £7.99	
4	Moodah Brook Estate Verdelho, 1993, Western Australia £5.99	
4	de Redcliffe Rhine Riesling, 1993, Marlborough, New Zealand £7.49	
11	Côteaux de Mascara, 1987, Algeria £5.25	
12	Ch. Beaumont, Haut-Médoc, 1989, Bordeaux, France £8.49	
12	Cyril Henschke Cabernet Sauvignon 1988, Barossa South Australia £10.99	
13	Côtes du Rhône Valvigneyre, Alain Paret, 1991, Rhône, France £4.99	
16	Copertino Riserva, Cantina Sociale Copertino, 1991, Puglia Italy £4.75	
19	Anjou Moulin Touchais, 1969, Loire, France £23.99	
21	Seppelt Para Liqueur Tawny, Bottling No. 115, Australia £15.99	

COR Corn Road Vintners ★★★

The Cellar, Bridge Street, Rothbury, Morpeth, Northumberland NE65 7SE (Tel 0669 20240). By the case, but hopefully introducing bottle sales at the end of 1994. **Opening Hours:** Flexible, but in general Mon, Weds, Thurs, Fri, Sat 10am-4pm, Sun 12-3pm **Delivery:** free for 3 cases or more. **Tastings:** regular on site, three roadshow tastings a year, plus sessions for groups on request. **Services:** mail order, gift mailing, glass hire.

A clear and simple list, organised by grape variety and refreshingly free of the sort of 'tired old fogey' wines too frequently found lurking in the cellars of other wine merchants up and down the land. Graham Hodgson and his team were surprised by the 'phenomenal response' generated by their first wholesale list last year, but with wines from Charles Melton and Mt Langi Ghiran in Australia, South Africans Hamilton Russell, Klein Constantia and Simonsig and Champagne from Michel Gonet we can see what all the fuss was about.

4	Regatta 1991, Valley Vineyards Twyford England £4.99	
4	Klein Constantia, Sauvignon Blanc 1993, Cape South Africa £5.60	
9	Niersteiner Pettenthal Riesling Spätlese 1990, Anton Balbach Rheinhessen, Germany £9.40	
12	Rustenburg Estate Cabernet-Sauvignon 1988 South Africa £7.55	
15	Hautes Côtes de Nuits, Dom. Thevenot-le-Brun et Fils, 1990, Marey-les-Fussey Burgundy, France £8.95	
16	Grignolino 1991, G.L. Viarengo & Figlo, Piedmont, Italy £6.20	
20	Antonio Barbadillo, 'Jerez Dulce', Pedro Ximenèz Jerez, Spain £10.99	

C&B Corney & Barrow ★★★

12 Helmet Row, London EC1V 3QJ (Tel 071-251 4051). **Opening Hours:** Mon–Fri 8.30am-6pm. **Delivery:** free locally, nationally for over 3 cases. **Tastings:** regular in-store plus tutored tastings for customers on request. **Services:** cellarage, en primeur, mail order, gift mailing, glass hire.

Corney and Barrow, one of London's leading traditional wine merchants have been forced to come to terms with post-recession trading and an erosion of the good old fashioned wine styles and values that they represent. The response of Mr Brett-Smith, one of the managing directors, is to introduce a 'highly sophisticated computer system' so that customers can instantly discuss their requirements with staff who have access to a network of screens connected to head office. Among the laurels on which Corney's currently rest are the exclusive agencies for Ch. Pétrus and the Domaine de la Romanée Conti, two of the very finest in Bordeaux and Burgundy respectively. These wines are notoriously expensive. So, in their way, are many of the other bottles on the Corney's list, some of which are rather more affordable elsewhere. Console yourself instead with a choice from the rather slim section of the C&B wine list entitled 'Wines under £7.50'.

1	Champagne Delamotte Brut, France £16.69
3	Bourgogne Blanc Les Setilles ,Olivier Leflaive 1992, Burgundy, France £7.50
4	Corney and Barrow's House White £4.00
4	Aotea Sauvignon 1993, New Zealand £6.90
12	Ch. Richotey, Fronsac, Ets JP Moueix 1990, Bordeaux, France £6.32
12	Ch. de Lamarque, Haut-Médoc, 1990, Bordeaux, France £11.20
12	Parker Estate First Growth, 1990, Coonawarra, South Australia £17.82
12	Ch. Pétrus, 1983, Pomerol, Bordeaux, France £194.76
21	Corney & Barrow 10 year old Tawny, Martinez, Douro, Portugal £13.75

CWM   Cornwall Wine Merchants Ltd   ★★★

Chapel Road, Tuckingmill, Camborne, Cornwall TR14 8QY (Tel 0209 715765). Wines by the case only. **Opening Hours:** Mon–Fri 9am-5pm, Sat 10am-1pm. **Delivery:** free locally, nationally at cost. **Tastings:** occasional in-store, also through own wine club. **Services:** en primeur, mail order, gift mailing, glass hire.

A wholesome and satisfying mixture of the reliable and the eccentric; bankers like Antinori, Louis Latour and Berberana provide the meat in the pasty, while agencies for unusual wineries like Willespie in Margaret River, Te Kairanga from Martinborough N.Z., and McGuigan Brothers in the Hunter Valley add a touch of seasoning. There is a merciful lack of stodgy pastry and overcooked root vegetables commonly found in inferior variants from the West Country.

1	Pinot di Pinot, Gancia, Italy £6.92
3	Chablis, William Fèvre 1991, Burgundy, France £9.14
12	Casillero del Diablo Cabernet Sauvignon, 1990, Chile £5.89
12	Château la Fleur Peyrabon, Pauillac, 1989, Bordeaux, France £10.76
13	Hermitage, Cuvée Marquis de la Tourette, Delas Frères, 1986 Rhône, France £13.41
16	Regaleali Rosso, 1990, Sicily, Italy £6.06
16	Brunello de Montalcino, Val di Suga, 1981, Tuscany, Italy £12.18
16	Tignanello Vino da Tavola, Antinori, 1989, Tuscany, Italy £22.13
20	Don Zoilo Fino, Jerez, Spain £5.35 (half)
21	Quinta de la Rosa, £1992, Douro, Portugal £4.74

CEB   Croque-en-Bouche   ★★★★★

221 Wells Road, Malvern Wells, Worcester WR14 4HF (Tel 0684 565612). Wine by the case only. **Opening Hours:** Any reasonable hour by appointment. **Delivery:** free locally for over two cases . **Tastings:** occasional for groups. **Services:** mail order.

Not so much a wine list, more a pocket encyclopedia. Or two encyclopedias, to be precise, given restaurateur Robin Jones's decision to offer a red and a white wine list. We could fill pages here with offbeat examples, ranging from the 1944 Ferreira Reserva Portuguese red ('A very rare, excellent vintage, not tasted but the colour and levels look splendid') to Clos Réné 1978 ('GREAT WINEMAKING'), Rouge-Homme Coonawarra Claret 1976 and Ridge Monte Bello Cabernet 1981. With wines like these for special occasions and a raft of Provence reds for everyday, it's easy to see why others find it so hard to keep up with the Joneses.

1	Iron Horse, Brut, 1986, Sonoma, California £16.00
1	Jacquesson ChampagneBlanc de Blancs Brut N.V, France £19.40
2	Hillebrand Chardonnay, 1990, Canada £6.80
2	Chablis, Dauvissat, 1990, Burgundy, France £7.50
2	Vin de Paille, La Vignière, Henri Mair,e Jura, France £9.50 (half)
2	Condrieu, Côteaux de Veron, Vernay, 1989, Rhône, France £25.00
3	Villa Mount Eden Chardonnay, 1989, Napa, California £8.60

3	Saint Aubin, Prudhon, 1988, Burgundy, France £11.90
3	Lake's Folly, Hunter Chardonnay, 1986, Hunter Valley, Australia £17.60
3	Blanc de Lynch-Bages, 1990, Bordeaux, France £17.90
3	Bâtard-Montrachet, Vincent Leflaive, 1981, Burgundy, France £51.00
4	Savennières, Coulée de Serrant, 1978, Loire, France £21.40
8	Riesling, Frédédric Émile, Trimbach, 1985, Alsace, France £15.90
9	Dorsheimer Goldloch Riesling Spätlese, 1971, Schlossgut Diel, Germany £24.00
11	Saumur-Champigny, Vielles Vignes, Filliatreau, 1990, Loire, France £10.80
12	Ch. Labégorce Zédé, 1985, Margaux, France £13.50
12	Mayacamas Napa Cabernet, 1982, California £18.40
12	Barca Velha 'Ferreirinha', 1982, Portugal £32.70
12	Heitz 'Martha's Vineyard' Cabernet, 1982, Napa, California £51.00
12	Ch. Cos D'Estournel, 1959, St. Éstephe, France £54.00
12	Ch. Vieux-Château-Certan, 1983, Pomerol, France £1983
13	Quinta Da Carmo, 1987, Portugal £8.90
13	Ridge Santa Clara, Paso Robles Zinfandel, 1985, California £10.30
13	Dom. de Trévallon, 1985, Midi, France £20.70
13	Ch. Rayas, Châteauneuf du Pape, 1985, Rhône, France £29.60
15	Vosne Romanée, Clos des Réas, J. Gros, 1988, Burgundy, France £29.60
15	Aloxe-Corton, Tollot-Beaut, 1985, Burgundy, France £32.00
19	Cloudy Bay Late-Harvest Riesling, 1991, Marlborough, New Zealand £10.50 (half)
19	Ch. Nairac, 1983, Sauternes, France £17.90
19	Bonnezeaux, Ch. les Gauliers, 1935, Loire, France £75.00

CUM The Cumbrian Cellar ★★★

1 St. Andrew's Square, Penrith, Cumbria CA11 7AN (Tel 0768 63664). **Opening hours:** Mon-Sat 9am-5.30pm. **Delivery:** free locally, nationally at cost. **Tastings:** occasional in-store, plus events for clubs and societies. **Services:** mail order, gift mailing, glass hire.

If you've ever had a hankering to sample the vinous offerings from such outlandish outposts as Morocco, Peru, Brazil or Zimbabwe then you need look no further than Kenneth Gear's 'The Cumbrian Cellar' based in Penrith. These more esoteric examples are backed up by a solid core of wines of rather more classic origin, particularly from regional France, Italy and Australasia.

1	Russian Sparkling Golden Duke Brut, Russia £7.50
2	Tsingtao Chardonay, 1989, China £6.99
3	Palomas, Chardonnay, Santana do Livramento, 1988, Brazil £5.25
11	Sidi Brahim Rouge, Morocco £4.55
11	Ch. de Blomac, 1989, Minervois, France £5.00
11	Marondera Pinotage, 1991, Zimbabwe £5.85
11	Tacama, Gran Tinto Red, 1990, Peru £6.05
14	Fleurie, Trenel et Fils, 1992, Burgundy, France £9.20
16	Valpolicella Classico, Masi, 1991, £5.20
16	Venegazzù della Casa, Loredan-Gasparini, 1988, Veneto Italy £9.70
19	Jurançon Moelleux 1990, Clos Girouilh, South West France £9.10

D Davisons Wine Merchants ★★★★

7 Aberdeen Road, Croydon, Surrey CR0 1EQ (Tel 081-688 5939). **Opening Hours:** Mon-Sat 10am-2pm, 5-10pm, Sun 9am-12-1pm, 7-9pmpm. **Delivery:** free locally, nationally at cost. **Tastings:** occasional in-store. **Services:** gift mailing, glass loan, ice.

Still one of the little-known sources of mature classic wines, Davisons remains a favourite with wine buffs in the home counties. Over the years, we have often wondered how this family firm could maintain its policy of buying and cellaring wine until it is ready to be drunk. Well, reading between the shelves, we suspect that the answer is 'with great difficulty'. This year saw the closure of Davison's Master Cellar wine warehouse in which those wines were often sold, and an apparent general slimming down of the stocks. Even so, the younger wines are not to be sniffed at with anything other than pleasure and the shops generally are among the most genially staffed — if you don't get thirsty at lunchtime.

1	Cuvee Prestige Pinot Noir Chardonnay, Yalumba, South Australia £7.99	
1	Killawarra Brut, Penfolds, Australia £4.99	
2	Chablis Moreau, 1993, Burgundy, France £6.50	
3	St Romain, Clos Sous Le Chateau, Jean Germain, 1991, Burgundy, France £10.95	
3	Rothbury Estate, Hunter Valley Chardonnay, 1993, Australia £6.00	
3	Chassagne Montrachet, Premier Cru Chaumes, Jean Marc Morey, 1989, Burgundy, France £22.50	
4	Cooks Discovery Sauvignon Blanc, 1993, New Zealand £4.99	
4	Babich Semillon-Chardonnay, 1993, New Zealand £6.80	
12	Wirra Wirra Church Block Red, 1992, South Australia £6.99	
12	Chateau de Cardaillan, Graves , 1986 Bordeaux, France £6.95	
13	Rothbury Estate Shiraz, 1992, Hunter Valley, Australia £5.95	
13	Domaine Font de Michelle, Châteauneuf du Pape, Les Fils d'Etienne Gonnet Frères, 1990, Rhône, France £10.75	
13	Penfolds Bin 28 Kalimna Shiraz, 1991, South Australia £6.49	
14	Fleurie, Domaine des Quatre Vents, Georges Duboeuf, 1993, Burgundy, France £6.00	
15	Savigny Les Beaune, J M Pavelot, 1989, Burgundy, France £12.45	
17	El Coto Rioja Crianza, Bodegas El Coto, 1991, Spain, £4.99	
18	Brown Brothers Late Picked Muscat Blanc, 1993, £5.50	

ROD   Rodney Densem Wines   ★★★

Stapeley Bank, London Road, Nantwich, Cheshire CW5 7JW (Tel 0270 623665). **Opening Hours:** Mon–Fri 9am-6pm, Sat 9am-5.30pm. **Delivery:** free locally, nationally at cost **Tastings:** regular in-store plus occasional tutored tastings by arrangement. **Services:** en primeur, mail order, gift mailing, glass hire.

Rodney Densem offers the residents of Nantwich a service that a good many towns up and down the country would look on with envy – good wines at good prices, with a clear and unstuffy approach. Big name French producers like Louis Latour, Jaboulet, Krug, Dopff 'Au Moulin' (Alsace) and Drouhin are featured alongside decent house wines at £2.99 (watch out though when considering prices; all are prices are quoted ex VAT) and a range of such reliable Aussies labels as Brown Bros and David Wynn.

3	De Redcliffe Chardonnay, 1989, New Zealand £7.40	
11	David Wynn Dry Red, 1993, South Australia £5.40	
11	Negru de Purkar, 1986, Moldavia £5.75	
12	Chateau Potensac, 1983, Bordeaux, France £9.50	

DIR   Direct Wine Shipments   ★★★★

5-7 Corporation Square, Belfast BT1 3AJ (Tel 0232 238700/243906). **Opening hours:** Mon, Tues, Wed, Fri 9am-6.30pm, Thurs 9am-8pm, Sat 9.30am-5pm. **Delivery:** free locally, nationally at cost. **Tastings:** regular in-store, plus two six-week courses a year plus various illustrative tastings. **Services:** cellarage, en primeur, mail order, glass hire.

If our Belfast sources are to be believed, Corporation Square in the centre of town is not to be visited without a lengthy exploration of Direct Wine Shipment's 'dark and dusky cellar'. For an Irishman to describe the management as 'affable' must make them among the easiest people in the world to aff. This particular visitor was kitted out with half a dozen bottles of venerable port for his dear old Pa's birthday. DWS faxed us a proof of their forthcoming wine list and suffice it to say that when dangled out of the window of a three storey Clapham house, it reached the ground with no trouble at all, at all. What is more, every inch is covered in such tempting names as the ones which follow:

3	Hunters Chardonnay, 1991, New Zealand £10.50
8	Riesling Jubilee, Reserve Personelle, Hugel, 1983, Alsace, France £13.95
12	Château Puygueraud, Côtes de Francs, 1988, Bordeaux, France £9.50
12	Pavillon Rouge, Margaux, 1990, Bordeaux, France £17.95
13	Cornas, Auguste Clape, 1991, Rhône, France £14.50
15	Stonier's Pinot Noir, 1992, Victoria, Australia £8.95
16	Barolo Monprivato, Mascarello, 1987, Piedmont, Italy £14.50

DD Domaine Direct ★★★★

29 Wilmington Square, London WC1X 0EG (Tel: 071-837 1142). Wines by the case only. **Opening Hours:** Mon-Fri 8.30am-5.30pm. **Delivery:** free locally. **Tastings:** regular in-store. **Services:** cellarage, en primeur.

Apart from Domaine Direct's agency for Leeuwin Estate in Western Australia, this by-the-case merchant concentrates exclusively on bringing a range of top red and white Burgundy straight from the producer to the consumer. As you might expect, this means keener prices than you might find in most retail shops, and with Domaines such as Michel Juillot, Etienne Sauzet, Guy Roulot, and Domaine de la Pousse d'Or, non-Bransons will need to make those savings. There is a good range of magnums offered and over 50 wines available in half bottles.

2	Chablis 1990, Jean Durup, Burgundy, France £8.00
3	Leeuwin Estate Art Series Chardonnay 1989, West Australia £14.00
3	Meursault Clos de la Barre 1991, Comtes Lafon, Burgundy, France £24.00
15	Bourgogne Rouge 1991, Guy Roulot, France £9.50,
15	Clos de la Roche 1989, Armand Rousseau, Burgundy, France £28.00

DWC/WHC The Dorking Wine Cellar Ltd ★★★

Glebelands, Vincent Lane, Dorking, Surrey RH4 3YZ (Tel 0306 885711). **Opening Hours:** Mon-Fri 9am-6pm. **Delivery:** free locally, nationally at cost. **Tastings:** regular in-store. **Services:** cellarage, en primeur, mail order, gift mailing, glass hire, ice.

Since last year, wholesalers Whiclar & Gordon have sold the retail shop in their bunker – hence its change of name – but they continue to supply its range of Aussie wines (notably from BRL Hardy) and well-chosen offerings from southern France where Andrew Gordon still runs the imaginative vine-share scheme which provides thirsty Brits with a guaranteed liquid return on their investment.

1	E&E Sparkling Shiraz, Valley Growers Co-Op, South Australia £12.50
2	Mâcon Blanc Villages Les Chazelles, Cave De Vir,é 1993, Burgundy, France £3.99
4	Gaillac Blanc, Cave de Labastide de Levis, 1993, South West France £3.49
4	Phillippe De Baudin Sauvignon Blanc, Domaine de la Baume, 1993, Vin de Pays d'Oc, France £3.99

6	Moondah Brook Estate Verdelho, 1993, Western Australia £4.99
12	Hardy's Nottage Hill Cabernet Sauvignon, 1992, South Australia £4.39
13	Chateau Reynella Basket-Pressed Shiraz, 1991, McLaren Vale, Australia £6.75
13	St Joseph, Cuvée Médaille d'Argent, Cave de St Désirat, 1990, Rhône, France £7.85
13	Ebenezer Shiraz, BRL Hardy Wine Co, 1991, South Australia £8.99

ECK   Eckington Wines   ★★★★

2 Ravencar Road, Eckington, Sheffield S31 9GJ (Tel 0246 433213). Wines by the case only. No credit cards. **Opening Hours:** Mon-Fri 9am-9pm, Sat 9am-6pm, Sun 9am-3pm. **Delivery:** free locally, nationally at cost. **Tastings:** regular in-store, plus tutored sessions on the first Tuesday of each month. **Services:** mail order.

If you are tired of popping in to the offie every time you want a bottle of wine and irritated by the fact that the selection keeps changing, it is wise to cultivate a relationship with a wholesale case merchant like Dr Andrew Loughran at Eckington. All you have to do is choose twelve bottles from his list and with a generally sound selection, you cannot go too far wrong. Australia, California and Chile are particularly well-represented, and if you have trouble making up your mind, just sign up for Eckington's quarterly wine scheme – they will send you a mixed case at a special price and you can re-order your favourites.

3	Neil Ellis Chardonnay, 1992, South Africa £6.24
4	Peteroa Sauvignon/Semilon, 1992, Chile £3.29
11	Taltarni, Fiddleback Terrace Dry Red, 1991, Victoria, Australia £4.99
12	Yarra Yerring No. 1 Cabernet Sauvignon Australia £4.58
12	James Irvine Grand Merlot, Yaldara, 1988, Australia £11.75
12	Clos du Marquis, 1985, Bordeaux, France £11.90
12	Robert Mondavi Reserve Cabernet Sauvignon, 1989, California £16.95
13	Jade Mountain Syrah, 1990, California £17.39
16	Cepparello, Isole e Olene, 1988, Italy £15.86
17	Chivite Reserva, 1989, Spain £4.95

EV   El Vino   ★★★

47 Fleet Street, EC4Y IBJ (Tel 071-353 6786/7541), 30 New Bridge Street, EC4V 6BJ (Tel 071-236 4534/071-248 5548), 6 Martin Lane, Cannon street, EC4R ODP (Tel 071-626 6303/6876) **Opening Hours:** Mon-Fri 8.30am-8.30pm. **Delivery:** free nationally for two cases or more. **Tastings:** weekly. **Services:** cellarage, en primeur, mail order, gift mailing, glass hire, ice.

'Old established City wine merchant and shipper' is the unabashed heading to the El Vino newsletter, correctly calling to mind what to expect from this long-time haunt of lawyers and journalists. The 80s have arrived with the addition of two dozen or so New World wines, but it is easy to see that the management and customers are really rather happier with the (own-label but from such good *negociants* as Jaffelin) Burgundies and (often toughly traditional) claret. The Fleet Street shop will not only sell any bottle from the list but also serve it in the attached Wine Bar and lunch room, both of which are now sadly (for El Vino's if not for some of the other more sober customers) often almost journalist-free zones.

3	Mercurey Blanc 'Domaine de la Croix Jacquelet' Faiveley, 1991, Burgundy, France £13.20
4	Babich Semillon-Chardonnay, 1992, New Zealand £6.50
15	El Vino Chorey-lès-Beaune, 1986, Burgundy, France £8.65
12	Ch. Pitray, Côtes de Castillon, 1987, Bordeaux, France £5.90
12	Torreon de Paredes, Merlot, 1990, Chile £5.95

188 Merchants

EP   Eldridge Pope   ★★★

Weymouth Avenue, Dorchester, Dorset DT1 1QT ((Tel 0305 258300). **Opening Hours:** generally Mon–Fri 9am-5.30pm, Sat 9am-5pm, with local variations up to 9pm. **Delivery:** free locally, nationally at cost. **Tastings:** regular in-store; also runs the Dorset Wine Society with lectures/tastings from October to May. **Services:** cellarage, en primeur, mail order, gift mailing, glass hire

Eldridge Pope have been shipping wine since 1833 and now have eight retail outlets in the Dorset/Hampshire area. A deeply traditional company (the Chairman is Christopher Pope, a descendant of the founder) there is a heavy bias towards France, although the range of House Wines now includes 'The Chairman's exuberently fruitful New World Sauvignon' made for them by the excellent Redwood Valley Estate in New Zealand. Bordeaux is reliably represented by traditional wines of the Cissac ilk, and Moulin Touchais from the Loire and Reichsgraf von Kesselstat from the Mosel are well worth a second look.

2	The Chairman's White Burgundy, 1991, France	£5.88
4	The Chairman's New World Sauvignon Blanc, 1993, New Zealand	£7.34
11	Chateau Canet Minervois, 1991, Languedoc Roussillon, France	£3.82
12	Chateau Cissac, 1985, Bordeaux, France	£11.93
19	Moulin Touchais, 1970, Loire, France	£32.31

EVI   Evington's Wine Merchants   ★★★

120 Evington Road, Leicester LE2 1HH (Tel 0533 542702). **Opening Hours:** Mon–Sat 9.30am-6pm. **Delivery:** free locally, nationally at cost. **Tastings:** occasional in-store, plus local evening classes (standard and advanced) and courses for clubs, societies, etc. **Services:** cellarage, en primeur, gift mailing, glass loan, ice.

A glance at the sparkling wine selection gives a clue to Evington's intentions – Linduaer and Deutz from New Zealand, Seaview and Salinger from Australia, Brédif Vouvray Brut and a Blancs de Blancs from Claude Leger: a small but well chosen selection featuring wines from a wide range of sources, at realistic prices. L.A. Cetto from Mexico, Gamla from Israel and Portugal's Perequita are among the more unusual choices in a thoroughly reliable list.

2	Montana Marborough Chardonnay ,1993, New Zealand	£5.29
3	St. Aubin 1er Crû, Dom. G. Thomas, 1991, France	£12.00
4	L.A. Cetto, Fumé Blanc, 1992, Mexico	£4.79
6	Sylvaner, Trimbach, 1990, Alsace, France	£6.85
9	Berncasteler Doctor Riesling, Deinhard, 1985, Mosel, Germany	£30.85
11	Brown Bros, Tarrango, 1992, Victoria, Australia	£5.29
12	Ch. Palmer, Margaux, 1983, Bordeaux, France	£41.00
13	Ch. Fortia, Châteauneuf du Pape, 1988, Rhône, France	£10.70
15	Chambolle-Musigny, P. Bourée, 1986, Burgundy, France	£18.20
16	Badia a' Coltibuono, Sangioveto, 1982, Tuscany, Italy	£11.90
17	Bairrada, João Pato, 1985, Portugal	£6.15
17	Marques de Griñon, Cabernet Sauvignon, 1986, Spain	£10.65
19	Tamaïioasa Romaneasca, 1960, Romania	£7.19
19	Quarts de Chaume, Dom. de Baumard, 1986 Loire, France (Half)	£7.65

PEY   Philip Eyres Wine Merchant   ★★★

The Cellars, Colehill, Amersham, Bucks. HB7 OLS (Tel 0494 433823). **Opening Hours:** Mon–Fri 8am-10pm, Sat/Sun 9am-9pm. **Delivery:** free locally, nationally at cost. **Tastings:** regular in-store. **Services:** cellarage, en primeur, mail order, glass hire.

To make up for the lack of a shop, Philip Eyres, father of Harry the well-known wine writer, takes account holders' orders from his extensive list over the telephone from 'Breakfast time to Late Supper time'. Those who can only deal face-to-face can call round, but only by appointment. The visit would be worthwhile though, partly for the name-strewn portfolio (Guigal, Jaboulet, Conterno, Cape Mentelle, Trefethen, Fetzer), compiled with assistance from SH Jones (qv), and partly for the range of wines from Mr E's first love, Germany, where the team includes Dr Loosen, Bassermann-Jordan and host of estates whose names read like a typist going face-down on the keyboard.

FAR Farr Vintners ★★★★★

19 Sussex Street, Pimlico, London SW1V 4RR (Tel 071-828 1960) Wines by the case only. **Opening hours:** 10am-6pm **Delivery:** nationally at cost. **Tastings:** occasional in-store, plus tastings and dinners for regular customers. **Services:** cellarage, en primeur, mail order.

Don't bother looking for agreeable House Wines at £3.50 or the 'Directors Selection Mixed Christmas Case' when you peruse Farr's list. The minimum order is a mere £250 and discounted prices are available if you are spending over £2,000! Farr's are Fine Wine Brokers, and they are very good at it indeed, receiving countless accolades in their short history. Pretty well every wine estate that they deal in would find its way into any self-respecting list of the World's Top 100, and because they source their wines direct from producers and play the Fine Wine market like a futures index, they frequently offer the best prices anywhere in London. One of their specialities is to snuffle out really rare special cuvées, and they have been known to ring up customers to whom they have sold a wine and offer them a healthy profit in order to buy it back and sell it to someone else, often on another continent...

3	Ch. de Fieuzal, Pessac-Léognan, 1992, Bordeaux, France	£14.00
3	Chassagne Montrachet Caillerets, Dom. André Ramonet, 1992, Burgundy, France	£16.00
4	Wairau River Sauvignon Blanc, 1993, New Zealand	£8.00
12	Ch. Haut-Batailley, 1985, Bordeaux, France	£13.00
12	Ch. Pétrus, 1955, Bordeaux, France	£400.00
12	Ch. Lafite, 1874, Bordeaux, France	£2,000.00
15	Pommard Vignots, Dom. Leroy, 1991, France	£35.00
19	Ch. d'Yquem, 1893, France	£1,250.00 (limited stock)

FV Fernlea Vintners ★★★

7 Fernlea Road, Balham, London SW12 7RT (Tel 081-673 0053). **Opening hours:** 10.30am-6pm, Sat 10am-6pm. **Delivery:** free locally, nationally at cost. **Tastings:** occasional in-store.

Situated in the area of London that the nouveaux pauvres refer to as 'B'lahm', Peter Godden supplies wines as varied as the offerings of the local markets; from top Burgundies to Mexican reds, from Sauternes to Swiss whites. Refill your cocktail cabinet too, although the farmers' trick of expense-deducting an order of Sheep Dip (the Malt) may fail in this none-too-rural location.

3	Dom. William Févre, Chablis 1er Cru, 'Montmains' 1991, Burgundy, France	£10.00
3	Goldwater Marlborough Chardonnay, 1992, New Zealand	£9.00
3	Mountadam Chardonnay, 1991, High Eden, South Australia	£11.75
12	Ch. Cantenac-Brown, Margaux, 1989, Bordeaux France	£11.03
12	Opus One, 1988, California	£41.88
13	LA Cetto Zinfandel 1992, Mexico	£4.09
15	Gevrey-Chambertin, Rossignol-Trapet, 1989, Burgundy, France	£12.00

AF Alexr Findlater & Co Ltd ★★★★

8 Freegrove Road, London N7 9JN (Tel 071-607 0114) Wines by the case only.
Opening Hours: Mon–Fri 10am-5pm. **Delivery:** free locally, nationally for three
cases or more. **Tastings:** occasional in-store. **Services:** cellarage, mail order, gift
mailing, glass hire, ice.

Alex Findlater can truly claim to have pioneered the Australian invasion before
Oddbins brought the Wizards of Oz to public attention. If you want to get in on the
ground floor of the South African vinous revolution, you would do well to pop
down to Freegrove Road. His list is mercifully free of the ubiquitous KWV and
largely disappointing Zonnenbloem, and instead offers you Villiera, Thelema, Neil
Ellis, Warwick, Rustenberg and Kanonkop. New Zealand and Australia are still
extremely well served both by famous names and small boutiques and the slim 'Old
World' selection emphasises Mr F's commitment to quality.

1	Jacquesson, Blanc de Blancs, Champagne, France	£16.99
3	Dieu Donné, Chardonnay, 1992, South Africa	£7.99
4	Pierro, Semillon-Chardonnay, 1992, Western Australia	£7.49
4	Brokenwood Semillon, 1992, Hunter Valley, Australia	£7.99
12	Palmer Vineyards, Cabernet Sauvignon, 1988, Long Island, New York State, USA	£5.99
12	Negru De Purkar, 1978, Purkar Winery, Moldova	£8.99
12	Ch. La Lagune, Ludon, 1985, Bordeaux, France	£19.99
15	Ata Rangi, Pinot Noir, 1991, Martinborough, New Zealand	£14.35
15	Corton, Doudet Naudin, 1955, Burgundy, France	£65.49
16	Le Sassine, 1992, Le Ragose, Veneto, Italy	£5.89
17	La Rioja Alta, Gran Reserva 904, 1981, Spain	£13.99
21	Stanton & Killeen, Liqueur Muscat, Victoria, Australia	£9.59
21	Quinta de la Rosa Vintage Port, 1990, Douro, Portugal	£10.49

FDL Findlater Mackie Todd & Co Ltd ★★★

Deer Park Road, Merton Abbey, London SW19 3TU (Tel 081-543 0966) Information
only – not premises. Wine by the case only. **Opening hours:** Mon-Fri 9am-5.30pm.
Delivery: nationally at cost. **Tastings:** tutored tastings by invitation. **Services:**
cellarage, en primeur, mail order, gift mailing, glass hire.

The news that Waitrose had bought this long-established mail-order merchant took
most of the wine trade by surprise; it was almost as though the maiden aunt of
supermarketeering had decided to elope with the somewhat younger man next door.
Whether this description would apply to the distinctly tweedy FMT is another
question; it was just that, as part of the John Lewis group which eschewed such 20th
century novelties as advertising, marketing and credit cards, the idea of taking over
a firm which was responsible for selling wine to Visa cardholders came as a shock.
Today, though, the relationship seems to be a highly successful one, providing the
southern-based supermarket chain with the means to offer a national service
including a solid range of wines, cellarage and even an advice-line.

2	Bourgogne Blanc 'Clos de Chenôves' Cave de Buxy, 1991, Burgundy, France	£7.45
4	Pouilly-Fumé, Jean-Claude Chatelain, 1992, Loire, France	£7.25
4	Redwood Valley Estate Sauvignon Blanc, 1992, New Zealand	£8.95
6	Tokay Pinot Gris d'Alsace, Blanck Frères, 1992, Alsace, France	£5.25
11	Philippe de Baudin Merlot, 1992, Languedoc Roussillon, France	£4.45
12	Avontuur Cabernet-Merlot, 1993, South Africa	£3.99
12	Ch. La Tour St. Bonnet, 1990, Bordeaux, France	£5.95
12	Ch. Sociando-Mallet, 1990, Bordeaux, France	£11.95
12	Bahans-Haut-Brion, Graves, 1988, Bordeaux, France	£14.35

12	Ch. Pape-Clément, 1989, Bordeaux, France £25.00
13	Cartlidge & Browne Zinfandel, California £4.35
13	Ch. Reynella, Stony Hill Shiraz, 1990, South Australia £5.95
13	St. Joseph, Cave de St.-Désirat, 1991, Rhône, France £7.85
17	Viña Albali Reserva, Bodegas Felix Solis, 1987, Valdepeñas, Spain £4.95
17	Tinto da Anfora, João Pires, 1990, Portugal £4.95
19	Ch. Bastor-Lamontagne 1990, Bordeaux, France £14.25

LEF   Le Fleming Wines   ★★★

9 Longcroft Avenue, Harpenden, Herts AL5 2RB (Tel 0582 760125). Wines by the case only. No credit cards. **Opening Hours:** 24-hour answerphone. **Delivery:** free locally, nationally at cost. **Tastings:** regular in-store, plus tutored sessions for local clubs, schools, etc. **Services:** mail order, gift mailing, glass hire, ice.

Cheerful Cherry Jenkins approaches the business of single-handedly running her small wholesale wine company with energy and enthusiasm, and has built up a loyal following of regular customers who appreciate her personal service. Her list, built up over the past few years, continues to impress us with new finds and old favourites, all liberally spiced with a sprinkling of chatty, exclamatory tasting notes.

4	Klippenkop Chenin Blanc, 1993, South Africa £3.99
4	Lugana, Ca dei Frati, 1990, Italy £6.16
4	Sancerre, Guy Saget, 1992, Loire, France £6.50
13	Côtes de Ventoux, Vieille Ferme, 1991, Rhône, France £4.50
13	Rockford Basket Press Shiraz, 1990, South Australia £8.90
15	Vosne Romanée, Domaine Rion, 1989, Burgundy, France £18.05

JFD   John Ford Wines

See York House Wines

F&M   Fortnum & Mason   ★★★★

181 Piccadilly, London W1A 1ER (Tel 071-734 8040). **Opening Hours:** Mon-Sat 9.30am-6pm. **Delivery:** free locally for orders over £40. **Tastings:** regular in-store. **Services:** cellarage, mail order, gift mailing.

It may not come as a surprise that the shop with the clock can offer eleven vintages of Yquem or eight of Mouton Rothschild. But in addition to the classic claret, vintage port and fine Burgundy, Annette Duce has put together an excellent array of Californian, Rhône and Australian wines. In fact, since her arrival, this has become a very impressive wine shop in its own right with top quality emphasised by the presence of such names as Au Bon Climat, Ridge, Petaluma, Cloudy Bay, Paul Jaboulet and Zind Humbrecht. Even more surprisingly, considering the premium to be paid for many of the other items on sale here, Fortnum's prices are generally quite close to those asked in far less august surroundings.

1	Daniel Le Brun Brut NV, Cellier Le Brun, New Zealand £11.99
1	Champagne Pol Roger, Blanc de Chardonnay, 1986, France £35.00
1	Champagne Taittinger Cuvée Prestige Brut Rosé, France £25.00
2	Chardonnay, Vino da Tavola, Jermann, 1992, Italy £12.50
3	Moss Wood Chardonnay, Margaret River, 1993, Western Australia £11.00
4	Pinot Blanc, Kuentz Bas, 1992, Alsace, France £7.60
8	Jackson Estate Marlborough Dry Riesling, 1993, New Zealand £6.49
8	Adgestone English Table Wine, Adgestone Vineyard, 1991, £5.95
12	Hollick Coonawarra Red, 1991, South Australia £7.99

12	Meerlust Rubicon, 1988, South Africa £10.00
12	Ridge Santa Cruz Cabernet Sauvignon, 1992, California, £17.19
12	Fortnum & Mason St Emilion Grand Cru, Château Grand Mayne, 1989, Bordeaux, France £12.50
12	Fortnum & Mason Margaux, Chateau Palmer, 1989, France £14.75
13	St Hallett Old Block Shiraz, 1991,South Australia £9.49
15	Robert Mondavi Pinot Noir Reserve, 1991, California £16.99
15	Pinot Noir, Domaine Parent, 1990, Burgundy, France £6.95
17	Fortnum & Mason Rioja Reserva, La Rioja Alta, 1989, Spain £6.75
18	Setubal Superior Moscatel, Jose Maria da Fonseca Succs,.1966, Portugal £9.99
20	Fortnum & Mason Amontillado, Lustau, Jerez, Spain £6.45
21	Blandys Vintage Malmsey Madeira, 1964, Portugal £63.00
21	Fortnum & Mason LBV Port, Burmester, 1989, Portugal £9.75
21	Quinta Do Noval Colheita, 1976,Portugal £9.99
21	Calem Quinta da Foz, 1982, Portugal £13.80

FUL Fuller's   ★★★

The Griffin Brewery, Chiswick Lane, London W4 2QB (Tel 081-994 3691). **Opening Hours:** Mon-Sat 10am-10pm, Sun 12-3pm, 7-10pm. **Delivery:** free locally. **Tastings:** regular in-store. **Services:** glass hire, ice.

Quietly competing with Davisons and Unwins over the last couple of years, this independent chain has tidied up the look of its shops, trained its staff and built up a list which includes such top quality producers as Roumier, Chave, Chapoutier, Tedeschi and Dr H Thanisch, as well as a first class selection of French Country wines from La Serre. With all this on offer, Fuller's deserves to be better known beyond the immediate neighbourhood of its shops. One way to spread the word might be to print a price list excluding the cartoons whch seem to have been drawn by shop managers on quiet Monday afternoons.

1	Killawarra Brut, Penfolds, Australia £4.99
1	Omar Khayyam, Indian Sparkling Wine 1987, £6.99
1	Champagne Brossault Brut Rosé, F. Bonnet, France £9.99
2	Tasmania Wine Company Chardonnay, Pipers Brook Vineyard, 1993, Australia £8.25
3	Penfolds Chardonnay, 1993, South Australia £6.99
3	Auguste Couillaud Chardonnay, Vin de Pays du Jardin de la France, 1991, Loire, France £7.49
3	Crichton Hall Chardonnay, 1991, Napa, California £10.00
3	Ch. de Sours, Bordeaux Blanc, 1992, France £5.99
3	Oxford Landing, Chardonnay, Yalumba, 1993, Australia £4.99
4	Fortant De France Sauvignon Blanc, Skalli 1993, £3.89
4	Nobilo Marlborough Sauvignon Blanc, 1993, New Zealand £6.50
4	Muscadet de Sèvre et Maine sur Lie, Domaine du Magasin, Martin-Luneau 1992, Loire, France £4.99
4	Pinot Grigio Trentino, i Mesi, Casa Girelli, 1993, Italy £4.19
8	Hardy's RR, Riesling, 1993, Australia £3.99
11	Ch. De Cabriac Corbières, Jean De Cibeins, 1992, France £3.50
12	Vina Undurraga Cabernet Sauvignon Reserva, 1990, Chile £5.75
12	Dieu Donné Cabernet, 1992, South Africa £5.00
16	Castelbravo, Brunello di Montalcino, Paccini, 1989, Italy £7.49
17	Señorio de Nava, Ribera del Duero Crianza, 1989, Spain £5.99
17	Vina Albali, Valdepeñas Reserva, Bodegas Felix Solis, 1987, Spain £3.79
18	Stanton and Killeen, Rutherglen Liqueur Muscat, Victoria, Australia £5.65
21	Noval LB Port, Quinta Do Noval, Portugal £8.49

G   Gateway

See Somerfield

GON   Gauntleys of Nottingham   ★★★★★

4 High Street, Exchange Arcade, Nottingham NG1 2ET (0602 417973). **Opening Hours:** Mon-Sat 8.30am-5.30pm. **Delivery:** free locally, nationally at cost. **Tastings:** regular in-store plus frequent tutored tastings given by wine growers (especially from the Rhône). **Services:** cellarage, en primeur, mail order, gift mailing, glass hire.

1993s award-winning Rhône Ranger continues to delight (under 'Northern' & 'Southern' headings) with such august names as Guigal, Perrin, Clape, and Verset whose various wines should perfectly match some of the aromas of their fine Cigar selection. Gauntleys now bring Ch. Pibarnon Bandol, Ravenswood Zinfandel and Vilmart Champagne to Nottingham, continuing the tradition of spreading the riches amongst the locals. (True Rhônophiles should ask about availability of the almost-impossible-to-find-on-this-side-of-the-Channel Châteauneuf du Pape 'Hommage à Jacques Perrin, of which Mr G might be able to find a bottle or two...)

3	1988 Puligny-Montrachet, Champ Canet, Carillon, Burgundy, France £24.70
5	Vouvray, Clos du Bourg Demi-Sec Huët, 1982 Loire, France £10.50
12	Domaine du Puget, Merlot, Vin de Pays, 1990, France £4.20
12	Ch. Certan-de-May, Pomerol, 1988, Bordeaux, France £33.90
13	Ravenswood 'Vintners Blend' Zinfandel, California £8.70
13	St Joseph, Clos de l'Arbalestrier, Florentine, 1991, Rhône, France £11.90
13	Cornas, Les Ruchottes, Colombo, 1989, Rhône, France £17.90
13	Hermitage, Graillot, 1990, Rhône, France £23.90
13	Châteauneuf-du-Pape, Ch. Rayas, 1989, Rhône, France £27.90
17	Vega Sicilia Unico 1975, Ribera del Duero, Spain £52.30

JAG   J A Glass   ★★★

11 High Street, Dysart, Kirkcaldy, Fife KY1 2UG (Tel 0592 651850 Fax 0592 654240). **Opening Hours:** Mon-Fri 9am-6pm; Sat 9am-6pm Sun 'possibly'. **Delivery:** free locally 'for larger orders', nationally at cost. **Tastings:** regular in store, plus wine club and regular tutored tastings, including a November event at which over 100 wines are shown. **Services:** cellarage, en primeur mail order, gift mailing, glass hire.

There are many things in stock at this Kirkcaldy merchants of which we would certainly pour a tumbler. The French range has three vintages of Mouton Baronne Philippe, Faiveley Burgundies, Alsace from Dopff 'au Moulin' and the Provence wines of Domaine Rimauresq. Affordable Italians come from Le Veritière, while tops in the New World are the Aussies from Green Point and Penfolds and the Hamilton Russell South Africans. Glass-conscious malt whisky fans will also find several versions of their favourite medicine.

1	Champagne Canard-Duchêne, Brut Rosé, France £16.99
2	Principe de Viana Chardonnay, 1993, Spain £3.54
3	Stonier's Chardonnay, Winery Selection,1991, Victoria, Australia £8.75
4	Villiera Merlot, 1990, South Africa £8.75
12	Michel Lynch, Bordeaux Rouge, 1989, France £5.99
13	Evans and Tate Gnangara Shiraz, 1986, Western Australia £7.49
12	Opus One 1990, California, £45.00
17	Principe de Viana, Cabernet Sauvignon, 1990, Navarra, Spain £3.54

MG   Matthew Gloag & Son Ltd   ★★★

Bordeaux House, 33 Kinnoull Street, Perth PH1 5EU (Tel 0738 621101 Fax 0738 628167). **Opening Hours:** Mon-Fri 9am-5pm. **Delivery:** free locally, nationally at cost. **Tastings:** for wine clubs. **Services:** gift mailing, glass hire.

There's a hint of this merchant's area of special interest in its address. More clues? Have a wee gander at their pocket (or sporran) sized list and you'll find a serious range of clarets and malts the conjuncture of which would have delighted Queen Victoria who allegedly found a blend of wine, spirit and a tincture of cannabis used to give her a welcome fit of the giggles. Complementing these are fine Rhônes, Burgundies and a selection of the rest of Europe with a dash of Australasia and South Africa. Sassanachs and Highland Scots alike, avail yourself of their mail order service – you'll nay find a better selection of malts outside of the Tokyo Golf Club.

1	Cuvée Flamme Brut, Gratien & Meyer, Loire, France £8.75	
2	Tim Adams Semillon, 1991,Clare, South Australia £9.99	
11	Cuvée Mythique, Val D'Orbieu, 1991, Languedoc Roussillon, France £3.99	
12	Ch. Cissac, 1986, Bordeaux, France £11.70	
16	Cumaro, Umani Ronchi 1990, Marches, Italy £9.95	
20	Barbadillo Oloroso Seco, Jerez, Spain £11.99	

GH   Goedhuis & Co Ltd   ★★★★

6 Rudolf Place, Miles Street, London SW8 1RP (Tel 071-793 7900). Wine by the case only. **Opening Hours:** Mon-Fri 9am-6pm. **Delivery:** free in London for over three cases, nationally over five. £7.50; over 5 cases free **Services:** cellarage, en primeur, mail order, glass hire, ice.

This year, Jonathan Goedhuis (pr. 'Goodhouse') has chosen the minimalist path for his name, price & drinking status-only list, eschewing the trend for prosaic descriptions. Whilst it is true that some lists induce adjective-fatigue or claim 'all their geese as swans', a few words can work wonders. Criticism aside, this is a fine list with valuable names and promising discoveries in Burgundy (especially) & Bordeaux, together with deals such as the sensible Bottle Bank scheme (a monthly-instalment Cellar plan) and renowned trade offer/bin end deals. Mr G is apparently very well regarded among overseas wine buffs, though we hate to think of the difficulties some of them must have when trying to order a case of Latricières Chambertin over the phone; the fax line to Tokyo must run the risk of overheating.

2	Chasan, Cuvée du Domaine, Dom Boyer, 1992, France £4.33	
3	Bourgogne, Vieilles Vignes, Antonin Rodet ,1991, France £6.41	
3	Morey St Denis Blanc 1er Cru Montluisants, 1988, Burgundy, France £22.08	
4	Ch Thieuley, Bordeaux 1992, France £5.58	
12	Ch. Sociando Mallet, Haut Médoc, 1988 Bordeaux, France £11.83	
15	Bourgogne Passetoutgrains, Michel Lafarge 1990, France £8.17	
15	Nuits St Georges, Dom Méo Camuzet 1989, Burgundy, France £23.08	
19	Ch de Fargues, Sauternes 1985 Bordeaux, France £43.75	

NGF   Norman Goodfellow   ★★★

70 Wigmore Street, London W1H 9DL (Tel 071-224 1994). **Opening Hours:** Mon-Fri 9am-7pm, Sat 11am-7pm. **Delivery:** free locally, nationally at cost. **Services:** mail order, gift mailing.

Setting up its stall as 'The South African Wine Centre' with more than a casual nod at a certain establishment on the Strand, this newly established London outpost of one of South Africa's leading specialist merchants bravely offers 'From Allesverloren to Zandvliet - all your favourite South African wines, spirits, beers and liqueurs under one roof.' Those interested in finding out more might care to join Goodfellow's Wine Club (cost currently £15) and benefit from 7.5% discounts, regular tastings and frequent special offers and trips.

1	Kaapse Vonkel Brut, Simonsig Estates, 1991, South Africa £8.50	
4	Blanc de Blanc, Moreson Vineyards, 1993, Franschhoek, South Africa £4.80	
12	Simonsig Cabernet Sauvignon, 1988, South Africa £7.99	
13	Simonsig Shiraz, 1990, South Africa £6.99	

G&M   Gordon & MacPhail   ★★★

George House, Boroughbriggs Road, Elgin, Moray IV30 1JY (0343 545110). **Opening Hours:** Mon-Fri 9am-5.15pm Sat 9am-5pm (half day closing on Wed during Jan, Feb, May, June, Oct and Nov). **Delivery:** free locally, nationally at cost. **Tastings:** occasional in-store. **Services:** mail order, glass hire.

Northern exposure atop o' bonny Scotland has caused David Urquart to seek out some of the world's most Southerly wines in South America and – with greater success – South Africa. Closer to home, Germany can provide ideal Haggis-accompaniment, should you prefer a change from G&M's extraordinary range of malts and Scottish wines (fruit other than grapes).

3	John Martin, Backsberg, 1991, South Africa £5.99
4	Santa Carolina Sauvignon Blanc, 1993, Chile £4.29
12	Sunnycliff Coonawarra Cabernet Sauvignon, 1992, South Australia £4.95
13	Mitchell Peppertree Shiraz, 1992, Clare, South Australia £6.79
19	Neetlingshof Weisser Riesling, Noble Late Harvest, 1991, South Africa £8.49

GI   Grape Ideas   ★★★

3-5 Hythe Bridge Street, Oxford OX1 2EW (0865 722137). **Opening Hours:** Mon-Fri 10am-7pm Sat 10am-6pm. **Delivery:** free locally, nationally at cost. **Tastings:** regular in-store, tutored sessions on request for wine clubs, societies, colleges, etc. **Services:** mail order, glass hire, ice.

Located a mere Bolly cork's pop from Worcester college and a electronic beep from the Quasar Lazercentre, Alastair Stevens successfully walks the tight-rope between the conflicting demands of Oxford's wine-buying populace – impecunious students (& dons) who have ransacked their sofa backs for beer tokens, and Domestic bursars seeking vintage wines to celebrate their latest bequest/Norrington table position/round of college fines. Flippancy aside, the list is generally strong (especially in South America), although some other countries are represented solely by one producer. Ask for the vintage wine list (colleges often trade stocks).

3	Chardonnay 'Oak Cask' Reserve, Trapiche, 1993, Argentina £5.45
4	Côtes de Duras Sauvignon Vieilles Vignes, Berticot, 1993, South West France £4.99
4	Bairrada Branco, Quinta de Pedralvites, Sogrape, 1993, Portugal £4.99
12	Trapiche Cabernet Sauvignon 'Oak Cask', 1990, Argentina £5.45
13	Plantagenet Shiraz 1990, Western Australia £7.95
15	Chorey-lès-Beaune, Edmond Cornu, 1990, Burgundy, France £11.45
16	Barbaresco, Azienda Agricola Guiseppe Cortese, 1988, Piedmont, Italy £12.06
17	Barca Velha, Ferreira, 1985, Portugal £24.99

GNW   The Great Northern Wine Co   ★★★★

Granary Wharf, The Canal Basin, Leeds, W. Yorks. LS1 4BR (0532 461200).
Opening Hours: Mon-Fri 9am-6pm, Sat 9.30am-5pm. **Delivery:** free locally,
nationally at cost. **Tastings:** regular in-store, monthly tutored sessions, annual wine
fair in October. **Services:** cellarage, mail order, gift mailing, glass hire.

Although the name is all colliery bands and Hovis-ads, Great Northern operate out
of a smart Granary wharf in Leeds and Blossomgate in Ripon, so leave that cloth cap
at home for the whippet to chew on. A great spread of New World wines (close on
three dozen Australian producers and two dozen Americans, including rarities from
New York State), blend with the Old World offerings to form an eclectic list that
provides drinking across the price range. Some prices are high enough to smack of a
more southern attitude to value for money (are the bottles expensively shipped up
by canal?) but the range is one of the best on either side of the divide. Surprisingly,
their 'Desert' section (referred to on page 4) neglects bottled water; perhaps it was to
be Sue Lawley's selection.

1	Champagne Joseph Perrier Cuvée Josephine Brut, 1985, France £39.50	
2	Bellefontaine Chardonnay, Paul Boutinot, 1993,France £3.99	
3	Cervaro Della Sala, Antinori, 1992, Italy £19.70	
4	Brown Bothers King Valley Sauvignon Blanc, 1993,Victoria, Australia £6.90	
12	Preece Cabernet Sauvignon, Mitchelton, 1992, Victoria, Australia £6.99	
12	Amiral de Beychevelle, St Julien, Chateau Beychevelle, 1989, Bordeaux, France £12.99	
13	Peter Lehmann Shiraz, 1990, Barossa Valley, South Australia £5.49	
13	Foppiano Petite Syrah, 1990, California £7.99	
18	Campbells Rutherglen Liqueur Muscat, Victoria, Australia £5.65	
18	Essencia, Quady Winery, 1992, California £5.99	
20	Dos Cortados Oloroso, Williams & Humbert, Jerez, Spain £8.50	
21	Smith Woodhouse Traditional Late Bottled Vintage Port, 1981, Portugal £12.99	

GRT   The Great Western Wine Company   ★★★

2-3 Mile End, London Road, Bath, BA1 6PT (0225 448428). **Opening Hours:** Mon-
Fri 9am-7pm Sat 10am-7pm. **Delivery:** free locally, nationally at cost. **Tastings:**
regular in store, plus tutored events by winemakers, 'beginners'' courses and
tastings of Bordeaux crus classés. **Services:** Cellarage, en primeur, mail order, gift
mailing, glass hire, ice.

Perhaps as British Rail is privatised, Wine merchants with historic railway
influenced names will switch too; this company to become Network West Wines.
Meanwhile, board your own train of thought here with an inspection of the rolling-
stock Philip Addis and Rachel Tully have joined together and assemble a mixed-case.
Ride on the footplate through an ever-changing landscape of French regional wines,
perhaps alighting at Mas de Daumas Gassac or staying on through Burgundy for a
whistle-stop tour of the rest of the world. Better still, book a season ticket for their
day-trip tastings.

3	Goundrey Langton Chardonnay, 1993, Western Australia £6.99	
13	Gigondas, Chateau Du Trignon, 1991, Rhône, France £7.99	
17	Vina Real Rioja Reserva, CVNE, 1986, Spain £7.99	
20	Barbadillo Principe Amontillado Seco, Jerez, Spain £10.59	
21	Dow's 20 Year Old Tawny Port, Portugal £20.99	

GWC   The Greek Wine Centre   ★★★

48 Underdale Road, Shrewsbury, SY2 5DT (Tel 0743 364636 Fax 0743 367960).
Opening Hours: Mon-Fri 9am-5pm. **Delivery:** free nationally over 7 cases.
Otherwise £6 per case **Tastings:** by arrangement **Services:** mail order..

Until recently a merchant who specialised in Hellenic wines was about as
recommendable as a fishmonger who only sold rubbery squid. But Jordanis
Petridis's range provides a fascinating insight into what Greek winemakers can do
when they try. And if you want to compare ancient and modern, he can offer you
vintages of Chateau Carras from the 1970s.

4	Ambelon, Hatzimichalis, 1992, Greece £7.00
11	Cava Hatzimichali, Hatzimichalis, 1990, Greece £8.50
11	Cava Tsantalis, 1987, Greece £4.50
12	Domaine Hatzmichalis Merlot, 1992, Greece £12.50

PTR   Peter Green & Co   ★★★★

37 A/B Warrender Park Road, Edinburgh EH9 1HJ (031 229 5925). no credit cards,
Switch only. **Opening Hours:** Mon-Fri 9.30am-6.30pm, Sat 9.30am-7pm. **Delivery:**
free locally, nationally at cost. **Tastings:** occasional in-store, monthly tastings in local
hall; other groups on request. **Services:** mail order.

There are so many wine regions in which Peter Green could be considered a
specialist, that it's difficult to know which to mention. Suffice it to say that if you're
after wine from Alsace, Bordeaux, the Loire, Germany, Italy, Spain, Australia, New
Zealand, Chile or South Africa, this is the place to come. And if you're after
something from beyond those areas, well, you'll probably find something tasty in
stock too. Quite simply an excellent wine (and malt whisky) merchant.

1	Champagne Canard-Duchêne Brut Rosé, France £16.99
3	Hamilton Russell Vineyards Chardonnay, 1993, Walker Bay, South Africa £7.75
4	Domaine De Laballe, Vin De Pays De Terroirs Landais Blanc, Noel Laudet, 1993, France £4.49
4	Marquès de Alella Classico, 1993, Spain £5.99
6	Gewürztraminer, Trimbach, 1991, Alsace, France £7.99
12	Venegazzù della Casa, Loredan Gasparini, 1989, Italy £8.99
16	Barolo, Fontanafredda, 1989, Piedmont, Italy £7.99
17	Pago de Carraovejas Ribera del Duero, 1992, Spain £5.99
17	Guelbenzu Navarra Crianza Tinto, 1990, Spain £5.99
17	Masia Barril Tipico Priorato, Hermanos Barril, 1991, Spain £6.99
21	Noval 10 Year Old Tawny Port, Quinta do Noval, Portugal £11.99

GRO   Grog Blossom   ★★★

253 West End Lane, West Hampstead NW6 1XN (071 794 7808). **Opening Hours:**
Mon-Fri 11am-10pm. Sat 10am-10pm Sun 12am-3pm, 7pm-10pm. **Delivery:** free
locally, nationally at cost. **Tastings:** every Saturday, in store. **Services:** mail order,
glass hire, ice.

'We're still here. For the moment'. The slightly forlorn tone of voice is quite
understandable from the manager of a three-shop chain which has been cut back to a
single link. Notting Hill residents miss the alternative to Majestic and Oddbins their
branch used to offer, so we only hope that North London wine lovers are more
appreciative of the efforts Paul O'Connor makes to buy up worthwhile bin-ends and
stock interesting parcels of wine and beer. It would be a great pity if there were no
room even in London for a budding Oddbin.

1	Omar Khayyam, Indian Sparkling Wine, 1987, £6.99
2	Chandlers Hill Chardonnay, Normans, 1993, Australia £5.89
12	Monteviña Cabernet Sauvignon, 1991, California £6.99
13	Brown Brothers King Valley Shiraz, 1991, Australia £6.00
15	Nuits St Georges 1er Cru Clos de la Maréchale, Faiveley, 1989, Burgundy, France £23.00
17	Navajas Rioja Tinto Riserva, 1985, Spain £6.99
19	Tokaji Aszu 6 Puttonyos, Hetszolo, 1981, Hungary £19.95
21	Rutherford & Miles, Old Artillery Malmsey, Madeira, Portugal £8.00

HLV   Halves

See The Wine Treasury.

HAM   Hampden Wine Company

Jordan's Courtyard, 8 Upper High Street, Thame, Oxon OX9 3ER (Tel 0844 213251 Fax 0844 261100). **Opening Hours:** Mon-Wed 9.30am-5pm; Thurs-Fri 9.30am-5.30pm, Sat 9am-5pm. **Delivery:** free within 15 miles. **Tastings:** regular in-store, plus tutored events at local restaurants. **Services:** mail order, gift mailing, glass hire.

The compact selection put together by Ian Hampden Hope-Morley and Lance Foyster MW contains much to croon about. We'd head for the Dr Loosen Mosels, Marcel Deiss Alsaces, Huët Vouvrays and the excellent French country wines, particularly the K de Krevel Montravel. We might also find ourselves detained by interesting ranges from Italy, Australia and Portugal.

1	Seppelt Pinot Rosé Cuvée Brut, Australia £6.50
8	Moyston Australian Riesling, B Seppelt & Sons, 1993, Australia, £3.99
9	Dr Loosen Wehlener Sonnenuhr Riesling Spätlese, 1992, Mosel, Germany £10.79
13	Rouge Homme Shiraz-Cabernet, 1991, South Australia £4.99
13	Fairview Estate Shiraz, 1992, South Africa £4.95
17	Quinta de la Rosa, Douro, 1992, Portugal £4.90
21	Quinta de Eira Velha, Single Quinta Vintage Port 1987, Portugal £15.99

HPD   Harpenden Wines

68 High Street, Harpenden, Herts AL5 2SP (0582 765605). **Opening Hours:** Mon-Fri 10am-10pm, Sat 9am-10pm, Sun 12-3pm, £7-10pm. **Delivery:** free locally. **Tastings:** regular in-store. **Services:** gift mailing.

Paul Beaton goes further than most modern wine merchants when dealing with organic wines; he marks those in which no animal-derived fining agents have been used as 'suitable for Vegans'. Organic producers such as Eden Ridge (Australia), Millton (New Zealand), Pierre Frick (Alsace) and Domaine Richaume (Southern France) can be found here, amongst others. This is not, however, to say that callers to his shop will be asked to remove their leather shoes –– he stocks wines for the unenlighted too –– heady clarets and smoky Rhônes that would help provide palatibility to the heaviest and least seasoned nut cutlet or spinach roulade.

8	David Wynn Eden Valley Riesling, 1992, South Australia £6.10
11	Minervois, Campagne de Centeilles, P Boyer-Domergue, 1990, Languedoc Roussillon, France £6.95
11	Mas de Gourgonnier Reserve du Mas, 1990, Midi, France £7.50
12	Eden Ridge Cabernet Sauvignon, 1992, South Australia £7.30
19	Sainte Croix du Mont, Baron Philippe De Rothschild 1990, France £10.39

ROG   Roger Harris Wines   ★★★★

Loke Farm, Weston Longville, Norwich, Norfolk NR9 5LG (Tel 0603 880171). Wine by the case only. **Opening Hours: Mon-Fri** 9am-5pm. **Delivery:** nationally at cost. **Tastings:** tutored sessions on request from customers. **Services:** mail order.

Apart from the intrusion of a Champagne and a Vin de Pays des Côtes de Gascogne, Roger Harris sticks to his last, focusing his attention exclusively on Southern Burgundy, and in particular on Beaujolais. Should you wish to know anything about the world's friendliest but potentially most disappointing wine Mr H's beautifully produced monthly newsletters are the perfect place to begin your quest.

2	Beaujolais Blanc, Cave de Sain Bel, 1992, France	£6.00
2	Mâcon Vinzelles, Cooperative de Loché, 1993, France	£6.10
14	Beaujolais Villages, Jean-Charles Pivot, 1993, France	£6.25
14	Moulin à Vent, Le Vieux Domaine, 1992, France	£6.25
14	Chénas, Dom du Maupas, 1993, France	£6.35

HAR   Harrods   ★★★★

Knightsbridge, London SW1X 7QX (071-730 1234). **Opening Hours:** Mon, Tue, Sat 10am-6pm; Wed, Thu, Fri 10am-7pm. **Delivery:** Free within M25 for orders over £50. **Tastings:** regularly for members of the Gourmet Club and people on the mailing list. **Services:** gift mailing and mail order. Cellarage and en primeur to be offered 'shortly'.

As Harvey Nichols, Fortnum & Mason and Selfridges steadily develop top class wine departments, this sleepy little corner shop near an army barracks has, after several false starts, recently begun to overcome its narcolepcy. The buyer cast in the role of Prince Charming is Nicholas Mason, a passionate Rhône fan who has already begun to introduce a broad range of the sorts of wines Harrods ought to have been selling for years.

1	Daniel Le Brun Brut NV, Cellier Le Brun, New Zealand	£11.99
1	Champagne Nicolas Feuillatte, Reserve Particulière Brut 1er Cru, France	£15.00
1	Champagne 'R' de Ruinart Brut, France	£22.00
2	Chardonnay 'Buchholz', Alois Lageder, 1992, Italy	£7.99
3	Chardonnay Le Veritière, Gruppo Italiano Vini, 1993, Italy	£5.50
3	Au Bon Climat Chardonnay, 1992, California	£12.50
3	Wakefield Chardonnay 1992, Clare, Australia	£5.99
4	Pinot Bianco, Jermann, 1992, Italy	£12.00
4	Dry Reserve, Hidden Spring Vineyard, 1990, England	£7.50
8	Steiner Hund Riesling Kabinett, Fritz Salomon, 1990, Austria	£7.49
8	Petaluma Clare Riesling, 1993, South Australia	£9.21
12	Santa Rita Medalla Real Cabernet Sauvignon, 1990, Chile	£6.99
12	Torres Gran Coronas, Mas La Plana, 1988, Penedes, Spain	£20.99
13	Ridge Geyserville, 1992, California	£15.75
15	Pinot Noir 'La Bauge Au-dessus', Au Bon Climat, 1991, California	£18.00
16	Solaia, Antinori 1990, Tuscany, Italy	£46.00
17	Negre Scala Dei Priorat Priorato, Cellers de Scala Dei, 1991, Italy	£5.99
17	Baron de Ley, Rioja Reserva, 1987, Spain	£6.95
18	Campbells Old Rutherglen Liqueur Muscat, Victoria, Australia	£12.99
19	Denbies Wine Estate Noble Harvest, 1992, England	£17.50
20	Don Zoilo Very Old Fino, Jerez, Spain	£8.00
21	Blandys' 10 Year Old Dry Sercial, Madeira Wine Company Portugal	£15.75

HWM   Harvest Wine Group   ★★★

Clocktower Mews, Stanlake Park, Twyford, Reading, RG10 0BN (Tel 0734 344290) **Opening Hours:** Mon-Sat 10am-5pm, Sun 12-3pm. **Delivery:** nationally at cost. **Tastings:** phone for details. **Services:** mail-order.

The motto is 'English wines of distinction with an Australian accent'. Since his arrival from the Antipodes five years ago, John Worontschak has done more for English wine than the combined industry had done in the previous quarter-century. Harvest consists of a dozen or so vineyards who all benefit from the Worontschak winemaking skills. All the releases, including the Heritage range (a blend from the various vineyards), are at least good, but the wines from Wickham, Pilton Manor, Boze Down, Valley Vineyards and Sharpham are currently very good.

1	Heritage Brut N.V., England	£7.99
3	Pilton Fumé, 1992, England	£6.99
8	Valley Vineyards Regatta, 1992, England	£4.99
8	Boze Down Dry, 1993, England	£5.50
8	Sharpham Estate Selection, 1993, England	£6.50

HN   Harvey Nicholls   ★★★★

Knightsbridge, London SW1 (Tel 071 235 5000). **Opening Hours:** Mon-Fri 10am-8pm, Sat 10am-6pm. **Delivery:** £50 order is free locally. **Tastings:** regular in-store plus tutored sessions. **Services:** mail order, gift-mailing (gift-wrapping in-store).

Fashionable, yet understated, this miniature wine boutique counterpart to the Fifth Floor food hall is as innovative and alluring as its clientèle, not to say as well-heeled. It offers the latest collections from Italy, France, the US and Australia; the majority are quality prêt-à-porter producers. There's some scrumptious little numbers in the stickies and halves, and then there's those with a more classic taste, the Bordeaux and Fine Wine room will suit. Every Monday the Fifth floor Restaurant and café will serve your wine purchased from the shop with no charge for corkage. Absolutely fabulous.

1	Champagne Pol Roger Blanc de Chardonnay, 1986, France	£35.00
2	Tasmania Wine Company Chardonnay, 1993, Australia	£8.25
3	Au Bon Climat Chardonnay, 1992, California	£12.50
4	Pinot Bianco, Jermann, 1992, Friuli, Italy	£10.99
7	Ca Del Solo Malvasia Bianca, Bonny Doon, 1992, California.	£7.50
11	Madiran Bouscassé, Alain Brumont, 1991, S.W. France	£6.25
12	Opus One, Rothschild/Mondavi, 1990, Napa, California	£45.00
13	Cape Mentelle Shiraz, 1991, Australia	£8.49
13	Orlando Lawsons Padthaway Shiraz, 1989, Australia	£9.99
13	Qupé Syrah, 1992, California	£9.90
15	Neudorf Vineyard Moutere Pinot Noir, 1992, New Zealand	£11.95
15	Georg Stiegelmar Pinot Noir Barrique Trocken, 1990, Austria	£15.00
17	Guelbenzu Navarra Crianza Tinto, 1990, Spain	£5.99
19	Ruster Beerenauslese, Weinkellerei Burgenland, 1981, Austria	£5.99

HHC   Haynes, Hanson & Clark   ★★★★

Sheep Street, Stow on the Wold, Gloucs GL54 1AA (Tel 0451 870808). **Opening Hours:** Mon–Fri 9am-7pm, Sat 9am-6pm. **Delivery:** free locally, nationally at cost. **Services:** en primeur, mail order, gift mailing, glass hire, ice.

HH&C have moved their offices from Fulham to the decidedly more pleasant environs of Stow-on-the-Wold, although the London link remains with the Kensington Church Street shop. The firm is known as a Burgundy specialist, and the likes of Olivier Leflaive, Gagnard-Delagrange and Michel Lafarge will not disappoint. However, the rest of the range has also been well chosen, so do try the many regional French wines, the Murphy-Goode and Saintsbury Californians and the Kiwis from Palliser Estate and C J Pask.

3	Palliser Estate Chardonnay, 1992, Martinborough, New Zealand, £9.99	
4	Cape Mentelle Semillon Sauvignon, 1993, Australia £7.99	
12	Cape Mentelle Cabernet Merlot, 1991, Australia £7.99	
15	Saintsbury Pinot Noir Reserve, 1991, California £18.00	
18	Morris Liqueur Muscat, Victoria, Australia £8.49	
21	Warres Traditional Late Bottled Vintage Port, 1981, Douro, Portugal £12.49	

H&H   Hector & Honorez Fine Wines   ★★★

7, East Street, Kimbolton, Cambridgeshire PE18 0HJ (Tel 0480 861444). **Opening Hours:** Mon-Sat 9.30am-5.30pm. **Delivery:** free locally, nationally at cost.. **Tastings:** occasional. **Services:** cellarage, en primeur, mail-order, glass-hire.

Eclectic has always been the style for this pair of merchants. In France, go for the reds and whites from Alain Brumont, the great range of Burgundies and Rhônes, an impressive set of red Loires and Marc Kreydenweiss's Alsace wines. Elsewhere, there's an expanding New World selection and the Kracher Austrians which offer a rare treat.

1	Chardonnay - Pinot Noir Brut, Domaine De l'Aigle, France £7.50
3	Brokenwood Chardonnay, 1993, Hunter Valley, Australia £7.00
3	Domaine De l'Aigle, 'Les Aigles' Chardonnay, 1992, France £6.75
4	Brokenwood Cricket Pitch Sauvignon Blanc/Semillon, 1993, Hunter Valley, Australia £6.50
11	Madiran, Montus, Alain Brumont, 1991, South-West France £9.50
12	Brokenwood Cabernet Sauvignon, 1991, Hunter Valley, Australia £7.00
13	Brokenwood Shiraz, 1991, Hunter Valley, Australia £7.00
13	Domaine du Mas Crémat, Côtes Du Roussillon, 1991, France £5.00

HW   Hedley Wright & Co Ltd   ★★★★

11, The Twyford Centre, London Road, Bishop's Stortford, Herts CM23 3YT (Tel: 0279 506512). **Opening Hours:** Mon-Wed 9am-6pm, Thu-Fri 9am-7pm, Sat 10am-6pm. **Delivery:** free locally, nationally at cost.**Tastings:** regular in-store, plus tutored events. **Services:** en primeur, glass hire, gift-mailing, ice.

Watch out for Hedley Wright's 'very exciting' new list which was due to appear just after we went to press. Joining old (and not so old) favourites such as the Churchill Graham ports, Montes Chileans, Kiwis from Jackson Estate and Daniel Le Brun, and Burgundies from Fougeray de Beauclair will be some innovative Spaniards, Italians and the wonderful Henschke Aussies.

1	Daniel Le Brun Vintage, Cellier Le Brun, 1990, New Zealand £19.95
1	Gosset Grand Reserve Champagne, N.V., France £25.99
2	Montes Chardonnay, Cuvee Ryman/Montes, 1993, Chile £4.99
3	Jackson Estate Sauvignon, 1994, Marlborough, New Zealand £7.95
4	The Warden Abbot, Warden Abbey Vineyard, 1993, England £5.40
10	Chinon Rosé, 1993, Ch. de Grille, Loire, France, £9.95
15	Santenay Clos de la Confrerie, Vincent Girardin, 1992, Burgundy, France £12.50
16	Chianti Rufina, 1991, Villa Vetrice, Tuscany, Italy £4.45
20	Olorosa Viejo, Manuel De Argueso, Jerez, Spain £8.45
21	Churchill's Quinta da Agua Alta, 1987, Douro, Portugal £14.50

DHM Douglas Henn-Macrae ★★★

81 Mackenders Lane, Eccles, Aylesford, Kent ME20 7JA (Tel 0622 710952; Fax 0622 791203). Wine by the case only. Not a shop – mail order and telephone enquires. **Delivery:** free locally, nationally for ten cases or more. **Tastings:** tutored sessions on request. **Services:** mail order.

Mr H-M would be certain of being nominated for any award for Britain's oddest wine selection. He clearly enjoys a challenge, representing fewer than a dozen producers, half of which are in the States – Oregon, Texas and Washington State, to be precise – and half of which are in Germany. And those German wines come in virtually every colour, sweetness and fizziness possible. If you want to expand your horizons without resorting to drugs or New Age claptrap, give the man a call.

2	Aligoté, 1987, Covey Run Wines, Washington State £5
7	Trittenheimer Altärchen Riesling Hochgewâchs Halbtrocken, 1992, Mosel, Germany £6.40
7	Erbacher Marcobrunn Spätlese Staatsweingûter Kloster Eberbach, Rheingau, Germany, £12
9	Grûnstadter Höllenpfad Scheurebe Auslese, 1976, Rheinpfalz, Germany £11.75
12	Cabernet Sauvignon 1987, Llano Estacado, Texas £8.30
15	Traisener Rotenfels Blauer Spätburgunder Rotwein Spätlese Trocken, 1989, Nahe, Germany £6.70
15	Willamette Valley Pinot Noir, 1987, Elk Cove Wines, Oregon £6.95
15	Grûnstadter Höllenpfad Spätburgunder Spätlese, 1989, Rheinpfalz, Germany, £9.50

H&D Hicks & Don ★★★★

The Brewery, Blandford St Mary, Dorset DT11 9LB (Tel 0258 456040). **Opening Hours:** Mon-Fri 9am-5pm plus answerphone. **Delivery:** free for three cases or more. **Tastings:** four or five every year. **Services:** cellarage, en-primeur, mail order, gift-mailing, glass hire, .

Hicks & Don, the firm which takes the credit/blame for more or less inventing 'en primeur' in this country is now the mail order arm of Woodhouse Wines, and offers a personal selection from the core list of that wholesale merchant. However, additional wines are available on an ex-cellars basis via regular special offers, whereby customers pay for half the wine up front and the remaining half after shipping. H&D thereby know exactly how much to ship and, from eliminating the need for storage facilities, can pass on savings to the customers.

1	Mountadam Eden Valley Sparkling Wine, 1990, South Australia £16.95
1	Champagne Joseph Perrier Cuvee Royale Brut Rosé, France £22.50
2	David Wynn Chardonnay, 1993, South Australia £6.10
3	Montes Nogales Estate Chardonnay, Discover Wines, 1994, Chile £5.49
4	Reserve du Reverend Corbières Blanc, CGC, 1991, France £3.99
13	St Joseph Grande Reserve, Guyot SA, 1990, Rhône, France £6.05

JEH J E Hogg ★★★

61, Cumberland Street, EH3 6RA, Edinburgh (Tel 031 556 4025). **Opening Hours:** Mon-Fri 9am-1pm; 2:30pm-6pm, Sat & Wed 9am-1pm. **Delivery:** free locally in East Lothian. **Tastings:** for groups on request. **Services:** glass hire.

Hamilton Russell, Olivier Leflaive, Hunter's, Antinori, Rothbury, Jaboulet Aîné ... wherever you're looking in the wine world, Mr Hogg should be able to come up

with virtually any wine you want, or even a better alternative. However, if you want
to bring a smile to his face, ask him to give you a guided tour through his wines from
Alsace and Germany.

3	Houghton Swan Valley Dry White, 1991, Australia £4.79	
4	Sancerre Comte Lafond, de Ladoucette, 1992, Loire, France £12.50	
8	Riesling Cuvee Frederic Emile, F E Trimbach, 1988, Alsace, France £15.99	
21	Noval LB Port, Quinta Do Noval, £8.49	

HOL   Holland Park Wine Company   ★★★★

12 Portland Road, London W11 4LA (Tel 071-221 9614). **Opening Hours:** Mon-Fri
10am-8.30pm, Sat 9am-8.30pm. **Delivery:** free locally, nationally at cost. **Tastings:**
regular in-store, plus a series of tutored tastings beginning in October. **Services:**
cellarage, en primeur, mail order, gift mailing, glass hire, ice.

With the minimum of fuss, James Handford MW is establishing his company as one
of London's best. Olivier Leflaive Burgundies, toothsome clarets, Trimbach Alsace,
Kracher Austrians and some excellent Italians and Aussies are just some of the
reasons to give his Notting Hill, sorry, Holland Park establishment a visit.

2	Stonier's Chardonnay, 1992, Mornington Peninsula, Australia, £7.50
2	St. Andrews Estate Chardonnay, 1990, Napa Valley, California, £7.95
2	Moss Wood Chardonnay, Margaret River, 1993, Australia, £11.00
11	Chateau Pech de Jammes, 1989, Cahors, France £7.99
12	Michel Lynch Bordeaux rouge, 1989, France £5.99
12	Niebaum Coppola Cabernet Franc, 1990, California. £9.95
15	Stoniers Pinot Noir, 1992, Mornington Peninsula, Australia, £7.50
17	Rioja Belezos Tinto, Bodegas Zugober, 1993, Spain £4.29
16	Brunello Di Montalcino, La Magia, 1988, Tuscany, Italy £11.99
19	Kracher Traminer Beerenauslese 'Nouvelle Vague', 1989, Austria £19

HOU   Hoults Wine Merchants   ★★★

5 Cherry Tree Walk, The Calls, Leeds LS2 7EB (Tel 0532 453393). **Opening Hours:**
Mon-Sat 10am-6.30pm, Sun 12-3pm. **Delivery:** free locally, nationally at cost.
Tastings: regular in-store plus occasional tutored sessions for organisations.
Services: mail order, gift mailing.

The Huddersfield establishment is opposite a branch of Tesco, while the recently-
opened Leeds outlet (see above) competes with Oddbins. However, enthusiasm,
hard work and good wines ensure that Hoults survive and even prosper. Italy,
Australia and New Zealand are the source of the most interesting wines, but there is
more than enough from other parts of the globe to warrant a visit.

1	Champagne Lang Biemont Cuvee d'Exception, 1985, France £22.00
3	Rouge Homme Chardonnay, 1992, Australia, £6.99
3	Santa Carolina Chardonnay, 1993, Chile £4.49
3	Fetzer Vineyards Barrel Select Chardonnay, 1992, California £9.21
3	Moondah Brook Estate Chardonnay, BRL Hardy, 1993, Australia £5.49
4	Palliser Estate Sauvignon Blanc, 1993, New Zealand £8.75
10	Santa Carolina Cabernet Sauvignon Rosé Special Reserve, 1992, Chile £5.49
12	Preece Cabernet Sauvignon, Mitchelton, 1992, Australia £6.99
12	Santa Carolina Merlot Special Reserve, 1992, Chile £5.49
21	Old Trafford Tawny, B Seppelt & Sons, Australia £7.49

HOT · House of Townend · ★★★

Red Duster House, 101 York Street, Hull, N Humberside HU2 0QX (Tel 0482 26891). **Opening Hours:** Mon-Sat 10am-10pm, Sun 12-2pm. **Delivery:** free locally, nationally at cost. **Tastings:** regular in-store, tutored sessions for groups plus monthly tastings for own wine club. **Services:** cellarage, en primeur, mail order, gift mailing, glass hire, ice.

This Hull-based chain with 15 outlets is as solid as they come, though less conservative than in the past. Clarets from good reliable châteaux abound, there are familiar names among the Burgundies, Rhônes come from Jaboulet and Chapoutier and you'll find some excellent Germans. Outside the traditional areas, the Australians from Henschke and Mitchells, and the Klein Constantia South Africans are the wines to look for.

1	Varichon Et Clerc Carte Blanche Blanc de Blancs, France £6.50	
1	Rowlands Brook Sparkling Rosé Wine, Penfolds, Australia £4.99	
2	Domaine des Manants, J-M Brocard, 1992, Burgundy, France £7.20	
11	Cotes Du Roussillon, De Mare, South-West France £3.75	
12	C J Pask Cabernet/Merlot, 1992, New Zealand £8.39	
13	Mitchell Peppertree Shiraz, 1992, Australia £6.79	
16	Chianti Ruffina Villa di Vetrice, Fratelli Grati, 1991, Tuscany, Italy £3.99	
17	Orla Dorada, Faustino Rivero, 1990, Spain £4.25	
20	Wisdom & Warter Fino, Jerez, Spain £3.99	
21	D'Oliveira 5 Year Old Dry Madeira, £8.70	

TOJ · Tony Jeffries Wines · ★★★

69 Edith Street, Northampton NN1 5EP (Tel 0604 22375). **Opening hours:** Tues-Fri 10am-3pm, Sat 9am-5pm. **Delivery:** free locally, nationally at cost. **Tastings:** occasional in-store plus tutored tastings on request from local wine clubs, etc. **Services:** glass hire.

As well as importing six of Vincent Girardin's fine Burgundies direct from the producer, and majoring on Beaujolais from Depagneux, Tony Jeffries has recently become highly (and understandably) excited by the potential offered by red Rhônes from 1989 and 1990, and now lists a number of juicy numbers from Guigal, Jaboulet etc as well as a more adventurous selection from the likes of Pouzin, Rostaing and Sabon. Australia is a real strength, as is South Africa, although we would advise sticking to Warwick, Fairview, Saxenberg and possibly Backsberg rather than some of the more pedestrian estates that also feature.

13	Gigondas, Domaine Raspail Ay, 1990, Rhône, France £7.50	
17	Rioja Eduardo Garrido Garcia, Vina Joven, 1991, Spain £4.25	

SHJ · S H Jones & Co Ltd · ★★★★

27 High Street, Banbury, Oxon OX16 8EW (Tel 0295 251177). **Opening hours:** Mon-Fri 8.30am-6pm, Sat 9am-6pm. **Delivery:** free locally for one case or more. **Tastings:** regular in-store plus tutored sessions (please check). **Services:** cellarage, en primeur, mail order, gift mailing, glass hire, ice.

If only every town had a merchant like S H Jones. Wines ancient and modern abound, and if France receives the lion's share of attention, the rest of the world does very nicely thank you with the portion left for the remainder of the jungle. Traditionalists will head for the von Schubert Germans, Droin Chablis, Vieux Télégraphe Châteauneuf, Huet Vouvray, clarets dating back to 1970 Cos d'Estournel and multiple vintages of Rieussec. Others might try the Santadi Sardinians, Rothbury Aussies, Weinert Argentinians and Palliser Estate Kiwis.

1	La Grande Marque, Saumur Co-Op, France £6.79
1	Champagne St. Honore, Duval Leroy, France £10.69
2	Domaine 'Virginie' Chardonnay, Vin de Pays d'Oc, 1992, France £4.75
2	Chablis Premier Cru 'Montmains', Domaine des Manants, Jean-Marc Brocard, 1992, France £9.50
8	Dr Loosen Riesling, 1992, Mosel, Germany £5.99
11	Cotes Du Roussillon, De Mare, Sout-West France £3.75
11	Ch. Roc de Montpezat, Cotes de Castillon, J P Moueix, 1990, South-West France £5.70
12	Viña Undurraga Cabernet Sauvignon Reserva, 1990, Chile £5.75
12	Ch. Lagarosse, Première Côte de Bordeaux 1989, France £6.95
13	Côtes du Rhône Chateau Du Grand Moulas, Rykwaert, 1993, Rhône, France £5.05
13	Mitchell Peppertree Shiraz 1992, Australia £6.79
16	Chianti Classico, Castello Di Volpaia 1988, Tuscany, Italy £6.45
17	Crianza 89, Vina Salceda, 1989, Spain £4.25
17	Conde de la Salceda Rioja Gran Reserva, 1985, Spain £11.00

J&B   Justerini & Brooks Ltd   ★★★★★

61 St. James's Street, London SW1A 1LZ (Tel: 071-493 8721). **Opening Hours:** Mon-Fri 9am-5.30pm (open Sat during December). **Delivery:** free for two cases or more on UK mainland. **Tastings:** occasional in-store plus special tastings for selected customers on request. **Services:** cellarage, en primeur, mail order, gift mailing, glass hire, ice.

Regional Wine Merchant of the Year; London and the South East Wine Merchant of the Year

Of course you could blow £3,000 on a bottle of 1895 Haut-Brion, but you could also spend it on several dozen of the many halves on offer. Whatever your preference, J & B will be able to provide something rather tasty, and if it isn't actually in stock in the newly refurbished (and now much friendlier) St James's shop, it will be within 24 hours. Highlighting the excellent German, Bordeaux, Rhône and Burgundy selections only detracts from the quality of the rest of the range. The Loire, regional France, Italy, Spain and the New World are covered efficiently and effectively, whether your taste is for vin de pays or Vega Sicilia. Definitely worth making a J & B-line for.

2	Mâcon-Uchizy, Domaine Talmard, 1992, Burgundy, France £6.60
3	Meursault Clos Des Perrieres, Albert Grivault, 1990, Burgundy, France £35.00
9	Bernkasteler Badstube Riesling Spatlese, Dr Thanisch, 1989, Germany £9.80
12	Ch. Laplagnotte-Bellevue, St Emilion Grand Cru, 1990, France £9.45
12	Ch. Canon, St Emilion Grand Cru, 1985, France £29.00
13	Vacqueyras, Cuvee des Templiers, Domaine Le Clos des Cazaux, 1990, Rhône, France £6.60
13	Crozes Hermitage, Domaine Pochon, 1992, Rhône, France £6.95
13	Côte Rotie, Bernard Burgaud, 1991, Rhône, France £17.90
15	Gevrey-Chambertin Clos St Jacques, Domaine G. Bartet, 1989, Burgundy, France £28.00
19	Clos d'Yvigne, Saussignac, Atkinson, 1990, South-West France £10.90

KS   Kwiksave   ★★★

Warren Drive, Prestatyn, Clwyd, LL19 7HV (Tel 0745 887111, Fax 0745 882504). **Opening Hours:** Mon-Sat 8:30am-5:30pm (late opening 8pm selected stores).

Angela Muir MW continue to massage the Kwiksave wine range into something which, outside the obligatory Liebfraumilch, Lambrusco and British wine sectors, represents some of the very best value on the High Street. For example, in 1993, Ms Muir felt that the Beaujolais and Côtes du Rhône were not up to scratch for the prices asked, so they have been displaced from the range until the value improves. Not the most fashionable place to be seen shopping, but one which deserves a big pat on the back for the combination of common sense and good wines. Great for early risers.

1	Champagne Louis Raymond Brut, France £7.89	
2	Jacobs Creek Chardonnay, 1993, Australia £3.97	
3	Pelican Bay Semillon, Australia £2.79	
4	Comtesse de Lorancy, EEC Blend £2.29	
5	Leziria Medium dry white, Portugal £1.99	
6	Burgas Ugni Blanc and Muscat, Bulgaria £2.39	
7	Kwik Save Morio Muskat, St. Ursula, 1993, Germany £2.29	
10	Côtes de Ventoux Rosé, France £2.69	
11	Minervois, 1993, S.W. France £2.59	
12	Lovico Suhindol Reserve Merlot, 1990, £2.99	
13	La Miracle Ventoux Blanc, U.V.C.V, 1993, France £3.29	
22	Piemontello Light, Santero, £1.99	

L&W   Lay & Wheeler Ltd   ★★★★★

6 Culver Street West, Colchester, Essex CO1 1JA (Tel 0206 764446). **Opening Hours:** Mon-Sat 8am-8pm. **Delivery:** free locally, nationally for two cases and over. **Tastings:** regular in-store, plus tutored tastings and workshops. **Services:** cellarage, en primeur, mail order, gift mailing, glass hire, ice.

Bordeaux and German Specialist Wine Merchant of the Year

This is the sort of wine list that you would expect to find in the downstairs loo of any self-respecting country house, among a pile of back issues of The Field, Country Life and Tatler, or slipped behind the accumulated debris of Labrador leads, spent shotgun cartridges and half-used tins of wax Barbour proofing. You would however be making a big mistake if you assumed that purveying agreeable claret to the luncheon tables of the landed gentry was all that Lay & Wheeler is good for. This is, quite simply, a brilliant all-round merchant. In addition to the huge list of top notch French wine (and there is not a famous name that does not justify its presence by the quality of its current wines), there is the full range of superb Henschke wines from South Australia, magnificent Italians from, among others, Prunotto, and a large well-balanced and adventurous South African range headed by the wonderful reds from Kevin Arnold's Rust-en-Vrede. We sincerely hope that L&W's customer base remains sufficiently conservative to appreciate the stunning range of Mosel Rieslings which most of the rest of the 'sophisticated' wine buying public appear to have thrown out along with a good deal of German bathwater.

2	Chablis, Etienne & Daniel Defaix, 1990, Burgundy, France £10.65	
3	Henschke Tilly's Vineyard Semillon-Chardonnay, 1991, Australia £5.99	
3	Rully 1er Cru Les Clous, Olivier Leflaive, 1992, Burgundy, France £9.19	
3	Peter Michael Clos du Ciel Chardonnay, 1991, California £15.25	
8	Henschke Eden Valley Riesling, 1990, Australia £6.69	
8	Traiser Rotenfels Riesling Spätlese Trocken, Crusius, 1992, Rhineland, Germany, £9.95	
8	Brauneberger Juffer-Sonnenuhr Riesling Auslese, 1992, Fritz Haag, Mosel-Saar-Ruwer, Germany, £18.95	
12	Henschke Abbotts Prayer Merlot/Cabernet, 1990, Australia £11.65	
12	Ch. Leoville Barton, St-Julien, 1989, France £19.19	
13	Henschke Mount Edelstone Shiraz, 1991, Australia £10.65	
13	Henschke Hill of Grace Shiraz, 1990, Australia £20.45	

L&S   Laymont & Shaw Ltd   ★★★★

The Old Chapel, Millpool, Truro, Cornwall, TR1 1EX (0872 70545, Fax 0872 233005) mail order by the case only. **Opening Hours:** Mon-Fri 9am-5pm **Delivery:** Free, mainland UK, minimum 1 case. **Tastings:** Occasional in-store plus tutored events. **Services:** cellarage, mail order, gift mailing, glass hire.

Spain provided many people's introduction to wine, but the country in recent years has often disappointed those who have sought further. However, if it's good and it's Spanish, long-time defender of the Hispanic faith John Hawes is likely to have it.. Rioja, Navarra, Valdepeñas, Priorato, Rias Baixas and other appellations are available in depth, and the ranges of sherry and Cava are also good. All credit to Mr H for sticking to what he knows best, and to what he is extremely good at.

3	Armonioso, Valdepenas Blanco, Los Llanos, 1992, Spain £3.95
3	Montenovo Blanco, Valdeorras Bodegas Senorio, 1992, Spain £4.95
12	Jean Leon Cabernet Sauvignon, 1987, Spain £7.45
17	Agramont Tinto, Bodegas Principe De Viana SA, 1990, Spain £3.99
17	Montenovo Tinto, Bodegas Senorio S.A.T., 1992, Spain £4.95
17	Yllera Tinto, S.A.T. Los Curros, 1990, Spain £6.75
17	Vina Arana Rioja Reserva, La Rioja Alta SA, 1986, Spain £8.75
17	Vina Ardanza Rioja Reserva, La Rioja Alta SA, 1986, Spain £10.25
17	Gran Reserva 904, La Rioja Alta SA, 1983, Spain £14.50
20	Malaga Solera 1885, Scholtz Hermanos S.A., Spain £8.49
20	Amontillado Fino (Pilar Aranda y Latorre), Emilio Lustau SA, Spain £5.99
20	Malaga, Moscatel Palido, Scholtz Hermanos, Spain £7.85

LAY   Laytons   ★★★★

20 Midlands Road, London NW1 2AD (071 388 5081, Fax 071 383 7419). **Opening Hours:** Mon-Fri 9am-5:30pm, Sat 10am-4pm. **Delivery:** Free nationally for orders over £100 ex VAT; otherwise £7 per order. **Tastings:** Occasionally. **Services:** cellarage, en Primeur, mail order, gift mailing, glass hire, ice.

There is a main list for customers of Laytons and the Andre Simon shops, but the real joy of dealing with the company is through the many special offers which all exude the seductively eccentric personality of Graham Chidgey. Some of which are handwritten, some of which contain far too much bold type and far too many exhortations of the 'it is imperative that you buy NOW' type, yet all of which contain something of interest. Burgundy, Bordeaux and, to a lesser extent, the rest of France are the main enthusiasm, but don't ignore the Italians, the Portuguese, the Tui Vale New Zealanders and the Australians from Taltarni.

1	Clover Hill Sparkling, Taltarni, 1991, Australia, £9.99
2	Pinot Blanc, Paul Blanck et ses Fils, 1992, Alsace, France £5.75
4	Taltarni Sauvignon Blanc, 1993, Australia £6.99
12	Ch. D'Armailhac, 1989, Pauillac, Baron Philippe De Rothschild SA Bordeaux, France £16.29
13	Crozes Hermitage Les Launes, Delas Freres, 1990, Rhône, France £6.49
16	Barbaresco, Az Ag Giuseppe Cortese, 1985, Piedmont, Italy £13.74
21	Dow's 20 Year Old Tawny Port, Douro, Portugal £20.99

LEA   Lea & Sandeman   ★★★★

301 Fulham Road, London SW10 9QH (Tel 071-376 4767). **Opening Hours:** Mon-Fri 9am-8.30pm, Sat 10am-8.30pm. **Delivery:** free locally, nationally on orders over £120. **Tastings:** regular in-store plus special tastings for small groups of customers. **Services:** mail order, gift mailing, glass hire/loan, ice.

One might be excused for mistaking Lea and Sandeman's Fulham Road shop for another boutique purveying expensive wedding presents, such was the profusion of hand-painted watering cans and ornate aprons last time we passed by. Resist the temptation to pop across the road to Oddbins (how Charles Lea must hate that word) and immerse yourself in studying the pastel-painted shelves of this redoubtable and impressive establishment. Burgundy, red and white is a big feature here as well as a very fine range of red Italians and Spaniards. They are also the only wine merchant we know to have mounted an exhibition of erotica, so they're not likely to be shocked if you ask if they have any really special bottles hidden beneath the counter.

1	Seppelt Pinot Rosé Cuvee Brut, Australia £6.50
2	Tasmania Wine Company Chardonnay, 1993, Australia £8.25
12	Niebaum Coppola Cabernet Franc, 1990, California £9.95
12	Clos Du Val Merlot, 1990, California £13.50
16	Camartina, Agricola Querciabella, 1988, Tuscany, Italy £19.95
17	Pago de Carraovejas Ribera del Duero, 1992, Spain £5.99
18	Campbells Old Rutherglen Liqueur Muscat, Australia £12.99
20	Pedro Ximenez Solera Superior, Valdespino, Jerez, Spain £9.75
20	Inocente Fino, Valdespino, Jerez, Spain £7.95
21	Henriques & Henriques, 10 Year Old Bual Madeira £15.00

LWE London Wine Emporium Ltd ★★★★

86 Goding Street, Vauxhall Cross, London SE11 5AW (Tel 071-587 1302). Wines by the case only. **Opening Hours:** Mon–Fri 10am-7pm, Sat 10am-5pm. **Delivery:** free within UK mainland. **Tastings:** occasional in-store plus tutored tastings on the third Monday of the month (except July, August and December). **Services:** mail order, glass hire.

The New World is very much the thing at Colin Barnes's railway arch, with stunning ranges from Australia, South Africa and New Zealand. The rest of the range is competent rather than exciting, although the mature Moldovans and the southern French range are worth a look.

1	Boschendal, Le Grand Pavillon N.V., South Africa £6.49
1	Champagne Jacquesson Brut, 1986, France £20.49
3	Ngatarawa, Alwyn Chardonnay, 1992, New Zealand £9.99
4	Pierro, Semillon / Sauvignon, 1992, Australia £6.49
4	Villiera Sauvignon Blanc, 1992, South Africa £6.99
4	Platts Semillon, 1992, Australia £7.49
4	Amberley Estate, Sauvignon Blanc, 1991, Australia £7.99
4	Tim Adams Semillon, 1991, Australia £8.99
4	Amberley Estate, Premier Selection Sauvignon / Semillon, 1990, Australia £9.99
11	Botobolar, St. Gilbert Dry Red, 1991, Australia £6.79
11	Quinta Do Cotto Grande Eschohla, 1985, Champalimaud, Portugal £10.49
12	Vavasour, Dashwood Cabernet Sauvignon, 1992, New Zealand £7.79
12	Seville Estate, Cabernet Sauvignon, 1988, Australia £9.49
12	Meerlust Merlot, 1987, South Africa £10,49
13	Alain Paret, Valvigneyre Syrah, 1991, France £5.39
13	Best's Shiraz, 1990, 'Concongella Vineyard', Australia £8.49
13	Brokenwood Shiraz, 1990, Australia £8.59
15	Stonier's, Pinot Noir, 1992, Australia £8.39
15	Wignalls, Pinot Noir, 1992, Australia £9.79
15	Ata Rangi, Pinot Noir, 1991, New Zealand £15.39
17	Bodegas Felix Callejo, Callejo Tinto, 1990, Spain £5.29

WL   Wm. Low & Co plc   ★★★

P.O. Box 73, Baird Avenue, Dundee DD1 9NF (Tel 0382 814022). **Opening Hours:** Mon–Sat 9am-8pm, Sun 10am-5pm. **Tastings:** occasional in-store plus sessions for wine clubs and societies on request. **Services:** glass hire.

As we go to press, William Low is the subject of a fight between Tesco and Sainsbury, both of whom are eager for a slice of Scottish pie. And so, yet another keen wine buying department seems set to be assimilated into one or other of the giants' maws. We fear that the following list of wines may have to serve as a memento of the efforts which were being made to turn a once dull chain into one of the most enterprising on either side of the border.

1	Wm Low Champagne Cuvee Selection Brut, Cooperative Le Brun De Neuville, France £12.49
1	Codorniù Napa Pinot Noir-Chardonnay, California £8.99
2	Chardonnay Teresa Rizzi, Gruppo Italiano Vini, 1993, Italy £3.79
2	Bel Arbors Chardonnay, Fetzer Vineyards, 1992, California £5.73
3	Martinborough Vineyard Chardonnay, 1992, New Zealand £10.90
4	Fortant De France Sauvignon Blanc, Skalli, 1993, France £3.89
4	Viognier, Vin de Pays de l'Ardeche, Cevenne, 1992, France £4.99
6	Gewurztraminer, Cooperative de Beblenheim, 1992, Alsace, France £5.49
8	Penfolds, Bin 202 Riesling, 1993, Australia £3.99
9	Riesling, Lingenfelder, 1992, Rheinpfalz, Germany £4.99
10	Ch. Thieuley Clairet, F Courselle, 1993, Bordeaux, France £4.99
11	Wm Low Vin du Pays de Vaucluse, Cellier de Marrenon, France £2.59
12	Fetzer Valley Oaks Cabernet Sauvignon, 1991, California £6.99
12	Les Forts de Latour, Pauillac, Chateau Latour, 1986, France £17.95
13	Penfolds Bin 128 Coonawarra Shiraz, 1991, South Australia £6.99
13	Cartlidge & Browne Zinfandel, Stratford Winery, California £4.39
15	Fleur de Carneros Pinot Noir, Carneros Creek, 1992, California £6.99
16	William Low Chianti, Marchesi de Frescobaldi, 1992, Italy £3.29
17	Navajas Rioja Sin Crianza, 1992, Spain £3.99
17	Priorato Negre Scala Dei, Cellers de Scala Dei, 1988, Spain £4.99
19	Ch. Bastor Lamontagne, 1988, Sauternes, France £12.49
20	William Low Amontillado, Perez Megia, Jerez, Spain £3.99
22	Piemontello Light, Santero, Italy £1.99

LU   Luigi's Delicatessen   ★★★

349 Fulham Road, London SW10 (071 352 7739). **Opening Hours:** Mon-Fri 9am-9:30pm Sat 9am-7pm. **Delivery:** Free locally. **Services:** Mail order, Gift mailing.

'Do you sell wine from anywhere else?' asked our (former) intrepid reporter. The answer was admirably direct. 'No – just Italian'. But if you're not looking for a Barossa red or a Burgundy, and if you fancy the idea of roast garlic, tasty salami and 12 types of olive oil, this could be your kind of place. Take loads of cash though. Credit cards have yet to reach this corner of the Roman empire and those olive oils cost more than a fairly serious bottle of claret.

1	Bellavista Cuvee Brut Franciacorta, Italy £13.30
3	Poncanera Collio Chardonnay, Conte Attems, 1991, Italy £7.45
4	Vernaccia Di San Gimiganano, Geografico, 1993, Italy £4.99
16	Cabreo Il Borgo Capitolare di Biturica, Ruffino, 1988, Italy £15.75
16	Malbech Del Veneto Orientale, Santa Margherita, 1987, Italy £8.95
16	Collio Cabernet Franc, Conte Attems, 1991, Italy, £7.45
16	Aglianico Del Vulture Riserva, D'Angelo, 1988, Italy £8.65

MWW Majestic Wine Warehouses ★★★★

Odhams Trading Estate, St. Albans Road, Watford, Herts WD2 5RE (Tel 0923 816999). Wine by the case only. **Opening Hours:** Mon–Sat 10am-8pm, Sun 10am-6pm. **Delivery:** free locally, nationally at cost. **Tastings:** regular in-store, plus tutored sessions for local wine groups and clubs. **Services:** mail order, glass hire, ice.

One of the most obvious features of the way in which Majestic has grown up in recent years has been the apparent sobering of its list. Long-gone are the rag-week leaflets with their red and blue print; today's list is a monochrome affair. Until you begin to read it and discover just how colourful a range it contains. The selection below gives a pretty good idea of some of what's on offer, but we'd recommend you head down to one of the shops, because, as in the past, one of the joys of shopping at Majestic lies in the unpredictability of what you are likely to find. And take a good look at the fizz. Distressing though it must be to Oddbins, this is often the best source of bargain Champagne in town, offering as we go to press, vintage Roederer for the same price as the non-vintage.

1	Champagne De Telmont, Grande Reserve, France £10.99
3	Ch. Thieuley, Bordeaux, Cuvée Barrique, 1992, France £7.89
3	Chablis 1er Cru Vaillon, Domaine Vocoret & Fils, 1992, France £8.99
4	Coopers Creek Marlborough Sauvignon Blanc, 1993, New Zealand £4.99
4	Pouilly Fumé 'Les Loges', Guy Saget, 1993, Loire, France £6.79
8	Cuvée Constantin, Max Ferd Richter, 1992, Germany £4.79
9	Riesling, Grans-Fassian, 1991, Mosel, Germany £5.99
11	Monastère de Trignan, Coteaux du Languedoc, 1992, France £3.99
12	Dom. Baury, Margaux, 1989, Bordeaux, France £8.49
13	Côtes de Rhône Villages Carte Noire, Beaumes-de-Venise, 1990, £4.99
15	Vosne-Romanée, Mongeard-Mugneret, 1990, Burgundy, France £15.99
16	San Crispino Sangiovese di Romagna, Ronco, 1990, Italy £5.99
17	Quinta da Bacalhôa, Joao Pires, 1990, Portugal £5.99
17	Marques de Murrieta Rioja Tinto Reserva, 1988, Spain £7.49
19	Farina Bianco Semi-Dulce, Bodegas Farina, Spain £3.69
20	Hidalgo Manzanilla La Gitana, Jerez, Spain £5.39
21	Skeffington Ruby Port , Douro, Portugal £5.99

MAR Marco's Wines ★★★

13 Ferrier Street, Wandsworth, London SW18 1SN (Tel 081-871 3233). **Opening Hours:** Mon–Fri 11am-10pm, Sat 10am-10pm, Sun 12-3pm, 7-10pm. **Delivery:** free locally. **Tastings:** regular in-store. **Services:** glass hire, ice.

Now, with dominion over six shops in and around London, His (would-be) Majesty Marco, pretender to the Wine Warehouse throne continues to expand simply by offering familiar wines at good prices. This is the place to go for cru bourgeois, Torres, Antinori, Santa Rita, a large set of Penfolds/Lindemans Aussies and some of the cheapest beers in London. And if you want to save a bit more, buy precisely the same stuff in Marco's first mainland venture on the other side of the Channel.

1	Great Western Brut Seppelt, Australia £4.99
1	Champagne Joseph Perrier, Brut, France £13.99
3	Labouré Roi, Chassagne-Montrachet, 1990, France £19.49
4	Libertas Chenin Blanc, 1993, South Africa £3.69
12	Ch. Ramage La Baptisse 1989, France £8.99
12	Ch. Cissac, 1985, Bordeaux, France £11.99
13	Penfolds, St. Henri, 1989, Australia £9.99
15	Alain Constant, Gevrey Chambertin, 1988, France £14.99
19	Drouet Fréres, Côteaux du Layon, 1990, Loire, France £6.99

M&S   Marks & Spencer plc   ★★★

47 Baker Street, London W1A 1DN (Tel 071-935 4422). No credit cards, except M&S account card. **Opening Hours:** vary from store to store. **Tastings:** regular in-store. **Services:** mail order.

Catering skilfully for the nation's private parties and private parts, M&S has had a strangely schizophrenic attitude towards its wine department. Presumably it was reckoned that customers who were ready to try the exciting new oven-ready casseroles and silk cami-knickers would balk at the challenge of an unfamilar Cabernet Sauvignon. Hence the tendency to bore these same customers' to death with dull available-everywhere wines like the Duboeuf Beaujolais and Mondavi Woodbridge wines with M&S own-labels and a commensurate premium on the price. But a light has evidently dawned in Baker Street, possibly following the arrival of a new face in the buying department.

This year, there are some far more interesting wines, as the list below shows. But M&S could do far better; winewriters' and others' intelligence is still being insulted by the pretence to exclusivity of some of M&S's wines. The only thing, for example which differentiates their Bin 65 Chardonnay from the Lindemans version on sale everywhere else is the label which, if licked, may admittedly have a flavour of its own. There is far too much evidence of lazy one-stop shopping on the shelves: nine of the 14 Aussies come from Lindemans and McWilliams; only two of the Italians do not come from Girelli and Martini.

On the other hand, we were pleased to see the creation of a proper M&S wine shop in the Muswell Hill branch which provides further evidence that fermented grapes are beginning to be taken as seriously as the fresh ones which go into M&S's brilliant salads and sandwiches.

1	St. Michael Australian Brut Sparkling Wine, de Bortoli, Australia £4.99
1	St. Michael Desroches Champagne, Cave Co-Op Chouilly, France £12.99
2	St Michael Chardonnay Del Veneto, Girelli, Italy £2.99
2	St. Michael Jeunes Vignes, La Chablisienne, Chablis, France £4.79
3	M&S/Lindemans Bin 65 Chardonnay, 1993, Australia £4.99
3	St. Michael Chardonnay, Len Evans, 1992, Australia £5.99
3	Puligny-Montrachet, Maroslavac-Leger, 1991, Burgundy, France £14.99
4	St. Michael Craighall Chardonnay-Sauvignon, 1993, South Africa £3.99
4	St. Michael Marlborough Sauvignon Blanc, Corbans, 1992, New Zealand £4.99
5	St. Michael Châteauneuf du Pape Blanc, Quiot, 1991, Rhône, France £7.99
11	St. Michael Fitou, Caves du Mont Tauch, 1991, Languedoc, France £3.49
11	St. Michael French Full Red, Vignerons Catalans, France £4.29
12	St. Michael Merlot/Cabernet Sauvignon, Jan Coetzee/Neil Ellis, 1993, South Africa £4.99
12	St Michael Bordeaux Merlot, J P Moueix, 1989, France £5.49
12	Coldstream Hills Cabernet Sauvignon, 1990, Australia £9.99
12	Ch. Gazin, Pomerol, 1989, Bordeaux, France £14.99
13	St. Michael McLaren Vale Shiraz, Andrew Garrett, 1992, Australia £4.99
14	St Michael Beaujolais Villages, Georges Duboeuf, 1992, France £4.99
15	Gevrey-Chambertin, J-M Boillot, 1989, Burgundy, France £18.99
16	St. Michael Montepulciano D'Abruzzo, Girelli, 1992, Italy £2.99
17	St. Michael Valencia, Schenk, 1991, Spain £2.99
17	Aliança Dão, 1989, Portugal £3.99
20	St. Michael Rich Cream Sherry, Williams & Humbert, Jerez, Spain £4.79
21	St. Michael Vintage Character Port, Morgan Bros, Douro, Portugal £6.49
21	St. Michael 10 Year Old Port, Morgan Bros, Douro, Portugal £9.49

MYS   Mayor Sworder   ★★★★

381 Kennington Road London SE11 4PT (071-735 0385, Fax 071-735 0342). **Opening Hours:** Mon-Fri 8:30am-5:30pm. **Delivery:** Free locally, nationally for six cases or more.**Tastings:** regular in-store. **Services:** cellarage, en primeur, mail order, gift mailing, glass hire.

The take-over last year of Russell & McIver, another City-based merchant, has hardly put the 'rad' into 'tradition' – the by-word for this established firm. As most of its customers are City and corporate institutes who buy by the case and their employees who buy bottles through Cuddefords wine-bar, this is not surprising. However, the R & McI stock of French regionals, German, Spanish, Italian, and restricted New World, together with classic fortified wines has dovetailed neatly with Mayor Sworder's French-oriented range (clarets and Burgundies in particular and Loire & Rhône in general). The result is a (now VAT-inclusive) list to make pinstripes and tweedies alike quiver with pleasure and the rest of us re-appraise the fascinating Changing of the Guard in the Old World.

2	Mâcon Clessé, Jean Thevenet, 1991, Burgundy, France £11.28
3	Chardonnay Domaine Gibalaux, Jean Bonnet, 1992, France £5.66
3	Bourgogne Chardonnay, Dom. Gerard Chavy & Fils, 1992, France £7.21
3	Hillstowe Chardonnay, McLaren Vale, 1991, South Australia £7.42
4	Sancerre, Roger Millet, 1992, Loire, France £8.31
11	Merlot Dom. de la Serre, M Tobena, 1991, France £4.32
12	Ch. du Moulin Rouge, Haut-Médoc, 1989, Bordeaux, France £7.98
12	Mendoza Cabernet Sauvignon, Navarra Correas 1988, Argentina £8.27
16	Chianti Classico, Poggerino Ginori Conti, 1991, Tuscany, Italy £6.79
19	Ch. La Borderie, Monbazillac, 1990, South West France £12.27

MM   Michael Menzel Wine   ★★★★★

297-299 Eccleshall Road, Sheffield, S. Yorks. S11 8NX (Tel 0742 683557). **Opening Hours:** Mon-Sat 10am-9pm, Sun 12-2pm, 7-9pm. **Delivery:** free locally, nationally at cost. **Tastings:** occasional in-store. **Services:** glass hire, ice.

While wine merchants in the more fashionable southern counties and East Anglia hog the limelight, this Sheffield company quietly concentrates on putting together one of the best, most *classic* ranges of wines around. All the big names are here – but not just for show. Someone is clearly taking a lot of trouble to assemble as good a team of superstars as they can, but they're having fun while doing it. How else can anybody explain that sparkling red Burgundy?

1	'Maufoux' Red Sparkling Burgundy, France £12.00
2	Joseph Drouhin, Mâcon Villages, 1992, France £7.50
3	Montrachet, Marquis de Laguiche, Drouhin, 1987, France £135.00
4	"Baron de L" Pouilly Fumé, 1990, Loire, France £25.00
9	Deinhard, Bernkastel Bratenhofchen, Riesling Auslese, 1988, Mosel, Germany £15.00
12	Ch. Beaumont, Haut-Médoc, 1989, Bordeaux, France £10.00
12	Meerlust, Cabernet Sauvignon, 1986, South Africa £12.00
12	Ch. Leoville Barton, St Julien, 1985, Bordeaux, France £19.00
12	Jermann, "Where The Dreams Have No End", 1989, Italy £28.00
12	Ch. Cheval Blanc, St Emilion, 1985, Bordeaux. France £58.00
13	Côte Rôtie, Chapoutier, Brune et Blonde, 1990, Rhône France £23.00
15	Joseph Drouhin, Pernand-Vergelesses, 1989, Burgundy, France £13.00
15	Dom. Faiveley, Charmes Chambertin, 1988, France £45.00
16	Fontanafredda, Dolcetto d'Alba, 1992, Piedmont, Italy £7.50
19	Ch. Rieussec, 1983, Sauternes, France £48.00

MTL — Mitchells Wine Merchants Ltd ★★★★

354 Meadowhead, Sheffield, S. Yorks. S8 7UJ (Tel 0742 745587/740311). **Opening Hours:** Mon-Sat 8.30am-10pm, Sun 12-2pm, 7-10pm. **Delivery:** free locally, nationally at cost. **Tastings:** weekly in-store plus tastings and talks for groups and members of own wine club. **Services:** cellarage, mail order, gift mailing, glass hire, ice.

John Mitchell is definitely your man if you want good wines, beers and whiskies mixed in with infectious enthusiasm. In particular, there are strong selections from Bordeaux, Australia and Spain, and intrusions in other vinous areas from the likes of Moreau Chablis, Trimbach Alsace, the New Zealanders Vidal and Goldwater, and five different Châteauneufs.

4	Cape Bay Chenin Blanc, 1993, South Africa	£3.75
4	Conde de Valdemar Rioja, 1991, Spain	£6.99
4	Vidal Sauvignon Blanc, 1992, New Zealand	£7.89
4	Cape Mentelle Semillon-Sauvignon Blanc, 1991, Australia	£7.99
4	Ch. de Tracy, Pouilly Fumé, 1991, France	£11.89
11	Dom. Le Puts, 1991, France	£3.99
11	Ch. Val Joanis, Côtes du Lubéron, 1989, France	£5.69
12	L A Cetto, Cabernet Sauvignon, 1986, Mexico	£5.39
12	Robert Mondavi Cabernet Sauvignon, 1983, California	£12.59
12	Ch. Haut Marbuzet, 1986, Bordeaux, France	£14.79
13	Ch. Fortia, Châteauneuf du Pape, 1988, France	£10.95
21	Taylors, 1970, Douro, Portugal	£46.75

MOR — Moreno ★★★★

2 Norfolk Place, London W2 1QN (Tel 071-706 3055 Fax 071-724 3813). **Opening Hours:** Norfolk Place Mon-Sat 10am-8pm; Marylands Road Mon-Sat 10am-9pm, Sat 12pm-3pm. **Delivery:** free locally, nationally for six cases or more. **Tastings:** regular in-store, plus the Spanish Wine Club on the last Friday of every month. **Services:** mail order, gift mailing, glass hire, ice.

Spanish Specialist Wine Merchant of the Year

Developments behind the scenes with the Moreno wholesale business should spell good news for customers of the two retail shops. The Iberian range will continue to be one of the country's best, with Navajas Riojas, Scala Dei Priorato, Barbadillo sherries, Ribera del Duero from Protos and CVNE Riojas very much to the fore. But watch out for new intrusions from South Africa, Australia, Bordeaux, Burgundy and many other regions.

2	Marquès de Alella Classico, 1993, Galicia, Spain	£5.99
3	Navajas Rioja Blanco Crianza, 1989, Rioja, Spain	£5.99
4	Viña Porta Chardonnay, 1993, Chile	£4.99
6	Casablanca Santa Isabel Estate Gewürztraminer, 1994, Chile, £6.29	
17	Pago de Carraovejas, Ribera del Duero, 1992, Spain	£5.99
17	Negre Scala Dei Priorat Priorato, 1991, Spain	£5.99
17	Guelbenzu Navarra Crianza Tinto, 1990, Spain	£5.99
17	Masia Barril Tipico Priorato, Hermanos Barril, 1991, Spain	£6.99

M&V — Morris & Verdin ★★★★★

The Leathermarket, Weston Street, London SE1 3ER (Tel 071 357 8866, Fax 071 357 8877). Wines by the case only. No credit cards. **Opening Hours:** Mon-Fri am-6pm. **Delivery:** free locally, nationally at cost. **Tastings:** occasional in-store, plus tutored tastings. **Services:** cellarage, en primeur, mail order, glass hire.

When the *Guide* went to press, Jasper Morris MW was still presiding over his Pimlico wholesale shop with the enthusiasm (and some might kindly say the looks) of an overgrown red setter puppy, from a desk squashed in between towering stacks of wine cases. By now, however, he should have the run of new premises four times as big somewhere near London Bridge. Most of the business is to the trade, but there is a substantial base of discerning private customers who reap the benefits of Mr Morris's expertise in developing good relationships with a number of excellent Burgundy producers and a clutch of maverick Californians who attend increasingly frequent get-togethers, giving customers the chance to sink a few glasses while witnessing the interpersonal relationships between the likes of Dominic Lafon of Meursault and Jim Clendenen and Randall Grahm, of the planet Betelgeuse.

3	Mâcon La Roche Vineuse Vieilles Vignes, Domaine Du Vieux Saint-Sorlin, 1992, Burgundy, France £7.50
3	Vita Nova Chardonnay, 1992, California £12.50
3	Au Bon Climat Chardonnay, 1992, California £12.50
4	Pyramus, Château Routas, Côteaux Varois Blanc, 1992, France £6.40
7	Ca Del Solo Malvasia Bianca, Bonny Doon, 1992, California £7.50
11	Cuvée Agrippa, Château Routas, 1992, France £8.50
12	Ch. Poitou, Lussac St Emilion, 1986, Bordeaux, France £7.20
12	Château Tour du Pas St Georges, 1990, Bordeaux, France £7.90
12	Vita Nova Cabernet Sauvignon, 1990, California £9.90
13	Bonny Doon, Clos de Gilroy, 1993, California £7.30
13	Qupé Syrah, 1992, California £9.90
15	Pinot Noir 'La Bauge Au-dessus', Au Bon Climat, 1991, California £18.00
15	Vosne Romanée Premier Cru Les Beaux-Monts, Domaine Daniel Rion, 1989, Burgundy, France £24.00
17	Quinta de la Rosa, 1992, Douro, Portugal £4.90
19	Riesling Vendange Tardive Muenchberg, André Ostertag, 1990, Alsace, France £25.00
21	Finest Reserve Port, Quinta de la Rosa, Douro, Portugal £9.50
21	Quinta de la Rosa Vintage Port, 1988, Douro, Portugal £12.00

MRN   Wm Morrison Supermarkets   ★★★

Hilmore House, Thornton Road, Bradford BD8 9AX (Tel 0924 870000). **Opening Hours:** vary between: Mon–Fri 8.30am-8pm, Sat 8.30am-6pm, Sun 10am-4pm. **Tastings:** occasional in store and for selected customer groups. **Services:** glass hire/loan.

Not a spectacular place to buy wine, but if you want a reasonable set of sparklers, Denbies English wine, Aussies from Brown Bothers and Wolf Blass, Murrieta Riojas and a large set of French country wines, there are certainly as the chain's customers have so often been told, 'More reasons to shop at Morrisons'.

1	Champagne Nicole D'Auriny Reserve, Union Auboise, France £8.99
2	Petit Chablis, Domaine De L'Orme, 1993, Burgundy, France £5.49
4	Muscadet de Sèvre et Maine sur Lie, La Sabliere, Alban St-Pré, 1992, France £3.49
12	San Pedro Merlot, 1991, Chile £4.29
12	Ch. Cap Leon Veyrin, Listrac-Médoc, 1990, Bordeaux, France £7.99
13	Châteauneuf du Pape, Dom. du Vieux Lazaret, 1990, France £7.99
14	Regnié, Georges Duboeuf, 1992, Beaujolais, France £5.59
16	Merlot Vigneti del Sole, Grave Del Friuli, Pasqua, 1992, Italy £2.49
16	Montepulciano D'Abruzzo, Cortenova, 1992, Italy £2.75
17	Morrisons Rioja, Bodegas Navajas, 1992, Spain £2.99
17	Bairrada Reserve, Borges, 1987, Portugal £2.99
20	Inocente Extra Dry Sherry, Macharnudo, Jerez, Spain £5.95

NAD Nadder Wines (Salisbury) Ltd ★★★★

Hussars House, 2 Netherhampton Road, Harnham, Salisbury Wilts. SP2 8HE (Tel 0722 325418). **Opening Hours:** Mon-Fri 9am-6pm Sat 9am-1pm. **Delivery:** free locally, nationally at cost. **Tastings:** Occasional in-store, plus on request for customers and local wine societies. **Services:** mail order, gift mailing, glass hire, ice.

Chris Gilbey soldiers on, inspired perhaps by the refurbishment of his Hussars House base within which are to be found Leon Beyer Alsace wines, J M da Fonseca Portuguese, Brown Brothers Aussies, beefy Californian reds from Foppiano and some gentler ones from Carneros Creek. Add in some some reasonable clarets, and you have a place well worth popping into if Stonehenge is closed.

1	Champagne Duval Leroy Brut Tradition, France £13.89
3	Ch. St. Jean Chardonnay, 1991, California £10.09
3	Elston Chardonnay, 1993, New Zealand £10.95
4	Quinta de Camarate Branco, 1993, Portugal £6.49
12	Ch. Terry Gros Cailloux, Margaux, 1982, France £14.95
15	Fleur de Caneros Pinot Noir, 1993, California £7.75
21	Quady 'Starboard, Batch 88', 1988, California £4.55 (half)
21	Quarles Harris, 1980, Portugal £17.99

JN James Nicholson ★★★★★

27a Killyleagh Street, Crossgar, Co. Down, Northern Ireland (Tel 0396 830091). **Opening Hours:** Mon–Sat 10am-7pm. **Delivery:** free locally, nationally at cost. **Tastings:** regular in-store, plus tutored sessions by visiting winemakers, seminars, dinners, etc. **Services:** en primeur, mail order, gift mailing.

Northern Ireland Wine Merchant of the Year

Not only the best merchant in Northern Ireland, but one of the best in the UK. The company is the agent for many familiar estates – Mondavi, Huet, Guigal, Jaboulet, Dubouef, Drouhin, Château Palmer, Schlumberger, Dr Loosen, Louis Roederer, Martinez Bujanda, Rosemount and many more – but wherever there is a gap in the portfolio, it has been filled with great wines. We particularly recommend the southern French wines from Chemins de Bassac and Château Grand Moulin (Corbières), and any of the tasty Italians. Mainlanders should take a look at the reasonable prices and consider dealing with the company by mail order.

1	Vouvray Mousseux, Gaston Huët, 1990, Loire, France £9.60
1	Heemskerk Jansz, Tasmania, Australia £13.25
1	Pelorus, 1989, Cloudy Bay, Marlborough, New Zealand £11.99
2	Soave Classico Pieropan, 1992, Veneto, Italy £6.69
2	Pinot Blanc Schlumberger, 1991, Alsace France £6.59
3	Cape Mentelle Chardonnay, 1992, Margaret River, Western Australia £8.99
3	Marsannay, Alain Guyard, 1990, Burgundy, France £10.25
3	Puligny Montrachet, JM Boillot, 1992, Burgundy, France £23.50
4	Ch. de la Jaubertie Bergerac Blanc, Henry Ryman, 1992, France £6.70
6	Gewürztraminer Grand Cru Kessler, Domaines Schlumberger, 1989, Alsace, France £14.70
8	Wehlener Sonnenuhur Riesling Kabinett, JJ Prum, 1989, Mosel, Germany £9.65
12	Claret, Sichel, 1990, France £4.29
16	Barolo 'Bussia Soprana' Aldo Conterno, 1988, Piemonte, Italy £20.95
17	Duas Quinta Douro Tinto, Ramos Pinto, 1991, Douro, Portugal £5.25
19	Ch. La Nère Loupiac, 1988, France £7.75
21	Quinta da Noval, 1963, Douro, Portugal £49.50

N&P — Nickolls & Perks Ltd ★★★

37 High Street, Stourbridge West Midlands DY8 1TA (Tel 0384 494518). **Opening Hours:** Mon-Sat 9am-6pm. **Delivery:** free nationally for five cases or more. **Tastings:** regular in-store, plus for the company's own Stourbridge Wine Society. **Services:** cellarage, en primeur, gift mailing, mail order, glass hire, ice.

Take our advice: don't ask this long established Midlands merchant which New World wines they stock. It would be a bit like requesting a rendition of U2's greatest hits from Mr Rattle's band down the road. N&P are good at the classics, with Champagne in particular being offered in just about every form, with plenty of old vintages, half-bottles, Methuselahs and special cuvées.

2	Chablis, 'les Clos' Grand Crü, Dom. Pascal Bouchard, 1989, Burgundy, France £22.50	
3	Bienvenues-Bâtard-Montrachet, Dom. Henri Clerc, 1985, France £45.00	
15	Rully, Dom. d'Ermitage, Dom. Chanzy Frères, 1989, France £7.95	
15	Vosne Romanée, Dom. René Engel, 1988, France £14.95	
21	Fonseca Vintage Port, 1985, Portugal £25.00	
21	Taylor 1960, Portugal £49.00	
21	Cockburns 1904, Portugal £260.00	

NIC — Nicolas UK ★★★

71 Abingdon Road, London W8 6AW (Tel 071-937 3996). **Opening Hours:** Mon-Sat 10am-10pm, Sun 12-3pm, 7-9pm. **Delivery:** free locally, nationally at cost. **Tastings:** regular in-store plus courses (ring 071-586 1196 for details). **Services:** en primeur, mail order, gift mailing, glass hire, ice.

The eight well-appointed (and rather expensive) Nicolas shops in London and the south-east give us Brits a chance to buy wine as the French do. Which of course explains why the 'Cartes Fines Bouteilles' includes a very impressive set of claret and Sauternes, DRC Burgundies, and many tasty regional wines, but excludes such wines as Opus One, Chateau Musar and Green Point which we know are in stock. All of the printed material is translated directly from the French, so all the most obscure names get their circumflexes and cedillas while 'Burgundi' features (twice) as a description for a style of wine available by the 'dobble magnum'.

1	Champagne Henriot Souverain Brut, France, £19.60	
2	Chablis Premier Cru Côtes de Lechet, Bernard Defaix, 1989, France £11.60	
4	Jurançon Sec Grain Sauvage, Cave Des Producteurs, 1993, France £6.50	
11	Marcillac, Cave Des Vignerons Du Vazlon, 1992, France £5.70	
11	Cahors, Clos La Coutale, 1990, France £6.90	
12	Madiran Cru du Paradis, M. Maumus, 1985, France £10.80	

NRW — Noble Rot Wine Warehouses Ltd ★★★

18 Market Street, Bromsgrove, Worcs B61 8DA (Tel 0527 575606). Wines by the case only. **Opening Hours:** Mon-Fri 10am-7pm, Sat 9.30am-6.30pm. **Delivery:** free locally, nationally at cost. **Tastings:** regular in-store plus occasional tutored sessions and 'wine fair-type tastings' in May and November. **Services:** glass hire.

The role of botyris – or 'noble rot' – is to concentrate the flavour and quality of the juice in a grape. Which pretty well describes this small range of wines. Good value abounds through the range – hardly any table wines creep above £10 – which puts particular emphasis on French country wines, Italians and Australians, many of which can be sampled at wine fairs in May and November.

NI Nobody Inn ★★★★★

Doddiscombsleigh, Nr. Exeter, Devon EX6 7PS (Tel 0647 52394). **Opening Hours:** Mon-Sun 11am-2.30pm, 7-11pm, other times by arrangement. **Delivery:** free locally, nationally at cost. **Tastings:** regular in-house, tutored tastings once a month between Ocotber and March. **Services:** mail order, gift mailing, glass hire.

Small Independent Wine Merchant of the Year; West of England Wine Merchant of the Year

If you can't make it down to the Nobody Inn to sample the hundreds of cheeses, whiskies, wines and Doddiscombsleigh hospitality, take an hour or two to browse through the entertaining list. Specialities are California, Australia and anything sweet, particularly from the Loire, although the Italian, southern French and English ranges are also pretty good, and no areas suffer from weakness. The recommended wines below are mostly new additions to the range which Nick Borst-Smith and Martyn Jones discovered too late for inclusion in an already-out-of-date-but-most-up-to-date list, thicker than the file of press clippings on Lord Archer. There's a lot to be said for – and about – inventive nobodies.

1	Roederer Cristal Champagne, 1982, France £59.65
3	Newton Vineyard Chardonnay, 1991, Napa, California £10.95
3	Amberley Estate Margaret River Semillon, 1993, Western Australia £9.90
3	Wellington Chardonnay, 1992, Tasmania £7.90
3	Mâcon Clessé, Domaine De La Bon Gran, Cuvée Tradition, 1991, Burgundy, France £13.95
3	Sharpham Barrel-Fermented White, 1993, England £7.95
3	Hardy's Moondah Brook Estate Chardonnay, 1993, Western Australia £5.49
8	Goundrey Langton Australian Riesling, 1991, Western Australia £5.49
9	Martinborough Vineyard Riesling, 1993, New Zealand £7.99
11	Beenleigh Cabernet Sauvignon-Merlot, Beenleigh Manor Vineyard, 1991, England £12.75
12	Mayacamas Cabernet, 1982, Napa, California £19.43
12	Ch. Lynch-Bages 1985, Pauillac, Bordeaux, France, £37.73
13	Hermitage, Chave, 1978, Rhône, France £82.59
13	Penfolds Grange, 1983, South Australia £39.75
15	Kent Rasmussen Carneros Pinot Noir, 1989, California £20.26
17	Vinha do Monte, Sogrape, 1991, Portugal £5.29
17	Torres Gran Coronas Black Label, 1982, Penedes, Spain £16.43
18	Rutherglen Show Muscat DP 63, B Seppelt & Sons, Victoria, Australia £10.49
18	Bailey's Founder Liqueur Muscat, Victoria, Australia £9.95
19	Ch. d'Yquem, 1976, Sauternes, France £97.91

RN Rex Norris Wine Merchants ★★★

50 Queens Road, Haywards Heath, West Sussex RH16 1EE (Tel 0444 454756). **Opening Hours:** Mon-Fri 9am-5.30pm. Sat 9am-4.30pm. **Delivery:** free locally, **Tastings:** occasional in-store, plus around two big tastings per year. **Services:** gift mailing, glass hire, ice.

Traditionalists at heart, these commuter-line merchants are prepared to venture well beyond the comfort zone of agreeable claret and fine mature Burgundy in search of their ever-changing range. The New World is far better served than in the past, though the top value wines come from some of the more esoteric areas of France and Italy. Prices are unusually fair – with an emphasis beneath £5, thanks possibly to the poverty inflicted on commuters by the Great Southern Railway.

| **OD** | Oddbins | ★★★★★ |

31-33 Weir Road, Merton, London SW19 8UG (Tel 081-944 4400). **Opening hours:** vary between: Mon-Sat 10am-9pm, Sun 12-3pm, 7-9pm. **Delivery:** free locally. **Tastings:** in all stores every Saturday, as featured on television, plus tutored tastings and two wine fairs per year. **Services:** en primeur, glass hire, ice.

National High Street Chain Wine Merchant of the Year; Wine List of the Year; New World Specialist of the Year

The wine buyers at Thresher haven't got a pin-encrusted wax effigy of Oddbins' chief buyer, John Ratcliffe. But they'd love to find one if they could. It is easy to see why Oddbins so infuriates its competitors. However hard they train, the lads at Wine Rack, Bottoms Up and Majestic will never quite match the playing style of the iconoclastic Merton wanderers. This year, for example, Threshers shops throughout the land suddenly sprouted Oddbins lookalike blackboards covered with colourful handwriting.

At first glance it all looked a bit like the real thing, but it wasn't. Threshers managers don't come up with lines like the 'No Spain, No Gain' which was briefly plastered over the window of one of the firm's Fulham road stores. The rather prissy illustrations in Wine Rack's list really cannot compete with the wilder excesses perpetrated by Ralph Steadman, a cartoonist who, like Randall Grahm in California, was created by God to work with Oddbins.

No other merchant has managed to hold an annual tasting which is attended by a team of superstar winemakers; none can offer wine-bored customers such a mouthwatering range of beers. What must be uncomfortable for traditionalists is the way Oddbins has so skilfully moved into the field of fine wine, offering bargain-price Bordeaux and one of the best ranges of white burgundies on offer anywhere. It is rather like the way the Japanese motor manufacturers have managed to take on Rolls Royce and Mercedes at their own game.

1	Yalumba 'D', 1990, Australia £9.99	
1	Cuvée Napa, Pinot Noir Chardonnay, 1989, California £9.99	
1	Champagne Billecart-Salmon Brut, 1982, France £27.99	
2	Casablanca White Label Chardonnay, 1993, Chile £4.99	
2	Fetzer Sundial Chardonnay, 1992, California £5.49	
2	Alain Geoffroy, Chablis 1er Crû Vaulignot, 1991, France £7.99	
3	Agramont Barrel Fermented Viura-Chardonnay, 1993, Spain £3.99	
3	Tim Knapstein Chardonnay, 1990, Lenswood Australia £7.49	
3	Coldstream Hills Chardonnay, 1992, Australia £7.99	
3	Montana McDonald Church Road Chardonnay, 1992, New Zealand £7.99	
3	Franciscan Chardonnay Sauvage, 1991, California £9.99	
3	Dom. Michelot-Buisson, Meursault, 1er Cru Le Limozin, 1991, France £17.99	
4	Ch. Tahbilk Marsanne, 1992, Australia £4.99	
4	Giesen Rapaura Road Marlborough Sauvignon Blanc, 1993, New Zealand £6.49	
4	Sancerre Les Fredins, Silex, Gitton, 1992, France £8.49	
4	Cullens Sauvignon Blanc, 1992, Australia £8.99	
5	Dom. des Aubuisières, Vouvray Demi-Sec, 1992, France £6.99	
6	Bonny Doon, Bloody Good White, 1993, California £5.99	
8	Brüder Dr. Becker, Dienheimer Riesling Kabinett Halbtroken, 1992, Germany £5.99	
9	Kurt Darting, Ungsteiner Herrenberg Riesling Spätlese, 1992, Germany £5.99	
9	Grans Fassian, Piesporter Goldtröpfchen Riesling, Germany £5.99	
9	Müller-Catoir, Haardter Mandelring Scheurebe Spätlese, 1992, Germany £8.99	

11	Mark Robertson, Le Radical, 1993, France £3.49
11	Garnacha Veganueva, 1993, Spain £3.99
11	Ch. Paul Blanc, Costières de Nimes, 1992, France £4.99
12	Ch. Bertinerie, 1992, Bordeaux, France £4.99
12	Seaview Limited Release Cabernet Sauvignon, Padthaway, 1988, Australia £4.99
12	Errazuriz Merlot, 1993, Chile £4.99
12	Yalumba Menzies Cabernet Sauvignon, 1990, Coonawarra, Australia £6.99
12	Ch. Lilian Ladouys, 1990, Bordeaux, France £9.99
12	Pavillon Rouge du Ch. Margaux, 1991, France £11.99
12	Ch. Le Bon Pasteur, 1989, Pomerol, Bordeaux, France £19.49
13	Bonny Doon, Bloody Good Red, 1993, California £5.99
13	Bonny Doon, The Catalyst, 1992, California £5.99
13	Fetzer Eagle Point, Petite Sirah, 1991, California £5.99
13	Peter Lehmann, Clancy's Shiraz-Cabernet, 1990, Australia £6.49
13	Alain Graillot, Crozes-Hermitage, 1991, France £8.49
15	Coldstream Hills Pinot Noir, 1993, Australia £7.99
15	Dom. Rossignol-Trapet, Gevrey Chamberlin, 1991, France £9.99
15	Coldstream Hills Reserve Pinot Noir, 1992, Australia £11.99
15	Dom. Louis Trapet, Le Chambertin, 1991, France £26.99
16	Chianti Ruffina Riserva, Castello di Nippozzano, 1990, Italy £5.99
16	Barbaresco, 1988, Castello di Nieve, Italy £7.99
17	Sogrape, Douro Vila Regia, 1990, Portugal £3.69
17	Campo Viejo Crianza, 1990, Spain £3.99
17	Agramont Oak-aged Cabernet-Tempranillo, 1990, Spain £3.99
17	Hermanos Lurton Tempranillo, 1992, Spain £3.99
17	Campillo Crianza, 1988, Spain £4.99
17	Ferreirinha, Barca Velha, 1985, Portugal £24.99
18	Plantagenet Muscat, 1993, Mount Barker, Australia £4.99
19	Kiona Late-Picked Riesling, 1993, Washington State £5.99
19	Torcolato, Maculan, 1990, Italy £9.99 (half)

P   Parfrements   ★★★★

68 Cecily Road, Cheylesmore, Coventry CV3 5LA (Tel 0203 503646). wines by the case only. **Opening Hours:** Mon-Fri 9am-6pm, Sat 9am-1pm, Sun 9am-6pm; may also be available at other times – 'we never refuse a sale'. **Delivery:** free locally, nationally at cost. **Tastings:** regular in-store, plus tutored sessions on request. **Services:** mail order, gift mailing, glass hire.

The wines which Gerald Gregory shows at his regular tutored tastings must have customers queueing up to place orders. Apart from the expanding range of classy clarets, we'd find space in our mixed case for the Jackson Estate Kiwis, Manuel de Argueso sherries, Gundlach Bundschu Californians and Prieur Brunet Burgundies.

2	Chablis 1er Cru Fourchaume, Durup, 1990, France £10.93
3	Shaw & Smith Chardonnay, 1991, South Australia £12.82
12	Ch. Richotey, Fronsac, 1990, Bordeaux, France £7.31
13	LA Cetto Petite Sirah, 1991, Mexico £6.86
21	Gould Campbell, 1977, Douro, Portugal £18.00

THP   Thos Peatling Ltd   ★★★★★

Westgate House, Westgate Street, Bury St Edmunds, Suffolk IP33 1QS (Tel 0284 755948; Mail order: 0284 714466). **Opening Hours:** vary from shop to shop **Delivery:** free locally, nationally for two cases or more. **Tastings:** regular in-store, plus tutored sessions 4-6 times a year at the Bury St. Edmunds and Clerkenwell Road (London) branches; others as required.

With 30 retail shops scattered around East Anglian market towns and a penchant for the finest claret, this country merchant might be expected to be the embodiment of conservatism, but Thos Peatling avoids all the pitfalls commonly threatening other rural firms. In fact, our 1993 Bordeaux specialists of the year have been flirting with a rather more racy image of late. Their 'Pressings' newsletters resembles a Soho 'lifestyle' magazine, supporting the notion that there is more to life in sleepy Bury St Edmunds than flicking the dust off turn-of-the-century claret bottles in time to the ticking of the grandfather clock. In fact, while Peatlings have resolutely maintained the tradition of English-bottling for fine wine made by the likes of the Domaine de l'Arlot and Ch. le Pin. When it comes to the New World, they race almost neck-and-neck with Adnams and Lay & Wheeler.

1	Champagne Joseph Perrier Cuvée Royale Brut, France £15.00
2	Chablis Domaine de L'Eglantière, Jean Durup, 1992, France £8.99
3	Ch. Charmes Godard, Bordeaux Blanc, 1990, France £7.99
3	Dry Creek Vineyard Barrel Fermented Chardonnay, 1992, Sonoma California £9.35
3	Krondorf Show Reserve Chardonnay, 1992, South Australia £9.99
3	Mâcon Viré, Domaine de Roally, 1991, Henri Goyard, France £9.99
4	Cape Mentelle Semillon-Sauvignon, 1993, Western Australia £7.99
4	Ch. Couhins-Lurton, Pessac-Leognan, 1990, France £12.99
4	Selaks Marlborough Sauvignon Blanc, 1993, New Zealand £7.99
4	Sancerre Les Roches, Jean Louis Vacheron, 1992, Loire, France £8.99
4	Pouilly Fumé, Baron De L, de Ladoucette, 1990, Loire, France £28.99
8	Riesling Kappelweg, Rolly Gassmann, 1989, Alsace, France £13.49
9	Wehlener Sonnenuhr Riesling Auslese, Dr F. Weins-Prum Erben, 1983, Mosel, Germany £12.99
11	Côtes du Roussillon Villages, Domaine Gauby, 1990, France £8.49
12	Ch. Lafite-Rothschild, Pauillac, 1990, France £50.00
12	Ch. la Lagune, Haut-Médoc, 1990, France, £13.39
12	Wirra Wirra Church Block Red, 1992, South Australia £6.99
12	Cape Mentelle Cabernet Merlot, 1991, Western Australia £7.99
12	Santa Helena Directorio Cabernet Sauvignon, 1990, Chile £5.29
12	Fairview Estate Merlot Reserve, 1991, South Africa £6.95
13	Coteaux du Tricastin, Domaine de St Luc, 1991, France £7.99
15	Mercurey, Andre Delorme, 1990, Burgundy, France £9.49
15	Nuits St Georges, Domaine De L'Arlot, 1992, Burgundy, France £11.99
16	Nebbiolo, L.A.Cetto, 1986, Mexico £8.99
18	Brown Brothers Late Picked Muscat Blanc, 1993, Australia £5.50
18	Elysium, Quady Winery, 1993, California £5.99
21	Gould Campbell Vintage Port, 1980, Douro, Portugal £17.50
21	Taylor Vintage Port, 1980, Douro, Portugal £18.99

PST   Penistone Court Wine Celllars   ★★★

Railway Station, Penistone, Sheffield S30 6HA (Tel 0226 766037). **Opening Hours:** Mon-Fri 9am-6pm Sat 10am-3pm. **Delivery:** free locally, nationally at cost. **Tastings:** regular in-store. **Services:** cellarage, mail order, glass hire.

When asked to list his areas of expertise, Christopher Ward would not be drawn further than 'Austria', but his range of French and Italian classics – including Delas Frères' Hermitage Cuvée Marquise de la Tourette and three different Brunello di Montalcinos from Banfi – proves him to be unnecessarily modest.

4	Fumaio Sauvignon Blanc, Banfi, 1993, Italy £8.50
12	Mandrielle Nerlot, 1991, Italy, £10.00
13	Hermitage Cuvee Marquise de la Tourette, Delas, 1990, France £18.00
16	Col-di-Sasso Sangiovese-Cabernet, 1992, Italy £6.00
18	Forteto Della Luja, Scaglione, 1990, Italy £18.20

PHI   Philglas & Swiggot   ★★★★

21 Northcote Road, London SW11 1NG (Tel 071-924 4494). **Opening Hours:** Mon-Fri 11am-9pm, Sat 10am-9pm, Sun 12-3pm, 7-9pm. **Delivery:** free locally, nationally at cost. **Tastings:** regular in-store, tutored sessions for groups and wine clubs on request. **Services:** mail order, gift mailing, glass hire, ice.

Phil D. Glass, Paul Unchtime-Claret, Will Swiggot and their associate Karen Rogers, make no excuses for specialising in Antipodean producers such as Henschke, Petaluma, Wairau River, Rothbury, Martinborough Vineyards and Balgownie. Resolute Old Worldians are not completely neglected however. There are also some very decent Italians, clarets, Burgundies, French country wines and South Africans.

1	David Wynn Brut, South Australia £8.30
1	Yellowglen Brut, Mildara, Australia £8.99
3	Yarra Ridge Chardonnay, 1993, Australia £10.99
3	Preece Chardonnay, Mitchelton, 1993, Australia £6.99
4	Mitchelton Marsanne, Mitchelton, 1993, Australia £5.99
12	Balgownie Estate Cabernet Sauvignon, 1988, Australia £9.49
12	Preece Cabernet Sauvignon, Mitchelton, 1992, Australia £6.99
12	Krondorf Cabernet Sauvignon, 1990, Australia, £7.75
12	Mildara Alexanders Dry Red, 1988, Australia £12.49
13	Campbells Bobbie Burns Shiraz, 1992, Australia £6.99
13	Roo's Leap Shiraz Cabernet, Mildara, 1992, Australia £5.85
13	St Joseph, Les Larmes Du Pere, Alain Paret, 1991, France £7.99
15	Tunnel Hill Pinot Noir, TarraWarra Vineyards, 1993, Australia £7.99
15	Balgownie Estate Pinot Noir, 1989, Australia £11.99
21	Fine Ruby, Martinez, Douro, Portugal £6.85
21	Churchill's 10 Year Old Tawny Port, Churchill-Graham, Portugal £12.99

CPW   Christopher Piper Wines Ltd   ★★★★

1 Silver Street, Ottery St. Mary, Devon, EX11 1DB (Tel 0404 814139). **Opening hours:** Mon-Fri 9.30am-1pm, 2-6pm, Sat 9am-1pm, 2.30-5pm. **Delivery:** free locally, nationally for six cases or more. **Tastings:** regular in-store plus numerous tastings throughout the year (including three major ones and three wine-weekends). **Services:** cellarage, en primeur, mail order, gift mailing, glass hire.

Wine merchant and Beaujolais maker Chris Piper manages to shoehorn hundreds of good and great bottles (and half-bottles) into his tiny Devon shop. All regions look impressive, Bordeaux, Burgundy and Beaujolais particularly so. The trepidation with which the bubbly Piper introduced 'Les Vins du Terroir et Cépage', has apparently proved unfounded. They, like his tasty Italians and Germans should be plundered, while the New World is represented by Coldstream Hills, Domaine Drouhin, Ridge and Rongopai. All worth paying the Piper for.

3	Hunter's Oak-Aged Marlborough Sauvignon Blanc, 1992, New Zealand £9.99
3	Rockford Local Growers Semillon, 1990, Australia £8.99
4	Brown Bothers King Valley Sauvignon Blanc, 1993, Australia £6.90
12	Cuvée du Cepage Cabernet Sauvignon, Vin de pays d'Oc, Domaine St Hilaire, 1992, France £4.65
12	Villa Montes Cabernet Sauvignon, Discover Wines, 1992, Chile £4.49
12	Ch. Le Bourdieu Vertheuil, Haut Médoc, 1990, Bordeaux, France £7.95
13	Campbells Bobbie Burns Shiraz, 1992, Australia £6.99
14	Moulin-à-Vent, Paul Janin, 1991, Beaujolais, £8.50
18	Campbells Rutherglen Liqueur Muscat, Victoria, Australia £5.65
20	Barbadillo Amontillado de Sanlucar, Jerez, Spain £5.49
21	Churchill's Finest Vintage Character Port, Portugal £8.99

TP   Terry Platt Wine Merchant   ★★★★

Ferndale Road, Llandudno Junction, Gwynedd LL31 9NT (Tel (shop) 0492 872997
(office) 0492 592971 **Opening hours:** (shop) Mon-Sat 10am-8pm, Sun 12-2pm;
(office) Mon-Fri 8am-5.30pm. **Delivery:** free locally, UK for five cases or more.
Tastings: regular in-store plus special tasting sessions and dinners. **Services:** mail
order, gift mailing, glass hire.

Business is good in North Wales, or so it seems from a glance at Platt Jr's
introduction to the 1994 Wine list which sets out the percentage change in sales of a
number of key areas of their range. Most regions, with the revealing exceptions of
Germany, Alsace and Champagne, have shown a healthy growth on the year before,
with the notable performer being 'the New World' which was up by 110%! Over 150
new wines are introduced this year, with Bordeaux featuring strongly and Spanish
reds looking tempting. There are also some interesting Californians from Wile and
Son, and Monteviña while d'Arrenberg and Cape Mentelle keep the Aussie flag
flying. The appearance of Platt's from Mudgee is apparently a coincidence...

1	Gloria Ferrer, Freixenet Somoma Caves, California £12.50
3	Platt's Mudgee Chardonnay, 1992, Australia £8.35
4	Platt's Semillon, 1992, Australia £7.75
4	Domaine de Montmarin, Vin de Pays des Côtes de Thongue, Philippe de Bertier 1993, South-West France £4.20
4	Chenin Blanc, 1993, Vinas del Vero Covisa, Chile £3.99
12	Taltarni Cabernet Sauvignon, 1988, Australia £8.99
12	Monteviña Cabernet Sauvignon, 1991, Chile £6.99
12	Platt's Cabernet Sauvignon, 1991, Australia £8.35
12	Montes Merlot, Discover Wine, 1993, Chile £4.79
13	Taltarni Shiraz, 1991, Australia £6.99
13	d'Arenberg Ironstone Pressings, 1991, Australia £8.75
13	Monteviña Zinfandel 1989, California £5.99

PLA   Playford Ros Ltd   ★★★

Middle Park House, Sowerby, Thirsk, N. Yorkshire (Tel 0845 526777). **Opening
Hours:** Mon-Fri 8a.m.-6p.m.. **Delivery:** free locally, nationally at cost. **Tastings:** 3-4
trade tastings per annum. **Services:** cellarage, mail order, gift-mailing.

With a set of Domaine Leflaive Burgundies, Alsace from Trimbach, Aussies from
Yarra Yering and Cape Mentelle, South Africans from Dieu Donné, plus a good
range of regional French offerings, putting together a representative international
mixed dozen would be a doddle.

1	Yaldara Brut Pinot Noir-Chardonnay 1990, Australia £7.99
3	Moss Wood Chardonnay, 1993, Margaret River, Australia £11.00
3	Montes Nogales Estate Chardonnay, 1994, Chile £5.49
3	Dieu Donné Chardonnay 1993, South Africa £6.00
4	Pikes Polish Hill Sauvignon Blanc, 1993, Australia £6.20
8	Goundrey Langton Australian Riesling, 1991, Australia £5.49
10	Ch. de Sours Bordeaux Rosé, 1993, Bordeaux, France £5.99
11	Domaine De Lauziers, Minervois, 1992, South-West France £3.89
12	Ch. de Sours, 1991, Bordeaux, France £4.99
12	Collection Privada, Bodega J E Navarro Correas, 1988, Argentina £9.75
12	Mountadam 'The Red', Adam Wynn, 1991, Australia £15.90
13	Yaldara Shiraz, 1992, Australia £5.49
13	Riverside Farm Zinfandel, 1992, Foppiano, California £5.99
20	Oloroso Viejo, Manuel De Argueso, Jerez, Spain £8.45
20	Dry Amontillado, Manuel D'Argueso, Jerez, Spain £6.45
21	Grahams Crusted Port, Douro, Portugal £11.99

PON   Le Pont de la Tour   ★★★★

The Butler's Wharf Building, 36D Shad Thames, London SE1 2YE (Tel 071-403 2403
Fax 071-403 0267). **Opening Hours:** Mon-Sat 12p.m.-8:30p.m., Sun 12p.m.-3p.m.
Delivery: free locally, nationally at cost. **Tastings:** occasionally **Services:** mail
order, gift-mailing, glass hire, ice.

Open rather more often than the architectural feature after which it is named, the
ubiquitous Mr Conran's retail wine merchant generates much of its trade from the
clientele of the restaurant with which it shares the premises. With over a thousand
wines on offer you should not be short of either breadth or depth; this is one of the
best, all-embracing, ranges in the country. There are few bargains here, though the
prices will seem ludicrously cheap if you compare them with those asked for the
same wines on the restaurant wine list.

1	Champagne Alexandre Bonnet Cuvée Prestige Brut, France £12.95
3	Chardonnay 'Buchholz', Alois Lageder, 1992, Italy £7.99
3	Palliser Estate Chardonnay, Martinborough, 1992, £9.99
3	Tim Adams Semillon, 1991, Australia £9.99
3	Capitel Croce, 1991, Anselmi, Veneto, Italy £10.50
3	Pinot Bianco, 1992, Jermann, Friuli Venezia Giulia, Italy £10.99
3	Ch. La Tour-Martillac, 1989, Pessac-Léognan, Bordeaux, France £17.99
3	Where The Dreams Have No End, 1989, Jermann, F-V-G, Italy £29.50
4	Verdicchio 'Casal Di Serra', 1993, Umani Ronchi, Italy £5.99
4	Soave Classico Superiore, 1993, Anselmi, Veneto, Italy £6.75
12	Niebaum Coppola Cabernet Franc, 1990, California £9.95
12	Katnook Cabernet Sauvignon, 1990, Australia £8.99
12	Niebaum Coppola Rubicon, 1982, California £19.75
13	Châteauneuf du Pape, Chante-Cigale 1990, France £11.50
16	Cumaro, 1990, Umani Ronchi, Marches, Italy £9.95
16	Roccato, 1990, Rocca Delle Macie 1990, Tuscany, Italy £8.99
21	Muscat de Rivesaltes, 1992, Domaine Cazes, France £10.50

POR   The Portland Wine Company   ★★★★

16, North Parade, Sale, Greater Manchester (Tel 061 962 8752). **Opening Hours:**
Mon-Sat 10a.m.-10p.m.. Sun 12p.m.-3p.m. & 7p.m.-9:30p.m. **Delivery:** free locally.
Tastings: tutored events, regular tastings in Hale. **Services:** gift-mailing, glass loan,
ice.

Despite following up his trip to Australia with a visit to California, Geoff Dickinson's
passion remains firmly in the land of Oz where he has been adventurous enough to
list wines from Henschke, Chapel Hill, Mount Langi Ghiran and Penley Estate.
Those Californians did get a foot in the door, though, in the shape of the eminently
recommendable Newton and Au Bon Climat. As for the Old World, there are Italians
from Altesino and Allegrini and impressive sets of Burgundies and Spanish wines. A
friendly welcome is assured at any of the four shops, but for the full range, it's worth
heading to Hale. And for a chance to taste your way through the range, ask about the
event Mr D holds every year with the Great Northern Wine Co. (qv) at Old Trafford.

1	Champagne Gosset Brut Reserve, France £18.99
2	Bellefontaine Chardonnay, 1993, Paul Boutinot, £3.99
2	Goldwater Chardonnay, 1993, New Zealand £8.99
2	Mâcon La Roche Vineuse Vieilles Vignes, 1992, Domaine Du Vieux Saint-Sorlin, Burgundy, France £7.50
6	Ca del Solo Malvasia Bianca, 1992, Bonny Doon, California £7.50
12	Ch. D'Armailhac, 1989, Baron Philippe De Rothschild, Pauillac, Bordeaux, France £16.29
13	Lindemans Bin 50 Shiraz, 1992, Australia £4.99

13	St Joseph, Les Larmes Du Père, 1991, A. Paret, Rhône, France £7.99
15	Mercurey 1er Cru Les Combins, 1991, Juillot, Burgundy, France £12.35
16	Palazzo Altesi Rosso, 1990, Altesino, Italy £14.99

PMR   Premier Wine Warehouse   ★★★

2 Heathmans Road, London SW6 4TJ (Tel 071-736 9073). Wine by the case only **Opening Hours:** Mon-Fri 10.30am-7.30pm, Sat 10am-5pm. **Delivery:** free locally, nationally at cost. **Tastings:** regular in-store. **Services:** en primeur, mail order, gift mailing, glass hire.

A single-branch wine warehouse stuck away down a pot-holed alley off Parson's Green in Fulham, a mere spit from the lair of the famous ethnologist, author and wine buff, Professor Robert O'Clarke, Premier offers a sensible range of small grower Burgundy and petit-chateau claret, as well as good Spanish and reliable Australian (Rosemount) selections. Good service and reasonable prices ensure its continued popularity with the locals, many of whom stop in here while shopping for BMWs at the showroom opposite.

17	Navajas Rioja Sin Crianza, 1992, Spain £3.99
17	Vina Oro Tinto, 1992, Co-Op Vinos Del Bierzo, Spain £3.99
17	Torres De Casta Rosada, 1993, Spain £4.25
17	Navajas Rioja Blanco Crianza, 1989, Spain £5.99
17	Guelbenzu Navarra Crianza Tinto, 1990, Spain £5.99

R   R S Wines   ★★★

32, Vicarage Road, Southville, Bristol BS3 1PD (Tel 0272 631780). **Opening Hours:** Mon-Fri 9am-7pm **Delivery:** free locally. **Tastings:** regular in-store. **Services:** cellarage, en primeur, glass hire.

A case-sales operation with a list so packed with wines from France (half the list), Australasia and Spain that pictures are confined to the front & inside cover. Although some of the text reads like publicity blurb from the particular wineries and regions, the choice is extensive and tempting, and it is hard to find a dull wine. Value-conscious wine lovers should be aware that bottles on offer at larger merchants can be a little dearer here once VAT is added, but none of those giants can offer such serious Californians as Shafer, Niebaum Coppola and Clos du Val (including 'Le Clos' the second label).

1	Champagne Grand Cru Chardonnay Brut, Dom. M.Gonet, France £15.50
3	Chateau Reynella Chardonnay, 1993, Hardy, Australia £6.75
4	Moondah Brook Estate Chenin Blanc, 1993, Hardy, Australia £4.99
12	Ravenswood Cabernet Sauvignon, 1990, Hollick, Australia £15.00
13	Chateau Reynella Basket Pressed Shiraz, 1991, Hardy, Australia £6.75
16	Nebbiolo, L.A.Cetto 1986, Mexico £8.99

RAE   Raeburn Fine Wines   ★★★★★

21-23 Comely Bank Road, Edinburgh EH4 1DS (Tel 031 332 5166). **Opening Hours:** Mon-Sat 9.30am-6pm. **Delivery:** free locally, nationally at cost. **Tastings:** occasional in-store, plus tutored tastings at The Vaults in Leith. Details on application. **Services:** cellarage, en primeur, mail order, glass hire.

Joint Scottish Wine Merchant of the Year

Every month seems to bring another tempting offer from Edinburgh's finest. Recent months have seen top 1992 Burgundies, en primeur Bordeaux, Port from Niepoort, and old Vouvray from Huët. At first glance the prices seem so low that one could imagine them to be be VAT exclusive. But no, savings made by importing directly are passed on to the customers. The new list which was being prepared as we went to press seems sure to build on the successes of the past - all of France, select Germans, a sprinkling of Italians & Spaniards and some unusual Aussies (Who else sells 1984 Redgate Cabernet Sauvignon?). America is principally a battle between Bonny Doon and (similarly rare) Joseph Swan, though there are other vineyards represented on an exclusive basis for Scotland. It is hard to believe that a one-time corner store is now bottling its own scotch.

1	Billiot Brut, Cuvée Reserve, Champagne, France £18.30	
3	Kistler 'Dutton Ranch' Chardonnay, 1989, California £14.95	
4	Cloudy Bay Sauvignon Blanc, 1992, New Zealand £9 (limited stocks)	
8	Forster Ungeheur Riesling Spätlese, 1986, Basserman-Jordan, Rheinpfalz, Germany £9.50	
12	Vieux Ch. Certan, 1987, Pomerol, France £19.50	
13	Cornas, 1989, Noel Verset, Rhône, France £12.50	
17	Beronia Reserva, 1985, Bodegas Beronia, Rioja, Spain £6.95	
21	Ruby Port, Niepoort, Douro, Portugal £6.99	
21	Framboise, Infusion of Raspery, Boony Doon, California £5.99 (half)	

RAM   The Ramsbottom Victuallers Co Ltd   ★★★

16-18 Market Place, Ramsbottom, Bury, Lancs. BL0 9HT (Tel 0706 825070). **Opening Hours:** Wed-Sat 10am-5.30pm, 7.30-10pm, Sun 12.30-3pm. **Delivery:** free locally, nationally at cost. **Tastings:** wine of the week every Saturday, plus tutored tastings with supper in the adjoining restaurant (next series: Sept-Nov)

Like a eunuch selecting novitiates for a harem, the teetotal Chris Johnson has overseen the gathering of over 800 wines from across the world to join the home-made and natural food-stuffs available in this Aladin's cave. If you lack the time to inspect them all, or find your attention wandering to the delicatessen counter, concentrate on the Rhône, Alsace, French regional, wines, Spain or Italy. Just the stuff to make you want to enjoy a vinous harem of your own.

3	Katnook Estate Chardonnay, 1991, Coonawarra, Australia £9.99	
3	Newton Vineyard Unfiltered Chardonnay, 1991, California £17.50	
4	Eden Ridge Dry White, 1993, South Australia £5.20	
12	Pikes Polish Hill Cabernet Sauvignon, 1991, Australia £8.10	
12	Mitchelton Reserve Cabernet Sauvignon, 1991, California £7.49	
12	Newton Unfiltered Merlot, 1991, California £15.05	
13	Riddoch Shiraz, Katnook, 1992, Australia £6.99	
13	Eden Ridge Shiraz, 1992, Australia £7.30	

RAV   Ravensbourne Wine Company   ★★★

6.0.2. Bell House, 49 Greenwich High Road, London SE10 8JL (Tel 081-692 9655). **Opening Hours:** Mon-Fri 9am-5pm., Sat 10am-1pm. **Delivery:** free locally and surrounding boroughs, nationally at cost. **Tastings:** occasionally in-store, wine workshop for clubs/groups on request (charge only for wine). **Services:** mail order, gift-mailing, glass hire, ice

Ravensbourne's list starts out with a time-honoured mystery: what is that black object perched beneath the nose of the Frenchman pictured on the cover? Are those a pair of slugs or is it a moustache?

Within, in a style reminiscent of a fifth-form Geography field-trip handout complete with maps, potential customers may not only identify locations of their wines, but also plan their next European itinerary. Ravensbourne may not have put Bulgaria on the vinous map, but they've put the map in anyhow. Flip through, and try the bargain-priced French regionals and Eastern Europeans. Or pick up slightly higher-priced affairs from Domaine Cauhapé, Concha y Toro, Cousiño Macul, or a set of organic producers, warm in the knowledge that margins have not been squandered on Graphic Designers.

1	Champagne Philipponnat Grand Blanc, 1986, France £29.99
2	Domaine de la Batteuse Chardonnay, 1993, Bernard Delmas, South-West France £4.95
3	Miguel Torres Chardonnay de la Cordillera, 1993, Chile £5.70
4	Mauzac Vin de Pays de l'Aude, La Batteuse, 1993, Bernard Delmas South-West France £4.55
21	Finest Reserve Port, Quinta de la Rosa, Douro, Portugal, £9.50

RD   Reid Wines 1992 Ltd   ★★★★★

The Mill, Marsh Lane, Hallatrow, Nr. Bristol BS19 3DN (Tel 0761 452645) **Opening Hours:** Mon–Fri 10am-6pm, Sat by arrangement. **Delivery::** free locally and central London, national at cost. **Tastings:** occasional in-store plus 'vertical/horizontal, regional and comparative' tastings at The Mill or in a local restaurant. **Services:** cellarage, mail order, gift mailing, glass hire.

Bill Baker's reconstituted firm continues to thrive as a vinous treasure chest; one of the country's very best sources of old and rare Bordeaux, Burgundy, Rhône and Loire wines. However we would be just as happy to make up a Baker's dozen from Reid's range, starting with some Italians from Jermann and Mascarello, Californians from Bonny Doon and Jade Mountain, a Cape white from Warwick, reds and fizz respectively from Yarra Yering and Taltarni in Australia and a sticky and a Sauvignon from Redwood Valley and Wairau River in New Zealand.

2	Vintage Tunina, 1992, Jermann, Friuli-Venezia-Giulia, Italy £17.99
3	St Hallett's Chardonnay, 1993, Australia, £7.49
3	Wairau River Chardonnay, Marlborough, 1992, New Zealand £9.95
3	St. Andrews Estate Chardonnay, Napa Valley, 1990, California, £7.95
3	Pouilly Fuissé, Domaine Corsin, 1991, Burgundy, France £11.55
4	Taltarni Sauvignon Blanc, 1993, Australia £6.99
4	Wairau River Sauvignon Blanc, 1993, New Zealand £7.95
11	Madiran, Montus, Alain Brumont, 1991, South-West France £9.50
12	Niebaum Coppola Cabernet Franc, 1990, California £9.95
12	Clos Du Val Merlot, 1990, California £13.50
13	St Hallett's Old Block Shiraz, 1991, Australia £9.49
13	Clos Du Val Zinfandel, 1989, California £9.75
17	Contino Rioja Reserva, Vinedos Del Contino CVNE, 1988, Spain £10.99
20	Puerto Fino, Emilio Lustau SA, Jerez, Spain £3.29
20	Los Arcos Dry Amontillado, Emilio Lustau SA, Jerez, Spain £3.99
21	Banyuls Tradition, Domaine De Baillaury, 1985, Southern France £9.25

RES   La Reserve Group   ★★★★

56 Walton Street, London SW3 1RB (Tel 071-589 2020). **Opening Hours:** Mon-Sat 9:30a.m.-9p.m. **Delivery:** Free within 5 miles, nationally at cost (free for orders over £200). **Tastings:** regular in-store and tutored. **Services:** en primeur, cellarage, mail order, gift-mailing, glass hire, ice.

Uniting those incompatible beings who live in Belgravia, Fulham and Paddington, with his La Réserve, Sac à Vin and Le Picoleur shops, Mark Reynier has put together a good range of smart, mature clarets, ports, Burgundies and Italian wines as well as recommendable sets of younger wines from these regions, the Loire, Alsace and the Rhône. Also worth trying are the Calera Californians, Brokenwood's & Stonier's Australians and the expanding selection from South Africa and New Zealand.

3	Chablis, Jean Collet, 1992, France £9.50
2	Brokenwood Chardonnay, Hunter Valley, 1993, Australia £7.00
4	1992 Domaine D'Augeron, Vin De Pays De Terroirs Landais Blanc, Bubola, 1992, France £4.24
12	Stonier's Cabernet 1991, Australia £7.50
12	Brokenwood Cabernet Sauvignon 1991, Australia £7.00
13	Brokenwood Shiraz 1991, Australia £7.00
13	Lirac Cuvée Prestige La Fermade, 1989, Maby, Rhône, France £8.95

RIB Ribble Vintners ★★★★

93-97 Lancaster Road, Preston PR1 2QS (Tel 0772 884866). **Opening Hours:** Mon–Fri 10am-6pm, Sat 9am-5pm. **Delivery:** free locally, nationally at cost. **Tastings:** Saturday in-store, plus Thursday and Friday evening sessions and wine tours. **Services:** cellarage, mail order, gift mailing, glass hire, ice.

Howard Roche (aka 'Big H') continues to find excellent wines to impress the good folk of Preston. His list is laid out by grape variety, revealing that, should you so wish, you could compare Pinot Noirs from Alain Burguet in Gevrey Chambertin, Trapiche in Argentina and Rex Hill in Oregon; Chardonnays from Jean-Marc Boilot in Burgundy, Kistler in Sonoma and Kumeu River in New Zealand; Rieslings from Renaissance in California, Boschendal in the Cape and Dr Loosen in the Mosel. and Syrahs from Alain Paret in the Rhône, Dalwhinnie in the Australian Pyrenées and Klein Constantia in South Africa. However, for Tempranillo, you'll just have to stick to the excellent Spanish range.

12	Joseph Phelps Insignia, 1990, California £27.97
13	Seppelt Gold Label Shiraz, 1992, Australia £4.99
16	Barolo Riserva, Giacomo Borgogno & Figli 1988, Piedmont, Italy £8.76
21	Campbells Rutherglen Liqueur Muscat, Australia £5.65
21	Fine Ruby Port, Martinez, Douro, Portugal £6.85
21	Martinez Vintage Character Port, Douro, Portugal £8.49

RWW Richmond Wine Warehouse ★★★

138 Lower Mortlake Road, Richmond, Surrey TW9 3JZ (Tel 081-948 4196). **Opening Hours:** Mon-Sat 10a.m.-7p.m.. **Delivery:** free locally. **Tastings:** regular in-store. **Services:** en primeur, mail order, gift-mailing, glass hire, ice.

This year, we promise, there will be no education-related humour for this merchant housed in a former school. Forget the hurly-burly & frayed tempers of Waitrose or Safeway on Saturday and instead park on the playground and select a case or two whilst enjoying the day-long tasting (11am-6pm) in spacious surroundings. One sure to benefit from the opening of the Channel tunnel, Stephen Addy has gone long and big on France – the range includes an 18 litre Behemoth of Bordeaux – and does all the buying himself. While Italy and Australia may provide the familiar and tempting names and Spain the bargains, we feel that California has seen the best improvement this year. Addy is the tru skule swot, as any fule kno.

3	Goundrey Windy Hill Mount Barker Chardonnay, 1991, Australia £9.49
3	Chardonnay Fermentado en Barrica, 1992, Bodegas de Crianza de Castilla La Vieja, 1992, Spain £5.80
4	Bornos Sauvignon Blanc, 1993, Bodega de Crianza de Castilla La Vieja, Spain £5.80
13	Yaldara Shiraz, 1992, Australia £5.49
13	Domaine des Anges Clos de la Tour, Domaine des Anges, 1991, Rhône, France £7.99
17	Quinta Folgorosa Red, Carvalho, Ribeira & Fereira, 1989, Portugal £3.79

17	Vinadrian Rioja Tinto, Bodegas Gurpegui, 1993, Spain £3.50
17	Vina Berceo, Rioja Tinta Crianza, Bodegas Berceo, 1990, Spain £4.50
19	Tokaji Aszu 6 Puttonyos, Hetszolo, 1981, Hungary £19.95
19	Denbies Wine Estate Noble Harvest, 1992, England £17.50

RWC   Rioja Wine Co.   ★★★

Argoed House, Llanfwrog, Ruthin, Clwyd LL15 1LG (Tel 0824 703407). **Opening Hours:** Mon-Fri 9am-6pm, Sat 9am-12 noon plus answerphone. **Delivery:** free locally, nationally at cost. **Tastings:** regular instore and tutored for societies, etc.

It's a foolhardy idea restricting yourself to selling Rioja – which is why we're relieved to find such excellent non-Spanish wines as Niepoort's wonderful ports, J M da Fonseca's table wines and the tasty Minervois from Château Villerambert Julien as represented as well.

11	Ch. Villerambert Julien, Minervois, 1992, France £7.00
17	Dão Terras Altas tinto DO, 1989, Douro, Portugal £3.41
17	Garrafeira TE, Jose Maria da Fonseca Succs., 1988, Portugal £6.50
17	Viña Ardanza tinto Reserva 1986, Rioja, Spain £7.70
21	Colheita 1978, Niepoort, Douro, Portugal £25.40

HR   Howard Ripley Select Domaine Imports ★★★★★

35 Eversley Crescent, London N21 1EL (Tel 081-360 8904). Wines by the case only. No credit cards. **Opening Hours:** Mon-Fri 9am-10pm, Sat 9am-4.30pm, Sun 9-11.30am. **Delivery:** free locally, nationally at cost. **Tastings:** occasional in-store, tutored sessions to groups on request. **Services:** en primeur, mail order, glass hire.

Burgundy Specialist of the Year

Former dentist and obsessional Burgundy-lover turned wine merchant, Howard Ripley has now extracted anything remotely foreign from his list, filling it instead with an amalgam of top class wines from a wide range of estates. Fellow Pinophiliacs – sufferers from what one might call Ripley's Disease – will be pleased to find bottles on offer which do not reach second mortgage level, though they will find it hard not to order heavily from a fairly-priced range which includes Gérard Thomas's St Aubin, Jean-Marc Boillot's Puligny, Pierre Morey's Meursault, Ramonet's Chassagne, Pommard from Comte Armand, Volnay from Michel Lafarge, Gevrey Chambertin from Armand Rousseau, Morey St Denis from Dujac and Vosne-Romanée from Leroy. Just a small cheque... now that didn't hurt did it?

3	Morey St Denis Blanc, Domaine Dujac, 1991, Burgundy, France £16.80
3	Meursault 1er Cru Charmes, 1992, Burgundy, France £19.00
3	Nuits St Georges Blanc 1er Cru, Domaine de l'Arlot, 1991, Burgundy, France £22.00
3	Chassagne Montrachet 1er Cru Morgeots, 1992, Burgundy, France £24.00
15	Chambolle Musigny, Hudelot-Noellat, 1992, Burgundy, France £11.50
15	Gevrey Chambertin Vieilles Vignes, Denis Bachelet, 1992, Burgundy, France £13.00
15	Nuits St Georges 1er Cru Clos de l'Arlot, 1989, Domaine de l'Arlot, Burgundy, France £15.00
15	Gevrey Chambertin, Vieilles Vignes, A. Burguet, 1988, Burgundy, France £18.30
15	Volnay 1er Cru Dom. Michel Lafarge, 1991, Burgundy, France £19.00
15	Corton Bressandes, Chandon de Briailles, 1989, Burgundy, France £21.00

RBS   Roberson   ★★★★

348 Kensington High Street, London W14 8NS (Tel 071-371 2121). **Opening Hours:**
Mon-Sat 10am-8pm, Sun 12-3pm. **Delivery:** free locally, nationally at cost.
Tastings: regular in-store, plus tutored sessions with producers or suppliers.
Services: en primeur, mail order, glass hire, ice.

If you ever fancied buying wine in Gaudi's Barcelona cathedral (what, you mean the
idea never occurred to you?) Roberson is your kind of shop. Weirdly sited close to
the Olympia exhibition hall on a piece of road where illegal parking is a capital
offence, this shop has 'designer' written all over it. It comes as a surprise to discover
that within all that form, there's some very impressive content. Clarets go back to
1924, Burgundies to 1928 and ports to 1927, and the most up-to-the-minute New
World wines are here aplenty. Sadly the wine courses which used to be run
downstairs are no more, but the wine range is an education in itself.

1	Croser Brut, 1990, Petaluma, Australia £12.95
2	Chablis, 1989, Etienne Defaix, Burgundy, France £12.50
2	'Y' d'Yquem, 1980, Bordeaux, France £33.50
3	Sonoma-Cutrer Chardonnay, Les Pierres, 1990, California £17.95
3	Puligny Montrachet 1er Cru Les Champs Gains, 1988, Henri Clerc, Burgundy, France £25.85
4	Fendant Réserve des Administrateurs, 1991, Caves St. Pierre Switzerland £8.50
4	Carmenet Sauvignon Blanc, 1987, California £9.95
4	De Ladoucette, Pouilly Fumé Baron de'L', 1988, France £27.75
8	Inniskillin Riesling, 1988, Canada £6.50
9	Schlossgut Diel, Grauburgunder, 1988, Germany £14.35
10	Bardolino Chiaretto Classico, 1992, Guerrieri-Rizzardi, Italy £5.75
11	Ch. de Lastours, 1989, Fûts de Chêne, France £7.75
12	Hess Collection Cabernet Sauvignon, 1990, California £14.95
12	Ch. Léoville-Poyferré, 1989, Bordeaux, France £18.75
12	Ch. Léoville Lascasse, 1955, Bordeaux, France £105.00
13	Ravenswood Vintners Blend Zinfandel, 1992, California £8.95
13	Ch. de Beaucastel, Châteauneuf-du-Pape, 1988, Rhône, France £17.50
14	Jacques Dépagneaux, Juliénas, 1992, Beaujolais, France £7.95
15	Bannockburn, Pinot Noir, 1990, Australia £9.95
15	Ruchottes-Chambertin, Grand Cru Clos des Ruchottes, 1988, Armand Rousseau, Burgundy, France £33.50
16	Isole e Olena, Chianti Classico, 1989, Italy £8.75
17	Quinta de la Rosa, 1992, P.D E. Bergqvist, Portugal £4.95
17	Juvé y Camps Reserva de la Familia, 1989, Spain £9.95
17	Vega Sicilia Valbuena 3rd. Year, 1987, Spain £22.50
19	Recioto dei Capitelli Recioto di Soave, 1988, Anselmi, Italy £9.45 (half)
19	Ch. Filhot, 1976, Sauternes, France £32.50
19	Marc Brédif, Vouvray, 1959, Loire, France £49.50

RTW   The Rose Tree Wine Co Ltd   ★★★

15 Suffolk Parade, Cheltenham, Glos. GL50 2AE (Tel 0242 583732). **Opening
Hours:** Mon-Fri 8.30am-7pm, Sat 9am-6pm. **Delivery:** free locally, nationally at
cost. **Tastings:** regular in-store plus sessions for local wine clubs. **Services:** en
primeur, mail order, gift mailing.

Messrs Brown and Maynard must be glad to see their business begin to bloom after
the thorny years of the recession when they had to prune it back quite tightly. They
are to be congratulated for putting together what might be termed a very fragrant
range. We'd happily order a big bunch of their clarets, Burgundies, Italians and
Spaniards.

3	Vinos del Vero Chardonnay, 1992, Spain £5.49
4	Ch. La Verrerie, 1992, Blanc de Blancs, Cotes du Lubéron, France, £8.38
11	Ch. La Verrerie, 1989, Bastide La Verrerie Rouge, Cotes de Lubéron, France £6.29
15	Vinos del Vero Pinot Noir, Cia Vitivinicola Aragonesa, 1990, Spain, £6.59
15	Fleur de Carneros Pinot Noir, 1992, California £6.99
17	Ochoa Tempranillo, 1990, Bodegas Ochoa, Spain £5.99
20	Añada Oloroso, Emilio Lustau SA, Jerez, Spain £5.99

SAF   Safeway Stores plc

Safeway House, 6 Millington Road, Hayes, Middlesex UB3 4AY (Tel 081 848 8744). **Opening Hours:** Mon-Sat 8am-8pm, Sun 10am-4pm **Tastings:** occasional in-store **Services:** glass hire, ice.

If the last 12 months have not seen quite as dramatic a development of the Safeway range we found so impressive a couple of years ago, Liz Robertson and her crew have continued to break new ground. This was the first chain to introduce Fetzer's excellent organic wines (which, we have to say, did not precisely tumble into shoppers' baskets) and a pioneer of the 50cl bottle (a clever wheeze to bring in the under-£1.80 bottle). We were pleased too to see the success of the 'Young Vatted Tempranillo' (third in the line invented by this chain) and the arrival of some flavoursome alternative fizzes. Flying winemakers are doing as much here as elsewhere, but not always to the greatest effect (some of Nick Butler's wines made us coin the term, 'low-flying' winemaker) and there are too many pleasant but characterless whites at the bottom end of the price scale. Even so, we'd happily recommend all of the wines listed below – and a lot more besides.

1	Le Grand Pavillon, Boschendal, South Africa £6.49
1	Maison La Motte Sparkling Chardonnay Brut, James Herrick, South West France £7.99
1	Safeway Albert Etienne Vintage Champagne, 1988, France £14.99
2	Chardonnay del Salento, 1993, Cantele, Puglia, Italy, £3.99
2	Pouilly-Fuissé, 1991, Luc Javelot, Burgundy, France £6.99
3	Danie De Wet Chardonnay Sur Lie, 1993, South Africa £4.39
3	Millton Vineyard Chardonnay, 1992, New Zealand £6.99
4	Riva Trebbiano DOC, Ronco, 1993, Italy £2.99
4	Villa Montes Sauvignon Blanc, 1993, Discover Wines, Chile £3.99
4	Wairau River Sauvignon Blanc, 1993, New Zealand, £7.49
5	Black Country Gold, Medium English Table Wine, 1992, Halfpenny Green Vineyards, England, £4.99
8	Van Loveren Special Late Harvest Gewürztraminer, 1993, South Africa £4.49
9	Safeway Rheinpfalz Auslese, 1992, St. Ursula, Germany £3.99
10	Safeway Cabernet Sauvignon Rosé, 1993, Nagyrede, Hungary £2.99
11	Ch. de Belesta, 1992, Côtes du Roussillon Villages, Les Vignerons Catalans, South-West France £3.49
11	La Cuvée Mythique, 1991, Vignerons Val D'Orbieu, South-West France £4.99
12	Dom. La Tuque Bel-Air, 1989, Côtes de Castillon, Jean Lavau, Bordeaux, France £5.59
12	Margaux, 1989, Barton & Guestier, Bordeaux, France, £7.99
13	Fetzer Zinfandel, 1991, California £4.99
13	Châteauneuf du Pape La Source aux Nymphes, 1991, Les Fils d'Etienne Gonnet, Rhône, France £7.69
15	Safeway Bourgogne Rouge, 1992, Cave Vignerons d'Igé, Burgundy, France £4.99

15	Hamilton Russell Pinot Noir, 1991, South Africa £7.49
15	Chambolle-Musigny, 1991, C. Masy-Perier, Burgundy, France £11.99
16	Puglian Red, 1993, Cantele/K.Milne, Puglia, Italy £2.99
16	Villa Pagello Merlot, 1992, Co-op Breganze, Italy £3.49
16	Copertino, 1990, Cantine Sociale Copertino, Italy £3.59
17	Young Vatted Tempranillo, 1993, Vinicola De Castilla, Spain £3.19
17	Safeway Oak Aged Valdepeñas, 1987, Felix Solis, Spain £3.39
17	Tinto Da Anfora, 1990, J. P. Vinhos, Portugal £5.35
19	Ch. de Berbec, 1989, Premières Côtes de Bordeaux, France £3.49
19	Seewinkler Impressionen Ausbruch, 1991, Austria £6.99
20	Lustau Old Dry Oloroso, Jerez, Spain £3.29
20	Cream of Cream Sherry, Argueso Valdespino, Jerez, Spain £8.99
21	Smith-Woodhouse Tawny Port, Oporto, Portugal £5.39
21	Safeway Fine Ruby Port, Calem, Oporto, Portugal £5.41
21	Fonseca Guimaraens Vintage Port, 1976, Douro, Portugal £19.99

JS   Sainsbury's   ★★★★

Stamford House, Stamford Street, London SE1 9LL (Tel 071-921 6000). **Opening Hours:** Mon-Fri 8am-8pm, Sat 8am-6pm, Sun 10am-4pm. **Tastings:** occasional in-store, plus tutored tastings around the country 2-3 times a year. **Services:** mail order via Sainsbury's magazine, ice in some stores.

Supermarket Wine Merchant of the Year

Last year, the editors of another guide decided that Sainsbury's deserved the prize of Supermarket of the Year. We were not so certain, feeling that there were still too many signs of the heavy-handed buying of the previous couple of years. Well, this year, as he left the wine department to work in Homebase (such are the ways of supermarkets) Simon Blower could congratulate himself on having left behind him a range which really does deserve that prize. There are all sorts of signs of the good old Sainsbury spirit at work in the wines of two 'new' flying winemakers, in the shape of Peter Bright and Geoff Merrill, whose efforts in Spain and Italy respectively yielded first class results, as well as in the arrival of an Australian range to rival that of Oddbins.

Sainsbury was also the first major UK wine retailer to cross the Channel, incidentally introducing the bemused burghers of Calais to the delights of Chilean Cabernet Sauvignon. The next development is a long-term project with Hugh Ryman and others to plan the production of the staples of their range, ensuring that, over the next few years the chain's customers will be offered such wines as Bordeaux, Côtes du Rhône, and Beaujolais that have been produced to standards required by Sainsbury, rather than the often lax authorities and inefficient producers of these regions. Watch this space.

1	Madeba Brut, Graham Beck Wines, South Africa £6.95
2	Mâcon Domaines les Ecuyers, 1992, Duboeuf, Burgundy, France £6.69
3	Sainsbury's Chardonnay delle Tre' Venezie, 1993, Geoff Merrill, Italy £3.59
3	Santa Sara, Fernão Pires, JP Vinhos, 1993, Portugal £3.95
3	Sainsbury's Chardonnay, Vino Da Tavola, 1993 Geoff Merrill/GIV, Italy £4.75
3	Casablanca Santa Isabel Estate Chardonnay, 1992, Chile £7.95
3	Tasmanian Wine Company Chardonnay, Pipers Brook Vineyard, 1992, Australia £7.99
4	Sainsbury's Vino de la Tierra Blanco, Peter Bright, Spain £2.59
4	Sainsburys Italian Grechetto, 1993, Geoff Merrill / GIV, Italy £3.95
4	Rueda Sauvignon Blanc, 1993, Hermanos Lurton, Spain £3.99
4	Muscadet de Sevre et Maine sur Lie 'Première', 1992, Domaine Jean Douillard, Loire, France £5.45

4	Jackson Estate Sauvignon Blanc, 1993, New Zealand £7.95
6	Hugel Gentil, 1992, ALsace, France £4.95
7	Lily Farm Vineyard Muscat, 1993, Grant Burge, Australia £3.95
10	Sainsburys do Campo Rosado, Peter Bright, Spain £2.99
10	Mount Hurtle Grenache Rosé, 1993, Geoff Merrill, Australia £4.99
12	Sainsbury's Chilean Merlot San Fernando, 1993, Canepa, Chile £3.99
12	Clancy's Red, 1990, Peter Lehmann, Australia £6.45
12	Ch. La Vieille Cure, 1989, Fronsac, France £7.95
12	Devil's Lair Cabernet Sauvignon, 1991, Australia £9.45
12	Les Forts de Latour, 1987, Pauillac, Bordeaux, France £16.95
14	Sainsburys Gamay Vin de Pays des Coteaux de Barronnies, 1993, Jean Claude Boisset, South-West France £3.35
15	Gevrey Chambertin, 1983, Antonin Rodet, Burgundy, France £12.95
16	Sainsburys Copertino Riserva, 1991, Cantina Sociale Co-op Copertino, Italy £3.95
17	Sainsburys El Conde, Vino de Mesa Tinto Santiago Vinicola SA, Chile £2.79
17	Sainsburys do Campo Tinto, Peter Bright, Spain £2.99
19	Clos St Georges, Graves Supérieur, Gallaire et Fils, 1990, Bordeaux, France £6.95
19	Ch. Bastor Lamontagne, 1989, Sauternes, France £8.99
20	Sainsburys Palo Cortado, Gonzalez Fernandez, Jerez, Spain £3.39
20	Sainsburys Aged Amontillado, Bodegas del Ducado, Jerez, Spain £3.39
20	Sainsburys Pale Dry Fino, Morgan Brothers, Jerez, Spain £4.39
21	Sainsburys Vintage Character Port, Taylor Fladgate & Yeatman, Douro, Portugal £6.09
21	Sainsburys LBV Port, 1987, Croft, Douro, Portugal £6.59

SAN Sandiway Wine Company ★★★★

Chester Road, Sandiway, Cheshire CW8 2NH (Tel 0606 882101). **Opening Hours:** Mon–Fri 9am-1pm, 2-10pm, Sat 9am-10pm, Sun 12-2pm, 7-10pm. **Tastings:** regular in store, 'seasons' of tutored tastings with visiting speakers, plus sessions for local companies and groups. **Services:** gift mailing, glass loan.

Quite how Graham Wharmby manages to entice so many top notch winemakers to talk to the customers of his middle-of-nowhere shop in Cheshire we do not know, but over the last few years, both Franco Conterno and the eccentric Randall Grahm have presented evenings, and future bookings include Francois Billecart (of Billecart Salmon) and Andre Ostertag from Alsace. News and views from Sandiway arrive in the form of a quarterly newsletter which – there being no wine list – is well worth receiving.

2	Mâcon La Roche Vineuse Vieilles Vignes, 1992, Domaine Du Vieux Saint-Sorlin, Burgundy, France, £7.50
6	Ca Del Solo Malvasia Bianca, 1992, Bonny Doon California £7.50
11	Mas du Gourgonnier, Reserve du Mas, 1990, South-West France £7.50
12	Bellefontaine Merlot, 1993, Paul Boutinot, South-West France £3.29
12	Niebaum Coppola Rubicon, 1982, California £19.75
12	Ch. Tour Du Pas St Georges, 1990, Bordeaux, France 7.90
13	Rouge Homme Shiraz/Cabernet, 1991, Australia £4.99
13	St Joseph, Les Larmes Du Père, 1991, A. Paret, Rhône, France £7.99
15	Bourgogne Rouge Bons Batons, 1992, Domaine Patrice & Michele Rion Burgundy, France £7.50
15	Pinot Noir 'La Bauge Au-dessus', 1991, Au Bon Climat, California £18.00
17	Quinta de la Rosa, 1992, Douro, Portugal £4.90

SWB Satchells of Burnham Market ★★★

North Street, Burnham Market, Norfolk PE31 8HG (Tel 0328 738272). **Opening Hours:** Mon-Fri 9:30a.m.-6p.m., Sat 9:30a.m.-7p.m. seasonal Sundays 12p.m.-2p.m. **Delivery:** free locally. **Tastings:** regular in-house and tutored, plus organised events. **Services:** mail order, gift-mailing, glass loan, ice.

Set in the heart of Norfolk's answer to Sloane Square (in Season), Satchells provides the local squirarchy and weekend refugees from London with a comprehensive range of impressive and unusual wines.

SK Seckford Wines ★★★

2 Betts Avenue, Martlesham Heath, Suffolk IP5 7RH (Tel 0473 626681). **Opening Hours:** Tue-Sat 10a.m.-6p.m. **Delivery:** free locally. **Tastings:** regular in-store and tutored, plus organised events. **Services:** en primeur, glass loan, gift-mailing.

At last, the case-only wine shop without that 'Boeing-hanger' feel. Yet, despite the limited size, there are several wines open for tasting every day. If you do buy anything untasted, Seckford will exchange the remaining bottles for something more to your liking but we would be surprised if your tastebuds were other than delighted by the late-80s Bordeaux, the Italians and Australasians on offer here.

4	Vendange Blanc, Vin de Pays des Côtes Catalanes, 1993, Les Vignerons du Roussillon, France £3.95
12	Joseph Phelps Insignia, 1990, California £28.00
12	Ravenswood Cabernet Sauvignon, 1990, Hollick Wines, Coonawarra, South Australia, £15.00
13	Ch. de Beaucastel, 1990, Châteauneuf-du-Pape, J P & F Perrin Rhône, France, £17.50
21	Campbells Old Rutherglen Liqueur Muscat, Victoria, Australia £12.99

SEL Selfridges ★★★★★

400 Oxford Street, London W1A 1AB (Tel 071-629 1234). **Opening Hours:** Mon-Sat 9.30am-7pm (Thurs until 8pm). **Delivery:** free nationally for orders over £100 **Tastings:** regular in-store; introducing wine club and tastings with wine producers. **Services:** mail order, gift mailing, glass hire.

This Oxford Street Emporium does not immediately feature on most wine buffs' list of places in which to buy wine, but it should. Given the store's address which is equidistant from all London's ethnic clusters, the breadth of a range that unites bottles from Israel, Lebanon, Turkey, Switzerland and Canada is perhaps unsurprising. Even so, 1966 Dom Perignon is hard to find on a fine wine list; to pick it from a shelf rather than in a merchant's (distantly-sited) cellar is a miracle. The spirit of discovery is abroad (or is that the other way around?) Shop from home and spend an extra £100 it would otherwise cost you to unclamp your car.

1	Bouvet Ladubay Saphir Brut Vintage, 1990, Saumur, France £9.99
1	Champagne Charles Heidsieck Brut Vintage, 1985, France £24.00
1	Taittinger Comtes de Champagne, Blanc de Blancs, 1985, France, £60.00
3	Beringer Fumé Blanc, 1992, California £5.95
3	Gramps Chardonnay, 1993, Orlando Wines, Australia £7.19
3	Crichton Hall Chardonnay, 1991, California £10.00
3	Babich Irongate Chardonnay, 1991, New Zealand £11.75
3	Where The Dreams Have No End, 1989, Jermann, Italy £29.50
4	Domaine de Subremont Sauvignon, 1993, Vin de Pays d'Oc, Domaine La Tour Boisée, South-West France £3.65

4	Dieu Donné Sauvignon Blanc, 1993, Du Lucque & Dieu Donné, South Africa £4.00
4	Pouilly Fumé, 1992, de Ladoucette, 1992, Loire, France £12.49
4	Soave Classico Costeggiola, 1993, Guerrieri-Rizzardi, Italy, £6.00
6	Trimbach Riesling, 1991, Alsace, France £7.50
7	Yarden Muscat, 1990, Golan Heights Winery, Galilee, Israel, £4.99
10	Beringer White Zinfandel, 1993, California £5.95
11	Chinon, Ch. de la Grille, Antoine Gosset, 1992, Loire, France £8.90
12	Ch. Du Cartillon, 1990, R Giraud SA, Haut-Médoc, France £7.00
12	Columbia Merlot, 1988, Columbia Winery, Washington, U.S. £7.50
12	Simonsig Tiara, 1990, South Africa £11.49
12	Torres Gran Coronas, 1988, Mas La Plana, Penedès, Spain £20.99
13	Côtes du Rhône, 1991, E. Guigal, Rhône, France £5.49
13	Rosemount Shiraz, 1992, Australia £5.99
15	Georg Stiegelmar Pinot Noir Barrique Trocken, 1990, Austria £15.00
16	Chianti Classico Riserva La Prima, Castello Vicchiomaggio, 1988, Tuscany, Italy, £15.10
17	Artadi Viñas de Gain Rioja Crianza, 1991, Cosecheros Alaveses, Rioja, Spain £5.49
17	Gran Reserva 904, La Rioja Alta SA 1983, Rioja, Spain £14.50
19	Tokaji Aszu 5 Puttonyos, 1981, Tokaji Hegyalja, Hungary £12.00
19	Denbies Wine Estate Noble Harvest, 1992, England £17.50
19	Ruster Beerenauslese, 1981, Weinkellerei Burgenland, Austria £5.99
20	Dos Cortados Oloroso, Williams & Humbert, Jerez, Spain, £8.50
21	Delaforce Special White Port, Douro, Portugal £7.59
21	Quinta Do Noval Colheita 1976, Douro, Portugal £9.99

ES   Edward Sheldon Ltd   ★★★

New Street, Shipston-on-Stour, Warwickshire CV36 4EN (Tel 0608 661409). **Opening Hours:** Mon-Fri 9am-7pm, Sat 9am-5pm. **Delivery:** free locally, nationally at cost.. **Tastings:** regular in-store. **Services:** en primeur, mail order, gift mailing, glass hire.

This is where actress and coffee-advertiser Cherie Lunghi, discovered wine while she was on stage in nearby Stratford on Avon, so male wine-buffs who'd like to rub shoulders or bottles with similarly beautious thespians should do their shopping here in person. Both shop and list are distinctly old style. This is where to find 'hunting port' presumably for use in hip flasks. Apart from New Zealand, the New World selection reveals a less than committed attitude towards the former colonies. But perhaps luvvies favour the old rather than the new world.

1	Segura Viudas Cava Brut Reserva, Spain £5.99
1	Champagne Joseph Perrier, Cuvée Royale Brut Rosé, France £22.50
4	Coopers Creek Gisborne Sauvignon Blanc, 1993, New Zealand £6.49
12	Cabernet-Merlot, Coopers Creek, 1991, New Zealand £7.99
12	Ch. Cissac, Médoc, 1986, Bordeaux, France £11.70
17	Periquita Reserva, J M Da Fonseca Succs, 1985, Portugal £7.50
17	Muga Rioja Reserva, 1988, Spain £7.89
21	Graham's Six Grapes, Douro, Portugal £11.49
21	Grahams 10 Year Old Tawny Port, Douro, Portugal £14.99

SAS   Sherston Wine Company   ★★★

97 Victoria Street, St Albans, AL1 3TJ (0727 858841). **Opening Hours:** Tues-Fri 11:30am-7pm, Sat 9:30am-6pm. **Delivery:** free locally, nationally at cost. **Tastings:** regularly. **Services:** glass hire.

In 13 pages, the earnest Mr Jacoby spans £3.29 (French House Red & White) to £99 (Castillo Ygay 1952) in a list that includes comments here and there, although a reference to Corton Charlemagne 1985 (Dubreuil-Fontaine) as 'le pi-pi de Dieu' may simultaneously stretch 'O'-level knowledge and some wine lovers' sensibilities. You want to buy a Richebourg 1982? I know a man who's got one. You want Spanish without a trip to Cornwall (Laymont & Shaw q.v.) or Italian without tears? St Albans beckons; complete the feast with coffee and chocolates.

1	Carr Taylor Sparkling Wine, England £9.50	
2	Chablis Grand Cru Vaudésir, Domaine Des Malandes, 1992, France £15.50	
2	Chablis 1er Cru Montmains, Domaine Des Malandes, 1992, France £9.00	
5	Carr Taylor Medium Dry, 1992, England £4.85	
16	Chianti Classico Riserva, Banfi, 1988, Italy £9.00	

SV Smedley Vintners ★★★★

Rectory Cottage, Lilley, Luton, Beds. LU2 8LU (Tel 0462 768214). Wine by the case only. No credit cards. **Opening Hours:** Mon-Fri 9am-6.30pm, Sat, Sun 9am-6pm. **Delivery:** free locally, nationally at cost. **Tastings:** occasional in-store, plus three major courses and two wine dinners a year. **Services: cellarage,** en primeur, mail order, gift mailing, glass hire, ice.

The modest Derek Smedley whose business, located near the Vauxhall works at Luton, is justly popular with its workers, remains one of our very favourite small wine merchants. The £1.20 discount offered as an inducement to leave cases unmixed reveals that Mr S adds distinctly uncavalier margins to a range of wines which are all of the right calibra. The recent severing of a link with Antinori may mean that Tignanello will no longer sell here for a fiver less than at Winecellars (qv) but we're confident that Mr Smedley will introduce alternative high-powered Italian winners in its stead. Do test-drive this range (0-50-miles: delivery free of charge). Per Vino ad Astra (police-permitting).

1	Daniel Le Brun Vintage, 1990, New Zealand £15.20
3	Montes Chardonnay, 1994, Chile £4.99
3	Jackson Estate Chardonnay, 1992, Marlborough, New Zealand £6.96
3	Dieu Donné Chardonnay, 1992, South Africa £6.74
4	Warden Vineyard, English White Wine, 1992, England £5.80
5	The Warden Abbot, Warden Abbey Vineyard, 1993, England £5.40
12	Montes Cabernet Merlot Special Cuvée, 1992, Chile £4.60
16	Chianti Classico Riserva, Badia a Passignano, 1990, Antinori, Tuscany, Italy £9.00
16	Tignanello, 1990, Antinori, Tuscany, Italy £17.00
16	Solaia, 1990, Antinori, Tuscany, Italy £37.00
20	Fine Dry Fino, Manuel D'Argueso, Jerez, Spain £4.76
20	Fine Amontillado, Manuel D'Argueso, Jerez, Spain £4.76

SMF Somerfield Stores Ltd ★★★

Somerfield House, Hawkfield Business Park, Whitchurch Lane, Bristol BS14 OTJ (Tel 0272 359359). **Opening Hours:** Mon-Sat 8.30am-6pm (some stores open until 8pm during the week), Sat 8.30am-6pm, Sun 10am-4pm. **Tastings:** regular in-store.

Life in the high street can be very confusing. Peter Dominic, Augustus Barnett, Gough Brothers... Where are they now? And whatever happened to Gateway? Well, in answer to the third question, it's still there but has changed its name by deed poll to the rather more 90s Somerfield. Fans of wines like Black Tower and Piat d'Or will be pleased to know that going up-market hasn't led to their expulsion; those who prefer 1er Cru Chablis or Château Haut-Marbuzet will be just as well served. And between the two, there's a growing range of own-label wines which offer far better value than pricier versions on ofer elsewhere. Whether Somerfield 'Prince William' Champagne will enjoy a better cachet in Belgravia than the Gateway version remains to be seen. What's in a name?

1	Somerfield Cava, Conde de Caralt, France £4.99
1	Prince William Champagne, Marne et Champagne, France £11.95
2	Moldova Chardonnay, Hincesti, Hugh Ryman, 1993, Moldova £2.99
2	Somerfield Chardonnay del Piemonte, 1993, Araldica, Italy £3.75
2	Somerfield Chablis, 1993, La Chablisienne, Burgundy, France £6.19
3	Meursault, 1990, Georges Désire, Burgundy, France £9.59
4	Domaine de la Roche Côte de Duras, Hugh Ryman, 1993, South-West France £3.99
4	Pinot Blanc d'Alsace, 1992, Caves de Turkheim, Alsace, France £3.99
4	Sancerre Les Côteaux Domaine Michel Brock, 1993, France £6.99
9	Somerfield Morio Muskat, 1992, St Ursula Wenkellerei £2.99
9	Scharzhofberger Riesling Kabinett, 1990, R. Müller, Germany £4.59
11	Somerfield Côtes du Rousillon, Maison Jeanjean, South-West France £3.85
12	Somerfield Oak-Aged Claret, 1990, Louis Eschenauer, Bordeaux, France £4.45
12	Santa Rita Reserva Cabernet Sauvignon, 1989, Chile £4.99
12	Château Musar, 1987, Serge Hochar, Lebanon £7.99
12	Beringer Cabernet Sauvignon, 1989, California £8.25
12	Ch. Haut Marbuzet, 1988, St Estèphe, Bordeaux, France £14.25
13	Cape Selection Pinotage, 1993, Vinimark Trading, South Africa £3.35
13	Somerfield Shiraz, Penfolds, Australia £3.99
13	Sebastiani Zinfandel, 1988, California £5.49
13	St Joseph, 1989, Caves de Saint Désirat, Rhône, France £7.95
13	Châteauneuf du Pape Domaine de La Solitude, 1990, Pierre Lançon, Rhône, France £8.75
14	Brouilly, 1992, Georges Duboeuf, Beaujolais, France £5.65
15	Somerfield Red Burgundy, 1991, Caves de Buxy, Burgundy, France £4.75
15	Nuits St Georges, 1991, Georges Désire, Burgundy, France £9.99
16	Copertino, 1988, Copertino Co-op, Italy £3.85
16	Ciro Rosso Classico, 1990, Librandi, Italy £4.35
16	Barolo, 1988, Vinidea, Italy £6.95
17	Leziria Tinto, Vega Co-operativa Almeirim, Portugal £2.49
17	Somerfield Rioja Tinto Almenar, 1990, Spain £3.79
17	Vina Albali Tinto Gran Reserva, 1984, Felix Solis, Spain £4.99
17	Campo Viejo Rioja Gran Reserva, 1981, Spain £7.69
18	Somerfield Moscatel de Valencia, Gandia, Spain £3.25
19	Ch. Bastor-Lamontage, 1989, Sauternes, Bordeaux, France £7.59
20	Somerfield Fino Sherry, Luis Caballero, Jerez, Spain £3.89
21	The Navigators Tawny Port, Real Vinicola del Norte, Douro, Portugal £5.45
21	The Navigators Late Bottled Vintage Port, 1988, Real Vinicola del Norte, Douro, Portugal £6.59
22	Bucks Fizz, Muller & Co. Germany £1.99

SOM   Sommelier Wine Co Ltd ★★★★

The Grapevine, 23 St. George's Esplanade, St Peter Port, Guernsey GY1 2BG (Tell 0481 721677). **Opening Hours:** Mon-Fri 10am-5.30pm, Sat 9.30am-5.30pm. **Delivery:** free locally **Tastings:** regular tastings for clubs, etc. plus an evening class. **Services:** en primeur, mail order, gift mailing.

There's a lot to be said for living in a place where fictional policeman are named after French wine regions. There's no income tax, no excise duty, no VAT – and all the more reason to take advantage of the Sommelier Wine Co. There may be a few wine-buying islanders unaware of this firm's existence, but then they either can afford to ship wine in from merchants on one or other mainland or enjoy a glass of dry white from the pub's wine box. Addressing the unenlightened but willing remainder and the holidaying buffs, the chatty Sommelier list features Pol Roger's entire range (White Foil for a third less than U.K. price), Neudorf Semillon, Ca del Solo Malvasia and Charles Melton's Rosé of Virginia amongst lesser-known wines. An amazing selection from a trio of enthusiasts who boldly confess to buying only wines they like – we assume they've hardly had a dry glass in the house to get a list like this.

1	Yalumba D, 1991, Australia £9.99
1	Pol Roger White Foil, France £13.50
3	Wairau River Chardonnay, 1992, Marlborough, New Zealand £9.95
3	Martinborough Vineyard Chardonnay, 1992, New Zealand £10.90
3	Newton Vineyard Unfiltered Chardonnay, 1991, California £17.50
4	Eden Ridge Dry White, 1993, Australia £5.20
4	Sancerre Les Baronnes, 1992, Henri Bourgeois, Loire, France £7.30
11	Clos Centeilles, Minervois, Daniel Domergue 1990, South France £9.50
12	The Angelus Cabernet Sauvignon, 1992, Wirra Wirra, Australia £9.00
12	Wirra Wirra Church Block Red, 1992, Australia £6.99
12	Newton Vineyards Cabernet Sauvignon, 1990, California £10.95
13	David Wynn Shiraz, 1992, Australia £6.10
14	Morgon, 1992, Marcel Jonchet, Beaujolais, France £7.95
15	Martinborough Vineyard Pinot Noir, 1992, New Zealand £10.90
15	Mercurey 1er Cru Les Combins, Juillot, 1991, Burgundy, France £12.35
19	Yalumba Museum Show-Reserve Rutherglen Muscat, Australia £6.99

SPR Spar ★★★

32-40 Headstone Drive, Harrow, Middlesex HA3 5QT (Tel 081-863 5511). **Opening Hours:** vary between: Mon-Sun 8am-10/llpm. Credit cards at discretion of individual stores. **Delivery:** at discretion of individual stores. **Tastings:** occasional in-store, tastings available on request. **Services:** glass hire, ice (selected stores).

Philippa Carr MW has a job which every other professional wine buyer would die for. And from. Choosing wine for 2000 shops, one of the biggest chains in the world sounds wonderful, until you wander into some of those shops and look at the wine shelf and the manager resposible for it. Persuading him or her to stock Villeneuve de Cantemerle would be like wondering whether he couldn't possibly order in salsify or kumquats. But Ms Carr likes a challenge and the quality of wine she is easing into those stores shows how successful she is being at it.

1	Spar Marquis de Prevel Champagne, Marne et Champagne , France £11.69
3	Chablis, 1990, Union Des Viticulteurs La Chablisiene, 1990, Burgundy, France £6.49
4	Vina Mocen Rueda Sauvignon, 1992, Bodegas Antano, Spain £4.99
6	Spar Viognier Cuxac, Val d'Orbieu, South-West France £3.99
9	Mainzer Domher Spatlese, Müller, 1992, Germany £3.45
10	Rosé de Syrah, Vin de Pays d'Oc, Val d'Orbieu, £2.99
11	Spar Cabernet Sauvignon & Cinsault Country Wine, Russe Winery, Bulgaria £2.79
11	Spar Fitou, Val d'Orbieu, South-West France £3.49
12	Spar Claret, Dulong, Bordeaux, France £3.19
12	Sable View Cabernet Sauvignon, 1991, Stellenbosch Farmers Winery, South Africa £3.99
12	Spar Oak Aged Merlot, Val d'Orbieu, South-West France £3.99
17	Senorio de Nava Ribera Del Duero Crianza, 1987, Spain £5.99

SPG Springfield Wines ★★★

Springfield Mill, Norman Road, Denby Dale, Huddersfield HD8 8TH (Tel 0484 864929).
Opening Hours: 9:30a.m.-7p.m., Sat 9a.m.-5p.m. **Delivery:** free locally, nationally
at cost. **Tastings:** regularly in-store. **Services:** mail order, glass hire.

Brooks & Higgs are not BBC TV's new female detective duo (you know the style,
Brooks is short & sassy & wears trousers; Higgs is tall & attractive, yet has boyfriend
trouble for three series before marrying and having husband trouble). No, these two
are wine-sleuths; fearlessly tracking down wines that even the locals are unaware of
and bringing them back to the precinct (of Denby Dale). As some wines are listed by
region alone or declassified, best try before you buy.

11	Nemea Kouros, 1988, D. Kourtakis S.A., Greece £3.95	

FSW Frank E Stainton ★★★

3. Berrys Yard, Finkle Street, Kendal Cumbria LA9 4AB (Tel 0539 731886). **Opening
Hours:** Mon-Sat 8:30a.m.-5:30p.m. **Delivery:** free locally, nationally at cost.
Tastings: regular in-store **Services:** cellarage, mail order, gift-mailing, glass hire.

It must be difficult for a wine merchant when deciding on stocks – does (s)he
concentrate on particular countries or regions? Should (s)he choose names that sell
well, wines that taste exquisite but are not cheap or good-value wines that come
from regions and producers no one has ever heard of? (Thinking) caps off to Mr
Stainton, who has developed the Odyssean ability to skirt the Scylla of overpricing
and Charybdis of unfamiliarity in his world-wide quest for value. From Alsace by
Hugel to Zinfandel by Ridge (and aalborg Akvavit to vodka). He might even find
you an accompaniment for Kendall's other speciality (but not the Yquem 1975).

1	Clover Hill Sparkling, Taltarni 1991,Tasmania, Australia £9.95
3	Tasmania Wine Company Chardonnay, 1993, Pipers Brook Vineyard Australia £8.25
3	Waipara Springs Chardonnay, 1992, South Island, New Zealand £9.49
3	Aldridge Estate Chardonnay, Cranswick Estate 1993, Australia £4.49
7	Riesling, 1990, Hugel, Alsace, France £7.95
12	Ch. Lamothe De Haux, 1990, Premières Côtes de Bordeaux, Fabrice Néel, Bordeaux, France £6.99
12	Simonsig Cabernet Sauvignon, 1988, South Africa £7.99
12	Simon Hackett Cabernet Sauvignon, 1992, Australia £6.49
13	Aldridge Estate Shiraz Cabernet, Cranswick Smith & Sons 1992, Australia £3.99
13	Ridge Zinfandel, 1990 Paso Robles, California £8.95
13	Hermitage 'La Chapelle', 1986, Jaboulet-Aîné, Rhône, France £22.50
17	Viña Real Rioja Reserva, 1986, CVNE, Spain £7.99
19	Ch. d'Yquem 1975, Sauternes, France, p.o.a.
20	Capataz Andres Cream, Emilio Lustau, Jerez, Spain £3.99

SUM Summerlee Wines Ltd ★★★★

64 High Street, Earls Barton, Northampton NN6 0JG (check code) (Tel 0604 810488).
No credit cards. **Opening Hours:** Mon-Fri 9am-1pm. **Delivery:** free locally (plus
London, Oxford and Cambridge) for two cases or more, nationally for five cases or
more. **Tastings:** occasional in-store. **Services:** cellarage, en primeur, mail order,
gift mailing, glass hire.

Freddy Price has sited his operation with his biggest customers in mind – the
Oxbridge colleges who buy Claret, Burgundy, Sancerre and Alsace and benefit from
his experience in, and enthusiasm for, German wine. Although, since Peterhouse

Senior Common Room recently spent time debating the installation of a sun-dial on the grounds of technological innovation, some dons may take a little persuading to drink hock until we've made peace with the Kaiser. But there's nothing old fashioned about the stock. Summerlee has the best of the new-wave Germans, with an emphasis on the Rieslings. Try Max Ferd Richter's Erdener Treppchen Riesling Kabinett and take a break from all those New World Chardonnays. Then, as an alternative to another merchant's anorexic German red or muscle-bound Barossa Shiraz, our tip is the well-defined Crozes-Hermitage from Domaine des Entrefaux.

1	Richter Estate Riesling Brut, 1990, Max-Ferd Richter, Mosel, Germany £10.49
8	Erdener Treppchen Riesling Kabinett, 1989, Max-Ferd Richter, Mosel, Germany £5.17
8	Brauneberger Juffer Riesling Auslese, 1990, Max-Ferd Richter, Mosel, Germany £11.31
12	Undurraga Cabernet Sauvignon, 1989, Maipo, Chile £4.50
13	Crozes-Hermitage, 1990, Domaine des Entrefaux, Rhône, France £8.97
15	Chassagne Montrachet Rouge Vieilles Vignes, 1990, Bernard Morey, Burgundy, France £13.34
19	Ch. Filhot, 1988, Sauternes, France £15.75
21	Croft 1963, £110.78 (Magnum)

DWL Sunday Times Wine Club ★★★

Paddock Road, Reading, RG4 0JY (Tel 0734 461953 'Customer services'). **Opening Hours:** (by telephone) Mon-Fri 9a.m.-7p.m., Sat-Sun 9a.m.-4p.m. **Delivery:** free for orders over £50. **Tastings:** National Tastings - next is 17-18 March, Westminster **Services:** mail order, gift-mailing.

Maybe value for money isn't everything. After all, we've never roasted some of the City traditionalists for charging more than Tesco. And the Sunday Times Wine Club *does* offer its members a very enjoyable annual tasting and lots of jolly bits of printed material. And the initiative of putting together 'discovery' cases through which novices can find their own way into wine. It's just that lots of these things are provided by other merchants whose lists are more exciting and prices keener.

3	Babich Chardonnay, 1992, New Zealand £7.80
4	Babich Semillon-Chardonnay, 1993, New Zealand £6.80
4	Babich Marlborough Sauvignon Blanc, 1993, New Zealand £7.25
12	Ch. Segonnes, 1991, Ch. Lascombes, Margaux, Bordeaux, France £9.00

T&W T & W Wines ★★★★

51 King Street, Thetford, Norfolk IP24 2AU (Tel 0842 765646). **Opening Hours:** Mon-Fri 9.30am-5.30pm, Sat 9.30am-1pm. **Delivery:** free locally, nationally at cost. **Tastings:** regular in-store **Services:** cellarage, en primeur, mail order, gift mailing, glass hire.

Fine and Rare Wine Merchant of the Year

Thetford is an unlikely candidate for vinous capital of the UK, but it should make the short-list. T&W Wines of King Street offer a simply extraordinary range of enticing examples from all of the best sources. Primarily a wholesale operation majoring on agencies, they also sell retail (although their prices are quoted exclusive of VAT). Alsace producers Trimbach and Hugel are listed extensively, many in half bottles, and including vintages from as far back as 1973. T&W are also agents for the wonderful sweet wines of Willi Opitz, and hold a fine range from Angelo Gaja, possibly the best and, certainly most expensive, producer in Piedmont. From

California there is a quirky mixture of top superstars featuring Silver Oak, Kent Rasmussen, Flora Springs and Duckhorn. The Rhône too is a bit of a hobby horse for Trevor Hughes; as well as Guigal and Jaboulet, you will find Bernard Gripa, Jean-Michel Gerin and Condrieus from Georges Vernay and Domaine Chèze. Rest assured, the Claret and Burgundy section is every bit as good and even more extensive.

6	Riesling Reserve, 1989, Trimbach, Alsace, France £11.69	
6	Condrieu, 1992, Domaine Georges Vernay, Rhône, France, £22.21	
12	Silver Oak Cabernet Sauvignon, 1989, California, £21.09	
13	Saint Joseph, 1991, Bernard Gripa, Rhône, France £12.69	
13	Côte Rôtie Les Grandes Places, 1991, JM Gerin, Rhône, France £26.79	
16	Rosso Conero Le Terazze, 1988, Marches, Italy £8.17	
19	Ch. Loupiac Gaudiet, 1990, France £10.05	
19	Blauberger Trockenbeerenauslese, 1991, Willi Opitz, £44.12 (half)	
20	Grahams 1979, Douro, Portugal £19.86	

TAN   Tanners Wines Ltd   ★★★★

26 Wyle Cop, Shrewbury, Shropshire SY1 1XD (Tel 0743 232400). **Opening Hours:** Mon-Sat 9am-6pm. **Delivery:** free locally, nationally at cost. **Tastings:** regular in-store, plus tutored sessions with the likes of Gerard Jaboulet, Ernst Loosen. **Services:** en primeur, mail order, gift mailing, glass hire, ice.

The Shrewsbury headquarters of this four-shop West Midlands chain is the Dickensian premises at Wyle Cop, ably reflecting the company's deep-seated rural tradition and history. Tanners' range of wines, hower, reveals this to have become one of the more modern country merchants, fully conversant with New World wines while keeping up with such go-ahead French producers as Château de Sours and Domaine de Limbardie. Of course claret and Mosel feature in abundance, as well as some excellent selections bottled under Tanner's own label (try the Champagne and sherry).

1	Tanners Cava Brut, Conde de Caralt, Spain £6.49	
4	Domaine des Salices Sauvignon Blanc, 1993, Vin de Pays d'Oc, J & F Lurton, South-West France £4.65	
8	Riesling Auslese Trocken, 1989, Weingut Schales, Rheinhessen, Germany £8.99	
11	Dom. Saint Martin de la Garrigue, Cuvée Reserve, 1991, France, £4.85	
11	Minervois Château Villerambert Julien, Cuvée Trianon, 1990, £7.45	
16	Barbera d'Alba, Luciano Sandrone, 1991, Piedmont, Italy £8.32	

CT   Charles Taylor   ★★★★

64, Alexandra Road, Epsom, Surrey KT17 4BZ (Tel 0372 728330). **Opening Hours:** Mon-Fri 9am-5pm **Delivery:** free locally, nationally for four cases or more). **Services:** en primeur, mail order.

Despite his comparative youth, Charles is a remarkably traditional off-the-peg Taylor. He'll have no truck with the meretricious cut favoured by some of his more fashion-conscious competitors. He prefers the styles which have stood the test of time: Loires, clarets and, above all, his first love: Burgundies from producers like Boyer-Martinot, Carillon and Ancien Domaine Auffray, Charlopin-Parizot, Rossignol Trapet and Bertrand Ambroise. Where he has listed man-made wines from the New World, have no fear, they are sufficiently soberly cut to satisfy the most conservative of tastes. Once again, Ruskin provides a fitting end (see Avery's q.v.).

1	Champagne Bonnet Carte Blanche Brut, France £12.50	

2	Saint-Aubin 1er Cru La Chatenière, 1992, Domaine Gérard Thomas Burgundy, France £9.50
2	Chablis 1er Cru Fourchaume, 1992, Ancien Domaine Auffray, Burgundy, France £11.00
2	Meursault 1er Cru Les Perrières, 1992, Domaine Yves Boyer-Martenot, Burgundy, France £15.50
3	Two Vineyards Chardonnay, 1993, Evans & Tate Australia £6.75
3	Ch. Thieuley Cuvée Francis Courselle, 1992, Bordeaux, France, £7.50
4	Pouilly Fumé, 1993, Domaine Jean Claude Chatelain, Loire, France £6.75
6	Riesling Grand Cru Rosacker, 1985, Domaine Jean-Luc Mader, Alsace, France £8.00
12	Ch. Tour Du Haut Moulin, 1989, Bordeaux, France £7.95
13	Hermitage Rouge, 1990, Domaine Marc Sorrel, Rhône, France, £16.00
15	Nuits St Georges, 1990, Domaine Bertrand Ambroise, Burgundy, France £12.50
19	Coteaux du Layon Rochefort Moelleux, 1990, Domaine de la Motte, Loire, France £9.00

TO   Tesco   ★★★★

Wines & Spirits Department, Tesco Stores Ltd, P.O. Box 18, Delamere Road, Cheshunt, Waltham Cross, Herts EN8 9SL (Tel 0992 632222). **Opening Hours:** vary. **Tastings:** occasional in (selected super)stores, tutored and organised events.

In the annual penalty shoot-out between Tesco and Sainsbury's, it is often almost impossible to compare the relative merits of a particular shot or save. Sainsbury's got to Calais first, but Tesco secured the better site. Sainsbury's introduced a red from Uruguay; Tesco brought in a made-to-measure wine from Brazil.

There's a lot going on in the background here. The Guide's editor has, for example, to declare an interest in appearing in an experimental touch-screen, food-and-wine-matching computer system which will go into a few stores at around the same time as this book hits the shelves. The mail-order service is building up nicely too, offering better value than many a specialist. Perhaps the greatest compliment paid to Tesco came from one of its suppliers: 'They buy keenly – they have to – but they really do their damndest to offer their customers the best value they can'.

1	Tesco Vintage Cava, Marquès de Monistrol, Spain £6.99
2	Tesco Mâcon Blanc Villages, 1993, Cave de Viré, Burgundy, France £4.49
2	Tesco Chablis, Cuvée Claude Dominique, 1992, Vaucher, Burgundy, France £5.99
2	Tesco White Burgundy, 1993, Cave de Viré, Burgundy, France £9.99
3	Tesco Western Australian Chenin Blanc, 1993, Moondah Brook, Australia £4.99
3	Tesco McLaren Vale Chardonnay, 1992, Ryecroft, Australia £5.99
4	Tesco Domaine Saint Alain, 1993, Vin de Pays de Côtes de Tarn Blanc, Alain Gayrel, South-West France £3.29
4	Tesco Californian Sauvignon Blanc, Stratford Winery, California £4.29
4	Tesco Sancerre, 1993, Alphonse Mellot, Loire, France £6.99
9	Tesco Golden Harvest, Zimmermann Graeff, 1992, £4.49
10	Tesco Californian White Zinfandel, Stratford Winery, California £4.29
11	Tesco Vin de Pays des Côtes de Gascogne Rouge, Yvon Mau, South-West France £2.89
11	Tesco Domaine Beaulieu St Saveur 1990, Côtes du Marmandais, Univitis, South-West France £3.49
11	Buzet. Domaine de la Croix, 1989, Vignerons de Buzet, South-West France £3.99
12	Tesco Cabernet Sauvignon, Lovico Suhindol, Bulgaria £2.89

12	Tesco Australian Cabernet Sauvignon, Mildara Blass, Australia £3.99
12	Tesco Vintage Claret, 1990, Yvon Mau, Bordeaux, France £4.79
12	Tesco Pauillac, Borie Manoux, 1990, Bordeaux, France £6.99
12	Tesco Margaux, Yvon Mau, 1990, Bordeaux, France £9.99
13	Tesco Australian Red Shiraz-Cabernet, Penfolds, Australia £2.99
13	Tesco Australian Mataro, Kingston Estate, Australia £5.99
13	Châteauneuf du Pape Rouge Les Arnevels, 1992, Vignobles Jerome Quiot, Rhône, France £7.99
16	Tesco Chianti Classico, 1992, Ampelos, San Casciano, Italy £3.99
17	Tesco Viña Maria Rioja Reserva, 1987, Bodegas Arisabel, Spain £4.99
18	Tesco Moscatel De Valencia, Gandia, Spain £2.99
19	Tesco Botrytis Semillon, 1992, Wilton Estate, Australia £6.99
20	Tesco Superior Manzanilla, Sanchez Romate, Jerez, Spain £2.99
20	Tesco Finest Solera Fino Sherry, Sanchez Romate, Jerez, Spain £4.99
21	Tesco LBV Port, Smith-Woodhouse, Douro, Portugal £6.59
21	Tesco Finest Madeira, Madeira Wine Co, Madeira £6.99
21	Tesco Australian Aged Tawny Liqueur Wine, Australia £7.49
21	Tesco 10 Year Old Tawny Port, Smith Woodhouse, Douro, Portugal £9.49

TH/TDS Thresher/Thresher Drink Stores ★★★★

Sefton House, 42 Church Road, Welwyn Garden City, Herts. AL8 6RJ (Tel 0707 328244). **Opening Hours:** Mon-Sat 9am-10pm, Sun 12-3pm, 7-10pm. **Delivery:** free locally, nationally at cost. **Tastings:** occasional in-store plus sessions for local organisations. **Services:** glass loan, ice.

After the publication of last year's Guide, we were taken to task for suggesting that there was even the tiniest smidgeon of confusion in the public mind between the corner beer 'n fag emporia which call themselves Thresher Drink Stores and the far more serious Thresher Wine Shops. Apparently, any such confusion was all in our journalistic imagination – which makes all the more surprising the recent trade survey which revealed the fourth most popular wine merchant in Britain to be Peter Dominic, a chain whose name disappeared from the high street two years ago.

As for the Wine Shops, these are the places which, through a festooning of blackboards, are beginning to look like Oddbins' less wayward cousin. If Wine Rack has slightly lost speed this year; Thresher has, if anything, slipped into a higher gear. At their best, these stores are like Michelin one-star restaurants – forever trying harder. The staff are better trained with every year and the range is generally good if rarely the cheapest in town. There are creditable innovations too, in the shape of food-and-wine matching lists and free taster sachets of particular promoted wines.

And even if you are clear on the difference between the two kinds of Thresher, don't be too sniffy about the Drink Stores; behind the Sol 'n Skol, you could find some pretty decent wine.

1	Champagne Piper Heidsieck Brut, £14.99
1	Champagne Francoise Descombes Grand Cru Vintage Brut, 1985, Le Mesnil, France, 1985, £19.75
2	Mâcon Villages, 1992, J.P. Bartier, Burgundy, France £3.99
2	Chablis Vieilles Vignes, 1991, La Chablisienne, Burgundy, France £7.89
3	Tollana Black Label Chardonnay, 1993, Penfolds, Australia £4.99
3	Marquès De Murrieta Rioja Reserva, 1987, Spain £7.69
3	Chassagne Montrachet, 1989, Louis Jadot, Burgundy, France £25.29
4	Le Cordon, Lot 39, Vin de Pays d'Oc Blanc, 1993, Gabriel Meffre, South-West France £3.99
4	Vouvray, Cuvée Des Fondraux, 1992, Champalou, Loire, France £6.85
4	Pouilly Fumé Domaine Buisson Menard, 1992, Didier Dagueneau, Loire, France £14.99

5	Viognier, Vin De Pays D'Oc, 1992, Fortant de France Collection, South-West France £6.95
5	Saint Joseph Blanc, 1992, Pierre Coursodon, Rhône, France £9.69
6	Gewürztraminer Herrenweg Turckheim, 1990, Zind Humbrecht, Alsace, France £12.99
6	Condrieu, 1992, Domaine Du Chêne, Rhône, France £15.29
7	Tollana Dry White, 1993, Penfolds, Australia £3.49
8	Riesling Reserve, 1991, Rolly-Gassmann, Alsace, France £8.29
9	Kreuznacher Bruckes Riesling Auslese, 1989, Schloss Von Plettenburg, Germany, £8.99
10	Domaine de l'Hortus, 1993, Côteaux du Languedoc, J Orliac, South-West France £4.99
11	Fitou Terroir De Tuchan, 1991, Tuchan, South-West France £7.55
12	Château Bonnet Reserve, 1992, Bordeaux, France £6.49
12	Clos du Marquis, 1988, St Julien, Ch. Léoville Lascases, Bordeaux, France £14.69
13	Penfolds Tollana Cabernet Shiraz, 1992, Australia £3.99
13	Sablet La Ramillade, 1991, Côtes du Rhône Villages, Ch. du Trignon, Rhône, France £5.85
13	Crozes-Hermitage, 1992, Domaine Barret, Rhône, France £6.99
13	Saint Joseph L'Olivaie, 1992, Pierre Coursodon, Rhône, France £11.29
13	Côte Rotie 1990, Domaine Gerin, Rhône, France £17.99
15	Hautes Côtes De Nuits, 1990, Cave Des Hautes Côtes, Burgundy, France 1990, £6.99
15	Palliser Estate Pinot Noir, 1991, New Zealand £9.99
15	Vosne Romanée, 1989, Domaine Jean Gros, Burgundy, France £20.99
15	Nuit St Georges Premier Cru Clos de l'Arlot, 1990, Domaine de l'Arlot, Burgundy, France £25.99
16	Chianti Classico Riserva, 1989, Villa Antinori, Tuscany, Italy £6.49
16	Le Volte, Tenuta dell'Ornellaia, 1992, Tuscany, Italy £7.99
17	Albor Rioja, 1992, Campo Viejo, Rioja, Spain £3.49
17	João Pato Tinto, Luis Pato, 1989, Portugal £6.39
17	Conde de Valdemar Rioja Gran Reserva, 1985, Martinez Bujanda, Rioja, Spain £10.49
19	Château Climens, 1991, Barsac, France £21.49
20	Don Cavala Pale Cream, Blazquez, Jerez, Spain £4.39
21	Skeffington Vintage Port, 1977, Douro, Portugal £19.99
21	Rutherford & Miles Jubilee Selection Verdelho, 1952, Madeira £69.00

TVW   Turville Valley Wines   ★★★★

The Firs, Potter Row, Great Missenden, Bucks, HP16 9LT (Tel 0494 868818). **Opening Hours:** Mon-Fri 9a.m.-5:30p.m. **Delivery:** free locally, nationally at cost. **Tastings:** n/a **Services:** cellarage, en primeur, mail-order.

Don't even think of coming here for Chilean Merlot or Côtes de Gascogne; they don't sell either. Turville Valley are strictly blue chip traders and brokers of fine wines who, in addition to the usual range of First Growth Claret, Grand Cru Burgundy and Vintage Port, also prove a useful source of such rarities as older vintages of Dominus, Penfold's Grange and Tignanello. The Yquems go back to 1861 and the list of vintage Madeiras is perhaps the most impressive ever. It is not clear how Turville managed to exhume and recruit Lord Kitchener, but his famous digit & moustache appear on page seven, demanding the conscription of your surplus wines (though not, we'd suggest, Chilean Merlot). Useful tip: wine lovers having difficulty with 21st birthday presents from the 1974 vintage should seek out Vega Sicilia Unico at £752 a case; it's one of the few European wines of real merit of that vintage which are still in good shape.

UBC   Ubiquitous Chip Wine Shop   ★★★★

8 Ashton Lane, Hillhead, Glasgow G12 8SJ (Tel 041 334 5007). **Opening Hours:** Mon-Fri 12-10pm, Sat 11am-10pm. **Delivery:** free locally for three cases or more. **Tastings:** occasional tutored tastings, sometimes followed by lunch/dinner in adjacent restaurant. **Services:** cellarage, mail order, glass loan.

Joint Scottish Wine Merchant of the Year

Please forgive us for indulging our interest in beer, but occasionally a chilled Chimay discovered at the back of the fridge at 2 am reaches parts denied to even the most insistent Chardonnay. The Chip Shop's Belgian Witbiers and an 8.5% brew named Skullsplitter may well be first in the shopping trolley, but they would quickly be followed by a Hunters Sauvignon and a bottle or two of Dr Prum's efficacious Wehlener Sonnenhur Riesling. Truly fine German wines, reliable and well-priced clarets and a better range of malt whiskies than the nineteenth hole of St Andrews Old Course make this more of an attraction than Charles Rennie Mackintosh's architecture.

3	Tim Adams Semillon, 1991, Australia £9.99	
4	Vendange Blanc, Vin de Pays des Cotes Catalanes, 1993, Les Vignerons du Roussillon, South-West France £3.95	
4	Soave Classico Superiore, 1993, Anselmi, Veneto, Italy £6.75	
12	Pikes Polish Hill Cabernet Sauvignon, 1991, Australia £8.10	
12	Newton Vineyards Cabernet Sauvignon, 1990, California £10.95	
16	Amarone, 1985, Le Ragose, Veneto, Italy £16.99	
16	Ser Gioveto, 1989, Rocca delle Macie, Tuscany, Italy £7.85	
16	Barolo Di Serralunga, 1988, Fontanafredda, Piedmont, Italy £9.50	
16	Cumaro, Umani Ronchi, 1990, Marches, Italy £9.95	
16	Roccato, 1990, Rocca delle Macie, Tuscany, Italy £8.99	

U   Unwins Wine Merchants   ★★★★

Birchwood House, Victoria Road, Dartford, Kent DA1 5AJ (Tel 0322 272711). **Opening Hours:** varies between: Mon–Fri 9am-10pm, Sat 9am-10.30pm, Sun 12-3pm, 7-10pm. **Delivery:** free locally. **Tastings:** regular in store, occasional tutored tastings. **Services:** mail order, gift mailing, glass hire, ice.

Something is happening at Unwins. Fresh from its 150th birthday, this chain looks rather like a suburban spinster who's just spent the day shopping for clothes in Covent Garden. The shops have been smartened up, the list is as modern and colourful as all but the best recent offerings from some of Unwins' neighbours and the range has been spruced up impressively too. More than one industry observer has suggested that the new wardrobe indicates that the family-owned company has marriage on its mind (we can think of at least a couple of potentially eager suitors).. For our part, we'd be sorry to see Unwins lose its identity; we need independent merchants like this, particularly now they're looking so good.

1	Duchatel Brut, A Thienot, 1985, Champagne, France £14.99	
3	Chardonnay, Cartlidge & Browne, California £4.99	
4	Frascati Superiore 'Tullio', 1993, San Marco, Latium, Italy £3.99	
5	Vouvray Demi-Sec, 1989, Ch. Moncontour, Loire, France £6.49	
6	Gewürztraminer Grand Cru Côtes du Brand, 1988, Cave de Turckheim Alsace, France £7.49	
11	Minervois, Domaine de L'Estagnol, 1992, Les Chais Beaucairois, South-West France £3.49	
12	Ch. Mingot, 1990, Côtes de Castillon, Yvon Mau, South France £4.99	
12	Ch la Tour de By, 1989, Médoc, Bordeaux, France £8.49	
13	Cartlidge & Browne Zinfandel, Stratford Winery, California £4.99	

14	Fleurie, 1993, Domaine Meziat, P. Dumont, Beaujolais, France £6.99
15	Pinot Noir, 1992, Bichot, Burgundy, France £5.49
15	Beaune 1er Cru Domaine de la Salle, 1991, Burgundy, France £10.99
16	Barbera Del Piemonte, 1992, Giordano, Piedmont, Italy £3.99
16	Rocca Suena, Amarone Recioto Della Valpolicella, 1986, Produttori Associati Soave, Veneto, Italy £8.49
16	Terre Brune, Santadi 1989, Italy £13.85
17	Borba, 1992, Adega, Portugal £3.99
17	Rioja Crianza, 1990, Faustino Rivero Ulecia, Rioja, Spain £4.79
21	Smith Woodhouse Tawny Port, Douro, Portugal £6.49

V&C Valvona & Crolla Ltd ★★★★

19 Elm Row, Edinburgh EH7 4AA (Tel 031 556 6066). **Opening Hours:** Mon, Tues, Wed, Sat 8.30am-6pm, Thurs, Fri 8.30am-7.30pm. **Delivery:** free locally, nationally at cost.**Tastings:** regular in-store, informal weekly tastings, plus yearly programme of tutored sessions. **Services:** mail order, gift mailing, glass hire.

If it's Italian and V&C don't stock it – you don't need it. With help that extends to all facets of Italian cooking as well as wine choice and a list that refreshes the parts 'O' level geography failed to reach, it's almost worth a trip nor'o'the border just to pick up a few bottles. It is always a tough decision to call the toss between them and Winecellars when choosing 'Italian Specialist of the Year'. So there's no brickbats for Philip Contini and ragazze in coming second this time in a very close race.

1	Gancia Pinot Di Pinot, Fratelli Gancia, Italy £5.99
3	Chardonnay 'Buchholz', 1992, Alois Lageder Alto Adige, Italy £7.99
3	Capitel Croce, 1991, Anselmi, Veneto, Italy £10.50
3	Where The Dreams Have No End, 1989 Jermann, F.V.G., Italy £29.50
4	Verdicchio 'Casal Di Serra', 1993, Umani Ronchi, Marches, Italy £5.99
4	Soave Classico Superiore, 1993, Anselmi, Veneto, Italy £6.75
12	Solaia, 1988, Antinori, Tuscany, Italy £47.00
16	Rosso Conero, Umani Ronchi, 1992, Marches, Italy £4.19
16	Ciro Rosso Classico, 1991, Librandi, Calabria, Italy £4.99
16	Ser Gioveto, Rocca Delle Macie, 1989, Tuscany, Italy £7.85
16	Aglianico Del Vulture Riserva, 1988, D'Angelo, Basilicata, Italy £8.65
16	Tignanello, 1990, Antinori, Tuscany, Italy £22.49
21	Morsi di Luce, 1990, Moscato De Pantelleria, Florio, Sicily £12.50

HVW Helen Verdcourt Wines ★★★★

Spring Cottage, Kimbers Lane, Maidenhead, Berks. SL6 2QP (Tel 0628 25577). wine by the case only. No credit cards. **Opening Hours:** anytime — with the help of the answerphone. **Delivery:** free locally, nationally at cost. **Tastings:** sessions arranged for local clubs. **Services:** cellarage, en primeur, mail order, gift mailing, glass hire.

With hardly a token wine in sight, Helen Verdcourt - one-woman-band, continues to satisfy a large audience of wine enthusiasts around her Maidenhead base – people who enjoy choosing from a fairly priced range which includes the Rhône wines of Château de Beaucastel, Vincent Girardin's Santenays, Paul Draper's Ridge Californians, and all things good and Australian. Life is not easy for merchants like Ms Verdcourt; since last year's Guide appeared, Gill Reynolds, with whom she shared the award for best Small Independent Merchant, has closed the doors of her shop, the Hermitage. Support Ms V. to protect her from the same fate.

12	Cyril Henschke Cabernet Sauvignon, Henschke, 1988, Australia £9.65
12	James Irvine Grand Merlot, 1989, Australia £14.99
13	Gigondas, Domaine Raspail Ay, 1990, Rhône, France £7.50
17	Rioja Eduardo Garrido Garcia, Viña Joven, 1991, Spain £4.25

VW Victoria Wine ★★★★

Brook House, Chertsey Road, Woking, Surrey GU21 5BE (Tel 0483 715066).
Opening Hours: varies between Mon–Sat 10am-10pm, Sun 12-3pm, 7-10pm.
Tastings: occasional in-store. **Services:** gift delivery (a bit like Interflora with bottles), glass hire, ice.

After several years when this subsidiary of the Allied Breweries never quite found a way to compete with the evidently more committed team at Threshers, Victoria Wine finally seems to have digested Augustus Barnett, the chain it bought last year, and sunk its incisors firmly into the bullet of serious wine retailing. The range looks better than ever (proportionally outscoring Thresher in the International Wine Challenge), prices are fair and the new Victoria Wine Cellars offer an appealingly approachable alternative to Wine Rack. Declaring an interest (the editor of the *Guide* appears in an Australian video given away in October 1994, free with bottles of wine) we have to say that Victoria Wine really should be a name to watch in 1995.

1	Champagne Paul D'Hurville Brut, Champagne de Hours, France £9.99
1	Victoria Wine Vintage Champagne, Marne et Champagne, 1986, £18.59
2	Victoria Wine Chablis, 1993, La Chablisienne, France £5.99
3	Basedows Barossa Valley Semillon, 1993, Australia £4.99
3	Moondah Brook Chenin Blanc, 1993, Hardy's, Australia £4.99
3	E & J Gallo Reserve Chardonnay, Northern Sonoma 1991, £19.99
4	Cuvée Madame Claude Parmentier sur Lie, Vin de Pays d'Oc Blanc, Les Producteurs Réunis, France £3.69
4	Cape View Sauvignon Blanc, 1993, Kym Milne, South Africa £4.29
9	Kiedricher Sandgrub Kabinett Riesling, 1988, Schloss E. Groenestyn Germany £6.29
9	Serriger Heiligenborn Riesling Spätlese, 1983, Germany £6.39
9	Trittenheimer Apotheke Riesling Auslese, Friedrich Wilhelm Gymnasium, Germany, 1988, £10.19
10	Ch. La Jaubertie Bergerac Rosé, 1993, Hugh Ryman, France £4.99
12	Ch. Vrai Caillou, 1989, M. Pommier, Bordeaux Supérieur, France £4.79
12	Krondorf Limited Release Cabernet Sauvignon, 1989, Australia £7.39
12	Corbans Private Bin Merlot, 1992, Australia £8.99
12	Domaine de Bigarnon, St Julien, Ch. Léoville Las Cases, 1983, Bordeaux, France £12.99
12	Château Latour, 1983, Pauillac, France £59.49
13	Santa Julia Argentinian Red, La Agricola, Argentina £3.59
13	Penfolds Woodford Hill Cabernet/Shiraz, 1993, Australia £3.99
13	Stratford Zinfandel, Stratford Winery, California £4.69
13	Rothbury Shiraz, 1991, Australia £6.99
13	Ch. de Vaudieu Châteauneuf-du-Pape, 1992, Gabriel Meffre, Rhône, France £8.59
15	Stratford Pinot Noir, California £4.99
16	Barolo Terre Del Barolo, 1988, Terre De Barolo, Italy £6.99
16	Chianti Classico Riserva di Fizzano, 1987, Rocca Dell Macie, Italy £8.99
17	Leziria Red, Adega Co-Op De Almeirim, 1993, Portugal £2.59
17	Jumilla, Carchelo 1990, Spain £3.59
17	Chivite Reserva, Chivite, 1989, Spain £4.49
18	Muscat de Rivesaltes Mimosas, 1990, Salses le Château, France £2.99
19	Stellenzicht Weisser Riesling Noble Late Harvest, 1992, South Africa £3.99
19	Les Cypres de Climens, 1984, Ch.Climens, Sauternes, France £10.29
21	Starboard Batch 88, Quady, California £4.99
21	Quinta Da Eira Velha, Martinez Gassiot, 1987, Douro, Portugal £14.99
21	Fonseca Vintage Port, 1985, Douro, Portugal £21.15
21	Quinta Do Noval Vintage Port, 1975, Douro, Portugal £22.69
21	Warre's Vintage Port, 1983, Douro, Portugal £22.79

LV   La Vigneronne Fine Wines Ltd   ★★★★

105 Old Brompton Road, London SW7 3LE (Tel 071-589 6113). **Opening Hours:** Mon-Fri 10am-9pm, Sat 10am-7pm. **Delivery:** free locally, nationally at cost. **Tastings:** regular in-store plus an average of two evening tutored sessions given by Liz Berry MW. **Services:** cellarage, en primeur, mail order, gift mailing.

Liz and Mike Berry's small shop on the Old Brompton Road has become as much of an institution as the nearby Conran shop. And for much the same reasons. Neither has ever been the place to look for a bargain; both have excelled at the art of offering something stylish & desirably different. Unlike Tel's store, though, this shop doesn't limit itself to the up-to-the-minute. Here, there's the opportunity both in the shop and at tutored tastings, to compare such wines as current Mondavis with ones which were harvested when Habitat was still trying to persuade us to be brave enough to have a non-chrome loo roll holder. Whatever the age of each individual bottle, the selection of Loires, Rhônes, Alsaces, French country & New World wines is stunning.

4	Mas Jullien Les Vignes Oubliées, Coteaux de Languedoc Blanc, Olivier Jullien, 1992, France £8.95
4	Vouvray Sec Aigle Blanc, Prince Poniatowski, 1985, Loire, France £8.95
4	Kritt Klevner, Marc Kreydenweiss, 1992, Alsace, France £9.95
5	Vouvray Aigle Blanc Vin de Tris, Prince Philippe Poniatowski, 1989, Loire, France £16.95
6	Tokay Pinot Gris Grand Cru Moenchberg Vendages Tardives, Marc Kreydenweiss, 1992, Alsace, France £13.95

VDV   Vin du Vin   ★★★★

Colthups, The Street, Appledore, Kent TN26 2BX (Tel 0233 758 727). **Opening hours:** Mon-Sun 9am-6pm. **Delivery:** free locally, nationally at cost. **Services:** mail order, gift mailing.

Do not even think of asking for Piat d'Or - unless you really want to take up the offer of a pointer towards 'something further up the evolutionary ladder'. This quote comes directly from their Aussie-packed list, which has a much in common with other merchants' offerings as 'Have I Got News for You' has with the 'Nine O'Clock News'. Irreverent but by no means irrelevant, we'd love to know what mind-altering substance they took before writing it; our money's on The Grange 1983.

1	Yalumba Cuvée Prestige Sparkling Cabernet, Australia £8.75
3	Botobolar Organic Marsanne, 1992, Australia £6.75
4	David Wynn Dry White, 1992, South Eastern Australia £4.40
4	Jackson Estate Sauvignon, 1993, New Zealand £6.75
6	Mount Langi Ghiran Riesling, 1993, Australia £5.95
12	Ryecroft Flame Trees Cabernet/Merlot, 1992, £3.99
13	Charles Melton Nine Popes, 1992, Australia £8.85
13	Yarra Yering Underhill Shiraz, 1990, Australia £15.95
13	Penfolds Grange Bin 95, 1983, Australia £49.95
17	Torres Gran Coronas Reserva, 1987, Spain £6.99

VER   Vinceremos Wines & Spirits   ★★★

65 Raglan Road, Leeds LS2 9DZ (Tel 0532 431691). Wine by the case only. **Opening hours:** Mon-Fri 9am-5.30pm, Sat: occasionally open – call first. **Delivery:** free locally, nationally at cost. **Tastings:** two a year in Leeds: call for details of events elsewhere. **Services:** mail order, glass hire (locally).

Jem & Jerry are purveyors of organic and vegetarian wine and therefore not to be mistaken for Ben & Jerry, purveyors of ice-cream. This is not to say that the same 'feel-good factor' cannot be shared between the two. Vinceremos show that no cork has been left unpulled in the quest for quality organic wines, and their list reads like a Body Shop guide to right-on countries of the world. All we're waiting for now is for the new South Africa to join Morocco, Zimbabwe and the Ukraine.

3	Millton Vineyard, Chenin Blanc, 1992, New Zealand £5.99
4	Czech Dry White, Nick Butler, Vinium , 1993, Czech Republic £2.05
6	Jacques Frelin, Costières de Nîmes Viognier, Jacques Frelin, 1993, South France, £5.99
6	Gewürztraminer Grand Cru Steinert, 1992, Pierre Frick, Alsace, France £8.75
11	Domaine du Soleil, 1993, Vegetarian Syrah, Vin de Pays de L'Aude, France £3.49
11	Ch. les Pins, 1991, Côtes de Roussillon Villages, France £4.99
13	Domaine Richeaume Syrah, 1992, South-West France £7.99
19	Tokay 5 Puttonyus, 1988, Interconsult, Hungary £6.49

VR   Vintage Roots   ★★★★

Sheeplands Farm, Wargrave Road, Wargrave, Berks. RG10 8DT (Tel: 0734 401222). **Opening Hours:** Mon-Fri 9am-6pm, plus answerphone. **Delivery:** free locally, nationally at cost. **Tastings:** occasional in-store. **Services:** mail order, gift mailing, glass hire.

Organic wine is set to become the politically correct tipple of New Age Aqua Librans and the population of Islington and Hampstead, not to mention the genuinely sulphur-sensitive. Messrs Palmer, Piggott and Ms Belsh's Wargrave store does for experiment with green wine what Fergie and David Mellor did for toes.

2	Petit-Chablis, 1993, Jean Goulley et Fils, Burgundy, France £8.00
3	Puligny-Montrachet, 1992, Guyot et Fils, Burgundy, France £14.35
11	Ch. Roubia Minervois, 1991, SCEA Mestre Grotti, France £4.25
12	Ch. Pouchaud-Larquey, 1990, M Piva, France £5.60
14	Morgon, 1991, Gerard Belaid, Beaujolais, France £7.25
15	Beaune, 1992, Jean-Claude Râteau, Burgundy, France £13.50

W   Waitrose   ★★★★

Doncastle Road, Southern Industrial Area, Bracknell, Berkshire RG12 4YA (Tel 0344 4244680). **Opening hours:** vary from store to store. **Tastings:** occasionally.

The commercialisation of Waitrose continues apace. This year, for example, the chain which famously never even allowed itself to advertise its wares, rather like a shy monarch meeting his subjects, went so far as to participate in the BBC Good Food Show at Olympia. By all accounts the experience was enjoyed by all concerned. With its combination of range and trained staff, Waitrose probably remains the supermarket with the most loyal wine-loving customers.

1	Comtesse de Die Clairette de Die Tradition, 1992, Cave Cooperaive de Die, France £5.95
1	Krone Borealis Brut, 1988, Twee Jonge Gezellen, South Africa £7.95
2	White Burgundy, 1992, M. Michelet & Fils, Burgundy, France £4.99
2	Mercurey Blanc Tastevinage, 1992, J C Boisset, Burgundy, France £7.75
3	Backsberg Chardonnay, 1992, Paarl, South Africa £5.95
4	Vin du Pays Du Gers Blanc, 1993, Producteurs Plaimont, South-West France £2.99
4	Dom.des Fontanelles, Vin de Pays d'Oc, 1993, Foncalieu, South-West France £3.49

4	Sauvignon de Touraine, 1993, Domaine Gibault, Loire, France £3.99
6	Santa Julia Torrontes Riojano, La Agricola, 1993, Argentina £3.75
6	Tokay Pinot Gris, 1992, Blanck Frères, Alsace, France £5.25
11	Domaine de Beausejour, 1992, Archambault, France £3.45
12	Waitrose Good Ordinary Claret, Ginestet, Bordeaux, France £2.99
12	Santa Julia Malbeck, La Agricola, Argentina £3.75
12	Ch. Segonzac, 1990, Première Côte de Bordeaux, France £4.95
13	Cartlidge & Browne Zinfandel, Stratford Winery, California £4.35
13	Fairview Shiraz Reserve, 1991, Australia £5.95
20	Waitrose Montilla Cream, Perez Barquero, Jerez, Spain £2.99
20	Waitrose Cream Sherry, Antonio Romero, Jerez, Spain £4.35
20	Waitrose Fino Sherry, Luis Caballero SA, Jerez, Spain £4.35
21	Waitrose 10 year Old Tawny, Skeffington, Douro, Portugal £10.45

WAW   Waterloo Wine Co Ltd   ★★★★

59-61 Lant Street, Borough, London SE1 1QL (Tel 071-403 7967). **Opening Hours:**
Mon–Fri 10am-6.30pm, Sat 10am-5pm. **Delivery:** free very locally, nationally at cost.
Tastings: regular in-store and tutored sessions on request. **Services:** glass
hire, ice.

Appropriately located in Vine Yard, London SE1. Waterloo imports a remarkably
well chosen bunch of wines, including Champagne from Le Brun de Neuville, the
stunning Stoniers reds and whites from Australia and the wines of Central Otago's
Waipara Springs from New Zealand. That is, of course, besides a really strong
selection of Loire including Mme de Jessey's Savennières and a number of wines
from Couly Dutheil and Gaston Huet. No Napoleon brandy though.

1	Champagne Le Brun de Neuville Blanc de Blanc, France £13.99
3	Waipara Springs Chardonnay, 1992, New Zealand £9.49
10	Domaine La Tour Boisee Rosé, 1993, Domaine La Tour Boisee, South-West France £3.75
11	Corbières, Ch. Hélène, 1989, Cuvée Hélène de Troie, South-West France £6.81
15	Stoniers Pinot Noir, 1992, Victoria, Australia £7.50
16	Dolcetto D'Alba, 1992, Aurelio Settimo, Italy £5.55

WAC   Waters of Coventry   ★★★

Collins Road, Heathcote, Warwick, Warwickshire CV34 6TF (Tel 0926 888889).
Opening hours: Mon–Fri 9am.-5pm, Sat 9am.-12.30pm **Delivery:** free within 30
miles. **Tastings:** occasional in-store. **Services:** glass loan, ice.

Perhaps this by-the-case merchant might consider renaming itself the Warwick Wine
Shop, as they relocated a year or two ago. Robert Caldicott has gone in at the deep
end with his choice of New World wine with a good range from Australia, New
Zealand and California. We'd be happy with any of those but would be just as happy
to splash out on one of his selections from regional France. A very passable merchant.

1	Clover Hill Sparkling, 1991, Taltarni, Australia £9.99
4	Vouvray Sec Aigle Blanc, 1985, Prince Philippe Poniatowski, Loire, France, £8.95
4	Vouvray Clos Baudoin, 1992, Prince Philippe Poniatowski, Loire, France £9.50
5	Vouvray Aigle Blanc Vin de Tris, 1989, Prince Philippe Poniatowski, Loire, France £16.95
12	Caliboro Cabernet Sauvignon, 1993, Vina Segu-Olle, Chile £3.89
14	Fleurie Domaine des Quatre Vents, 1993, Georges Duboeuf, Beaujolais, France £6.00

WES Wessex Wines ★★★

197 St Andrews Road, Bridport, Dorset DT6 3BT (0308 423400); Wine Warehouse: Unit 88, St Michaels Estate, Bridport, Dorset D16 3RR. Wine by the case only. **Opening Hours:** Mon–Sat 9am-12.30pm, Sun 'on call'. **Tastings:** regular in-warehouse, plans for tutored tastings. **Services:** gift mailing, glass hire, ice.

Mike Farmer continues to gather in a crop of dependable wines from often unfamiliar sources, as anyone who ploughs their way through this list will discover. Wines like Tarrawarra Pinot Noir and Niepoort port are far from commonplace. Surprisingly, the Australian list contains nothing from the locally-apt Thomas Hardy, though that pioneer's McLaren Vale is well represented by Blewitt Springs. Value throughout is good and you have to make an effort to spend over a tenner.

13	Ryecroft Flame Tree, Shiraz, 1992, Australia £5.36	
15	Hamilton Russell Pinot Noir, 1992, South Africa £6.99	
15	Tarrawarra Tunnel Hill Pinot Noir, 1990, Australia £7.69	
21	Niepoort Colheita Port, 1980, Douro, Portugal £12.79	

WHC Whiclar & Gordon Wines Ltd

See Dorking Cellars

WWT Whitebridge Wines ★★★

Unit 21, Whitebridge Estate, Stone, Staffs ST15 8LQ (Tel 0785 817229). **Opening hours:** Mon-Fri 9am-5:30pm, Sat 9:30am.-1pm **Delivery:** free locally, nationally at cost. **Tastings:** regular in-store. **Services:** mail order, gift-mailing, glass hire.

If you want a taste of the wine produced in England's most northern vineyard at Halfpenny Green, this is the place to come. Whitebridge likes to support its local growers, but it's pretty supportive towards its customers too, bringing many prices down over the last year while expanding the range. All the basics are here, but there are sufficient unusual wines for anyone with a spirit of adventure not to need them.

2	Chablis 1er Cru Fourchaume, 1990, La Chablisienne, France £9.70	
8	Brown Brothers King Valley Riesling, 1993, Australia £5.99	
11	Ch. Pech de Jammes, Cahors, 1989, South-West France £7.99	
13	Foppiano Petite Sirah, 1990, California £7.99	
15	Carneros Creek Pinot Noir, 1991, Los Carneros, California £11.99	
17	Berberana Rioja Gran Reserva, 1975, Spain £11.99	
18	Brown Brothers Liqueur Muscat, Australia £8.99	
18	Muscat Beaumes de Venise, 1992, Vidal-Fleury, Rhône, France £15.95	
21	Bailey's Founder Liqueur Tokay, Australia £9.95	
21	Quarles Harris 20 Year Old Tawny Port, Douro, Portugal £9.99	

WOC Whitesides of Clitheroe Ltd ★★★★

Shawbridge Street, Clitheroe, Lancs. BB7 1NA (Tel 0200 22281). **Opening Hours:** Mon-Sat 9am-5.30pm. **Delivery:** free locally, nationally at cost. **Tastings:** regular in-store. **Services:** gift mailing, glass hire.

What is it about this one-horse, two wine merchant town? There are hundreds of places all round the country full of thirsty residents who'd love to have a wine merchant half as good as Whitesides or David Byrne (qv), but there you go. Life's like that. Once again, we appreciate the helpful notes alongside wines on the list such as 'Excellent', 'Good Value' and 'Fruity Style', though are less certain about the 'Well Presented' De Venoge pink fizz. As the selection below shows however, finding good wines here could not be easier.

1	Green Point Vintage Brut, Australia £10.45
2	Chablis 1er Cru Vaudevey, 1990, Laroche, Burgundy, France £10.75
3	Babich Hawke's Bay Chardonnay, 1992, New Zealand £7.25
3	Willespie Margaret River Verdelho, 1990, Australia £5.99
8	Hochheimer Konigin Victoriaberg Kabinett, 1989, Deinhard, Germany £9.49
15	Beaune 1er Cru les Teurons, 1987, Jacques Germain, Burgundy, France £18.50
16	Amarone della Valpolicella Classico, 1986, Allegrini, Italy £11.05
17	Campo Viejo Gran Reserva 1981, Spain £7.89

WDW   Windrush Wines Ltd   ★★★★

The Ox House, Market Square, Northleach, Cheltenham, Glos. GL54 3EG (Tel 0451 860680). **Opening Hours:** Mon--Fri 10am-8pm, Sat 10-7pm, Sun 12-2pm. **Delivery:** free locally, nationally for five cases or more. **Tastings:** regular in-store plus special sessions on request. **Services:** mail order, glass hire.

Despite the departure of Mark Savage MW and their installation into what was the Hungerford Wine Company's eponymous headquarters, this Cheltenham merchant continues to offer a well-thought-out list of reliable wines with such gems as Ceppi Storici Barbera, Ponzi from Oregon, Sonoma's Laurel Glen and Quinta de la Rosa from the Douro as well as five wines from Jurançon and a selection of six cuvées of Bandol from Domaine Tempier.

3	Montes Nogales Estate Chardonnay, 1994, Chile £5.49
17	Yllera Tinto, 1990, S.A.T. Los Curros, Spain £6.75
18	Malaga, Moscatel Palido, Scholtz Hermanos, Spain £7.85
21	Churchill's Port, Quinta da Agua Alta, 1987, Douro, Portugal £14.50

CRL   The Wine Centre/Charles Steevenson   ★★★

Russell Street, Tavistock, Devon PL19 8BD (Tel 0822 615985). **Opening hours:** Mon-Sat 9am-7pm **Delivery:** free locally, nationally at cost. **Tastings:** tutored tastings at cost on group request **Services:** cellarage, gift-mailing, glass hire, ice.

Charles Steevenson (whose name we, unlike his local newspaper, have spelled correctly) blends wholesale and retail wine selling seemlessly. He produces no retail list because the range in the shop changes so frequently, but we'd be happy to walk in and find any of the following selection we have chosen from his current stock.

4	Domaine Hilaire, 1993, Côtes de Gascogne, France £3.59
12	Mas de Daumas Gassac Rouge, 1990 Midi, France £10.99
13	Domaine Font de Michelle, Chateauneuf-du-Pape, 1991, £10.49
13	St Joseph, les Larmes du Père, Alain Paret 1991, France £7.49

WR   Wine Rack   ★★★★

Sefton House, 42 Church Road, Welwyn Garden City, Herts. AL8 6RJ (Tel 0707 328244). **Opening hours:** Mon-Sat 9am-10pm, Sun 12-3pm, 7-10pm. **Delivery:** free whenever possible. **Tastings:** occasional in-store plus special sessions for local organisations. **Services:** glass loan, ice.

After winning the big prize of Wine Merchant of the Year twice running, this, the up-market niche of the Thresher empire had a lot to play for this year. Before going any further, we have to stress that this remains a first class place to buy wine. If you have one nearby, you should count yourself lucky. But... this year there was a distinct feeling that it wasn't quite on top of its game. It's all very well listing a dazzling

252 Merchants

range, but rather less use if customers wanting three bottles of a particular wine in a hurry have to visit two or three branches to find them. Oddbins manages to stock the wines it lists. Prices are another concern. The 1989 Volnay Champans from the domaine de la Pousse d'Or is a nice wine. It is not a £31.50 nice wine. These criticisms aside, the staff are generally well-informed and when questions reveal gaps in the encyclopedic 'Book of Knowledge' they have all been given, they do their best to satisfy even the trickiest customer. (See also wines listed under Threshers.)

1	Champagne Moët & Chandon Brut Imperial Vintage, 1986, France £22.99
1	Dom Perignon, 1985, Moet et Chandon, France £56.80
2	Chablis Premier Cru Vaillons, 1990, Louis Michel & Fils, France £10.99
3	Vavasour Oak-Aged Sauvignon Blanc, 1993, New Zealand £9.99
3	Hermitage Blanc, 1991, Guigal, Rhône, France £16.99
3	Chassagne Montrachet, 1989, Louis Jadot, Burgundy, France £25.29
4	Hunters Sauvignon Blanc, 1993, New Zealand £9.49
7	Valley Vineyards Hinton Grove, 1993, Thames Valley Vineyard 1993, England £4.99
8	Riesling Turckheim, 1990, Zind Humbrecht, Alsace, France £9.39
10	Esk Valley Merlot/Cabernet Franc Dry Rosé, 1992, New Zealand £6.49
11	Madiran, Montus, 1991, Brumont, South-West France £9.50
11	Beenleigh Cabernet Sauvignon/Merlot, 1991, England £12.75
12	Lindemans Pyrus, 1991, Australia £9.99
12	Les Tourelles De Longueville, 1989, Pauillac, France £15.99
13	Chateau Grand Prebois, 1992, Perrin, Rhône, France £5.79
13	St Hallett's Old Block Shiraz 1991, £9.49
14	St Amour, Domaine Pirollette, 1992, Duboeuf, Beaujolais, France £6.99
15	Vosne Romanée, 1989, Domaine Jean Gros, Burgundy, France £20.99
17	Bairrada, 1990, Luis Pato, Portugal £6.99
19	Pilton Manor West Holme, 1992, England £14.95
21	Cossart Gordon 5 Year Old Malmsey, Madeira, £10.99
21	Blandys Vintage Bual 1954, Madeira, £65.00

WSC The Wine Schoppen Ltd ★★★★

1, Abbeydale Road South, Sheffield S7 2QL (Tel 0742 365684). **Opening hours:** Mon-Fri 9:30a.m.-6p.m., Sat 9a.m.-5p.m. **Delivery:** free locally, nationally at cost. **Tastings:** regular in-store, plus wine-tasting circle. **Services:** cellarage, mail order, gift-mailing, glass hire, ice.

Germany is the real speciality of this Sheffield Shipper and Merchant as the moniker might suggest. If the Mosel selection looks a little thin on the ground, it is only by comparison to the massive range from the Rhine and Franken. There is no better place in Britain for anyone who wants to learn more about Germany's various regions and styles. Other countries are well served, though in a slightly eccentric manner; there are as many wines on offer from Russia as there are from Australia.

1	Deutscher Sekt Privat, Germany £7.00
8	Alte Vogtei, Kabinett, 1990, Franken, Germany £4.00
8	Binger St Rochuskapelle Kabinett, 1993, Rheinhessen, Germany £3.10
8	Boetzinger Kaiserstuhl Silvaner (Organic), 1991, Weingut Zimmerlin, Baden, Germany £4.00
8	Forster Stift Riesling Auslese, 1989, Rheinpfalz, Germany £7.00
8	Schlossböckelheimer Kupfergrube Riesling Kabinett 1989, Nahe, Germany £10.00
8	Walporzheimer Klosterberg, QbA, 1990, Ahr, Germany £5.29
11	Unteruerkheimer Herzogenberg, 1990, Wurttemburg, Germany £6.00
21	Churchill's Finest Vintage Character Port, Douro, Portugal £8.99
21	Churchill's Quinta da Agua Alta Port, 1987, Douro, Portugal £14.50

WSO The Wine Society ★★★★★

Gunnels Wood Road, Stevenage, Hertfordshire SG1 2BG (Tel 0438 741177 - Enquiries; 0438 740222 - Orders). **Opening hours:** Mon-Fri 9am-5:30pm, Sat 9am-1pm **Delivery:** free nationally. **Tastings:** regular in-store and tutored, plus organised events and customers' club. **Services:** en primeur, cellarage, mail order, glass hire.

Bordeaux Specialist Wine Merchant of the Year

There is something wonderfully English about The Wine Society. On the one hand, it's non-profitable (what could be more English than that?); on the other it embodies a spirit of exploration. So members who want to find out what happens beyond the Old World are led through the list, regular mailings & tastings to obscure corners of the New one such as Wirra Wirra. The Society was also, it should be remembered, the first British wine merchant to plant itself on Gallic soil – with such success that it has had to expand its Hesdin operation to cope with unexpected demand.

1	Champagne Alfred Gratien Brut, 1985, France £19.50
2	Chablis Grand Cru Vaudésir, 1992, Domaine Des Malandes, Burgundy, France £15.50
2	The Society's White Burgundy, Mâcon Villages, 1992, Jacques Depagneux, Burgundy, France £4.95
2	Chablis Grand Cru 'Les Clos', 1992, Moreau Burgundy, France £10.90
3	Wirra Wirra Chardonnay, 1992, Australia £8.49
3	Hunter's Oak-Aged Sauvignon Blanc, 1992, New Zealand £9.99
3	Navajas Rioja Blanco Crianza, 1989, Spain £5.99
4	Marquès de Alella Classico 1993, Spain £5.99
12	The Angelus Cabernet Sauvignon, 1992, Wirra Wirra, Australia £9.00
12	Ch. Carteau, Saint-Emilion Grand Cru, 1989, France £9.25
12	Clos Du Val Cabernet Sauvignon, 1989, California £12.75
13	Rockford Basket Press Shiraz, 1990, Australia £9.99
13	Lindemans Bin 50 Shiraz, 1992, Australia £4.99
15	Pinot Noir, Domaine Parent, 1990, Burgundy, France £6.95
15	Saintsbury Pinot Noir 1992, California £11.00
17	Navajas Rioja Tinto Crianza, 1989, Spain £5.99
17	Tinto Callejo Ribera del Duero Crianza, 1989, Felix Callejo, Spain £7.40
20	Malaga Solera 1885, Scholtz Hermanos S.A., Spain £8.49
20	Viejo Oloroso Dulce 30 Year Old, Valdespino, Jerez, Spain £7.95
21	The Society's Celebration 20 Year Old Tawny Port, Martinez Gassiot Douro, Portugal £13.50
21	Churchill's Traditional LBV, 1988, Douro, Portugal £9.99

WLA Wine Talk of Lytham St Annes ★★★

50 Wood Street, Lytham St Annes FY8 1QS (Tel 0253 714140). **Opening hours:** Mon-Sat 10am-6pm. Sun 12am-2pm. **Delivery:** free locally, nationally at cost. **Tastings:** regularly in store, plus the annual wine festival. **Services:** glass hire.

Until the sale of Peter Dominic to Thresher, John Dunkerley was manager of the former chain's branch in this quiet town just down the coast from Blackpool, the resort where wine lovers wear 'Taste-Me-Quick' hats. Now, local residents have the choice of buying their wine in Mr D's old shop or in the one he started up himself. Having watched large numbers of them enjoy themselves sipping their way through the range at the Dunkerley-organised wine festival, we readily understand their loyalty. Italy, France and Australia are the strongest sections of the range but there are no real areas of weakness.

11	Ch. de Lastours, 1986, Corbières, France £18.99

12	Ch. de Pez, 1986, St Estephe, Bordeaux, France, £12.99
15	Vosne Romanée, 1989, Daniel Rion, Burgundy, France £19.99
16	Barolo Montanello, 1970, Piedmont, Italy £14.99

WTR The Wine Treasury ★★★★

899-901 Fulham Road, London SW6 5HU (Tel 071-371 7131). **Opening hours:** Mon-Sat 11am-9pm, Sun 12-3pm. **Delivery:** free locally, nationally at cost. **Tastings:** regular in-store, currently developing wine courses. **Services:** cellarage, en primeur, mail order, gift mailing, glass hire, ice.

Arising phoenix-like from the ashes of the Fulham Road Wine Centre, The Wine Treasury has upped sticks from Pimlico to offer Fulhamites serious Burgundies (with help from ex-Windrush boss, Mark Savage) top Californians and cheerful, knowledgeable service. Additionally, it houses Halves, Tim Jackson's less-than-pint-sized company with one of the country's best range of half bottles. Look out in particular for the selections of port, Burgundy, Bordeaux (red and white), Italians, Californians and the excellent Chinon from Couly-Dutheuil. Remember, however though that half bottles are just about the least economical way to buy wine, so don't expect any bargains. The Treasury is also planning to restart the previous tenant's highly-regarded wine courses and will even deliver a single bottle (locally) in the evening without charge. Yes, we were amazed too!

3	Penley Estate Chardonnay, 1992, Coonawarra, Australia £8.85
3	Dalwhinnie Chardonnay, 1992, California £12.49
5	St Péray, Marcel Juge, 1992, Rhone France £9.99
6	Gewürztraminer Grand Cru Steinert, 1988, Joseph Riefle, Alsace, France £9.79
11	Les Chemins de Bassac Vin de Pays d'Oc Rouge, 1992, Isabelle & Remi Ducellier, South-West France £5.89
12	Petroso Merlot, Vigneto Delle Terre Rosse, 1990, Italy £8.49
12	Shafer Merlot, 1991, California £11.99
13	Cornas Cuvée 'SC', 1991, Marcel Juge, Rhône, France £13.99
13	Côte Rôtie Champin Le Seigneur, 1991, Gerin, Rhône, France £15.99
15	Olivet Lane Russian River Pinot Noir, 1992, Pellegrini Family Vineyards, California £8.99
15	Morey-St-Denis 'En la Rue de Vergy', 1990, Domaine Henri Perrot-Minot Burgundy, France £13.89

WCE Winecellars ★★★★★

153-155 Wandsworth High Street, London SW18 4JB (081-871 3979) **Opening Hours:** Mon–Fri 11.30-8.30pm, Sat 10am-8.30pm. **Tastings:** regular in-store, plus tutored tastings and dinners. **Services:** gift mailing, glass hire, ice.

Italian Specialist Wine Merchant of the Year

When the news broke that one of British Italophiles' two favourite haunts had been taken over by a wholesaler, there was, if not a wailing and a gnashing of teeth, a serious worry that Winecellars would close its doors. For a while, all sorts of southerners began to consult their atlases to check the whereabouts of Valvona & Crolla's Edinburgh base. Well, fortunately, Enotria, the wholesaler in question have turned out to be as ideal a partner as Winecellars could have wished for. Today the Italian list continues to grow and improve, deftly sidestepping the traps of hype and misplaced historic reverence, introducing countless people to the extraordinary range of flavours to be found from one end of Italy to the other.

But, as Winecellars fans know, Italy is only part of the story. Over the last few years, Messrs Belfrage, Gleave and Brown have built up a impressive ranges of wines from Australia and the Rhône. Very much an all-round specialist.

1	Asti Spumante, Araldica, Italy £5.99
4	Pinot Grigio, Collio, 1993, Enofriulia Italy £6.89
4	Shaw & Smith Sauvignon Blanc, 1993, Australia £7.99
4	Poggio alle Gazze, 1992, Tenuta dell'Ornellaia, Italy £9.79
5	Soave Superiore, Vigneto Calvarino, 1992, Pieropan, Italy £7.59
8	Mount Langi Ghiran Riesling, 1993, Australia £5.99
12	Salisbury Estate Show Reserve Cabernet, 1992, Australia £6.99
12	Ornellaia, 1991, Vino da Tavola, Tuscany, Italy £22.79
16	Salice Salentino, 1989, Candido, Italy £4.99
16	Chianti Rufina Riserva, 1990, Villa Di Vetrice, Tuscany, Italy £4.99
16	Ceppi Storici Barbera d'Asti, 1991, Araldica, Piedmont, Italy £4.99
16	Parrina Rosso Riserva, La Parrina, 1990, Italy £6.99
16	La Grola Valpolicella, 1990, Allegrini, Veneto, Italy £8.99
16	Barolo, 1990, Ascheri, Italy £9.39
16	Bric Mileui, 1992, Ascheri, Italy £9.95
16	Chianti Rufina Riserva Vigneto Bucerchiale, 1988, Fattoria Selvapiana Tuscany, Italy £11.39
16	Amarone Recioto della Valpolicella, 1985, Allegrini, Italy £17.19
16	Cepparello, 1990, Isole e Olena, Tuscany, Italy £17.25

WMK Winemark ★★★

3 Duncrue Place, Belfast BT3 9BU N. Ireland (Tel 0232 746274). **Opening hours:** Mon-Sat 9.30am-9.30pm. **Delivery:** free locally. **Tastings:** regular in-store, plus tutored tastings for wine club. **Services:** mail order, gift mailing, glass hire,

The largest retail off-licence chain in Northern Ireland with 71 outlets, forges ahead with a high proportion of International Wine Challenge medal-winning wines & plenty of own-labels, sourced & shipped direct. Add a set of 15 wines from Mitchelton, lots of stuff from Geoff Merrill (the wizard of Oz) & Trapiche in Argentina. We would suggest, however, that their buyers pay a visit to South Africa to see if they can come up with wines more interesting than Delheim and Bellingham.

2	Winemark Pouilly Fuissé, 1992, Paul Boutinot, France £6.99
3	Bourgogne Aligote, 1992, Dufouleur, Burgundy, France £5.29
4	Montevina Fumé Blanc, 1992, California £5.29
8	Muller Catoir Riesling Trocken, 1991, Germany £8.49
9	Riesling Spatlese Dienheimer Kreuz, Bruder Dr Becker, 1991, Germany £7.99
9	Haardter Mandelring Scheurebe Kabinett, 1991, Muller Catoir, Germany £8.59
12	Ch. St Didier-Parnac, 1990, Cahors, France £5.99
12	St Supery Cabernet Sauvignon, 1988, California £9.99
12	Ch. Grand Puy Ducasse, 1986, Pauillac, Bordeaux, France £17.95
16	Contessa Marini Chianti, 1992, Fratelli Martini, Italy £3.29
17	Vina Albali Reserva, Felix Solis 1987, Spain £3.99
17	Vina Albali Valdepeñas Tinto Gran Reserva, 1984 Felix Solis, Spain £5.99

WIN The Winery/Les Amis du Vin ★★★

4, Clifton Road, Maida Vale, London W9 1SS (Tel 071 286 6475). **Opening hours:** Mon-Fri 10.30a.m.-8.30pm, Sat 10am-6pm **Delivery:** free locally. **Tastings:** regular in-store. **Services:** mail order, gift mailing, glass hire, ice.

Just over a ball's throw from Lords, The Winery is a former pharmacy which now offers the only opportunity to buy wines from the Les Amis du Vin list over the counter. Apart from these, there is a good range of Burgundies, Rhônes, Alsaces,

Champagnes, clarets and hard-to-find mature Californians (if that isn't a contradiction in terms). As for Les Amis du Vin, don't try to read the seemingly compact A5 list on the tube; it folds out to ania, is particularly well-represented with Ridge, Joseph Phelps, Cuvaison and Carmenet. Don't ignore New Zealand with Delegats and Cloudy Bay, or Yalumba and Petaluma from Australia, but pay some attention to the Italian selection; Superb old Barolos from Borgogno (the 1974 at £27.50 is tempting) and fine Barbarescos by Gresy as well as an excellent range wines from the Veneto.

1	Argyle Brut, 1987, Oregon £9.95
1	Cuvée J. Schram 1987, California £25.00
3	Fetzer Barrel Select Chardonnay, 1990, California £8.95
3	St. Romain, 1990, Olivier Leflaive, France £9.95
3	Clos du Bois 'Calcaire' 1991, California £13.50
4	Delegat's Sauvignon Blanc, 1992 New Zealand £4.95
4	Barbera Oltrepò Pavese, 1988, M & G Fugazza, Italy £5.50
8	Firestone Riesling, 1991, California £5.95
11	La Vieille Ferme, 1990, Côtes de Ventoux France £4.75
12	Ch. Gazin 1983, Bordeaux, France £17.25
13	Ridge Zinfandel, Geyserville, 1991, California £11.25
15	Acacia Pinot Noir St. Clair Vineyard, 1987, California £13.95
15	La Tâche, Dom. de la Romanée Conti, 1982, France £79.95
16	Cirò Classico Rosso, 1990, Librandi, Calabria, Italy £4.50
16	Montesodi, 1988, Chianti Ruffina, Frescobaldi, Italy £15.95
19	Tedeschi Recioto Classico Monte Fontana, 1988, Italy £14.85
19	Ch. Raymond-Lafon, 1984, Sauternes, France £17.95
21	Clocktower Old Australian Tawny Australia £6.95

WOI Wines of Interest ★★★★

46, Burlington Road, Ipswich, Suffolk IP1 2HS (Tel 0473 215752). **Opening hours:** Mon-Fri 9am-6pm, Sat 9am-1pm **Delivery:** free throughout much of Suffolk & North Essex and over one case in London; six cases nationally. **Tastings:** occasional in-store & tutored, plus sampling club. **Services:** mail order, gift mailing, glass loan.

Despite its hostage-to-fortune name, this is a merchant which really is of interest to anyone who wants to try a taste of something a little different. Take our advice and join the Sampling Club whose members receive wines monthly at half retail price. The effort taken to choose these cases is just as evident in the way the list has been compiled. Each of nearly 300 wines is given a sentence or two of description, and there is a separate collection of fine wine. Amazingly, Tim Voelker and his team still find time to run tastings (food included) in London, Clacton and Norwich once a month.

1	Yaldara Vintage Brut Pinot Noir/Chardonnay 1990, Australia £7.99
2	Chablis 1er Cru Vau de Vey, 1992, Domaine Des Malandes, Burgundy, France £8.00
3	Wirra Wirra Church Block White 1993, Australia £6.99
12	The Angelus Cabernet Sauvignon, 1992, Wirra Wirra, Australia £9.00
13	Wirra Wirra R.S.W Shiraz 1992, Australia £8.00
13	*Blaauwklippen Zinfandel 1989, South Africa £6.60
13	Fairview Estate Shiraz/Merlot 1992, South Africa £4.25
17	Langunilla Rioja Crianza, Bodegas Lagunilla 1988, Spain £4.49

WNS Winos Wine Shop ★★★

63, George Street, Oldham, Lancs, OL1 1LX (Tel 061 652 9396). **Opening hours:** Mon-Sat 9am-6pm **Delivery:** free within 30 miles. **Tastings:** tutored. **Services:** gift mailing, glass loan.

A company that has the chutzpah to give itself this kind of name in a down-to-earth town like Oldham deserves support - especially when it offers its customers an ever-changing stock of over 800 generally interesting wines. There is no list. Pop in and take a gander - you may happen acrosss one of Winos's popular local wine fairs.

WGW   Woodgate Wines   ★★★

Lowick, Nr. Ulverston, Cumbria LA12 8ES (Tel 0229 885637). **Opening Hours:** Mon-Sat 10am-7pm, Sun by appointment. **Delivery:** free locally, nationally at cost. **Tastings:** occasional in-store. **Services:** gift mailing, glass hire.

As the name might lead you to suppose, this is a country case-merchant operating out of an old farm outhouse. The list is full of good, solid, dependable fare at keen prices; there are no great surprises, yet no obvious disappointments. Particularly of note are the Jura wines, the Antipodeans, French country reds & various Italians.

2	Côtes du Jura, 1983, Vin Jaune, Jura, France £13.00 (half)
3	Salisbury Estate Chardonnay/Semillon, Australia £4.00
4	Cloudy Bay Sauvignon Blanc, 1992, New Zealand £7.00
12	Ch. Ramage la Batisse, 1986, Bordeaux, France £9.00
13	Hermitage, 1989, Cave de Tain l'Hermitage, Rhône, France £11.00
16	La Grola, Valpolicella Classico, 1990, Allegrini, Italy £7.00

WWI   Woodhouse Wines

See Hicks & Don

WRW   The Wright Wine Company   ★★★★

The Old Smithy, Raikes Road, Skipton, N. Yorks. BD23 1NP (Tel 0756 700886). No credit cards. **Opening hours:** Mon-Sat 9am-6pm. **Delivery:** free locally, nationally at cost. **Tastings:** occasional in-store. **Services:** gift mailing, glass hire, ice.

Do not be dissuaded by the Amish plainness of their list - start reading and discover a very Catholic range of alcohol. Indeed, in addition to a comfortable range of Burgundies and mid-to-late eighties Bordeaux, one will find every spirit known to a cocktail barman, Madeiras back to 1842, a useful list of halves and a range of malts that makes one believe that Scotland's Distilleries must now be empty.

11	Mas de Daumas Gassac, 1985, South-West France £20.45
12	Ch. d'Angludet 1985, Margaux, Bordeaux, France £17.30
13	Côte-Rôtie, 1989, Domaine Jamet, Rhône, France £18.45
15	Chambolle-Musigny, 1988, J. Faiveley, Burgundy, France £23.70
21	1842 Terrantez, Madeira £185

PWY   Peter Wylie Fine Wines   ★★★★

Plymtree Manor, Plymtree, Cullompton, Devon EX15 2LE (Tel: 0884 277555). No credit cards. **Opening Hours:** MonFri 9am-6.30pm, Sat 9am-2pm. **Delivery:** free locally, nationally at cost. **Services:** cellarage, en primeur, mail order, gift mailing.

If you are the kind of person who enjoys perusing the lists of antiquarian booksellers, you will feel completely at home with Mr Wylie's offering, which contrives to have all the charm and professionalism of a parish newsletter, complete with type from an ancient Remington and handwritten additions. Struggle through and find Bordeaux from 1910 and Burgundy from the 1960s, together with vintage port and Champagne. Ask nicely and Mr W might do us all a favour by selling you the typewriter.

YAP Yapp Brothers ★★★★★

Old Brewery, Mere, Wiltshire BA12 6DY (Tel 0747 860423). **Opening hours:** Mon-Fri 9am-5pm, Sat 9am-1pm plus answerphone at other times. **Delivery:** free locally, nationally at cost. **Tastings:** occasional in-store & tutored. **Services:** gift mailing, glass hire.

Rhône Specialist Wine Merchant of the Year

This year sees the husband and wife team of Robin & Judith Yapp celebrate both 25 years in the trade and the — some might say belated - acknowledgement by the Wine Merchant of the Year judges of their Rhône range and expertise. This is not, as Loire and regional styles know, to the exclusion of the rest of France, The beautifully illustrated list (with watercolours to make HRH weep) is an informative read, heightening the sense of exploration and is packed with evocative evidence of Mr and Mrs Y's love of France. A perfect counterpoint to Mayle or Balzac.

6	Condrieu, 1993, Georges Vernay, Rhône, France £18.75	
11	Bourgueil, 1992, Pierre-Jacques Druet, Loire, France £6.75	
13	Brézème, 1990, Dom Jean-Marie Lombard, Rhône, France £7.50	
13	Crozes Hermitage, 1993, Alain Graillot, Rhône, France £8.25	
13	Châteauneuf du Pape, 1989, Père Caboche, Rhône, France £9.25	
13	Dom de Trévallon, 1990, Côteaux des Baux, Provence, France £13.25	
13	Hermitage, 1992, Grippat, Rhône, France £15.95	
13	Cornas, 1990, Auguste Clape, Rhône, France £16.95	
13	Hermitage, 1992, Gérard Chave, Rhône, France £22.25	

YHW York House Wines ★★★

8, Richardson Road, Hove, East Sussex BN3 5RB (Tel 0273 735891).**Opening hours:** Mon-Sat 9am-9pm, Sun 12pm-2pm, 7pm-9pm. **Delivery:** free within 10 miles, nationally at cost. **Tastings:** regularly in-store. **Services:** cellarage, gift mailing, glass hire, ice.

Whilst the owners remain unchanged this shop has returned to its previous incarnation as 'York House Wines'. Fortunately for the inhabitants of Hove, this retrograde step will not be matched in the list, which continues to improve. As long as one is not partial to premium Burgundy, it is easy to keep quality high and price low. Petits Châteaux, solid Rhônes (Chapoutier, Jaboulet), top Australians (Wolf Blass) all under £10. Exceed this and the wonderful world of Drouhin beckons, as do examples of Brunello di Montalcino from the early 80s.

NY Noel Young Wines ★★★

56, High Street, Trumpington, Cambridge CB2 2LS (Tel 0223 844744). **Opening hours:** Mon-Sat 10am-9pm, Sun 12pm-2pm. **Delivery:** free within 20 miles. **Tastings:** regular in-store, plus 'winemaker evenings'. **Services:** en primeur, mail order, gift mailing.

This Cambridge merchant deserves far wider attention then he currently receives. The business has only been in operation for three years, but the quality and depth continues to grow impressively. While we'd be happy to recommend virtually anything from the range, we'd particularly point you towards the Kracher Austrians, the Aussies (including Noel's own Magpie Estate wines), Italians and Californians. Very much a 'watch this space'.

11	Blaufrankisch & Zweigelt 'Blend II', 1992, Kracher, Austria £7.99	
19	Pinot Gris Eiswein, 1992, Kracher, Austria £15.99 (half)	
19	Kracher Traminer Beerenauslese 'Nouvelle Vague' 1991, £18.99	

Index **265**

WINE
MAGAZINE

A Special Offer for Readers of
The Sunday Telegraph Good Wine Guide

If you enjoy the *Sunday Telegraph Good Wine Guide*, you are sure to find similar pleasure in *WINE*, Britain's most popular monthly wine magazine.

Since its launch in 1984 by Robert Joseph, *WINE* has, with each issue, shared many of the qualities for which the *Guide* has been so widely acknowledged. The recommendations from its blind tastings, the in-depth profiles of regions and producers, the features on food and wine, the detailed information on fine wine values, the photography and design and, above all, the impartial and often irreverent style of every issue, have made this the world's best-selling monthly wine magazine.

WINE is published every month at £2.50. As a reader of the *Sunday Telegraph Good Wine Guide*, you are invited to sample a copy of the magazine at the special price of £1.50 (inc postage), or to subscribe for just £20 for 12 issues, including the special *International WINE Challenge* results edition which includes descriptions of over £4,000 award-winning wines.

If you would like to take advantage of either of these offers (which apply exclusively to the UK and only until March 31 1995), please write to Sophie Wybrew-Bond, Publishing House, 652 Victoria Road, South Ruislip, Middx HA4 0SX, enclosing a cheque for £1.50 (for the sample copy) or £20 (for a year's subscription) made out to Quest Magazines, and state that you are a reader of the *1995 Sunday Telegraph Good Wine Guide*.